Katherine Fitzgerald m.(1) Hon. (2) Gen. W.   'Governor' Thomas m. Jane
Viscountess Grandison   Edward   Stewart   Pitt (1653-1726)   Innes
                           Villiers

-enville m. Hester, Countess   Lady Harriet m. Robert Pitt   John   Lucy
728) | Temple (1690-1752)   Villiers   (1680-1727)   m.   m.
-er   Mary   James,
                                                                       Belasyse   1st Earl
                                              Thomas, cr.   Essex,   Stanhope
                                              Earl of   m.   (1673-1721)
                                              Londonderry   Charles
                                              m.   Cholmondeley
                                              Lady F.
                                              Ridgeway

  Hester m. WILLIAM PITT   Thomas   Elizabeth   Mary
) (1721-1803) 1ST EARL OF   (1705-61)   m.   (b.1725)
              CHATHAM   m.   John Hannan
              (1708-78)   Christian   Philip, 2nd   6 others
                      Harriot   Lyttelton   Catherine   Ann   Earl Stanhope
                      (b.1704) (q.v.)   m.   (1712-81)   m.
                        m.   Robert Nedham   Grizel Hamilton
                     Sir W. Corbet

  William   James Charles   Hester m. Charles, Lord Mahon,   Philip,
  (1759-1806)   (1761-80)   (1755-80) 3rd Earl Stanhope   Lord Mahon,
                                               (1753-1816) m.(2)   (1746-63)
                                               Louisa Grenville (q.v.)

-Hester Stanhope   Lucy (3)   Griselda (2)
(1776-1839)   m.
                    Thomas   Philip, 4th Earl Stanhope   3 others
                    Taylor   (1781-1855)

                       Philip,   George   Catherine   m.(2)
                    Lord Mahon,   m.(1)   Lord H. Vane,
                    historian,   Lord   Duke of
                    5th Earl Stanhope   Dalmeny   Cleveland
                    (1805-75)

  Editors
  of the   5th Earl
  Chatham   W. S. Taylor   Rosebery
  Correspondence   (1847-1929)

THE ELDER PITT

By the same author

GEORGE THE THIRD

THE ELDER PITT
Earl of Chatham

Stanley Ayling

COLLINS
St James's Place, London

1976

William Collins Sons & Co. Ltd

London · Glasgow · Sydney · Auckland

Toronto · Johannesburg

First published 1976

© Stanley Ayling 1976

ISBN 0 00 216202 4

Set in Bembo

Made and Printed in Great Britain by

William Collins Sons & Co. Ltd, Glasgow

Contents

Illustrations

MAPS

ACKNOWLEDGEMENTS

I wish to thank Mr J. D. G. Fortescue, of Boconnoc, for allowing me to photograph and reproduce his Kneller portraits of Pitt's parents, and also Mr B. H. Tweedale for his assistance. I am indebted to the Somerset County Library at Yeovil for the print of Burton Pynsent from Collinson's *History and Antiquities of the County of Somerset*. Illustration No. 9 is reproduced by kind permission of the Administrative Trustees of the Chevening Estate; No. 30, and Nos. 23 and 27, respectively by that of the Trustees of the Tate Gallery and of the British Museum. No. 8 is from an original in the Mansell Collection, and No. 31 from the Mary Evans Picture Library. All the remaining illustrations, including the portrait of Pitt by William Hoare on the jacket, are by courtesy of the National Portrait Gallery.

Preface

'The life of Chatham is exceedingly difficult to write, and strictly speaking can never be written at all . . . The fact is that the materials do not exist . . . The intimate facts are wanting . . . He revealed himself neither by word nor on paper, he deliberately enveloped himself in an opaque fog of mystery'. And so 'posterity sees nothing but the stern effigy representing what he wished, or permitted, or authorized to be seen'. Thus Lord Rosebery in 1910, discouragingly enough – in a preface to a book on Pitt which, after five hundred or so pages, ends abruptly at the very point where Pitt reached high office.

Only three years after Lord Rosebery had refused at this first big fence, Basil Williams finished the course in style, publishing what remains by far the most authoritative of Pitt biographies. Masterly as it is, however, it cannot fail to reflect the mood of a vanished world. Confessedly it was written to show 'what Pitt meant and still means to the people of England' – a man who not only won an empire but 'united a people'. The overtones are unmistakably didactic and imperial. Pitt emerges as the patriot hero standing high above the intriguing, corrupt, puny figures around him; the statesman-seer.

Historians (if not biographers) have on the whole over the past forty or fifty years developed less reverential attitudes. The Namier school laid upon him much of the blame for the political chaos of the 1760s. Richard Pares found in him a good deal of the 'exceedingly artful demagogue, who took the credit for anything popular, and often . . . shirked the responsibility for things that would not go down'. Few would deny that, when he wanted, he could intrigue as subtly as any. Not many would now be found to claim that his statesmanship, for all its conciliatory imaginativeness, could have held America long within the Empire.

Happily we do not have to worship at the shrine to feel the man's extraordinary qualities. Even those many among his contemporaries who disapproved of his style and mistrusted his judgement seldom denied him marks of greatness. And no one could take from him those shining laurels of his few years of wartime triumph.

Lord Rosebery was perhaps somewhat exaggerating. Some of his 'fog' was penetrable even in 1910, and much peering and probing has gone on since. However, it is true that it has generally proved easier to explain and interpret Pitt's tactics and policies than to elucidate his character and personality. The label of 'manic-depressive' is doubtless a correct one, but a label is not necessarily an enlightenment. Pitt frequently puzzled his contemporaries, admirers and detractors alike. With his ambiguities and contradictions he can still baffle and perplex. For all his lordly and often overbearing manner, he was at many points, mental and physical, a very vulnerable man, and his camouflages and smoke-screens were sometimes devices to afford a degree of self-protection. Like Churchill, with whose career Pitt's provides so many parallels, he will continue to elude facile diagnoses or flip judgements. In his middle years he was more than once accused of being a chameleon. No doubt estimates of him will equally prove chameleons, as the generations re-colour, while they rewrite, the lives of the nation's great men.

CHAPTER ONE

———◆◈◆———

Governor Pitt and his Family

On 15 November 1708, Robert Pitt, member of Parliament for Old Sarum in Wiltshire, and son of Thomas Pitt, once East India buccaneer and 'interloper' but by now East India Company 'Governor' in Madras, was writing to his father one of those letters which, so the Governor grumbled, were far too infrequent and uninformative. Robert Pitt, who had himself spent four years as commercial adventurer in the East, was now acting as his father's principal agent in English affairs, managing his estates and investments, trying vainly to find a purchaser for his monster diamond (which its owner reckoned would be 'cheap as neck beef' at £200,000)[1], and suffering periodic blasts of parental vituperation which blew in with the mail from India. He had little alternative to enduring these with philosophy, for his whole existence as a gentleman, sitting in Parliament, maintaining a fine establishment in Golden Square to the north of Piccadilly – currently the politest square in town[2] – was dependent on the wealth his father had acquired in his merchant-venturing, and on a continuing degree of paternal goodwill, however testy.

On this particular day, towards the end of Thomas Pitt's decade or so of the Madras governorship, his son was reporting to him what he had learned of the pressure building up against him in London. It was considered that the Governor had seriously mismanaged recent inter-caste disturbances: 'what they most resent is your threatening to whip and hang one whom they had named of their Council'. The Company seemed very ready to take advantage of their truculent Governor's frequent protestations that he wished to return home. (In the end they dismissed him.)

Robert Pitt's letter appended a few morsels of domestic and political news. His mother, the wife whom Governor Pitt had renounced, had given up occupation of his manor house at Stratford-sub-Castro, near Salisbury, and Robert himself had taken possession of it. He was about, so he continued, to place his youngest brother John, on the Governor's instructions, at Eton. The troop of horse for his next brother Thomas 'proving too dear', was not bought. 'He is now thinking of a troop of dragoons which, as he writes, will cost 1100 guineas'[3]. The nations reported Robert, was in general mourning for Prince George of Denmark, the husband of Queen Anne. There seemed but distant prospect of peace in the long war with France and Spain, and hence little immediate hope of finding a European monarch to lay out the £1500 per carat that Thomas Pitt was demanding for his 130-carat diamond. Parliament was due to meet; 'Mr Harvey and I were chosen at Old Sarum, *nemine contradicente*, by the old legal votes' – just now these numbered ten. And then a final crumb of news, almost as an afterthought:

> My wife intended to have written to you this day, but early in the morning was suddenly prevented by the birth of another son. We now have two boys and two girls.[4]

The eldest son had been named Thomas after his grandfather; the girls were Harriot and Catherine, later to be joined by three more sisters, Ann, Elizabeth, and (by thirteen years the youngest) Mary. On 13 December 1708, at St James's Piccadilly, the Governor's new grandson was christened William.

It was an inharmonious family among which the baby made his appearance. Governor Pitt alternated erratically between benevolent solicitude for his dependants at home and a very choleric contempt for them. Certainly there was seldom a time when they for their part were not quarrelling among themselves. Indeed in this very year of William Pitt's birth, his father combined with his uncles and aunts, in a brief interval of buried hatchets and remorseful good intentions, to send a letter to their father in Madras, expressing sorrow for their unnatural discords.[5]

On occasion the Governor could sound full of wisdom and goodwill. 'Remember', he counselled from Madras,

> that wee are not borne only for ourselves, nor has God Almighty bestowed this plentiful fortune on me to give it only amongst my own children, but also necessitous relations and friends . . . If ever you intend to be great, you must be first good . . . Nothing so

chagrins me as when I have a doubt upon me of the welfare of my children. I send two pieces of cloth of gold and silver as a present to your wife, and the like to your sisters Essex and Lucy, also casks of arrack and mangoes to be distributed among friends . . .[6]

Politically, too, the Governor's advice could have a ring of sturdy honesty and patriotism. 'If you are in Parliament', he wrote when his son Robert was first returned for Old Sarum in 1705,

show yourself on all occasions a good Englishman, and a faithful servant to your country. If you aspire to fame in the House, you must make yourself master of its precedents and orders. Avoid faction, and never enter the House prepossessed; but attend diligently to the debate and vote according to your conscience . . . I have met with some diamonds and consign them to you . . . Do not let any money of mine lie idle or unemployed.[7]

Most of the Governor's communications, however, were couched in terms of the tartest censure: 'I trouble you with no news of these parts, because you write none; not as much as to be civil to those who intrusted you with their concerns!'[8] 'Did ever mother, brother, and sisters study one another's ruine and destruction more than my unfortunate and cursed family have done?' Not a letter from England reached him, he declared, but bore accounts of the 'hellish confusion' in his family. 'Having, by God's blessing, acquired such a competency as I never expected or could hope for . . . and now to have all blasted by an infamous wife and children, it is such a shock as man never mett with'. He ranted against his son Robert's ostentation and extravagance, and the inconsiderateness he showed to his sisters and his mother:

I cannot but think of your turning your mother and sisters out of doors, and your frivillous and pittifull excuses for it; and I think their resentment just. [In your fine house], as I suppose, four or five storeys high, it was hard you could not spare them one storey . . . What hellish planet is it that influences you all? . . . My letters from several friends are full of your extravagances, and in what vaineglorious manner you went down to the election at Old Sarum, and what charge you put me to in house-keeping whilst there . . . Where was the need for this? It never cost me above 10 *l*., which was for a dinner the day of the election . . . I find you have exhausted your own fortune and your wife's too; and are you now broaching mine? Have a care what you doe, for I assure you if I find a just cause, I will cutt you off and all your family . . .

In 1700 Governor Pitt had still been writing to his wife with 'hearty love and affection', reminding her to look carefully after the younger children's education and his Old Sarum plantations and gardens. Stories however had begun to reach Madras of her being intimate with some 'scoundrell rascally villain'. 'I make noe distinction', he accordingly announced to Robert, 'between women that are reputed ill and such as actually are so; wherefore I have discarded and renounced your mother for ever.' She was extravagant too; 'if she can't live upon the income of my land', he wrote, 'let her starve, and all her children with her'.[10]

During the London smallpox epidemic of 1706, in which the Governor's youngest son died, Robert Pitt moved his family, for safety, to Forty Hill near Enfield, where he rented a house standing in fifty acres, while his mother and sisters retreated to Bath. Eventually (though 'in a very od surly sort of way' as she put it), the Governor did make provision of £200 a year for his wife. It would serve, she hoped, to go towards the rent for a house in 'Pell-Mell' or 'Twitnam'; 'for the rest he shall find I can live upon the aire as well and better than I ever did in my life, for I won't disgrace him by living meanly, no longer'.[11]

Politics gave fresh food for the Governor's complaints. He was an emphatic Whig and supporter of the proposed Hanoverian succession, and to his disgust his son Robert turned Tory. 'I have been thinking what box you have gott into in the House of Commons', he ruminated in February 1707; and just nine days after the birth of his new grandson William he wrote, 'It is said you are taken up with factious caballs, and are contriving amongst you to put a French kickshaw upon the throne againe'.[12] Six years later, when the Jacobites were preparing their attempt to dislodge the new dynasty, the Governor (back in England from 1710) was alarmed and disgusted to hear reports that his son was hobnobbing with potential rebels. There came news of arrests, and of the attempted suicide of Edward Harvey of Salisbury, a close friend of Robert Pitt and at that time Governor Pitt's own fellow-member for Old Sarum. 'I hear', he wrote to his son in alarm and indignation, that letters from his friends have been found among his papers, and hope there are none that can compromise you. I have heard since I came to towne that you are strooke in with your old hellish acquaintance . . .[13]

When there appeared to be danger of a Jacobite attack from the south-west, Governor Pitt proclaimed his readiness to provide 'arms for one hundred foot and accoutrements for twenty horse', if only his son would put himself at the head of an 'association' for Wiltshire and Dorset, and Robert Pitt did labour to demonstrate his loyalty by assisting his father in the arming of the Dorset militia, though as usual he got no thanks for it. And certainly he showed no enthusiasm for the Hano-verians. The good offices of his sister Lucy's husband, Secretary of State for the Southern Department, General Stanhope, had obtained for him the promise of a Clerkship of the Green Cloth in the Prince of Wales's establishment, a sinecure worth some £500 a year, but he showed prolonged reluctance to pay his respects to the Prince (the future George II) and clinch the appointment – which however in the end he does appear to have accepted. Stanhope seems tactfully to have found a use for his brother-in-law's political sympathies, and to have employed him as a secret intermediary to persuade the Jacobite Duke of Ormonde to flee the country.*[14] Robert Pitt attended Parliament as a staunch Tory churchman to vote against his brother-in-law's government on the repeal of the Occasional Conformity and Schism Acts, but lay low while the Whigs were busy securing their own future with the Septennial Act.

Governor Pitt continued employing his eldest son as agent-in-chief while maintaining his running fire of complaint and abuse. Robert had 'wasted the estate'; there was so much 'neglect and ill management', the Governor declared, that it would be a relief for him to go abroad again. Indeed at one point he kissed hands upon, but failed to take up, an appointment as Governor of Jamaica. 'When I receive any letters from you,' he moaned, 'write you, or thinke of you, it is *renovare dolorem*.'[15] One might have nothing but sympathy for this son of so

* After the 'Fifteen' had failed and Bolingbroke claimed to have accepted the Hano-verians, Stanhope made similar use of his father-in-law too. Governor Pitt, who happened to be in Paris, was asked by Stanhope to see Bolingbroke and discuss conditions for his return from exile (J. H. Plumb, *Walpole*, i. 251).

tetchy and tyrannical a father, were it not that Robert Pitt appears to have fallen out also with the rest of his relations, and as time went on turned into a paler and less positive version of his father, less stormy but equally complaining, and eventually as critical of his own eldest son Thomas as his father had been of him, and in terms of anxiety and censure remarkably similar.[16]

When all allowances are made for his relationship with this impossible father, Robert still emerges as drab and unlovable. He bore grudges. He quarrelled with his mother and sisters. Once at a family gathering under the Governor's roof in Pall Mall he refused to move into an adjoining room to meet one of his sisters 'who was that moment come to towne', and when the Governor himself carried her new-born baby among the company, all except Robert 'took notice of the child'. General Stewart, Robert's stepfather-in-law, pointing out the offence this kind of conduct gave, thought it friendly to warn him of the strong danger of the Governor being moved to disinherit him.

On the other hand, Robert does seem to have got along in tolerable harmony with his wife. True, the Governor had once written from India, 'I hear that among the many ill things you are guilty of, you ill-treat your wife',[17] but that might well have been malicious repetition of rumour and the Governor's customary readiness to believe the worst. From the first he had disapproved of his son's rushing into wedlock 'before hardly he knew the woman's name'[18]; but when various acquaintances reassured him upon his daughter-in-law's virtues and accomplishments, he had somewhat relented. One must suspect that these testimonials on behalf of the bride were not altogether unsolicited by the anxious bridegroom. 'Your son, my opposite neighbour in Golden Square', declared one, 'lives very handsomely and in esteem with all good men, and also very happily with a good lady'; and another affirmed, 'it is a great dispute whether her beauty, understanding, and good humour be the most captivating' – or, he might well have added, the £2000 which she brought with her upon her marriage (with the promise of a further £1000 in a legacy).[19]

Robert Pitt himself had written nervously to his father and purse-master, 'I hope I shall not be abandoned by you at a time when I have no other support but yourself, since my alliance with the greatest families in England is as much to your credit, as my wife will be a comfort to you when you know her . . . Her age is 21 . . .; and I hope to obtain some genteel employment by the intercession of her relatives'.[20] The Governor, so anxious for the social prestige of his family, could hardly have objected on grounds of birth. Harriot Pitt's father was the Hon. Edward Villiers; *his* father, whom he predeceased, was the third Viscount Grandison, nephew of Charles II's Duchess of Cleveland. On her mother's side Harriot descended from the stormy Irish Fitzgeralds. As an infant her mother had been 'married' to the future Earl of Tyrone, then aged seven, but repudiating this somewhat premature contract had defied her family and taken as her first husband Edward Villiers. After his death she became Viscountess Grandison in her own right. Her second husband was that same General William Stewart who was always trying to promote better relations between Robert Pitt and his family; who was one of William Pitt's two godparents (the other being cousin George Pitt of Stratfield Saye); and after whom the boy was named.

Indeed on grounds of social status the Governor should have been pleased with the marriages made by all five of his surviving children: the second son Thomas to Frances Ridgeway, co-heir to the Earl of Londonderry; the third, John, to Mary Belasyse, the sister of Viscount Fauconberg; the elder daughter to Charles Cholmondeley; the younger, Lucy, to James, later Earl, Stanhope, soldier and statesman, First Lord of the Treasury from 1717.

Though Governor Pitt was a self-made man, the Pitts themselves were by no means an impoverished or obscure family. A point has often been made of William Pitt's humble extraction compared with that of the Whig magnates among and against whom he worked. At different times different factors were to tell against him – intransigence of temper, infirmity of body, vulnerability of mind – but never the poverty or insignificance of his ancestors. In the counties of Dorset and Hampshire particularly, the Pitts had long been of some substance. Pitts from Dorset had been among the Exchequer officials of both Elizabeth I and James I. An Elizabethan Thomas Pitt was Chamberlain of Bristol. A William Pitt, knighted in 1618, was Comptroller of the Royal Household, represented Wareham in the Commons, and by buying the manor of Stratfield Saye in Hampshire became the founder of what Governor Pitt in 1700 was still regarding as the senior branch of the family. It was presided over by five consecutive George Pitts; the second of them was one of William Pitt's godparents and the fourth in 1776 became Lord Rivers.

The Dorset Pitts too were of some standing. One had built alms-houses at Wareham; another founded a school there; two more bequeathed sizable sums for charities at Blandford. Governor Pitt's grandfather had been one of the seven 'capital burgesses' of Blandford at its original incorporation. His uncle was mayor of Dorchester. His father, inheriting the advowson, took holy orders and became rector of Blandford. Such origins, if not aristocratic, were decidedly respectable; but it was through Governor Pitt himself, with his legendary diamond, his notorious wealth, his investment in broad English acres and parliamentary boroughs, that the family gained admittance to the social platform from which a man of ability and ambition, such as his grandson William, might reasonably essay to climb the greasy pole of political power.

Robert and Harriot Pitt disposed of the comfortable income of £1400 a year and lived, as all the Governor's children did, amid confident hopes of a share of his fortune upon his death. In 1717 he had at last succeeded in selling the great diamond that he had bought fifteen years earlier from an Indian merchant for some £24,000, modestly hoping to translate it into cash at 1000% profit. Robert Pitt had been entrusted with it, returning to England in 1702 after his years in the East Indies and China; and until 1710, when the Governor himself returned home, he had been ceaselessly admonished and badgered by his father concerning the caretaking and offering for sale of this great jewel:

> I charge you that you never take the stone out upon any occasion, but that you yourselfe weigh it when you take it out and when you put it in; and that it never be out of your eye as much as in shifting from one hand to another; and if there be any occasion to shew it to the Queen, or any great man, you ought to have the charge of it.[21]

'God send me a good chapman for it', he prayed, 'which will put me in a position to provide for you all'.[22] Governor Pitt was certainly churlish and cantankerous, and he worried endlessly over his money and possessions. But he was not crudely avaricious. His goal had indeed been to make a fortune, but his dream was to found a notable family, to establish a house of Pitt that should count for something considerable in the world. 'What I want a good purchase for is chiefly to settle you', he declared. 'I wish it could be contrived that [the diamond] may be bought by the Crown of England for the honour of me and my posterity'.[23] Failing that, 'I believe, whenever peace comes, the King of France or Spain will be the fairest chapman for it, being the greatest jewell in the world'. 'Let any potentate buy it', he affirmed hopefully, 'and the next day it is worth a million pounds sterling'.[24] Having persuaded himself of this, it became natural for him to consider that to let so precious a brilliant go for a mere quarter of a million would be simple charity.

During a period of warfare, however, when the potentates of Europe were not easy to approach, still less to milk of a quarter of a million, the diamond's fortunes had sailed into the doldrums. In 1707 the Governor was still hopeful that Parliament would 'have a heart great and gratefull enough to present it to her Majesty', but Queen Anne's ministers failed to oblige.[25] Seven years later he personally showed it to George I and the Prince of Wales, who expressed admiration but did not prove buyers.[26] At last he managed to unload this 'great concern' of his upon the Regent of France for the nominal sum of two million *livres* (about £125,000), though only one-third of that was cash down. Since the balance was never fully paid, Thomas Pitt's profits cannot be calculated. Some alternative investment of his original purchase price of £24,000, which had remained dead money so long, might well have brought him better gains for less anxiety. However, the money realized in 1717 was adequate for the purchase of the Mohun estates in Cornwall, including Boconnoc, near Lostwithiel, for £53,000.

With other Cornish manors which he purchased and Okehampton in Devon, he expected to find himself advantaged both in status and pocket. And disposing valuable parliamentary assets, he did not intend to waste them. If gentlemen wanting seats were not inclined to pay up, 'I will give them all the trouble I can imagine . . . and I will be at no other expence than a bottle of wine, a barrell of ale, and a dish of meat'.[27] In fact, living most of the time in his house in Pall Mall, and dependent on his son Robert and his other agents to transact his business, he discovered that Okehampton and his Cornish properties brought him little but worry. The Governor's latter years were uncomfortably full of a sort of spluttering, tyrannical impotence. 'I am the most unfortunate man in my sons . . . My resentments against you all have been justly and honourably grounded, and that you will find when my head is laid . . . Money I have none, for that all my bags are emptied'. In this emptying the South Sea Bubble had played a considerable part, and Governor Pitt was one of the most violent and vocal of those Whigs who combined with the Tories in Parliament to demand punishment for the South Sea Company's directors.[28]

More than ever now he imagined every man's hand against him; he was being robbed and abused by rogues and swindlers. There was such 'villany at Boconnock', such 'dirty work', that he repented buying it. At Swallowfield too, the estate south of Reading which he added to his purchases in 1718 and where he spent some of his last years, there were 'villains' at work disobeying his instructions, who should 'pay for it, by the living God'. 'I have mett with foul play all around me', he raged, 'and being grown old I cannot struggle with it'.

The centrepiece of the Pitt properties remained Old Sarum. When he was still a highly successful 'interloper' and the bane of the East India Company, Thomas Pitt had bought Mawarden Court at Stratford-sub-Castro,* just below the ancient earthworks which were all that was left of Celtic–Saxon–Norman Salisbury. Though for the most part a ruined hill-top encircled by great banks and ditches, Old Sarum remained a parliamentary borough sending two members to Westminster. It was at Mawarden Court that several of Thomas Pitt's children were born; it was here that Robert Pitt, born in India, spent most of his childhood, as his son William was to do later. As the years went by, the Governor from afar, and his son on the spot, developed the estate, shrewdly buying up more properties as they became available – including the hill-top site of the old 'castle' itself† – until the constituency of Old Sarum became wholly at the disposal of the

* Now generally called Stratford-sub-Castle. A mile or two from Salisbury, a Wiltshire Stratford-upon-Avon, it lies between the river and the Old Sarum ruins. The grey stone manor house still bears over its porch the modest motto engraved by the owner preceding Thomas Pitt: *Parva sed apta domino, 1673:* 'small but suited to its master'. A hundred yards away is the village church, the rebuilding of whose tower by Governor Pitt in 1711 is boldly advertised, THO: PITT ESQ. BENEFACTOR.

† Thomas Pitt bought this from Lord Salisbury in 1691 and had ambitious designs to level it. Fortunately they were never put into execution.

Pitts. Either Governor Pitt or Robert, and frequently both, sat for it in the Commons for, in all, twenty-five years. (They both added a few more years as member for New Sarum or Salisbury, 'represented' at one time by Governor Pitt from rather beyond commuting distance at Madras.) In 1722 there was a seat to spare when father and son elected to sit for their other property of Okehampton, and the second Old Sarum seat was taken by George Morton Pitt, a cousin. Such easy-going parliamentary practice was not yet the occasion of much public criticism, and it was to be many years before Old Sarum became nationally notorious as a symbol of parliamentary anachronism.

Governor Pitt knew the value, social as well as practical, of a good education. From Madras in 1702 he had written to Robert:

> Your brothers William [who died in 1706] and Thomas . . . I would have sent to Holland to learne that language and French, mathematics and merchants' accounts, and write an excellent hand; or putt to the best schooles in England to learne the before-mentioned and all other accomplishments. I would also have you putt your mother in mind that she gives her daughters good education, and not to stick at any charge for itt.[29]

The youngest son John was sent to Eton. Ten years later it was the turn of Robert's sons Thomas and William to follow him there.

CHAPTER TWO

———◆◆◆———

Beginnings

What earlier education William received is not known. It cannot all have come from the swift streams, chalk hills, and grassy meadows round Stratford-sub-Castle, though it is pleasant to consider that much of it did. But the environs of Salisbury were not likely to have lacked clergy ready to supplement their stipend by instructing the young in that groundwork of a classical education then indispensable for a gentleman. When the child was six, the expected Jacobite rising in the west country must have brought a temporary break in the Stratford regime. Robert Pitt went to Blandford to help organize the militia, and his wife joined him there, dispatching the children to the care of their grandmother Lady Grandison in St James's, where the Governor too was enabled to have a better look at the progeny of his unsatisfactory elder son. Apparently he took something of a fancy to young William, and later when the boy was at Eton he had him for short periods to stay at Swallowfield. In the Governor's letters to his son Robert there are five brief references to his grandson:

> 1721, August 10. Pall Mall . . . Tomorrow morning I sett out for Swallowfield, and shall call at Eaton to take your two boys with me, and some of their comrogues; and will sett them down there again on Monday.
>
> 1724, March 31. Pall Mall . . . I set out hence for Swallowfield Friday next; your son William goes with me.
>
> 1724, May 12. Pall Mall . . . Your son William is a hopefull lad and doubt not but he will answer yours and all his friends' expectations.
>
> 1724, June 23. Swallowfield . . . I shall be glad to see Will here as he goes to Eton.
>
> 1724, July 5. Swallowfield . . . Monday last, I left Will at Eton.[1]

It seems that young Will's grandfather may well have liked his company, though whether or not he told him tales of the distant Indies or fired him with imperial visions must remain conjecture. Certainly the adult William Pitt grew to have little liking for East India 'nabobs' in general.

Whatever the holiday interludes at Swallowfield or Pall Mall, or back home at Stratford-sub-Castle, existence at Eton seems to have offered more unpleasantness than enjoyment. William was sent there with his elder brother Thomas at the age of ten. Probably he was too young and sensitive to be exposed to the rigours Eton then offered, without suffering painful and perhaps lasting damage. He neither forgot nor forgave. (Yet the poet Gray, following at Eton a few years after Pitt, remembered only his own extreme happiness there, 'the sunshine of the breast'.) Pitt enlarged on his schooldays as little as on the other events of his childhood, but once, many years later, remarked to Shelburne that he 'scarce observed a boy who was not cowed for life at Eton; that a publick school might suit a boy of turbulent forward disposition but would not do where there was any gentleness'.[2] Eton, like the other public schools of the day, managed to combine a bleak academic severity in the classroom with very lax control out of it. Pitt would have agreed with the 'gentle' William Cowper, who pleaded for private tuition, remembering his own years at Westminster:

> Would you your son should be a sot or dunce,
> Lascivious, headstrong, or all these at once . . .
> Train him in public with a mob of boys,
> Childish in mischief only and in noise . . .
> The rude will scuffle through with ease enough;
> Great schools suit best the sturdy and the rough.[3]

Scholarly boys at Westminster or Eton could obtain a precocious proficiency in classical grammar and literature and in ancient history. Subjects however which bore any stigma of utility tended to be relegated to holidays and half-holidays. Mathematics and geography were two such; perhaps even the utility of geography we may question, the principal author studied for it at Eton being one Pomponius Mela, of the first century AD. Writing many years later as a man of forty-five to his sixteen-year-old nephew Thomas, Pitt, after earnestly recommending 'the study of the French language, to speak and write it

correctly . . . indispensable if you would make a figure in the world',
went on to inquire if the boy 'had been taught geography and the use
of the globes by Mr Leech [the parson at Boconnoc]? If not, pray
take a geography master [at Cambridge] and learn the use of the globes;
it is soon known'. He recommended him 'Euclid; a course of logic, a
course of experimental philosophy; Locke's *Conduct of the Understanding*'; and also 'to acquire a clear and thorough notion of what is
called the solar system, together with the doctrine of the comets' –
studies unlikely indeed to have been pursued at Eton.

As a scholar, he himself did well, if not so sensationally as to
proclaim a prodigy or genius. In February 1723, when Robert Pitt's
two sons were respectively seventeen and fourteen, he received a
letter from their tutor, William Burchett, concerning their progress.
Thomas had obviously had an earlier bad report, for Burchett's letter
explains that he had not meant to write him off entirely, as Robert
Pitt seems to have understood, but merely to advise on what was best.
Thomas had been generally negligent and was especially deficient
in Greek. However, since at the university 'most of the books he will
read are wrote in Latin', he might just be expected to cope there.
By contrast

> yr younger son has made a great progress since his coming hither,
> indeed I never was concerned with a young gentleman of so good
> abilities, and at the same time of so good a disposition, and there is
> no question to be made but he will answer all yr hopes.[4]

The tutor's phrases are very close to the grandfather's: a hopeful
lad; 'doubt not but he will answer yours and all his friends' expectations'.

With neither is there mention of illness, or of 'that hereditary
malady' to which 'he was already a martyr', and which is supposed to
have 'cut him off from the sports of the school' and thus 'impelled
him to study'[5] – as though academic distinction must merely be a
by-product of athletic deprivation. A boy of his sharp intelligence
hardly needed any such fortuitous stimulus to proceed up the school,
as he did, by regular promotions. And he was not so 'martyred' a
bookworm as to be unable to go on bird's-nesting expeditions, which
he remembered and reminisced about to his wife forty years later.
His father was suffering at Bath 'a severe fit of the goute' in 1723, but

William in writing to him makes no mention of any of these sufferings of his own which figure so prominently in later accounts of his school and Oxford days:

> I write this to pay my duty to you, and to lett you know that I am well, I hope you and my mama have found great benefit from the Bath, and it would be a very great satisfaction to me to hear how you do . . . My time has been pretty much taken up this three weeks in my trying for to gett into the fiveth form, and I am now removed into it; pray my duty to my mama . . . I am with great respect,
> Hon^ed. Sir, your most dutiful son,
> W. Pitt.[6]

There are in fact no reliable grounds upon which to base the conventionally accepted picture of William Pitt at Eton as 'a sickly boy . . . deprived of all the pleasures of his age . . . an invalid, and so disabled for games, a recluse'; or to give substance to the romantic 'shadow of the lean, saturnine boy as he limped by the Thames, shaping a career, or pondering on life and destiny, dreaming of greatness where so many have dreamed, while he watched, half enviously, half scornfully, the sports in which he might not join'.[7] Whether Pitt played the newly fashionable game of cricket at Eton is not known, but he was certainly playing it a few years later among Lord Cobham's circle at Stowe, and 'very well' too, by his own account.[8] There seems to be no good reason why one who later revelled in horse-riding and other outdoor pursuits should not as a youngster have taken part in some at least of Eton's active amusements.

What Pitt was obliged to endure at Eton, and at whose hands he suffered it, may only be conjectured. It is significant that he was to educate his own sons privately at home. When he was first sent away to school at the age of ten, although he was accompanied by his thirteen-year-old brother, he was unlikely not to have been homesick at first. Perhaps at some stage he was bullied. Certainly life in Lower School presented rigours difficult for a 'gentle' boy to support. 'The horrors and hardships of Long Chamber, the immense dormitory of those lads', as Lord Rosebery wrote, 'have come down to us in a whisper of awful tradition'.[9] There was a *tradition* too that he once underwent an unusually severe flogging for having been caught out of bounds. But it is impossible to credit that he was one of those whom

Eton 'cowed for life'. He survived to become so very much more cowing than cowed.

It is generally supposed that he was lonely and thrown in upon himself. But at Swallowfield Governor Pitt was pleased to welcome young William and his unnamed 'comrogues'; and this pleasant expression seems to connote a measure of natural boyishness and high spirits. The tough and censorious old gentleman would not be likely to open his house or his heart to some juvenile invalid, full merely of 'a fund of useful and premature knowledge'. This phrase of Lord Chesterfield's might better fit the one Etonian of whom it is known that Pitt was a close friend, George Lyttelton. Lyttelton, first cousin of the five Grenville brothers and their young sister Hester (born while Pitt was at Eton; one day to be his wife) was much of an age with Pitt, and grew to look like a woebegone caricature of him – lean, lank, hook-nosed; a figure whose appearance was always to be the subject of uncharitable jest. Delicate and precocious, he suffered the misfortune of having his schoolboy compositions held up as models to the class. He was to go with Pitt to Oxford, see his sister Christian marry Pitt's unsatisfactory brother Thomas, engage in politics first as Pitt's ally and later as his opponent, and be remembered as a conventional but mellifluous minor poet. He became a historical biographer too; of his *Henry II*, Horace Walpole wrote, 'How dull one may be, if one will but take pains for six or seven-and-twenty years together!'[10]

It would of course be strange if there were not occasions at Eton when Pitt was ill. Indeed, one of the half-yearly bills for his first year there, 1719, contains two items which indicate as much: 'To the surgeon, for attendance, bleeding, etc.', two guineas; 'To the other surgeon, for going to visit him', one guinea. So far no one has deduced from this document that Pitt was sickening for gout at the age of *ten*; but ever since John Almon first set down in print that the great statesman 'before he left Eton was afflicted with the gout, which increased during his residence at Oxford, and which at length obliged him to quit the university without taking a degree',[11] Pitt's biographers have repeated the story, often with ingenious embellishments – though one of the latest, perhaps sensing improbabilities, will allow him only 'twinges' at the schoolboy stage.[12]

Concerning gout in general, and Pitt's alleged early gout in particular, some observations and reservations are necessary. First, gout is extraordinarily rare before puberty and still rare in adolescence.[13] 'Young men', Hippocrates recorded, 'do not take the gout until they have sexual experience' – adding usefully that eunuchs 'do not take the gout or become bald'. In England it was Dr Thomas Sydenham (1625–89), himself a victim, who first popularized an explanation of the supposed nature of the disease; and after his day, during the eighteenth and much of the nineteenth century, the term 'gout' was employed with such astonishing freedom and vagueness that it must always be met with scepticism and often with disbelief. (No understanding of the physiological causes, in the bodily excess of sodium urates or 'uric acid' was even begun until the discoveries of Scheele and Wollaston during the last quarter of the eighteenth century.)

Following Sydenham, a distinction was drawn between the 'regular' and 'irregular' version. The regular variety, with pain and swelling usually in the extremities and especially in the joint of the big toe, was in fact regarded as a favourable indication for driving out the more ubiquitous irregular or 'flying' variety, a sort of Robin Goodfellow of a disease which might assume the character of almost anything – intestinal disorder ('gout in the bowels'), neuralgia or practically any kind of arthritis, dyspepsia ('gout in the stomach'), and a great deal more – even mental derangement ('gout in the head'). 'I have been extremely ill indeed with the gout all over,' wrote Horace Walpole to his friend William Cole, 'in head, stomach, both feet, both wrists, and both shoulders';[14] and a friend of Pitt's wrote to him in 1756, 'I have narrowly escaped sinking under repeated attacks of gout in my stomach, lungs, etc., where good Dr Duncan had been so kind as to throw it'.[15] Such references are legion. By Pitt's day 'gout' might cover practically any otherwise undiagnosable rheumatic or digestive or renal or pulmonary or mental ailment. The fortunes of Bath, Tunbridge Wells, and numerous other spas were constructed very largely on it. Like the Deity, if it had not existed, it would have had to be invented. This does not mean that the adult Pitt did not later suffer, chronically and severely, from true gout; the description of his symptoms and of the various devices he employed to palliate them suggests that he indeed did; but it is another reason for being wary of the traditional story of the nature of his youthful ailments.

As a correspondent, except in a few early letters to his sister Ann and occasionally later in letters to his wife, Pitt gave very little, indeed infuriatingly little, of his private self away. But once or twice in letters written when he was in his forties to his nephew Thomas,* to whom he was then standing *in loco parentis*, he begs him, in the midst of a good deal of general educational and other moral advice, to beware of youthful 'excesses' of an unspecified kind in which he clearly indicates that he *thinks* his own 'gout and the rest of Pandora's box' originated:

> Give me leave, therefore, my dear nephew, who have gone before you, to point out to you the dangers in your road; to guard you against such things as I experience my own defects to arise from.[16]

More explicitly, in April 1755 when Pitt was forty-six, still a bachelor, and his nephew aged eighteen was in his second year at Cambridge:

> My own travels at present are none of the pleasantest. I am going through a fit of the gout, with much proper pain, and what proper patience I may. *Avis au lecteur*, my sweet boy: remember thy Creator in the days of thy youth: let no excesses lay the foundations of gout and the rest of Pandora's box; nor any immoralities or vicious courses sow the seeds of a too late and painful repentance. Here ends my sermon; which, I trust, you are not fine gentleman enough, or in plain English, silly fellow enough, to laugh at.[17]

He was conscientiously anxious to be the means of preserving this nephew from 'the taints of a corrupted world'; from 'wits and rakes', and what 'those unhappy young gentlemen . . . are pleased to call pleasure'. He wished him to read the right books, admire the best authors, develop a correct style ('"I received yours" is vulgar and mercantile . . . Inclose your letter in a cover; it is more polite'); but above all he wished to save him having to wait for wisdom till 'experience, that dear-bought instructor', taught it to him too late.

To that disease of biographers which manifests itself in idolatrous adulation Macaulay gave the name *Lues Boswelliana*, a condition in

* His brother Thomas's son Thomas, the future politician, connoisseur, and amateur architect Lord Camelford.

which he pronounced his contemporary Pitt-worshipper, the Rev. Francis Thackeray (the novelist's uncle), to be 'far gone'.* In general few of Pitt's biographers have been entirely unmarked by this distemper, and those of them who have not ignored these muted confessions of his have ridiculed any idea of taking them seriously, and turned indignantly on the only one among them who thought Pitt had something real to talk about. That odd man out was the German, von Ruville, who reasonably enough concluded that Pitt, probably at Oxford, though Pitt himself ascribes no time and place, felt himself guilty of 'immorality and excess', and 'not only had he given way to these temptations – weakness which in early youth is easy and to some extent excusable – but he had seriously damaged his health in consequence'.[18] In preaching to his nephew against 'your young gentlemen of pleasure', it is perhaps significant that Pitt directly associated 'a tainted health and battered constitution' with 'a whore and a bottle'; and even if we limit the possible contents of his 'Pandora's box' to arthritic consequences of some kind, there would be plenty of candidates for consideration besides gout – in particular the various infective forms of the disease.

Whatever the skeletons rattling behind these oblique references to indulgence and folly (indeed, if any), Pitt's youthful indiscretions and any possible penalties he paid for them would matter no more than 'What porridge had John Keats?' – were it not that from his middle thirties onwards his health, or lack of it, came to loom very large, not merely in his own life but later in the political life of the nation itself. Probably we shall discover the truth of it no more completely than we may fully uncover the inmost man within the cocoon of mystification in which he later learned so successfully to conceal himself.

William Pitt left Eton in the summer of 1726, at seventeen and a half. It was two or three months after the death of his grandfather the Governor, who bequeathed him £100 a year, together with certain reversionary claims which never came to anything. Death, indeed, knocked repeatedly on the family door during 1726–7. William's grandmother Grandison died in January 1726, and was magnificently interred in the Duke of Buckingham's vault in Westminster Abbey,

---

* Essay on *William Pitt* (1834). 'What greater boon can any writer ask than to be trounced by Lord Macaulay?' asked Virginia Woolf, who, learned as she was, had perhaps never come across Thackeray's uncle.

being attended thither by four pall-bearing dukes and double that quantity of earls, together with a mourning procession becarriaged and servanted and ceremonious enough to impress all here below and to give fair notice above that one of the Villiers connection was on her way. The only recorded comments however of the Governor, whose own life had at that juncture a little over three months remaining, were that it was 'a great burial'; that the widowed General was already thinking of remarrying; and, more cryptically, that as for Lady Grandison, 'all that were her friends are glad she is out of this world'.[19] Instead of marrying again, General Stewart himself died five months after his wife. A little before that, in April, Governor Pitt had finally departed from a scene that he had for many years viewed through jaundiced misanthropic eyes, and from a family he had long ranted and railed against – the 'cockatrice brood' of Pitts. He died suddenly, of 'a mixture of apoplexie and palsie'.[20] Seven months later his estranged wife was dead too, though not before she had descended upon her son Robert at Stratford-sub-Castle and, by his account, 'staid there 2 days, rhodomontading and talking like a mad woman, and stirring up strifes with my tenants against mee'. Unlovable, unfilial, and self-justifying to the last, Robert Pitt expostulated to his lawyer, 'You see what people I have to deal with'.[21] Within six months he had followed his parents to the grave.

The Governor's fortune, and with it his sons' great expectations, had suffered serious shrinkage. Much the greater part of what remained rested in real estate; and most of Robert Pitt's last year of life, which largely coincided with William's time at Oxford, had been occupied with bitter argument, and the preliminaries of litigation, between himself as residuary legatee and the will's executors. While these fraternal feuds were entering on their career in Chancery, William was preparing to pursue his at Trinity College, Oxford, which he joined in January 1727, following a hiatus of half a year after he left Eton. His brother Thomas,* meanwhile, on a continental tour, was being visited in the traditional Pitt manner by his father's rancorous displeasure. Upon the

---

* The Thomas Pitts are confusingly numerous. William Pitt had a grandfather Thomas, Governor Pitt (1653–1726); an uncle Thomas, Lord Londonderry (d. 1729); a cousin Thomas who succeeded the preceding as Lord Londonderry (d. 1734); an elder brother Thomas, the borough-monger (1705–61); a nephew Thomas, the first Lord Camelford (1737–93); and a great-nephew Thomas, the second and last Lord Camelford (1775–1804).

Governor's death, Robert Pitt announced at first that he had decided to forget Thomas's 'past slighting and disobedient conduct' and to allow him £700 a year. He then alleged he had intended the £700 only while Thomas was travelling abroad; and that it was in any case too much and must be reduced to £500, which was 'more than many noblemen of twice my estate allow their sons'. Thomas of course proceeded to acquire substantial debts which, so he claimed, threatened him with arrest in Lunéville and, if his father did not relent, he would be driven 'to the last extremities'.[22]

As the younger brother, William could hardly vie with Thomas in expenditure, but he too received his share of paternal complaint. Could, for instance, his laundry bill at college really amount to *over two pounds*? William had already made precautionary noises concerning his previous, initial, account (sum total £84-18-8, including caution money £10, and £10 for a benefaction to the college required of every gentleman-commoner). The tutor, the Rev. J. Stockwell, had written to Robert Pitt that many mere commoners also paid their £10 college benefaction; 'but I know Sr that you will excuse me for mentioning that several young gentlemen of Mr Pitt's gown [gentleman-commoners] have besides made the college a present of a piece of plate of 10 or 12 *l*. I am thus particular only in obedience to your orders'. He further represented that he had turned down many previous requests to act as tutor to young gentlemen of fortune; 'but the great regard that every Salisbury man must have for your family, and the character I hear of Mr Pitt from all hands, put it out of my power to decline a proposal of so much credit and advantage to myself and the college'.[23]

'Honoured Sir,' William had written to his father, professing shame at the sum his account required:

. . . I have too much reason to fear you may think some of these articles too extravagant, as they really are, but all I have to say for it is humbly to beg you would not attribute it to my extravagance, but to the custom of this place; where we pay for most things at a too high rate.

In April 1727, three weeks before his father's death, this 'most dutifull son' attempted some explanation of the condition he found himself in:

. . . I find with the utmost concern the dissatisfaction you express at my expences. To pretend to justify, or defend myself in this case would be, I fear, with reason thought impertinent; tis sufficient to convince me of the extravagance of my expences, that they have met with yr disapprobation, but might I have leave to instance an article or two, perhaps you may not think 'em so wild and boundless as with all imaginable uneasiness I see you do at present. [He then itemizes his laundry bill.] One considerable article is a servant, an expence which many are not at, and which I shall be glad to spare if you think it fitt . . .[24]

Robert Pitt, a stranger to the customs and traditions of universities, had been apprised by Mr Stockwell that it was 'customary and creditable to a gentleman of family to be attended by a footman . . . who may live here at a very easy rate (I believe very well for 15 *l.* p.am.)', and he had never been one to allow himself to be considered other than 'a gentleman of family'. However, his death in May 1727 cut short these exchanges with his sons over their allowances; and the family finances were certainly not eased by the subsequent behaviour of his son Thomas, who succeeded to the estate – including of course the important parliamentary properties. Thomas had not, after all, been driven to the 'last extremities' by debt, and he now proceeded to treat the rest of the family, including his mother, with little consideration.

It is altogether more probable that lack of money rather than 'an acceleration of his gout' was a principal cause of Pitt's leaving Oxford after only one year; and if the climate of the place was to blame at all, being we are told 'bad for his gout',[25] it is far more likely to have been the intellectual rather than the geographical variety. Pitt would not have wished to remain at Trinity as a poor relation, and although Thomas later assured him that 'nothing that the estate can afford shall be denied' for his 'advantage and education', that was after William had abandoned Oxford and settled upon Utrecht, which Thomas was acquainted with and may well have thought cheaper.

Better value, perhaps, too; and in this William may not have disagreed. Utrecht had a good reputation as a centre of studies, especially legal studies. Pitt is not on record with as harsh a judgement upon Oxford as upon Eton; but he never showed the place any affection. There is no evidence that he regretted his failure to stay for a degree – and it was to Cambridge that he was to direct his nephew and his son William.

As a scholar – which then meant, almost exclusively, Latin scholar – Pitt is reckoned to have been tolerable. He was at Oxford when George I died, and to commemorate that event and compete for a prize (which was won by the young Christ Church graduate William Murray, the future Lord Mansfield) he had put together some Latin hexameters which do not impress even those searching for early traces of genius, and brought from Macaulay a dismissal of both the undergraduate Latinist and the dead monarch:

> They prove the young student had but a very limited knowledge even of the mechanical part of his art . . . the matter of the poem is as worthless as that of any college exercise that was ever written before or since. There is, of course, much about Mars, Themis, Neptune, and Cocytus. The Muses are earnestly requested to weep over the urn of Caesar; for Caesar, says the Poet, loved the Muses; Caesar, who could not read a line of Pope, and who loved nothing but punch and fat women.[26]

Nevertheless, it was the opinion of Lord Chesterfield and others (according to Francis Thackeray, who was willing to give his hero the benefit of every doubt) that Pitt 'had he applied himself to poetry, would have greatly excelled in it'.

This is not the only observation of Chesterfield concerning Pitt during these years that must be met with scepticism. 'His constitution', Chesterfield wrote, 'refused him the usual pleasures, and his genius forbade him the idle dissipations of youth'. Such small evidence as exists, in Pitt's letters to his nephew already cited, implies the contrary, but does suggest that neither physically nor psychologically was he constituted to fall in contentedly with the conventional pleasures and pursuits of his fellow undergraduates. It is a fair surmise, too, that he developed a distaste for the intellectual and conversational atmosphere of the high table where as a gentleman-commoner he would be privileged to dine. One does not readily imagine Pitt's restless intelligence being satisfied with the lazy, self-indulgent Oxford of the 1720s, as torpid a decade as any during its prolonged Georgian slumbers.

However, there is no conclusive explanation of Pitt's premature departure – perhaps no *single* explanation either. Possibly he would have stayed on if his father's death had not brought further disruption to the already disturbed family. The good-for-nothing Thomas, now at the head of it, failed to answer his letters; failed to let anybody know where he was: 'what part of the world my brother is in or when he will be in town, I know not'.[27] Pitt may reasonably have thought that Thomas was not to be relied on for funds sufficient to maintain the Oxford life-style his status as a gentleman demanded. That he came to despise his brother is plain.

Thomas, as the inheritor of the estates, was required to look for no occupation beyond that of gentleman. William needed a career, and it seems that at one time he was headed towards the Church. At the Hampshire village of Abbots Ann, one of Governor Pitt's purchases, the incumbent was understood to be 'in a very declining way', and Robert Pitt's cousin Elizabeth, of Blandford, suggested to him in March 1726 (while William was still at Eton) that since the living – which she heard was 'destined' for William – was likely soon to be vacant, *her* son Christopher, who was already installed at Pimperne, near Blandford, should hold Abbots Ann too and keep it warm until William was of an age to take over. The livings of Abbots Ann and Pimperne, she considered, were 'within distance' – they were in fact forty miles apart – and in any case her son was 'qualified to hold both by being chaplain to Lord Stanhope' – surely one of the stranger arguments to be advanced in favour of clerical pluralism. However, after William's leaving school, although we never once hear from him of religious doubts, we equally hear no more of his settling down in a quiet country rectory. Lack of vocation would hardly then have been thought a bar – at least it would have been considered an eccentrically high-minded objection; but obviously there was a lack of inclination.

It was towards the army that he was eventually to gravitate; but that was not till early in 1731, when he was twenty-two. His movements in the interim are obscure. By February 1728, in a letter written from Utrecht to his mother discussing a possible return to England, he seems to imply that he had already been in Holland some time – and incidentally was not anxious for a repetition of the crossing: 'Nothing less than the pleasure of seeing you should prevail upon me to repeat so much sickness and difficulty'. 'Sickness' means of course sea-sickness; not once in his letters over these years does he mention any illness he is suffering. If he had indeed been 'tortured by gout' at Oxford, surely he might be expected to have at least made some passing reference to a cessation, continuation, or abatement of the agony.

How long he remained at Utrecht is uncertain. He was still there in April 1728, writing to reassure his mother that 'supplies' were coming through Thomas, who was promising to behave well; but reporting at the same time that 'this place affords . . . little matter of entertainment'. It did appear, however, that one of Pitt's companions in Utrecht, his cousin Lord Villiers, had discovered rather too *much* entertainment, and consequently been recalled for what Pitt (sorry for the loss of a companion) described as 'a little indiscretion arising from too much vivacity'. Cousin Villiers obviously had his sympathy. Perhaps they had enjoyed one another's company in some of the vivacity. There are, after all, fair reasons for supposing that William Pitt was not born middle-aged, and that he was not always the intolerably and eternally lofty-minded hero that biographers managed later to construct.

Unlike his friend George Lyttelton, Pitt did succeed in keeping an intact heart, though Lyttelton wished it were otherwise; 'Would to God', he wrote, 'Mr P. had a fortune equal to his brother's, that he might make a present of it to my pretty little M.!' M. was for Molly, one of Lyttelton's sisters; another, Christian, had just married Pitt's brother Thomas. And if Lyttelton himself could only have carried off Pitt's handsome eldest sister Harriot, his cup would have brimmed over. He confided the 'madness' of his love for her to Pitt in Utrecht. 'Sure', Pitt commented to his mother, 'there was never so much fine sense and extravagance of passion jumbled together in any one man. Send him over to Holland: perhaps living in a republick may inspire him with a love of liberty, and make him scorn his chains'. Poor Lyttelton: Pitt was 'in pain' for him: 'I wish there were leagues of sea between him and the charms of Miss Harriot. If he dies I shall sue her for the murder of my friend'. Harriot's conquests seem to have been numerous; according to the tradition handed down to her nephew Lord Camelford, she 'was one of the most beautiful women of her time' – but died young, after making a 'private' marriage which was frowned on by the families of both parties.

The sister whom Pitt was closest to in temper and spirit was Ann, four years his junior. In too many ways, in the end, for comfort, she was his counterpart. There was to come a time when they fought like cat and dog; but now they corresponded more like lovers, and there is a springtime gaiety and a spontaneity in his letters to this favourite sister, his 'dearest Nanny', his beloved 'little Jug', that was too seldom to show itself once he had donned the garb and assumed the disguises of the public man. It is indeed from those of his letters to Ann which have been preserved, and a few more to his mother, that what little is known of him over these years may be discovered. Even so, from April 1728 to January 1730 there is a void.

Thereafter, and probably during those blank months also, he divided his time between the family's town house in Pall Mall and its country houses at Swallowfield, Blandford, and Boconnoc, with an occasional visit to Bath, where his mother often repaired in pursuit of health, and his sisters, as befitted unattached virgins (the 'poor vestals' or 'poor nuns' as Pitt called them) accompanied her and made what they might of the town's restorative and social amenities. If he was nursing political or military ambitions, they are nowhere evident; but it is likely that he was reading widely during all this apparently aimless period of leisure. Already at Oxford he had begun to take lessons in French and 'experimental philosophy', and in his letters to Ann he seizes every chance to break into French, mainly for practice, one judges, if possibly also on occasion for a shared intimacy. Amusements were by no means to be neglected, though sometimes they were in too short supply; at Boconnoc, for instance, in deepest Cornwall, only to be reached after an 'execrable journey' – this 'cursed hiding place', where the state of the roads and a spell of bad weather as early as October might hold one prisoner for weeks. Yet even Boconnoc might offer its isolated festivities: 'We are to have a ball this week', he announced in January 1730, 'at Mr Hawky's love-feast (a heathen name for the Christian institution of baptism), where the ladies intend to shine most irresistably'.

The 'shining' of his own sister Nan was a subject that afforded him a fraternal protectiveness. He wished to give his little Jug some elder-brotherly advice. Flirtation was all very well, indeed a fine thing, but health was finer, and she must remember she had not been well. He manages to convey his solicitude with the lightest of touches:

Blandford. October the 13th, 1730.
. . . I cannot help suggesting to you here a little grave advice, which

is, not to lett your glorious thirst of conquest transport you so far, as to lose your health in acquiring hearts . . . In God's name, when the waters [at Bath] have had their effect, give no quarter, faites main basse upon all you meet . . . Spare neither age nor condition; but like an unskilfull general don't begin to take the field till your military stores are provided and your magazines well furnish'd . . .[28]

Even when they had 'nothing to say' to one another, letters became precious: 'I know not how it comes to pass, one has a pleasure in saying and hearing very nothings, where one loves'. And again: 'What shall I talk of to my dear Girl? I have told her I love her, in every shape I cou'd think of: we'l converse in French and tell one another the same things under the dress of novelty'.[29] Another of his more-than-brotherly protestations claims to have been written while he was being noisily pursued by some 'sportly' girls at Lyttelton's – one of them perhaps George's sister Molly:

London. March the 13th, 1731.
I am now lock'd into George's room; the girls thundering at the door as if Heaven and Earth would come together: I am certainly the warmest brother, or the coldest gallant in the universe, to suffer the gentle impertinencies, the sportly sollicitations, of two girls not quite despicable, without emotion, and bestow my time and spirits on a sister . . . Tis impossible to say much, amidst this rocking of the doors, chairs and tables . . . Let the winds roar, and the big torrent burst! I won't leave my Nanny for any lady of you all . . .[30]

Ann Pitt, said Camelford, equalled her brother 'in quickness of parts, and exceeded him in wit and in all those nameless graces and attentions by which conversation is enlivened and endeared'; and Lord Shelburne described her later as 'a very uncommon woman of great insinuation, and great force of character'.[31] When William felt lonely amid 'muzzy conversation' and the rowdiness of Northampton on market day (after joining the army), he longed for 'the restless tongue of dear little Jug'.

Brother and sister exchanged not only a mutual tenderness, but an understanding of one another's sarcasms. When she at eighteen turned down a proposal of marriage from the Rev. Dr Francis Ayscough (pronounced Askew, hence his nickname 'Skew'), who was later to become the Prince of Wales's Clerk to the Closet, preceptor to the future George III, and in the ripeness of time Dean of Bristol* – but who had apparently prefaced his proposal with some ungallant observations on Ann's appearance – Pitt mingles his implied congratulations to her with amused ironies:

> Why shou'd I mention Ayscough's overthrow?... I can assure you, child, a man can *think* that declares his passion by saying tis not a set of features I admire etc. Such a lover is the ridiculous Skew, who instead of whispering his soft tale to the woods and lonely rocks, proclaims to all the world he loves Miss Nanny – faith – with the same confidence he wou'd pronounce an heretical sermon at St Mary's.[32]

When Ann feared that it was William who was in danger of making an unwise marriage (with whom does not appear) she must have sent him some serious advice of her own. 'What shall I say to my dearest Nanny?' he replied. 'My dear girl, suspend your inquietudes ... Love me and preserve your own happiness'.[33] During most of this period of his early manhood, and indeed until the time they quarrelled sharply, when Pitt was in his late thirties, there is no doubt who was the most important woman in his life. When he was abroad in 1733 and confessing to her (and of course to her alone) a passing love affair at Besançon, he was still trying to analyse and explain his older and steadier attachment: '*Il est vrai que je vous aime à un point qui passe bien souvent dans le monde pour aveuglement; mais je prétens vous aimer en connoisseur, je veux que le goût et la raison fassent ici ce que l'entêtement fait d'ordinaire ailleurs*'.[34]

Of his male friends, George Lyttelton was not only the closest, but also the most influential. Lyttelton's mother was sister to Richard Temple, Viscount Cobham, the immensely rich owner of Stowe in Buckinghamshire, distinguished veteran of the wars of Marlborough, political opponent of Sir Robert Walpole, and Colonel commanding the King's Own Regiment of Horse, a dragoon regiment known as 'Cobham's Horse'. It was naturally through Lyttelton that Pitt gained his introduction to Lord Cobham, and thereby to a cornetcy in Cob-

---

* It was *Lyttelton*'s sister Anne that Ayscough married; and it was this same 'ridiculous Skew' who was one day to officiate at the private marriage ceremony of William Pitt and Hester Grenville on 16 November 1754.

ham's regiment; and it was the Cobham connection that was to provide the springboard from which Pitt leaped into political prominence.

In 1730 he had no money of his own beyond the £100 a year left him by his grandfather, and his share under the terms of his father's will of the rents coming in from the family properties. In all, his income may have amounted to rather more than £200 a year. By the standards of a Georgian gentleman it was near poverty. He thus had no prospect of buying his commission, for which the going price was then £1000, and it had until recently always been assumed that the first of the services that Cobham rendered to his nephew's friend was the cost of the cornetcy. But this was not so. The charge was defrayed in characteristic manner by the Walpole administration, presumably as recognition of past and expectation of future support from Pitt's brother Thomas, who had brought four members, himself included, into the 1727 parliament. The cornetcy must thus be viewed as a favour tendered to Pitt jointly by his brother and by Walpole.[35]

CHAPTER THREE

Cornet of Dragoons

Pitt took his military duties as seriously as could be reasonably expected in an age when a young officer did not reckon to be enslaved by the demands of his profession. No difficulty was made after a couple of years over their interruption by a private continental tour lasting eight months or so. His initial complaint to Ann of the boredom of military life in the provinces – only to be relieved, or perhaps worsened, by bouts of tipsy conversation – are not necessarily incompatible with his later claim, to Shelburne, that at this time he read every military treatise that he could lay hands upon, ancient and modern. And it would be surprising if this serious-minded and intermittently studious young cornet of horse had not also read and pondered a great deal of the history of the recent past, the age of William III and Louis XIV, of Charles XII of Sweden and of Marlborough. He was studying to be a cavalryman, not a naval officer or a merchant overseas, but he could hardly have neglected to notice the role of sea power in that recent history, or to have forgotten that the age of Marlborough was also – as it happens almost precisely – the age of his own buccaneering grandfather.

Pitt joined his regiment at Northampton in January 1731, and at various times over the next five years was quartered either there, or at Towcester or Newbury. At first in Northampton he reported to his sister,

the wings of gallantry must be terribly clip'd, and can hope to soar no higher than to Dolly, who young at the bar is just learning to score – what must I do? My head is not settled enough to study; nor my heart light enough to find amusement in doing nothing . . . I entreat you . . . send me witty letters or I must chear my heart at the expense of my head and get drunk with bad port to kill time.[1]

Happily this existence at Northampton, where you might become involved in 'a course of drunken conversation' even for 'some days', or where you were liable to be inconvenienced by 'swearing butchers and drunken butter women, and in short all the blessings of a market day', might be frequently punctuated and rendered tolerable by the joys of London, where he could discover a more 'agreeable set of acquaintance'; and when his regiment later came to be based on Towcester, conveniently there lay at a mere ten miles distance Stowe itself; Stowe, the Cobham fountain head, and increasingly as the 1730s progressed the headquarters of those wits and poets and ambitious young hopefuls of the political opposition who accepted this lively and incisive young man as one of them. 'In a very short quarter of an hour', Lord Cobham was to discover, 'Mr Pitt can persuade a man of anything'.

Whether it was Lord Cobham, Thomas Pitt, or some other source of subsidy that helped foot the bill, Pitt was able during 1733, while Cobham and his friends were enjoying a short-lived triumph over Sir Robert Walpole in their defeat of his unpopular Excise Bill, to afford the luxury of a continental expedition – not quite the conventional grand tour of the full-blown English milord, but a leisurely solo peregrination through Paris to Besançon (where he stayed three months); then on to Marseille and Montpelier; through Lyon, Geneva, and Strasbourg to Lunéville in Lorraine, where his brother had lodged and run into debt six or seven years before; where George Lyttelton had more recently found much 'foppish ignorance' and contempt for what he had been 'taught to value'; and where Pitt now spent the months of October and November. Lyttelton's much grander tour made between 1728 and 1731 had discovered 'abject slavery' in France, and 'decay of learning' in Italy; yet, like the man of conscience he was, he had striven (we have his word for it)

> The useful science of the world to know
> Which books can never teach not pedants show.[2]

From France Lyttelton had reported home to his father the great 'number of hands that are employed in the military service, the swarms of idle ecclesiastics, and above all, the chimerical distinction between a gentleman and a merchant'. Pitt may have noticed such things; his eye was surely no less observant; but his few letters home are not concerned with that kind of social observation. Apart from one or two rather formal, dutiful communications to his mother, Pitt's letters from the continent, written largely in a French which is idiomatic but far from flawless, tell rather of the state of his heart. He protested to Ann from Paris that he loved her better than ever at so great a distance. He would not mind her failing to reply in French: 'j'aime autant que votre coeur s'explique avec moi en bon Anglais'. He proposed, he wrote, to banish 'la sagesse et la raison; c'est de notre vie le poison'. These however were rather different sentiments from the high-flown moralizings he had recently been proffering when she had asked for his advice upon her taking up a position as Maid of Honour to Queen Caroline. Then he had had much to say about 'le secours du bon sens et de la prudence'.[3]

These latter qualities did not desert him when he suddenly fell in love with one of the young ladies of Besançon. A letter from Lord Waldegrave, ambassador at Paris, had introduced him to the best Besançon society, and there he had discovered this enchanting 'Madamoiselle de —, fille cadette de Monsr de —, écuyer de Besançon'. Ann very naturally demanding a 'portrait de la belle', he replied that 'sa taille etoit grande' – by then the tense was already past, though the memory still acutely present; her manner was simple, 'avec quelque chose de noble', while her features announced 'quelque chose des qualités d'une ame admirable'. But the voice of good sense, while it allowed the surface waters of the heart to be ruffled, did not permit the projected itinerary to be disturbed. Nor was the voice of prudence silent: 'Elle n'a point de titre ni de grand nom qui impose; et c'est là le diable'. He was soon persuaded that it had been a passing flame merely, 'un eclair qui a passé si vite qu'il n'en reste pas le moindre vestige . . . N'allez pas m'accuser de légèreté, voilà comme il faut être en voiage'.

When Pitt left England in May 1733 the fierce political struggle over Walpole's Excise Bill had just passed crisis point. The measure to bring tobacco within the operation of the fiscal and warehousing arrangements which had already been successfully applied to tea, coffee, and chocolate had encountered the united and vociferous opposition of merchants, smugglers, and vested interests of every kind; of Tories and dissident Whigs looking for any stick to beat Walpole with; of a noisy press and noisier mob element always just below the surface of Georgian urban life; of patriotic citizens alarmed at the alleged threat to individual liberty posed by the hated exciseman, with his right of entry and search of private premises. In the Commons Pulteney had pitched into the Excise Bill, 'that monster . . . that plan of arbitrary power'. Walpole's Commons majority sank to 56, to 16; worse still, there was a real possibility of actual defeat in the Lords, where even the episcopal lobby-fodder began to look perishable. The honest Englishman, it was put about, would end up no better than a servile Frenchman, shod like him in clogs: 'Excise, wooden shoes, and no jury'.

A week or so before Pitt sailed for France Walpole saw that 'this dance it would no further go' and sounded the retreat. But that was by no means the end of the matter. Sir Robert Walpole, accustomed now for well over a decade to rely on an acquiescent Parliament; the scourge of Jacobites and Tories; the politician who had survived the scandals and disasters of the South Sea Bubble and presided over the recovery from them; who had kept England at peace and taxes at a level to satisfy even Tory squires; who had handled so dextrously the reins of patronage and power and so dominated court and cabinet, Lords and Commons, that the opposition had long spent their brilliant talents in impotence – this consummate political manager had tasted defeat, and it was an experience he could not be expected to relish. He had been saved from downfall only by loyal support from two vital quarters: from his inner group of advisers, the 'old corps' of Newcastle, Pelham, Devonshire, and Harrington, and from the Court, where George II declared him 'a brave fellow' – for him, extravagant praise.

Walpole's reaction to his misfortunes of 1733 was threefold: to promote loyal and able juniors such as Philip Yorke, who became Lord Chief Justice Hardwicke; to reward waverers who had not yet turned against him, such as Lord Wilmington, who acquired a Garter; and to strike at those powerful peers who had deserted him. Foremost among these was the Earl of Chesterfield, whom George II dismissed from his Lord High Stewardship in April 1733. With him went Lord Clinton and, by the summer, the Dukes of Montrose and Bolton, the Earls of Stair and Marchmont, and Viscount Cobham. All these found themselves banished from Court and parted from their offices and emoluments. That in addition Cobham and Bolton were deprived of their regiments was regarded as the most unscrupulous cut of all, since a colonel's regiment was bought for cash and was therefore considered his personal property, inviolable as his house or land. Indeed, such treatment as was now meted out to Bolton and Cobham would not have been possible unless the King, angry with the opposition, had actively wished it.

By the time Pitt had rejoined the dragoons at Newbury, their ex-Colonel Lord Cobham was in full opposition in the Lords, and looking to build up his connection in the Commons. After the parliamentary session ended in April 1734, a general election would be due. Cobham's eldest Grenville nephew, Richard, was of an age to enter the Commons, and the Cobham interest could without trouble provide him with a seat at Buckingham. Then there was Cobham's politico-literary Lyttelton nephew, by now twenty-five and ready for parliament. Conveniently, George Lyttelton's sister was married to Thomas Pitt, who, in full control of Old Sarum and partial control of Okehampton and Camelford, was worth at least four seats if he could be attached. One of the Okehampton seats was destined for George Lyttelton. And now too there was Thomas Pitt's brother and Lyttelton's close friend, William Pitt, anxious it appeared to follow family tradition and enter the Commons, and as aware as Lord Chesterfield or anyone that 'you must first make a figure there if you would make a figure in your country'. Merely among the ramifications of Lord Cobham's family alliances there obviously lay useful potential for a parliamentary connection.

In the election of 1734 Thomas Pitt, fearing that his return for Okehampton might not be wholly assured, caused himself to be returned for Old Sarum too. Being in fact elected at Okehampton, together with George Lyttelton, he had a 'spare' seat at Old Sarum and at first appeared to be offering it unequivocally to his brother William, who was very ready to accept. (The other seat there went to their brother-in-law Robert Nedham, Catherine Pitt's husband.) A suggestion was then made deviously, through Harriot Pitt, that William should take a money payment for withdrawing in favour of a Colonel Thomas Harrison, who had sat for Old Sarum since 1728, when he defeated Henry Fox in a by-election (Fox managing to muster one vote).

What puzzled Pitt was that his unfathomable brother should have anything to do with Harrison's offer, which seemed wholly opposed to Thomas's interest. He apprehended, he said, 'no difficulties from this affair; if I have any to encounter they'l come from another quarter.

I wrote to a certain gentleman [Thomas] above a month ago, without any answer, so judge of his kind disposition towards me'. In October he wrote to his 'dearest Nanny':

> You may conceive I was a good deal surprised at Mr Harrison's *modest* proposal . . . I cannot conceive how poor Harriot cou'd think of employing herself in such a message . . . My first astonishment is a little abated by hearing he was encouraged to it by my brother at Paris . . . for the latter, I have done wondering at any the most inscrutable of his proposed designs . . . I can talk no more of him; I'll endeavour to put him out of my mind till January . . . All I have of happiness is confined to you and my friend George; you may easily judge of my impatience to be with you; I suppose he's still at Stowe . . .[4]

In several of Pitt's letters to Ann over this period there is criticism of his brother, and a good deal of oblique sarcasm at the expense of 'a certain gentleman', the usually unnamed but easily identifiable 'person'. The Pitts as usual were deep in family quarrels. One of these concerned the ailing and unfortunate Harriot, whose marriage Thomas opposed (as did the bridegroom's father, Sir William Corbett), and Pitt was bitterly critical of what he reckoned the shabby treatment Harriot was receiving. 'Poor girl,' he wrote, 'what unnatural cruelty and insolence she has to suffer from a certain person that shou'd be her support and comfort in this distress'.[5] William, the unpropertied younger son, felt that he also had to contend with an unsympathetic and unreliable head of the family; yet on occasions he had to acknowledge Thomas's financial assistance. He was dependent on him for an easy passage into Parliament. He had no wish to incur his hostility by seeming to side against him and with his mother in the all-but-endless litigation arising out of the wills of Governor Pitt and his son Robert.* Yet if Thomas must not be 'disobliged' he could still be despised: 'I am seriously ashamed of him', wrote Pitt to Ann. 'That man's whole life is a sort of consolation to me in my poor little circumstances. He gives me occasion to reflect too often that I wou'd not act his part one month for twice his estate'.[6]

---

* Lord Camelford wrote of his father Thomas Pitt that 'he seized whatever fell into his hands . . . keeping at arm's length every demand upon him, till somehow or other these litigations seem to have worn themselves out and slept by the acquiescence of all parties'.

On 18 February 1735 Pitt was returned by the half dozen or so electors remaining at Old Sarum. He was twenty-six; still an officer of dragoons, but with military duties not too burdensome. The new Colonel of the King's Own Regiment, Lord Pembroke, was, wrote Pitt, 'very good in leaving it in my power to come to town'. Once in the Commons, the new member wasted little time in showing his colours, making a maiden speech in April against the administration in a debate upon a place bill. He was one of a group of young members, including George Lyttelton and the two sons of the Earl of Marchmont, who were reckoned to have made a promising début on this occasion from the opposition benches.[7] Towards the end of the following year's session he again spoke, against the universities being allowed to increase the number of benefices at their disposal. Too many livings in the hands of Oxford and Cambridge, it was argued, 'only made the Fellows lazy, whereas when pinched in their circumstances and without prospect of college livings, they would study hard and go out in the world'.[8]

If he spoke on other matters during these early months of his parliamentary career nothing is known of what he said. But at least within fifteen months or so of his arrival at Westminster, he was being judged 'a very pretty speaker'; he was, so Lady Irwin added, 'a young man of no fortune . . . one the Prince is particular to, and under the tuition of Lord Cobham'.[9]

These, the Prince and Cobham, were to be two key figures in the future opposition to Walpole and the rise of Pitt to political importance. 'The Prince' was George II's heir Frederick, Prince of Wales, who had been brought up in Hanover according to the instructions of his grandfather George I, and had only recently been allowed to emerge into the daylight of British politics. His father detested and despised him, and his mother Queen Caroline viewed him with a most unmaternal loathing that has never been fully accounted for. As for Frederick, perhaps he was not merely the frivolous and ineffectual clown that Hervey's memoirs have handed down. As well as political ambitions he had artistic leanings. He was musical. He enjoyed posing as the friend of poets and painters, and indeed Joshua Reynolds considered that had he survived to become king he would have proved an outstanding royal patron. True, his private behaviour was not responsible or seemly – after sociable evenings he and his companions might well fall foul of the watch, or amuse themselves by pitching stones through the windows of some of the best houses in St James's. 'This night', wrote Egmont in March 1738, 'between twelve and one o'clock the Prince in a frolic broke the windows of Dunoyer, his dancing master, only to frighten and disturb his rest . . . a silly demeanour (and of ill example) for an heir of the Crown, thirty years old and married'.

But it was more than the Prince's irresponsible skylarking that caused offence at court. He had slipped into the role vacated by George II on his accession – a focus of opposition, a magnet to draw malcontents together. Carlton House in Pall Mall, which he had bought of Lord Chesterfield, and his White House at Kew became, in the manner of Cobham's house at Stowe, a rendezvous for many of the 'outs' who hoped one day to be 'ins' – and perhaps one day soon, for George II was already past fifty. Walpole himself, so long and profitably 'in', was well acquainted with the subtleties of this game. He had been in his time a habitué of both camps. Fifteen years or so earlier he had frequented Leicester House himself, in the company of his brother-in-law Townshend, after they had fallen out with George I's chief minister, Pitt's uncle Stanhope, in the days when George II and Caroline had been Prince and Princess of Wales and presided over just such a lively opposition society as they were now vexed to see repeated.

Viscount Cobham's 'tuition' of Pitt was conducted amid the elegant splendours of Stowe in Buckinghamshire, which for about three years became Pitt's second home. 'Direct me to Stow,' he wrote to his sister in September 1735. 'I am more here than [with the regiment] at Touster. You must say "member of Parlt". They make me pay always else'.[10] Cobham, it was usually reckoned, was hungry for a dukedom (as his descendants continued to be until at last they arrived at one in 1822). Certainly he lived in a setting as princely as any provided by the great Georgian grandees: the palatial mansion built by Vanbrugh and James Gibb, to be refashioned by Robert Adam during the 1770s; the 400 acres of park and gardens which Bridgeman, Gibbs, William Kent, and Capability Brown each took a turn in shaping; great lawns and landscaped vistas; rotunda, Palladian bridge, and grotto; pavilions, shrines, temples; every classical embellishment that money could buy or the fashion demand. Cobham's fame lay in his military achievements, but he was pleased also to be a patron, to take intellectuals under his wing and entertain poets among his politicians. Pope was one of the guests with Pitt at Stowe in 1735; the poet's compliment to 'brave Cobham' was repaid with a garden temple to his honour. James Thomson, author of *The Seasons* (but not for a year or two yet of *Rule Britannia*), spent a good deal of the years 1734 and 1735 at 'the fair majestic paradise of Stowe', composing an ambitious extended poem on *Liberty*, which was dedicated to the Prince of Wales and later 'improved' by Lyttelton.* Of Stowe and its Temple of Virtue, and of Pitt whose 'pathetic eloquence' was destined to 'shake Corruption on her venal throne', Thomson sang:

> And there, O Pitt, thy country's early boast,
> There let me sit beneath the shelter'd slopes;
> Or in that temple, where, in future times,
> Thou well shalt merit a distinguish'd name;
> And with thy converse blest, catch the last smiles
> Of Autumn beaming o'er the yellow woods . . .

Lyttelton himself, of course, was a man of letters. Among his early poems were some vapid laudatory couplets upon his friend Pitt, as well as eclogues and pastorals which, so Dr Johnson pronounced, 'cant of shepherds and flocks, and crooks dressed with flowers'. (In general, Johnson judged that Lyttelton's verse had 'nothing to be despised, and little to be admired'.) Another of Cobham's politician-poets was James Hammond, who like Pitt proceeded to the service of the Prince of Wales, but died at the age of thirty-two – at Stowe. Of Pitt and Cobham he wrote flatteringly:

> To Stowe's delightful scenes I now repair
> In Cobham's smile to lose the gloom of care . . .
> There Pitt, in manners soft, in friendship warm,
> With mild advice my listening grief shall charm,
> With sense to counsel, and with wit to please,
> A Roman's virtue with a courtier's ease.

---

* Lyttelton also made 'great corrections . . . in the diction of *The Seasons* before sending to Mrs Doddridge "a new, compleat, and correct edition" with "not a line in it which a lady of virtue and modesty may not safely read" ' (Phillimore, *Lyttelton*, i. 322). There was a good deal of the Victorian evangelical in Lyttelton.

When Pitt first went to Stowe Cobham was in his middle sixties. Chesterfield was forty. Pulteney, next to Cobham the senior of the dissident Whigs, had passed fifty. But the energies of the Stowe circle emanated chiefly from its young men, all in their twenties: George Lyttelton, the Grenville brothers, particularly Richard, George, and James; Pitt; Hammond; Lord Polwarth and Alexander Hume Campbell, sons of the Earl of Marchmont; and Lord Cornbury, a great-grandson of Clarendon. All these men were much of an age – and it happened too to be the same age as the Prince of Wales.

There were also the Stowe ladies. One might say that, for this narrative at least, principal among them was Cobham's niece, an intelligent-eyed, slightly tilt-nosed girl of thirteen or fourteen, Hester Grenville, visiting Stowe frequently at this time from her father's home twelve miles away at Wotton. She presumably would have been surprised if they had told her that in twenty years' time she would be marrying the tall, animated, commanding-looking Mr Pitt, who talked a great deal and was it seemed much listened to – 'with sense to counsel and with wit to please' – but on subjects that were not yet for her. Of an earlier generation there was Lady Suffolk (sometime Mrs Howard), who for twenty years had been mistress of George Prince of Wales and later the Second, and 'long borne his Majesty's contempt, neglect, snubs, and ill humour' – so Hervey wrote – 'with a resignation that few people . . . could have suffered so patiently'. Now she 'resolved to withdraw herself from these severe trials'. In her latter days at St James's she had proved a kind friend to Ann Pitt, then newly arrived as a Maid of Honour to the Queen. Now, from Stowe in September 1735, a letter from William to his sister went in tandem, with a paragraph in Lady Suffolk's hand. Like all the others at Stowe, Cobham himself, Hammond, Thomson, Lyttelton, Cornbury, she is witness to the liveliness of Pitt's company:

> How often, my dear child, have I wished you here . . . I know you wou'd like it, and I know two who think even Stowe wou'd be still more agreeable. They talk of you. I believe both love you. But one can pun and talk nonsense . . . more elegantly . . .[11]

Then there was the irrepressible Kitty, Duchess of Queensberry, Lord Cornbury's sister, who had exiled herself from court for impudently soliciting subscriptions, almost under the King's nose, for John

Gay, whose *Polly* had been proscribed for overstepping the limits of tolerable libel upon Walpole. She too was on intimate terms with Ann Pitt, and both she and her brother Cornbury only a little less so with William.

Not often *of* the company at Stowe but aggressively *with* it in spirit was the ageing, immensely rich, and still formidable Sarah, Duchess of Marlborough, who loathed Walpole and all his works so vehemently, and was to signify her approval so tangibly of those opposing him, that two of them, Chesterfield and Pitt himself, were eventually to become beneficiaries under her will. Chesterfield had offended by marrying George II's illegitimate daughter against the known royal wishes. The Duchess went one better: she promoted a plan for uniting her own granddaughter secretly to the Prince of Wales, with a dowry of £100,000, which to Frederick would have been a godsend. The scheme itself was soon scotched. The Duchess, however, promised to be indestructible.

George II had always ridden his 'scoundrel' and 'puppy' of an heir on a tight rein. While the Prince remained a bachelor the King paid him £24,000 a year from the Civil list. As Duke of Cornwall Frederick enjoyed also some supplementary revenues which his father could not touch; his Cornwall property provided him too with some parliamentary patronage – and incidentally soon brought him in contact with Pitt's brother Thomas, that important figure upon the Cornish borough scene. In all, his income made a grand total of something between £36,000 and £38,000, not nearly enough for his requirements. Its insufficiency, to which his princely debts bore witness, was a constant source of complaint. George II (who as a married Prince of Wales had had £100,000) ignored and snubbed his son by turns, tried to maintain a right of veto over appointments to his household, and rebuffed his application for an independent establishment to coincide with a marriage settlement. Frederick, already twenty-eight when Pitt and Lyttelton entered Parliament, was not slow to perceive the advantage of having his case taken up in a public arena. From their side, disaffected politicians saw a disgruntled Prince as a useful stick to beat the government with and as a hopeful source of benefits to come. When Bubb Dodington lent Frederick the wherewithal to pay for Carlton House we may doubt whether it was an act of pure philanthropy, even though Dodington, a lord of treasury, was for the time being very intent on avoiding offence at St James's. (There is equally reason for thinking the Prince had no very brisk intentions of paying the money back.) It was in the Prince of Wales's service in 1734 that the newly dismissed Lord Chesterfield saw his principal hope of political recovery. Pulteney, of course, was prominent in the Prince's counsels. And not surprisingly most of Cobham's young men – Cobham's Cubs, as they were being called – looked towards Carlton House for their promised land.

Sometimes Queen Caroline tried to persuade herself that her son was not wholly wicked, and then she would attempt to reason with him. As Hervey reports her saying:

> What concerns me most is to see you can be so weak as to listen to people who are trying to make a fool of you . . . and would sacrifice not only your interest, but the interest of our whole family to pursue what they think their own, or to gratify their personal resentment.

In general, however, the association between opposition politicians and the Prince was liable to produce in George and Caroline pure rage.

The growing popularity of the Prince relative to his father – a further cause of the Queen's anger – was assisted by his obvious anxiety to be as nearly an Englishman as any German who had spent his first twenty-two years in Hanover could hope to be. His father, on the other hand, preferred his palace of Herrenhausen to St James's and habitually enjoyed long sojourns there, of late refreshed by the company of a new Hanoverian mistress, Madame Walmoden or Wallmoden (or Valmont, or Vormale, as rumour picked up her name in England – she eventually became Lady Yarmouth). Every kind of report was credited on this subject, and many slurs published. Egmont wrote:

> A paper was fixed on St James's door, advertising that a little gentleman had escaped from his wife and whoever brought him back should have 100 *l*. . . . The Queen, I am told, has writ him a very pathetic letter, acquainting him with the daily disaffection . . . Reports come to my ears occasioned by the King's absence in Hanover, as that his Majesty kept Madame Vormale's birthday with

great magnificence . . . Again, the people will have it that the King has writ for 200,000 *l.* from England to give her; others that he does not design to come this winter; others that she has poxt him; others talk almost treason . . . In the meantime the Prince grows more popular.[12]

In the end Walpole persuaded the Queen to encourage George to set up his new mistress in England, which Caroline was realist enough to concur in, declaring that she was 'sorry for the scandal it gave others, but for herself she minded it no more than his going to the close stool'.[13] This was the time when 'an old, lean, lame, blind horse was turned into the streets, with a broken saddle on his back and a pillion behind it, and on the horse's forehead this inscription was fixed: "Let nobody stop me – I am the King's Hanover equipage going to fetch his Majesty and his whore to England"'. At least of the Prince of Wales it could be said that his mistresses were English.

The word 'patriot' itself was soon to connote 'follower of the Prince' and hence 'opponent of the government'. However, that Pitt should have begun his career as a patriot in this special sense should not be taken necessarily to detract from the genuineness of his wider patriotism. Trifles of personality and circumstance may decide which way political cats jump; and a sight of the main chance may determine embarkation upon the most memorable of journeys. In considerable measure Pitt's future course was laid out for him by his present chances in the mid-1730s; and these indicated that he should turn his back on the setting and face the rising sun. 'We have a prospect of the Claude Lorraine kind before us,' wrote Chesterfield to Lyttelton in 1737, 'while Sir Robert's has all the horrors of Salvator Rosa. If the Prince would play the Rising Sun, he would gild it finely'. Pitt turned hopefully towards this prospective morning glory. As usual, of course, the future was incalculable. As it turned out, George II's sun was a long time setting, and went down at last in the blaze of glory that Pitt himself had done so much to create, whereas the sun of Frederick Prince of Wales was to disappear in early cloud. But the development of divisions and tensions between King and Prince just at the moment when Pitt entered Parliament was to affect his political career at least for the next twenty years. His championing of the Prince's cause and the notoriety of his subsequent dismissal from the army; his oratorical retaliation upon the Walpole administration; his playing up of purely British 'patriotic' interests and corresponding vilification of the Hanoverian connection; the King's consequent resentment and veto upon employing him as a major minister – all these found their beginnings among the court feuds and seeming trivia of the years 1735-7. For Pitt's future these constituted 'the shape of Cleopatra's nose'.

Before the end of 1735 a suitable bride was at last agreed upon for the Prince of Wales. Before George II left Herrenhausen that autumn, 'to undergo', as Hervey put it, 'the mortification of returning to his British dominions', it was arranged that, 'as by accident', he should take a look at Princess Augusta of Saxe-Gotha. He pronounced her suitable, and Frederick obediently accepted his father's choice of bride. Augusta was then brought over and the wedding solemnized on 27 April 1736, in time for George to set off again for Hanover in May. On 29 April congratulatory addresses to the King were moved in both Houses. Ministers, in view of the state of affairs at court and the known wishes of the King, were for letting the occasion pass on the basis of least said, soonest mended; but opposition members had different ideas. Thus it was Pulteney, Walpole's old rival and foremost spokesman among the Patriot Whigs, who introduced the Commons motion. After him, Richard Grenville, Lyttelton, and Pitt made supporting speeches which even the Walpolian Lord Hervey considered 'remarkable'. These three, he reports,

> got up one after another in the House of Commons to compliment the Prince's character and the Princess's family and to insinuate, not in very covert terms, that the King had very little merit to the nation in making this match, since it had been owing to the Prince demanding it of his father, and the voice of the people calling for it too strongly not to be complied with.[14]

Pitt's contribution, as recorded in the *Gentleman's Magazine*, reads in fact remarkably unremarkably:

> How great soever the joy of the public may be, and very great it certainly is, in receiving this benefit from his Majesty, it must be inferior to that high satisfaction which he himself enjoys in bestowing it . . . the paternal delight of indulging the most dutiful application and most humble request of a submissive and obedient son . . .

the justice and goodness of his Majesty in the measure now before us . . . etc.

Only by reading heavily ironic inflections into Pitt's voice can the reception accorded to the effusion be accounted for. Until recently this was wrongly thought to have been Pitt's *maiden* speech, and therefore all the more worthy of note; and historians have been at pains to explain the mark it undoubtedly made and the strong reaction it provoked. Macaulay, reading it 'straight', reckoned it 'just as empty and wordy as a maiden speech on such an occasion might be expected to be', and imagined that its undeniable effect must have been gained from 'the fluency and personal advantages of the young orator', which 'instantly caught the ear and eye of the audience'; his figure 'strikingly graceful and commanding, his features high and noble, his eye full of fire'.

Certainly Pitt's performance in the Commons – and all of Pitt's speeches were essentially performances – earned him much praise and some strong resentment. At least he had made a mark, in an age when the merit of speeches in the House of Commons was weighed seriously, and views of a man's stature were formed by his success or failure there. The pro-administration *Gazetteer* was soon to accuse him of trying 'to rank himself with the first in reputation and experience' and 'assuming the character of a great man, which he is no way able to support'. He had had the vanity to think himself another Cicero. Perhaps his neck was as long and his body as slender, but 'such a one may . . . not see that he is raised by a party as a proper tool for their present purposes, and whom they can at any time pull down when those purposes are served'.[15]

A more tangible rebuke came at the end of the parliamentary session, when Pitt found himself suddenly dismissed from his cornetcy. 'The King two days ago', wrote Lady Irwin to her brother Lord Carlisle, 'turned out Mr Pitt from a cornetcy for having voted and spoke in Parliament contrary to his approbation . . . The army is all alarmed at this, and 'tis said that it will hurt the King more than his removing my Lord Stair and Lord Cobham, since it is making the whole army dependent, by descending to resent a vote from the lowest commission'.[16] Presumably Walpole's celebrated remark (if indeed it was ever made) about the need to muzzle 'this terrible cornet of horse' was as ironical as Pitt's original speech, for it is difficult to envisage Walpole, that tough and still powerful veteran, cowering before this new portent in the heavens. Government money had bought Pitt his commission in the days when the Thomas Pitt connection looked to be worth cultivating; but ever since the 1734 election all Thomas Pitt's members with the single exception of Lyttelton senior (Sir Thomas, M.P. for Camelford), had voted steadily against the government. Walpole may reasonably have thought that a tacit bargain had been broken. He certainly remained quite unrepentant on the issue and, when subsequently attacked upon it, declared that a minister acting otherwise would be 'the most wretched of creatures'; for himself, he 'left the practice as a legacy to his successors'. However, many judged the cashiering of Pitt as harsh and vindictive; even some within the court party. Hervey disapproved in particular of the timing:

> At the end of the session Cornet Pitt was broke for this [his speech], which was a measure at least ill-timed, if not ill-taken; since the breaking him at the end of the session looked as if it had been done on account of the general tenor of his conduct during the session, to avoid which interpretation . . . he ought certainly to have been turned out the night after he made the speech, to mark out the crime that drew the King's indignation upon him.[17]

Pitt's histrionic bent and his ability to attract the limelight were further shown during the summer recess. Deprived of his military pay, he was now by genteel standards a poor man, dependent on his meagre private means, and he ostentatiously proceeded to advertise his poverty and proclaim his martyrdom by driving a one-horse chaise servantless upon his journeys. In friendly territory he was even the object of sympathetic demonstrations, and he admitted that it tickled his vanity 'to be the object of the hatred of a minister hated even by those who call themselves his friends', and was 'obliged to Sir Robert' for honouring him 'with so distinguished a mark of his resentment'.[18]

'I was surprised at Billy Pitt's disgrace,' wrote Lady Lyttelton. 'I hear he seems easy about it; I hope he has reason to be so'. His friends certainly made what capital they could out of his abrupt dismissal; publicly and privately, in prose and in verse, they sang his praises. Cornbury enclosed some laudatory stanzas with a letter: 'Thou gallant youth! whom storms unshaken find' . . . etc.[19] Lyttelton was another who enshrined his admiration in high-toned verses which incorporated some ironic praise for Walpole too:

> Long had thy virtues marked thee out for fame
> Far, far superior to a Cornet's name;
> This gen'rous *Walpole* saw, and grieved to find
> So mean a post disgrace that noble mind.
> The servile standard from the free-born hand
> He took, and bad thee lead the patriot band.

Both Pitt and Lyttelton now became unofficial advisers to the Prince of Wales. The King was once more in Hanover, and the Queen as Regent made a written request to her son that he should remain at Kensington Palace, rather than 'aller vous établir à Londres' – that is, he should stay under the parental eye, according to the King's instructions. Frederick's reply expressed a filial compliance, 'malgré tous les inconvéniens que j'y trouve', though in fact he continued to spend most of his time 'at Kew or London'. Commenting on how well written was Frederick's letter, Caroline asked Hervey who he thought had written it.

> Lord Hervey said . . . Lord Chesterfield would have written better French . . .; that Mr Lyttelton would have been more verbose; and therefore that he should imagine it was the work of young Pitt, who was now perpetually with the Prince, and at present in the first rank of his favour.[20]

With Pitt and Lyttelton at his elbow, the Prince was busy during the latter months of 1736 courting likely support, in particular among the London merchants, whose Common Council had for a dozen years been foremost in the fight against Walpole, and for whom Frederick now gave a grand dinner at Carlton House with speeches and toasts in 'patriot' vein in honour of the City itself, of the navy, and of 'Liberty and Property' – all of which popularity-hunting, said the Queen, made her *vomit*. Thus already, through the Prince of Wales, a sort of alliance was being built between Pitt and the City of London, which would be reinforced over the next year or two and play eventually a major part in his political career.

Between Caroline and her son there was war. With an exaggeration born, no doubt, of over-anxiety, she claimed at this time that Frederick's party 'talked of the King being cast away with the same sang-froid as you would talk of a coach being overturned', and that 'her good son strutted about as if he had already been King'.

Upon his marriage the Prince of Wales's allowance from his father rose to £50,000, but this still left it at only half the sum George II had himself received as Prince, and did nothing to soften Frederick's sense of grievance. Lyttelton in 1735 had strongly advised him not to press this matter,[21] but now he and Pitt and the rest of the 'patriot band' concerted measures to spring suddenly upon the Court a parliamentary motion demanding a fixed income of £100,000 payable from the Civil List. A motion upon Pulteney's 'humble address' to this effect was lost, but only by thirty votes, with forty-odd Tory abstentions. The King and Queen were already 'wishing a hundred times a day that the Prince might drop down dead of apoplexy' when he finally precipitated a rupture with the Court by defying his father's instructions that the Princess of Wales, expecting her first child, should lie in at Hampton Court, where the King and Queen were in residence. Frederick, who had twice before attempted to remove his wife and her belatedly publicized pregnancy from the suspicious attentions of Queen Caroline, at last, in George II's own angry words, brought to a climax 'a series of the most insolent and premeditated indignities offered to me and the Queen', by whisking his wife away from Hampton Court to his quarters at St James's actually after labour had begun. Specifically for this 'extravagant and undutiful behaviour in a matter of such great consequence as the birth of an heir to my Crown, to the manifest peril of the Princess and her child', but in general because of 'the whole tenor' of his conduct, the Prince was expelled from the Court in September 1737.

For Pitt this development was significant. After the rupture some of the Prince's household resigned their places, not wishing to incur the consequences of the Crown's displeasure – which allowed Lyttelton and Pitt to assume officially the situation of adviser to the Prince that they had held unofficially for some time. Lyttelton became Principal Secretary at £700 a year, and Pitt a Groom of the Bedchamber at £400, which for a space gave an altogether healthier appearance to his income. Now an acknowledged placeman, he was at pains to refute the criticism that this must affect the independence of his judgement. He considered it an honour to hold his place, so he claimed in the

Commons, but he would think differently if it did not leave him free to give honest opinions on all topics.²² Although, to say the least, it was convenient for him to have views which ran parallel with the public attitudes of the Prince of Wales, the charge of mercenary place-hunting would never be one that could easily be levelled against him.

His association with the Prince's court did bring complications. Was it proper for instance for his sister, with her own place in the opposite camp as Maid of Honour to the Queen, to be visited by her brother? Lady Suffolk advised no; Ann Pitt protested why not? And the Duchess of Queensberry observed an elegant inability to dogmatize: 'You, my Lady Suffolk, are quite in the right to advise Mrs Pitt against seeing her brother at Hampton Court . . .; you, Mrs Pitt, are quite in the right in seeing your brother where you please'.²³ This was in October 1737; but the Queen's death next month, a severe shock to Ann, greatly altered her situation and brought brother and sister eventually under the same roof. That November Pitt was still heading his correspondence 'Stow' and hoping merely to be with his sister for a week at Christmas. His duties as Groom of the Bedchamber were undemanding, beyond an occasional presence at the Prince's country seats at Kew or Cliveden, or rather more frequently at the subsidiary town residence which he now rented in St James's Square from the Duke of Norfolk. It was convenient for Pitt to be near Norfolk House, and necessary to be in Westminster for that half of the year in which Parliament was sitting – and Ann Pitt had lost her employment at Court. The two of them therefore set up house together in Pall Mall. They made the third consecutive generation of Pitts to have lived in Pall Mall. For a few more years these two fiery particles managed to share a roof there in amity.

CHAPTER FOUR

The Campaign Against Walpole

Once Pitt had put all his eggs in the opposition basket by joining Cobham's group, and then compounded his commitment by accepting a place at Norfolk House, his hostility to government policies became almost automatic. Several of his speeches over the years 1737 to 1742, while he was closely tied to the Prince of Wales, seem to have neither judgement nor merit, but to have been designed merely to make a mark in the Commons. He already had the reputation of being clever, and also of being given to theatricality and an excess of rhetorical gesture. Attacked on these scores by Horace Walpole the elder (Sir Robert's brother), he was well able to counter with energetic self-approbation and sarcastic wit. Age, he remarked, always brought one privilege, that of being insolent and supercilious without punishment. As for

> the atrocious crime of being a young man, which the honourable gentleman has with such spirit and decency charged upon me, I shall neither attempt to palliate nor deny, but content myself with wishing that I may be one of those whose follies may cease with their youth, and not of that number who are ignorant in spite of experience.

Theatricality? That might imply either gesturing or insincerity.[1] The first charge was 'too trifling to be confuted'. The second: 'If any man shall, by charging me with theatrical behaviour, imply that I utter any other sentiments than my own, I shall treat him as a calumniator; nor shall any protection shelter him from the treatment he deserves'.[2]

In his speech of February 1738 in favour of reducing the army by a third of its strength, there were clear echoes of Pitt's resentment against Walpole for the loss of his cornetcy, though these were tactfully transposed to the alleged grievances of some hypothetical 'old officer, who has often ventured his life and often spilt his blood in the service of his country', who might be reduced to starvation 'at the arbitrary will and caprice of a minister'.[3] In his less personal line of attack, he is open to the charges of factiousness and irresponsibility; especially when it is remembered that, quite apart from the brewing quarrel with Spain, there was always the chance (which Walpole never failed to take most seriously) of another Jacobite rising, very likely with French assistance. 18,000 men should be a minimum limit, Walpole considered; but Lyttelton, Pitt, and the Patriots now unconvincingly argued for 12,000.

'The keeping up of an army', Pitt premised, 'was the first cause of our discontents; and those discontents, we now find, are made the chief pretence for keeping an army. Remove, therefore, the army', he argued, 'or but a considerable part of it, and the discontents complained of will cease'. At least three-quarters of non-commissioned ranks in the army 'never went under any fatigue except that of a review, nor were ever exposed to any danger, except in apprehending smugglers or dispersing mobs'. There would therefore be 'not the least ingratitude' to complain of if they were 'all turned adrift tomorrow morning'. As for the officers, 'in case of a reduction, there is a handsome provision for every one of them' – and British half pay was in any case better than full pay anywhere else in Europe.

The whole speech amounted to little more than a clever debater's contribution to the popularity-hunting of the Prince of Wales and his followers. As Hervey had himself observed three years before, 'a standing army was the thing in the world that was most disliked in this country, so the reduction of any part of it was a measure that always made any prince more popular than any other he could take'.

It was to this parliament of 1738 that William Beckford, West India merchant of the City of London, future alderman, Lord Mayor, and close ally of Pitt, introduced Robert Jenkins, who had been captain seven years earlier of the *Rebecca* when it was boarded and ransacked by Spanish coastguards who had at the same time slit off (so it was alleged) one of Jenkins's ears with a cutlass. No one in the Commons was ungentlemanly enough to ask Captain Jenkins to raise his wig in order to prove the story, on which Beckford himself afterwards cast a sceptical aspersion;[4] and there certainly was *an* ear exhibited. The furore created by this notorious organ, and the state of Anglo-Spanish relations which it was witness to, gave Pulteney, Lyttelton, Pitt, and the rest of the Patriots something much more substantial upon which to attack Walpole than anything that had arisen since the Excise Bill.

Both before and after the Asiento, or Contract, agreed at Utrecht in 1713 – which gave the British South Sea Company the monopoly of selling black slaves to Spanish America and allowed in addition *one* British ship a year to unload at Porto Bello – British merchants and shipmasters had been striving, and with some success, to break through the tight restrictions with which Spain surrounded her South American trade. Where the Elizabethan pirates had once seized treasure-ships and looted the precious metals travelling from Peru, English freebooters now pursued a profitable if risky contraband business with the Spaniards of South America, the *criollos*, whom Spain's mercantilist policies kept chronically starved of legitimate imports. Apart from slaves, hungrily demanded by the *criollos* and legally supplied by the British, a host of other goods, manufactures especially, could be provided according to law only laboriously and expensively through Porto Bello, Spain's compulsory port of entry and regulation, the bottleneck whence they were distributed, via the great fairs at Vera Cruz, Cartagena and Porto Bello itself, and from there by pack-horse or mule-train, to the remotest corners of the Spanish dominions, then extending from California to Cape Horn. French and Dutch merchants, and particularly British, many operating from the West Indies and New England, were more than ready to take their chance of obliging the *criollos* and their own fortunes.

Even the legal trade laboured under difficulties exasperating to both Spaniards and British. Between 1717 and 1739 only eight of the 'annual' ships reached Porto Bello; and even those sometimes met, from ingenious port officials, delays sufficient to make the goods too late for sale at the fairs. Resenting both these annoyances and the dues they had to pay, the British contrived some ingenuities of their own. More than once the 'annual' ship arrived with accompanying fully laden tenders to replenish the holds as the cargoes went ashore, so that a multiple cargo could be sold. Meanwhile the risks of the illegal trade brought many desperate little incidents as the running war developed between the Spanish coastguards and the freebooting smugglers. 'Sloops from this island [Jamaica] on that illicit trade', wrote Rear-Admiral Charles Stuart, 'have more than once bragged to me of having murdered seven or eight Spaniards on their own shore'. In Spain it was claimed that Spaniards captured by British pirates had been sold as slaves. Certainly by 1738 some scores of British sailors were being held in Spanish prisons – and was not that enough, cried Alderman Wilmot in the Commons, 'to fire the coldest'?

Under the Treaty of Utrecht and by the generally accepted criteria of contemporary commercial behaviour, Spain had a very strong case. All European powers managed their colonial trade in their own interests or supposed interests. Equally all colonials were eager when it suited them to encourage foreign smuggling. French and Dutch West Indian traders were at this time building a profitable and extensive business in cheap sugar and tea supplied to the British colonists in America – of which not a little was to be heard in years to come. Walpole, with a lifelong experience of smuggling (even including some early ventures in Norfolk on the wrong side of the law), was realist enough to see that Britain's own colonial trade regulations could never be fully enforced without excessive vexation and expense; but the Spaniards, after a slack period in the middle 1730s, laboured prodigiously after 1737 (as in England George Grenville was to labour after 1763) to secure enforcement.

Pitt approved, at least in theory, of trade regulation. The control by the British government of the external trade of British America and the restriction of its manufactures were subjects on which, later, he was never to concede the justice of the colonists' demands. But what was to be sauce for the gander in the 1760s and '70s was by no means sauce for the goose in 1738 and '39. It was clear to him that Spain had acquired in the sixteenth century much more than she could manage in the eighteenth. Unless France was prepared to rescue her, he judged that she was in no position to defend all her vast properties. She could be made, if not to disgorge territory, at least to abandon claims to commercial monopoly. It was no time in 1738 or 1739 to be talking of Spain's legal rights, which she could be regarded as having forfeited by her arrogant and violent behaviour; no time to go meekly into conference with her when her officials were imprisoning or murdering British sailors, and British merchants were 'despairing' for their seized merchandise and blocked markets: 'Sir, Spain knows the consequences of a war in America; whoever gains, it must prove fatal to her'.[5]

Moreover, this anti-Spanish line of attack provided a heaven-sent weapon against Walpole – an increasingly unpopular minister trying to work towards a negotiated compromise. While demanding redress from the Spaniards, he nevertheless requested their ambassador in London to explain to Madrid that the warlike noises being made by the Prince of Wales's party in England should be somewhat discounted. He did, however, dispatch a squadron to cruise in the Mediterranean, and a regiment to sustain British claims on 'the parts of Carolina southward of Georgia'. Unfortunately for Walpole, it was not only the opposition who were banging the drum and raising cries of indignant fury. Within his own inner cabinet some of his hitherto closest supporters, his Secretaries Newcastle and Harrington in particular, sensing the ground-swell against Spain and against the government, began to weaken in their support. So too did the military-minded George II.

Hard bargaining brought the original British claim for £200,000 compensation down to £95,000, against which there also had to be set an outstanding Spanish claim for £68,000 against the directors of the South Sea Company – strongly contested by them, though they declined to produce their books and made counter-claims. Naturally the Spaniards would not consider abandoning their rights of search in what they still regarded as the exclusively Spanish main, and Walpole had had to leave this matter with others in dispute – including the right of the British to continue their settlement in Georgia, a tender young plant[6] – to be decided later by plenipotentiaries. Meanwhile, on the strength of the preliminary agreement, he withdrew the naval squadron threatening the Spanish coast.

Whether such an indeterminate convention, accompanied by such unpopularly pacific gestures, would be accepted by parliament was doubtful enough to make Walpole pull out all his well-tried stops to ensure a majority. However, Lord Egmont was writing in his diary on 25 February, after attending the King's levee, 'Some privately told me they looked on Sir Robert Walpole to be lost'.[7]

When the Commons debated the issue a week later, Pitt was one of twenty-five speakers attacking the Convention from the opposition benches. In the gallery, encouraging his supporters and 'applauding all abuse' of the government, sat the Prince of Wales. 'I know who hears me', declared George Lyttelton somewhat gratuitously, 'and for that reason I speak'. And the Prince greeted Pitt's own 'very pretty and most scurrilous' speech afterwards with a public kiss.[8] The opposition lost the day, but only by 260 votes to 232 in a remarkably full House; and as Egmont observed, 'Sir Robert Walpole has no other reason to rejoice that he has carried the question than that he has put off the day to another session; for it is universally believed he will not be able to stand his ground next year'.[9]

In this speech or in any other that he made, Pitt's precise words can never be known, the reporting of debates being forbidden, and such accounts as were printed necessarily containing paraphrases and abridgements; tidyings-up and improvements no doubt too, as Samuel Johnson modestly implied, when a fellow guest remarked that a certain speech of Pitt's was unequalled even in Demosthenes, and Johnson (once a parliamentary reporter for the *Gentleman's Magazine*), waiting till the praise had subsided, then observed to the company, 'That speech I wrote in a garret in Exeter Street'. In the account of Pitt's onslaught upon Walpole and the Pardo Convention, the 'author' is not Johnson but Chandler, whose version, being followed later by John Almon and (with trifling alterations) by Francis Thackeray, became standard. Its substantial, if not stylistic, faithfulness is not in doubt:

Our trade is at a stake, it is our last entrenchment; we must defend it, or perish . . . If this union [of the Bourbon powers] be formidable are we to delay only till it becomes more formidable, by being . . . more strongly cemented? But be it what it will, is this any longer a nation, or what is an English parliament, if with more ships in your harbours than in all the navies of Europe, with above two millions of people in your American colonies, you will bear to hear of the expediency of receiving from Spain an insecure, unsatisfactory, dishonourable convention? . . . Sir, as to the great national objection, the searching your ships, [this represented] on the part of Spain, an usurpation, an inhuman tyranny, claimed and exercised over the American seas . . . Sir, as to treaties, I will take part of the words of Sir William Temple, quoted by the honourable gentleman near me: it is vain to negotiate and make treaties, if there is not dignity and vigour to enforce the observance of them . . . We'll treat with you [say the Spaniards] but we'll search and take your ships; we'll sign a convention, but we'll keep your subjects prisoners,

prisoners in Old Spain; the West Indies are remote; Europe shall
be witness how we use you . . . Spain stipulates to pay to the crown
of England £95,000 . . . But how does it stand then? The Assiento
contract is to be suspended. You are to purchase this sum at the price
of an exclusive trade, pursuant to a national treaty, and of an immense
debt of God knows how many hundred thousand pounds due from
Spain to the South Sea Company . . . Can any verbal distinctions,
any evasions whatever, possibly explain away this public infamy?
To whom would we disguise it? To ourselves and to the nation. I
wish we could hide it from the eyes of every court in Europe: they
see Spain has talked to you like your master . . . This convention,
Sir, I think from my soul, is nothing but a stipulation for national
ignominy . . . The complaints of your despairing merchants, the
voice of England, has condemned it. Be the guilt upon the head of
the adviser . . .[10]

Several of the often-to-be-iterated Pitt themes are to be heard in this
philippic: the value of naval supremacy, the precious asset of the
Englishness of two million Americans, the equation of overseas trade
with national greatness, the need for a warlike stance in a world of
arrogating Bourbons. Perhaps not all the facts deployed could have
been literally substantiated: 'more ships in your harbours than all
the navies of Europe' was at least doubtful. And not all the disasters
envisaged would now be thought disastrous – for example the loss of
the slave trade monopoly. But the ring of patriotic belligerence was
absolutely in tune with the national temper of 1739 – the prevailing
spirit of 'Britons never shall be slaves'. ('When Britain first, at Heaven's
command . . .') The expression 'My country right or wrong' could
never have made much sense with Pitt, for his country's aims and ambitions had of necessity to be right. Considerations of international
morality raised their confusing and debilitating challenge no more with
him than with Frederick the Great or Choiseul or the Tsarina Catherine
II or any of their statesman contemporaries. *Raison d'état* was sufficient
right, and never more so than in the international jungle of the
approaching 'age of enlightenment'. For Pitt it was as uncomplicatedly
right to raise Britain up as to bring Spain or Walpole down. When
Admiral Vernon, an opposition M.P., won a victory – his only victory
– it was perfectly natural for Pitt and Lord Gower to congratulate one

another upon 'our honest Admiral's triumph *over Sir Robert and Spain*'.[11]

As Walpole's likely retirement or supersession drew closer, some of the Patriot Whigs began sensibly to soften their anti-ministerial tone. It was concluded that Pulteney, until now their Commons leader, and Lord Carteret, excluded by Walpole from cabinet office since 1724 but still only just turned fifty, might both be hoping for leading roles in a reconstructed ministry. There remained the 'ultras' in the assault upon 'the sole minister', 'the corrupt minister', the fount of evil, Walpole. Prominent among them were Cobham and Chesterfield in the Lords, and in the Commons the Grenville brothers, Lyttelton, and Pitt.

The conduct of the war gave them plenty to attack. The campaign against Spain which was to have easily provided Pitt's 'war of plunder' petered out in confusion and mutual recrimination between army and navy, while tropical fevers halved the numbers of fighting effectives. Admiral Vernon, given *carte blanche* to 'commit all sorts of hostilities' against the Spaniards, proved a short-lived hero, acquiring a permanent fame upon tavern signboards that his initial much-blazoned success in capturing Porto Bello hardly justified. Subsequent attempts upon Cartagena and Santiago de Cuba were both resounding failures, largely because of the inability of General Wentworth's army to co-operate with Vernon's fleet. And the navy, despite the preponderance in numbers that Pitt had recently claimed for it, proved unable to prevent the Spaniards from sailing convoys across the Atlantic. As for the governmental direction of the war, Newcastle's innocently honest explanation to Hardwicke of the reason for the delay in reinforcing Vernon is a classic: 'You ask me, why does not Sir Chaloner Ogle sail? I answer because he is not ready. If you ask another question, why is he not ready? to that I cannot answer'. Walpole in the Commons washed his hands of responsibility: 'As I am neither general nor admiral, as I have nothing to do either with our navy or army, I am sure I am not answerable for the prosecution of the war'.[12]

On 13 February 1741 Pitt spoke at length in support of an address to the King to remove Walpole 'from his presence and councils for ever'. There was much delving back into the alleged iniquities and incompetences of the past twenty years' conduct of diplomacy 'calculated only for the advancement of the House of Bourbon'. Spain had been courted 'only to the ruin of our trade'. In the 'last war with Spain

[1726–8] . . . the Plate fleet was spared, our ships sacrificed to the worms, and our admiral [Hosier] and his sailors poisoned in an unhealthy climate'. As for the Convention of the Pardo, it had been an 'artifice to amuse the people with an idle appearance of a reconciliation'. 'He who has doomed thousands to the grave and has co-operated with foreign powers against his country: who has protected its enemies, and dishonoured its arms, should be deprived not only of his honours but his life'. Astounded at their own moderation, however, the opposition desired 'nothing further than that the security of the nation may be restored, and the discontents of the people pacified, by his removal from the trust he has so long abused'.[13] This debate was an occasion when the still far from moribund Walpole appears to have given better than he got. Even the voting this time was emphatic in his favour, 290 to 106. 'A patriot, Sir?' he demanded of the Speaker in the course of his counter-attack. 'Why, patriots spring up like mushrooms. I could raise fifty of them within the four and twenty hours. I have raised many of them in one night. It is but refusing to gratify an unreasonable or insolent demand, and up springs a patriot'.

1741 was election year, and Pitt's return for the family property of Old Sarum, for the second and last time, was assured. His brother Thomas was more arduously employed as the Prince of Wales's election agent in Cornwall, where there were altogether forty-four seats and more decayed boroughs than in any other county, and where the common people 'think they have as much right to sell themselves and their votes as they have to sell their corn and their cattle'. 'The freemen [of Camelford] cannot have less than 10 or 12 *l.* each', Newcastle's agent was told in 1759, the men of Tintagel having just received like sums; and by 1818 Camelford freemen could expect some £600 each.[14] In 1741 votes for the Prince of Wales's candidates were relatively cheaply bought. From 1741, twenty-seven of Cornwall's M.P.s represented the Prince's interest. Thomas Pitt, with high hopes of rank and reward under King Frederick, received as an appetizer the Wardenship of the Stannaries in the Duchy of Cornwall. Nationwide, the 1741 election brought substantial advances to the opposition parties.

William Pitt gave some assistance in this Cornish electioneering,[15] but his brother's part was much the greater. Jockeying and trafficking amid the boroughs of the west country was to become Thomas Pitt's special, precarious, and ultimately desperate line of business. Shortage of ready money had already driven him to secure a private act of parliament permitting the sale of Governor Pitt's old Swallowfield estate.[16] The Prince's business helped to keep him afloat for a while, but the time was coming when, undermined by the agents of the Dukes of Bedford and Newcastle, he would be obliged to pawn his assets to the government for cash. His brother William – in attacking Walpole, and in later years in condemning the abuse of royal influence – made much play with his own hatred of corruption. Nevertheless he always found it convenient to be returned himself for undeniably 'corrupt' boroughs, whether his family's own or those of his political allies of the moment. He never knew what it was to fight an election, nor ever represented a constituency of more than a few score electors. Details of borough management always bored him; such tiresome trivia were for small men like his brother, or for that matter like the Duke of Newcastle, that least negligible of small men. Briefly in 1754, on the death of Pelham, he seemed to be thinking of the Pitts, Grenvilles, and Lytteltons as a family connection (never including Thomas Pitt, though John Pitt of Encombe came into the reckoning). Between them they controlled something like fifteen seats, an appreciable nucleus; but the tendency towards fission always proved incurable.

While the new Parliament was waiting to meet, Pitt spent the summer and autumn of 1741 in his now accustomed round of visits to the country seats of his friends and political associates. One of the most important of these, Chesterfield, being beyond visiting distance in France to mend his health, Pitt did not fail to keep in touch with him too by correspondence, over whose correctness of expression and grace of phrase (it appears from the many corrections in his rough draft) he took the care which so distinguished a recipient merited; nor did he neglect the requisite touch of flattery:

I think with your Lordship, the scene abroad a most gloomy one. Whether day is ever to break forth again, or destruction and darkness is finally to cover all – *impiaque aeternam meruerunt saecula noctem* – must soon be determined . . . France, by her influence and arms, means, to be sure, to undo England and all Europe; by her air and climate she may do the reverse, if they confirm the health of the only man who can save us.[17]

While Chesterfield was in France getting into condition for the final assault on Walpole, Pitt's English itinerary included Cliveden (with the Prince), Stowe (with Lord Cobham) and Hagley (with Lyttelton). He stayed with Lady Queensberry and Lord Cornbury too, and Lady Suffolk at her new and delightful house of Marble Hill, Twickenham – whither he was *not* accompanied by Lady Suffolk's old friend Ann Pitt.

Ann had gone to Spa, ostensibly for the good of her health, and the brother-and-sister ménage at Pall Mall had broken up, while Pitt took new London lodgings in Cork Street, behind the gardens of Burlington House. He was at such pains to protest that he approved of his sister's move that it seems fair to wonder whether he perhaps did not.[18] Certainly when she proposed to stay on in France, setting up on her own in Paris (though under the 'protection' of Lady Boling-broke), he expressed strong disapproval. Bolingbroke's second wife was herself French (the niece of Mme de Maintenon), and her protection would, Pitt allowed, be 'the most reputable advantageous thing imaginable'. But the fact remained, Paris was 'the most improper place for a single woman to live at'; and – Pitt emphasized to Lady Suffolk, who as a retired royal mistress of indisputable respectability might be regarded as an authority on the proprieties – the world would not see Lady Bolingbroke's protecting reputation, but only that William Pitt's sister Ann 'was living at Paris, a single woman'.[19] In the event she was persuaded not to, but she remained abroad. George Grenville found her living with the Bolingbrokes at Argeville in the autumn of 1742, 'pretty well, because she is extremely happy with Lady Bolingbroke, who is equally so with her'.[20]

The rift between brother and sister had probably been developing before it was thus openly visible. Ann Pitt was a woman of indifferent health,* warm temper, and strongly independent spirit. In fact, she resembled her brother altogether too closely – it was Horace Walpole who said '*ils se ressemblaient comme deux gouttes de feu*'[21] – and like William she was in the future to suffer wretched distress from mental illness. (At least four of the seven Pitt brothers and sisters were from

---

* Presumably, however, it was Ann to whom Richard Grenville was referring when he wrote to his brother George in January 1745 of 'the most potently vigorous dancer of these parts, Mrs Pitt'. (*Grenville Papers*, i. 34.)

time to time so afflicted.*) Already she made sudden and perhaps capricious decisions, and was certainly not the sort of self-immolating woman who would have her life directed by a managing elder brother, attached to him though she was. In years to come she did indeed accuse him of demanding 'absolute deference and blind obedience' – he wanted her, she said, to be *his slave* – a charge which, though he found the language unreasonably strong, he did not wholly reject:

> I have certainly declared to you [he admitted] that I cou'd not be satisfy'd with you, and I could no longer find in you any *degree of deference towards me*. I was never so drunk with presumption as to expect *absolute* deference and *blind submission to my will*. A degree of deference to me and my situation, I frankly own, I did not think too much to expect from you, with all the high opinion I really have of your parts. What I expected was too much . . . In our former days friendship had led me into the error . . .²²

The 'situation' he was referring to was presumably his political situation; his sister's friendships, especially with the Bolingbrokes, may have embarrassed him. But the tone of this letter (not written until 1751) indicates tellingly enough the difficulties that had already arisen between brother and sister ten years earlier. 'I have infirmities of temper,' he admitted, 'blemishes and faults, if you please of nature, without end'; and he had, he said, no desire to sharpen his pen. Plainly Ann's letter had been passionate and accusing. He wrote in reply (still in 1751 a bachelor) of the 'friendship that was my very existence for so many years' – understandably he exaggerated – and of 'the quickest sensibility and tenderest jealousy of friendship' that had disturbed their happy relations and 'embittered' much of his life since.²³

---

* The fourth and most eccentric sister Elizabeth, who (her nephew Camelford wrote) had 'the face of an angel and the heart of all the furies', lived for a time with her brother Thomas – Horace Walpole thought even, perhaps, in *both* senses; then openly as mistress of Lord Talbot; and finally, having failed in her design to capture a rich British merchant in Leghorn, as wife to a lawyer much younger than herself – he being possessed of a fortune superior to her own, as she aggressively informed her brother William. After travelling in Italy she changed her forenames to Clara Villiers (or Villiers Clara as the whim dictated) and her religion to Roman Catholic. She alternated between raging against William, who allowed her money but she thought not enough, and calling him 'the best of brothers and of men'. Augustus Hervey, finding her at Lisbon in 1753, thought her 'a very extraordinary woman – clever, but mad'.

From 1741 the colonial war with Spain in the West Indies subsided into relative insignificance with the fresh outbreak of the old European dynastic struggle. This had been re-activated the previous year by the death of the Habsburg Emperor Charles VI, the accession of his daughter Maria Theresa,* and the simultaneous arrival upon the Prussian throne of that new force in Europe, Frederick II, France's ally, who lost no time in attacking Maria Theresa, the ally of Britain. Thus, although Britain was not officially at war with France, each of these powers was as an auxiliary actively helping its ally (or that ally's allies) against the other's. Into this vortex of European war, Bavaria, Saxony, and other German states, as well as Holland, Spain, and Sardinia (which included Piedmont and Savoy) were inevitably sucked; and long before March 1744, when Britain and France at last made their mutual hostilities official, their fleets and armies had been engaged against one another in what Carlyle called that 'unintelligible, huge English-and-Foreign-Delirium' which British historians – since wars have somehow to be designated and distinguished – have in general agreed to call the War of the Austrian Succession.

It was not Walpole's war at all, though of necessity it was George II's as Elector of Hanover; and when the French, dispatching one army into Bohemia to occupy Prague, sent another into Westphalia to threaten the Electorate, George in alarm took what precaution he could by declaring Hanoverian neutrality. It was a question however of how long Britain could afford to limit her part in this continental war merely to subsidizing Maria Theresa and assisting her with minor contingents of German and Danish mercenaries.

Walpole was unreasonably cheerful when the newly elected parliament met in December 1741. He still expressed confidence that he could cling on to office – it could hardly any longer be called power; yet at the same time, in face of the opposition's increased numbers and the feeling against him within his own cabinet, he was busy making such dispositions as would enable him, if it came to defeat, to ensure his safety from those vindictive proceedings which his most implacable enemies, Pitt included, were freely talking about. 'I look upon it now,

---

* As a woman, she could succeed only to the hereditary Habsburg dominions. The imperial throne was disputed between two principal candidates – the French-supported Elector of Bavaria (Emperor 1742–5) and Maria Theresa's husband Francis of Lorraine (Emperor 1745–65).

that the question is, Downing Street or the Tower,' wrote his son Horace to Sir Horace Mann; 'will you come to see a body, if one should happen to lodge at the latter?' And a little later, 'As to impeachment, I think they will not be so mad as to proceed with it . . . For a bill of pains and penalties, they may if they will, I believe, pass it through the Commons, but will scarce get the consent of the King and the Lords'.[24]

In a last bid to hold on, Walpole persuaded the King in early January 1742 to make the following offer to the Prince of Wales (who could influence nineteen votes in the Commons): the grant of his long-demanded extra £50,000 a year, payment of his debts, and admittance of his supporters to Court, in return for acknowledgement of his past offences. But the Prince, expecting his £50,000 in any case from a new ministry, refused this olive branch so long as Walpole should continue in office.*[25]

A major trial of strength came on 21 January, when Pulteney moved for the setting up of a secret committee with full powers to inquire into the conduct of recent affairs. After what Horace Walpole thought 'glorious speeches' on both sides, including that of 'W. Pitt', and after both sides had fetched out their sick and dying to vote – men on crutches, and one at least 'brought in like a corpse', 'with a blister on his head and a flannel hanging out from under his wig' – the Government scraped home by 253 to 250, 'the greatest number that ever was in the house, and the greatest number that ever *lost* a question'.[26] By the last day of January, however, a most reluctant Sir Robert had been persuaded by his friends and relatives that the game was up. He was defeated, in all, in seven divisions, and 'the panic was so great', so he reported to Devonshire, '*they all* declared my retiring was become absolutely necessary'.[27] By early February – but not before he had to a large extent satisfactorily settled the succession – he had arranged to be translated to the Lords as the Earl of Orford.

Walpole would have had no power to keep a finger in the new pie if there had been a united opposition; but there was of course no such thing. The opposition comprised every kind of so-called Tory and so-called Whig. There were some Tories near to Jacobitism, others more

---

* Unstable as ever, he was soon promising Walpole that he would discourage attacks on his life or fortune – at the very moment when Pitt and other of the Prince's supposed following were planning tactics to bring Walpole to 'condign punishment'.

than half way to becoming Whigs of a kind, others whose 'Toryism' merely signified the independence of the country gentleman. Then there were opposition Whigs of every shade of dissidence – individuals and shifting groups manoeuvring suspiciously against one another as men counted their chances and held up straws to catch the latest change of wind. Carteret and Pulteney, the two most prominent among the opposition, were known to be secretly and separately negotiating with important figures within the government, more particularly with such members of the 'old corps' as Newcastle and Hardwicke, and indirectly through them with the King. As Chesterfield, another dissident, whose views were close to Pitt's own, wrote bitterly to Dodington: 'Those who will lead the opposition will make it their business to break and divide it, and they will succeed. I mean Carteret and Pulteney'.[28] Promises were being made and deals done (Dodington was of course trying to negotiate his own) which were likely to exclude from office many of those who had stood out most strongly in opposition – the Tories naturally, but also the more extreme of the Stowe House set and those of the Prince's party who disapproved of his flirtations with Carteret and Pulteney. Pitt and Lyttelton fell into both these categories.

In the new administration-making Pulteney was outmanoeuvred. He was given a seat in the cabinet but, being awarded the equivocal honour of an earldom, lost his Commons influence without gaining any compensating regard in the Closet. Without the one or the other no one, either in this reign or the next, could hope to reach the headship of affairs, and without *both* no one could long retain it – as Carteret was soon to find, and Pitt himself in the course of time.

The new First Lord was a nullity, Lord Wilmington, 'very servile to his Majesty's intentions'. Regarded by all as first minister was the new Secretary, Carteret, generally allowed to be 'a very considerable man as to capacity, parts, and experience'. Excluded from cabinet office by Walpole for the past eighteen years, but still little over fifty and full of energy – despite a trifling touch of gout, he declared, he was 'for vigorous measures both as to Mars and Venus' – he was a classicist, wit, *bon viveur*, diplomatist, and linguist. Best of all from the King's point of view he not only spoke excellent German but was expertly conversant with the complications of German politics. Unfortunately for his hopes of political success, his personal arrogance matched his intellectual distinction – he treated his far from negligible

73

colleagues in a manner almost as Olympian as Pitt later was to treat his – and in the long run the King's enthusiastic backing was to prove no specific against the lack of solid parliamentary backing. 'Had he studied Parliament more and Demosthenes less,' his Paymaster, Winnington, said of him, 'he would have been a more successful Minister'.

Carteret had no intention, so he told Lord Egmont, 'of coming in as a screen to Sir Robert Walpole, or that Sir Robert should . . . play still the game behind the curtain'. Conversely, he was not going to accommodate those extremists among the opposition who were even now pressing, like Pitt, for the punishment of 'the corrupt minister'. 'Considering his Majesty's temper', Carteret told Egmont, 'it would have been impossible to make the intended changes if all at once a number of gentlemen whom Sir Robert Walpole had possessed his Majesty with an ill opinion of, had offered to force themselves upon him before the aspersions cast on them were removed'.[29] Patriots were going to have to work their passage and, as it turned out, Pitt would be working his longest of all. 'The Prince will be reconciled, and the Whig Patriots will come in', Horace Walpole wrote at the beginning of February 1742; and indeed the Prince *was* reconciled to the new regime of Carteret, and was officially received again by the King – all of which pleased Pitt and his friends not at all. He continued for some years yet – until 1745 – to draw his welcome salary as Groom of the Bedchamber, but from 1742 he can no longer be regarded as the Prince of Wales's mouthpiece. Repeatedly he now spoke in the Commons against the Princes's known attitudes and wishes.[30]

In later years Pitt allowed that he had been as mistaken in his condemnation of Walpole as in many more of his youthful judgements. ('A young man of fine parts', said Bolingbroke; but 'narrow, did not know much of the world, and was a little too dogmatical'.)[31] But now, further prompted by his own chagrin at having failed to gain even minor recognition, he was among the least yielding of those demanding the fallen minister's punishment. When a first attempt to get a parliamentary committee of inquiry into the past twenty years' conduct of affairs was lost by two votes, a second motion, reducing the span to ten years but no less punitive in intention, was narrowly passed. Pitt attacked on both occasions, belabouring corruption and again making repeated play with 'the voice of the people' – indeed the attempt to win popularity may have been no less strong a motive with him than a desire to punish. As a member for a family borough Pitt was not in need of constituency votes, but he was well aware of the tone and language of petitions flowing in from the constituencies, demanding not merely stringent action against Walpole but also such reforms as shorter parliaments and a reduction of places, and he managed to include support for both of these in his speech of 9 March. In addition, he rehearsed once again all the old grievances against Walpole's policies at home and abroad, even suggesting his connivance in the hostile actions of France and Spain; he repeated the old grudge against dismissing army officers from political motives; and insisted (with some justice) that Walpole had not in fact genuinely retired at all. He was 'our late, and I fear still, our present minister'. 'Though he be removed from the Treasury, he is not from the King's closet, nor probably will be, unless by our advice or sending him to a lodging at the other end of the town [to the Tower, that is] where he cannot do so much harm to his country'.[32] Pitt's peroration of 9 March leaves no doubt that he had already anticipated the committee's findings and pronounced the defendant guilty:

> Let us be as merciful as we will . . . when we come to pronounce sentence; but sentence we must pronounce; and for this purpose we must inquire, unless we are resolved to sacrifice our own liberties and the liberties of Europe to the preservation of one guilty man.[33]

This last phrase, flung accusingly across the House, was an unconscious echo of what, from within the cabinet, Newcastle had just been saying privately to Hardwicke: 'The fatal obstinacy of one single man "resolved to ruin, or to rule, the state" '.[34]

Pitt managed to get elected to the committee of inquiry, but only just. The investigation, however, soon ran into every kind of obstacle, and at last into a dead end. Walpole's Cornish election agent was hastily given a barony to put him out of the committee's reach; the Treasury Solicitor surrendered to imprisonment in Newgate rather than disclose secrets; and when the Commons passed a bill giving indemnity to witnesses who might without it have incriminated themselves, the Lords, with Carteret's encouragement, threw it out. Pitt and his fellow inquisitors were frustrated at every turn, to the amused delight of Horace Walpole, who reported one particular rebuff to Pitt's 'abrupt' questioning in June 1742, when John Scrope, Walpole's Secretary to the Treasury, was so incensed that he was with difficulty restrained from challenging his persecutor to a duel:

> The Committee are in great perplexities about Scrope . . . He wants to fight Pitt. He is a most testy little old gentleman, and about eight years ago would have fought Alderman Perry . . . The Committee have tried all ways to soften him, and have offered to let him swear to only what part he pleased . . . but the old gentleman is inflexible, and answered, 'that he was fourscore years old, and did not care whether he spent the few months he had to live in the Tower or not; that the last thing he would do should be to betray the King, and next to him the Earl of Orford.[35]

Scrope was the 'immovable object' and Pitt still rather less than the 'irresistible force'. Others beside the ex-Secretary to the Treasury found the manner and approach of this admittedly vigorous and brilliant Mr Pitt in fact very resistible. Bolingbroke, that elder Tory statesman (back in England again intermittently after 1738), thought him lacking in 'deference'. Deference, except on the written page, where it became sometimes unconvincingly excessive, was never to be Pitt's most notable characteristic. But Bolingbroke added a perhaps more substantial criticism. Mr Pitt, he considered, was altogether too prone to 'mingle passions with business' and 'act out of anger to one or to another man'.[36]

CHAPTER FIVE

---◆◆◆---

The Assault on Carteret

Carteret's first moves upon the continent of Europe looked promising. While the Austrians threw back the French in Bohemia, Carteret added to Maria Theresa's subsidy of £300,000 an extra £200,000 for her ally the King of Sardinia; encouraged her to make peace with Frederick, so setting free more of her resources to fight France; and persuaded George II as Elector of Hanover to sign a defensive treaty with Frederick, who thus left the French in an over-extended position and France's Bavarian ally vulnerable to Austrian invasion. Carteret himself travelled to Holland to try rousing the Dutch to more active war measures which might attract Saxony and perhaps other German states into a grand anti-French alliance. At the same time a British fleet off Naples persuaded the Bourbon Don Carlos (the future Charles III of Spain), under threat of bombardment, to withdraw his contingent from the forces attacking Austria. In Flanders a large allied force – the so-called Pragmatic Army – of British, Dutch, Austrians, Hessians, and Hanoverians was being assembled under the command of Lord Stair, a fiery veteran eager to be allowed to conduct a swift campaign towards Paris itself.

Pitt, equally eager to launch his attack on this administration that had turned its back on him and his friends, had so far had little to get his teeth into. Parliament would in any case not be meeting till November. By then, although there had been grumbles at the inactivity of the allied army and at British money being paid to support Hanover's troops, vigorous British diplomacy did seem to have helped to rescue Maria Theresa (though at the price of Silesia), forced the French out of Westphalia, and revived something that began to resemble the Duke of Marlborough's Grand Alliance. When Parliament met it was observed that all the members of the Prince of Wales's party sided with the administration, except only two, Pitt and Lyttelton; and after Pitt spoke on the address following the King's Speech, Henry Fox, that once

77

favourite pupil of Walpole and rising star now among junior ministers, noted that 'the Prince labour'd and labours for us as much as he [earlier] did for his own question, and says Pitt might as well have spit in his face as spoke as he did'.[1] It was only a little over three years since the Prince kissed him in the House; now it was assumed that both Lyttelton and he must soon be dismissed from their places. It was agreed too that Pitt must now be regarded as the real leader of the Commons opposition. With his 'pompous and sarcastical oratory', wrote Richard Glover, 'he was the most distinguished among the younger sort . . . and took the lead'. And Lord Hardwicke's son Philip Yorke considered him 'the most popular speaker in the House of Commons and at the head of his party'.[2]

What Pitt actually said on this occasion is unrecorded, though Richard Grenville, reporting to his brother George, thought 'he spoke like ten thousand angels'. Richard Grenville, not at all put out by the size of the government's majority, was characteristically appreciative, too, of his own performance in the debate, and delighted to note 'how colloguing and flattering all the ministers are to us, notwithstanding our impertinence'. But the *pièce de résistance* would have to wait for the coming tussle over the Hanoverian troops: 'We shall then see who are Hanoverians and who Englishmen'.[3]

This was the issue which would give Pitt and his friends a chance to pillory the government and wring the maximum advantage from their countrymen's endemic xenophobia. That George II should be a German, with German habits and speech, a German wife and mistress, German tastes, and long absences in Germany,* had to be accepted as a minor misfortune attendant upon the blessings belonging to a free and protestant England. That the King of England was also Elector of Hanover was acceptable so long as Hanover was kept in its subordinate place. That wars should have to be fought against Spain or France was part of the nature of things, and if in order to fight them Britain needed allies, then her traditional and 'natural' allies would be the Dutch and Austrians together with such other European states as could be bought or persuaded into the arrangement – and after 1714 it was only

* Once when 'in a good humour', George II pointed out to the Prussian ambassador 'that the people here were angry at his going to Hanover, when they went all out of town to their country-seats; but it was unjust, for Hanover was his country-seat, and he had no other' (Marchmont Papers, i. 54).

reasonable to include Hanover. What would not be reasonable was for Britain either to be encumbered with a war to please Hanover, or to pay honest British taxes to satisfy Hanoverian interests.

When the French in the spring of 1742, deserted by Prussia, had withdrawn their army from Westphalia, a relieved George II had decided to cut his Hanoverian expenditure by reducing the number of his troops. Carteret, and at this stage a still more or less united cabinet, had agreed that this would serve to weaken the alliance, and offered to take the Hanoverian forces into British pay and

> to advise his Majesty to order sixteen thousand of his Electoral troops to march forthwith with the six thousand Hessians in the pay of Great Britain, to join the sixteen thousand British troops and the Austrian forces at such rendezvous as shall be thought proper to support the Queen of Hungary and the interest of the common cause.[4]

From a military point of view it was common sense; but British opinion was touched on a sensitive spot. Chesterfield ('Jeffrey Broad-bottom') was one of those who had already hastened into print with several magazine articles and an anonymous pamphlet on the subject* – a 'detestable' production, old Horace Walpole said, which had been 'very industriously dispersed among the people', and was aimed at 'inflaming the lowest classes'.[5] The prevalent popular anti-Hanoverianism was well summarized by George Grenville:

> It is therefore not only certain that these troops, these boasted and important troops, have not yet been of any use; but probable that no use is intended for them, and that the sole view of those who have introduced them into our service is to pay their court by enriching Hanover with the spoils of Great Britain.[6]

When the Commons debated the issue on 10 December 1742, Pitt rose immediately after Fox, who had been arguing that though it was a pity to have to rely on mercenaries, surely at least *Hanoverian* mercenaries, owing allegiance to a prince who was also the British monarch, were

---

* *The Case of the Hanover Forces in the Pay of Britain*, of which Chesterfield is the most likely author, though Horace Walpole thought that Dodington, Lyttelton, and Pitt all had a hand in it. It was answered by Horace Walpole the elder in *The Interest of Great Britain Steadily Pursued*.

likely to provide a better purchase than any other. He would therefore vote for the continuance of the government's measures until he heard of superior proposals. This gave Pitt, that now very dextrous debater, his opening, typically at once gracious, neat, and 'sarcastical':

> Sir, if the hon. gentleman determines to abandon his present senti-
> ments as soon as any better measures are proposed, I cannot but
> believe that the ministry will very quickly be deprived of one of
> their ablest defenders; for I think the measures which have hitherto
> been pursued so weak and pernicious that scarcely any alteration
> can be proposed that will not be for the advantage of the nation.

The sarcasm continued, with careful touches imputing incompetence and cowardice to these foreign troops, willing, he implied, to fight to the last Austrian soldier and British taxpayer:

> The troops of Hanover, whom we are now expected to pay,
> marched into the Low Countries indeed, and still remain in the same
> places; they marched to the place most distant from the enemy,
> least in danger of attack, and most strongly fortified . . . They left
> their own country for a place of greater security.

Britain had hired Hanoverians, in fact, 'to eat and sleep'. 'Neither justice nor policy' required Britain to engage in the quarrels of the Continent; the confidence of the people was 'abused by making alliances'. 'We are told the Dutch would join us, but they say that was never their intention'. In any case if honour did commit this country to assisting the Queen of Hungary, was not the Elector of Hanover committed no less than the King of Great Britain? Why then was he seeking to escape his obligations? Of course he *would* without doubt have sent his proportion of troops to the Austrian army, had not the temptation of financial profit been laid before him by the 'pernicious counsels' of his ministers. Here Pitt was having recourse to the well-known fiction that the King's misdeeds were always the work of his advisers, but there was no diluting the vitriol in the long unforgiven words that followed:

> It is now too apparent that this great, this powerful, this formidable
> kingdom, is considered only as a province of a despicable Electorate
> . . . To dwell upon all the instances of partiality which have been

shown; the yearly visits that have been made to that *delightful* country; to reckon up all the sums that have been spent to aggrandize and enrich it, would be an irksome and invidious task.[7]

'*Hanover* is the word given out for this winter,' wrote Horace Walpole. The political scene was dominated by it as decidedly as were fashionable card tables by the current craze for 'whisk'. Because of the Hanover troops Lord Gower refused to attend cabinet meetings. Lord Cobham, who had been promoted to field-marshal on the fall of Walpole and had had the colonelcy of a Horse Guards regiment restored to him, resigned his new command over the Hanover issue. Anxious, as he said, to 'blow the Hanover flame to the height', Chesterfield spoke as violently against the Hanoverians in the Lords as Pitt in the Commons – and outside parliament even more strongly: 'If we have a mind', he said, 'effectually to prevent the Pretender from ever obtaining this crown, we should make him Elector of Hanover, for the people of England will never fetch another king from thence'.[8]

Inside the cabinet the Pelhams* and Hardwicke, who had in the summer of 1742 resisted Lord Stair's 'wild scheme' of a march on Paris, now felt that it was George II and Carteret who were over-cautious and irresolute. 'The King', wrote Newcastle, 'was unwilling to expose his Hanover troops' to the risk of crossing the Rhine into Germany to winter there, and 'thus the whole campaign was sacrificed once more to the alarms for Hanover'.[9] When the allied army did make contact with the French in June 1743 it found itself not upon the road to Paris but at Dettingen by the banks of the Main near Frankfurt, and under the personal command of George II, who had set out the previous month for the Netherlands and Germany, accompanied by his second son the Duke of Cumberland, his Hanoverian mistress Lady Yarmouth, and Lord and Lady Carteret. Dettingen was a battle which the French, in superior numbers and with a tactical advantage, ought to have won but threw away by rash errors. Early on, the King's horse took fright and bolted, but the King himself, sword in hand

---

* The Pelhams: that is, Thomas Pelham-Holles, among the richest and most powerful of the Whig magnates; supremely diligent political manager; by 1743 already in his twentieth year as Secretary of State; and his younger brother Henry Pelham, no less a ministerial veteran – a lord of treasury under Walpole as far back as 1721, and then successively his Secretary-at-War and Paymaster General. First the younger, and then the elder, brother were of course in time to become First Lord of the Treasury.

and trusting eventually to his feet, emerged with credit and a sort of victory – which Pitt nevertheless insisted on describing later as merely 'a fortunate escape'. At least it caused the French to recross the Rhine and retire out of Germany, even if the allied army left its wounded on the field (as again Pitt did not fail to remind the public)[10] and did not follow up its advantage. George's alleged heroism, enthusiastically reported upon by Carteret, who observed the battle from his coach, proved unhappily a nine days wonder. It was true that he had led the British and Hanoverian infantry to beat back the rash advance of the French; that there were thanksgivings in St Paul's and a new Handel *Te Deum*; and that the town was briefly mad with 'drums, trumpets, bumpers, bonfires!'[11] But it later appeared that the King, however unflinching under fire, had throughout preferred the advice of his Hanoverian to his British generals, and had undeniably and unpardonably, and no doubt proudly, gone into battle wearing his yellow Hanoverian sash. The Duke of Richmond, Colonel of the Blues, complained of 'our dear Master's venal partiality for those damned Hanoverians', and many more officers wrote home in the same strain. The Hanoverian General Ilten had 'hindered the [British] Guards from engaging', reported Walpole; these 'maiden heroes... call him "the Confectioner", because he says he *preserved* them'.[12] Preference for Hanoverian advice during the battle, and the resumed inactivity of the army after it, which was attributed to the desire of the King to play German politics and above all to safeguard Hanover, were the chief causes of the disgruntled resignation of Lord Stair two months after the battle. Newcastle himself, Carteret's fellow Secretary, complained that the notion seemed to be 'to prefer the welfare of the Germanick body to all other considerations';[13] and Carteret, as Robert Pelham wrote to Pelham, 'gains the King by giving in to all his foreign views'.[14] In fact, after Dettingen, during the summer and autumn of 1743, Carteret saw himself as subservient to nobody, but rather in the majestic role of one 'knocking the heads of the kings of Europe together, and jumbling something out of it that may be of service to this country'.[15] While the Pragmatic Army vegetated by the Rhine at Hanau, Carteret, manoeuvring the promise of subsidies and the projects of treaties with half Europe, was trying to square the diplomatic circle. And upon his return he 'carried all with a high hand, and treated the rest as ciphers'.[16]

So long as Carteret was dominant, Pitt's chances of forcing his way into office were negligible. If, however, the tensions within the cabinet should become insupportable, the Pelhams and their friends might well have need of Pitt and those around him, such as Chesterfield. Already, as early as July 1743, political bricks had been loosened by the death of the apparently irrelevant First Lord of the Treasury, Wilmington. (He had gone off to Bath six months earlier, but that, as Horace Walpole's bland brutality had it, was only to pass away the time till he died.)[17] In his place the King, privately advised by Robert Walpole (Lord Orford) chose to appoint Henry Pelham in preference to Carteret's candidate, Pulteney (Lord Bath); and Pelham was one of those who saw advantage in coming to an accommodation with those members of the opposition who could be, as Chesterfield put it, 'softened'. A chink of promise appeared to be opening for Pitt, and between July and November 1743 there were several private meetings between the Pelhams, the 'Cobham squadron' and other members of the opposition. Things proved for the time being too difficult to arrange, and the Pelhams resolved to live with the 'insolence' of Carteret a little longer.[18] Meanwhile, Pitt was chosen as one of a committee of six, three Whigs and three Tories, to concert opposition tactics. As Parliament prepared to reassemble, Horace Walpole managed to sound at once despondent and detached:

All is distraction! no union in the Court; no certainty about the House of Commons: Lord Carteret making no friends, the King making enemies: Mr Pelham in vain courting Pitt etc., Pulteney unresolved. How will it end? No joy but in the Jacobites.[19]

From the session's opening day Pitt threw himself into a full-scale assault on Carteret. He began with a long and magisterial review of foreign and military policy over the past three or four years. Ministers had made every possible mistake. They should at the start, under Walpole, have encouraged Maria Theresa to settle for the loss of Silesian territory and thereby earned the opportunity to gain the powerful alliance of Prussia. (Instead, 'having led that Princess upon the ice . . . we left her there to shift for herself'.) They should have attempted to establish a German confederacy opposed to France, while themselves concentrating on the 'just and necessary war against Spain'. Then Carteret had burst upon the scene:

Our new minister . . . ran into an extreme quite opposite to that of the old. Our former minister thought of nothing but negociating, when he ought to have thought of nothing but war; the present minister has thought of nothing but war, or at least its resemblance, when he ought to have thought of nothing but negociation.[20]

This last might well have seemed quite outrageous to Carteret, who had just spent the months after Dettingen in a depressing morass of negotiations and been generally blamed (as he was later in this same speech to be blamed again by Pitt himself) for failing to follow up Dettingen with active measures of war.

During a later debate Pitt gave the House his general view of the sort of foreign policy Britain ought to have been pursuing. Though time and circumstance would force him to modify his doctrine and rob it of its neat simplicity, a belief in the essential correctness of a blue-water strategy was always to remain with him:

I lay it down, Sir, as a certain maxim that we should never assist our allies upon the continent with any great number of troops. If we send our troops abroad, it should be rather with a view to improve them in the art of war than to assist our allies . . . The only manner in which we ought to support [Maria Theresa] and our other allies upon the continent is with our money and our ships. My reason for laying this down as a maxim is, not only because the sea is our natural element, but because it is dangerous to our liberties and destructive to our trade to encourage great numbers of our people to depend for their livelihood on the profession of arms . . . For this reason, we ought to maintain as few regular soldiers as possible, both at home and abroad. Another argument on this subject presents itself: our troops cost more to maintain them than those of any other country. Our money, therefore, will be of most service to our allies, because it will enable them to raise and support a greater number of troops than we can supply them with for the same sum. I shall prove my assertion, Sir, with figures – stubborn obstinate figures, which neither bend nor vary at the will of a minister and his friends . . .[21]

But Pitt was far from confining himself to such general principles. All the venom which he had turned on Walpole two years before was now concentrated on Carteret, 'the Hanover troop minister', 'an execrable, a sole minister, who had renounced the British nation, and seemed to have drunk of the potion described in poetic fictions which made men forget their country'. On 6 December he was called to order for attacking persons, and not speaking to the motion, when he referred to the King as being on the brink of a precipice, in need of being snatched 'from that gulph where an infamous minister has placed him'. Undeterred, he insisted that at Dettingen, where Lord Stair had not been consulted and General Ilten, the Hanoverian, had been promoted 'out of his turn', the King had been 'hemmed in by German officers and one English minister without an English heart'. The little finger of Lord Carteret, that 'desperate and rodomontading minister', had 'lain heavier upon the nation than the loins of an administration which had continued for twenty years'. His only party were 'the 16,000 Hanoverians, the placemen by whom he has conquered the Cabinet . . . the source whence these waters of bitterness flow'.[22]

In these polemical pyrotechnics Pitt was both careful and reckless: careful to see that it was only Carteret who was singled out for attack, while the Pelham contingent was either ignored or, on one occasion, given honourable mention as 'the amiable part of the administration'; reckless, in that some of the rockets fired at Carteret could hardly fail to land in the King's lap. And while Carteret, weak in parliamentary backing, rested his security upon the King's approval, the King saw in Carteret the most capable and sympathetic of possible ministers. If Pitt had been unambitious for office, such onslaughts as he now made would have mattered not at all. He could have thundered away to his heart's content and enjoyed the shocked admiration of his audience in the Commons and the delighted applause of his public outside. But he had no mind to become a mere *enfant terrible*; he was hungry for advancement; and if Carteret committed the mistake of imagining the key to the Closet the talisman of power, Pitt now fell into an opposite error. The day would indeed come when he might 'storm the Closet' by virtue of his indispensability in a national crisis, but it was not to be for a long time yet. He was far from indispensable in 1743 and '44; and he allowed his exuberant oratory not only to attack the policies of the minister but also to impugn the character of the monarch – offensively enough in George II's judgement to cause Pitt to be disqualified from high office for more than a decade.

By January 1744 he had implicitly charged the King with inattention to British interests, with favouritism to foreigners, and with military incompetence. And he had added to the untenable charge of cowardice on the part of the Hanoverians an imprudent belittlement of the King's own personal courage, touching him on his proudest and tenderest point: 'Suppose', he suggested, 'it should appear that his Majesty was exposed to few or no dangers abroad but what he is daily exposed to at home, such as the overturning of his coach or the stumbling of his horse . . .' It was an unworthy and unprofitable supposition; but the desire to make a trenchant effect, the passion to strike fire, often overpowered his cooler judgement, and there was long to remain with him the sort of problem faced by an author who has difficulty in living down the *succès de scandale* of his youth.

Serious national danger threatened in February 1744, when the French were observed to be making preparations for a descent upon the Channel coast. One squadron was reported already to have left Brest and to be heading for the Dover Straits, while at Dunkirk, together with transports and an army under de Saxe, was the Pretender's son Charles Edward. On 15 February the King sent a message to Parliament announcing that the Pretender was planning an invasion 'in concert with disaffected persons in England'. One of the most suspect of these, Lord Barrymore, was arrested.

The opposition used the opportunity to demand why the fleet was unready; and according to Egmont their leaders 'spoke with passion to inflame the House'; he specially named Dashwood and Pitt, who 'railed according to his usual manner'.[23] Horace Walpole mentions Waller and Dodington, 'supported in the most indecent manner by Pitt'.[24] Pitt did in fact speak and vote with the opposition, but he protested against any suggestion of disaffection to the dynasty – still however managing an anti-ministerial flourish:

If there are any grounds for asserting it, what could be more impolitic than to animate the French with such an encouragement to prosecute their design? If there are none, as I am inclined to believe, how monstrous is it in any minister to poison the fountains of truth, and fill the nation with mutual jealousies and mistrust?

There was in fact no reason to complain of the Admiralty's sluggishness, or of any inaction on the part of Sir John Norris, in vigorous command of the fleet at the age of eighty-four. There was a week or two, however, of acute fright, and when the government proposed the precaution of suspending habeas corpus, Pitt showed his sentiments by ostentatiously leaving the Chamber while an opposition member was speaking against the measure. And he won praise from Pelham when he deprecated alarmism. The fleet was out, he said, and might intercept the embarkation (it was 24 February, the same night that Norris's fleet, in superior numbers and position, came within eight miles of the retreating French off Dungeness); and should the French land, he could not 'think any so desperate, or so mad as to think of joining in the attempt . . . If confidence was ever to be placed in ministers, it was at the present crisis'.[25]

Though this was a new sort of language to come from him, it by no means excluded fresh attacks on Carteret and his 'impracticable' war – which was now at last formally and mutually declared, and on land going strongly in favour of the French. The allied army, its British, Dutch, and Austrian generals in dispute and disarray, performed ignominiously against them in the Netherlands; the British subsidy to Sardinia reaped only defeats; and Frederick of Prussia, France's ally once again, invaded Bohemia. While Carteret prepared new subsidies, together with fresh contingency plans for the defence of Hanover and still wider coalitions to involve Saxony, Poland, and Russia, the foundations of his authority were crumbling, as coalitions of another kind were planned at home by those, both inside the government and among the opposition, who were anxious to bring him down.

CHAPTER SIX

Manoeuvres and Accommodations

Manoeuvres against Carteret came to a head in the autumn; but long before that, while many of the participants were enjoying the summer season on their estates, Pitt was suffering the first serious attack of the illness which was to dog him intermittently for the rest of his life – or rather one should say illnesses, for no simple diagnosis will easily fit the variety of his symptoms. One of his enemies was undoubtedly gout – 'regular' gout, that is, in the terminology of the eighteenth century. During the second half of his life Pitt suffered much acute pain and very frequent disability from the inflammatory condition of the feet, hands, and elbows which may properly be called gout.[1] But the trouble that attacked him in the spring of 1744 was gouty in no acceptable modern sense. His friends referred to it as 'gout in the stomach' – a designation in accord with the current medical orthodoxy, that peripatetic gouty humours were liable to settle upon the internal organs and would not be defeated until they were either excreted or driven into the extremities, from where they might be better eliminated. Hence many of those endless miseries of purging and blistering that accompanied eighteenth-century medical treatment. In Pitt's case the gastric and intestinal disorders that constituted 'gout in the stomach' were usually associated with the depressive states that incapacitated him, often for protracted periods. It may well be that during 1744 he experienced a first taste of these, together with the fever, insomnia, loss of appetite, and nervous prostration that accompanied later attacks. But the very sketchy nature of the evidence imposes some caution. When a modern interpretation of Pitt's various breakdowns suggested that he was a manic depressive, it became rather too easy to fit accounts of his condition and behaviour into a preconceived pattern of the disease. Thus it is reasoned that the anti-Carteret outbursts of 1743–4 must have marked the manic phase,[2] to be inevitably followed by the depressive sequel of 1744. But there seems to be no

convincing evidence to support this thesis, either in the speeches themselves (Pitt's speeches were seldom *under*-emphatic) or in the reported
manner of delivery (with Pitt this was always liable to be stagy), or
indeed in anything unusual in his behaviour over these months. Pitt
railed, Egmont had written, according to his *usual* manner. Moreover,
the theory itself seems to be based on the preconception that the type
of depression he suffered from must necessarily be preceded by a
manic phase marked by over-confidence and hyper-activity. This
appears not to be so; the peak preceding the trough, or even a succession of peaks, is not unusual; but commoner is the trough on its own,
or a succession of troughs.[3]

Certainly Pitt had had an active session. As well as repeatedly
intervening on issues of European politics and war, he had taken part
in several debates on fiscal and commercial policy. In February he
made the first of what were to be many defences of West Indian
mercantile interests, opposing on behalf of his City friends – these were
to be a growing company – an increase in the duty on sugar; and in
April he spoke in favour of opening up the privileges of the Levant
Company to all merchants prepared to pay £20 as entrance fee. None
of this, however, can be reckoned to argue 'manic excitement'; and it
is questionable whether it was the intensity of his parliamentary
activities that 'nearly killed him'.[4]

Nevertheless, he was ill, and at the beginning of the summer recess
in May he went off to Bath for a course of the waters. If, as seems
likely, he was suffering from a depression every bit as genetic in
origin as the gout which punished him so severely later, it is not
surprising that Bath failed to work any magic. But he remained there,
through the summer into the autumn, and little is heard of him while
the campaigning season on the continent saw nothing but success for
the French and Prussians, and up in London the Pelhams struggled
with Carteret for control of the government, and wheels revolved
within wheels in the complicated negotiations and intrigues for a
Carteret-free ministry 'on a broader bottom'. Everyone assumed that
Pitt, despite his mysterious indisposition, must become a member of
such an administration. Nevertheless, as late as October, James, third
of the Grenville brothers, found him 'in a very bad way, having never
been able to get rid of the gout in his bowels ever since it first seized
him . . . in the spring'. This, commented George Grenville, was 'a

grievous misfortune' for him; it might 'perhaps disable him, and make a cripple of him for ever'; possibly even 'affect his life'. This last expression can hardly have meant less than 'kill him', though Grenville adds that he 'cannot help thinking that his youth and ease are most likely to get the better of it in a great degree'. Plainly 'gout in the bowels' was something much worse than regular gout.[5]

To 'youth' Grenville added 'ease'; and if Pitt's physical condition remained distressful, his worldly situation that autumn did receive considerable ease. The Duke of Marlborough's aged widow had long been contemplating how best to dispose of her great possessions, and had decided that there might be worse ways than by rewarding her enemies' enemies, and thus combining a judicious philanthropy with a last snort against latterday iniquities in general and Walpole's in particular. In 1740 she had pressed £1000 on Hugh, Earl of March-mont (Pitt's fellow-'patriot' Lord Polwarth), whom she appointed one of her executors and to whom she spoke about a bequest to Pitt. Marchmont must then have consulted Chesterfield, whose reply shows which way the wind was blowing:

> My dear Lord, I share the marks of your friendship to Mr Pitt, looking upon everything that concerns him as personal to myself. I have not yet had the opportunity of speaking to him on the subject, and when I have I shall break it gently, knowing his delicacy; but in the meantime encourage her Grace in so right and generous a measure.[6]

Perhaps therefore, although the relevant codicil to the Duchess's will is dated as late as August 1744, two months before her death, Pitt had had the pleasure of dreaming of his fruit upon the bough before the wind blew it into his lap. The Duchess had been generous. Chesterfield, hardly a pauper already, received £20,000, and 'William Pitt . . . upon account of his merit in the noble defense he has made for the support of the laws of England, and to prevent the ruin of his country',[7] £10,000 in cash, and the potentially much more valuable gift of the reversion (jointly with Chesterfield) to the Duchess's very extensive unsettled estates, on the failure of the line of her grandson John Spencer. She further had persuaded this John Spencer, in the event of his own son dying without issue, to bequeath his Sunderland estates to Pitt too. When John Spencer did in fact die in 1746, only twenty months after his grandmother, there remained this one child's life between Pitt and two princely inheritances – only birds in the bush, certainly, but birds of brilliant feather. As things turned out, the Spencer child survived to have legitimate issue, so that these greatest prizes were never netted. But the bird in the hand was plump enough.

Plump enough, some in fact considered, to encourage Pitt to be unconscionably independent, and hence prickly, in his political attitude. One who found him so was Bolingbroke – an old man by now, but still busy and influential; once the inspiration and still the doyen of the Tory opposition, yet on good terms with important Whigs such as Hardwicke. During the summer and autumn of 1744 he exercised all his energies and charm in trying to find some set of formulae which might satisfy the maximum number of party groups and important private individuals, in order to oust Carteret and forge a new coalition. (No doubt, despite his claims to have put ambition by, he would not have refused some recognition for himself.) When Bolingbroke now arranged to see Pitt, he found his attitude altogether 'less reasonable' than before he had been left his legacy. Pitt, it seemed, difficult and puzzling as he was, had hardened his view of the old corps of Whigs, particularly of Pelham, and 'thought any union with them quite impossible'. They must concentrate instead on an intact *opposition*, and 'he hoped his Lordship would assist 'em to make their conduct systematical'. This distressed Bolingbroke, who could see no prospect of any such group ever becoming the majority.[8]

When Bolingbroke told Pitt his latest piece of inside information, that the Pelhams with the backing of most of the Cabinet, had gone to the King with an ultimatum, offering a choice between Carteret and themselves, Pitt reacted 'superciliously' – and failed moreover to show Bolingbroke the respect which as an elder statesman he expected. They ought to wait, Pitt pronounced, for 'some conjunction as would form a new epocha, such as the death of the King'.[9] Pitt seems, if only temporarily, to have felt that with his new-found financial solidity he could afford to wait for the next reign. After all, as the Prince did not fail to point out to Lord Harrington, 'My lord, remember the King is sixty-one, and I am thirty-seven'.[10] If this *was* Pitt's mood, it certainly did not last.

By the end of November the King, much against his will, was obliged to accept the Pelhams' terms. Carteret (now Earl Granville), with his friends, departed; Harrington became the new Secretary. Gower was again Lord Privy Seal; his son-in-law Bedford took the Admiralty, and their ally Sandwich had a place on the Admiralty Board. Hardwicke's son-in-law Anson, newly returned from the disasters and triumphs of his voyage round the world, was another of those given a seat on the Board. Most of the chief aspirants among the previous opposition were provided for. The deafness of Edmund Waller did not disqualify him from becoming Cofferer of the Household. Dodington's hunger for place and profit was quieted with the Treasure-ship of the Navy. Jacobite Tories were not excluded: Sir John Cotton became Treasurer of the Chambers, and Sir John Philipps and John Pitt of Encombe in Dorset, Pitt's cousin, became Lords of Trade. Of the Cobham squadron, Lyttelton had a place at the Treasury and George Grenville at the Admiralty. ('Do what you will', Cobham had said, 'provided you take care of my boys'.) Chesterfield, though the King bucked and jibbed, was given the important mission of ambassador to the Dutch, and simultaneously solaced with the Lord Lieutenancy of Ireland, a cabinet post; he chose Ireland, he said, because 'it was a place wherein a man had business enough to hinder him from falling asleep, and not so much as to keep him awake'.[11]

Surveying their handiwork, the 'old corps' might justifiably con-gratulate themselves. 'If your Majesty looks round the House of Commons', said Hardwicke to the King, 'you will find no man capable of heading or conducting an opposition'.[12] He omitted to mention Pitt, the obvious name of consequence missing in the new dispensation. 'The great Mr William Pitt,' explained Horace Walpole, 'to preserve his character and authority . . . was unwilling to accept anything yet: the ministry very rightly insisted that he should; he asked for Secretary at War, knowing it would be refused – and it was'.[13] Bolingbroke had heard a different tale, 'that Harrington prevented Pitt's being Secretary at War because of my Lady Young'[14] – that is, because Sir William Yonge already held the post and his wife's in-fluence with the new Secretary of State prevailed. Even Bolingbroke, who had so recently been listening to Pitt's talk of waiting for 'a new epocha', did not suggest that he would have refused the War Office if it had been offered. There cannot be much doubt that he strongly desired it; and perhaps the simplest explanation of his being left in the cold is also the likeliest – that the King refused to have him then, as he certainly refused later. And Pitt's complaisant mildness under the rebuff, his genuine or assumed lack of chagrin, his praise for Pelham and Pelham's government and Pelham's policies (even where these were remarkably little different from Carteret's) suggest that Pelham had engaged to keep Pitt's case before the King and support his claims, if Pitt on his side would be prepared to back the administration and thus help shorten his sojourn in limbo.

Only Lyttelton seems to have suggested that Pitt's poor health had been a factor in his exclusion; that, and as he cryptically hinted, 'some other little difficulties which he has seen fit to give way to'.[15] He undoubtedly remained ill and was unable to attend parliament until 23 January. When he then resumed his place, it was with the first of those self-dramatizing presentations of suffering for which he was to become so celebrated and in the eyes of the sceptical so suspect. 'He came down', reported Philip Yorke, 'with the mien and apparatus of an invalid'. When he spoke, his words demanded sympathy equally with his appearance; he compared his ailing condition to the country's own; and on this first occasion at least, even Horace Walpole denied himself his usual drollery and judged him 'very ill'. More; he allowed that Pitt's speech in support of the new government was 'very strong and much admired'.[16] Yorke, too, reported 'much grace both of action and elocution', and noted the disdain with which he rounded on the Tory squire Sir Roger Newdigate, who had ventured that though the ministry might be new, the measures were the old measures of Carteret. Pitt swept aside this thesis and Sir Roger with it, and generally carried off his *volte-face* with what Yorke considered 'fulminating eloquence'. He now *supported* the employment of 28,000 troops in Flanders; distinguished between Pelham's war and the 'capital errors' of Carteret, which he once again rehearsed; praised the new administration's 'moderate and healing measures'; and, in fine, 'thought a dawn of salvation to this country had broke forth'.[17]

A few weeks later Pitt gave further evidence of this new vein of brazen tact. The King had agreed to discontinue the direct payment of Hanoverian troops from the British exchequer, but parliament was being asked to approve a £200,000 increase in Maria Theresa's subsidy, and it was not denied that this was to enable her to employ the Hanoverians, or at least half of them. There can be little doubt that any such ingenious device used by Carteret a year before would have met the

93

pulverizing scorn of Pitt's invective. Now he was all mild reasonableness. The only objection to the earlier use of Hanoverian troops, it now appeared, had been that they and the British could not work *together*. Challenged on this by Sir Henry Liddell, 'Pitt carried himself in his reply with all the art and temper imaginable; he soothed and complimented Sir H. Lyddel, and at the same time put the question on a more just and acceptable light: that the hon. gentleman had quoted his words exactly, but mistook his meaning . . .'[18] The new arrangement was evidence of his Majesty's wisdom and goodness. There was no more suggestion of Hanoverian 'cowardice'; and 'God forbid', he said, 'that those unfortunate troops should by our votes be proscribed at every court in Europe'.

As if to burn his boats Pitt now resigned his place at the Prince of Wales's court – which, wrote Walpole, it was expected that out of solidarity with Lyttelton 'he would have done long ago'. (Lyttelton had been dismissed by the Prince on taking government office.) 'Winnington [the Paymaster] says, "Pitt is turned deist, and has renounced the Son for the Father"'.[19]

In 1745 the war brought only one victory of consequence, the capture from the French, by American colonial forces, of the fortress of Louisbourg, on Cape Breton Island; but there came a succession of defeats and alarms nearer home. At Fontenoy the British component of the allied force fought fiercely but unavailingly, and the French went on to capture Ghent and Ostend, and became masters of most of Flanders. In Lombardy they and their Spanish, Neapolitan, and Genoese partners carried all before them. Maria Theresa failed in an attempt to wrest back Silesia from Frederick the Great, who however was sufficiently alarmed by the successes of his French allies to reinsure his position by making a treaty with the British. But these same successes encouraged young Charles Edward Stuart, though himself unsure of French assistance, to gamble everything on a Highland rising, which he hoped would snowball southward and, given a dash of fortune, tumble down the house of Hanover – whose reigning representative, when Charles Edward came ashore on Eriskay towards the end of July, was enjoying his customary pleasures at Herrenhausen and did not get back to England until the last day of August.

When he returned, it was with the settled intention of changing his administration and restoring to office men who would pursue policies closer to what he thought proper; and in particular that meant Lords Bath (Pulteney) and Granville (Carteret), whom he had never ceased to consult in private.[20] Newcastle and his brother Pelham meanwhile, when he allowed himself to speak to them at all, had to put up with his growls and insults. 'The conduct of a certain person', observed a pained Henry Pelham, 'is worse than ever'. Ministers were in a quandary. The war was going badly; the storm cloud of the Jacobite rebellion hung over them. They would have liked to confront their ill-tempered master and show him that his partiality for Granville and Bath could not prevail against their own strength in both Houses; but so long as the rebellion remained undefeated, they decided that they must continue to bear their cross in the Closet, 'even with such foul language that no one gentleman could take from another'. They would continue to 'serve the King, to save him from destruction whether he will or no'.[21] Parliament was reconvened early on account of the emergency, in October, by which time the Jacobites had beaten the redcoats at Prestonpans and were heading south for Carlisle.

However unloved, at least George II was not a papist. Neither was he a tyrant, except of a petty and personal kind. A strong tide of patriotic sentiment was running therefore in favour of the regime; but there was no corresponding groundswell in favour of the government. Many members of parliament felt that so long as Bath and Granville monopolized the royal confidence 'there was in effect no administration to support'; hence poor attendance, erratic voting patterns, and Lord Strange's comment in the Commons that 'the House might as well adjourn for three months till the rebellion was over'.[22]

Pitt's tactics continued unpredictable. At first he spoke up as patriotically as anyone for the established order and the ministry, condemning an amendment in favour of 'freer and fairer representation of the people'. It was no time to 'render ministers odious in the eyes of the people', he declared. 'When thieves have burst into the mansion, the fool, only, would plan out methods to prevent the frauds of his servants'.[23] But a week later he moved that the King be requested to recall the entire British force from the continent, though presumably he knew that his motion must embarrass the government.

As a focus of opposition Pitt thus once more posed a problem for the Pelhams, and once more they tried to win him for the government.

At a conference with them on 25 October, Pitt and Cobham made three stipulations: first, there must be a place bill to exclude junior officers from the Commons – those 'puppy subalterns' who used their votes to gain promotion;[24] second, there must be a clean sweep of the remnants of Granville's supporters from the King's Household; and, infinitely more important, Britain must inform the Dutch that she was limiting her Netherlands commitment to 10,000 men and concentrating on a naval war. The King, strongly rejecting the second and third of these demands, urged upon the Pelhams that their parliamentary majority was not seriously in jeopardy from Pitt; and indeed another harassing Commons motion that he backed, for an inquiry into the *causes* of the rebellion, was very comfortably thrown out.

But when again the Pelhams came near to defeat on a suggestion that jobbery was involved in a proposal of the Duke of Bedford's for loyal private noblemen to be allowed to form their own regiments (and have the King's commission at their disposal for the officers), they once again approached Pitt. On this last issue he had in fact supported them, against the defection of many of their own adherents. There was exceptional parliamentary confusion.

This latest negotiation also collapsed, again over the question of disengagement from the continental war. And when in the Commons Pitt urged the immediate expansion of the navy – with his eye still on a maritime war – but failed to gain more than 36 votes against 81, he appeared to Horace Walpole to be left with nothing but 'his words and his haughtiness, his Lytteltons and his Grenvilles'.[25] In the course of this debate Pitt (so recently all mildness and tact) treated Pelham, in the opinion of Henry Fox, so harshly as to leave it 'hardly reputable for the latter ever to agree with him' in future.[26] He continued to give ministers no peace, pressing again for the rapid return of the remaining cavalry from the Netherlands and fulminating against the proposed import of *German* troops to meet the domestic crisis. Fox was always ready to praise Pitt's oratory; superior to his own, he allowed, though *he* had 'more common sense'; but over the troops from Germany, 'Pitt spoke ill', he wrote,

> and abus'd the City [of London] for being [in favour of] Hessians and Hanoverians too, as necessary for our security. He called them *shopkeepers* . . . To divide against both courts [the King's and the

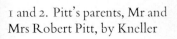

1 and 2. Pitt's parents, Mr and Mrs Robert Pitt, by Kneller

3. Sir Robert Walpole, by J. B. Van Loo

Prince's], abuse the City, leave the D. of Bedford, Ld Gower and ev'n Cobham, who in the Cabinet was for the Hessians . . . knowing that he should not divide more than he did, which was 44 only; making thus a bad figure and blinking his own ambitious views . . . is a conduct difficult to guess the motives of.[27]

By this time, the Jacobite tide had reached its full at Derby; hesitated while, for a few days, alarm in London was prodigious; and then begun to recede. The chief fears after the first week in December, as Lord Hardwicke wrote to his son Joseph, were of a less panicky sort, that the Highlanders would get back to Scotland unchastised, and join that growing army of rebels in the north; though there were nervous rumours too 'that the French were actually landing at Pevensey Bay, in Sussex', and an invasion, Hardwicke thought, was 'too reasonably apprehended'.[28]

During this year 1745 Pitt seems to have tried everything. He had 'alternately bullied and flattered Mr Pelham';[29] at times all apparent acquiescence, only to turn subsequently stubborn. 'To bring Mr Pitt in against his will', Newcastle remarked, 'is impossible'. The Pelhams reported at one moment 'great civility and good humour', and then, at the next, coldness and reserve. But neither humility nor arrogance, neither concurrence in ministerial policies nor presentation of stiff terms, neither singing of loyal praises nor the sudden sharp attack, had produced a satisfactory arrangement. Pitt was always a man of mysteries. On some of his qualities, however, everyone seemed to agree: his ability, his ambition, his masterfulness, his unpredictability. Horace Walpole was writing at this juncture of

> Pitt's wild ambition . . .; and he has driven Lyttelton and the Grenvilles to adopt all his extravagances. But then, they are at variance within themselves: Lyttelton's wife hates Pitt, and does not approve his governing her husband and hurting their family; so that, at present, it seems he does not care to be a martyr to Pitt's caprices, which are in excellent training; for he is governed by her mad Grace of Queensberry.*

* Walpole to Mann, 3 January 1746. In April 1747 Walpole was still imagining, or indulging the fancy of imagining, that he saw his *bête noire* the Duchess prompting from the wings: 'The majority was 233 against 102. Pitt was not there. The Duchess of Queensberry had ordered him to have the gout'.

Whatever the caprice, the ambition would not sleep. Office he must have. At the end of the year, therefore, he tried yet once more, initiating negotiations through the agency of Cobham. The insistence on a merely naval war was now abandoned, together with the other earlier stipulations. All that was now demanded was that the Cob-hamite Lord Barrington should have the Admiralty, Pitt the War Office, and James Grenville 'any employment worth £1000 a year'. These terms the Pelhams were prepared to accept, and they conveyed them to the King.

However, they were not yet masters of the situation. The King, tired of being managed by his ministers – 'forced or threatened', as he complained to Hardwicke – tried to construct, from the nucleus provided by Bath and Granville, a new government which would be wedded to active continental measures. And after his audience on 6 February Bath was delighted to be able to inform Harrington (whom the King had vainly tried to lure away from the Pelhams) that he, Bath, had 'put a negative on Pitt's being Secretary at War'. George had declared that if they made him take Pitt, he promised to use him badly and would never admit him to his presence. Four days later Hardwicke, Harrington, and the Pelhams decided upon a trial of strength. They resigned.

Bath's projected ministry was never more than a royal mirage. Backing for it in the Lords did not exceed 30, and in the Commons 80. The 'shopkeepers' of the City withdrew their offer of a loan to the Treasury. At Pelham's levee 192 members attended, in a demonstration of support.[30] The King, snowed under with Pelhamite resignations, declined to accept any more, acknowledged defeat, and invited his conquerors back. 'The King hated the people about him,' observed Chesterfield, 'but after having made a vain attempt to get rid of them, finding they had the Parliament, he was resolved to be quiet, and let them do what they thought fit'.[31]

When he heard that Bath and the King had agreed to put a 'negative' upon him, Pitt volunteered to relinquish his claim to be War Secretary. He had no desire, he protested, to force himself upon an unwilling monarch.[32] But Pelham *redivivus* needed him and was determined to have him.

When he again put Pitt's name forward for Secretary at War,

George again declined to accept it. The next best arrangement had therefore to be settled for, and Pitt received instead the sinecure post of joint Vice-Treasurer of Ireland. This did not involve contact with the King; it did not necessitate going to Ireland; and it was worth a handsome £3000 a year. 'I don't doubt but you will be surpris'd that Mr Pitt should be thought on for so high and so lucrative an employment,' wrote Pelham to Lord Ilchester, 'but he must be had, and kept. This will do it . . .'[33] For Pitt it brought not only governmental office at last, at thirty-seven; it offered also a prospect of something like opulence. But in several ways it marked a come-down. 'Patriotism', sneered Walpole, 'has kissed hands on accepting a place'. The stance of the disinterested patriot, the claim to an individual judgement uncorrupted by party or financial bonds, would for a time be more difficult to sustain – at least without a show of sublime impudence.

Impudence, however, was a quality Pitt never lacked. Certainly he was now lampooned and vilified, often from the quarters that had earlier given him loudest support. Cartoonists made much play with his decline from virtue. The Duchess of Marlborough's resentful ghost, for instance, was now depicted visiting him and declaiming vengefully against him, as his forehead was branded. That he was not insensitive to these attacks is perhaps to be argued from the care he subsequently took to advertise his scrupulousness in treating public money when he became Paymaster; but at least he contrived now to appear unabashed. When there had to be a defence made in the Commons for the expenditure of £300,000 upon 18,000 *Hanoverians* for the allied army regrouping in Flanders, it was Pitt who refused to assent in silence, but carried the thing off with elegant effrontery and assured members of his 'unembarrassed countenance'. That phrase became the title of one of many satires upon his conduct circulating at this time:

> . . . Whilst Balaam was poor, he was full of renown;
> But now that he's rich, he's the jest of the town.
> Then let all men learn by his present disgrace,
> That honesty's better by far than a place . . .

Pitt, Lyttelton, three Grenvilles and Lord Barrington all voted for the Hanoverians, Horace Walpole tartly observed –

though the eldest Grenville [Richard], two years ago had declared in the House that he would seal it with his blood that he would never give his vote for a Hanoverian. Don't you shudder at such perjury? . . . Pitt was the only one of this *ominous* band who opened his mouth, and it was to add impudence to profligacy.[34]

'Profligacy' is perhaps rather an odd expression to be coming from Walpole, for the accepting of a sinecure; from his glass house perhaps an imprudent stone. But undoubtedly Pitt had given the cynics an outing. And was it possibly George II's sense of mischief that prompted him now to suggest Pitt as the best person to move the additional parliamentary grant of £25,000 a year to the Duke of Cumberland for his services in quelling the Jacobite rebellion, which perished that month on the blood-soaked moors of Culloden? And what sentiment persuaded the Duke himself to decline, not of course the grant, but the honour of its being proposed by Mr Pitt?

A few weeks after Culloden, in May 1746, following the death of Winnington, the Paymaster, Pitt was promoted to take his place. This bringing with it membership of the Privy Council, George was at last obliged to receive him in audience at the ceremony of installation. After Pitt's recent display of renewed loyalty and tact the King was even ready to meet him without the hostility he had earlier shown on a like occasion to Chesterfield.

But a most cynical suspicion greeted the appointment, as earlier the Irish treasurership. Of all governmental posts the Paymastership of the Forces – in addition to providing a net annual salary of a little over £4000 – was the most notorious for furnishing perquisites and opportunities for heavy personal gains, especially in time of war. Paymasters had by custom become possessed of the right to invest for their private profit the very substantial public balances held by their departments, and also to take one quarter per cent upon all subsidies to foreign powers. In Marlborough's wars the Duke of Chandos had accumulated enough to build for himself the vastly fine palace of Canons, and have plenty to spare to sustain it majestically. Robert Walpole had taken the Paymastership to get, so he said, some fat upon his bones, and provided evidence of how well he succeeded by turning his manor house at Houghton into another palace. What Henry Fox later, and after him Richard Rigby, were to make of their tenure of the office became the subject of hot scandals. It was not unreasonable that in 1746 men of the world should be sneering at Pitt as one who had apparently mislaid his well-advertised principles and shown himself to be a hypocrite, as self-seeking as the next man. Lord Leicester, after listening to a fine dignified speech from Lord Kilmarnock, one of the Jacobite rebels then awaiting execution, remarked slyly to the Duke of Newcastle that he had never heard so great an orator; 'if I was your Grace, I would pardon him and make him *Paymaster*'. 'Whenever we become posterity and forefathers,' wrote Horace Walpole to Henry Conway, 'we shall be in high repute for wisdom and virtue. My great-great-grandchildren will figure me with a white beard down to my girdle; and Mr Pitt's will believe him unspotted enough to have walked over nine hundred hot ploughshares, without hurting the sole of his foot'.[35]

CHAPTER SEVEN

—◦◦—

The Pitt Style

'I have seen nothing of Pitt for some time,' Pelham told Lyttelton in October 1748. 'He has been a rambler, and among the various places he has visited, I am sure he cannot have forgot Hagley [the Lyttelton estate in Worcestershire]; which, though you call a farm, all your impartial friends tell me is an exceeding fine place'. At least until Pitt's late marriage, few men can have lived bigger slices of their lives as 'rambler', or guest at large. Nowhere was he anchored. To Richard Grenville in the summer of 1749 he confesses as much, referring to himself in a sort of serious banter as a 'changeling', and going on, 'When do you think of being at Wotton? Let me know, for I am at present on the parish'.[1] Whenever parliament was not sitting, which usually meant for the greater part of every year, from May perhaps to November and again over the Christmas recess, he was to be discovered peregrinating between the houses of his friends: at Hagley with the Lytteltons; at Wotton with the Grenvilles; at neighbouring Stowe – he was still 'in raptures' there on a 1749 visit; with his cousin John Pitt at Encombe, where the Purbeck hills ran finely down to the Dorset coast; at Prior Park, with that great man of Bath and philanthropist Ralph Allen, who quarried one fortune from local stone and another from improved postal services, served as the original for Fielding's Squire Allworthy, and became one of Pitt's great champions and admirers; at Wickham in Kent, with Gilbert West, Cobham's nephew, and his young sister Molly, who admired Pitt to a degree perhaps more than strictly platonic; at Radway in Warwickshire, with his friend the architect and antiquary Sanderson Miller;* or in company with Lyttel-

---

* Pitt called Miller 'the great master of Gothick'. Among his works were a new Hagley Hall for Lyttelton (this 'in the Italian style') and the rebuilt Great Hall of Lacock Abbey. Above his own Radway, on a hill-top overlooking the field of the battle of Edgehill, he built a commemorative 'castle'. 'Fertile Radway', wrote Pitt, 'where the sweet and the romantick meet the eye in looking up to your tower-cap't Edge Hill'. Fielding dedicated

ton again, to see the Peak Country, where 'the ground rolls and tumbles so finely' and from there to 'make a visit to my Lord Gower'. To Sanderson Miller in 1752 Pitt writes, 'Wotton and the Aylesbury Races have pravail'd over Lord Cobham's [Richard Grenville's] desire to see Radway and Hagley, and your humble servant is at present an appendage to his Lordship's motions'.[2] 'If I am an irregular correspondent,' he apologizes to William Lyttelton in 1750, 'you must impute it to my rambling about; for I lead so vagabond a life, that no letter scarcely reaches me so soon as it might'. Even after his marriage, in his forty-eighth year, Pitt was still writing to his nephew of his 'wandering Scythian life'.[3] He was just, as ever, coming from Stowe and proceeding to Wotton.

During those months when Westminster debates or Pay Office routine did not claim him, if he were not to be discovered on the estates of his friends, he might be looked for at one of those mineral spas whose reputations, supposedly therapeutic and undoubtedly social, were then at their fashionable height. Bath, of which he had been a freeman since 1738, he eventually made his own even in a parliamentary sense, though he did not have his own house there in the Circus until 1754. Bath saw him repeatedly, both before and after that, in search of relief from his gout and his more mysterious and less easily discussed maladies (as a puzzled Lyttelton described them, 'real or imaginary'); pursuing also, when his limbs and his disposition agreed, the town's polite amusements, and enlivening his friends with the animation of his talk, his 'most manly sense, and the fine sallies of a warm and sportive imagination'. He frequented other springs too: Astrop Wells in Northamptonshire; Sunninghill in Windsor Forest; fashionable Tunbridge; and he came to regard himself as an expert on these various waters, of whose virtues, despite the chronic persistence of his complaints and their resistance to treatment, he never appeared to grow sceptical. 'I have almost experience enough of the Bath waters to be a physician with regard to them,' he wrote to George Grenville in 1750. 'I advise Mrs Grenville to discontinue them a little, and try them again in small quantities . . . before she entirely gives up the use of them. I have done what I advise many times and with great benefit'.[4]

In August 1748 Pitt was writing, 'I have just returned from Tun-

---

Tom Jones to Miller, and it is thought that it was at Radway that he read some of it in the summer of 1748 to a company that included Lyttelton and Pitt.

bridge, and set down for a few days at my Lodge'. As usual, it was for 'a few days' only. His 'Lodge' was at Enfield, at an hour's drive from London, and it was his first venture in proprietorship. Since becoming Paymaster he had had an official residence in Whitehall, but he felt the need to stretch his wings and find a country establishment of his own, where he could indulge his architectural tastes and his growing passion for landscape gardening. In Enfield Chase he found South Lodge, set in sixty-five sylvan acres. He bought the lease in 1747 and immediately set about enlarging and improving the house, and creating in the grounds what his friend West pronounced to be 'a little paradise opened in the wild'. There were two lakes, one with a wooded island; a rustic bridge; such fashionable fancies as a Pyramid and a Hexagon; and in particular a much-admired Temple to Pan, in the Doric style, encompassed by a colonnade.[5]

Pitt modestly allowed himself as a gardener to possess 'the prophetic eye of taste'. His acquaintances were charmed and delighted by his verdurous vistas and classical rusticities, his oak dingles and bosky bowers. Henry Legge looked pleasurably forward to the winter prospect of war upon snipe and woodcock, and sessions when 'we will discuss politics, poetry, and that greatest of all the *Nepenthes*, nonsense *pro re nata*'.[6] Legge's tense was future; there exists no account of any of these shooting parties or feasts of sense and nonsense. There was a dissatisfaction of spirit in Pitt which forbade rest and turned him adrift from Arcadia. He once told Mrs Montagu he was never at Enfield a whole week at a time, and after five years he sold the place. With him the supreme pleasure was in the envisaging and planning. After he had constructed his little heaven it proved a heaven no longer. Much the same was to happen later at his Kentish home of Hayes; and not until his paradise was lost did he pant to regain it.

He became an acknowledged connoisseur of gardens and constructed landscapes, and his 'prophetic eye' was in steady demand upon his travels. At Gilbert West's Wickham he supervised the making of a garden walk. Noble opportunities offered themselves at the Lytteltons' Hagley Park in Worcestershire and in September 1747 Lyttelton and Pitt were busy 'contriving some considerable new improvements' to this 'British Tempe', of which Lyttelton was 'as proud as Lord Cobham of Stowe, especially since the honour Mr Tompson has done it in the new edition of his Seasons'.[7] Lyttelton was 'vexed' in March 1748 that fencing had not been found 'to enclose the plantation that Pitt marked out for the Cottage' – one of their new 'improvements', together with a Rotunda and 'Castle'. Pitt too would be disappointed: 'I won't answer for Pitt's coming to Hagley at Whitsuntide, especially as there will be no cottage built nor trees planted there; but in the summer I hope we are sure of him'. Indeed, in August Pitt was there, and writing to Lyttelton's brother Billy, then in Germany, 'I would not quit the Dryads of your father's woods for all the charms of Westphalia'.[8] Almost a neighbour of the Lytteltons, at The Leasowes, Halesowen, five miles away, lived the poet William Shenstone, whose little park and gardens Lyttelton exhorted all his guests to visit and admire. At Leasowes Pitt,

> Tho' form'd for Courts, vouchsafed to move
> Inglorious through the shepherd's grove;

and moreover, seeing 'several possible improvements which Mr Shenstone could not afford', vainly tried to persuade him to accept £200 to execute them.[9] At Radway it appears he was more successful in putting money with his advice, if the owner's doggerel says true:

> A Window there to take a peep
> Of Lawns and Woods and Cows and Sheep,
> And Laurel Walk and Strawberry Bank
> For which the Paymaster I thank,
> The Paymaster well-skilled in planting
> Pleased to assist when cash is wanting.
> He bid my Laurels grow, they grew
> Fast as his Laurels always do.[10]

He himself did nothing by halves, and he expected others to follow; 'Throw about your verdant hills some thousands of trees this planting season,' he wrote to his cousin by the sea at Encombe. 'Group away, my dear Pitt . . .' He loved this place of his cousin's as well he might. At 'dear unknown, delightful, picturesque Encombe', the fancy persuaded him that he could 'kick his heels and look like a shepherd in Theocritus'.[11]

With Pitt, a thing worth doing had better be done in style. It was during a stay at Tunbridge Wells with the Wests, in quest of a recovery in the summer of 1753 from one of his worst depressions, that Pitt and his friends conveyed Mrs Montagu and hers, with whom they had formed a holiday coalition, to drink tea *al fresco*

> in the most beautiful rural scene that can be imagined, which Mr Pitt discovered in his morning's ride about half a mile from hence; he ordered a tent to be pitched, tea to be prepared, and his French horn to breathe music like the unseen genius of the wood.[12]

To hire a tent and musicians for a little picnic was in the authentic Pitt manner. And as his nephew wrote, when he thought it worth while to exert his abilities 'as a private man he had especially in his youth every talent to please'.

The picture from his years of fame, of a man aloof and Olympian, prickly, haughty, affected, intimidating, is not false. He did thunder and lighten, flash his terrible eye, and seek those stage effects which only a formidably respected man could have carried off without absurdity – but even then behind the public façade and the parade of genius there were other more vulnerable, more fallible, though not always more accessible, Pitts. In these earlier years of his thirties and forties, though he was already practising his lofty Ciceronian manner, there is testimony enough of his sociability and charm, when his health and temperament allowed the sun to shine. It was true, said Chesterfield, that he showed 'too great a consciousness of his own superior talents'; but he was nevertheless 'a most agreeable and lively companion in social life, and had such a versatility of wit that he could adapt it to all sorts of conversation'.

No Boswell ever recorded his talk; and even the public speeches through which posterity has to guess at his eloquence are mere jobs of reconstruction and summary by fellow members of parliament or by reporters who were not officially allowed even to take notes. Some part of his compulsive power lay in his physical presence. Though his invalidism became chronic, he was tall, elegant, and upright in carriage; his voice was clear and musical; his gestures studied and graceful; his general appearance commanding.

He prepared rough drafts of some of his speeches but seldom delivered an ordered set piece.* He digressed. His argument would turn

---

* He 'much disapproved' the making of too many notes, except for intending authors. 'A common-place book . . . tends to impair the memory, and to deprive you of a ready, extempore use of your reading . . . My advice to you is not to common-place upon

in its tracks to stress a point made earlier. And sometimes he would
be desultory and rambling. 'When my mind is full of a subject,' he
admitted, 'if I once get on my legs it is sure to run over'.[13] His voca-
bulary was remarkably wide, and he laboured consciously to enlarge
it. Waldegrave, a peer, would not have heard Pitt in his own element,
the Commons, and he was certainly not prejudiced in Pitt's favour,
but his cool and judicious-sounding appraisal accords with most
contemporary opinion.

> Mr Pitt [he wrote] has the finest genius, improved by study and all
> the ornamental parts of classical learning . . . He has a peculiar
> clearness and facility of expression, and has an eye as significant as
> his words. He is not always a fair or conclusive reasoner, but
> commands the passions with a sovereign authority, and to inflame
> or captivate a popular assembly is a consummate orator. He has
> courage of every sort. He is imperious, violent, and implacable;
> impatient of even the slightest contradiction, and, under the mask
> of patriotism, has the despotic spirit of a tyrant . . .[14]

'His diction', wrote his nephew Thomas, another who was a long way
from being a blind admirer, 'flowed like a torrent, impure often, but
always varied and abundant'. His delivery was more often conversational than declamatory, yet on occasions he would work himself up
to a tearing passion, genuine or contrived; he seemed 'sometimes like
the lion to lash himself with his own tail to rouse his courage, which
flashed in periods and surprised and astonished rather than convinced
by the steady light of reason'.[15] He turned frequently to ridicule, and
his sarcasm was biting; but his touch could be light too – he could
tickle to death, said Horace Walpole, with a feather.

If his wit was sharp, flippancy was foreign to him. He was passionately serious: serious about himself and his career; seriously concerned
for the well-being and success of the nation; intellectually serious. He
never gave much of himself away; but during his forties, following a
fashion of the times, and somewhat in the manner of Lord Chesterfield writing to his son, he enshrined something of his views and
beliefs in the score or so of letters he addressed to his schoolboy and
subsequently undergraduate nephew Thomas, his unsatisfactory and

paper, but . . . to range and methodize in your head what you read . . .' (Pitt to Thomas
Pitt junior, 5 September 1754.)

unloved brother's son, who if Pitt had remained a bachelor was to have become his heir. The letters are earnestly affectionate, comprising partly an educational regimen, partly advice upon behaviour, taste and morals; didactic, stilted sometimes, solicitously avuncular. And the counsel for the nephew tells something, at least, of the uncle, when he is away from politics.

What books should a thirteen-year-old scholar be directed to? Of course, before any others to the *Iliad* (also Pope's translation of it) and to the *Aeneid* 'from beginning to ending'. Homer and Virgil were

> not only the two greatest poets, but they contain the finest lessons for your age to imbibe; lessons of honor, courage, disinterestedness, love of truth, command of temper, gentleness of behaviour, humanity, and in one word virtue in its true signification. Go on, my dear nephew, and drink as deep as you can of these divine springs . . .

Pitt's devotion to the classical, and in particular Roman, masters was conventional, but no sham. They formed the bedrock of his culture, and his speeches and letters are even more thickly bespattered than most others of his day with classical allusions and Latin quotations. Despite his eulogy of Homer, he clearly thought Greek a less useful study than Latin; a seventeen-year-old, at least, should not 'meddle' with it overmuch, 'otherwise than to know a little the etymology of words in Latin, English or French'. Nor should he bother with Italian. French was an important secondary study, with priority in its literature being awarded to Molière. But the practice of writing *English* verse he plainly regarded as a youthful self-indulgence (though he begged 'a copy of your Elegy on your Mother's Picture'); and he requested his undergraduate nephew for the present to desist: 'plunge deep into prose and severer studies'.

Of the great oratorical models, Cicero and Demosthenes towered above the rest: 'Arm yourself with all the variety of manner, copiousness and beauty of diction, nobleness and magnificence of ideas of the great Roman consuls; and render the powers of eloquence complete by the irresistible torrent of vehement argumentation, the close and forcible reasoning, and the depth and fortitude of mind of the Grecian statesman'. In history, both ancient and more particularly recent, Pitt was well versed, and his recommended reading for his nephew correspondingly thorough. Among philosophers, as might be expected, Locke came first.

Pitt was not closely bound to religious forms or much concerned with doctrinal niceties. He would never have agitated himself, as George Lyttelton did, over a doubt whether their friend Thomson, the poet, had or had not died a Christian. In general he fell in with the tolerant latitudinarian spirit of his day. 'Enthusiasm' he mistrusted, and strongly disliked what he called 'church spirit', that High Church intolerance of the sort that erupted, for instance, after Pelham's bill of 1753 seeking to permit naturalization of Jews. As for the 'errors of Rome', they stood for 'rank idolatry – a subversion of all civil as well as religious liberty, and the utter disgrace of reason and of human nature'. The errors of the Nonconformists, which 'turn upon the use of the surplice, the cross in baptism, and upon church government', were in an altogether less obnoxious category;[16] and he once, on an occasion just after his years of wartime triumph, went out of his way to correct Bishop Warburton for appearing in his book *The Doctrine of Grace* to equate them with what Pitt called 'the horrors of Rome'. Warburton, a fervent admirer of Pitt, had already 'altered and softened' his manuscript once to come more in line with what he dutifully described as Pitt's 'more precise ideas', and he prefixed the published version with a fulsome 'advertisement' in praise of 'our illustrious Modern'. (A second edition, while accepting another of Pitt's corrections concerning the liberty of the press, still however failed to satisfy him in differentiating properly between the venial heresies of Nonconformity and the detestable errors of Popery.)[17]

There is indeed, Pitt affirms, 'an all-wise and almighty Father constantly watching over his earthly children'. Man's duty is to hold him in 'reverential awe', though by no means in 'superstitious fear'. If you are not right towards God, he tells his nephew,

> you can never be so towards man . . . 'Remember thy Creator in the days of thy youth' is big with deepest wisdom . . . Nay, I must add of this religious wisdom 'Her ways are ways of pleasantness, and all her paths are peace.'

And later to his sister Ann, then ill with a 'sickly constitution of thought' likely to have been the twin of his own depression, he preaches the only remedy he supposes can cure: 'that mild and generous philosophy which teaches us the true value of this world, and a rational firm religion that anchors us safely in the confidence of another'.[18]

Pitt to his nephew is much like Polonius to Laertes: a similar conventionality of sentiment and solemnity of presentation, a similar worthiness of motive and precept. On the few occasions that he essays to be 'light' and 'literary', he pirouettes with lamentably flat feet. Thus, hoping that Thomas's health is recovered with the better weather and that he has abandoned the writing of verses:

> As the season of humidity and relaxation is now almost over, I trust that the muses are in no danger of nervous complaints, and that whatever pains they have to tell are beyond the reach of Esculapius, and not dangerous, though epidemical to youth at this soft month,
> > 'When lavish nature, in her best attire,
> > Clothes the gay spring, the season of desire'.[19]

Similarly, when writing to wish his friend Miller and the company at Radway a pleasant morning on the banks of the lake at Wroxton, Pitt makes heavy weather of his literary conceits:

> May the great landskip painter, the sun, spread his highest colouring o'er the sweet scene, and the fairest naiad of the lake frisk all her frollick fancy at the cascade, and be, what you must ever think a pretty girl, most charming in her fall.[20]

Humour was never his forte. Indeed, on the whole he did not think it wholly proper, being too insistent on the necessity of preserving dignity and elegance to be caught in the vulgarity of laughing. 'It is rare', he writes, 'to see in anyone graceful laughter'; 'it is generally better to smile than to laugh out; . . . the trick of laughing frivolously is by all means to be avoided: *risu inepto, res ineptior nulla est*'.[21]

'Mr Pitt', wrote Mrs Montagu to Gilbert West, 'mixes the elegant with the sublime'. Doubtless it was elegance that so frequently demanded ten words where plain speech would have managed with two; 'The post is going,' he writes to George Grenville in 1750, 'so adieu! It is impossible to be more sensible than I am of the manner in which you and Mrs Grenville are so good to accept my most sincere wishes for your health and happiness'. In the same manner that he tended sometimes to converse in private rather as though rehearsing a parliamentary speech, picking each word, as Chesterfield remarked, with elaborate correctness, his manner of writing became as ornate an artifact, and sometimes as opaque a mystery, as his private persona. 'I am still apprehensive', he writes to his nephew recovering from illness at Brighton,

> till I have the satisfaction of hearing from you, that your course of sea-bathing has been interrupted by such gusts of wind as must have rendered the sea too rough an element for a convalescent to disport in. I trust, my dearest nephew, that opening scenes of domestic comfort and family affection will conform and augment every hour the benefits you are receiving at Brighthelmston, from external and internal medical assistances . . .[22]

Gentility of style, correctness of behaviour, 'true politeness', 'grace of mind and limb' – these were the ideals of a gentleman. 'Genteel' for Pitt and his day was an epithet still entirely laudatory, with none of its later hints of the emasculated or the pretentious. For Pitt, to be un-genteel was to be awkward, 'revolting', 'offensive'. 'You are to qualify yourself', he told his nephew, 'for the part in society to which your birth and estate call you. You are to be a gentleman . . .' Proper behaviour, he was pleased to note, was a subject upon which Thomas had 'surprisingly little to learn', considering he had seen little outside Boconnoc, and been reared amid 'the very savage rocks and moors, and yet more savage natives' of Cornwall. Towards such inferiors, 'gentleness, condescension, and affability, is the only dignity. Towards servants never accustom yourself to rough and passionate language'. The better among them must be regarded as humble fellow Christians, the worse must be pitied, admonished, or dismissed if incorrigible.* 'On all occasions beware, my dear child, of anger, that daemon, that destroyer of our peace'. 'Towards equals, nothing becomes a man so well as well-bred ease, polite freedom, generous frankness, manly spirit . . .' Towards 'superiors in dignity, age, learning, or any dis-tinguished excellence, be full of respect, deference, and modesty'.

Even such counsels of conventional perfection tell their tale. It

---

* Later, Pitt's nephew (by then Lord Camelford) remembered that his uncle when he first knew him was as 'intemperate' towards servants as Camelford's own father Thomas Pitt. He allowed however that it was to his uncle's honour 'that when he owed a better example to his children he got the better of that habit'.

occurred to Pitt as little as to the overwhelming majority of his contemporaries that strong distinctions of class and rank and wealth were in any way to be deplored. One had superiors, and if one could climb to join them, well enough. One had equals. One had inferiors – how many inferiors! The natural order of society was not a subject for argument. Liberty was a fine and precious thing, which Englishmen must be proud and jealous of, and Frenchmen deserved pity for lacking. Fraternity was a respectable Christian theory, but not to be pressed too hard or far, even on Sundays. Equality had not yet raised its troublesome head. For Pitt the 'finest lessons' for the age to imbibe were still those he claimed were taught long ago by Homer and Virgil: 'honour, courage, disinterestedness, love of truth, command of temper, gentleness of behaviour, humanity, and in one word, virtue . . .'[23]

CHAPTER EIGHT

———◆◆◆———

The Pelhams' Paymaster-General

'Consideration of weight in the House of Commons arises generally but from one of two causes – the protection and countenance of the Crown, visibly manifested by marks of royal favour at Court, or from weight in the country, sometimes arising from opposition to the public measures'. This was Pitt's own reading of affairs; and, he went on, it was along the second of the two paths that he had proceeded until it became a dead end or, as he put it, 'as soon as I became convinced there might be a danger . . . from pursuing opposition any further'.[1] This is a clear enough acknowledgement of motive. Taking office in 1746, he deliberately chose to risk disappointing his public and losing some 'weight in the country' in order to acquire some 'countenance' from the Crown. He would not, however, if he could avoid it, throw away all the advantages of popular support. He therefore countered the cynicism which greeted his promotion to the Paymastership by openly denying himself the usual perquisites of the office. It was soon generally known that he had lodged the Pay Office balance with the Bank of England, adjured his personal commission on the £200,000 subsidy to Sardinia, and capped this by turning down the alternative of an equivalent amount offered by the Turin court as a gift. Such lights were not to be hid under bushels; Pitt had no sort of objection to the world's hearing that the Paymaster was bringing the highest standards of honesty and self-denial to the handling of public funds. Throughout his nine years' tenure of the Paymastership – which would have given time enough to add a second and greater fortune to his windfall from the Duchess – he continued to refuse the use of public balances for his private investment or to touch a penny of the foreign subsidies. In respect of his future standing with the nation his conduct afforded in fact the shrewdest of investments. He laid up for himself incorruptible treasures in the public mind, at the same time labouring conscientiously to gain the countenance of the King. The thousands of pounds forgone were a lesser consideration. Pitt was far from despising money. He spent freely, as befitted a gentleman; much too freely for wisdom, as time went by. But he had no avarice. Against 'weight in the country' and the esteem of his true constituency, the British people, the acquisition of a fortune would be a trifle.

In 1747 he had to find a new constituency, in a stricter sense. In that year Frederick Prince of Wales, who had for the past five years preserved broad support for his father's government, decided to resume hostilities, making an alliance with the Tories and issuing a sort of election manifesto which among much else promised 'to abolish for the future all distinction of party'. His chief election managers were now Francis Ayscough, tutor to his children, and Ayscough's brother-in-law Thomas Pitt, his impecunious and cantankerous Warden of the Stannaries, who was still of course master of the Old Sarum seat for which his brother William had come in for the second time in 1741. The two brothers were not only on cool terms personally but also now on opposite sides of the political fence. It was to the Pelhams therefore that William had to turn for a seat in 1747, and the Duke of Newcastle offered him one at Seaford, amid his own rich political pasture-lands of Sussex. The Duke's nod towards the rate-paying householders of that little borough, a small company of seventy or eighty, was by tradition electorally sufficient, and doubly so when graced by the civility of a bowl of punch or round of beer. Newcastle's recommendation to the voters of Seaford to recognize 'Mr Pitt's zeal for his Majesty's service' was duly dispatched, together with an indication that Mr Pitt, in the company of the Duke himself, proposed that week-end to be in Bishopstone, Newcastle's property near Seaford, when the intended new member would 'have an opportunity of being personally known' to the electors. Suddenly, however, upon this peaceful and secure fold ravening wolves appeared in the form of two of the Prince of Wales's men, Lord Middlesex and William Hall Gage, sons respectively of the Duke of Dorset and Viscount Gage, the latter of whom in particular was prepared to spare no expense to secure his son's election. Newcastle was bothered exceedingly by this 'impertinence' (his brother's expression; Pitt went so far as to call it 'persecution'); he assured Pitt that no quantity of Lord Gage's money should frustrate him; and gave him the exactest instructions in respect of their coming joint descent upon Seaford: '. . . if you would be so good as to be at my lodgings at Kensington in your riding dress at one o'clock I hope we may get away soon after and then we shall be in time . . . I hope you have sent your horses to East Grinstead'. Pitt's reply to the Duke indicates at the same time a proper awareness of their respective stations, and proffers the sort of soothing reassurances Newcastle always found necessary, together with a seemly gratitude – 'ten thousand thanks' from the beneficiary to benefactor

for the honour of your letter and for the trouble you are so good as to give yourself . . . I never can enough express the high sense I have of the honour of your Grace's friendship and goodness to me . . . I shall with great pride meet any persecution in which I have the honour to be joined with your Grace and Mr Pelham. I have sent on horses to East Grinstead and a post chaise, in case of rain, which I am too infirm to venture to stand. I will be sure to attend your Grace at the time appointed.

The Duke travelled to Seaford with Pitt on Saturday 27 June; gave the voters a dinner and a personal canvass on Sunday; sat improperly close to the returning officer upon the hustings on Monday, bending a ducal eye towards the votes as they were cast; and was thus able to congratulate Pitt and his fellow candidate Mr Hay on their being freely chosen to represent the popular will of Seaford in time for the new member to return to London on Tuesday. It was the nearest Pitt ever came to fighting an election campaign.[2]

His brother Thomas was less fortunate. As owner, he could without trouble put in at Old Sarum one of the defeated Seaford candidates, Lord Middlesex; but his failures elsewhere, especially upon his home pitches in Cornwall, were too numerous for comfort. 'I shall be ashamed to look the Prince in the face', he moaned, 'after the hopes I have raised in him'. He had been outspent and outmanoeuvred, and was 'most damnably mortified . . . I am vexed to the soul. What can I say?' His answer was given in the same strain of querulous fury that his grandfather and namesake had been used to employ forty years before, and his own father too in his latter days: 'I have been betrayed by villains,' he miserably protested; 'I shall hide myself at Boconnock, for I am ashamed of making appearance in the world'. He was 'full of passion and resentment', wrote his Cornish Vice-Warden, Hawkins, 'but I am so long acquainted with Mr Pitt's constitution that no behaviour of this kind either surprises or affrights me'.[3] Even Oke-hampton let him down, and elected George Lyttelton against the Prince's candidate.

From this time on, Thomas Pitt's chronically embarrassed fortunes grew steadily more desperate. His creditors pressed him hard, and he spent the years 1749 and 1750 in various abortive schemes for staving off ruin, like trying, jointly with Ayscough, to lease the farm of the Duchy of Cornwall tin mines, and unsuccessfully attempting to persuade Ayscough, a trustee, to release some of the funds held from the sale of Governor Pitt's estate of Swallowfield, where the boy William Pitt had once spent holidays from Eton. However, as George II approached seventy and must surely be succeeded by Frederick before much longer, Thomas Pitt could still survive upon expectations, which indeed were great. The Prince, even after the election results, thanked him for his 'zeal and trouble' and hoped he would be seeing him soon at Cliveden with his gun; and when Frederick began allocating among his supporters the satraps of his future empire, was not Thomas Pitt promised the rich Vice-Treasurership of Ireland (the very office William had briefly held before the Paymastership) – and with a peerage too?

In general, the elections went well for the Pelham party and their associates. Their confirmation in office persuaded even the King that since he had to have Henry Pelham and the Duke, he had better try to get on with them, and even like them. When parliament reconvened, Pitt's own election for Seaford gave rise to an unsuccessful Commons petition from the defeated candidates – such challenges were a regular feature of post-election sessions – on the grounds of Newcastle's corrupt interference before and during the poll, 'in order to awe and influence the voters'. Perhaps unwisely for one who had previously stood, and would often wish in the future to stand, against corrupt influence, Pitt decided to treat the petition as a subject for contemptuous fun – and was loftily rebuked for his cavalier attitude by one of the Prince of Wales's new members, Thomas Potter.*

Except when he felt impelled to pose as the champion of political purity – in his youth against Robert Walpole for instance, or in later

* Potter (1718–59), son of an Archbishop of Canterbury, is thought to have been the original author of the *Essay on Woman* that Wilkes later refurbished. During the middle 1750s he was to become one of Pitt's chief allies and associates.

years against George III's alleged abuse of power – Pitt in general accepted without much demur existing practices concerning influence and patronage. Some small part of the rewards of even such limited power as a Paymaster commanded lay in the opportunities it afforded to oblige one's friends; and with Pitt as with most of his contemporaries, it was only when opponents obliged *their* friends that one hinted at jobbery. One of those he could now take pleasure in gratifying – though the opportunity did not arise until 1754 – was his friend Gilbert West, for whom he found a comfortable place as paymaster of Chelsea Hospital. It was worth £1000 a year, wrote a delighted Mrs Montagu: 'it is in the gift of Mr Pitt and was given with a grace that few know how to put into action . . . Mr Pitt dined with [the Wests] on Saturday'. What a fine thing it was 'to act the part of Providence and bless the good'.[4]

West, a nephew of Cobham, constituted an extension of the Cousin-hood; the more politically active members of it, Lyttelton and the Grenvilles, Pitt continued to treat over these years as fellow members of a clan. Throughout his years at the Pay Office his Deputy Paymaster was James Grenville. And Grenvilles at this time always had his energetic support even when their conduct seemed to most others dubious and their ambition overweening. He flew to their defence when an angry little local quarrel escalated from Buckinghamshire to the House of Commons. (The matter occupies 44 columns of the *Parliamentary History*.) What the Grenvilles were fighting to reverse was a decision to move the summer assizes from Buckingham to the more convenient Aylesbury, where the jail was; but to have thus down-graded *their* Buckingham would have been regarded by the Grenvilles as an infraction of the sovereign rights of the kingdom of Stowe. The matter occasioned impassioned denunciations in the Commons of this 'all-grasping' family. But Pitt defended his friends – 'Sir, I take it to be no job, and I will prove it to be none'; and the status of the Grenvilles and of the Buckingham assizes were alike sustained.[5]

When Lord Cobham died in 1749, his hungry Grenville nephews lost no more than a few days before applying for an earldom for Cobham's widow, to devolve upon her death to Richard Grenville. Whether the title were to be 'Buckingham' or merely 'Temple' should not, the prospective earl considered, be allowed to constitute an obstacle. 'We will not kick down an excellent pail of milk by a wrong-headed obstinacy', he wrote to his brother George, 'but desire the title of Countess Temple . . . It will be proper to fix something exactly about Hetty as it will be necessary to know what to call her'. (She would duly be styled Lady Hester Grenville; although now twenty-eight, she was still unmarried.) For his part, the Hon. Richard Temple-Grenville, as he chose to be designated, would be able pending his aunt's demise to enjoy the courtesy title of Viscount Cobham.* Pitt was applied to for advice, and used such persuasion as he could in support; and although Newcastle thought, not unreasonably perhaps, that there should be a delay of, say, 'three weeks or a month', as the King had 'lately had a good deal of solicitation about peerages, etc.', the Grenvilles' thirst for grandeur was assuaged without untoward delay.[6]

Pitt's cousinly support was exercised also on behalf of John Pitt of Encombe, whose election for Wareham in 1747 was another of those unsuccessfully challenged by petition. Pitt never liked lawyers, and it seems that he handled the petitioners' advocate so harshly that the affronted man 'flung down his brief in a passion' and retreated with a vow he would never come to that place again. When in 1750 John Pitt, aspiring to climb, solicited for 'a new mark of his Majesty's favour' in the shape of a place to compensate him for making his Wareham seat available, Pitt supported him, Pelham was sympathetic, and John Pitt became the first member of the Commons to receive the sinecure stewardship of the Chiltern Hundreds – which having been awarded, he was returned unopposed for the neighbouring seat of Dorchester; as tidy a little job as could be.[7]

By contrast, however, there was little to be done for Pitt's brother Thomas, that 'bad man', as Horace Walpole called him ('never was ill-nature so dull as his, never dullness so vain').[8] When the Prince of Wales died in 1751, Thomas Pitt had to give up to Lord Waldegrave the Wardenship of the Stannaries that had stood between him and ruin. He opened negotiations with the Pelhams for his last remaining assets – Old Sarum, Okehampton, and Camelford – which he finally succeeded in pawning to the government for £2000 and a pension of

---

* Lady Temple died three years later. 'Lord Cobham will now be the richest man in England,' wrote Lyttelton, 'so you may expect to see new beauties at Stowe . . . I beg his pardon; I should have called him Earl Temple' (George Lyttelton to Sanderson Miller, October 1752).

£1000 during pleasure. But the downward slide was not arrested. After sending his son Thomas to Cambridge, his plight was such that in 1755 he was obliged to flee abroad from his creditors. He took with him his two daughters and at first intended taking his son too. The younger Thomas, towards whom Pitt already saw himself virtually *in loco parentis*, then informed his uncle that his books and rooms were about to be sold off; whereupon Pitt, having first consulted Sir Richard Lyttelton, another of young Thomas's uncles, intervened to take over responsibility for his nephew's education. Young Thomas did not however in his mature years remember with any affection the uncle who had come to his rescue and proffered him so much virtuous advice. He himself seems to have behaved honourably towards his luckless father, cutting his own entail upon the estate in order to settle debts and provide for his sisters, so that Thomas Pitt senior was eventually to return to England (and to remarry) before his death in 1761. But young Thomas clearly thought that his father had been hard done by. He obviously considered that Pitt, rising 'to the top of everything' at the time that Thomas was 'shipwrecked' should have done more for him; should have given him perhaps the post of minister to the Swiss Cantons that he once desperately begged. Pitt, however, set limits on the claims of family loyalty. He turned his brother down – no doubt on the reasonable grounds that the nation deserved to be represented abroad by those more dependable. When the young Shelburne met Thomas Pitt after this, living at Utrecht, he stayed up half one night listening to a violently bitter and perhaps half-crazy man pouring forth abuse against his by then dominant brother.[9]

By the time Pitt was appointed Paymaster most of the spirit for the war that had begun amid national jubilation in 1739 had already disappeared. However, after the capture of Louisbourg in 1745, Pitt was for a time excited by a prospect originating with Governor Shirley of Massachusetts and William Vaughan of New Hampshire, a wealthy fishing merchant, for an attack on Canada to be launched in 1746 by New Englanders with the aid of a British naval squadron and eight regular battalions. Shirley and Vaughan, together with Admiral Warren, who had led the squadron attacking Louisbourg, succeeded in selling the idea to the Duke of Bedford at the Admiralty, and Pitt strongly supported him. 'The nation is certainly with you', he wrote hopefully to Bedford; 'with such a second, your Grace can surmount all obstacles'. Naval and military forces were indeed prepared – those in New England fretted with impatience – but the project was deemed too ambitious and risky by Pelham and Newcastle; and in the end (to save appearances, so the elder Horace Walpole claimed) the ships and regiments that Bedford and Pitt would have liked to see sailing against Quebec were diverted to an assault, mismanaged, upon the Breton coast at Lorient. But the plans put forward by Shirley and Vaughan went on working within Pitt's mind. They were 'great and practicable', he decided; and in the light of events to come they are worth a closer scrutiny here.[10]

As Bedford set them out in a memorandum to Newcastle, five main arguments stood out. First, the conquest of the French North American colonies must mean 'the whole fish and fur trade, by both of which the French gain yearly such vast sums, besides the means of training up great numbers of seamen. Secondly, by this they will be debarred supplying sugar islands with provisions, lumber, and all things necessary for carrying on their sugar and indigo works, which must in the end prove their ruin, or at least enable our sugar planters to undersell them . . .' Thirdly, if France lost Canada and her West Indian islands she would lose a large export market for her domestic manufacturers. 'Fourthly, France will no longer have it in her power to build ships of war in America, and will be obliged to furnish herself with great masts and other things absolutely necessary for the building of great ships from [the Baltic] only, which will be a great means of keeping her naval force within due bounds'. Fifthly, Britain's own American colonies would never be secure until the French were expelled.[11]

All this remained for the time being a memorandum only. As Paymaster, Pitt had the task of compensating the colonial captains for their out of pocket expenses when the 1746 project withered away (to the disgust of the New Englanders). On the European continent, military fortunes continued during 1746 and 1747 to smile only on the French. Anson off Cape Finisterre, and Hawke off Belle Isle, gained important naval successes in 1747 (it was in the Finisterre action that Thomas, fifth of the Grenville brothers, was killed); but de Saxe's armies once again called the tune in the Netherlands and by early 1748, having invaded Holland, were laying siege to Maastricht. 'Mr Pitt and I', wrote Pelham, 'both see our condition so bad that nothing can be thought of but to take the lesser evil' of seeking peace. 'We fight

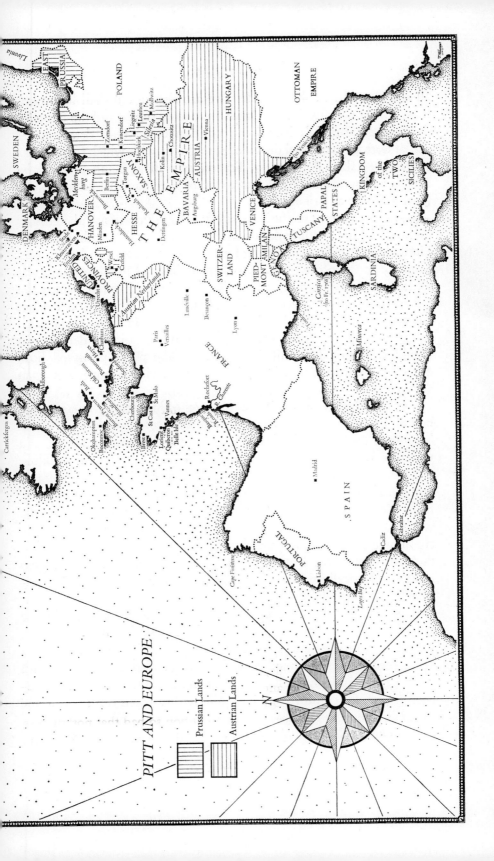

PITT AND EUROPE

Prussian Lands

Austrian Lands

N

all and pay all . . .' he said, 'but we are beaten and shall be broke'. If, as Pitt thought likely, the Dutch were to be ruined and the Emperor dispossessed, Britain's bargaining position could only deteriorate;[12] and at least the navy had provided some cards with which to go to the conference table. Fortunately, France, as well as being deserted by Prussia and weakened by the accession of Ferdinand VI in Spain, was quite as broke as Britain.

After nine years of confusing wars, few Englishmen remembered how they had begun, with Jenkins's ear and the right of search, and with Pitt and the Patriots clamouring for a war to teach Spain a lesson. And certainly at the peace of Aix-la-Chapelle in 1748 nothing much was settled; certainly nothing concerning the right of search, which the peace terms did not even mention. Madras was returned to Britain, and Cape Breton Island, with Louisbourg, to France. The French restored their European conquests and undertook to demilitarize Dunkirk. Prussia kept Silesia. In Europe the peace promised little other than a truce and a breathing space; outside Europe, not even that.

Pitt, who had always seen the greatness of his country as essentially bound up with mercantile expansion and colonial strength – the 'empire of trade' – was obliged to learn, over the ensuing decade, of a variety of unpleasant developments across the Atlantic: the building of a strategic chain of French forts which hemmed the British colonies in upon the Atlantic, and would give when completed a through-way from New Orleans in the South to Canada in the north, along the waterways of the Mississippi and the Ohio and the Great Lakes; the continuing growth of the French sugar business in the West Indies, to the detriment of the British, whose products it could undersell even in the theoretically protected British colonial market; the refortification by the French of Louisbourg, with its dominance over the St Lawrence estuary and its threat to the New England fisheries, of whose crucial importance Pitt had become almost fanatically convinced; and, associated with this last, the deteriorating British position in Nova Scotia, ceded after the wars of Marlborough and confirmed as British territory at Aix-la-Chapelle, but containing far too many unassimilated French for comfort, and increasingly threatened from both Cape Breton Island to the north-east and from new forts built on the mainland to the north-west.

It was American and West Indian affairs that most concerned Pitt; the situation in India, grandparental association notwithstanding, never exercised him so much. He did not maintain links with the nabobs of Leadenhall Street like those that kept him in touch with the City merchants involved in the Atlantic and Caribbean trade. In any case, the peace treaty had put Madras back under British control; and, for the rest, Pitt considered that Britain's best contribution to the East India Company's fortunes must be to dominate the oceans, keep open the channels of British trade and reinforcement, and be able when necessary to block those of the French. Above all, he was impressed by the immense advantage which Britain ought to enjoy in North America in any war waged between Britain and France. British settlers vastly outnumbered French. It was volunteers raised in America that had taken Louisbourg. Who could tell what similar forces, properly stiffened and given naval support, might not do in Canada or the West Indies? As long ago as 1739, when the immediate enemy was not France but Spain, Lord Stair had written: 'The Havannah could be taken by troops raised in America. I mention the Havannah only, because *cela décide de la guerre* . . . By the means of our colonies in America Britain should get the better of any nation in a war in America'.[13] These views corresponded exactly to Pitt's, and he did not fail to put them before the Duke of Newcastle, whose principal attention however remained concentrated upon the shifting complications of the European scene.

When Pitt looked in that direction, he thought he saw one thing very clearly. Britain continued to cling to the old Austrian alliance; but things had changed since the Duke of Marlborough's days. A new power, and a protestant power at that, had arisen in Europe; and this new Prussia of Frederick the Great ought to provide Britain's best security against France. In December 1747, Pitt expressed agreement with Newcastle that in view of Britain's 'melancholy prospects', a negotiated peace was immediately prudent, but at the same time he ventured to 'tease' the Duke with views he knew would not be shared: 'I will sum up my whole political creed in two propositions: this country and Europe are undone without a secure, lasting peace; the alliance as it now stands has not the force ever to obtain it without the interposition of Prussia'. Frederick had reason, Pitt thought, to 'take umbrage at the language of the court of Vienna ever since the cession of Silesia'. Britain must not encourage the irredentism of Maria Theresa; for, once Frederick's fears of Austria subsided, 'it is his interest and therefore his inclination to see Europe pacified and France contained within some bounds'. It was as the elder Horace Walpole had said when the war was going badly in 1746: 'You will say, where is the remedy for this calamitous situation? To which I reply, Prussia, Prussia, Prussia!'[14]

Pitt found himself rather more self-consciously on the same side as Horace Walpole senior in the Commons, when in February 1750 the question arose of Dunkirk, where the French had failed to fulfil their obligation under the recent peace treaty to dismantle the defences.[15] Pitt deplored the fact, but maintained that the only alternative to patient negotiation would be, in effect, war, and 'no nation ought to provoke a war when it is conscious of its being the weaker party'. 'Nations, as well as individuals, must sometimes forbear from the rigorous exaction of what is due to them'. To precipitate a war, with 'not one power on the continent that would be able to assist us' would be 'the height of imprudence'. This was undoubtedly not the kind of language members had been used to hear from Pitt in the old days, and he did not escape without some mockery. He acknowledged it but persisted:

> Gentlemen may make as merry as they please upon the word 'negociate'. I have formerly made as free with it as any gentleman in this House; but the circumstance of affairs are now very much altered . . . By negociation we keep our just claims alive.[16]

In general, during the first half dozen years of his Paymastership, Pitt took in a great deal of oratorical sail. He still spoke tellingly and trenchantly, but his lot was firmly thrown in with the Pelhams, and evidences of loyalty and solidarity were obligatory. Between 1746, and the renewed onset of his illness in 1752, it was, by contrast with what came before and after, a very sober, judicious Paymaster Pitt who rose in the Commons to justify the ways of the Pelhams to men. And his task was made no easier by the constant conflicts of personality and policy within the Pelham camp itself, between Henry Pelham and his allies, and the Duke of Newcastle and his.

Aix-la-Chapelle had not brought definitive peace between Spain and Britain. This had to wait till 1750, and when it was agreed, it was hardly of a kind that would have satisfied the Pitt who had cried havoc in 1739. He was now however obliged to accept the situation's realities. He regretted that the South Sea Company's claims were met only to the tune of £100,000 – but rather speciously argued that the nation, if not the Company, had been more than compensated by the profits of privateering during the war. As for the slave-trade monopoly – the *asiento* which Spain refused to recognize – it was in any case due to expire shortly. And the 'right of no search' of British merchant ships was a stipulation which it was 'ridiculous to insist on' since it was 'impossible to be obtained'. Once more, Pitt was conscious of being dogged by his earlier fighting words:

> I expect to be told that on a former occasion I concurred heartily in a motion . . . not to admit of any treaty of peace with Spain unless such a stipulation as this should be first obtained . . . I confess I did, Sir, because I then thought it right, but I was then very young and sanguine; I am now ten years older and have had time to consider things more coolly . . .[17]

The important thing for Pitt as for Newcastle, considering things coolly at the mid-century, must be to woo away from the French alliance Spain and such other powers as were susceptible to British advances. France always remained the arch enemy. Every diplomatic move must be directed towards limiting her great strength. For Newcastle this meant peace-time subsidies to various German states – Bavaria, Cologne, Saxony – in the not-too-reliable hope of their support in forthcoming diplomatic or military confrontations. Pitt, like Henry Pelham, had little faith in this casting of bread upon the waters. In any case, the one German power whose support would be most worth buying – Prussia – was not approached, partly because habit and conviction alike tied Newcastle to the Habsburg connection, and partly too because the King nourished an unrelenting detestation of his nephew Frederick of Prussia. Pelham, standing for economy and retrenchment, viewed his brother's European largesse sometimes with bemused fatalism, sometimes with resentful alarm.

'You see by the turn of my brother's letter', wrote Pelham to Hardwicke, 'that he regards no advice of a friend . . . I must declare to your Lordship . . . it is not in my will, it is not in my power, to undertake another session of Parliament upon the foot of expense we are now going into, and that only to preserve a bigotted notion of Old System and the House of Austria'.[18] From his side Newcastle insisted, with his unique mixture of fractious peevishness and dogged self-confidence, that he *must* be trusted and 'answer for the whole'; and it was 'unkind in my friends not to give as much credit to me as to every little Jackynepse that has been two months in a foreign court. I do act upon a principle of integrity to my country and some knowledge of my business'.

Both the brothers were inclined to run to Pitt for support, and he was careful to tread delicately between them. Newcastle's Bavarian subsidy received his unequivocal support in the Commons. It was wiser to subsidize allied armies abroad, he argued, than to maintain that essentially dangerous thing, a large standing army at home. 'By subsidies properly applied,' he said, 'we may secure such a confederacy upon the continent as must leave very little hopes for any prince in Europe to make an addition to his dominions by an alliance with France'.[19] And his backing for the economies practised by Pelham led him into fresh parliamentary reversals of old attitudes. In his speech on the Bavarian subsidy he did not fail to express the hope that an improving prospect abroad

> would be attended with measures of economy at home – perhaps by a different method of collecting the revenue – and he was not afraid to mention the odious word *excise* – (and then he mentioned Sir Robert Walpole with honour) – that the reduction of interest* was a great point gained for the public – and that the whole together made him hope that England would make as great a figure in a few years as it had done in any age.[20]

Pelham's influence was paramount in domestic policy. On the other hand, the Duke of Newcastle was the Duke of Newcastle, and Pitt's communications with him observed a proper, even an obsequious-sounding, regard for his power and position. There was an occasional hint of tension, when a flash of Pitt's notorious hauteur might alarm and offend. Once, according to Almon, he 'told his Grace [apropos of Saxony] that he engaged for subsidies without knowing the extent of the sums, and for alliances without knowing the terms';[21] but in general Newcastle was able to feel convinced that Pitt was his valuable

* The lending rate – reduced eventually to 3 per cent.

and loyal supporter. He himself wrote of the 'able and affectionate manner in which Mr Pitt has taken upon himself to defend me . . . when no other person in the house opened his lips in defence . . . I think myself obliged in honour and gratitude to shew my sense of it'; and Pelham too recognized that Pitt was 'the most able and useful man we have amongst us; truly honourable and strictly honest. He is as firm a friend to us as we can wish for'.[22]

Pitt even gained some recognition as a peacemaker between Newcastle and Pelham. After he had played what he called his 'poor little part' in patching up one of their numerous tiffs, he was surprisingly enough thanked by *both* parties. They were *too* good, he politely protested: 'I should be foolishly vain . . . if I ascribed the least part of the perfect union between you to anything but your own good hearts and understandings'. On his part, Newcastle vowed that he had 'acquainted the King with that proper zeal, satisfaction, and regard for his Majesty's honour and service' which Pitt had been showing; and Pitt, still ostentatiously wearing his best penitential sackcloth, continued pegging away 'to efface the pass'd by every action', and hopefully acknowledged Newcastle's 'good office in that Place, where I deservedly stand in need of it so much'.[23]

Occasions continued, right up to Pelham's death in 1754, when Pitt was prepared to speak and vote for ministerial policies he felt less than happy about. When for instance in 1753 Pelham's act to permit the naturalization of Jews roused such a fierce storm of ecclesiastical and vulgar opposition that (with an election pending) the cabinet decided it would be prudent to backtrack, Pitt, who had been strongly in favour of the original act, then proceeded to support its repeal, contenting himself with denouncing the unchristian popular prejudices that had made the reversal electorally necessary. 'I must still think', he explained, not very heroically, 'that the law passed last session in favour of the Jews was in itself right, and I shall now agree to the repeal of it merely out of complaisance to that *enthusiastic* spirit that has taken hold of the people'. All this ecclesiastical clamour he considered to have been 'only a little election art', which the government had been obliged 'to give way to genteelly'. However, when the church party went on to push their luck by trying to deprive Jews of their newly won naturalized status in British *colonies*, Pitt supported Pelham in defeating the moves. 'My maxim', he said, 'is never to do more for the Church than it now enjoys'. Its 'persecuting spirit' must be resisted, or it would be 'the Jew today, the Presbyterian tomorrow'.[24]

There were two matters upon which his judgement revolted strongly enough to take him into the opposition lobby. The more significant of these concerned the navy, whose strength Pelham, searching everywhere for economies, proposed to reduce to 8000 men. (It had been as high as 40,000 during the war.) Pitt, together with Lyttelton, three Grenvilles, and nine other rebels, voted in favour of a figure of 10,000. Aware of the need to justify so public a difference with Pelham, he showed what Horace Walpole described as 'great affectation of concern', and made 'great panegyrics' upon Pelham, who in his turn came to Pitt's defence when he was involved in an angry altercation with another member. All the signs were (so Walpole thought, and so the King suspected too) that 'W. Pitt, with his faction, was renewing his connection with the Prince of Wales, and impatient to be secretary of state, which he expected to carry . . . by storm'.[25] It is true that Pitt was chafing against the length of his stint, by then nearly five years, as Paymaster. Pelham and Newcastle had already changed Secretaries of State three times, and even consulted Pitt coolly enough concerning the changes. They would have had no lack of opportunity to promote him, assuming the King's veto was not absolute; Pitt, now forty-two, was finding it hard to be patient; and in common with every aspiring politician of the day he could not help keeping half an eye on the prospect of the 'new epocha' that would come in – must surely come in soon – with the accession of King Frederick. Richard Grenville 'cum suis', wrote Fox, had been 'making great court' with the Prince of Wales; Lyttelton too had patched up his quarrel with his brother-in-law the Prince's secretary, Ayscough; and even Newcastle himself, apprehensive of the Duke of Cumberland's suspected designs, began making discreet moves towards a tactical rapprochement with Frederick and his party, encouraging Pitt to do the same.

But the genuineness of Pitt's protest vote against naval economies can hardly be in doubt. He held passionately that maritime supremacy must always be an overriding imperative, and was unconvinced by Treasury and Admiralty arguments that, since the number of *ships* was not being reduced, the number of sailors could rapidly be made good from fishermen and merchant seamen in an emergency. The fleet, he declared, was Britain's true standing army.[26] The following year,

4. Frederick, Prince of Wales, by Philip Mercier

5. George II, by Thomas Worlidge

ridiculously enough – and, as Walpole has it, merely to 'cajole the Pitts and Lytteltons' – Pelham came round to accepting the larger figure of 10,000. Neither he nor the First Lord, Barrington, made any attempt to defend their change of opinion.

Pitt's vote in 1750 against the government on this issue had renewed old parliamentary talk of 'apostasy' and confirmed royal mistrust:

> The King on these votes commended the young men voting with the administration and said to the Duke of Newcastle before the Duke of Bedford, 'they are not like your Pitts and Grenvilles, whom you have cried up to me so much. You know I never liked them'.[27]

The Duke, however, continued this tactical 'crying-up'. In a circular letter to his parliamentary 'friends', he desired that none of them should yield to any 'clamour or run that may be made against [Pitt] . . . on account of his differing as to the number of seamen . . . after the kind part he has acted to me and . . . the meritorious one to the administration'. Newcastle of course was well aware of Pitt's potential as a rogue elephant; tranquillity in the herd was infinitely desirable. Frustratingly for Pitt, however, none of Newcastle's solicitous show of gratitude and amiability brought him any nearer those commanding heights of power upon which the eye of his ambition was always focused.

The second issue on which Pitt opposed the Pelhams concerned the British island of Minorca. In March 1751 he espoused the cause of a certain Don Juan Compagni, who had earlier been used ill by the then Governor, General Anstruther, and was petitioning parliament for a grant towards obtaining legal redress.

> Mr Pelham [reports Walpole] owned he had refused money from the Treasury and observed upon the impropriety of suffering such petitions, as it would encourage the like from all our governments and plantations . . . Mr Pitt spoke warmly for the petition, on the fitness of granting two or three thousand pounds to a poor man oppressed by military law, and of so good a family as the Compagnis (so deeply was Mr Pitt versed in Minorchese genealogies), and declared he would support such a cause to the last drop of his blood. Mr Fox ridiculed this warmth . . .[28]

This sarcastic parenthesis about 'Minorchese genealogies', taken together with Pitt's extravagance concerning the last drop of his blood and Fox's ridicule of his 'warmth', has induced some writers, again reasoning backwards from the imminence of a major onset of depression, to conclude that at this point he must have been already showing signs again of manic instability.[29] The supposition seems as mistaken here as in the earlier attack in 1744. We do not need to find a manic phase to precede every depression. Pitt was always prone to passion and hyperbole, and to parade too his command of recondite evidence. The Minorcan speech of 5 March does not show any particularly outrageous wildness. Over the next two months he spoke cogently both on this same subject and on the regency bill; and on 18 April even Horace Walpole conceded that Pitt 'spoke well' against the government on behalf of those he considered to have been 'oppressed and despoiled' by their Governor. The exposure of his misdeeds, said Pitt, should serve *pour encourager les autres*: 'other governors in our plantations and foreign garrisons' ought to take note that Anstruther was saved only by royal act of grace; they might well 'tremble for the future'. The language was strong, but not unusually excited, and certainly not irrational. It was consistent moreover with Pitt's genuine hatred of the abuse of power by petty tyrants, most of all when they were acting under the authority of the British flag.[30]

Everybody's calculations were upset in the spring of 1751 by the sudden death of the Prince of Wales. The happy expectations of his followers evaporated overnight. His son the new heir apparent, the future George III, was a boy only twelve years old, too young yet to form any party of his own. His nervously protective mother, Princess Augusta, was concerned to keep a watchful eye upon the boy's uncle, the Duke of Cumberland, who had his own parliamentary group, with Henry Fox as its chief spokesman, and whom some suspected of planning a military dictatorship in the event of a royal minority. Hence the battles over the Regency Act of May 1751, where Pitt was at pains to fight for the unimpaired authority of the Princess Regent presumptive, Augusta. In his references to the dead Frederick and his royal father he allowed himself the free use of conventional obituary insincerities and trod – dangerously perhaps, in view of his admitted need to placate the King – the ambiguous territory between brazen flattery and studied irony. Praising 'the most *patriot* prince that ever lived, to whom he had such infinite obligations' ('as if all mankind had forgot his ingratitudes to the Prince', Walpole indignantly interpolates) he promised his widow and her family the transference of his devoted attachment, and wondered – surely, tongue in cheek – at the King 'exerting a fortitude which Edward III had not been master of' upon the death of the Black Prince.

CHAPTER NINE

———◆◆◆———

'*An Indelible Negative*'

The last of the regency debates was in May 1751. In June Pitt was at the Pay Office, attending to business. Already ill by the late summer, he then remained an absentee from public life for over two years, not reappearing in the Commons until November 1753. Even then he soon fell ill again and was obliged for several more months to remain anchored to Bath by his gout.

The nature of his malady, when it was not simply gout, puzzled his contemporaries. It was most persistent, yet sufficiently intermittent to allow him, when it relented, to enjoy company, attend assemblies and balls, or go riding. When he was bad, his condition alarmed his friends; Lyttelton even spoke of it as 'dangerous'; yet some of his enemies were ready to believe he was merely suffering from a fit of political sulks – Horace Walpole wrote of his return to Westminster in 1753 'after a year of sullen illness'. At times when he genuinely had 'regular gout', everything appeared plain enough. But many months went by when he was quite free of gout, yet helplessly weighed down by a miscellany of symptoms, which included severe loss of appetite; intestinal troubles – 'disorders in my bowels, which have . . . reduced me to a weak state of health';[1] prolonged insomnia – at one stage Gilbert West reports him as entirely sleepless one night in two; and melancholia – that 'extreme dejection' of spirits which became for Pitt a darker enemy than his gout. Gout, though often acutely painful and disabling, was at least *discussable* and capable of providing some intelligible explanation to the world of his incapacity. Sometimes he might even exaggerate its effects, apologizing in a letter of perfect legibility for a scrawl enforced by swollen joints. No sufferer from gout would wish to underestimate its unpleasantness; yet Pitt, following the medical opinion of his day, taught himself to regard it as a visitor to be welcomed. Gout, if it behaved according to the physicians, would serve to bring his other maladies to a point of resolution, drawing off evil humours to the bodily extremities. And when gout did become superimposed upon his other afflictions, yet failed to relieve them, Pitt was understandably aggrieved: 'This gout', he complained, 'which I trusted to relieve me, has almost subdued me'.

There was little that eighteenth-century medicine could hope to do for his depressive state, with the physical disorders that at the same time resulted from it and aggravated it. There were, of course, the mineral spas, and he went his painstaking round of them, drinking widely of the waters of faith at Sunninghill and Tunbridge, at Astrop Wells in Northamptonshire, and most frequently at Bath, which increasingly became his chief headquarters outside London. He saw less and less of his 'little paradise' of South Lodge, which in 1753 he sold, buying instead for £1200 a fine new house, Number 7, The Circus, Bath, which was built by the two John Woods and completed in 1754. With Bath he was always to retain the closest connection; the place afforded its citizens and visitors the attractions of civilized intercourse and social entertainment, with the 'cure' for a bonus; next to London, it was the genteelest city in England. None of its advantages, however, in the summer of 1752, were able to do much for Pitt. It was 'quite destitute of amusement or resource', he lamented to his cousin John, whom he was trying nevertheless to persuade to come to join him there, solitude being 'in every way contrary' to his cure. In the autumn he had planned to visit Hagley and Encombe, but instead was obliged to stay on in Bath, where he had been prescribed 'as long a course of these waters as I can take, before necessary business of office will call me to town'. He remained ill all the winter of 1752–3, though by February was apparently back at the Pay Office, from where, writing to his sister Ann, he had however to report himself as 'still a good deal out of order'.

Ann was now living abroad again, and suffering too from troubles of mind and body which were akin to her brother's.[2] Briefly in 1751 she had held the appointment of Privy Purse to the Princess of Wales (the uncharitably minded had found in this Pitt's motive for seeking a reconciliation with her); but for reasons which remain uncertain she had soon parted company with her employment and returned to France. Horace Walpole declared that her removal arose from her intriguing nature and an 'impetuosity to govern her mistress', but it is well not always to accept Walpole as gospel, enormously well-informed as he was on political matters. Ann Pitt was never actually dismissed from her post and in the vicissitudes of her voluntary exile liked, as she said, to 'indulge her vanity' by having letters addressed to her with the addition of her 'title of Privy Purse to the Princess'.[3] Pitt, in his sickness, wrote several times to his sister, amid her own troubles, between February and May 1753. His tone in all of them is of anxious solicitude, and of regret for storms past.

> Believe me dear Sister, my heart is fill'd with the most affectionate wishes for your health, and impatient desire to see you return well and happy. I never can reflect of things passed (wherein I must have been infinitely in the wrong if I ever gave you pain) without the tenderest sorrow: and the highest aggravation of this concern wou'd be to think that, perhaps, you may not understand the true state of my heart towards you . . .[4]

The spirit of Ann's reply, 'affectionate and generous', removed a load of unhappiness from his mind. The quarrels of the past were to be buried.

Another pair of letters passed each way. Pitt was 'infinitely glad' that Ann's doctors held out hope that the Spa waters might offer some relief: 'May every day of spring contribute to the thing in the world I wish most ardently!' As for himself,

> I am now, in many respects, better, and seem getting ground, by riding and taking better nourishment. Warmer weather, I am to hope, will be of much service to me. I propose using some mineral waters: Tunbridge or Sunning Hill or Bath, at their proper seasons. As the main of my complaint is much abated and almost removed, I hope my horse, warm weather, and proper nourishment will give me health again. The kind concern you take in it is infinitely felt . . .[5]

A few months later he was **lamenting** to his youngest sister Mary – whom he was hoping to see again soon, 'after so very long an absence' – that Ann was not in England: 'her countenance, and her advice and instructions, superior to any you can otherwise receive, wou'd be the highest advantage to you. Supply it as well as you can', he added in the same paternal, hortatory vein which he used in addressing his nephew, 'by thinking of her, imitating her worth, and thereby endeavouring to deserve her esteem'. Mary, unmarried at twenty-eight, had before her, by contrast, the regrettable departures from propriety of her erratic sister Elizabeth – 'sad errors', Pitt wrote, which called attention to 'a high degree of prudence and exact attention to conduct' in his 'dear child' Mary.

Ann's health deteriorated rather than improved, and in March 1754 Pitt was writing to her (at Nevers now) of his concern: 'I hope you have spring begun at Nevers, which I pray God may relieve you'.[6] His own complaint, which he had hoped the previous spring was over the worst, had betrayed him. At Tunbridge Wells, where he had taken a house for a season, in company with Gilbert West, his wife, and West's sister Molly, Pitt became much worse. There was 'something intermitting' in his case, West noted, of which neither doctors nor patient seemed to be aware. On one of his worst days he had a visit from George Lyttelton, who promised to come again and might be persuaded, West hoped, to add his voice to West's own, urging a return to town to consult London physicians – to which, however, Pitt objected.

Writing to Mrs Montagu a few days later, West paints plainly enough Pitt's helpless wretchedness in one of the deep troughs of his trouble:

My spirits . . . were much sunk by the extreme dejection which appears today in Mr Pitt, from a night passed entirely without sleep . . . He began to drink the waters today, but as they are sometimes very slow in their operation, I much fear he . . . will suffer a great deal before the wished for effect will take place. For this *insomnium* his physicians have proscribed opiates, a medicine which . . . though they may procure a temporary ease, yet often after recoil upon the spirits. He seems inclined to take musk . . . I think the physicians have been to blame in giving all their attention to his bowels, and not sufficiently regarding the distemperature of his spirits, a disease much more to be apprehended than the other; while he continues under this oppression, I am afraid it will be impossible for me to leave him, as he fancies me of the greatest use to him as a friend and comforter . . .[7]

On 30 May West judged him 'somewhat better, tho' his spirits are too low to allow him to think so . . . his nights are still sleepless without the use of opiates'. But a little more than a month later Mrs Montagu was noting the 'favourable effect' of the dry season upon the Tun-

135

bridge waters, which she fancied had 'cured' Mr Pitt. And Lyttelton, who plainly had views on the autosuggestive causes of some of Pitt's ills, thought that 'Mr Pitt wants nothing of being quite well but to think himself so, and to sleep soundly at night. He has recovered his flesh, rides 15 miles a day, eats like a horse, and has as much wit as ever he had in his life'.[8] If this sounds a little superficial and over-cheerful, by midsummer Pitt was at least well enough to join his friends' excursions round the Tunbridge countryside. 'Instead of making parties at whist or cribbage', reported Mrs Montagu, 'and living with and like the *beau monde*, we have been wandering about like a company of gypsies, visiting all the fine parks and seats in the neighbourhood'.[9]

At the end of July Pitt undertook a five-day ride into Sussex, visiting Battle Abbey, Ashburnham Park, Herstmonceux ('very fine, curious, and dismally ugly'), Crowhurst ('Colonel Pelham's, the sweetest thing in the world'), and 'enchanting Hastings unique'. Despite this evidence of returning strength, however, he told his cousin John, 'my sleep continues very broken, and the irritation [is] not yet off my nerves and out of my blood'.[10] Back at Tunbridge he helped to occupy his mind by attending, together with Mrs Montagu, some lectures of 'philosophy, etc.', and apparently succeeded in keeping the lecturer on his toes, making him 'explain things very precisely'. And then in mid-September he was off on his wanderings once more, first to the Ayscoughs in Hertfordshire, then on to Stowe with West, then to stay with Lyttelton at Hagley.[11]

At Stowe in the early autumn – 'in good health and spirits', West declared – he was already looking ahead to the coming session of parliament and intending to resume his seat there; also making sure that he *would have* a seat after the election due the following year. The quarrel with his brother put Old Sarum (which he would have liked) out of the question, and he had again to be a suitor to Newcastle for one of his nominations. Newcastle promised him Aldborough in Yorkshire.

Towards the end of November parliament saw him again at last. However, in no time at all he was back at Bath and incapacitated again, not this time by his depression and its debilitating accompaniments, but by a sequence of sharp visitations of 'regular' gout. By February he was 'under the wholesome but painful discipline of fit the second . . . I was just beginning to use my feet when I lost them again, and have been . . . nailed to my great chair'. A month later he was still there, 'in the third fit of the gout in both my feet'.[12]

There could not have been an unluckier time for him to be out of action. Henry Pelham died on 6 March after a three days' illness. For over ten years he had been First Lord of the Treasury, Chancellor of the Exchequer, and leader of the House of Commons. Who was now to succeed in any or all of these positions?

There remained, of course, his brother the Secretary Duke; but Newcastle as a peer was disqualified at least for the Commons positions. On all sides it was considered that Pelham's successor in the Commons must be one of three outstandingly able parliamentarians – Murray, or Fox, or Pitt. To each, however, there were objections. Murray, though hardly the crypto-Jacobite some suggested, was an undeniable Scot, which was bad enough; and in the event he soon indicated an intention of concentrating on his legal career, being content to move up a step to Attorney General. Fox, though the King was at first inclined towards him, was personally disliked by the powerfully influential Hardwicke, and as the close associate of the Duke of Cumberland he was suspected of being too liable to befriend the supposedly dangerous ambitions of the King's favourite son. Here, so Hardwicke professed to fear, might be 'the Treasury and the House of Commons and the sword joined together'. (Without doubt this is what Princess Augusta genuinely feared, nervous for the rights of her son George.) There remained Pitt, in whose path lay the most formidable obstacles: his health was bad, his parliamentary connection was small, and worst of all he was *persona non grata* with the King.

Still at Bath, he reported himself 'extremely crippled', 'worn down with pain and confinement'. He longed to be in London, at the centre of the tangle of negotiation and intrigue; but, as he regretted to Newcastle, he was totally unfit to travel. His frustrated energies instead during the three weeks following Pelham's death poured forth a flood of letters to his associates, Lyttelton, Richard Grenville (now Lord Temple) and George Grenville, advising on aims and tactics. There should be no 'premature declarations' that might debar them from profiting 'from the mutual fears and animosities of different factions at Court'. They should certainly sit tight on their offices while awaiting events. If Fox were promoted, George Grenville ought to expect, and should accept, the War Secretaryship. They must work through

Hardwicke, who had 'wisdom, temper, and authority'; Newcastle without Hardwicke was 'feeble'. On the other hand, he trusted they would remember that his 'personal connection with the Duke of Newcastle' had 'a peculiar circumstance' which the rest of them were not bothered by – a typical Pitt obliquity; he meant that he depended on Newcastle for his seat at Aldborough.[13] They must all play their cards skilfully; Lyttelton in particular should be restrained from imprudence. (He should also be careful not to leave Pitt's letters in his pockets, 'or drop them. Pardon all these cautions; but we are beset with snares and dangers'.) The essence of their plans, as he explained tortuously, and not too coherently, to Temple ought to be

> to declare attachment to the *King's* government, and the future plans *under the Princess* [of Wales, Regent-Presumptive] . . . to give no terrors by talking big . . . to look out and fish in troubled waters, and perhaps help trouble them in order to fish the better: but to profess and to resolve bona fide to act like public men in a dangerous conjuncture for our country, and support Government when they will please to settle it; to let them see we shall do this from *principles of public good*, not as *the bubbles* of a few fair words . . . to leave them under the impressions of their own fears and resentments, the only friends we shall ever have at Court. Their fears will increase by what we *avoid saying concerning persons* . . . and by *saying very explicitly* . . . (but civilly), that we have our eyes open to . . . the foul play we have had offered us in the Closet . . .
>
> Give me leave to recommend to your Lordship a little gathering of friends about you at dinners . . . Some attention to Sir Richard Lyttelton I should think proper; a dinner to the Yorkes [Hardwicke's sons] very seasonable; and . . . any of the Princess of Wales's Court. John Pitt not to be forgot: I know the Duke of B[edford] nibbles at him . . . I mend a little. I cannot express my impatience to be with you.[14]

The situation demanded subtleties. One of the communications to Lyttelton contained two letters – one for Lyttelton alone and another ostensibly to Lyttelton but to be shown to Hardwicke; this second communication flattering Hardwicke with 'the great honour of my Lord Chancellor's good opinion', reminding him that Pitt had long ago abandoned factious opposition, yet perversely protesting his own consciousness of failings: 'Were my health restored and his Majesty brought from the dearth of subjects to hear of my name for so great a charge [as that sustained by Pelham], I should wish to decline the honour'. Decline *in any case*, he suggests, but especially in view of the King's hostility – a strange declaration, in complete opposition to his true feelings, and on the face of it invalidating his subsequent indignation on being rejected for cabinet office.[15]

Newcastle was to be the new First Lord of the Treasury, and it was intended that Fox should become Secretary of State. He did actually accept and for a day or so hold the Secretaryship, but Newcastle was persuaded by Hardwicke – indeed he needed little convincing – that it would not do to let the disposition of the secret service money and management of the Commons slip out of his own experienced hands; whereupon Fox declined 'to take this great office on the foot of being quite a cypher'. It would be better, he said, 'to remain Secry-at-War with, than to be Secry of State without, credit'.[16]

As late as 20 March – two days after the composition of the ministry had in fact been settled – Pitt was still half-hoping, against the odds and despite his ill health, for some recognition. As for disqualification from an 'office of fatigue' on grounds of health, *he* ought to be the best judge of that.[17] 'If they are in earnest to avail themselves of me against what they fear,' he wrote to Lyttelton, 'they will call me to the Cabinet', though it did (contradictorily) appear 'evident that I am never to be suffered to try to serve my country'. He was already feeling bitter, while intermittently professing to be resigned to the delights of a country retirement and 'the tranquil comforts of indolence and innocence'. 'The taste I find in me for quiet', he not at all convincingly declared, 'every hour takes deeper root in my mind'. 'What then remains?' he wrote to Temple, and found an answer to hand in Horace: 'the conduct of the much-enduring man, who by temper, patience, and persevering prudence, became *adversis rerum immersabilis undis*' (unsinkable amid the buffeting waves). 'I am so tired I cannot hold my head down to write any longer. A fine Secretary I should make'.[18] But the two-faced insincerities of Newcastle and Hardwicke nagged away at him. How could Hardwicke with one breath claim, as he had, to wish him back 'in town to take the lead', and in the next 'to plead the King's alienation of mind' against him? 'Who could his Lordship [Hardwicke] think he was talking to?'[19]

Pitt respected Fox's abilities, and had expected to see him Secretary. In any case, given enough rope, he thought, Fox might well hang himself. 'Fox is odious', he wrote to Temple (meaning 'generally disliked' rather than personally odious to Pitt); and he would 'have difficulty to stand in a future time'.[20] When, however, the disposal of posts in Newcastle's administration was made public, Pitt's hard struggle to bring his mortification under control shows well enough the insincerity of some of his earlier protestations to Hardwicke. Still at Bath, still lame and in pain, he now had a sense of outrage to add to his infuriating impotence. The key post in the Commons (Secretary of State and Leader of the House) had gone to none of the original contenders, not to Murray, not now to Fox, not of course to Pitt. Indeed it had ceased to *be* a key post, having been awarded to the merest puppet of Newcastle, a Court officer and minor ex-diplomat, Sir Thomas Robinson. Of the Cousinhood, George Grenville had been made Treasurer of the Navy and George Lyttelton Cofferer of the Household. Lyttelton's was largely a sinecure post: 'a good £2200 per annum', he was happy to say, which would allow him plenty of time to spend at Hagley and also power to give the place of Sub-Cofferer to his brother Billy at '5 or 6 hundred a year'.[21] Pitt's letters of congratulation did their best to sound pleased on his friends' behalf and to conceal his own bitterness.

To Newcastle and Hardwicke he wrote in a different strain, floridly polite as ever, yet resentfully barbed with protest. As so often with Pitt, the line between fulsome flattery and biting sarcasm was, in parts, very enigmatically drawn. 'Let me intreat your Grace', he begged Newcastle, '(if you can divest your mind of the great disparity between us) to transport yourself for a moment into my place'. He had, as he reasonably enough claimed, long and loyally supported the government on every issue but two – the strength of the navy and the Anstruther case.

For these crimes how am I to be punished? . . . An indelible negative is fix'd against my name . . . I will venture to appeal to your Grace's candour and justice whether I have not some cause to feel (as I do most deeply) so many repeated and visible humiliations . . . I will freely own I should have felt myself far less personally humiliated had Mr Fox been placed by the King's favour at the head of the

House of Commons. In that case the necessity would have been apparent . . . Could Mr Murray's situation have allowed . . . I should have served under him with the greatest pleasure. [But, he implies, Sir Thomas Robinson!] . . . My mortification arises not from silly pride, but from being evidently excluded by a negative personal to me (now and for ever) . . .[22]

'Indeed, my Lord,' he burst out to Hardwicke,

I am persuaded I can be of no material use under such circumstances; nor have I the heart or the presumption to attempt an active, much less a leading part, in Parliament. The weight of irremoveable royal displeasure is too heavy for any man to move under, who is firmly resolved never to move the disturbance of Government; it must crush any man; it has sunk and exanimated me; I succumb under it, and wish for nothing but a decent and innocent retreat wherein, by being placed out of the stream of Cabinet Council promotion, I may no longer seem to stick fast aground and have the mortification to see myself, and offer to others the ridiculous amusement of seeing, every boat pass by me that navigates the same river . . .[23]

To Lyttelton and the Grenvilles he was writing at this time, 'My plan continues fixt, not to quit employments'; but both to Newcastle and to Hardwicke he threatened resignation. 'Things standing as they do,' he told Newcastle, 'whether I can continue in office without losing myself in the opinion of the world is become a matter of very painful doubt to me'. And of Hardwicke he positively requested, 'as soon as practicable', a post of some honourable retirement, 'a retreat not void of advantages nor derogatory to the rank of the office I hold'. He would have been abandoning £4000 a year; but, as he hopefully observed, 'out of his Grace's immediate province accommodations of this kind arise'. Pitt's passion, however, as George Grenville rightly commented, was 'not money; it was ambition, power; of which he had no share'. His friends and correspondents were not taken in by his pose of the 'philosopher of Bath', with 'mind abstracted from what you gentlemen at London are pleased to call the great world', fixed instead 'on the contemplation of nature's system and intellectual and moral worlds'. Of course, neither did he convince himself; the pose was always half-humorous and self-mocking.[24]

Hardwicke's answer, 'the most condescending, friendly, obliging thing', Pitt called it, begged him to put away all thought of retiring. The reply from 'most unalterably yours, Holles Newcastle' – 'writ', Pitt said, 'with a condescension and in terms so flattering that it pains me' – offered explanations and justifications, and conveyed effusive assurances of sympathy and affection.[25] 'If I have not the fruit', Pitt wrote wryly to Lyttelton, 'I have the leaves of it in abundance: a beautiful foliage of fine words'; and proceeded once more to allege his wishes and intentions: 'Resolved not to disturb Government, I desire to be released from the oar of parliamentary drudgery . . . I am not fond of making speeches (though some may think I am). I never cultivated the talent but as an instrument of action . . .' He would, he said, be willing to 'sit there' and *wait*, 'ready to be called out into action when the Duke of Newcastle's personal interests might require'[26] – not quite the same thing as philosophically contemplating 'nature's system' in rural retirement.

Lyttelton, like George Grenville, had done well under the new arrangements.* Pitt wished him joy of his promotion and continued to preserve, for some time yet, this his oldest friendship. It had survived for over thirty years, despite some cloudy interludes. There had been frowns, for instance, back in 1744 when both George Grenville and Lyttelton had gained offices, but not Pitt. Lyttelton, clearly thinking Pitt had chiefly his own unreasonableness to blame for his misfortunes, wrote with some asperity then that Pitt 'as usual abuses the people to whom he accedes and befouls his own nest'.[27] And now he was to grow increasingly censorious of Pitt's tactics, and in particular of the 'personal malignity' Pitt was soon to show Newcastle (contrary to the intentions he declared to Lyttelton). In view of the bad feeling that was to develop, Lyttelton thought it necessary to commit to paper his own version of the transactions of 1754. As Pitt's intermediary he claimed to have played fair, and had moreover gained the clear impression that 'Hardwicke, to keep down Fox, his personal enemy, most ardently desired the advancement of Pitt as soon as the

* 'Sir George Lyttelton, whose warmest prayer was to go to heaven in a coronet, undertook to be factor for his friends. Unauthorized, he answered for Pitt's acquiescence under the new plan. He obtained a great employment for himself . . .' (Walpole, *Memoirs of George II*, i. 336).

obstacles in the Closet could be removed; but that was a work of much more difficulty than Pitt's impatience would believe'. On his side, Pitt was sure (as Grenville reported) that Hardwicke and the Pelhams 'had never taken the least care' to make him 'well with the King'; but Lyttelton obviously concurred with Hardwicke's opinion that if only Pitt had remained 'quiet and friendly to the Government the King would have been persuaded to give him the seals before the end of the year'.[28]

Certainly Pitt was soon to become very far from 'quiet and friendly'. However, he was for some months yet not well enough to give battle; and for a time he went on pretending to himself and the world that he could positively 'enjoy the absence of that thing called Ambition', and would be happy to live 'verdant days on verdant hills or sequestered valleys', indifferent to the news from London of 'Parliament assembling, and Speakers chusing, and all other great earthly things'.[29]

CHAPTER TEN

———◦◦◦———

Hester Grenville

Wanting 'a little repairs' after the 'so continual rains' of the summer, he visited Astrop Wells in August and September, and 'lodged in a dungeon called the Manor House of King's Sutton'; drinking the waters of a morning and riding 'in the dirt of Northamptonshire all the rest of the day'; hoping he was leading a life of *health*, 'for pleasure never found its way hither'. He claimed in fact by early September to be 'perfectly well, that is well cobbled up by Astrop waters and the life of a post-boy, always in the saddle'.[1]

From Astrop he had intended going to Henry Legge's, in Hampshire; from there back to Bath; and thence to Encombe to stay with his cousin John. However, he cancelled these plans, and returned unexpectedly to stay with George Grenville at Wotton. Perhaps he went there with resolutions already made; he had recently had leisure enough to take stock of his condition and find it wanting. It was a reasonable enough conclusion to arrive at that, approaching forty-seven, long an unsettled wanderer, he needed a wife. No doubt the emotions of a middle-aged semi-invalid bachelor provide an unprofitable subject for generalization; it does however seem inherently improbable that – the scales being, as it were, struck suddenly from Pitt's long-blinded eyes – he should all at once conceive so peremptory a passion for Hester Grenville (who he had known since her childhood, whose company he had enjoyed and whose virtues and charms he had been able to appraise on very many previous occasions) that within a few days of his now coming to Wotton it should have emerged spontaneous and entire as Aphrodite herself, and spurred him to an immediate proposal of marriage. Pitt calculated important moves rather more deliberately. But that is far from saying that his choice was cold or loveless.

As a matrimonial catch, Pitt now, with his poor health and dimmed prospects, was not quite what he had been ten years before. There had

been a time earlier still, when George Lyttelton had had lively hopes
for his sister Molly; and in 1737, when Pitt was thirty, Hester Lyttelton,
George's youngest sister, then seventeen, was thought to have got a
line aboard him. It was the year in which Thomas Pitt was being
obliged to sell Swallowfield to raise money, and Lady Lyttelton was
hoping that necessary business would keep William in town long enough
for the line to be secured. 'What you tell me of Hetty's conquest I
am pleased at', she wrote to her son Charles and asked to hear more of
it, being afraid that if Pitt, that inveterate nomad, went travelling
again before he saw her he might change his mind.[2] If Pitt's absorbing
passions were for power and fame, he was certainly not insensitive
to female charms, and there were plenty of women who were attracted
by his own. Mrs Montagu was one, albeit with never a smutch of
impropriety; and it was probably William Pitt (rather than one of his
cousins John or George) whom her twenty-year-old sister Sarah was
meaning when she sat the evening out at a ball in Bath in 1743, but
'did not regret it, having no inclination to dance with any man but
Mr Pitt', and since she had 'not acquaintance enough with him to
expect' *that*, she would only cherish hopes for the future.[3] Horace
Walpole even suggested that Lord Archibald Hamilton's wife Jane,
mistress of the Prince of Wales, abandoned the Prince for Pitt; an
'agreeable and artful' woman, he declared; but since he also writes
'neither young nor handsome' a little of the bloom is brushed off the
story.[4]

During the years before her marriage Hester Grenville's life had
followed a course superficially uneventful among the aristocratic
splendours and littlenesses of Wotton and London, Bath and Stowe.
Letters written to her by her brothers and by another Jane Hamilton
(later Lady Cathcart) disclose various approaches towards, and steerings
away from, the shores of matrimony. There is reference by Jane Hamilton to an unnamed 'happy man' that Hester is expected to marry, then
tactfully to a 'happy escape' when she is not. In 1748 there is a letter
passing on the information that Lord Pembroke, the architect earl,
holds Hester in flattering regard. Earlier, when she was twenty-one,
her brother Thomas (later drowned in action against the French)
was writing, 'You are either a little idle bitch or I am a sad unlucky
dog, for I have not seen a line from you this four months. I desire you
will tell me in your next what it is that takes your time up so. If it

is lovers I excuse you . . .'[5] Two years later a second brother, James, twits her with mock-brutality about one 'Simon Truelove' whose 'advantageous proposal' she really ought to close with: 'My dear Meg you grow old and it is time for you to think of a decent retirement from business . . . Therefore let me know by the very next post that the thing is concluded.'[6] Two years later again, her brother George appears to have been doing his best to steer her towards marriage with a Captain Geary, to coincide with suitable professional favours for the prospective bridegroom. 'Is not this good in me?' asks Grenville. 'See the advantage of having a brother in the Admiralty and make the best of it.'[7] The Captain did indeed progress to admiral, and to baronet too, but not as the husband of Hester Grenville who, by the time that Pitt came to Wotton in September 1754 to put his own proposal before her, had reached the advanced age, for so eligible a spinster, of thirty-three.

In every respect it appeared a fortunate match. Politically Hester helped to cement the connection of Pitt with the Grenville clan. Personally she was intelligent, capable, equable, gentle-mannered. If not a beauty, she was presentable enough; her portraits depict a calm, amiable face, a comely person; hair tending to auburn, a steady gaze, cheeks well-rounded, nose slightly tip-tilted – this last the most obvious of the physical characteristics she was to transmit to her brilliant second son. Mrs Montagu remarked on her reputed good humour, 'the principal article in the happiness of the marriage state', since 'beauty soon grows familiar to the lover'. Happily, Hester admired Pitt almost to idolatry and soon became utterly absorbed in his well-being; and his devotion to her, strong and true, only strengthened as the months and years went by.

The love letters[8] they exchanged in the few weeks of separation before their marriage mingle decorous protestations with the tenderest extravagances. Some have found these letters insufferably stilted. 'Pitt's love letters, alas! survive', wrote Lord Rosebery[9]; and sometimes his combination of the floridly formal and the sentimentally 'sweet' (an epithet he worked almost as hard as Miss Burney) does produce some odd effects. There is not more hyperbole than is proper to love letters; it luxuriates amid Pitt's usual crop of double negatives and elegant periphrases. Not every woman, it is true, would catch her lover's drift on being told, 'To me you turn'd poetry to prose, that is to reality'. Yet neither poetry nor passion was lacking. 'How often do I read and kiss the word [joy] you say you love to repeat, because I love to read it? Tell it me for ever, and let me thus be with you, in spite of cruel distance, with fondness, looking on your charms with my mind, and folding them with transport in my heart . . . I find no paper large enough for a heart that you permit to be yours'. On a ride near Bath at a spot where Hester had once been with him, 'the cascade, the river, the wood', he writes to her, 'was all delightfull, for I saw you in them all'. And again, 'To tell you that a heart all your own grows more so, may not be logick, but I am sure it is truth; I am sure it is love'.

However, the following missive, written to Hester on the Friday before their Saturday wedding, perhaps more fairly represents Pitt's amatory style:

> I fear this note, late as it is for my anxious impatience, may be too early in my loved Lady Hester's apartment. What joy will it be to hear she has slept well, and that she has waked free from every complaint: if so, may I tell myself that she does not disapprove my complaint that Friday is so long in moving out of the way of the sweet day that follows it?

Or this, a few weeks earlier:

> Was ever the most amiable goodness like that of Lady Hester Grenville, or felicity like mine? But a few delightful days have pass't since it would have surpassed all my hopes to be but suffered to tell the wishes my heart had presumed to form, and to have thought the smallest of yours not unfavourable to mine would have been the sum of all happiness.

He wrote like a man who could hardly believe his good fortune; who feared indeed it might be too good to be true. 'The tender delusion' could not last. But to this Hester was quick to answer: 'Never apply the term delusion to the dear and just idea I have form'd of your excellence . . . I have either so much or so little of the woman in me that it is an opinion I am determined never to recede from'. 'I think your nature of so noble a stamp,' she told him, 'so great and so amiable in its composition, that I shou'dn't esteem it less than a sin to wish the least particle of it alter'd. I look upon it . . . as some emanation of the All-beauteous Mind'. No wonder Pitt should reply, 'Fear mixes itself with my unspeakable delight to think how infinitely you over-rate me'. No such thing, she insisted:

> No joy can equal mine in having reason to believe your happiness depends on me . . . The thought that I am in possession of your heart is a pleasure and a flattery beyond every other . . . My fame, my pride, my glory is centred in you, and I every day approve myself for the admiration, adoration I had rather say, which my mind pays to your virtue and perfections.

Remembering times past and old associations amid all this new-found excitement, three or four weeks before the wedding Pitt asked Hester to write to his 'poor sister Ann', still in France and too unwell to return as he had hoped to England. He was clearly anxious to preserve the renewed but fragile harmony between his sister and himself. He would bless Hester 'a million of times' if she would be kind enough to write a letter showing goodwill, and he would forward it with one of his own. Hester obliged – though to a twentieth-century untransposing ear her phrases, intended to be friendly, sound frigidly formal – and Ann responded with immediate congratulations. They were all he needed, Pitt told her, to complete his happiness.

There was, of course, the business of the marriage settlement to be agreed and the consent to be obtained of Hester's brother Richard, Earl Temple, now head of the family. At first, these matters gave Pitt 'sensible sollicitudes'. He proposed to settle his reversionary Sunderland estates 'in the strictest manner' upon his wife; but, in the event of all his ships coming fortunately home to port, to reserve the Marlborough estates for his own disposal. This was in the first place in order to take care of John Spencer's debts, and then 'to have elbow-room for a town house of some expense, perhaps another one near town, and particularly to be in a condition to purchase Old Sarum' – which last, of course (it was still at this time his brother's property) would mean for him a permanently assured Commons seat, unbeholden to the Duke of Newcastle or anyone else. Both to Temple and to George Grenville Pitt felt obliged to justify himself carefully on these points which, he was afraid, might be considered as involving Lady Hester in 'infinitely too great a sacrifice of her establishment'.[10]

Happily, Temple gave ready consent to the arrangements, and seems to have been genuinely pleased over the forthcoming alliance. Hester herself expressed her gratitude to him with a formality that might seem severe in an affectionate sister; Pitt's thanks overflowed in a letter which protests rather *too* much; at once relieved, excited, and effusive towards his no longer *dear* but now *dearest* Lord Temple whose 'amiable delicacy of manner . . . even the best and kindest of friends cannot put into their actions unless their minds are truly Grenville':

> You sent me from Stow the most blessed of men, and every hour I live only brings me new and touching instances of the unceasing goodness and most affectionate and endearing partiality towards me of the kind, noble, and generous fraternity to which it is my glory and happiness to be raised . . . Your letter is the kindest that ever glowed from the best pen speaking the best heart . . . If it did not look like an expression more of a lover than a friend, I should say, I love, to the very pen that wrote it . . .[11]

Mrs Montagu was sure the engaged pair were ideally matched: 'there is an authority in the character of Mr Pitt that will secure him the deference and obedience of his wife; proud of him abroad, she will be humble to him at home'. However unemancipated or illiberal-sounding a prediction, that was to prove a just and shrewd one.[12] (Hester had already written to him, 'You never can have known the flattery of receiving applause from any-one superior to yourself, who had the superiority over all'.) Henry Legge, newly Chancellor of the Exchequer, writing to John Pitt, newly a father, was equally sanguine, and happy at the prospect of acquiring Pitt among 'the corps of us married men'. He thought the 'breed' must be good, and could not fail *to speak as soon as they were born*.[13] Henry Grenville was sure the Pitt alliance would do the Grenvilles honour; his brother James encouraged Hester by telling her that Pitt must make absolutely the best of all brothers-in-law. George Lyttelton wrote to her, 'As your friend I congratulate you, and as his I love you for the choice you have made'. (Pitt, having now 'much reserve' towards him, had let Lyttelton know of the impending marriage only indirectly, through William Lyttelton.) George Grenville, on whose Wotton territory the alliance had been concluded, wished it well and was friendliness itself, even though he did require to have the small print of the marriage settlement properly explained to him. Perhaps his wife Elizabeth, a long-established friend of Hester's, did have a few reservations. If only Pitt's health should not get worse – ; but even she looked on the bright side; 'happiness is so fine a medicine'.

In fact Hester, in accordance with her own instructions, was already receiving postings on the state of her lover's digestive and other ailments. As he had just written to Ann Pitt, 'My health is not good, but, as yet, it is not quite bad. I have gone on with the world (as I cou'd) with much worse'.[14] Now again he admitted to Hester that he was 'not quite well', but he was going riding and hoped to return better. He 'truly hoped' that his disorder was transient. Dr Wilmot had just now ordered him an emetic. He was as well as rhubarb would let him be and hoped 'to be better tomorrow for it'. Certainly in the matter of Pitt's health Hester was never misled. She entered upon her marriage to a chronically vulnerable man with her eyes open. Indeed Pitt had gone out of his way to stress to her his 'declined' or even 'shattered' condition. That she could accept him, maladies and all, made her for him more admirable and adorable than ever.

For Pitt no day could be too soon for the wedding. He hoped for the 6 or 7 November, a week before the opening of Parliament, when he was due immediately to introduce an uncontroversial bill, stemming from the initiative of the Duke of Cumberland, to secure prompter payment and fairer treatment for Chelsea Pensioners. Hester, however, pronounced – and had to repeat – that 'sooner than what I have named [15 November] it cannot be'; and they were in fact married on the sixteenth, two days after parliament had re-assembled. Pitt had asked for a quiet wedding; 'the less spectacle,' he urged, 'the less of everything but your lovely tender self, is surely best'. None of his relatives attended; only a handful of Grenvilles, and possibly Lyttelton and his wife. It was Lyttelton's brother-in-law Ayscough, the once 'ridiculous Skew', who conducted the ceremony at Lady Hester's in Argyle Street. Her cousin and Pitt's good friend Gilbert West, had offered them his house for a brief honeymoon. To West Wickham therefore, whose grounds Pitt had once helped to plan, he took his bride and what Mrs Montagu called his 'amorous impatience'. For a few days they had the place to themselves. And from closely neighbouring Hayes, within eighteen months to be Pitt's own, Mrs Montagu wrote, 'We have no communication by messages either to or from Mr Pitt', whom, she properly adds, 'we were un-

willing to disturb, or interrupt the free course of those pleasures which
. . . are most relished when private'.[15]

Propitiously begun, Pitt's marriage never faltered. For Hester,
'ever unalterably your most passionately loving wife', he was never
anything but 'my glorious love', 'my most loved love'. 'Nine o'clock,
the duties of our Sunday evening done, and the little ones retired to
bed, I musing by the fire, comes in my dearest love's letter'. Glorying
in the times of triumph that were soon to come, she supported stead-
fastly the burdens of the days of despair that arrived later. And in the
little personal messages and signing-off phrases of his letters the
strength of his devotion to his 'matchless Hetty' glints through his
fog of decorous circumlocutions. 'A thousand new circumstances
endear my love to me every day I live with her'. Her 'passionately
devoted husband', he discovered her 'all that the fondest passion has
been able to figure'. 'I will still indulge the hope', he writes, 'that . . . I
shall hold my tenderest and ever-adored love in my arms tomorrow'.
Perhaps the only two unqualified successes in Pitt's life – but they were
both resounding – were to be his conduct of the Seven Years War
and his marriage to Hester Grenville.

CHAPTER ELEVEN

Struggle for Power

While Pitt had been struggling back to something like health in the summer of 1754, and then courting and marrying Hester in the autumn, the power politics of Europe and the intrigues of Westminster had never for long moved out of his view. And events abroad, particularly in America, gave him no more confidence than Newcastle's handling of them.

The peace plenipotentiaries at Aix-la-Chapelle in 1748 had been quite content to relegate North American border problems to a boundary commission. While over the next few years this deliberated protractedly in Paris, the colonials were in effect left to take the law into their own hands. In the north, New France (Canada) faced a British colony in Nova Scotia upon her eastern flank and, upon her southern, the New England states and the thrusting territories of Pennsylvania and Virginia. Far away to the south lay French Louisiana; and between these two remotely separated dominions stretched the wilderness, pierced only by the great rivers of the Mississippi basin. These settlements along the St Lawrence and the Gulf of Mexico were sparse and poor, their inhabitants greatly outnumbered by the British colonies along the Atlantic seaboard, where the population was doubling every twenty-five or thirty years. But the strategic design of the French administrators was richly imaginative. Laying claim by right of discovery to the Mississippi and its tributaries, including the vital Ohio, they built along these natural highways a succession of fortified trading-posts, and thus planned both a link to join north with south, New France and the St Lawrence with New Orleans and the Gulf, and also a firm limit to British expansion beyond the Alleghenies or towards Lakes Ontario and Erie. Under two forceful Governors, the hunchback admiral Marquis de la Galissonière and the Marquis Duquesne, quick progress was achieved with this bold project, while from the British side traders and settlers continued to push to the

west and north-west towards the French barrier. Some of the deepest
penetration was made by agents of the British Ohio Company, moving
through Iroquois country towards the Great Lakes, with a royal
concession for the Indian trade.

It was in this area between Lake Erie and the head waters of the
Ohio that the ambitious French system was most vulnerable, and in
1753 the newly arrived Duquesne moved quickly to establish forts
along the Bull and Allegheny rivers, and to expel or take prisoner
the Ohio Company's men. Virginia, with strong interests in the Ohio
Company, replied by sending a force to attempt the establishment of
a fortified post (the beginnings of Pittsburg) at the head of the Ohio.
Surprised by the French in superior numbers, the Virginians were
obliged to surrender their fort only half completed. The French
finished the construction; named it Fort Duquesne; were in turn attacked
by troops commanded by young Lieutenant-Colonel George Washington; but forced his surrender at Fort Necessity and disarmed his men,
permitting them however to return home. What Americans call the
French and Indian War had begun. The date was July 1754. The
conventional English description 'Seven Years War' makes little enough
sense in the context of hostilities in America; and for Pitt America
was always the crucial theatre.

Newcastle was alarmed – 'everybody', he wrote to Granville, 'is
full of North America and our defeat there' – but he was anxious at
the same time to avoid alarmist talk of impending war. 'It is so difficult
to know what to do', he lamented. 'We cannot be too cautious, nor
too expeditious in determining something'; and then, with his unique
talent for sounding infinitely more fatuous than he was,* *that something
must be (if possible) effectual'.[1] Reasonably Newcastle reckoned that
he could hardly risk starting another general war at a time when he
was so unsure of the traditional British-Dutch-Austrian alliance,
which he rightly judged to be on the point of dissolution. Many
Englishmen, Pitt included, thought Austria had proved an expensive

* A characteristic which Walpole delightedly caricatures. From him of course derives
the legendary little anecdote of Newcastle's reply, 'with his evasive lisping hurry', to
General Ligonier's suggestion that Annapolis (in Maryland) must be defended. 'Annapolis must be defended. To be sure Annapolis should be defended. Where is Annapolis?'
Newcastle might justly be accused of timidity; but although his knowledge of America
was poorer than Pitt's, and much poorer than his own knowledge of Europe, the
implication of sublime ignorance is very unjust (*Memoirs of . . . George II*, i. 344).

and largely useless ally in the recent past, and had no enthusiasm for Newcastle's laborious attempts to bolster what seemed a moribund alliance by means of bribes to sundry Electors of the Holy Roman Empire; sending good money after bad. And with Kaunitz as her Chancellor from 1753 Maria Theresa approached steadily nearer to the détente with France that she hoped would enable her to achieve the isolation of Prussia and thus – her grand aim – the recovery of Silesia.

Newcastle was above all aware that Britain must not be seen to *initiate* a war. This might drive Spain, recently inclining towards neutrality, back into the arms of France; and although the British navy could outmatch the French, the combined fleets of France and Spain would be formidable. Holland, too, would admit no treaty obligations to Britain in a war aggressively undertaken. As for Frederick of Prussia, whose virtues as prospective ally Pitt and many more had so frequently and emphatically proclaimed, George II's hostility towards him still appeared insuperable, and Newcastle remained sceptical and reluctant. Instead, fearing that in a general war Prussia would pounce on Hanover, he spent several years trying to lure Russia into his alliance system as a means of deterring Frederick from any such enterprise.

Newcastle's problem was thus how to take strong enough action in America without precipitating a European crisis in which there were altogether too many unknown factors for comfort. 'Our friend Lord Granville,'* he privately grumbled, 'is always talking about our strength in America, and I don't see we are able to do anything'.[2] He did however eventually dispatch a naval squadron under Commodore Keppel, and two regiments from Ireland under the command of Major General Braddock, one of Cumberland's men, to reinforce American colonial troops; but not before some weeks of hesitancy, during the course of which, in early October, six weeks or so before Pitt's wedding, he ventured to consult the opinion of his difficult and resentful Paymaster. Pitt was at first sarcastically disingenuous: 'Your Grace, I suppose, *knows I have no capacity for these things* . . . and therefore I do not desire to be informed about them'.[3] But he ended by pressing Newcastle to be more decisive; to send more artillery; and

---

* Lord Granville (Carteret) had been Lord President of the Council since 1751. Newcastle over these years relied on the opinion of this most senior of his cabinet colleagues only a little less than on Hardwicke's.

to adopt Granville's proposal for raising further colonial contingents.

Newcastle's dilemma was real. To do nothing to assist the Americans might have meant closing the door for ever upon further expansion. Yet how might he manage to conduct a purely colonial war with France without risking everything in Europe? without losing Hanover and courting hostile control of the Netherlands coasts? And even if in a general war the British navy dominated the seas and great gains were made in America, might they not all be lost again at the peace as bargaining counters for the return of a newly lost Hanover? Newcastle therefore prudently determined to wage a strictly limited American war, calculated to contain French 'aggression'. Braddock was authorized to proceed against Forts Duquesne, Crown Point (on Lake Champlain) and Niagara. He was to break the French stranglehold, but to make no attempt to inflict an outright defeat or conquer well-established French territories (as activists like Governor Shirley of Massachusetts, in charge of the operations against Fort Niagara, wished passionately to do). 'You will try', wrote Newcastle to the British ambassador in Paris, 'to give such a turn to these defensive measures as may make the French ministers ashamed to complain of them'.

Long years of experience as postilion upon the coach of state had not diminished Newcastle's chronic fear of being struck by lightning, or ambushed by highwaymen at the next crossroads. By the autumn of 1754 the most menacing of the thunderclouds, the most alarming of the lurking desperadoes, was undoubtedly Pitt ('very much displeased with me', Newcastle noted, 'and thought he had been neglected'); but Fox and Legge also required careful handling. To Hardwicke Newcastle wrote: 'I will hope that we shall not suffer three ambitious men [Pitt, Fox, Legge] . . . to defeat all our good designs for the public, and to convince the King that we cannot serve him without their being our masters'. There was, he was sure, 'a most thorough combination in the *three* to get at once the House of Commons, and consequently the whole administration into their hands'.[4]

Newcastle was as puzzled as he was irritated by Pitt's attitude towards him. Legge had informed him that Pitt would be willing to come into the cabinet in some office other than Secretary of State, 'since the King did not like' the prospect of him as Secretary; but he must insist on being '*treated with confidence*'. Yet, so Newcastle claimed, when *he* had proposed just such an arrangement earlier, Pitt had 'treated it as *words* and mere *amusement*'.[5] No doubt Pitt, still smarting at what he reckoned hypocrisy and shabby dealing – snubs and fair words in equal measure – had taken up positions that were shifting and inconsistent. He deeply mistrusted Newcastle now and, if Horace Walpole is to be believed, rebuffed one of the Duke's exploratory propositions with 'Fewer words, my lord, if you please; for your words have long lost all weight with me'.[6]

The position of the Whig 'old corps' was still very strong, and there is something bizarre in the spectacle of so nervous and diffident a figure as Newcastle carrying as much political power as he did. He could perhaps hardly have managed without Hardwicke, the Chancellor, that altogether solider man, behind him. Though these two were by no means always united in judgement or uncritical of one another, they were tightly bound by habit, respect, and common interest, and as mutually complementary as bacon and eggs. 'I never had or ever shall have', wrote Newcastle, 'a friend whom I honour and love like yourself, and for whose opinion . . . I have and now for nearly thirty years have had, so great a deference'. After the occasions when they fell out, Newcastle was in torture until things had been put right. 'I cannot be easy', he would write, 'till I have . . . begged your Lordship's pardon and asked your forgiveness'. 'For God's sake, my dear Lord, 'don't harbour a thought of my want of gratitude, or the highest respect for you and submission to your advice'.[7] Yet, edgy as he was, Newcastle was in no danger of underestimating the strength that he and the 'old corps' wielded. He was well aware now, in September 1754, despite Messrs Legge, Fox, and Pitt, that 'we have as good a body of friends in the House of Commons as men ever had; we have the King' – *at present*, he warily added* – 'and we have, and shall have, the House of Lords'.

Soon after the beginning of the 1754–5 session of parliament Pitt, returning from his honeymoon in very tigerish mood, was ready to pounce, like one who had been sick and caged too long, on any unfortunate within reach.

---

* A month or two later, when the King smartly reminded him that he was only the chief *Treasury* minister – there was no such thing as prime minister – and he should not meddle in what did not concern him, he was in a flutter of apprehension at the thought that Fox, Cumberland's protégé, might be insinuating himself into a premier position in the royal favour.

Mr Pitt [wrote Walpole to Horace Mann] has broke with the
Duke of Newcastle, on the want of power, and has alarmed the
dozing House of Commons with some sentences extremely in the
style of his former *Pittics*. As Mr Fox is not at all more in humour,
the world expects every day to see these two commanders first
unite to overturn their antagonists, and then worry one another.
They have already mumbled poor Sir Thomas Robinson cruelly . . .
What will surprise you is that the Duke of Newcastle, who used to
tremble in the shadows, appears unterrified at Gorgons! If I should
tell you in my next, that either of the Gorgons has kissed hands
for Secretary of State, only smile: snakes are as easily tamed as lap-
dogs.[8]

Pitt's high-sounding invective had first fallen upon one Delaval,
who, in making a speech against a petition to invalidate his election
had employed just such unconcerned flippancy as Pitt himself seven
years before, in a like situation after his Seaford election, when *he* had
been rebuked by Potter. But now of course it was only indirectly at
Delaval that Pitt's fire was directed. The main target was Newcastle.
If members did not make an effort to recover their dignity, Pitt thundered – he had entered the Chamber to find laughter upon the subject
of bribery and corruption – they would soon be sitting 'only to register
the arbitrary edicts of *one too powerful a subject*'[9] – startling words to
use of the head of a government of which one was a member, even in
those days of less than complete governmental solidarity. It was later
the same day that he 'mumbled' Robinson, an exercise in which he
was joined by Fox. Softening the blow later to Robinson, 'to whom he
now spoke with respect, and with esteem of his integrity', he made it
clear that he regarded him merely as the agent of Newcastle. The Duke
had been put into 'the utmost fidget' by Pitt's onslaught, Fox reported
merrily; 'it spoiled his stomach yesterday'. Two days later Pitt used
the occasion of an army debate to deliver a wounding attack upon
another of his colleagues, the Attorney General, reviving the old
smear of Murray's alleged Jacobite sympathies, and coupling him by
implication with the 'treason' persisting in the heart of their common
university of Oxford – 'learned and respectable: so much the more
dangerous'.[10] Never directly accusing Murray, he fixed his intimidating
eye upon him at well-calculated moments; torture by innuendo.

According to Fox, who sat next to the victim, Pitt made him suffer for a whole hour; and to most present it seemed clear that he was bent upon pursuing Murray's humiliation.[11]

Either Fox or Pitt would have made a dangerous enough enemy for Newcastle; Fox with his sizable band in the Commons and the support of the Duke of Cumberland, Pitt with his smaller personal following, but formidably destructive in debate and oratory. In alliance, Fox and Pitt might well prove too strong for Newcastle and Hardwicke to handle.

> The Duke of Newcastle saw his mighty power totter; yet he could not determine to share it. The first thought was to dismiss Pitt. This was too bold a measure to have been the preference for long: the next more natural was to try to sweeten Fox.[12]

– which, wrote Walpole, put Lord Bath (Pulteney) in mind of a story concerning the Gunpowder Plot: 'The Lord Chamberlain was sent to examine the vaults under Parliament House, and, returning with his report, said he had found five-and-twenty barrels of gunpowder; he had removed ten of them, and hoped the other fifteen would do no harm'.[13] Newcastle rendered harmless the ten barrels by giving Fox a place in the cabinet and providing minor posts for his 'friends'. Fox remained in the relatively subordinate post of Secretary-at-War; did not obtain the leadership of the Commons; and gained no pecuniary advantage. Newcastle and Hardwicke thought him cheap at the price. Up to the moment of accepting a cabinet place Fox kept closely in touch with Pitt over tactics, and Pitt did nothing to dissuade him from dissolving their marriage of convenience. According to Hardwicke, moreover, Fox 'made it a kind of condition for himself that, if Mr Pitt should now be turned out, *he* must be excused from taking a personal part against him'. By Christmas 1754, however, Fox had effectively severed all connection with Pitt and privately resolved to have no further association with him. 'I do not desire to know,' he wrote to Lord Waldegrave, 'much less to determine, what Mr Pitt is to do or to be'. (Newcastle, Hardwicke and Granville had in fact agreed that Pitt should be left alone to stew quietly 'under the uncertainty where he now is'.)[14]

Fox could hardly be accused in fairness of betraying Pitt, but he had certainly parted company with him; and obviously resentment and jealousy resulted. It was the old story. Still Pitt had the mortification of 'seeing every boat pass by him that navigated the same river'. When in April the two men met by chance at the house of Lord Hillsborough there was something of a scene:

> Mr Pitt came to Lord Hillsborough's, where was Mr Fox, who stepping aside, and Mr Pitt thinking he was gone, the latter declared to Lord Hillsborough that all connection between him and Mr Fox was over – that the *ground was altered* – that Fox was of the Cabinet and Regent,* and he was left exposed, etc. Mr Fox rejoining the company, Mr Pitt, being heated, said the same and more to him; that if Fox succeeded, and so made way for him, he would not accept the seals of Secretary from him, for that would be owning an obligation and superiority, which he would never acknowledge: he would owe nothing but to himself . . .[15]

Once Newcastle had secured Fox, more or less – he never felt entirely sure of him – he had little trouble from the Commons during the early months of 1755. 'Things go very quietly this session', wrote Chesterfield. 'Fox has evidently the lead there. Pitt, though very angry, rather hints than declares opposition, unwilling to lose his employment and at the same time unable to stifle his resentment'.[16] The only noteworthy intervention Pitt made over these months was to warn against the dangers of arbitrary power in a speech arising from a debate on the continuing dependency of the Scottish sheriffs upon the pleasure of the Crown; 'one of the best worded and most spirited declamations for liberty', judged Horace Walpole, who despaired however of rendering the feel of it on paper. 'Like others of his fine orations, it cannot be delivered adequately without his own language . . . I cannot forget with what soul and grace it was uttered'.[17]

With both France and Britain nervous of the likely consequences of a new war, hostilities between them in Europe until August 1755 were restricted to the sparrings of diplomacy. Like two boxers intent upon their guard, the British and French governments bobbed warily round the ring, each too respectful of its rival's punch to risk the offensive. In America both countries were already committed to limited war, while at sea, where her superiority was considerable, Britain attempted to calculate to a nicety just how far action might go without

* Fox had recently been appointed a member of the Council of Regency.

the French being provoked into a war which must bring with it an immediate attack on Hanover.

At the end of April, George II left for his habitual summer sojourn in his German dominions – 'without one man about him', Pitt remarked indignantly, 'that has one English sentiment'[18] – and spent the next four and a half months there, with Secretary of State Lord Holderness at his elbow, negotiating treaties of subsidy and assistance with Hesse and Russia. The upshot of these was that in the event of war 8000 Hessians were to come to his assistance, and in return for an annual £100,000 the Tsarina Elizabeth undertook to provide a force of 55,000.

Before the King left for Hanover, Admiral Boscawen, newly in command of Atlantic naval forces, was given cabinet instructions to capture or destroy 'any French ships having on board troops or warlike stores'. In May two French squadrons, of warships and transports, left Brest for Canada, and managed, all but one warship and one transport, to elude Boscawen and reach port safely. Boscawen did not seem dissatisfied with his haul of one 64-gunner and eight companies of troops, but the politicians were far from sharing his pleasure. As Hardwicke wrote to his son-in-law Anson, First Lord of the Admiralty, 'It gives me much concern that so little has been done, since anything has been done at all. Voilà the war begun!'[19] – and since it seemed so, Newcastle was at first in favour of ordering the navy to prey on French shipping wherever it could be found. However, the still influential Granville successfully argued against such militancy – 'vexing your neighbours', he called it, 'for a little muck' – not on the grounds that war was undesirable but rather that if Britain waited a little longer, France would declare war and thus 'put us under the necessity of falling upon their trade in Europe' without any odium coming to Britain from neutral or allied states for her piratical behaviour. At first, therefore, the navy was instructed to confine its attentions to ships of the line, to prevent a junction between the French Atlantic and Mediterranean squadrons, and to bar the former's return from Canada to Brest; but, when the French broke off diplomatic relations and full-scale war appeared inevitable, Newcastle reverted to his original inclination, and the fleet was ordered to sweep up all the French shipping it could find. A great haul was made of over three hundred prizes.

The news from the American mainland meanwhile was very bad.

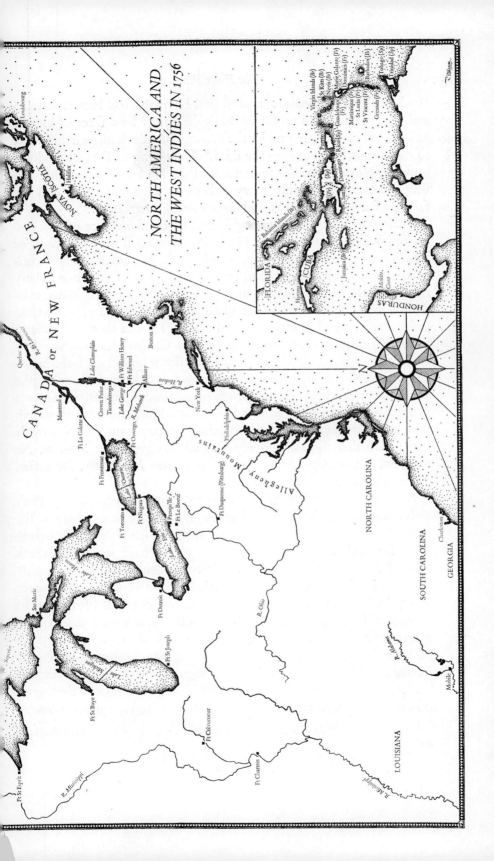

NORTH AMERICA AND
THE WEST INDIES IN 1756

CANADA or NEW FRANCE

NOVA SCOTIA

Louisbourg
Halifax

Quebec
R. St Lawrence
Montreal
Ft La Galette
Lake Champlain
Crown Point
Ticonderoga
Ft William Henry
Lake George
Ft Edward
Ft Oswego
R. Mohawk
Albany
Boston
R. Hudson
New York
Philadelphia
Allegheny Mountains
Ft Frontenac
Lake Ontario
Ft Niagara
Ft Toronto
Presqu'Ile
Ft Le Boeuf
Ft Duquesne (Pitsburg)
Lake Erie
Ste Marie
Ft Detroit
Lake Huron
Lake Superior
Ft St Joseph
Lake Michigan
Ft St Baye
Ft St Esprit
R. Mississippi
Ft Crèvecoeur
Ft Clartres
R. Ohio
NORTH CAROLINA
SOUTH CAROLINA
GEORGIA
Charleston
R. Alabama
Mobile
LOUISIANA
R. Mississippi

FLORIDA
CUBA
Havana
HONDURAS
Moskito Coast
Bahama Islands (Br)
Jamaica (Br)
San Domingo (Fr)
Puerto Rico (Sp)
Virgin Islands (Br)
St Kitts (Br)
Nevis (Br)
Guadeloupe (Fr)
Martinique (Fr)
St Lucia (Fr)
St Vincent (Fr)
Grenada (Fr)
Antigua (Br)
Ste Colombe (Fr)
Dominica (Fr)
Barbados (Br)
Tobago (Sp)
Trinidad (Sp)

Braddock's force advancing against Fort Duquesne had been ambushed and largely destroyed on the Monongahela river by a force of Indians and irregulars operating under the French, Braddock himself and most of his officers being among the dead.* The taking of Fort Beauséjour, opposite Nova Scotia, by volunteers of the New England militia was little recompense for this heavy setback in the Ohio valley and the failure of attempts upon Forts Niagara and Crown Point.

Their domestic position strengthened by the adherence of Fox and his following, Newcastle and Hardwicke were still very conscious of Pitt, hovering dangerously upon their flank. His parliamentary connection was small, smaller than ever since the loss of Lyttelton. Many members mistrusted him, much as conventional politicians mistrusted Winston Churchill over all his early and middle years. He had twisted and turned in the pursuit of power. He was thought brilliant, but strange; impressive, but arrogant. Like Cassius's his look was lean and hungry. Newcastle knew that Pitt's fire might catch light in the Commons. Given a popular rallying cry – in a House which despite all the arts and skills of election management and dispensation of loaves and fishes was still more impressionable and independent in its voting than latterday Houses – Pitt might indeed be dangerous, and Newcastle was aware that the rallying cry was all too available: *Sea-war, No continent, No subsidy* might prove as potent as *No slavery, No excise, No wooden shoes* had been in 1733.

Newcastle and Hardwicke resolved to make a serious bid for Pitt's active support, which became increasingly important for them as the news from across the Atlantic deteriorated. 'Whether the miscarriage upon the Ohio', wrote Hardwicke, 'may not have made him think himself the more necessary, your Grace . . . may best determine'.[20] Already in April Newcastle had tried, through the elder Horace Walpole, 'to bring Mr Pitt into temper', but Pitt (still Paymaster, of course; still a member of the administration) had shown that he was not to be had easily. He would not, he said, insist on a Secretaryship of State immediately, but 'when any vacancy happened he should have the seals'.[21] In the meantime the King must be persuaded to remove his 'proscription' and agree to deal with him on the same footing as other responsible ministers. And if he was cordially to support govern-

* George Washington was among the minority who escaped from this grim little action.

ment measures he must be clearly informed what those measures were.

A second attempt to *entamer* the great Mr Pitt', this time through Hardwicke's son Charles Yorke, brought no more amenable response. Newcastle then tried through Holderness, the Secretary attending the King in Hanover, to persuade their master to relax his veto upon Pitt at least to the extent of allowing him a seat in the cabinet, which would have meant winning Pitt on broadly the same terms as Fox. Despite 'the just reasons his Majesty has to be offended', the King did grudgingly agree to 'countenance' Pitt; but since he would not, when requested, enlarge upon the word 'countenance', Newcastle rightly concluded that there was no change of royal heart.

To treat publicly with Pitt, Newcastle was sure, would only 'raise his vanity and his terms, and make a ridiculous éclat'.[22] Nervous, however, of developments in the Commons, and noting moreover that Pitt had by midsummer come to an understanding with the Princess of Wales's party and was once more in favour at Leicester House, he now asked the Chancellor himself to make a discreet direct approach. After all, he wrote to Hardwicke, Pitt 'knows, and everybody knows, that your Lordship had . . . the principal hand in preventing his being turned out'. On 9 August, therefore, for an hour and three quarters Hardwicke proceeded to 'feel the pulse of the great Pitt', whose manner he discovered to be remarkably 'easy and frank', but whose terms remained obstinate. He must *be shown publicly* to have the King's confidence; and his friends – by which Hardwicke presumed 'he chiefly meant my Lord Temple' – must be embraced in any arrangement. However it was not *men* but *measures* that would provide the prime obstacle, Hardwicke saw. The maritime and American war, he reported, was fully approved by Pitt, however onerous it was likely to prove at over six millions a year. As for the continental war, Pitt 'allowed the principle, and the obligations on honour and justice . . . but argued strongly against the practicability of it'. The nation would not support it; neither would he. It would be by no means a tragedy, he considered, if Hanover were temporarily overrun, being

made the quarters of French or Prussian troops for a time, but there was no danger of the King or his family finally losing it, and he thought England ought never to make peace without restitution, and a full dédommagement to the King on that account . . . He had rather concur in giving the King five millions, by way of dédommagements, at the end of the war, than undertake the defence of it by subsidies.[23]

The government's foreign policy, in short, must be abandoned. Newcastle and Hardwicke were not yet so enfeebled as to swallow medicine such as this. Yet the problem of how to ensure acceptance of the subsidies remained. Indeed Newcastle was now faced with the more immediate and unexpected problem of getting them accepted by his own Treasury. Legge, the Chancellor of the Exchequer, an old friend of Pitt's, though recently in common with others 'crouching under the storm' of his invective,[24] now came back high into his esteem, for he flatly refused to put his counter-signature to the warrant for the Hessian subsidy. The sweetness of this move quite delighted Pitt. 'Legge is my guide, philosopher, and friend', he wrote enthusiastically to Hester. 'A less ludicrous comfort I should not taste a hundred miles from my lovely, adored wife'.[25]

Reluctantly Newcastle decided that he would have to try his own luck with Pitt face to face. 'I cannot say I have much *glee* in meeting Mr Pitt', he grumbled. 'I know it is necessary and I must do it, but I don't know how to talk to such a man, who has acted towards me as he has done'.[26] However, as Hardwicke had found, Pitt in conference, however firm and outspoken, could be personally disarming. 'The whole passed with the greatest decency, civility, openness, and seeming friendly disposition on his part', Newcastle reported. And yet 'at the same time there was such firm resolution, so solemnly declared . . . that, if complied with, must produce a total change in the present system, both as to measures and men'.[27] Pitt had been blunt. Newcastle must be prepared to part with some of his '*sole power*' (a wounding phrase Newcastle was at pains to rebut); he must be ready to accept a Secretary 'of ability' in the Commons. As things stood, Pitt reckoned that that House was no more than 'an assembly of atoms'; 'the great wheels of the machine were stop'd'. To be sure he did not actually demand the Secretaryship for himself in so many words, but he did stipulate that the existing Secretaries, Robinson and Holderness, should be 'provided for elsewhere' and his own new office, if he were to have one, must give him a genuine share in shaping and executing policy. He refused to speak like a mere lawyer from a brief. Above all, he must have, and be seen to have, the King's unequivocal confidence:

> He spoke with the utmost respect of Hanover; but he ridiculed extremely the notion of supporting Hanover with 8000 men, which was too little if Hanover was attacked, and a most unnecessary expense without it . . . No consideration should make him be for the Hessian and Russian treaties.[28]

Pitt had not gone to confront Newcastle without first sounding out his political friends and potential allies. He had strong hopes of the Duke of Devonshire (the third Duke – he died that December). The Duke of Bedford, though Pitt feared he was 'soft on measures', might prove another powerful ally. Legge was 'firm as a rock'. Then there was Leicester House, where Pitt had already accepted an invitation to 'enter in the closest engagements'. It was four years since the Prince of Wales's death, and the emerging force now, in the household of his widow, was the Earl of Bute, the politically ambitious Scotsman who had become tutor to the heir apparent and chief confidant and man of business to the Princess Dowager. In August Pitt was assuring Bute that he was 'counting every hour till he embraced him', and promising that he would not fail to act according to Bute's 'final will and pleasure'.[29] Both before and again after meeting Newcastle he consulted with that experienced trimmer Bubb Dodington, who was as ever prepared to sail towards the fishing grounds where the catch looked richest. 'We talked over whom we could engage', records Dodington's diary for 3 September. 'Lord Egmont seemed to enter into the thing . . . He [Pitt] desired me to apply to Lord Hillsborough and Sir Francis Dashwood . . .' What of Fox? asked Dodington. Pitt replied no, 'that he wished Fox very well, and had nothing to complain of, but that they could not act together . . . He, who was *sui juris*, could not act in connection with one who was not'. This insistence upon his complete independence was always to be a great and proud point with Pitt, even at a time like this when his very seat in parliament was dependent on the favour of the Duke of Newcastle. *Sui juris* or no, he was obviously quite ready at this stage to proposition Dodington. Seducible Dodington may have been, but not quite as gullible as perhaps Pitt hoped:

He professed a desire [writes Dodington] to unite himself with me in the strictest manner – he had ever the highest regard for my abilities – we had always acted upon the same principles: he had the honour to be married into my relations [by marriage again, the Grenvilles] . . . He added a great deal more, that surprised me very much, considering the treatment I have met with, for years past, both from him and those relations.[30]

But at this kind of game Newcastle was not easily worsted. He too began to make dispositions, on the assumption that Pitt's price would remain impossibly high. In mid-September the King returned from Hanover, and before the month was out Fox had accepted an offer of the seals of Secretary of State for the Southern Department, together with leadership of the Commons; Sir Thomas Robinson being awarded a £2000-a-year consolatory pension and restored to the recesses of the Great Wardrobe. (Still mistrustful of Fox and nervous of surrendering any substantial power to him, Newcastle tried to reassure himself that the King would 'not suffer Mr Fox to do anything *even in the House of Commons*' without first consulting Newcastle himself.)[31] The hint of a promotion to cabinet status served to whittle away Lord Halifax's objections to the subsidy treaties, and his ally Lord Hillsborough was won by the beckoning prospect of becoming Treasurer of the Chambers. Lord Halifax in turn was set to work upon another of his friends, Dodington, so recently and flatteringly wooed by Pitt, though it required the dangling persuasions of Newcastle finally to gain him. It was feared that Dodington's talents, though 'strangely betawdry'd', would have proved 'wonderfully mischievous' in opposition.[32] Finally abandoning Pitt, he eventually landed the Treasurership of the Navy. Horace Walpole the elder's prize for succumbing was a peerage, at last. Bedford proved content to see his brother-in-law, the newly succeeded Lord Gower, as Privy Seal, and two others of his followers, Rigby and Lord Sandwich, obliged with places, as the price of at least *not obstructing* the passage of the subsidy treaties, to the wisdom of which he remained unconverted. The Duke of Devonshire similarly disappointed Pitt and the Leicester House brigade, who had regarded him as a capture only less important than Bedford. Hume Campbell, once a fellow Patriot with Pitt, but one who had subsequently had brushes in parliament with him and was thought capable of standing up to him again now, was induced to give up his practice at the bar and brought in at £2000 a year to stiffen governmental ranks in the Commons. Thus Newcastle and Fox, with the wealth of patronage at their disposal, were able comfortably to win these preliminary rounds and come to the parliament of November 1755 with the prospect of easy majorities.

Pitt was far from down-hearted. He must have known that in the coming political conflict he was bound to be numerically the loser. Presumably too he was expecting dismissal, and thereby the loss both of his principal income and his Paymaster's residence. But he was clearly relishing the scent of battle ahead. Even his health, never wholly good, was at least for a time not altogether bad. Once, during the treaty debates of December, Walpole excuses the lifelessness of a long harangue of Pitt's by his being that day 'not well', but the following month Pitt declared himself on the whole 'pretty well, indeed quite so, the remains of a cold excepted' – though indeed 1756 had not progressed far before we learn of 'a troublesome pain' in his face and ear which caused him to be muffled up in flannel, and by the summer he was to be 'utterly unable to move for this ten days' – this time by 'a very awkward, uneasy, but not hurtful malady', its nature unspecified. Good health was always to be a strictly relative term with Pitt; at the very least, gout was now always lying in wait for him; but generally over this period he was physically active, and mentally free from depression. He was off on his own to Bath during the Christmas recess to see after the final stages in the building of his house there. Hester wrote wondering whether it did not mean that they were incurring too much expense – they were at the same time looking for a suitable town house to rent, which they found eventually in Brook Street – but Pitt, who seldom allowed himself to be deterred by such commonplace considerations, answered firmly, 'We are too advanced to recede'; as for himself too advanced *physically* also, he suggested, for him to be without a house in Bath: 'I have so made up my mind to it, for the evening of my day, that I should be grieved if my dearest love were brought to disapprove or dislike it'.[33]

Not content with two houses, and still quite heavily overdrawn at the bank, he was soon to be after a third, and launching out upon the purchase of a property which would be within riding distance of Westminster yet enjoy the blessings of the countryside. Early in 1756 he settled upon what had been Mrs Montagu's house at Hayes, near Wickham in Kent, where he had spent his honeymoon. He professed to see nothing but bankruptcy and ruin ahead for the nation but, politics and personal finances apart, his *private* prospects had not looked better for a long time. Shortly before parliament met, Hester had presented her 'ever passionate husband' (he signed himself so) with a baby daughter – another Hester – which greatly delighted him: 'little Blue-eyes', as he was soon describing her with a father's pride, 'a very growing personage in bulk and in favour, not to say in understanding'.[34] 'The mother and infant', he wrote at the end of October to his old friend Sanderson Miller, 'are both well as possible, and the father full of more happiness than he had even formed the idea of in his days of celibacy, when his imaginations were vain and his foolish heart darkened'.[35]

Pitt rose during the all-night debate of 13–14 November on the address to the throne following the King's Speech, to make his expected attack upon the policies of what was still, though for a few more days only, his own administration. The commanding impetuosity of his eloquence flowed, wrote Walpole, 'like a torrent long obstructed'. 'Haughty, defiant, conscious of irony and supreme abilities', he gave one of the most celebrated of all his performances:

> This speech, accompanied with variety of action, accents and irony, and set off with such happy images and allusions . . . (though one or two of the metaphors were a little forced), lasted about an hour and a half, and was kept up with inimitable spirit, though it did not begin till past one in the morning, after an attention and fatigue of ten hours.[36]

It ranged over all the current controversies. Hanover and the subsidy treaties – 'un-English measures . . . Will they not provoke Prussia and light up a general war?' And their cost: 'Within two years his Majesty could not be able to sleep for the cries of a bankrupt people'. Failure to give priority to the navy: 'Subsidies annihilated ten millions in the last war; our navy brought in twelve millions'. A continental land-war, which the government *must* be envisaging – 'how preposterously do they meditate it!' The plight of the British in America, 'long-injured, long-neglected, long-forgotten'.

Under this onslaught the men of the government suffered no less

sharply than its measures. Lyttelton, defending the steps to protect
Hanover, had cited 'the law of nations'. Pitt, half-turning towards him
'with an air of the greatest contempt' was ready to quote back at him
the greatest of all authorities upon the subject: 'Grotius declares it is
not necessary even *socium defendere si nulla spes boni exitus* [to defend
one's ally if the cause is hopeless]'. Granville was reminded of what had
happened in the late war thanks to his 'wicked counsels', when subsidies had been poured forth and the Dutch had been coerced into
Britain's struggle. 'Out of those rash measures sprang up a ministry . . .
I saw that ministry. In the morning it flourished; it was green by
noon; by night it was cut down and forgotten'. Murray as usual did
not escape Pitt's lash; nor Hillsborough, who had been persuaded to
move the address. For Fox, the man who had 'set himself at the head
of this measure', he professed only pity. There was a characteristically
sarcastic reference to Fox's patron Cumberland and his military
ambitions. Members would say the Carthaginians had a navy and yet
lost the war with Rome; 'ah, but not until they attempted a land war
and crossed the Alps – *and Carthage had, besides, a Hannibal!*' And then,
claiming to descry inconsistencies in the wording of the loyal address
under debate, he made one of his best-remembered sallies against the
peculiar union that had been contrived between the two leaders of the
government; that odd junction of the 'feeble and languid' Newcastle
and the impetuous Fox. The bald summary of the speech, which is all
we have, requires only a little imaginative filling out at this point
to put on live colours and give a momentary glimpse of the spell-
binder at work, the skilled actor commanding, with his 'variety of
action, accents, and irony', not indeed his auditors' votes (the government won the division by 311 to 105) but at least their wide-awake
attention and perhaps grudging admiration – at past two in the
morning.

I, *continued he*, who am at a distance from that *sanctum sanctorum*
whither the priest goes for inspiration, I who travel through a
desart and am overwhelmed with mountains of obscurity, cannot so
easily catch a gleam to direct me to the beauties of these negotiations
– but there are parts of this address that do seem to come from the
same quarter as the rest – I cannot unravel this mystery – yes, *cried
he, clapping his hand suddenly to his forehead*, I too am inspired now!

it strikes me! – I remember at Lyons to have been carried to see the conflux of the Rhône and Saône; this a gentle, feeble, languid stream, and though languid, of no depth – the other, a boisterous and impetuous torrent – but they meet at last; and long may they continue united, to the comfort of each other, and to the glory, honour, and security of the nation.

For once, it is perhaps possible to hear, in Walpole's bare synopsis, the transition, from the amused urbanity of the opening, through the well-meditated brow-slapping and the 'admired comparison' of the junction of the rivers, to the fierce sarcasm of the passage's close. It was never so much on the closeness of his reasoning, where both Murray and Fox were reckoned his superiors, as on imaginative and dramatic effects such as these that Pitt built his tremendous oratorical reputation.

A few days later the long-expected and in many ways overdue notice of dismissal arrived, for Pitt and also for Legge and George Grenville, who had spoken on parallel lines; for John Pitt too, from his Lordship of Trade. James Grenville resigned in sympathy. Legge's place at the Exchequer was given to Lyttelton, who would perhaps have been rather better suited to a university chair of divinity. Had they dragged Dr Halley from his observatory to make him Vice-Chamberlain, Walpole thought the choice would have been as judicious. 'Poor Sir George . . . not able to resist his devotion to the Duke of Newcastle or the impulse of his own ambition', was to come in for some unforgiving mauling from Pitt, who apparently suffered from no qualms in discarding the old friendship. Much hurt, Lyttelton at last complained that Pitt was using 'the language of Billingsgate against him', and turning the Commons 'into a bear-garden'. Lyttelton was an *innocent*, Pitt snapped back; *with his pen in his hand* nobody respected him more.

Pitt's now intimate rapport with Leicester House is seen by his immediately writing to acquaint Bute with the contents of his letter of dismissal and of his own reply, which signified his 'most respectful submission to his Majesty's pleasure'. He sounded very sanguine:

I trouble your Lordship with the words, because it is not impossible I may be misrepresented on this as I have been on so many other occasions. Good night my dear Lord: I believe I shall sleep very quietly and wake as happy as any minister now in England. Heaven defend and prosper the great cause we have the glory to serve.[37]

The loss of salary might have proved embarrassing; but not for the first or last time when money problems pressed, help was ready. This time it came from his 'best and noblest of brothers', Lord Temple, who immediately offered 'a thousand pounds a year till better times' and urged Hester to persuade her husband not to refuse. He perhaps need not have troubled. Pitt was never one to reject from false pride the financial assistance of friends or admirers, or to try and keep his dependence a secret. On this occasion, letting the world know of his indebtedness to Temple only served to underline the cleanness of the Paymaster's hands at the close of over nine years in the office. 'How decline', he replied to Temple's offer, 'or how receive so great a generosity, so amiably offered? We are both yours more affectionately than words can express'.[38]

On the day that he was dismissed Pitt promised that 'to add to England's strength' he would give daily and constant attendance in the Commons. Certainly over the ensuing months he was tirelessly on his feet, making speeches brilliant or laboured, witty or flat, floridly eloquent or pompously trifling, bitterly personal or passionately patriotic. During the first half of the session he was many times attacked and censured for the violence of his invective. Although he was at pains to justify himself, the protests did not finally go unheeded; for Walpole, while awarding the very highest praise to the best of these onslaughts, considered not only that in general 'he spoke too often, and he spoke too long', but also that 'being hurt at the reflections on his pomp and invective', he adopted in the latter part of the session 'a style of plain and scarce elevated conversation, that had not one merit of any of the preceding harangues'.[39] Fox too, though he many times expressed genuine admiration for Pitt as an orator, declared in January 1756: 'The four last times he has spoke he has made such violent speeches . . . upon such trifling matter, which I have been obliged to take advantage of, that he is lowered and I am raised by it . . .'[40]

The most vitriolic outburst of all was direct at Hume Campbell, the auxiliary whom Newcastle had specially introduced to stiffen the government's ranks against Pitt. Attacked by Campbell for his 'eternal invectives', for which the House ought to *exact punishment*,

Pitt, after 'taking time to collect his anger, rose at last, aggravating by the most contemptuous looks and action and accent the bitterest and most insulting of all speeches'. Walpole was so taken with the artistry of this 'annihilation', and 'the style of delicate ridicule and repartee' that followed it, 'flash after flash, for an hour and a half', that he promised his friend Richard Bentley he would gather up some of Pitt's 'glittering splinters' and post them off to him. Since he failed to, we are as usual left with the spare summary of the parliamentary reports, which recount, first, Pitt's carefully prepared parallel between Hume Campbell and another *servile lawyer* in James I's reign, who had called for the punishment of Sir John Eliot after he had insulted the Duke of Buckingham in the House. (There was a second parallel, Pitt said, driving home every damaging innuendo: now also, as 'in the profligate, prerogative reign of James I', they had *a great duke* in the seat of power.) Then, suddenly, the direct venomous personal attack:

> But, said he (turning and directly nodding at Hume Campbell, who sat three benches above him), I will not dress up this image under a third person; I apply it to him. His is the slavish doctrine, he is the slave; and the shame of his slavish doctrine will stick to him as long as his gown sticks to his back.[41]

There were certainly areas of Pitt's reputation and past record that rendered him vulnerable to attack. Murray on occasions and Fox frequently took full advantage of them. Perhaps where the accusation of having 'struggled for power' was concerned, with Fox and Pitt it was a case of the pot calling the kettle black; but when Fox said, 'What the motives of these struggles have been, *let those, who have struggled most and longest for power, tell*', there was such a general murmur of assent among members that Pitt felt obliged to rise there and then, and protest, 'If ever a man had suffered from the stilettos of a court which assassinate the fair opinion of a man with his master, he had'.[42]

In a debate upon the manning of the navy, why, demanded Fox, was Pitt only now crying up the alarms of war, and demanding immediately 50,000 sailors? Why not the previous years? Here Pitt, who had stood out in 1751 for 2000 more men, was better armed for counter-attack.

He asks why I did not call out sooner. *My* calling out was more likely to defeat than promote. When I remonstrated for more seamen [in Pelham's day] I was called an enemy to government: now I am told that I want to strow the King's pillow with thorns: am traduced, aspersed, calumniated from morning to night. *I* would have warned the King: did *he* [Fox]? . . . This whole summer I have been looking for government – I saw none . . . When his Majesty returned [from Hanover] his kingdom was delivered to him more like a wreck than as a vessel able to stem the storm . . . Let them show him how to contribute to the King's service, and then tax him with strowing the royal pillow with thorns.

Against Murray, who had claimed that 140,000 of Europe's best troops now stood ready to defend Hanover, Pitt declaimed:

Who boasts of what numbers are prepared for England? for America? . . . Two miserable battalions of Irish [Braddock's force], who scarce ever saw one another, had been sent to America, had been sent to be sacrificed.[43]

But Murray, whom on more than one earlier occasion Pitt had battered and browbeaten in the House, this time coolly held his own. Both men vied in professing their admiration for the late lamented premier, Pelham. Were he still alive, said Murray, perhaps they would have fewer struggles, 'if all who supported under him, did still'. Then he begged to ask one question. He believed that 'those sitting near' Pitt had understood him to say he had *refused* the office of Secretary of State; pray, had he? In an over-confident moment Pitt had indeed insinuated as much, but was now obliged awkwardly to concede that he had merely 'refused to come into measures'.[44]

There was a good deal of harking back, not only to Henry Pelham for whom respect was now *de rigueur*, but to that giant of earlier days, Robert Walpole, and *his* policies. It was a subject upon which Pitt would have perhaps been wiser to keep silent. Instead, once more he insisted on claiming that 'he had spoken, and all that minister's family had heard him speak, with respect of Sir Robert Walpole' *after he had fallen from power*. This could hardly fail to raise a laugh; whereupon Pitt 'angrily and haughtily told them, it was a blundering laugh'. Was it, or was it not, more honourable to respect a man after his power was ended?

Occasionally thrown back thus on the defensive, he was by no means yet the triumphant scourge of the government, whose majorities remained monotonously comfortable. Nevertheless, both hitting and missing, he maintained the attack to the end of the session, except when illness kept him briefly from his seat – which made Horace Walpole complain how sleepy the Commons seemed then. In February 1756 Walpole had been reporting: 'The House of Commons is dwindled into a very dialogue between Pitt and Fox . . . in which, though Pitt has attacked, Fox has generally had the better'. And so it might well have continued, if the accumulation of alarm at home (the fear of invasion) and one considerable catastrophe abroad (the loss of Minorca) had not thrust towards Pitt the opportunity of power.

Pitt's ridicule and rhetoric, endorsed apparently by his triumphs to come, made it altogether too easy for historians subsequently to put Newcastle and his policies in the dock, to write him off as a craven and inept bungler, and see in him merely the contemptible 'fixer', whom events were soon to sweep aside, by the grace of an Anglophile God, to make room for the hero and saviour of his country. In fact, while Pitt was belabouring Newcastle and his fellow ministers in the winter and spring of 1755–6, his conduct of affairs was far from foolish. Until disasters began to strike in the summer, his policies might reasonably have been thought to be holding their own well enough.

His treaty with Russia, ratified by parliament in December 1755, had been designed originally to ensure that if Hanover were attacked, Russia would move against France's ally Prussia. By this time, however, some deep diplomatic games were being played by all the major powers. Russia was intending to use her treaty with Britain as a pretext for assembling troops in the Baltic province of Livonia ready for an invasion of Prussia. George II, having at last agreed to accept the painful necessity of his nephew's friendship, had allowed his ministers to enter into secret negotiations for a Prussian alliance – the alignment of forces for which Pitt, with many others, had long been calling. The British then in effect used their Russian treaty to induce Prussia to come to terms; and by the secret Convention of Westminster (January 1756) each power agreed to give the other assistance against any invasion of its territories. The Russians, however, learning of the Convention of Westminster in February, themselves secretly undertook in March to assist Austria 'with the whole of their strength' in the war against Prussia for which both of these states were preparing. Austria's chief fear was that the Russians were being too precipitate. Frederick meanwhile continued to lull his ally France with fair words, and the Russians for a time with similar success misled the British, while joining with Austria in attempts to involve Sweden, Saxony, and Poland in their alliance. The final, vital, and sensational move in this grand reversal of alliances came with the diplomatic marriage between France and Austria, though this was not consummated until May 1756.[45]

In the last week of 1755 the French, still ignorant of Frederick's desertion, had sent to London confident demands for a full restitution of their seized shipping, which many (Granville, for instance, but not Newcastle or Hardwicke) wished to interpret as an invitation to Britain formally to declare war. By agreeing the Prussian treaty, and at the same time achieving an understanding in Madrid which promised the non-involvement of Spain, Newcastle's government had taken some of the initiative from the French. Unable now to attack England in Hanover, they were forced towards attempting an invasion across the Channel – a desperate undertaking in view of Britain's undoubted naval superiority.

Marshal Belleisle's plan was to assemble three expeditionary forces between Dunkirk and Cherbourg, one directed towards Scotland, one towards Ireland (both these diversionary) and one to aim the main blow at the west of England, using experienced smugglers as pilots, with the hoped-for blessing of a southerly wind to keep the British ships in port long enough to allow a bridgehead to be established. (There was no question of attempting at this stage any *conquest* of England; the most the French hoped for – and for this they were prepared to face heavy losses – was a campaign sufficiently damaging to force a favourable peace; to secure French America in Wessex.) A fourth expeditionary force was meanwhile assembled near Toulon, to attempt the seizure of the chief British Mediterranean base, Minorca.

Though they were lacking sufficient transports, the French were making 'tremendous' preparations in the north, reported Hardwicke's son Joseph Yorke, minister at the Hague; but he could not quite believe that the French would try to cross the Channel. Newcastle, however, thought it more than likely that they would, and 'risk 20,000 to 30,000 men to revenge themselves of this country'. 'For this reason', he added, 'we have sent for the Hessians'. As for British troops, there was no time to withdraw them from America; they must come from Ireland. He was still hoping too (vainly as it proved) that the Dutch would be obeying their treaty obligations and sending troops.[46]

There was anxiety, but hardly panic yet. Though Minorca was known to be threatened, Anson at the Admiralty, before whose professional judgement Newcastle bowed, thought it proper to take a calculated risk there, maintaining unquestionable supremacy in the Channel, where the maximum danger lay. The cabinet rejected Fox's proposal of early March to send a strong squadron to Minorca,* and it was not until 7 April, only three days before Galissonière, with his twelve of the line accompanying 15,000 troops, sailed from Toulon, that Admiral Byng was able to leave Spithead. His orders were to pick up military reinforcements from Gibraltar and use 'all possible means in his power' to protect or if necessary to relieve Minorca.

Shortage of sailors had been a further factor delaying Byng's departure, while the press gangs worked overtime. But shortage of soldiers for home defence was now a problem even more acute. Partly from a desire for low taxation, partly from civilian mistrust of the military, the British army was by statute limited to numbers which by continental standards were derisory. Rather, therefore, than 'waiting to see if the wind would blow' troops hired from abroad, Pitt argued for the establishment of a reformed 50,000–60,000–strong militia for home defence, to be organized by counties, officered by local gentry, chosen by lot, drilled every week by army sergeants on Sundays and one other day, and liable for service in an emergency anywhere in the kingdom. In association with George Townshend and Lord George Sackville he worked between December and May to get a bill on these lines through the Commons, many of Newcastle's own followers supporting it. The Lords however wasted little time in throwing it out, being persuaded, in particular by Hardwicke, that though a militia might well in principle be preferable to the hiring of foreign forces, this bill was too 'democratical'. It would, Hardwicke argued, take authority from the Crown by requiring parliament's approval before the militia could

---

* Later, when Fox was assuming an I-told-you-so tone, Newcastle reminded him, 'You must remember what was constantly said when this question was before us; that the *heart* must be secured in the first place' (Yorke, *Hardwicke*, ii. 290n.).

be called out – which must mean delay in an emergency; it would make for 'a nation of soldiers', which was undesirable;* and by introducing Sunday drilling it would 'turn the holy day into a fair'. Thus for the time being Pitt's militia scheme was frustrated; but he would be returning to it.

Dutch and Hessian troops had been imported against the Jacobite threat in 1745 without significant outcries. Now, however, the proposed introduction of continental auxiliaries served to stoke the fires of patriotic indignation which Pitt was lighting under the government. When in March Fox moved that his Majesty be requested to send to Hanover for his electoral forces, Pitt, with his face bandaged in flannel on account of a persistent ache in his face and ear, opposed vehemently. The only state, he declared, which deserved to call itself sovereign was one which could stand on its own feet; in which '*suis stat viribus, non alieno pendet arbitrio*'.[47] As for the Hessians, they would cost infinitely more than the same number of British troops. It was argued, he said, that the French employed mercenaries. 'But must we engage mercenaries because France does? She engages them because she has not blood enough in her own veins'. The waste on Hessians, he unconvincingly alleged, 'would have conquered America or saved Minorca', which he now 'despaired of'.

This Cassandra role which he now adopted might have been overplayed, if the loss of Minorca had not soon been coming to justify in retrospect every prophecy of woe. *Nothing* the government proposed was now acceptable to Pitt. He ridiculed the taxes proposed in Lyttelton's budget. When a scheme was put forward by one Prévost, a Swiss Protestant refugee, to raise four battalions in Pennsylvania largely from Swiss, Dutch, and German immigrants – this was the beginning of the Royal Americans, the first regiment to be raised specifically to fight a colonial war – Pitt opposed it, chiefly on the ground that foreign officers would be employed to command Englishmen. And how could ministers possibly claim to be *short* of English commanders, when they had just contrived the cashiering of Sir Henry Erskine, 'a brave officer, distinguished with marks of two wounds', merely because he had voted with the opposition?

* 'That which of all things I dread, it would breed up our people to a love of arms and military government, and divert them from their true business, husbandry, manufactures, etc . . .' (Newcastle to Devonshire, 10 April 1756).

When Lyttelton, for the Exchequer, asked for a vote of credit for £1 million, Pitt resisted it for lack of exact information on how it was to be spent; he would only support it if it could be guaranteed for a *naval* war. He attacked the amateurism and departmentalism of the administration. He would not in fact call it an administration at all, it was so unsteady:

> One is at the head of the Treasury; one, Chancellor; one, head of the navy; one great person, of the army – yet is that an administration? They shift and shuffle the charge from one to another. Says one, I am not general. The Treasury says, I am not admiral. The Admiralty says, I am not minister . . . A nullity results. One, two, three, four, five lords meet. If they cannot agree – oh! we will meet again on Saturday. Oh! but says one of them, I am to go out of town . . .[48]

This prompted Fox to demand whether he wished to see the executive dominated by one man – 'a sole minister'. A wholly frank reply might well have been yes, provided his name were to be William Pitt. Answering no, Pitt nevertheless allowed this much praise to Fox, that if *he*, Fox, were sole minister, they might at least then see some system and decision.

Against Newcastle himself, on 12 May (when the French had already got troops ashore on Minorca, which Byng would still need five more sailing days to reach), Pitt fired another of his broadsides. If – he said at one point – if he saw a *child* driving a go-cart on the edge of a precipice, 'with that precious freight of an old king and his family', surely he was justified in trying to take the reins from his hands – or at the very least (turning towards Fox) to admonish the child's nurse. He prayed to God that the King would not die with Minorca 'written on his heart'. A few days earlier he had been outrageous enough to suggest (making 'great compliments to my Lord Anson and the Admiralty all at my expense', complained Newcastle) that it was *designed* to lose Minorca 'in order to justify a bad peace'; an idea which was 'scouted and ridiculed by everybody'.[49] Even the Prussian treaty, which came before parliament in May, securing an alliance which Pitt had been advocating for years, now brought from him much more criticism than approval. The financial terms were ill negotiated, he alleged. 'We had bought a treaty with Prussia by sacrificing our rights. He would not have signed that treaty for the five great places held by those who had signed it'.[50]

On 8 May the French on Minorca began the siege of the citadel of Port Mahon, and on the same day Byng sailed from Gibraltar, having accepted without protest the refusal of the Governor, General Fowke, to supply troop reinforcements as ordered. A fortnight later Byng fought his indecisive battle with Galissonière's Toulon fleet off Minorca and, four days later again, held a council of war which resolved – to the astonishment of the harassed French ashore – that the proper course of action was not to risk his fleet further, since its possible loss would 'endanger Gibraltar and the Mediterranean trade'. On 28 June General Blakeney, the tough and tenacious octogenarian in command at Port Mahon, was obliged to sign a capitulation, news of which reached London on 14 July.

The loss of Minorca, though a serious blow, was not quite the strategic catastrophe it appeared at the time. Its chief value had been as a port of refuge for merchants and an advance base for the blockade of Toulon; but French reinforcement of Canada from the Mediterranean would still need to negotiate the Straits of Gibraltar. What Byng and General Fowke between them had done was to miss a very fair chance of putting a major French fleet out of action and of stranding a large French army upon an untenable island. But at home panic winds, which Pitt's violent speeches had undoubtedly done something to swell, now blew furiously. 'The rage of the people increases hourly', wrote Fox apprehensively, certain that he would receive, without deserving, much of the blame.[51] 'We are humbled, disgraced, angry', wrote Walpole, 'and extremely disposed to massacre somebody or other, to show we have any courage left'. There was 'no describing the rage against Byng'.[52] Newcastle, though like Hardwicke he was in general pessimistic, had hitherto comforted himself with the conviction that ministers were following the best professional advice available; but now for a time he quite lost his nerve. The defeat at Minorca had come hard upon the virtual collapse of the Anglo-Dutch alliance and the diplomatic bombshell of the Austro-French treaty of friendship – seismic shocks to Newcastle after his long years of painstaking negotiation and preparation. He now asserted that he had been 'for some time convinced' that the war was 'hopeless' and might be 'ruinous'; yet at the same time he called for new initiatives to offset Minorca, somewhere, anywhere – Corsica perhaps, Belle Isle, Louisbourg, Martinique, St Domingo, America; it was up to the naval and military gentlemen to find where; he had never claimed to be head of anything but the Treasury. Perhaps America would be best: 'let us begin there at once'. And an example must be made of Byng, whose 'trial and condemnation' ought to be begun immediately, 'if, as I think there can be no doubt, he deserves it'.[53] It was more than a possibility, he feared – and Newcastle was always one to run and embrace his fears – that there would be a demand for impeachment for 'justice against persons however dignified or distinguished' – Anson, for instance, Hardwicke possibly, very likely himself.

The patriot and the politician in Pitt were inevitably at odds as the bad news accumulated. Writing to George Grenville from amid the delights of the Kent countryside – in 'the pure air' of their village, where they were 'all well . . . and intend that our little colony shall, God willing, receive its increase'* – Pitt conceded that the tidings of calamity from the Mediterranean must bear for both of them some considerable, if selfish, consolation. They might rest at least relatively happy that though they shared the 'common ruin', they had no hand in the guilt of 'this administration without ability or virtue'. 'Distress, infinite distress, seems to hem us in on all quarters . . . If any among the ministry are disposed to be men, I hear they would be madmen; for the regret is that we have no continent war'. (Frederick of Prussia, in fact, not waiting for the Austrian attack, started the 'continent war' by invading Saxony early in September; declared war between Britain and France had begun with the invasion of Minorca.)

He dreaded to hear from America, Pitt added – with reason, as events happened, for news soon arrived of the capture and destruction by the new French commander in chief in Canada, Montcalm, of the three forts at Oswego on Lake Ontario, with 1400 prisoners and large stores of artillery and ammunition taken. 'Asia', he went on, 'perhaps may furnish its portion of ignominy and calamity to this degenerate helpless country'.[54] In fact, as he was writing, the Nawab

---

* A son, christened John, was born in October. 'My joy, my dear Grenville', wrote Pitt, 'will . . . easily be imagined . . . Dear Lady Hester is so happy with her offspring that her spirits would easily run away with her, if not beyond her strength, at least beyond the discretion of the sagest of the Sybils, Mrs Tyson . . . The young man meets with general applause for stature and strength. Nurse Cresswell looks with satisfaction, and Nurse Long with envy, upon his quality and quantity.'

of Bengal's capture of the station of Calcutta from the East India Company, and the subsequent incident of the 'Black Hole', were already facts, though it would be a full year before the news of them would arrive in London.

From Hayes in its summer purity Pitt could indulge the transient luxury of affecting to despise 'the great world – that least and most despicable of all little things', and of persuading himself that the rural paradise of Hayes or Wotton ('deep shades of oak, softening lawns, and tranquil waters, like a lively smile lighting up a thoughtful countenance') provided so much the 'better world to introduce youth to'.[55] Nevertheless, the great world beyond beckoned more and more vigorously as the summer of 1756 ran towards autumn and the imminent reassembling of parliament. The gales of national misfortune could hardly fail to blow some blue sky in the direction of Hayes. Pitt was the only leading politician whose reputation had been raised by the disasters, and even the extravagance of his earlier criticism of the government now seemed justified. The *Public Advertiser* called for him to join with Fox to form a new administration.[56] The City of London, and the merchant communities of the big provincial centres, especially those with interests in America and the West Indies, saw Pitt as their man. Alderman William Beckford, the Jamaica-born sugar magnate, had recently emerged as leading spokesman for City of London opinion, and his brother Richard had launched the weekly *Monitor* which, with the *London Evening Post*, during 1756 led the anti-Newcastle pack 'without doors' as Pitt led it inside the House. By November Alderman Beckford, who had earlier supported Fox, was writing to assure Pitt: 'In the militia [of Jamaica] during the last war I was no more than a common soldier: in our present political warfare I intend to act as one of your private soldiers without commission'.[57] He was to continue vociferously in that role through the remaining fourteen years of his life.

Strengthening his position further, the government's two leading men in the Commons, Fox and Murray, both now decided to abandon it. The Lord Chief Justiceship falling vacant, Murray claimed the succession as of right, with the peerage that would be expected to go with it. He could not be denied, and migrated to the Bench as Lord Mansfield. Fox had no mind to continue the task of sustaining so damaged a ministry, especially, so he complained, since he was neither trusted nor allowed power. Nor would he want to be 'turned out like a dog' to make way for Pitt if Newcastle and Hardwicke managed to agree terms with him.[58] The King, not relishing the prospect of having Pitt forced upon him, did his best to persuade Fox – the lesser evil – to remain; when he failed, he was angry, considering that Fox had used him ill.

Even before Fox's resignation Newcastle was half ready to contemplate throwing in the towel. Why was *he* to be blamed for naval setbacks when the Admiralty 'does not love to be controlled or even advised', or for military mishaps when 'the army is absolutely under other direction'? He was referring of course to the Duke of Cumberland. Hardwicke, writing to his son Joseph Yorke, confirmed just how far Newcastle was from being sole author of the nation's misfortunes: 'By the way, the D. of N. has had no more direction in the measures of the war than any one of seven of us'.[59] And Newcastle himself, writing to Hardwicke years later, immediately after Pitt's resignation in October 1761, though he did not exactly claim to have been made in the mould of a great war minister, was still maintaining that he could *prove* that

> our views of attack, both at home and abroad, were as active, as vigorous, and upon the same principle as Mr Pitt's, of annoying France in all parts; but we had not such good instruments as Mr Pitt had, or indeed (and that was our only fault) not the courage to insist upon them. A cowardly admiral gave up Minorca . . .; a mad unfortunate general [Braddock] occasioned the loss of our first attempt in North America; neither of them named, thought of, or indeed approved by me; representations from me in writing upon the advisability of attempting some operations on the [French] coast, rejected . . .; but above all forsook and abandoned by the then Secretary of State [Fox] . . .[60]

At the end of August Newcastle was applying to Hardwicke once more for reassurance: 'My dear Lord, pity me, alone as I am in my present distress; give me the comfort you only can'. And what were they to do about Pitt? There was, claimed Newcastle, nothing he would not yield to 'for the sake of the King and the public', and he 'rather thought' the King would in the prevailing circumstances accept *anything* they proposed to him; but 'what a figure shall we make with Pitt coming in in conquest over us?'[61]

Squaring up to this distasteful prospect, Newcastle asked Hardwicke once again to sound out Pitt, who was requested 'with civil excuses' to attend the Chancellor on 19 October. Half the political world suspected, with Newcastle – but mistakenly – that there must exist some secret alliance between Pitt and Fox; everybody knew there was certainly some kind of understanding between Pitt and Leicester House; and openly behind Pitt of course stood his 'family', the Grenvilles. But on this occasion Pitt was quite decided to speak for himself and no one else. His allies should be consulted afterwards. He asked Temple and George Grenville to hold themselves ready to come to Brook Street to discuss the *outcome* only; and he was 'resolved to go to this conference without previous participation with Lord B[ute]. I will report the issue afterwards'.[62]

He expected his interview with Hardwicke to be 'short and final'. From the Hardwicke-Newcastle standpoint it was certainly final. Pitt, though 'very polite', Hardwicke reported, 'and full of professions to me', blankly refused to serve in any administration that contained the Duke of Newcastle, against whom the nation was 'to the last degree incensed'. He presented further demands, one for a new militia, another that he should no longer be treated like a subaltern or a pariah. If he re-entered the King's service, he insisted on being 'in the first concert and concoction of measures', and have personal access to the Crown 'without going through the channel of any other minister'.

In the long run events and necessities would force Pitt to abandon his veto upon Newcastle, much as they were to compel his retreat in the matter of foreign subsidies and the 'anti-continental' policy generally. But for the moment he was uncompromising and intransigent. And when he saw no other means by which the King might, as he expressed it, 'be brought to open his eyes', he employed the directest tactics open to him. Sometimes when the door to the Closet was barred, the way to Lady Yarmouth's drawing-room might be open, and everyone knew that Lady Yarmouth, the Madame Walmoden whom Walpole had brought over from Hanover in 1737 to fill the vacuum in George II's life left by the death of Queen Caroline, remained now in her fifties his closest companion and confidante. Recently, Fox and Newcastle had each gone to her in the hope of enlisting her tactful persuasions. Now Pitt's carriage suddenly and unexpectedly appeared outside her quarters in St James's where he was a complete stranger. Presenting her with a list of ministers for a proposed new government, he tried to convince her, and through her to persuade the King, since Newcastle would never do it, that he *might be trusted.*

At the time this attempt to employ Lady Yarmouth's offices appeared to have failed. 'Mr Pitt', said the King, 'shall not go to *that channel* any more. *She* does not meddle, and shall not meddle'.[63] However, according to Shelburne, Pitt himself gave it as his opinion later that Lady Yarmouth had played a part in ending the King's indecision; 'she brought all about'.[64] As a Hanoverian herself, perhaps she did something, following hints dropped during the interview, to convince the King that Pitt would not prove quite so uncooperative on the subject of Hanover as his speeches had many times suggested. 'Mr Pitt won't do my German business',[65] had always been the most radical of George's objections to him, personal antipathy apart, and Pitt would soon be at pains to prove that the fear was exaggerated.

On 27 October the King asked Fox to form a government, which would of necessity have to include Pitt. The following day, taking him aside at the Prince of Wales's levee, Fox asked Pitt his intentions, and was unambiguously told them. He would not serve, wrote Fox, 'with me as [prime] minister. He foresaw, I suppose, that my place would be the Treasury. I can't much blame him...'[66] Fox, as combative and ambitious as Pitt himself, and always shrewdly perceptive, was better able to see Pitt's point of view than most of the Whig establishment. Than Devonshire,* for instance: 'Nothing has hurt Pitt so much as his having shown to the world that he did not value the confusion and distress that he might throw this country into, in order to gratify his resentment or satisfy his ambition . . . I do not think anything can justify such conduct'.[67] Or than Bedford: 'When I come to relate to you the impracticability of this man, it will amaze you', he wrote to his Duchess; Pitt seemed 'determined to place himself and family sole governors of everything'. Bedford entirely sympathized with the King, whom he found 'in great wrath . . . for the cavalier treatment he has received from Mr Pitt'. Only the weighty presence of Fox in the Commons and the influence of the Duke of Devonshire at the head

* The fourth Duke (1720–64).

of the Treasury (where he expressed patriotic willingness to serve) would be likely to 'restrain Pitt and his party from getting absolute ascendancy over the King himself and confine them to that proper degree of power they had a right to expect'.[68] Pitt had already, without consulting him, proposed Devonshire for the Treasury in the list he had submitted to Lady Yarmouth, it being thought 'necessary to place some great Lord there to whom the Whigs would look up'. A Devonshire-Pitt ministry, therefore, it was to be. By mid-November the thing was broadly settled.

CHAPTER TWELVE

The Pitt-Devonshire Ministry

The parliamentary weakness of this first of Pitt's administrations was patent from the beginning. The question was whether popular discontents would enable him to 'command such numbers without doors as may make the majorities within the House tremble'. 'Unless Mr Pitt joins with either Fox or Newcastle', wrote Horace Walpole, 'his ministry cannot last six months'.

> His success seems very precarious. If he Hanoverizes, or checks any inquiries [into governmental mismanagement], he loses his popularity, and falls that way; if he honours the present rage of the people, he provokes two powerful factions [Fox's and Newcastle's].[1]

'If the Duke of Newcastle would have joined Fox', Lyttelton wrote, 'Pitt and Company might have been safely turned out before Christmas'. But Newcastle would not join Fox; moreover, by temperament, habit, and conviction, he was disinclined to undertake systematic opposition. Sceptical of the new administration's chances, he preferred to await the resumption of the natural Whig order whose functioning had been momentarily disturbed. Meanwhile Pitt might be allowed to govern on sufferance.

Of Pitt's more positive sources of support, that which came from the Tories caused most stir. There were still, in 1756, about a hundred Commons members who might, if pressed, own up to the old-fashioned designation of 'Tory'. As a parliamentary force, Toryism had been dead for a generation. Ever since the arrival of the Hanoverians the most significant opposition to Whig government had always come from dissident Whigs, of whom Pitt had of course been one. Toryism was more a state of mind – close to the established Church; tending sometimes in its extremer or more nostalgic forms (notably in the university of Oxford) towards a sentimental Jacobitism; suspicious of Hanoverian ties; mistrustful of the power and wealth of the great magnates; standing for a militia as against an expensive and possibly dangerous standing army, and in general for 'Country' against 'Court'; to be found typically among rural squires and parsons, but strong too in those urban circles where it was felt that the Whig establishment was hostile, or corrupt, or insufficiently patriotic, or all these things together. (Hardwicke noted with some contempt that an address from the City of London in August 1756 attacking the Newcastle government was presented by fifteen aldermen, *not one of whom was a Whig.*)

Dissident Whigs and Whig 'patriots' had often in the past flirted with the Tories, and the tendency of these anti-ministerialists to appeal to 'the people' had always been distasteful to the ruling Whigs. But now it was a *government*, ostensibly Whig, which seemed to be looking towards 'the people' and the old opposition. 'Pitt flings himself upon the people and the Tories', wrote an indignant Newcastle as the new Devonshire-Pitt ministry faced the Commons. The two expressions – both of them, for Newcastle, disparaging – need a gloss: *people* implied, not of course the mass of humble folk, but the articulate ranks of society below noblemen or gentry, perhaps about one in six of the adult male population; and by *Tories* Newcastle was thinking of independent country gentlemen owing no obligation to the Whig factions. Pitt would not have disputed Newcastle's terms. He always claimed that his true constituency was 'the people', 'the nation'; and a few weeks after taking office he informed Hardwicke that he had the highest hopes of

> the country gentlemen; how well disposed they were to support government; how generous and candid their behaviour had been to him; and what assurances they had given him . . . No conditions at all; quite free and disinterested; merely to keep the ship from sinking . . .[2]

Thus most of the Tories and independents supported Pitt; and he had in addition the interested backing, first, of his own small connection of the Grenvilles and their immediate allies such as Legge, the two Townshends, and Potter – Walpole refers to 'the party of Mr Pitt and Mr Legge', and reckoned it at twelve to sixteen members; second, of the Leicester House following; and third, of those members such as Beckford, whose commercial interests favoured a vigorous policy in America and the West Indies. In the last resort, however, the fate of the government was obliged to rest upon the continuing tolerance of the Newcastle Whigs. 'Men of ordinary capacity', wrote Lyttelton, thought it very strange that if Pitt wished 'to set Mr Fox and his friends at defiance he did not unite to the Duke of Newcastle, and keep together that strength by which alone a faction could be kept down for any long time'; but, he reflected, 'great genius is not conducted by the rules of common prudence'.³ Whatever Pitt's merits as a statesman, he had few as a politician.

Lyttelton's own elevation to the peerage at this juncture afforded him the opportunity to do his sometime friend a good turn. As a new minister Pitt needed to be re-elected to parliament; and, having broken with Newcastle, he could hardly continue as his nominee at Aldborough. Lyttelton's peerage meant a vacancy at Okehampton, where the Ayscough (Leicester House) and Lyttelton interests concurred in offering the seat to Pitt. It was, of course, like Old Sarum, one of Governor Pitt's old purchases.

The new chief minister's immediate prospects in parliament would have looked brighter if he had enjoyed any support from the Crown. But the King, as Walpole observed, was disposed 'to communicate himself only to his old servants'. When he first received Pitt in audience on 1 December – Pitt had, as ever, been ill and was unable to attend earlier – he was at least civil. Pitt, who was at pains to be deferential, even to excess, thought the interview 'favourable, considering the long impression' against him, and seems to have been surprised to find it lasted as long as 'several minutes'. However, storms were brewing and, as late as three weeks after Newcastle's formal resignation, Pitt was still threatening to decline office, though parliament had already reassembled and heard the Speech from the Throne. He proposed to accept the Seals, he told Bute on 4 December, only if he found 'before hand that the Closet is subsided'.⁴ The irritations were many, the most troublesome being the introduction into the Lords' address following the King's Speech of a phrase expressing thanks to the King for having brought over his Hanoverian troops for the defence of England. Pitt wrote to Bute:

I told the Duke of Devonshire that if it had been attempted in our House I would have warmly opposed it; that if Lord Temple cou'd go to the House of Lords [he too was laid up with illness], I was

sure he wou'd think his honour concerned to resist it highly there.
He did not need my advice . . .*⁵

Pitt had taken some trouble with this his first King's Speech, hoping,
he said, that it might 'captivate the people'. In its first draft, which was
longer than was customary, it altogether failed to captivate the King,
who described parts of it as nonsense, and asked for cuts. What remained, if hardly as 'revolutionary' as has sometimes been claimed,⁶
certainly had the 'gravity and weight' that Pitt was aiming at. 'It is
in an high style *ad Populum*', wrote Lyttelton, 'and seems to promise
great things'.⁷ It declared for a militia, for sending the Hanoverian
troops back home ('relying with pleasure on the spirit and zeal of my
people'), warned of perils ahead and burdensome expenses to be borne,
acknowledged the 'sufferings of the poorer sort from the present high
price of corn' and, as a priority second only to the defence of the home-
land, pledged devotion to the 'succour and preservation of America'.

A point has often been made of the novelty of the stress laid upon
America in Pitt's first speech from the Throne. In the speech itself
there was little such novelty. In fact the King's Speech of 1755, composed by Hardwicke, had eighteen lines on the needs of American
defence, against Pitt's seven. The only novelty, the true 'revolution',
lay in the sense of urgency Pitt conveyed concerning American
preparations; in the thoroughness of his instructions and the decisiveness
of his plan of campaign (which, again, was of itself in no way original);
and in his manner of conveying that he understood what he wanted to
do and how it must be done. As he had soberly informed the Duke of
Devonshire, he knew that he and he alone could save the country;
and, gout notwithstanding, he embarked confidently, unsparing both
of himself and others, and in excellent spirits, upon a formidable task.
The absence of a parliamentary majority seemed to cause him small
worry, and inhibited him in planning the nation's affairs as little as the
want of a credit balance at the bank deterred him from embarking
on the most ambitious plans both for Hayes Place, which was to be
rebuilt in style, and for his estate, which he was already 'improving'
by the purchase or lease of adjoining farms and properties. Visitors
to Hayes found him half-crippled, but remarkably sanguine; 'as

* Temple found himself well enough to make a vehement protest in the Lords, walking
out immediately after delivering his speech.

cheerful as I ever saw him', wrote Gilbert Elliot.[8] When parliament adjourned on Christmas Eve Pitt had still not put in a single appearance, and in the Commons there had still not been one division. 'Mr Pitt's gout has *laid up* the nation', Walpole reported. But he was quite wrong. Although Pitt had been out of doors 'only for an airing', at Hayes time was not being wasted. The traffic upon the few miles of road to Westminster was busy over the mid-winter months of 1756–7 with the to-ing and fro-ing of memoranda and dispatches, and the carriages of officials and ministers. It seemed likely to prove a bedchamber ministry; even meetings of the cabinet and of the 'secret committee' were held at Hayes, where the ministerial bedroom, or the 'great chair' with its beflannelled prisoner, proved no bad place for concentrating the mind; and between December 1756 and February 1757 it became the 'operations room' of the war and the nerve centre of the nation.

By mid-December the decision was taken to send 'an expedition of weight' to America, and before Christmas the Earl of Loudoun, commander in chief there, had been sent an account of the general line of proposed action. The target was to have 17,000 men under Loudoun by April, after which, by June or if possible May, a combined naval and military assault was to be made on Louisbourg, giving time for an attack up the St Lawrence during the ice-free season with Quebec as the campaign's final objective.

At home, the immediate task was to fill the vacuum created by the return home of the Hessians and Hanoverians. Every available regular soldier would be needed in America; and England must be prepared to 'put herself on board her fleet'. Hence a reactivated militia as a safeguard against invasion became imperative, and the broad substance of the bill rejected the previous year was therefore put before the Commons again. This time it surmounted the hurdle of the House of Lords, though they did cut the county quotas to give a projected total of 32,000 men (to be paid for out of the rates and chosen by ballot) rather than the 60,000 Pitt wanted.*

It can hardly be held that Englishmen, of whatever class, sprinted

---

* The ballot was compulsory but, substitution being permitted, the well-to-do might pay the poor to serve for them, or pay a £10 fine to escape altogether. Colonels were chosen from volunteer landowners worth £444 a year or heirs apparent of those worth double that figure; junior officers from lesser landowners. The militia was a squirearchical institution, as its champions had always intended. It barely survived the war.

patriotically to the colours, and until the invasion alarm of 1759 the militia did not succeed in numbering more than half the 32,000 provided for. Implementation of the act in the summer of 1757 was to provoke rioting in many counties, when for a time the persons and property of magistrates, chief constables, and even lords lieutenant (the Duke of Bedford among them) went in danger from the militantly unmilitary populace. Well-intentioned promises proved insufficient to dispel a reasonable fear of being drafted overseas. Similar promises had been broken before. Ironically, some militia riots had to be put down by regular troops; others by volunteer corps of gentry. Nevertheless, however slowly and reluctantly it got into its stride, Pitt's scheme was made to work. Militiamen were enrolled for three years (four for officers); they were uniformed, drilled, and trained like a second regular army, but officered by amateurs. Captain Edward Gibbon considered his South Hampshire battalion 'rather a credit than a disgrace to the line . . . had the militia lasted another year we should not have yielded to the most perfect of our brethren' – whom he took to be the men of Dorset. 'Though the greatest part of the men were rather civilized than corrupted by the habits of military subordination' (which however never lost a certain 'looseness') the future historian admitted to finding his own temper 'soured by the society of our rustic officers' and blamed his own middle-aged gout on 'the daily practice of hard and even excessive drinking'. However, the militia made him, he said, 'an Englishman and a soldier'.[9] Although it never had to face the invader, there is no reason to doubt that, if it had, it would have given a patriotic account of itself.

The regulars were already being increased before Pitt came to power, and it is Newcastle's ministry rather than Pitt's that must be given credit for deciding in 1756 to create ten new regiments, for raising additional light forces eventually to be made into eleven regiments of light dragoons, for re-forming the Marines (now put under Admiralty control), and for enlarging existing regiments with new battalions.[10] Even the Royal Americans, later the sixtieth, which in time was to help to win Quebec, originated with Newcastle's administration,*

---

* The moving spirit in much of this expansion and modernization was the able and much respected General Ligonier, whom Newcastle sometimes called '*my* general' and consulted in preference to the Captain General, Cumberland (R. Whitworth, *Ligonier*, 206).

and *against* the criticisms of Pitt. The immediate contribution Pitt made
in 1757 to strengthening the regular army was limited to the augmen-
tation of certain battalions, including the Royal Artillery, and the
formation of two new regiments from those Scottish clans which only
a decade earlier had been rebels.

This move to enlist Highlanders had been mooted for the past year
or so – Newcastle himself had tentatively put the idea forward to the
King, who had dismissed it out of hand – and it was Cumberland who
now submitted the proposal anew. Pitt immediately accepted it. The
risks, he told Hardwicke, were much over-estimated. It would be
better to have 2000 clansmen fighting the French in Canada than nursing disaffection in the Highlands of Scotland. They were notably fierce
fighters; and besides, Pitt suggested, 'it would be a drain and not many
would return'. A charitable interpretation of this remark will give him
credit for envisaging the settlement of Highlanders in America at the
end of the campaigning – and indeed grants of land were then made.
It seems however that Hardwicke at the time understood Pitt more
cynically. Casualties could hardly fail to be high. But perhaps Pitt was
only using what seemed the best argument ready to hand for meeting
Hardwicke's objections. He always maintained not only that his
innovation won 2000 extra troops, 'who served with fidelity as they
fought with valour, and conquered for you in every part of the world',
but also that it helped to 'gain the Scotch' for King George. Ten years
later he was still lauding the move, of which it was then assumed, not
least by Pitt himself, that he had been the sole author; 'I sought for
merit wherever it was to be found . . . I found it in the mountains of
the north . . . I called it forth . . .'[11]

New ships were needed no less urgently than more troops. The
Admiralty under Anson had in 1756 assessed the navy's needs at 202
capital ships and frigates. The number theoretically available was 134,
but not all these were ready to put to sea. Specially serious was the
shortfall in light vessels – sloops, frigates, brigs, cutters – necessary
both for supporting ships of the line in action and for the protection
of commerce, where now merchants trading overseas were in some
cases suspending business for fear of capture. Of Anson, who had been
the major influence at the Admiralty since 1745, Pitt had earlier been
unjustly contemptuous, accusing him of being unfit to command a
cockboat on the Thames. Under him in fact much had already been

. John Carteret, Earl of Granville,
tudio of William Hoare

7. Richard Grenville-Temple, Earl
Temple, by William Hoare

8. George Grenville holding an Act
of Parliament. Mezzotint by James
Watson after William Hoare

9. Hester Grenville in 1750, by
Thomas Hudson

10. George, Lord Lyttelton, artist unknown

11. Henry Pelham, by William Hoare

12. Thomas Pelham-Holles, Duke of Newcastle by William Hoare

13. Henry Fox, Lord Holland, after Reynolds

done towards reorganizing and remodelling the navy. Now he and Pitt pressed ahead the building programme, in particular of frigates, whose effective strength soon rose from 82 to 120.

On Christmas Day 1756 Pitt summoned a cabinet to consider the tale of woe which had just arrived from India – though the tardiness of communication did not allow the story to include the disasters which had already overtaken the British in Calcutta. French influence was in the ascendant, and the English East India Company, to meet it, had only 2000 British and Indian troops, and five ships under Admiral Watson. Moreover, the colonel in command of the royal troops had fallen foul of the Company. Pitt directed the War Office to recall him, and the Admiralty to find four or five vessels to reinforce Watson. Watson himself was instructed to assist the Company in carrying out any practicable plans its officers might devise; but Pitt did not attempt, either now or at any time until within a few months of his resignation in 1761, any significant control of operations in this eastern theatre of war. He knew that the key to French strength in India must lie at their naval headquarters at Mauritius, whose capture if it could be effected would 'lay the axe to the root'; but whether that project were feasible or no he was obliged to leave to the concerted judgement of the naval commander and the merchants in Madras. For Pitt, events in India would continue to be of importance far below those in the West Indies and Canada. As things happened the one British success of note during Pitt's first frustrating year of office was to occur in Bengal, where Clive, having first recaptured Calcutta and the French fort of Chandernagore, went on to reverse the trend of events by his victory, at a cost of just eighteen dead, over Siraj-ud-Daula at Plassey.

An opportunity to vex the French and advantage the British at an intermediate point upon the long route to the East was laid before Pitt as soon as he became Secretary of State. Thomas Cumming, a merchant originally of New York and later of London, had for some time been trying to sell to British politicians and service chiefs his scheme for attacking the French in Senegal and Goree (the modern Dakar), where they conducted a profitable trade in slaves, in gum (used in the manufacture of linen and silk), and in gold dust and ivory. The enterprising Cumming, buccaneering 'interloper' and fighting Quaker, who seems to have shared at least some of the spirit and practical acquisitiveness of Pitt's grandfather the Governor, had already established friendly trade relations with the local 'King of the Legibbilli'; and having previously tried Fox, Anson, and Cumberland, he now approached Pitt, Temple, and Boscawen to enlist support for his project for destroying the French forts and capturing their trade.[12]

It was a sideline, but just the sort of sideline to attract Pitt. He accordingly composed a letter of greeting from George II to 'the High and Glorious Monarch, the Mighty and Right Noble Prince Amir Sultan, King of Legibbilli', inviting him to assist Cumming, and also the commander of 'the king's great ships of war' whom Cumming would introduce, to attack the French establishments at Senegal and Goree; and he set about preparing an expedition for the enterprise, writing also to his 'good and worthy friend' Cumming on 9 February 1757

> to repeat to you on paper, what I have often said with great sincerity to you in conversation, namely, that I have so good an opinion of your integrity, and think the service you are going upon to Africa so likely to prove beneficial to the public, that, in case success attends your endeavours, I promise you my best assistance in obtaining an exclusive charter in your favour for a limited terms of years . . . Averse as I always shall be to exclusive charters in general, I think your case a just exception . . .[13]

Pitt's removal from office in April was to cause the expedition to be put back a year; but in 1758 it would sail and win one of the first British successes of the war, ushering in the magical period when Pitt seemed gifted with a Midas touch.

There was no Midas touch yet. In particular, nothing was to go well for his first major undertaking, the 1757 expedition against Louisbourg. From the beginning, the planned timing threatened to go wrong. In New York, Loudoun did not receive his final orders from Pitt – dispatched on 4 February – until 1 May. Admiral Holburne's squadron – twelve ships of the line, with frigates – which was to escort the transports from Cork to the expedition's base at Halifax in Nova Scotia, and which Pitt had thought 'ought to set sail in February', did not manage to leave Cork before 8 May, a month in fact after Pitt had been temporarily removed from the Secretaryship. He had neglected no apparently trivial detail of prudent provision: 'orders to be sent by this night's post' for 'seynes to catch fish for the refreshment of the men with the proper cordage for them and lead for the fishing lines', in case Loudoun's commissariat should be insufficient on the expedition's arrival; reminders to the War Office about tents, about battering trains, about ammunition flints; precise directions to Bedford, Lord Lieutenant of Ireland, concerning the assembling of the Irish regiments at Cork. For at least some of the hindrances to his preparations Pitt blamed Cumberland. 'Using the plainness of a man who means right', he told Devonshire at the end of January that he would not 'acquiesce to a negative upon sending another battalion and a bigger battering train etc. to America, let the negative arise where it may. The ruin of the Kingdom shall not lie at my door but on those who obstruct and defeat a resource so obvious . . .'[14] He admitted that his heart was 'so fixed on the efforts of this summer not being frustrated' that he was in danger of becoming 'troublesome and tiresome'. That they were in fact frustrated was because, while the weeks and months slipped by, large reinforcements of the French navy succeeded in eluding the blockades and reaching Louisbourg.

Loudoun, unable even by the end of May to hear confirmation of the arrival at Halifax of Holburne, who was further delayed by adverse winds, was obliged to risk sending his contingents of the assault force from New York to Halifax without adequate cover. 'If [the French fleet] meet us', he warned Pitt, 'there is an end of the troops that go from hence'.*[15] They were fortunate not to be intercepted; but the failure of the expedition had already been determined: two squadrons from Brest and one from Toulon had arrived off Louisbourg by June. Holburne did not reach Halifax until 9 July; and Loudoun, seeing 'no probability of success at this advanced season of the year', and refusing to risk his 15,000 men, the force on which the future of British America depended, in a landing-and-assault operation in the face of a superior fleet, abandoned the enterprise and returned to New York. Not only had it failed to capture Louisbourg (let alone Quebec); its manning had meant withdrawing troops from the strategic valleys and lake-lands between the Canadian frontier and New York; and during Loudoun's absence at Halifax Montcalm captured the important Fort William Henry at the head of Lake George, his Indian auxiliaries slaughtering the British garrison. Thus Pitt's first attempt upon Canada ended not merely in failure, but with a marked debit balance.

* Pitt wrote to Bute: 'I have litterally hardly slept since this news'.

Loudoun was doubtless not an inspired commander. He had moreover been quite unable to preserve good relations with the Americans;
but Pitt's anger with him, privately and publicly expressed, was perhaps
excessive. To Hester, he even spoke of *treachery*. Why, Pitt wanted
to know, had Loudoun failed to send back more than one short dispatch
during the month following his arrival at Halifax? Why had he prepared no plans for the next campaign? For Loudoun there was no
next campaign. Before the year was out Pitt recalled him and never
employed him again. As for Holburne, Pitt's first hasty reaction was
to instruct him to seek out and destroy the French fleet, even if that
meant pursuing it back across the Atlantic; but second thoughts
prevailed. 'You are to consider', Pitt wrote to him in July on his return
to office, 'the conjunct operations of his Majesty's fleet and land forces
as the first and preferable service'.[16] Holburne was unfortunate. He
continued cruising between Halifax and Louisbourg until 24 September in the hope of catching the enemy, or tempting them to an
engagement. Then a hurricane all but destroyed him and drove him
off station; whereupon the French, desperate by then for food and
supplies, and reduced by fever and scurvy, made sail for Brest, to
which they brought back mixed gifts: good news of their defensive
victory, and to accompany it an epidemic of typhus, which raged
through the town and beyond, through Brittany. 'I long to come
instead of writing', Pitt wrote to Hester when he heard of the ruin
of Holburne's fleet, 'but alas! most calamitous news demands me this
night, and many . . . I fear we do not stand in the smile of heaven.
May a degenerate people profit in the school of misfortune'.[17]

Though little good was to come of it for many months, the direction
of maritime and colonial policy for a Pitt ministry had been generally
predictable. But how would so vehement an anti-continentalist act
towards the war in Europe?

He had of course already shown himself not unready to perform
somersaults in an honest cause – and honest causes embraced his own
fortunes and career, as well as the security and prosperity of his country.
He was, moreover, undoubtedly readier to change course than to
concede that a change had in fact been made; but on occasions he
had been at pains to justify past switches of direction – sometimes by
special pleading, sometimes by a bulldozing eloquence that consciously
ignored his own earlier arguments. He was on safer ground when he

depreciated, as he sometimes did, the very value of consistency, and claimed to have acquired wisdom with the years. And of course the nature of the *goals* he aimed at for his country never changed. The grand objective which he set, of commercial expansion and imperial conquest, which meant the reduction or destruction of the French position in America and the West Indies, which again meant British supremacy at sea and an essentially secondary regard for European continental interests, was never in doubt.

On coming to power in December 1756 Pitt made the most important turnabout of his career. Only very recently he had derided Newcastle's foreign subsidies, attacked the use of foreign troops, declared Hanover militarily indefensible, contested any notion of British forces fighting on the continent, even assailed the details of the treaty with Prussia. Almost all of this was now changed overnight, though it would be a year or two before he could bring himself to risk any drop of English blood being lost in Germany, in what he called 'that ocean of fire'. Plainly the advent of high office concentrated his mind wonderfully. The King's wishes, the views of the service chiefs and of the cabinet (for Pitt's power was as yet by no means uncircumscribed), the logic of the whole strategic situation faced for the first time realistically and responsibly rather than emotionally and polemically, forced him, while never openly retracting earlier views, simply to act as though he had never held them. It was no doubt well that he changed course. The front in Germany was to form the second of the two main pillars – naval supremacy being of course the first – upon which the edifice of victory was eventually built.

It is instructive to watch French politicians of the period confronting dilemmas and decisions exactly parallel to those which faced Pitt. A land campaign, argued Machault, the Minister of Marine, was folly. The sum of French resources would only just suffice to defeat Britain at sea and in the colonies. On the contrary, maintained d'Argenson, whose view was to prevail:

As the French conquests in the Low Countries in the previous war had forced England to return Louisbourg to France at the Peace of Aix-la-Chapelle, and as similarly that peace, so humiliating to France, has had to be accepted if Canada were to be kept, so in the coming struggle, '*On doit conquérir l'Amérique en Allemagne*'.[18]

Hanover therefore must be attacked. Similarly Pitt was obliged to see the force of the argument that, unless France were made to divert a large proportion of her great resources to fighting a continental war, she might well be able to outbuild, out-man, and ultimately defeat Britain in a colonial war. Hence the supreme importance of Prussia, as Newcastle, and even belatedly George II, had come to realize. With her modernized and (in proportion to population) massive army, she was the only state – now that Austria was allied to France – capable of drawing off enough French strength to be of much value to Britain or Hanover.

On his side, Frederick the Great, menaced by the four powers, Austria, France, Sweden, and Russia, had reason enough to be nervous, not least of the attitude Britain might adopt now that that notorious anti-continentalist Pitt was principal minister. Frederick had already been profuse in strategic advice to the previous British government, all the more interesting reading because so much of it coincides with what was to become the 'Pitt system'. Britain ought to supply the funds and organization to build up on the lower Rhine an army of Hanoverians, Hessians, and other available Germans (and if possible Dutch) to protect Hanover and Prussia's western flank. She should make 'descents upon the naked coasts' of Brittany and Normandy and thus draw off French troops from Germany. (This could perhaps be an alternative to an earlier proposal, which Britain found impracticable, that she should send a fleet to the Baltic to deter Russia and Sweden.) Britain might well, having lost Minorca, Frederick suggested, take Corsica instead, and perhaps also persuade the King of Sardinia to make a diversion against France, and the Sultan of Turkey against Austria. Overseas, Britain should take the initiative against the French in India, in Canada, in Africa.

To Frederick's considerable relief, Pitt showed himself to be a strategically changed character and very much a Frederician. Making in mid-February his first appearance in the House of Commons since taking the Seals two and a half months before, he now proposed a composite army, 50,000 or 60,000 strong, for the lower Rhine, its Hanoverians to be maintained from George's Hanoverian purse, its Hessians and Prussians from the British. Further, Prussia was to receive, the House consenting, a subsidy of £200,000. He lavished praise on Frederick himself, and insofar as he attempted any reasoned defence of his own change of front, based it on the high worth of the Prussian army, and the accomplished fact of the Anglo-Prussian treaty, to which Britain was bound both by honour and by self-interest. As for the allied German army, it was to be an 'army of observation', a description which implied an essentially defensive role unconnected with continental adventures. 'He attempted', wrote a still sceptical Walpole, 'to torture some consistence out of his conduct, sometimes refining, and when that would not do, glossing it over'.[19]

Only a few months previously, as Fox did not resist pointing out, such 'German measures' as Pitt was now promoting had been condemned as 'a millstone'. However, like most members and most of the public, Fox approved this new statement of war policy. He perceived, he said, *capacity*, and only hoped the new 'millstone' would prove to be 'an ornament round the minister's neck'. To all appearance Pitt now enjoyed the widest backing. He was practising consensus politics, conducting consensus strategy. The Commons vote on the Prussian subsidy was *nem. con.*

Outside parliament, effusive endorsement came also from Bute, not in parliament himself but tutor now and chief adviser of the eighteen-year-old Prince of Wales, and at this time Pitt's most reliable supporter after the Grenvilles. Bute hastened to congratulate Pitt on his 'great and most able conduct', and assured him of the goodwill of the young prince who was some day to reap the fruits of Pitt's 'unwearied endeavours for the public safety'.[20] In reply, vying with Bute's own florid fulsomeness, Pitt was careful to pay court to the future king, even at the expense of the reigning one. 'The reception today [by George II] was gracious', he wrote, but the 'whole devotion' of his heart was offered 'at another place'; and a few days later, with much affectation of humility, he continued:

> If my noble and kind friend had not bid me, I shou'd blush to notify to him my intention of having the honour to be presented to HRH the Prince of Wales tomorrow. My feet, thank God, hold out tolerably, and in default of feet, a heart truely penetrated with ardent gratitude and most dutifull affection will bear me to Saville House . . .[21]

Pitt had adapted his policies, partly at least to meet the King's needs and demands; but obviously a mutual mistrust persisted. For the moment Pitt was in harmony with the Commons and the public; but he knew well enough that the King, and many of his own cabinet too, would gladly be rid of him if they could. Meanwhile, firm alliance with the heir apparent and with his mentor and spokesman, Bute, that 'best and noblest of friends', kept a rod in pickle. 'My paper is at an end; till life is so', he wound up, 'I shall be warmly and devotedly yrs'.

If there was broad consensus upon war policy, there was certainly none in the notorious and tragic affair of Admiral Byng; and there proved to be at least a fraction of truth in the prophecy of a Commons member during the debate upon Byng's case in February 1757: Byng, he declared, had been the means of throwing out the old ministry, and would yet perform the same service for the new one.[22]

The condemnation of Byng was, for the late ministers widely accused of mismanagement, an essential corollary of their self-justification. Exonerating him of cowardice, a court martial had found him guilty, under a recently introduced Twelfth Article of War, of failing to do his utmost in the face of the enemy. The verdict, reached strictly upon the evidence, left members of the court with no option in the sentence, death; but they did add a recommendation to mercy. Only the King could sanction a commutation of the sentence; but he, like Newcastle, Hardwicke, Anson, and Fox, the ministers chiefly attacked, was strongly opposed to any interference with the law's rigour. The King in fact was 'horrid angry with the court martial who have shoved the odium of Byng's death, if he is to suffer, in some measure off their own shoulders'.[23] As to the late ministers, a parliamentary inquiry into their actions was likely to provide some vindication of them; Byng's execution would finally and spectacularly assign blame where it must be seen to belong.

When moves to save the admiral were made in the Commons by Sir Francis Dashwood, William Beckford, Bubb Dodington, and others, Pitt spoke in support of clemency; but he was in a difficulty. He had striven to observe the correctest deference in the Closet, where his standing remained so shaky. He badly needed to avoid any confrontation or collision there. He could hardly thump the table and *demand* a pardon for Byng; and at first therefore he contented himself with advising the House that, the prerogative of mercy being exclusively the King's, 'it was more likely to flow from his Majesty if he was left entirely free'.[24] Temple, on the other hand, always liable to thump tables in any company, so importuned and offended the King that he became more than ever determined to be rid of him at the first opportunity. Rather than live with him for another month, he declared, he would give his crown away to Temple. He was 'so disagreeable a fellow, there was no bearing him'; when he attempted to argue he 'was pert, and sometimes insolent; when he meant to be civil he was exceedingly troublesome; and in the business of his office he was totally ignorant'.[25]

The cabinet, certain members of the court martial, and a considerable majority of the Commons were for pardoning Byng; but the public had for the most part no more wish than the King or the late ministers that he should escape. Newspaper articles and anonymous letters began to threaten Pitt with the consequences of any mitigation of the sentence, at a time when he stood in much need of public support. 'Let the inconstant gale of public favour blow where it will', Bute wrote to him;[26] but the events of the next few weeks would show just how vitally he needed those fickle winds. He was aware, he said, he 'should probably smart' for any attempt to procure clemency; but 'thank God', he claimed when the matter finally came to the crunch, 'I feel something more than popularity; I feel justice'.[27]

When Pitt first went to the King to plead for Byng he was 'cut very short';[28] and when later he transmitted the Commons' request for a stay of execution while it was considered whether members of the court martial might be absolved from their oath of secrecy to testify on Byng's behalf, George is said to have come up with a tart rebuke: 'Sir, you have taught me to look for the sense of my subjects in another place than the House of Commons'.[29] The legal logic and powerful influence of Hardwicke and Mansfield in the Upper House helped to keep the unforgiving finger of justice pointing firmly towards the firing party. There was a respite, but it proved brief. On 14 March Byng met his end bravely on the deck of the *Monarque* at Portsmouth; in the words of Walpole, one of the most indignant and passionate of his would-be rescuers, 'put to death contrary to all equity and precedent'.[30] Pitt's efforts to save him, begun with mixed feelings but honestly and humanely pursued in the face of his own obvious interests, finished with the worst of both worlds. A little more than three weeks after Byng was shot Pitt was dismissed.

It was Fox and his patron Cumberland rather than Newcastle and Hardwicke who had brought the King to his intemperate decision. True, Newcastle had no intention of remaining excluded from power indefinitely, or Hardwicke of forgoing his still powerful influence (though he had abandoned thought of office); they were realistically aware, however, that despite their following, easily the largest in parliament, they could not hope to stand on their own. Looking at the two principal groups potentially coadjutor to them, on the whole they preferred the prospect of Pitt and Leicester House to that of Fox and Cumberland – the latter an unpopular pairing. Hardwicke, too, detested Fox personally, and Newcastle had not forgiven him his 'disloyal' conduct in 1756. It was obvious that Pitt commanded at least equal support with Fox in parliament, and much more outside, among Tory squires and the urban bourgeoisie. Pitt himself, conscious of Fox's machinations against his ministry from the beginning, professed himself 'ready to poll the House of Commons as well as the nation' against Fox; and if Fox and faction prevailed against him, he would clear out altogether, to a rural retirement, where he thought he should spend the happiest days of his life – the old story, told this time to Lord Barrington, Secretary at War, who probably smiled as sceptically as others on hearing these improbable suggestions of flight to Arcadia.[31] (The current Arcadia was of course Hayes, building and re-building and expanding fast.)

Fox had a convenient channel to the King in the Duke of Cumberland, who from the moment he took office Pitt had seen as the latent malignant influence working against him.[32] It was presumably through Cumberland that Fox had 'conveyed to the King that whenever it was proper to drive out these gentlemen, there should neither be wanting expedients nor courage to support his affairs'.[33] It was not long before George was 'constantly flinging in something in favour of Mr Fox' to Pitt's fellow Secretary of State, the Newcastle Whig, Lord Holderness, one of the ministers more acceptable in the Closet. Indeed, George told Lord Waldegrave 'he did not look upon himself as King while he was in the hands of these scoundrels', Temple, Pitt and company; and it was Waldegrave whom he employed on two occasions to sound out the chances of a union between Fox and Newcastle – for which the Duke showed no enthusiasm whatever.

Although Pitt had no war successes yet to report, Fox's anxiety was apparently growing. 'If these gentlemen remain two months', he said to Dodington in March, 'they are conquerors and Leicester House masters'. On 25 March Newcastle produced a memorandum for the King advising him not to dismiss Pitt. George was sorry; nobody, he grumbled, considered his troubles. He had been reciting some of them to Waldegrave: 'The Secretary of State made him long speeches, which possibly might be very fine, but were greatly beyond his comprehension;[34] and his letters were very affected, formal, and pedantic'. These complaints would certainly not seem serious enough to justify the dismissal of a minister still possessing, if only on sufferance, a parliamentary majority and (Byng notwithstanding) enjoying strong extra-parliamentary support; and George, irritable and testy as he was, was not usually irresponsible. Probably he would not have decided so summarily to evict Pitt and Temple if Cumberland had not pushed him into doing it.[35]

The Army of Observation for the defence of Hanover and Prussia's western flank was now in existence. The Duke of Cumberland, Captain General, was appointed to command it, and was due to sail. But he refused until there was a ministry at home under which he thought he might be reasonably expected to operate. That plainly excluded Pitt, and pointed towards Fox. In the spirit of Mr Micawber, the King acted. On 4 April he sent Holderness to deliver a notice of dismissal for Temple, and ordered Lord Winchilsea to take over the Admiralty. This, he hoped, would cause Pitt to resign. Pitt, however, as Waldegrave reported, 'did not choose to save his enemies any trouble, and attended his duty at court with unusual assiduity'.[36] When his own notice arrived two days after Temple's, he wasted less than an hour before calling upon Bute at Leicester House to concert future action.

CHAPTER THIRTEEN

——◆◆——

The War: June 1757 - January 1759

Legge, George Grenville, his brother James, and some further ministers resigned after the dismissals, while Devonshire, Holderness, and the merest ghost of a caretaker administration were left to carry on the nation's affairs. There then followed twelve weeks of inter-factional bargaining of a complication and protractedness rare even by the standards of eighteenth-century political intrigue; 'an amazing scene', Hardwicke commented, 'precipitated without reason or common sense'. In the midst of a war already going badly, from early April until late June there was a formidable shuttling to and fro of proposals, counter-proposals, memoranda, disclaimers; accusations of broken understandings; clandestine conferences specially arranged to be held where the place of meeting had 'a back door to the park';[1] rifts within factions, fallings-out between leaders and led (between Pitt, for instance, and the two Townshends, and to some extent Legge too); letters 'to be burned as soon as read';[2] a profusion of conjectural administrations, allowing for the King's known predilections and prejudices, assuming that Mr Pitt could be parted from his 'visionary' and 'impracticable' ideas, given that Fox must be somehow satisfied, that Newcastle and his following must be accommodated, that known irreconcilables could be by some means reconciled. At one stage Newcastle had a ministry almost ready for delivery. It omitted Pitt but included in his place the honourable but faded Robinson once again. It was still-born. In early June a Waldegrave ministry, with Fox as Chancellor of the Exchequer, was actually nominated, and its principal members were even assembled to receive the insignia of office. Lord Mansfield however persuading the King that only confusion could result from proceeding, the candidate ministers did not get past the ante-chamber.

The King, angry with Newcastle, demanded to know why he would not combine with Fox. Was he not in fact secretly negotiating with Pitt? Newcastle swore he was not, but jibbed at undertaking that he never would. At first Pitt turned up his nose at any sort of approach to Newcastle from his side, for 'all our public misfortunes were more imputable to him than to any other man'. But what Pitt would not do, Legge would, and did. Then from the Pitt camp Bute also took a hand; similarly Hardwicke from Newcastle's. A series of conferences ensued between Newcastle, Hardwicke, Pitt, and Bute during the weeks when the King was forming his abortive Waldegrave-Fox administration. Hard bargaining on behalf of 'friends' was complicated by knowledge of what the King would flatly refuse to accept – for one, Lord Temple in *any* post that involved his presence in the Closet. (He was eventually accommodated with the Privy Seal, which at least meant that George would be spared seeing him. Pitt did his best to secure him the Garter which Temple thought his due; this, however, the King absolutely declined, reserving that greatest honour as a consolation prize and token of gratitude for Waldegrave.) Pitt fought to have George Grenville at the Exchequer and Legge at the Admiralty, but was obliged to compromise upon Legge at the Exchequer, and Grenville as Navy Treasurer – an arrangement displeasing to both these men – with Hardwicke's son-in-law Anson back in charge of the Admiralty. James Grenville became a Lord of Treasury, Admiral Temple West a Lord of Admiralty (he was cousin to the Grenvilles, a brother of Gilbert West, and had been second in command at Minorca); the Cousinhood was thus well catered for. Lyttelton, who had deserted their ranks in 1754, now found he was among Newcastle's discards and did not like it. Newcastle himself of course was to head the new Treasury, Devonshire retreating to be Lord Chamberlain. Holderness returned as Secretary for the Northern Department, where theoretically he would deal with the King's 'German business'. In practice, Pitt would be largely directing him. The legal spoils were divided equitably between Leicester House, the followers of Pitt, and the Newcastle party. Sir Robert Henley (the future Lord Chancellor Northington and a Leicester House man) became Lord Keeper. Charles Pratt, the future Lord Camden, already one of Pitt's closest henchmen, was the new Attorney General – which left the post of Solicitor General for Hardwicke's son Charles Yorke. Pitt argued for Lord George Sackville, another Leicester House man, to become Secretary-at-War, but when it was learned that the King insisted on retaining Barrington, Bute prevailed on Sackville to withdraw. The problem of what to do with Fox was solved to the satisfaction of all parties. The King insisted that he must get the Paymastership that had been promised him; the royal honour was involved. This meant an office of profit rather than influence; hence neither Pitt nor Newcastle offered resistance. For Fox, if the Paymastership separated him from power and so from the choicest grapes on the vine (which he had already declared sour), at least he was assured of a handsome recompense: it is calculated that his perquisites over the next seventeen years, accruing according to the permissive customs of the day, amounted to about £400,000.

Above all, Pitt was adamant that for himself, together with his Secretaryship, he must have leadership of the Commons and unequivocal power to direct policy:

> Do not imagine that I can be induced to unite with [the Duke of Newcastle], unless sure of power; I mean power over public measures; the disposition of offices, except the few efficient ones of the administration, the creating deans and bishops, and every placeman besides, is quite out of my plan, and which I would willingly relinquish to the Duke . . .[3]

Nevertheless, when the Commons in April finally arrived at debating the conduct of the late ministers over Minorca ('a pantomine', wrote Walpole, 'from which nothing was intended, expected, or produced') he had been careful to forgo all philippics, and 'acquiesced in every softening term proposed by the advocates of the late criminals' – recollecting how useful Newcastle's majority might yet be to him in the future. This was one of the several occasions when Walpole enjoyed himself in his memoirs at Pitt's expense, describing the 'theatric valetudinarian' at his 'mummery', with his 'studied apparatus of specious debility' – riding stockings over his legs; old coat and waistcoat of beaver laced with gold; red surtout over it with *one* arm fur-lined and black-ribboned; crape sling supporting the same arm, which however 'with unlucky activity' he brandished in his speech as usual.

From *his* camp Newcastle graphically expressed and justified his own position in a memorandum for the King:

> I can't come in without bringing in my enemy, Mr Pitt. He turned me out. But I can't serve without my enemy. He will be unreasonable.

He is, Sir. Beat him as low as I can, if your Majesty won't approve it, I can't come in alone.[4]

Just how true this was had been underlined by Pitt's most demonstrative champions, the businessmen and merchants of the city corporations. The Common Council of London led by awarding him, and Legge with him, their freedom and a gold box worth £100; and an epigram of the day retailed by Walpole bears witness both to Pitt's current popularity and to the commonly held view of Fox's avarice:

> The two great rivals London might content,
> If what he values most to each she sent;
> Ill was the franchise coupled with the box;
> Give Pitt the freedom, and the gold to Fox.[5]

Ralph Allen and his friends on the Bath council soon followed London's example, and before long would be voting Pitt something he valued more highly still, one of the Bath parliamentary seats.* Then a score or so of towns joined in the presentation of gold boxes or similar testimonials of approval to the two dismissed ministers, which meant of course, conversely, votes of no confidence in Newcastle, in Fox, and in the King himself.

In its vociferous support for Pitt (and at this stage Legge) the City of London did not, it is true, speak with altogether united voice. He had become the darling of the majority; but there existed an influential inner group of big-fish financiers, bankers, government contractors, and directors of the great chartered companies, upon whom the Whigs had been in the habit of relying for loans by means of a jealously restricted list. This powerful moneyed interest was strongly resented by the 'popular' party, led by Beckford and reflected in the views of *The Monitor*, which fiercely attacked 'those harpies, called money-

* Pitt reassumed his old Secretaryship for the Southern Department when returning to office, and was therefore not bound to seek re-election; but he seized the opportunity to exchange Okehampton for Bath, the last of his five constituencies and the only one (apart from Old Sarum, with its ancestral associations) with which he felt any personal bond. From 1757 Thomas Potter, previously a Temple nominee at Aylesbury and currently one of Pitt's closest associates, sat for Okehampton, which allowed Potter's friend John Wilkes to have Aylesbury. Wilkes thus began in politics inevitably as a follower of Pitt and Temple.

jobbers, who, under the pretence of assisting government, become the plunderers of it'; while the pro-Pitt *Contest* ranted against 'exorbitant premiums to Jewish cormorants'. Legge as Chancellor of the Exchequer had openly favoured this popular party and attempted to raise supplies by open list and public lottery. Though the scheme failed dismally, it paradoxically brought Legge and Pitt much credit as champions of the many against the few. Devonshire, however – who was altogether a novice in these matters – was obliged to return to the time-honoured principle of plutocratic privilege, when Pitt and Legge left his administration in April; and four months later, when they were being feasted by the Grocers' Company, among the toasts was one 'to the downfall of monopolizers and infamous stockjobbing'.[6]

When at last the months of negotiation and compromise seemed to have achieved their end, Pitt still showed no enthusiasm. 'All is settled for kissing hands tomorrow', he was able to tell Bute on 28 June, but added, 'I go to this bitter but necessary cup with a more foreboding mind, even since last night'. At the last moment he had smelt treachery in Newcastle and Hardwicke. The Duke 'had the front to affirm' that there had been an agreement to make Lord Halifax Secretary of State for America and the West Indies, at which Pitt 'was enraged beyond bearing'. This suggestion concerning Halifax had indeed been made, but much earlier and by Legge not Pitt, who had declared strongly against it. Of course it was the last thing he could have agreed to surrender. America and the West Indies were his own particular provinces, which he would farm out to no one else. Now, on the eve of setting forth upon this most auspicious and eventually triumphant of coalitions, Pitt poured out to Lord Bute, that 'last and only support, a truly noble and generous friend', his rancour against the foremost of his new colleagues, Newcastle:

How hard is the lot of this vile age! . . . This is the wretch who draws the great families at his heels, and for whose elevation and power the pretended friends of the publick have so loudly pass'd sentence on my inflexibility. But no more of these exanimating heart-breaking reflections. I will . . . warm my heart and arm my mind to encounter every difficulty in that service to which I have the glory, in conjunction with your Lordship, to be unalterably and totally devoted.[7]

'All our friends are in raptures with [the new ministry]', Hardwicke wrote to Anson, 'the Court in general pleased, and the town more so. It is looked upon as the strongest administration that has been formed for many years, and by good conduct may become so'. As far as men, as distinct from measures, were concerned, the new ministry began to work more smoothly than Pitt expected. After five weeks he was reporting to Bute, 'I have nothing to complain of in my colleague [Newcastle]; we differ but his proceeding is fair and manly'.[8] The fact that they differed, and that a majority of the cabinet were rather of the Duke's way of thinking, did not however prevent Pitt from managing to run the war in his own way. The advice and instructions, for instance for the British ambassador to Prussia, signed by the Northern Secretary, Holderness (more of a cypher than ever, Newcastle admitted), have the very stamp of Pitt's views on them, and were indeed probably composed from Pitt's drafts. 'I am convinced', so Holderness-Pitt represented to the ambassador in mid-July, 'you will agree with me in one principle, that we must be merchants while we are soldiers; that our trade depends upon a proper exertion of our marine strength; that trade and maritime force depend upon each other; and that the riches, which are the true resources of this country, depend chiefly upon its commerce'.[9]

It was a Prussian crisis that immediately confronted the new coalition, for on the very day of its formation news arrived of disaster befalling Frederick at Kolin in Bohemia, where one-third of his army was destroyed. 'Oh, my dear friend, what dreadful auspices do we begin with', Bute lamented, remembering however to flatter Pitt and thank God that at the head of affairs happily there was now 'a soul fit for these rough times'.[10] Frederick, after his earlier censoriousness of Britain's 'want of union and steadiness' and fears that Pitt was too sick a man to be relied on as chief minister, alternated between a despondent defensiveness and a shrill insistence that Britain do something to relieve his desperate situation – order a fleet to the Baltic, raid the French coast, send reinforcements from England in order to set free for his own use the Prussian contingents in Cumberland's army: *something*, and something soon.

Among the cabinet Newcastle favoured the last of these options, fearing that otherwise there would be danger of Frederick concluding a separate peace. Pitt, his hopes still fixed on the Loudoun-Holburne expedition against Canada, and still standing firm by his commitment to send no *British* troops to Germany, laboured to convince Frederick of the impracticability of sending to the Baltic a British naval squadron powerful enough to match the combined strength of Denmark, Sweden, and Russia. But he did favour – against the opinion of the King, against most of his cabinet colleagues, and against a majority of military and naval experts – a descent upon the Biscay coast to draw off large French resources of men and materials.

Before this could be attempted, a second blow fell: Cumberland's Army of Observation had been defeated at Hastenbeck, where it had been thought he occupied a strong defensive position covering Hanover. As he retreated towards Stade and the mouth of the Elbe, the French again, as in the preceding war, proceeded to overrun the city and most of the state of Hanover, to the consternation of George II, who would have been glad at this point to make his own separate peace as Elector and disband the Army of so-called Observation. To help dissuade him, and to deprive Frederick of any justification for extricating himself from the general struggle, Pitt, while vetoing the proposal of Newcastle, Hardwicke, and Holderness to dispatch British reinforcements to the Elbe, offered the King an immediate grant, out of current supplies already voted, of £100,000 for Cumberland's army and £20,000 more for Hesse, whose Landgrave was by this time a refugee at Hamburg. If the King was pleasantly surprised at this, there were mumblings and grumblings from some of Pitt's close allies. It was certainly remarkable policy from a minister who not many months before had been arguing fiercely that Hanover was indefensible and not worth wasting British money on. To those of the Grenville group and Leicester House party who had followed him in those earlier attitudes he felt obliged to offer some self-justification:

> I wish extremely [he wrote to George Grenville] that it had been in my power to have consulted you, as I intended, before I took the step; but the moment of decision pressed. I trust that you and Lord Temple will be of opinion . . . I have not done wrong. My own lights assure me I have made the only tolerable option, in so violent and urgent a crisis; but be that as it may, your disapprobation will make me unhappy.[11]

Grenville, though 'sensible of the great difficulties' Pitt worked under, did indeed consider that the money should have come from '*some other* [i.e. Hanoverian] *quarter*'. He obviously disapproved[12] – and was to find, as the next few months and years progressed, more and more in the behaviour of his masterful brother-in-law to be critical and resentful of. He maintained that he 'never derived the least advantage' from his association with Pitt. He had resented Pitt's failure to make him Chancellor of the Exchequer in his first ministry, when 'contrary to those repeated professions of his' he had promoted Legge 'over my head'. Then, complained Grenville privately, Pitt had given him only a very 'shuffling account' of why he was not offered, alternatively, the Paymastership. Indeed, his brother-in-law's behaviour seemed 'contrary not only to friendship and alliance subsisting between us, but to the engagements of honour and good faith'. He began to repent that he had ever helped to bring 'an enemy instead of a friend into our family', and thus to alienate his sister's affection.[13]

Bute too, while still returning Pitt's professions of courtly admiration with protestations of the profoundest respect, was becoming fidgety. He might take what comfort he could from Pitt's assurance that 'your humble servant's negative has prevail'd to wa[i]ve' the dispatch of British forces to the Continent; but already he was beginning to admit his uneasiness with the way Pitt was going: 'I am not quite so satisfied with the Duke of Newcastle as you seem to be', he observed pointedly; 'one improper concession may prove fatal to us all'.[14]

There were a few days of hopeful expectancy in mid-August, by which time news had dawdled back across the Atlantic that Loudoun and Holburne were arrived safely at Halifax, poised ready for the great blows planned by Pitt the previous December. It proved an isolated morsel of good tidings. Soon followed Loudoun's account of the abandonment of his operations, not only against Quebec, which was half expected, but even against the initial target of Louisbourg. 'I find it hard to keep up my mind under this unhopefull state of things', Pitt wrote; 'I had my heart in America and our windbound expedition'.[15]

Miscarriage in America was succeeded depressingly soon by simultaneous misfortune in Germany and upon the French coast. On 19 September, while the expedition aimed at Rochefort was still making slow sail across the Bay of Biscay towards its target, news arrived from Hanover of an event so 'calamitous and ignominious' that Pitt, submerged in audiences at Kensington and in meetings with foreign ambassadors and cabinet colleagues at Westminster, begged Bute to come up immediately from Kew to confer.[16]

The Duke of Cumberland, with 40,000 men hard pressed by 100,000 French, and not waiting to prepare the defence of Hanover's emergency capital at Stade – which might have been supplied from the sea – had taken upon himself, by a convention agreed with the French commander Richelieu, at Klosterzeven near Stade, to arrange a cease-fire and the neutralization of the allied army. The Hanoverians were to be immobilized, the other German units dispersed, and this moreover at a moment when Frederick was marching hopefully eastward with the aim of linking up with Cumberland. To the French the advantage of the Klosterzeven agreement was that it offered an opportunity to withdraw large forces out of Hanover to reinforce their army facing Prussia in the south, and a possibility too of uniting with Austrian imperial troops and directly attacking Berlin. For Richelieu speed was essential; and luckily for the allied army and for Pitt's plans he moved away in such haste that some important points were left unresolved, in particular the vital matter of the disarming of the allied troops.

Most Hanoverians were only too pleased to think they had got the French off their backs. And their Elector, King George, had undoubtedly not long since given Cumberland discretionary authority to negotiate terms. Suddenly, however, his tune was remarkably changed – partly, one must assume, because the British government had now made itself liable for the extra money to finance operations. Directly he learned of Klosterzeven, the King heaped recriminations upon his son. Pitt had always seen Cumberland as a 'malignant influence' working against him, and he would be glad to be rid of him and have a commander-in-chief with whom there could be mutual trust; but his sense of fairness obliged him to show the King where some share of responsibility lay:

> When the King told him that he had given his son no *orders* for this treaty, Pitt replied with firmness, '*But full powers*, Sir, very *full powers*'. Yet this sincerity in a foe could infuse none into a father: two messengers were dispatched to recall the Duke . . .[17]

Pitt meanwhile was all for immediate renunciation of the convention and appointing the Hanoverian General Spörcken to take over temporary command of the operations. The Hessian contingent, which the

French found no time to disarm, had already been ordered by the Landgrave to stand fast. Although Lord Mansfield, co-opted at Newcastle's wish to the Secret Committee of the cabinet, advised on the illegality of abrogation, Pitt insisted on it, and persuaded his colleagues to assure the King that if he would authorize a resumption of hostilities, their entire cost should fall on the British exchequer. As things were to turn out, the Convention of Klosterzeven, ignominious as it began by seeming, was in the end, by discrediting Cumberland, to prove no small blessing to Pitt. He already began to visualize radical changes in the military command, with Ligonier, whose vigour belied his age, in charge at home, and the able Prince Ferdinand of Brunswick leading the army in Germany.

Before the about-to-be-humiliated Cumberland arrived back in London, the Rochefort expedition had suffered its own humiliation. The decision for such a diversionary attack, pleaded for by Frederick and strongly advocated by Pitt, had not been accepted by the Secret Committee without misgivings, or by the King without some derision. Even after it had been approved, the danger to Cumberland's army after the defeat at Hastenbeck had meant that George begged to have it diverted to the Elbe or to Friesland. Newcastle and Hardwicke, watching the retreat in Germany and learning too that French troops had recently taken over from Maria Theresa's along the Austrian Netherlands coast at Ostend and Nieuport, were again seriously afraid of invasion. The new militia was still in its troublesome infancy. Many of the best regiments were away across the Atlantic. 'For God's sake', wrote Hardwicke to the Duke, 'insist that the [Rochefort] troops should be back by the middle of or before the end of September'.

For Pitt, Rochefort offered the opportunity of combining high material damage to the French with maximum dislocation of their strategy and hence a measure of relief to hard-pressed German armies. He still refused absolutely to send British troops to Germany. Equally he refused to waste forces at home waiting for a possible invasion. Rochefort was an important naval base and arsenal. Moreover he had been encouraged by a report on its vulnerability presented in July by Ligonier – himself a French Protestant refugee,* who incidentally

---

* Jean-Louis Ligonier; born Toulouse 1680; came with his family to England, aged eleven; naturalized 1702; served under Marlborough, Argyll, Stair, Wade, and Cumberland.

claimed that the expedition might well meet Protestant sympathizers in that part of France. (The fleet carried a Huguenot pilot when it sailed.)

Orders had already been issued to Admiral Hawke 'to burn and destroy . . . all such docks, magazines, arsenals, and shipping' as might be found 'at or near Rochefort' (with discretion to extend depredations anywhere on the coast between Le Havre and Bordeaux) when at the last moment Newcastle again questioned the wisdom of the adventure. Pitt gave him what the Duke's jotted memorandum calls 'a strong answer': Pitt 'would defend it with his head. Whoever stopped it should answer for it'.[18]

Newcastle's jottings add, significantly: 'His suspicions of the land and sea officers'. Pitt had Ligonier on his side, but he knew that he did not yet have behind him a majority of the men in control of the services. Perhaps he was not wholly confident even of Hawke, and certainly less than wholly of Sir John Mordaunt, the general the King had appointed to command the expedition's troops. (Pitt's first choice had been Sackville, who begged to decline; his second Conway, who the King said was too young.) On 5 September, waiting it seemed interminably at Cowes for favourable winds, Hawke and Mordaunt each received a letter expressing the Secretary of State's impatient anxiety. 'The messenger that carries this', added an imperious postscript, 'has my orders to stay to bring an account of the fleet's sailing'.[19]

It was a very sizable undertaking. Finally, five days after Pitt's ill-received missives (and two days after Cumberland had put his signature to the Convention of Klosterzeven) an armada of 135 sail, including 16 ships of the line and 50 transports, sailed for Rochefort. On 23 September naval forces captured the fortified island of Aix, in the Basque Roads off the mouth of the Charente (Rochefort was ten miles up-river). They took soundings in the Roads, reconnoitred the coastline, and finally determined a suitable point for a troop-landing. But Mordaunt and most of his subordinate generals had become more than ever suspicious of the whole project's feasibility. He now refused to agree the navy's choice of landing place and timetable, and insisted to Hawke on the generals' right to hold a council of war, which after much tedious debate decided that, since Rochefort had now had five days' warning, it could not be captured 'by assault or escalade merely', as had been planned. For three more days Hawke waited for the generals to present alternative plans of attack. When none were forthcoming he informed them that he intended 'to proceed . . . for England without loss of time'. His orders had been to return promptly on the conclusion of operations.

The fiasco was complete. Anson wrote gloomily, 'There seems to be a fatality in everything we undertake'. Pitt received a bare notification of the 'afflicting news' at Hayes on 6 October, and was down there again ten days later, having 'been for some days in constant threatenings of gout' and feeling 'an absolute want of air in town'.* By then he had heard the whole story; 'I feel more and more I shall never get Rochefort off my heart,' he wrote to Bute on 17 October. 'Nor do I believe England (which is the misery) will cease to feel, perhaps for an age, the fatal consequences of this foul miscarriage'.[20]

On his return Mordaunt was met with cold anger by Pitt, yet (wrote Walpole) with 'greater decency' by him than by the King who, having earlier ridiculed the Rochefort project, now 'did the generals the honour of treating them as ill as his own son, the Duke'. Mordaunt requested a commission of inquiry, which sat during November, and as a result of its findings he had to face a court martial. More fortunate than Byng, he was honourably acquitted. 'The whole court', Walpole reported, 'treated the expedition as rash and childish', and remained unimpressed by the 'imperious speech' Pitt delivered them.[21]

Of course the débâcle at Rochefort gave a handle to all those who had opposed the strategy it represented. It had taken, it was said, large resources of ships, men, and materials which at best could only have sunk a few enemy warships, destroyed some docks and arsenals, and temporarily dislocated French troop dispositions. There were in fact at Rochefort fourteen ships of the line and eight frigates. Their destruction would have been a major blow. But, as things had gone, had the game been worth the valuable candle? Emphatically, Pitt claimed, it had. It had caused the diversion of seven (actually six) French and Swiss guards battalions and ten (actually eight) other regiments towards the west coast.[22] There had been great consternation in Paris, so he was reporting to Bute only one day before news arrived of the failure.

* 'In town' he had just taken a lease of 10 St James's Square, which remained his London residence until after his resignation in 1761. It is of course the modern Chatham House.

('Germany is redeem'd si l'on veut!')[23] If only the enterprise had been pursued with proper *élan* and with acceptance by the leaders of a reasonable degree of risk – so both Rodney, present at the council of war, and Wolfe, Mordaunt's Quartermaster General, agreed in considering – it ought to have succeeded.[24]

Pitt's first reaction to the commanders' empty-handed return was to contemplate ordering them straight back to occupy the Ile de Rhé. His colleagues pouring cold water on the suggestion, he did not persevere with it; but his resentment smouldered on. It was some time before he forgave Hawke; and in a long speech in the debate on army supplies in mid-December, at the time of Mordaunt's court martial, he asserted that nothing would be well until the army was properly subjected to the civil power. John Calcraft, the army agent, wrote to Lord Loudoun, 'Mr Pitt abused both land and sea officers exceedingly', Loudoun himself being singled out for special criticism;[25] and neither he nor Mordaunt would be further trusted by Pitt. He was determined that Ligonier should find him new men he could believe in – though any suspicion he might have harboured that Mordaunt had been in collusion with the King to thwart the Rochefort expedition seems to be invalidated by George's fury on hearing of the General's acquittal. It took some days to persuade him to give the necessary royal approval to the court martial's verdict.

When Cumberland arrived home – with written authority in his pocket, he told Fox, for everything he had done – his father greeted him nevertheless with rebukes both private and not so private. 'Here is my son,' he said before the company at cards, 'who has ruined me and disgraced himself'; whereupon Cumberland immediately resigned all his commands. Fox found him hurt, but 'cheerful and at ease', and admitting to be 'a little vexed to be obliged, as he must own himself to be, to Mr Pitt for his very honourable behaviour on this occasion'. Cumberland went out of his way to be seen chatting amiably with Pitt at the levee. It is difficult to forgive the kindness of enemies, and both men seem to deserve some credit in the affair – not that we should suppose that Cumberland overnight became an admirer of the man of whom only a few weeks earlier he had been characteristically complaining to the Secretary-at-War, 'I am surprised to hear that my orders . . . confirmed by his Majesty, are changed according to the whim and supposed improvement of every fertile genius'.[26] Neither, of course, was Pitt anything but delighted that Cumberland was out of the way.

He immediately proposed to Newcastle that Ligonier should be appointed Commander in Chief (with a peerage and the colonelcy of the First Regiment of Guards). He had already gained Bute's approval for this, and it was left to Newcastle's wheedling to extract that of the King, which came with the customary ungraciousness, somewhat lessened when, in audience, Ligonier was prudent enough to express approval of George's disposition of his military forces. Even then, Ligonier had for the time being to be content with an *Irish* peerage. Newcastle 'never saw a man more pleased' with the outcome than Pitt, who had been seriously afraid the King intended 'to be his own General'.[27] With the fall of Cumberland the title of Captain General lapsed, and the French-born Ligonier became the first British soldier to be officially styled Commander in Chief. (We would today call him Chief of the General Staff.) His place as Lieutenant General of the Ordnance was now taken by Lord George Sackville, later to be known as Germain, chief military man at Leicester House, and destined to gain an unhappy reputation under each of his surnames.

For Pitt a further source of satisfaction was that Ferdinand of Brunswick was confirmed at the head of the allied army in Germany. 'I am just setting out for Hayes', he wrote on 25 November, 'but cannot go without sending dear Lord Bute a line, to tell him things are ripen'd at Stade and the resolution taken. God be prais'd, Prince Ferdinand is to command'.[28] At the same time he was asking Ligonier to find him a new commander for the following year's resumption of the attack on Louisbourg and Quebec. Here the choice, contrary to routine promotion order, was Jeffery Amherst, aged a mere forty, who had been Ligonier's aide-de-camp at Fontenoy. However, on 19 December Pitt was complaining to Leicester House: 'The King refuses Amherst flat and peremptory. I wish the Duke of Marlborough.* What a consideration, that such commands should go a begging. We cannot be a country long'.[29] A few days later, the decision was made to replace Loudoun by Abercromby, of whom nevertheless Ligonier seemed to speak far from confidently; and this perhaps was why the new chief of operations was assigned a second-in-command 'stiffener' of exceptional energy and promise, the eldest of the three

* The third Duke (1706–58), soon to be given command of the St Malo raid.

Howe brothers: George, third Viscount, aged thirty-two. Their designated task would be to force the approaches to Canada from the Hudson Valley, via Ticonderoga and Crown Point. Leadership of the remaining, third, campaign projected in America – over the forests of the Alleghenies to the Ohio Valley and Fort Duquesne, was to be entrusted to another of Ligonier's men, Brigadier John Forbes.

At last, but only after the arts and persuasions of Newcastle and Lady Yarmouth had been persistently plied, the King unwillingly consented to have Amherst command the Louisbourg-Quebec operation; and he too was to be supported by one of the most highly regarded of the younger officers, James Wolfe. Some of the difficulties which Pitt and Ligonier had to surmount in preparing for these next campaigns in America may be surmised from reading an earlier report of the Secretary-at-War, Barrington, to the then Captain General, Cumberland. Barrington wrote that Ligonier had obtained royal approval for a draft of forty men from every battalion in Great Britain and Ireland, the Guards only excepted; but the King, added Barrington, consented 'with directions (as he afterwards told me in private) that the worst men be drafted' for America.[30]

1757 had been an altogether depressing year for British arms; only Plassey brought a belated flicker of remote triumphs. It was time, Walpole suggested, for England to slip her cables and float away into some unknown ocean. Diplomacy had brought no better return than warfare. Here the chief venture had been an offer by Pitt to restore Gibraltar to Spain, if she would assist Britain to regain Minorca. At a Secret Committee of 18 August ministers were unanimous upon this proposition. That it ever should have been made emphasizes the disparity of the relative values then set on Minorca and Gibraltar. Indeed, according to Gibraltar's very disgruntled Governor, Lord Tyrawley, the place in its 'fatherless and motherless defenceless state' was hardly worth giving away.[31] But Pitt was exceedingly cautious in his very detailed and precise instructions dispatched to the Madrid ambassador, Keene.[32] The offer was not to be left on the table, or construed as providing the basis for any future Spanish claim. The Spaniards must 'join their arms' to Britain, and the exchange would not be effective till 'Minorca, with all its fortresses and harbours', was restored to the crown of England.

Keene received only the dustiest of answers from Wall,* the Spanish chief minister, and was obliged to return to Pitt a 'long disagreeable letter' full of Wall's 'warm fluency of words' on the subjects of British 'usurpations' in Spanish America and 'insults Spain had met with from our privateers'[33] – language altogether too reminiscent of the 1730s and Jenkins's Ear to make pleasant music now in Pitt's. The insults from British privateers were real enough. As recently as 6 August Pitt had dispatched a stinging reprimand to Governor Pinfold of Barbados for failing to punish or report to Westminster 'some very extraordinary acts of violence and cruelty' complained of by Spain and committed upon the crew of a Spanish vessel 'under pretence that the ship and lading were French'. In future, Pitt demanded condign punishment and 'early and exact intelligence'.[34] The situation was not without its irony if one considers Pitt's own anti-Spanish broadsides of 1739, and the threats to impeach Robert Walpole, the last British minister to make the offer of Gibraltar to Spain; and the extent to which this 1757 offer was dictated by weakness is underlined by the rapidity with which, directly the first faint whiff of British victory drifted back across the Atlantic from Cape Breton Island the following year, Pitt instructed the new Madrid ambassador, Lord Bristol, to deny all knowledge of the proposal, which was 'totally at an end'.[35]

Towards the end of the year a few harbingers of victory came in from the continent. The brilliant and resilient Frederick, in two large-scale engagements fought respectively on 5 November and 5 December, routed first the southern French army and their allies at Rosbach in Saxony, and then a force of 80,000 Austrians at Leuthen (Lissa) in Silesia – and was excitedly and understandably, if a shade misleadingly, hailed as 'the Protestant Hero' by large numbers of relieved Englishmen lacking much else to shout about. Everybody kept his birthday, wrote Walpole, 'and the people, I believe, begin to think that Prussia is some part of *Old England*'.[36] Pitt, working fearsomely long and as yet unrewarding hours – 'full of gouty pains flying about' him, yet hoping, he said, 'not to fall down'[37] – had long been in sore need of some good news; and Rosbach did certainly send him 'to dinner with a better appetite'.[38] Hester, carrying by now their third child, sat down to write with unblushing effusiveness to her paragon of a husband (he combined, she told him, 'every amiable advantage that man can

* Don Ricardo Wall, of Irish Jacobite refugee descent.

have with every high capacity that makes a hero and a statesman'),
and to impute to him at least some part-share in Frederick's victory,
or even in Frederick himself – '*your* King of Prussia', she proudly
wrote.

Frederick's view was somewhat different. 'From your country', he
complained to the British ambassador Mitchell, 'I have had nothing
but good words'. He had, of course, had a good deal of money as well,
and would soon be getting much more; but he wanted men. He
constantly pressed to Mitchell the need for *British* forces to be sent to
the allied army, and as constantly Mitchell passed on his demands and
strategic recommendations to London. Pitt was quite ready to go to
parliament to ask for a Prussian subsidy bigger than any yet suggested –
four million crowns (nearly £700,000); and in fact he postponed the
opening of parliament to be able to make the most of Rosbach in the
King's Speech. But he irritably rejected the call for British troops;
attributed unpatriotic motives to Mitchell ('it is evident to whom he
belongs'); and to Newcastle resentfully indicated his angry suspicions
of *him*:

> Thus it is, my Lord, in every part of Government; the tools of
> another system are perpetually marring every hopeful measure of
> the present system. In a word, if your Grace is not able to eradicate
> this lurking, diffusive poison a little more out of the mass of Govern-
> ment . . . I think it better for us to have done. I do not intend for
> one that Andrew Mitchell shall carry me where I have resolved not
> to go.[39]

Another Anglo-Prussian agreement was being prepared; in return
for the subsidy, for a British garrison in Emden, and for further raids
upon the French coast, Frederick was to be required to pledge that he
would conclude no separate peace. Before negotiations ended, Pitt
insisted on Mitchell's recall, and his replacement *ad hoc* by the Hague
ambassador Sir Joseph Yorke. Frederick was to be made to see that
the British representative in Berlin spoke for the *British* government,
and with precise instructions. Just how precise these had to be Holderness painfully discovered over a five-hour session with his fellow
Secretary, finishing at three in the morning, while the draft was
polished and re-polished 'so as to be scarce legible' and Holderness
sank with 'fatigue and ennui'. He would not go through another such

experience, he said, 'for all the King's revenue, or for what is perhaps more valuable, Mr Pitt's abilities'.[40]

Such a feeling of exasperated admiration was general among Pitt's colleagues. He would let none of them rest. The commonly held view that his fellow-ministers stood aside and 'let Pitt run the war' is, at least at this juncture, largely false. He was inclined rather to insist on holding cabinets, sometimes when they found it least convenient; though, true, upon arrival they were very liable to be browbeaten into accepting his arguments and proposals. Immediately after Christmas 1757, for instance, Newcastle, entertaining at Claremont company which included the Bishop of Durham, was assuming that he might relax with his guests undisturbed for a while by political affairs. Most of the other ministers, too, would expect to be then at their country seats. But it was just the moment when Pitt and Ligonier were hoping to complete the plans and appointments for the 1758 American campaigns. From pressure of work, Pitt had already put off his own idea of getting away to Bath. He ventured to hope therefore that Newcastle would not think him

unreasonable or improper in wishing to have the sanction of a meeting of the cabinet and particularly of your Grace present there, concerning so important and extensive a scene as the campaign in America, where England and Europe are to be fought for.

Then, with that characteristic ambiguous touch of his, a subtle compound of ornate courtesy and sarcastic reproach, he added:

I cannot, however, after the desire your Grace has expressed not to break the agreeable engagements of Claremont, press any further your Grace's taking the trouble to come to town.[41]

The reproaches came from both, indeed from all, sides. Most cabinet members from time to time considered themselves put upon, or bullied, by Pitt; Newcastle in particular, who had vowed in the first days of the coalition, 'He shall not be *my superior*'.[42] Obstinate differences again arose in the early months of 1758 over a bill designed to strengthen rights of habeas corpus in cases of wrongful, or possibly wrongful, arrest by the press gang. Hardwicke, in common with most of the heavyweights of the law, reckoned the bill 'absurd', the work of inexperienced hands, 'entirely cooked up between [Pitt] and his new

Attorney General [Pratt]'; not even worth trying to amend.[43] Pratt, with Pitt's backing, piloted this measure through the Commons against negligible opposition, only to watch it emphatically thrown out by the Upper House. Newcastle, as usual when he had no strong views of his own, followed Hardwicke; and Pitt's furious anger with them all – the law lords in particular, leading lights of a profession for whom his contempt always flowed freely – distracted for a short space some of his attention from the conduct of the war. Descending one day unexpectedly upon a Newcastle again entertaining guests, he inflicted on him such a 'rhapsody of violence and virulence' (directed against Mansfield especially) as Newcastle felt he really ought not to be asked to tolerate.[44] 'I should think he will carry this point [over habeas corpus] to the utmost extremity', he wrote to Hardwicke, to whom he once more appealed for sympathy and succour:

> For my own part [he wrote] I am determined not to continue in business upon the present foot; obliged every day to be teazing and proposing disagreeable things to the King, and instead of being thanked for it, to meet with constant reproaches, jealousies, and an overbearing superiority; and (what is still worse) laid under the greatest difficulty every day, from proceedings in parliament without concert . . .[45]

Newcastle found Pitt hardly less easy to live with on the subject of financing the war. Finding that the Treasury estimates for the year's army expenditure amounted to nearly half a million more than he had been led to expect, Pitt expostulated to the Duke in indignantly outspoken terms. This 'mountain of expense' was 'prodigious . . . excessive . . . out of the question'; the cost of the forage for the Hessians was 'preposterous'. The House of Commons would be 'revolted' by such sums.[46] (In fact they were to swallow them very meekly, with only one dissentient vote, though the figure included the whole cost of the Hanoverian army, as well as Frederick's £700,000.)

Painstakingly polite, but not troubling to conceal his irritation, Newcastle pointed out that he had 'daily and hourly' tried to get the costs down. In any case, such matters were 'the business of the King's ministers collectively'; he refused to have sole responsibility loaded upon him simply because he was head of the Treasury. That he must have Pitt's backing in the Commons he knew 'too well' not to admit.

Pitt, however, should not forget that he did not have a monopoly of good intentions: 'whatever the public may think of me . . . to the best of my knowledge I act for the service of the King and the nation'.[47] As a rebuke it had a sort of forlorn dignity; as a statement, it deserves sympathy, and even perhaps simple acceptance. For Newcastle's doubtless still complaining shade it can have been no joke over the past two centuries to have been for so long cast in the role of the whimpering villain.

While these discords within the cabinet persisted, there were successes in the field. Before the new agreement with Prussia had been completed, Ferdinand of Brunswick, after only six weeks in winter quarters, resumed the initiative he had taken against the French in December and began winning swift successes in Hanover – news good enough, Pitt said, to chase the gout out of his 'lame' hand, and, if it only continued, might soon enable him to get on his legs again. For a time the dispatches from Germany continued to be quite exhilarating:

> By a courier arrived from Stade certain account is come that the French have evacuated, in the utmost consternation, not only Bremen, but Hanover, Brunswick, Wolfenbuttel, and it is thought Hesse Cassel. Prince Ferdinand is pursuing them on all sides. I write this note to dear Lord Bute with that sincere joy which he will feel on [this] so happy event.

Among the towns evacuated was Emden, which in March was occupied by a small British naval force that had managed to penetrate thus far up the river Ems. Ferdinand then asked the government for a *British* garrison to hold the place. For Pitt this meant making a decision small in itself but big in its implications. He hesitated, torn between the strategic attractiveness of the move and a fear that it might be taken as the thin edge of a wedge; but by the end of March he had been persuaded, and a battalion of redcoats took over duty from the men of Commodore Holmes's frigate and cutter. Once Pitt's so often and vehemently pronounced negative upon such continental involvement had been thus withdrawn it became progressively easier for the commitment to be extended; and every move he made in that direction was to mean more satisfaction for the Duke of Newcastle, but at the same time greater difficulty in retaining the support at Leicester House of the heir to the throne and his by now intimately close adviser and spokesman Lord Bute.

Another overseas operation launched at this time – the little African project which had had to be abandoned in 1757 – needed no such basic questioning as sending a handful of garrison troops to Emden. This time the small naval squadron with its 200 marines aboard, together with its only begetter, the Quaker Cumming, got under way for Senegal in early March, the earlier of two West African expeditions Pitt would be sending out in this year. Without much difficulty it succeeded in taking Fort Louis on the Senegal River, with a haul of prisoners, slaves, cannon, gold-dust, gum (400 tons of it) and other assorted booty.

The loss of Fort Louis would mean another blow to the already hard-pressed *Compagnie des Indes*. The loss of gum imports would affect Lyon silk and other French manufactures.* The denial of 500 slaves to the French West Indian islands would help to raise the price of labour there and hence the cost of French sugar, much of it traditionally but illegally imported into British America. Such nakedly mercantile considerations which would have produced hardly more than a well-bred yawn among the French ruling class (or, for that matter, among most of the British) were of prime importance to Pitt and his supporters among the wealthy bourgeoisie. Together, this alliance represented a force which had no parallel in France. Indeed it was very much of a novelty in Britain. There had, after all, never before been a chief minister hoisted back to power, as Pitt was in 1757, against the resistance of the King and his chosen government, largely by pressure from the commercial classes.

Colonial ventures and German subsidies apart, the chief British contribution to the war in 1758 was still to lie with diversionary raids. Despite Rochefort, Pitt's confidence in them was quite unshaken. With naval supremacy affording Britain the initiative and to some extent the advantages of surprise, he calculated that the French must be obliged to station along or near their coast such disproportionately large forces that the Prussian and allied armies could not fail to benefit.

* Previously, as the *Annual Register* of 1758 explained to its readers (p. 76n.), we were 'obliged to buy all our gum senega of the Dutch, who purchase it from the French; and they set what price they please on it'. Now 'the price of this valuable drug, which is so much used in several of our manufactures, will be much reduced'.

14. William Murray, later Lord Mansfield, by J. B. Van Loo

Philip Earl of Hardwicke
Viscount Royston appointed
Lord High Chancellor
Of Great Britain
20 Feb: 1736.

15. *above* Philip Yorke, Earl of Hardwicke, by Thomas Hudson

16. Admiral Lord Anson, after Reynolds

17. William, Duke of Cum-
berland, studio of Reynolds

18. Field-Marshal Lo
Ligonier, bust by Ro
biliac

At best a fortified foothold might be gained, and held perhaps for the war's duration; at least, there must be damage to enemy shipping and installations. And the raids were to be no pin-pricks. Each would employ scores of naval vessels, including the largest, and between 10,000 and 15,000 troops – not many fewer than the total of regulars employed at this time against Canada (though these were reinforced by larger numbers of American 'provincials'). For Pitt, coastal descents had the emphatic advantage of being wholly British based and controlled. They could to some extent be turned on and off at will, each situation being played according to the flow of fortune's tide. Behind them there would always ride the navy, to protect, sustain, or if necessary rescue. In brief, as he saw it, they would 'cause such a division of the forces of the enemy as may influence the grand operations of the campaign without going at too great a distance from this country'.[51]

St Malo was to be the first objective for 1758. By the end of May 13,000 men were encamped on the Isle of Wight, with an armada of 150 transports and smaller warships awaiting them offshore, and twenty-five ships of the line ready to welcome any offensive move from the Brest fleet. Command of the troops was given to Ligonier's choices, the Duke of Marlborough with Sackville as chief subordinate; that of the naval support to Richard Howe, an officer as highly regarded by the naval authorities as his brother Viscount Howe by the military. Hawke, however, took umbrage at the choice of this comparatively junior man and, thinking he was being slighted because of the Rochefort failure, struck his flag in a gesture of impetuous and rather risky protest. Now, he wrote, when (so he thought) 'every means to success is assured, another is to reap the credit'. He had mistakenly thought a *second* attack was to be made on Rochefort. The Lords of Admiralty reproved him for 'a high breach of discipline', but 'in consideration of his past services' let it go at that; 'whereupon, as the most proper measure on this occasion', they 'ordered Lord Anson to take upon himself that command'. So Hawke sailed under Anson with the covering force of heavy ships, while Howe's squadron attended more immediately upon the army.[52]

There was concern that Hawke's action might have occasioned some discontent in the navy; Anson, too, at sea again, discovered that his captains were not as well practised as they should have been. But 'the troops', Pitt wrote to Hester, 'are said to breathe nothing but ardor. Heaven go with them'.

Hester was regaining strength after the birth of her third child, Harriot, and in this same letter Pitt begged her to be careful of her 'dear, dear health'. His own, as usual, was wretched – Hardwicke recommended Newcastle to try to make allowances for their 'peevish colleague on that account': 'Your Grace certainly did right to leave him to cool'.⁵³ In mid-May Pitt had told Newcastle that his condition absolutely demanded that he must get some country air at Hayes; and by the 29th he was sending Bute a progress report of the *invalids* of Hayes: 'Lady Hester is better and I still muffled up with a swell'd face, which abates'.⁵⁴ Three days later, his 'enterprise' set sail; he wished not to use the word 'expedition' – it was associated too closely with Rochefort.

In these first days of June Pitt, back now at work in London, waited excited and anxious for dispatches from three fronts; in much better humour too, Newcastle found him; 'civil, some very unreasonable expressions, but at last rather good humour and joking than otherwise'. From Germany, news arriving on the 7th was excellent: Ferdinand had advanced beyond the Rhine near the Dutch frontier. From the vital American theatre, upon which Pitt's greatest hopes were pinned, a report had arrived from Abercromby of the successful concentration of forces preparing to attack Louisbourg. The prospect here, it seemed, must be favourable, the French being greatly outnumbered and British naval squadrons under Osborn and Hawke having already, between February and April, defeated attempts from Toulon and Rochefort to supply and reinforce the base. And from the French coast – at 12.30 a.m. on 8 June Pitt wrote, 'An officer is just arrived from Captain Howe, with news of a landing in Cancalle Bay, about 7 miles from St Maloes . . . Heaven send us a prosperous issue!'⁵⁵ He was so buoyed up by this exciting news of a St Malo landing coming together with Ferdinand's passage of the Rhine that he could not resist the highly unusual step of sending off letters to his two commanders in Halifax, Amherst and Boscawen (though he had 'no new orders to send you from his Majesty'), apprising them of 'this fortunate coincidence of events'.

By the time these messages were on their way, half a million pounds' worth of fire damage had been done in St Malo harbour to stores and shipping (four medium-sized to small warships on the stocks, some

privateers, and a large number of fishing boats); but Marlborough
and Sackville had decided that, with rumours of enemy forces approaching, the island detour necessary to reduce the town would be
too dangerous a proposition for their artillery and supply columns,*
and had therefore re-embarked, with the loss merely of some of
Marlborough's personal table silver, carelessly left behind but restored
with contemptuous civility, in a cartel-ship, by the Governor of
Brittany. No, scoffed Horace Walpole, it was *not* true that the town
of St Malo had been taken by storm or that 'the governor leaped into
the sea at the very name of the Duke of Marlborough', or that my
Lord Anson had 'ravished three abbesses, the youngest of whom was
eighty-five'. What did seem to be true was that 'the flower of our
troops and nobility' had 'performed the office of link-boys, made a
bonfire, and run away' – and that the Duke of Aiguillon had returned
Marlborough's teaspoons. A week or two later, our great fleet in the
meantime having 'dodged about the coasts of Normandy and Bretagne
. . . stepped ashore again at Cherbourg; I suppose, to singe half a yard
more of the coast'.[56] Owing to poor weather, a Cherbourg landing
had in fact been abandoned, although the troops had already been
assembled in landing craft. Then the armada returned from its three
weeks of desultory and unrewarded cruising, with some sickness and
lousiness aboard but otherwise unscathed – except by the criticism that
greeted its return. Pitt however continued to argue, to himself and to a
far from convinced cabinet, that there had been a great defensive
deployment of French troops along the coast, all the way from Dunkirk
to Rochefort, and that this amply justified the expedition. There were
indeed by then tens of thousands of French engaged in coastal defence,
but most of them seem to have been militiamen; the number of
regulars, though considerable, was never great.[57] And the French
remained puzzled at the British employing so impressive a
quantity of men, ships, and equipment when so little was finally
attempted; '*Les Anglais viennent nous casser des vitres avec des guinées*'.
   Marlborough and Sackville both indicated strongly that they did
not wish to be sent on further such 'buccaneering' expeditions. Like

---

* Ligonier's correspondence seems to show that a direct assault on St Malo must have
been part of the original plan; following its capture, an attempt was to be made to hold
the peninsula on which the port stood. Faulty intelligence, supplied by 'those Jersey
gentlemen', set the plans awry (R. Whitworth, *Lord Ligonier*, 254–6).

most British commanders (Wolfe ironically included)[58] they regarded Germany as the only true school of war; it was generally considered a misfortune to be relegated to America or one of the other colonial theatres, by French and English alike – and as for Pitt's raids, they had come to be regarded as ungentlemanly, unpleasantly amphibious, and accident-prone.

Pitt did not give in easily, and he was still strongly committed to further such expeditions; but the situation in Germany, grown suddenly tense, with Ferdinand's lines of communication threatened by French forces brought up from the south, seems to have shaken him into conceding that directer and more substantial British help must be given. Suddenly, 'in the best manner imaginable', he had approached Newcastle after a cabinet meeting, while the St Malo expedition was still at sea, and proposed that 6000 of its troops should be sent on their return to Germany. When immediately afterwards news arrived of Ferdinand's brilliant victory at Crefeld, which caused high rejoicing and suddenly seemed to make the idea of German campaigning positively popular in England, Pitt decided to dispatch *more*, rather than fewer, troops to him. He hoped soon, he said, to be sharing 'a sprig of Germanic laurel'.[59] Newcastle was as pleased as he was surprised: this would 'show our friends', he wrote, 'that we mean to do something in this war'. As for *Pitt's* friends, it was necessary to convince them that he was not on a slippery slope. It was only 2000 *cavalry* that they were sending, he informed them – which was initially true. He explained carefully to Bute that they had 'evidently an over-proportion of cavalry here at home'; and to Beckford that it was twelve squadrons of 'idle horse' that they would be ordering abroad. Both men returned their support and encouragement, Beckford's enthusiastic ('but keep your infantry') and Bute's wary ('a small body should not lead to a great one'). In fact, by the end of June, when the St Malo expedition arrived home, Pitt had already detailed fourteen cavalry squadrons and 3000 infantry for German service, and decided to reinforce the Emden garrison.[60]

Bute was emphatic that the raids should continue: 'I just learn . . . that the fleet is returned to St Helen's. For God's sake, let their stay be as short as possible!' Here, though he claimed that 'difficulties and obstructions swarmed' upon him from members of the cabinet, Pitt needed no persuading. He insisted on a new venture. Why not Rochefort again? Why not Flanders? argued the King; a landing there, being nearer to Ferdinand, could assist him more. Eventually it was the Normandy coast that was decided on. Marlborough and Sackville were given their German ticket and, three more senior generals having begged to be excused,* the 73-year-old General Bligh was sent out, under the protection of Howe's squadron again, to make an attempt upon Cherbourg. 'I like our General extremely', Pitt assured Bute, 'and never saw a more soldier-like man'.[61]

By 8 August Cherbourg surrendered. Its fortifications and a newly constructed basin were demolished, ammunition stores and two hundred guns destroyed, eighteen ships burned, and a quantity of brass cannon carried off. 'Soldier-like' Bligh, however, whose military incompetence shocked both Commodore Howe and Bligh's own brigadiers, failed to prevent his troops from marring their week's work by wholesale pillage and drunken brutalities which the population of Cherbourg and its environs long remembered with bitterness.

Pitt, elated at the town's capture, would have reinforced Bligh at once and tried to maintain a foothold there indefinitely, despite opposition among the rest of the cabinet; but he was eventually persuaded by Ligonier that what might have been possible at St Malo was impracticable at Cherbourg, which was not a peninsula with easily held landward defences. Pitt had to content himself with parading the captured brass cannon with victory pomp from Kensington Palace to the Tower. Bligh and Howe were within twelve days of their return sent out upon further marauding; but during that short interval the dispatches which Pitt had been awaiting with the most anxious hopes of all arrived at last from America. They came in two instalments, the earlier from Amherst good, the later from Abercromby telling of a severe repulse.

There was nothing new in the Pitt-Ligonier strategy against Canada. Indeed there hardly could be, given the geography. Two obvious main routes pointed straight at the colony's heart, one via Louisbourg and the St Lawrence estuary to Quebec, the other from New York via the Hudson valley and lakes George and Champlain, to Montreal and again Quebec. French southward expansion by lakes Ontario and

* 'The discipline among our military chiefs is not great when they must all choose their services', commented Newcastle. Fortunately for the British and Prussians, among the French at this time it was even worse, and their intrigues more destructive.

Erie towards the Ohio valley equally dictated the route of any supplementary British attacks over the Alleghenies towards Fort Duquesne or via Lake Ontario towards Fort Frontenac. Of these, Duquesne could be more easily attempted – though still with immense difficulty over that wild terrain – by a separate operation mounted from the 'southern' colonies, with Philadelphia as rear base; Frontenac by an operation subsidiary to the main Hudson valley advance.

If the outline of strategy allowed little argument, Pitt had taken immense care over every precise preparation or foreseeable contingency, and all the colonial governors in British America (except for Georgia) had been powerfully exhorted and pressed and reminded to stir their generally very reluctant assemblies to the maximum military effort. Pitt had already done his best in one respect, by ordering that colonial officers up to the rank of colonel should be given parity with their regular officer counterparts.[62] He hoped thereby to end the resentment arising from an order of 1754 under which any regular officer outranked all 'provincials'. However, even in Massachusetts, where enthusiasm to have a crack at the French had first won Louisbourg in 1745 (disgust at its return still rankled), and where a vigorous governor now took an active lead, voluntary enlistment with the offer of a bounty could find only 4460 men; the remainder of the state's quota of 7000 had to be obtained by pressing every fourth freeholder.[63] Most of the governors reported hard going. One of them, Lyttelton's brother William, Governor of South Carolina, was being instructed by Pitt, as early as 7 March, to be ready to co-operate with Amherst and Boscawen in possible operations against Louisiana after the northern campaigning season closed. (Letters to Charleston, which travelled via New York, were four or five months in arriving, so that such early dispatch was vital.) South Carolina was to prepare itself for an attack on 'the Albama Fort' (Fort Toulouse) 'as nearly as may be at the same time that the attempts by the King's forces are to be made . . . on the rivers Mobile and Mississippi'.[64] Nothing was to come of these particular plans, but they do indicate the span of Pitt's intentions and the scope of his preparations. Given bold enough ambition, efficient organization, vigour from colonial governors, initiative from state assemblies, harmony and co-operation between fleet and army, there was nothing that could not be achieved in America. The French were thin on the ground and precariously placed for reinforcement. Why should not their power throughout the continent be not merely checked, but utterly destroyed?

Canada was the first great objective of this ambition – 'New France', that is, the nucleus of modern Canada, the territories lying on each side of the St Lawrence and its estuary – and the key to Canada was Cape Breton Island with its fortress of Louisbourg. Pitt set immense store by its recapture, and recapture *early*, so that Amherst and Boscawen would be able to move on, up the St Lawrence, to concert with Abercromby in front of Quebec before the ice closed in. Boldness would be imperative, and a willingness to take risks:

> His Majesty, relying on your zeal for his service [he wrote to Boscawen] is persuaded, tho' no particular order is given . . . that you will not omit attempting to force the harbour of Louisbourg, in case you shall judge the same to be practicable, as the success of that operation will greatly tend to shorten and facilitate the reduction of that place . . .[65]

Such exhortation as this, however, did not dissuade Boscawen from taking time off, *en route* across the Atlantic, to secure a remunerative French prize. His crossing, further windbound, like Holburne's the year before, occupied in all eleven weeks.

The assault landing near Cape Breton, when it came on 8 June, was on one of the two alternative beaches agreed between Pitt and his commanders back in January. The directness and predictability of the attack, in fact, just west of the fortress, almost led to a bloody repulse, and it was troops under Brigadier Wolfe who with difficulty secured at last a beachhead. Eleven days later the harbour and shipping began coming under a bombardment which was to last for five and a half more weeks. The French squadron commander, with his five of the line and eight smaller vessels that had managed to slip through to Louisbourg, wished to try conclusions with the larger British force in a break-out, but was refused permission, so Boscawen, denied an engagement at sea, was able instead to demonstrate his zeal for inter-service co-operation, serving for a time ashore with some of his men. 'The Admiral and General', wrote Wolfe, 'have carried on public service with great harmony, industry, and union . . . Mr Boscawen has given all and even more than we could ask of him'.[66] Neither Amherst nor Boscawen, however, believed in taking undue risks, and it was not until 25 July that Boscawen sent boat-parties under cover of night bombardment to storm the principal enemy ships. When he did then threaten to do as Pitt had hoped, 'force the harbour' with his main fleet, capitulation of the fortress quickly followed. 3000 land troops were taken prisoner, and of the 2600 French seamen still alive, over half were found to be sick or wounded. The battle for distressed, outnumbered Louisbourg had essentially been won the previous winter by the blockading squadrons of Osborne and Hawke in the Mediterranean and Bay of Biscay.

The fall of this strategic bastion produced interesting reactions in London. Many like Lord Hardwicke and Horace Walpole thought its value would properly appear at the forthcoming peace (and the sooner the better) since it would be a fine counter with which to bargain for the return of Minorca. 'Now', wrote Newcastle, 'is our time to push, in order to make a safe and honourable end'.[67] On the other hand, news of the victory put George II into such a state of euphoria that he could already picture the French being driven out of America altogether, and Newcastle begged him to consider what that might cost.[68] Beckford of course was emphatic that it must be retained as a centre for the fishing industry. The nation, and the colonies too, celebrated with beer and bonfires, with fireworks and thanksgiving services and firing of cannon. At last the war had provided a victory worth shouting about. From the country Hester sent her almost idolatrous joy 'and that of the dear brothers [Grenville], the joy of my friend Mrs Boscawen', and – for good measure – 'of the people of England' to her 'most loved and admired husband'. Down at Bath Pitt's sister Ann (suffering 'pain of body and mind', trying the bathing 'which my brother advised . . . as thinking my troubles come from a want of perspiration') wrote to Lady Suffolk:

> I ordered a bonfire . . . upon a rising ground upon the Circus (where my brother's house is), ten hogshead of strong beer round it which drew all the company I could desire, and enabled them to sing 'God bless great George our King' with very good success, with the help of all the music I could get in the Circus. The whole town was illuminated.[69]

Pitt's own relieved delight at the news from Louisbourg was dampened when only two days later he learned of what had befallen

Abercromby's campaign through the lakelands to the north of the Hudson. The commander-in-chief had moved his 6000 redcoats and 9000 Americans, with their artillery and supplies, down Lake George in a six-mile-long flotilla of a thousand boats. As he advanced overland through virgin forests towards the fort of Ticonderoga commanding the entrance to the next lake highway, Champlain, one of his scouting parties led by Lord Howe (who ironically had done more than anyone to adapt British fighting methods to American conditions) stumbled upon a French patrol, and Howe was killed. By general consent he had been 'the soul of the army'; the 'complete model', wrote Pitt when he heard of the death, 'of the military virtue in all its branches'. 'The loss of Lord Howe', he added, 'afflicts me more than a publick sorrow . . . I have the sad task of imparting this cruel event to a brother [the then Commodore and future Admiral Earl Howe] that loves him most tenderly'.[70]

The British, in heavily superior numbers, moved impetuously forward after Howe's death to carry the breastworks of Ticonderoga by the bayonet, Abercromby unhappily and mistakenly calculating that time and terrain would not allow him first to bring up his artillery. Americans, English, and Highlanders thus ran alike into murderous fire from Montcalm's well dug-in defenders, and after six bloody hours were routed, leaving 2000 casualties. 'The General attempted, willingly, bravely,* and unfortunately', was Pitt's first judgement when he received these unhappy tidings; but he had little employment for failed generals, and Abercromby – 'Mrs Nabbercromby' to the Americans – was to go the way of Loudoun.

'I own this news has sunk my spirits', Pitt wrote to George Grenville. Still, he hoped, late as it was, Amherst might be able to proceed towards Quebec, and he was optimistic for Forbes, last heard of 'some miles west of the Susquehannah on his way to Fort Du Quesne'. There was Colonel Bradstreet also, the New Englander leading a detachment of 3000, mainly American 'provincials', to the wild north-west of Abercromby's main force, towards the forts on Lake Ontario. There were 'great hopes for the remaining campaign',[71] and at least the gain of Louisbourg was solid.

This qualified optimism proved to be justified. Bradstreet, against

* Abercromby's dispatch naturally did not disclose that personally he had not come within two miles of the carnage.

the inclinations of Abercromby, was nevertheless allowed to push westward with his provincials on the hazardous Ontario venture. He managed to reach the lake, ferry his men across it, and capture undermanned Frontenac before a French relieving force could arrive. It was a relatively small-scale but brilliant stroke – not, incidentally, envisaged in Pitt's original campaign plan for 1758, though it had been in Loudoun's the previous year – and its success in effect also settled the fate of Fort Duquesne which, if the French had clung on to it, must have had its line of communication strangled. The tough and resourceful Forbes meanwhile, with his force composed largely of raw American troops, hacked his way towards the Ohio, over mountains and through wilderness 'overgrown with brushwood', as he reported home to Pitt, 'so that nowhere can one see twenty yards'. Harassed as he went by French and Indians and abandoned by his own Indians, he took pains to avoid Braddock's mistakes on the same errand three years previously, and established fortified posts every forty miles or so, to reduce his dependence on supply wagons. Hampered by foul weather and at one point almost giving up in face of the impossible, often in torment from gastric pain and in fact a dying man, he finally reached Fort Duquesne on 25 November to find only charred ruins.* Renaming the fort after Pitt (in whose honour modern Pittsburg thus originated), he left behind only the smallest of garrisons to hold it over the winter. Then, burying first some of the skeletons remaining from Braddock's disaster, the doomed leader, borne on a litter, turned back with his column for Philadelphia. It is unlikely Pitt's congratulatory letter of 23 January 1759 ever reached him. A later one, of 15 March, conveying 'his Majesty's high satisfaction', and acknowledging 'the very great and undeserved honor you have done my name', certainly did not. Forbes died that same month.[72]

In this manner on both the left and the right flank the attack on Canada had in some degree prospered; it was only in the crucial centre that there had been outright failure. After taking Louisbourg Amherst at first had thoughts of pushing ahead towards Quebec. However, news reaching him of Ticonderoga meant instead that he must rush troops (as it turned out unnecessarily) to bolster Abercromby,

* Just nine months after the Marquis Duquesne himself had been captured, together with his 70-gun *Foudroyant*, by Admiral Osborn's squadron off the coast of Spain.

and of course abandon until 1759 any plans for invading Canada proper.

While Bradstreet was taking Frontenac, and Forbes was still in only the early stages of his arduous march, there took place the last and most seriously mismanaged of Pitt's forays upon the French coast. Bligh was once more in command, with Howe again directing the naval support; and, as on the Cherbourg raid, Howe took with him Midshipman Prince Edward, the Prince of Wales's brother. Bute had for some time been badgering Pitt to use his influence, such as it was, with the King, to get the Prince this privilege. Several of Bligh's staff officers also came from the Leicester House connection. The Prince of Wales's men, in fact, Pitt's allies still, and still resisting full British continental involvement, had managed to make this latest enterprise very much their own. Their reputation was hence closely bound to its fortunes.

Ligonier and Pitt seem not to have given Bligh any specific new orders beyond those he had received for the previous expedition, and surprisingly they both seem to have been ignorant of his intended target. Morlaix had been no more than *suggested*, but Bligh and Howe were persuaded instead, on Leicester House advice, to make another attempt on St Malo.[73]

Everything went wrong; the weather first, when a gale parted Bligh ashore near St Malo from his artillery afloat with Howe. Taking (as he hoped) no chances, Bligh therefore marched *away* from St Malo towards Matignon, the better to keep in touch with the navy – 'staring about the country', sneered Walpole flippantly, 'to see whether there were any Frenchmen left in France'. Then, deciding to re-embark, he ordered a retreat towards the beach at St Cast; conducted the operation with clumsy incompetence; and in the process lost at least 700, and perhaps as many as 1000, of his rearguard, who finally exhausted their ammunition and had to rush for the boats. Walpole's sardonic comments continued, 'I shall not be at all surprised if, to show he was not in the wrong, Mr Pitt should get ready another expedition by the depth of winter, and send it in search of the cannon and colours of these twelve battalions'. Bligh returned in ignominy and was cut dead by the King when he went to Kensington to pay his respects.[74]

This was not only the end of the road for Pitt's policy of diversionary descents on the French mainland. It also meant the end of the alliance with Leicester House that had helped to underpin his political position during the past seven years. Bute, in a letter passionately denying that he was in a passion, conveyed to Pitt his 'amazement and indignation' at the way Bligh had been treated. He railed against Newcastle and Ligonier. 'Excuse this long letter, my dear friend', he wrote,

> my heart is full, and feels for you as well as Bligh whom I never spoke to. This is in my firm opinion, the factious measures of men who abhor vigour and expeditions . . . Our Commander In Chief is now theirs, and co-operates in their revenge. Nothing has ever happen'd since we put the crown on that little Pelham's head that so thoroly opens my eyes. This is a trait a greater person than me [i.e. the future King] never will forgive.[75]

Pitt's reply exonerated Newcastle from any share in Bligh's disgrace and wondered why Bute, who had been swift enough to condemn General Mordaunt in the Rochefort affair, now sought to protect General Bligh. Bute replied by twice demanding promotion for Lieutenant-Colonel Clark, a Leicester House nominee on Bligh's staff, and was twice refused. He went on to accuse Pitt of knuckling under too easily to Newcastle (poor Newcastle, who never ceased complaining of being bullied by Pitt), and in particular objected to Pitt's apparent readiness to send more British troops to Germany. Echoing his mentor, the Prince of Wales was soon alleging that Pitt had 'given himself either up to the K[ing] or the D. of N. or else he could not act the infamous and ungrateful part he now does'.[76] Pitt's marriage of convenience with Leicester House was obviously at an end, and Bute's name must from this point be enrolled upon the eventually very long list of Pitt's *ex*-friends and allies. The sententious mutual protestations of undying affection, the lavish testimonials of loyal admiration, come suddenly to a halt. Pitt ceased troubling himself with consulting Leicester House, and the Prince wrote to Bute:

> As Mr P. does not now chuse to communicate what is intended to be done, but defers it till executed, he might save himself the trouble of sending at all . . . Indeed my dearest friend he treats both you and me with no more regard than he would do a parcel of children, he seems to forget that the day will come when he must expect to be treated according to his deserts.[77]

Pitt, who had had trouble enough over the years trying to wear away the hostility of George II, had until now taken assiduous pains to woo the court of the future George III, sometimes in the most unconvincing self-abasing accents. No doubt he felt, now that he had some substantial victories both in America and Germany to sustain him, that his need of Leicester House's support was less; but henceforth clouds certainly threatened to loom from that direction too. It was not long before the Prince of Wales was talking indignantly of Pitt's 'insolence', his 'want of regard' for Bute, 'and consequently of myself'. Pitt, Legge, and the Grenvilles were all lumped together as 'that faithless band'. 'My dearest friend,' wrote the Prince to Bute, 'we must look out for new tools, our old ones having all deserted us'.[78]

Meanwhile Pitt allowed himself to be argued out of organizing further coastal raids, while still claiming to justify their strategic value. The opinion of military historians remains divided on the validity of that claim; but whatever the truth of the matter strategically, the succession of failures and half-failures, culminating in heavy loss and unmistakable defeat at St Cast, effectively ended the controversy at the time. Pitt for a while clung to notions of an assault on Bordeaux, and at first countermanded Ligonier's orders that the returned troops on the Isle of Wight should go into winter quarters. They should, he said, remain there 'till they can get ready to go out again'.[79] But, both with the rest of the cabinet and with his military and naval advisers, he was conducting a losing argument.

Pitt's moves against the French in Africa raised no such controversy. On the very day in June that he had learned of the capture of Fort Louis on the Senegal river, with booty worth nearly a quarter of a million pounds, he gave orders for ships and men intended for Jamaica to be diverted to the West African coast. Anson concurred; the French, he said, 'would sit down very uneasy' with any losses there, and were soon known to be planning to restore their position. By early September Pitt and the Admiralty were engaged in organizing a further venture, aimed at the island of Goree, an important privateering base, which the earlier expedition had attacked but failed to capture. When Captain Augustus Keppel, in command, wrote the following month from Cork explaining his delay in sailing, Pitt's reply was in character, peremptorily urging haste, even at some risk. Getting away eventually in November and losing two ships in a storm on the way,

Keppel and troops under Lieutenant-Colonel Worge managed to take the forts on Goree on the last day of 1758. Pitt then appointed Worge governor, and directed him to give all assistance to those officers of the African Company who would be coming out to explore the area's commercial potentialities. These offered prospects of denying the French the 4000 to 8000 tons of gum-senegal they had been annually getting from Moorish traders in the interior. (The Moors now wished, so Worge was soon reporting to Pitt, to take from the English in exchange, 'blue Manchester goods, coarse brown sugar, sealing-wax, large size writing paper, arms, powder and ball' – but *not* brandy, which their religion forbade. He was suppressing attempts to encourage Negro spinning and weaving: 'as I found them in ignorance so I shall keep them, as it would be detrimental to our manufactures'.)[80] And Senegal would henceforth be contributing 1200 slaves a year to the British West Indies. Pitt's views on the Negro slave trade were entirely those of his generation, untouched by the humanitarian questionings which would in time be troubling his son. More slaves for British plantations and fewer for French could not fail to be good.

West Africa seemed important, but the sugar islands of the West Indies, where the slaves were transmuted into gold, immeasurably more so, and it was in their direction that Pitt's next enterprise was headed. He hardly needed pushing, but powerful City interests were at hand to give a jog to his intentions. His friend Beckford, the sugar magnate, was writing on 11 September: '*Verbum sat sapienti*, but to such a one as yourself half a word is sufficient'. Attack Martinique, he advocated. 'For God's sake', he begged Pitt, 'attempt it without delay and noise':

> The island I mentioned has but one town of strength [Port Royal]; take that, and the whole country is yours; all the inhabitants must submit for want of food, for they live from hand to mouth . . . The negroes and stock of that island are worth above four millions sterling, and the conquest easy . . .[81]

It did not prove so. The expedition arrived off Port Royal in January 1759, silenced the batteries and made a landing, but found the French too well prepared, both there and later at St Pierre. The commanders, Major-General Hopson and Commodore Moore, decided therefore to follow Pitt's alternative instructions and attack Guadeloupe, no less rich a prize. However, by March disease had killed half their 6000 men. Hopson himself died in February, when Brigadier John Barring-ton, brother to the Secretary-at-War, took over command. Though his supporting fleet then had to leave him in order to cover a threat from a French squadron to other British islands, Barrington and his survivors, after a punishing but a vigorous and tenacious campaign, managed to harass Guadeloupe into surrender by 1 May, only just in time. Barrington wrote to Pitt:

> I cannot help congratulating myself that I had just signed the capitulation . . . when a messenger arrived in their camp to acquaint them that Monsieur Beauharnois, the General of these islands, had landed . . . with a reinforcement [of 2600 men] from Martinico . . . As soon as he heard the capitulation was signed, he re-embarked again.[82]

Fevers continued to torment the British garrison, killing another 800 before 1759 was out, but for the time being at least Pitt was content enough with his West Indian expedition. Marie Galante fell to Moore and Barrington in June. Martinique and St Lucia could wait. Guade-loupe alone sent sugar worth £425,000 under its first year of British rule, and also began importing British wrought iron.[83]

CHAPTER FOURTEEN

The Year of Victories

An Anglo-French war inevitably involved repercussions upon the commerce and shipping of non-belligerents, and by now Pitt had to face the dangerous possibility of France being joined by hitherto neutral powers. French merchant traffic, largely paralysed by the British navy, did not always escape by transferring to neutral bottoms, Dutch or Danish or Italian. Even ships released from Admiralty prize courts were in constant hazard from British and American privateers, which on both sides of the Atlantic and in the Mediterranean did a thriving and often ruffianly business. In 1758 the port of Bristol alone fitted out 51 privateers. By the following year the Dutch were complaining that there were 110 of their vessels held in British ports.[1] The court of Madrid repeatedly protested at piratical attacks on Spanish ships. Pitt, even more seriously than before, was forced to take notice of the neutral threats that arose from these depredations. Strongly worded instructions to colonial governors and to British consuls in Europe proving ineffectual, he was eventually obliged in May 1759 to bring in a bill giving the Admiralty stronger powers to suppress the smaller privateering vessels which had been committing most of the outrages – one of the very few of his actions to meet with hostility from his usually strong and vocal supporters the merchant community. Even Beckford spoke against him on this in the Commons.

But the threat from the injured neutrals remained. Choiseul, chief minister to Louis XV from December 1758 and an altogether tougher and more capable antagonist than his predecessors, was straining to engage the uncommitted powers against Britain, and by March had at least the satisfaction of seeing Russia, Sweden, and Denmark form a league aimed at protecting neutral rights and excluding Britain from the Baltic. Meanwhile Choiseul persevered in Madrid. Without the Spanish navy's assistance he foresaw Canada lost, Britain totally dominant at sea and even pre-eminent in Europe. 'Urge them to make common cause with us,' he wrote to his Madrid ambassador . . . 'Moments are precious . . . Only the concerted navies of the two crowns can impose respect on our common enemies'.[2] From his side Pitt too looked hungrily for allies and auxiliaries. He had drawn blank in Spain and the Mediterranean, but there was still Bavaria. Every possibility must be explored. If a few thousand more men could be hired from Brunswick, he knew parliament could be persuaded to vote the money. 'He would forfeit his head rather than not take' any German offers that were available.[3] As for reinforcements from England, however, 'we must not think of any . . . whatever'. 'It would be dangerous in a country such as this to stretch the cord too much; the public must be humoured, and before all else sufficient forces must be kept here to put us beyond all reach of danger'.[4]

Parliament had reassembled in November 1758. It was, said Walpole, 'oppositionless'; Pitt was 'absolute master'. 'Our unanimity is prodigious – you would as soon hear *No* from an old maid as from the House of Commons – but I don't promise you', he added, 'that this tranquillity will last. One has known more ministries overturned of late years by their own squabbles than by any assistance from parliaments'. In view of the nagging resentments persisting within the government, this was pertinent comment.[5]

The war of course had to be financed, and here Pitt's dexterity in managing parliament matched his deviousness in dealing with colleagues. He was no doubt genuinely disturbed by the overcharging he was sure the Treasury was being subjected to by its German agents, and as in the previous year wasted no polite words in his protests to Newcastle: 'The burden is impossible to be borne . . . in the name of God, my Lord, how came such an idea on paper?'[6] Pitt's back bench supporters, independent or Tory gentlemen, were naturally concerned at the mounting cost of the war, in debt and taxation, and Pitt's awareness of their sentiments was hardly unconnected with his own complaints, public as well as private, against the financial administration of the Treasury. The money must be found, of course – he had little difficulty in carrying the House with him – but accusations in the Commons against his own colleagues did nothing to improve interministerial relations.

Pitt originally suggested a shop licence. The Treasury then came up with a sugar tax, which was of course anathema to the City's West India merchants. Lobbied by fifty of them, Pitt agreed to support, as a compromise, a tax on *all* dry goods. Rising in the House to speak on the subject, he began with: 'Sugar, Mr Speaker . . .' Some of the same derision which had been accorded to Beckford, during his speech which had just ended, spilled over into Pitt's opening words. It was as though upon entering the room the headmaster had caught the class sniggering. '"Sugar, Mr Speaker", thundered Pitt; and in the obedient silence that followed, "Sugar, Mr Speaker", he whispered in his most dulcet tone: "who will laugh at sugar now?"'. He proceeded with extravagant praise of Beckford, who *had done more to support the government than any minister in England.* When the Commons, who regarded Beckford as 'a wild, incoherent, superficial buffoon', actually laughed and groaned again, 'Pitt was offended and repeated his encomium'.[7]

Taxation, however, so he told the House later, was really not his province. His own inexpert preferences were for taxes on linen, or wines, or hops, or perhaps best of all for an excise such as had once been proposed by that excellent minister Sir Robert Walpole, who once again came in for posthumous commendation. But these were all matters beyond the competence of such a 'drudge' as himself; they concerned 'the department of another minister' – meaning Legge, whom he was at pains to snub and censure during the debates following, with a great show of contempt.

Britain's rapidly growing wealth, with a fiscal system far less inefficient than France's, enabled her to budget for thirteen millions in 1759 and service the rapid increase of the national debt, while France, with nearly two and a half times the population, was hard pressed to raise twelve millions. Pitt rejoiced in and intended to exploit this disparity. In general, government loans were being readily taken up, though he made Newcastle reduce one for what parliament, he said, would consider the inordinate sum of twelve millions to the more respectable figure of six. Money, since Pelham's economy drive, was cheap – too cheap at 3% in fact for one loan in the spring of 1759, and its failure to be fully taken up caused a sharp fall in the funds and acuter fears even than usual to flutter Newcastle; but the setback was temporary only. In all, the war in 1759 – Pitt's war – looked as if it might be costing twenty millions, a prodigious sum in those days. The Duke scribbled down his apprehensions before amplifying them for the King's ear. 'The country cannot support it . . . The Bank will shut up. The Exchequer next . . . The necessity of a peace this summer. My duty to tell his Majesty so'.[8] And the powerful and vastly wealthy Duke of Devonshire was committing to his diary that it would be 'impossible to carry on the war another year at this expense'.[9]

Pitt of course considered otherwise, but recognized the danger that he might be represented as a fanatical and ruinous warmonger. At the worst, if a peace were forced upon him, he was determined to ensure that British conquests would be rich enough to dictate an advantageous settlement. But he was pleased to notice that it was not only with himself that the appetite for victory grew with what it fed on. He had apparently an ally now even in the King who, first and last a soldier, while still protesting that he could never bring himself to *like* Pitt, fancied extremely the notion of his long reign culminating in a glow of glory.

Meanwhile Pitt, confined again for a time by his gout over the winter of 1758-9 and taking again to his 'great shoe',[10] but with his voracity for work unquenched, continued in a state of exasperation with his colleagues, and they both with him and one another. Mr Pitt, Newcastle complained, wished to be simultaneously 'Treasurer, Secretary, General and Admiral'; such treatment from one he had 'nourished and served' could not be borne.[11] At the same time Newcastle felt himself 'insulted every day by that *chit*' the other Secretary Lord Holderness ('he sneered at me when I turned my back!').[12] Hardwicke represented to the Duke that he was over-sensitive; but, philosophical for others, he had plenty of grumbles of his own. He too was unwell, getting old, and growing disinclined to attend cabinet meetings where he claimed he was constantly overruled. As for Legge, he had already resigned once in dudgeon at Pitt's behaviour, but had been persuaded by Newcastle to come back. Both Legge and Holderness seemed to Pitt to be studying to ingratiate themselves into his own earlier position of favour at Leicester House. Yet Holderness for his part declared he was having no part in 'the dirty court intrigues to lower Mr Secretary Pitt in the opinion of the King and public'.[13]

Then there were the Grenvilles, 'more violent and outrageous [i.e. outraged] than ever', reported the ever-knowledgeable Count Viry, 'against my Lord Hardwicke'. And not only against Hardwicke:

'Lord Temple's resentment to me is beyond expression', wrote New-castle.[14] Then, Horace Walpole was reporting in May 1759, 'There has been a great quarrel between Mr Pitt and Lord Anson, on the negligence of the latter' – adding a touch of his own light-hearted vitriol: 'I suppose they will be reconciled by agreeing to hang some admiral'.[15] If an *annus mirabilis* was about to dawn, as it indeed was, it could hardly be proceeding from the united efforts of a governmental band of brothers.

First prize for trouble-making ought probably to be awarded to Temple. Ever since September 1758 he had been importuning to be given one of the two Garters rendered disposable by the deaths of the Duke of Marlborough and the Earl of Carlisle – a demand in which he both expected and obtained Pitt's persistent support. In an age when soliciting for honours was common practice, Pitt, while affecting to disdain them for himself, pressed the harder as 1759 progressed on behalf of this prestige-hungry chief of the Grenville clan. Indeed the rather ridiculous campaign for Temple's Blue Ribband, sustained in a sort of war of attrition for more than a year, to the torment of Newcastle and against the stubbornly maintained refusal of the King, was to produce at last a full-scale cabinet crisis, with Pitt seriously threatening to resign if his brother-in-law, *and by association he himself*, were to be denied the honour.

Concerning these recurrent outbreaks of acrimony within the administration, Horace Walpole set down a shrewd observation. 'The ministers who don't agree', he forecast to Horace Mann, 'will, I believe, let the war decide their squabbles too. Mr Pitt will take Canada and the cabinet council together, or miscarry in both'.[16] Failure in the war, failure above all in Canada, would mean a patched-up peace and, more than likely, Pitt's demotion or exclusion. Uncertain as he was of his political associates at home, he knew how close he must cling to allies abroad; and there the importance of Prussia's survival was paramount.

Frederick the Great had again, in the summer and autumn of 1758, preserved his armies from seemingly probable annihilation. The powerful enemies that surrounded him lacked, fortunately for him and for Pitt, the ability or the will to co-ordinate or combine; and when news arrived in London that he was 'up to his eyes in dead Russians' after the critical and bloody battle of Zorndorf, he became more emphatically than ever a popular hero in England. The Austrians soon afterwards defeated him at Hochkirk, but even so he ended the campaigning season by squeezing them out of Dresden. 'It looks probable', wrote Charles Jenkinson, 'that his Prussian Majesty may extricate himself this year, as he did the last, and beat his enemies piecemeal'.[17]

With secret and to Pitt unwelcome peace overtures flying round the capitals of Europe, he went out of his way in a parliamentary speech of 6 December to pronounce a lavish panegyric upon Frederick and emphasize that they must ensure that no power suffered in any future treaty by having been Britain's wartime ally; at which Frederick (whose position was to remain intermittently desperate for two or three more years yet) expressed his relieved gratitude, and returned his own admiration for 'a great statesman and an honest man'. The exchange of flatteries and assurances continued warmly for some time, and Pitt promised Frederick – in a reference to Britain's desertion of her allies in 1713 – that '*no peace of Utrecht*' should ever 'again stain the annals of England'.[18]

Frederick might have favoured a settlement between France, Britain, and Prussia – if France could be induced to desert Austria – which would have left Prussia free to deal with Austria and Russia. What he feared was the sort of purely Franco-British bargain in which the French might be compensated for colonial losses by being allowed to acquire the western provinces of Prussia. But in May 1759 ambassador Mitchell reported ingratiatingly to Pitt how he personally had reinforced Frederick's conviction that in fact he stood in no such danger. 'Mr Pitt', said Frederick to Mitchell, 'is an honest man and firm; my interests are safe in his hands'. 'I took the liberty of saying', added Mitchell to Pitt, 'that, from a very long acquaintance, I was firmly persuaded his Majesty in the end would find you really was what he now thought you to be'. In order to contribute his share towards strengthening Pitt's domestic position, Frederick was persuaded – very probably by Pitt himself indirectly, though there is no proof – to send a letter 'for the record' to George II, publicizing the jointly virtuous intentions of Britain and Prussia and calling for a peace conference.[19] It was hardly likely to come about, but there was advantage to Pitt in having it demonstrated that he was not tied by unbreakable bonds to an insatiably militaristic and expansionist continental power.[20]

The fury of work, the hope of shining achievement, the challenge of power and fame, drove Pitt along during these his greatest years, and sustained him through recurrent attacks of physical disablement and mental depression – the latter, for the time being, not cripplingly acute. He was proud of triumphing over his afflictions: 'Sir', he once declared to an ordnance officer who was protesting that he was being asked to perform the impossible, 'I walk upon impossibilities'. His personal letters are full of references to his infirmities – 'much threatened by gout', 'lame in one foot', 'soreness and pain' in his legs, a 'painful swollen jaw', 'a slight eruption I had upon me', and a good deal more – usually however with some cheer to follow, such as 'I flatter myself that it may blow over, like an autumnal ruffle'.[21]

Work continued relentlessly. 'Your brother', writes Lady Hester to Ann Pitt, 'continues as usual overwhelm'd with business, and not entirely free from some notices of the gout', and again, 'Mr Pitt is this moment come to town . . . overwhelm'd with business'.[22] Often irritable, and sometimes preposterously difficult to work with, his moods would change with the speed of English weather. Expecting thunder, visitors would many times remark with relief upon his civility and charm – the 'decency' Hardwicke so frequently noted. And when Newcastle became once again, in 1759, thoroughly alarmed at the prospect of a French invasion, he was not a little shocked to find that Pitt was 'extremely gay . . . and laughs at everything the French can do'.[23] On the other hand, eruptions from the Pitt volcano were never to be taken lightly.

He continued to maintain his house in the Circus at Bath but seldom found the leisure to visit it over this period of his life. Hayes, ever-beckoning and growing steadily finer, was as far from London as he could usually find time to escape to, for an occasional week-end or just 'for some hours recess, that I want much'.[24] More than once, when he reached the sticking-point with irritations and frustrations in London, he retreated precipitately to Hayes for quiet and self-preservation. Fleeing to the country often meant, in addition, happy escape to Hester, though much of the time she shared his London existence and helped to soften its stresses. He had his Secretary of State's office in Cleveland Row, but much necessary business was done at his house in St James's Square. Not infrequently the cabinet itself would meet there – 'which always engrosses my apartment', Hester wrote, 'and banishes me to other quarters'.[25]

When in town and separated from Hester and his children in the country, whether she was at Hayes or, as sometimes, with her brothers at Stowe or Wotton, Pitt would regularly make time to dispatch by one of his grooms to his 'adored angel' and 'sweetest life' messages 'infinitely more interesting, and important too, than all I could ever address to all the potentates of Europe'. These intimate notes[26] sometimes merely post the latest news of politics and the war: 'I write before I go to bed, in order to open the morning at Hayes with the joyful tidings of this day' – a Prussian victory; 'here's enough to make one giddy'. Or they might share current military anxieties; 'Suspense, painful suspense, hold us still in the midst of solicitudes and gloomy doubts'. Rather too frequently the sharp taste of intimacies exchanged, and of hopes and fears shared, become diluted in a weak solution of insipid philosophizing – here Hester could outwilliam William – but then many times the sincere expressions of their mutual love quickly restore the writing's spontaneity and flavour, and reveal a Pitt easy to overlook amid the confusion of high policy and petty intrigue, and all but invisible in the shadows thrown by that larger-than-life marmoreal figure of the great and far-sighted statesman into which history soon transmogrified the living man: 'I will still indulge the hope that all will be well and that I shall hold my tenderest and ever adored love in my arms tomorrow'. 'Kiss the loved babes for papa', he writes; 'and may I find you all in perfect health tomorrow night'. And at the height of the triumphs of 1759:

> I wait with longing impatience for the groom's return, with ample details of you and yours. Send me, my sweetest life, a thousand particulars of those *little-great* things which, to those who are blessed as we, so far surpass in excellence and exceed in attraction all the *great-little* things of the busy, restless world . . . No news but what your faithful papers administer at breakfast . . .[27]

When, upon its being brought by Amherst's brother to London on 18 August 1758, news of the taking of Louisbourg was immediately forwarded by groom to Hayes, Hester's reply of the same day upon this 'most happy and glorious event' shows well enough that after four years of marriage, pride in her 'adored man' was still brimming

over. Not forgetting to apportion some share of the praise to 'the
Almighty Disposer of every event', her thrilled congratulations – not
yet dampened by the news of Ticonderoga to arrive in a day or two –
overflowed in an excited message to her 'most loved and admired
husband':

> I feel all your joy, my Life . . . I shall add the care of making our
> dear sweet Hayes testify by every outward mark of the inward joy
> with which its inhabitants are possessed. If my dearest Love can
> escape from the numbers who will congratulate his glory upon this
> occasion, I propose the brightness of our joy should reach him as
> soon as he gains Bromley Hill . . . A thousand kisses shall express my
> gratitude when I am blest with the happiness of receiving you in
> this joyful place made so by you, my glorious Love. Our bells are
> going to answer the guns, which just now speak their joy.[28]

On 28 May 1759, at Hayes, Hester gave birth to her fourth child, a
second son. 'After a labour rather severe', Pitt wrote the same day to
his sister Ann, mother and child were, 'thank God, as well as can be'.
(Ann was at Bath, taking the waters, her health still in poor way: 'I
can't help mentioning to you', her brother counselled in a postscript,
'the waters and bath of Buxton, which for a languid perspiration and
obstructions in the smaller vessels have done wonders'.)[29] Pitt continued
nervous for his wife's health. She was getting about 'with more courage
than conduct', he told her brother George nearly four weeks later,
asking him to become godfather-by-proxy.

The new arrival, William the second – or as he soon came to be
admiringly dubbed by his parents, from his kingly promise, William
the Fourth – was earmarked from the very beginning to become a
very considerable somebody: 'I cannot help believing', Hester wrote
within a few *weeks* of his birth, 'that little William is to become a
personage'.

Pitt was ever devoted to his 'infantry' – his 'little tribe', 'the dear
infants' – though when his nerves were taut and his sleep had been
bad, their noisy exuberance was liable to prove too much for him. He
therefore constructed new domestic arrangements at Hayes so that he
could isolate himself, when he wished, from their presence. When
work allowed, and the mood was right, he revelled in their high spirits.
'The young ones are so delightfully noisy that I hardly know what I

write', he tells Hester when she was on a visit to her brothers; and again on another occasion, 'Hetty is drunk with spring and joy. John, thank God, begins to mend his cheeks already and will soon be a ruddy yeoman of Kent. Harriot must not be forgot and looks round for applause. The old gentleman is as well as can be expected, he has been a-horseback for above two hours not a little tired'. Horace Walpole was perhaps pulling basically true facts a little out of focus when he wrote of Pitt at Hayes, 'His children he could not bear under the same roof, nor communications from room to room, nor whatever he thought promoted noise. A winding passage between his house and children was built with the same view'.[30]

Lord Camelford, the Thomas Pitt upon whom in his youth Pitt expended so much avuncular counsel, wrote later that outside his own immediate family circle, and excepting his early relationships with his sister Ann and George Lyttelton, Pitt never knew a genuine personal friendship; and Shelburne too, chief among Pitt's later protégés, vouched that he was 'incapable of friendship, or of any act that tended to it, and constantly upon the watch, and never unbent'.[31] Burke was another who declared that Lord Chatham had not 'one friend in the world'.[32] Camelford's distaste for his eminent uncle must be somewhat allowed for, and his stark comment – 'he lived and died without a friend' – is plainly not quite literally true; the Grenville brothers (James in particular), George Lyttelton, Gilbert West, Ralph Allen, Sanderson Miller, Thomas Potter, William Beckford, Thomas Hollis and a handful more might at one time or another have been gladly acknowledged as personal friends. Yet there is a deal of truth in Camelford's words. The intensity of affection of which Pitt was capable was reserved after his marriage exclusively for his wife and children. No mere friendship was ever strong enough to be allowed to interfere with his political judgement, or the pursuit of his own power and fame. In any case, pressure of work, chronically poor health, and the ever stronger pull of his family and of home combined to make a thing of the past his old 'Scythian life' of cultivating friends by end-lessly doing the rounds of their country houses.

Pitt's brother Thomas now lived abroad, ruined and more than a little mad. Pitt's dealings with him were long since over, though he had conscientiously tried to act as a sort of guardian to his son. A 'remarkable man', the young Shelburne judged Thomas Pitt when he met him in Utrecht in 1756: 'his temper resembled his brother's, but there was no bounds to his violence. He branded his brother with the most abusive epithets . . . Upon inquiry afterwards his brother did much the same by him, so that one or the other must have been ——'. It was 'no scandal', wrote Shelburne, 'to say there was a degree of madness in the family'.[33]

Pitt at this time was still paying out an annual £100 allowance to his sister Elizabeth, whose own draught of the family madness seems to have been laced with a dose of nymphomania. She had long disqualified herself from receiving the further hundred a year which Pitt had agreed to pay her on condition that she behaved herself. Horace Mann reckoned her 'still handsome', and possessed of 'wit and great art'; but of Pitt's requirement, correct behaviour, she was quite incapable. At one point she handed over some of his letters to an opposition newspaper, hoping to demonstrate that he had robbed her of her financial due, but (wrote Walpole) succeeded in showing only that 'he once allowed her two hundred, and after all her wickedness still allows her one'. This too ceased when in 1761 – the year of Thomas Pitt's death – at the age of fifty she married relative youth and substantial money in the person of a Mr John Hannan, of the Middle Temple. Pitt had no more dealings with her.

With his youngest sister Mary he remained on friendly elder-brotherly terms. She was unmarried, and quite frequently seems to have stayed in his house. Concerned that the world should treat her well, he 'seem'd to take every civility shown to her as a favour', Mrs Montagu thought. That, however, presented small difficulty, for she was 'a very sensible, modest, pretty sort of young woman'.[34] She lacked, declared Lord Camelford, the 'diabolical dispositions' of her sister Elizabeth, even if admittedly she was also without the 'wit and talents' of her other sister Ann.

Ever since his bachelor days when he and his sister Ann had kept house together, his relations with her had sailed in and out of storms and sunshine. Her remaining in France after war broke out in 1756 had been, she recognized, 'very disagreeable and embarrassing' to him and, weak as she then found herself 'in body and in mind', she was grateful for the goodness and 'delicacy' he had shown in eventually making special arrangements for a friend, a Mr de la Porte, once 'my Lord Stanhope's Governor', to travel to France and escort her back home from enemy territory. William, she told Lady Suffolk, had 'always seemed to guess and understand all I felt of every kind'. Immersed as usual in state affairs, he wrote that he hardly had *time* to write to tell Ann 'how impatiently and tenderly' he looked forward to embracing her on her return. Her health was better, he heard, which was good; 'at the same time let a veteran invalide recommend to you above all things, to use this returning strength and spirits very sparingly at first'.³⁵

Ann, now forty-eight and no less veteran an invalid, looked at first as though she might settle down quietly at Bath. She plainly hoped she might find a haven in her brother's long-unoccupied and only part-furnished house there, but Pitt was having none of this. An otherwise very amiable and sisterly letter from Hester, acknowledging gifts for herself and the children, declared firmly:

> I . . . wish extremely that [the house] was furnished and fit for your reception, but I find Mr Pitt thinks it is not proper to have hired furniture put into it, as well as that you cou'd not be so conveniently accommodated in a house so circumscribed as you will be in the very commodious lodgings which Bath affords.³⁶

Ann could at least celebrate the capture of Louisbourg on the green *outside* her brother's house.

But one never quite knew what Ann might not do next. That November (of 1758) she wrote to Lady Suffolk, wryly aware that what she was proposing sounded like the newspaper advertisement of 'a gentlewoman in distress': 'I hear that my Lord Bath [the now 74-year-old Pulteney] is very lively, but I have not seen him, which I am very sorry for, because I want to offer myself to him. I am quite in earnest, and have set my heart upon it . . . He could want nothing but a companion that would like his company'.³⁷ Would Lady Suffolk, she wondered, and certain of her friends, kindly reconnoitre the outworks of this substantial fortress in advance of a possible frontal assault?

No more was heard of this, and probably Pitt remained ignorant of the *non*-affair – as no doubt the Earl himself did also. But as the months went by, Ann's doings obviously caused Pitt embarrassment and irritation. She disappointed him by proving disinclined to take permanent root in Bath. One may guess, but not be altogether sure, why

Pitt grew so annoyed with her when she decided to accompany her nephew Thomas on his returning to London from Bath in 1759, and then stayed on there, first as the guest of the *other* Secretary's wife, Lady Holderness, and later in a house lent her by the Prince of Wales's Treasurer, Cresset. Was it simply that Pitt knew the world was saying that his sister was on occasion not quite right in the head, and did not relish being too closely encumbered with her society, that he could cherish her, and even feel to some extent responsible for her, but only if she observed a proper distance and did as she was bid?

His letters, and those that Hester wrote on his behalf when he was, as ever, 'overwhelm'd with business', do suggest so. Moreover the company Ann kept in London was no longer to William's taste, in particular that at Leicester House. And he may have already known, or guessed, that she was soliciting there for a pension. This touched a subject on which, for the present at least, he was righteously adamant. When she approached *him*, he excused himself on the grounds that, since he had never been 'a sollicitor for favours', to become one now would be 'contradicting the whole tenour' of his life.[38]

While silkily agreeing that of course he held her entirely free to live where she liked – 'I offer you no advice as to the choice of your residence' – Pitt made his opinion clear that she ought to go back to Bath and stay there: 'I am sorry to be forc'd to say this much, but saying less I should cease to be, with truest affection, dear Sister, ever yrs, W. Pitt'. Hester reinforced the message: 'Mr Pitt wou'd not set down to dinner without desiring me to let you know from him that this intention of yours [of taking lodgings in Lisle Street] gives him the greatest surprise and not less concern for *your sake*, being unalterably persuaded that retreat is the only right thing for your health, welfare, and happiness, and that Bath in your present state seems to be the fittest place'.[39]

To Ann's complaints that he was being unkind, Pitt protested, 'All idea of *quarrel* or *unkindness* (words I am griev'd to find you cou'd employ) was never farther from my mind'. Not quite convincingly, he begged her to put from her head any notion that his 'situation as a publick person' affected the matter: 'All I mean is that, *for your own sake*, you shou'd abstain from all desultory jaunts . . . I have refused myself the pleasure of seeing you, as considering your journey and hovering about London as too imprudent and restless, or as too mysterious . . .' Mysterious; in the circumstances an extraordinary adjective. Indeed, even when we recognize how little Pitt relished being *crossed*, his whole attitude in the affair remains itself mysterious.

Ann, in spite of her health and her brother, did in fact survive quite handsomely for a long time, with the aid of eventually *three* pensions. She was for a while Horace Walpole's near neighbour, entertaining expansively ('the prettiest ball that ever was seen at Mrs Ann Pitt's'); and then when she removed to Kensington, making good use of his expert opinion – on the propriety of bow windows, on latest French furnishing fashions, on 'designs of commodes'. Although, said Walpole, she was Pitt's sister and 'his very image', they were 'no dear friends'. Futher communication between them was limited to a few brief formal letters. When Chatham died in 1778 (again according to Walpole) she acted great grief for her brother, but by then she was 'in a very wild way'. By 1779 she was under restraint, and died two years later 'in one of Dr Duffell's houses' for the mentally disturbed.[40]

The taking of Louisbourg, of Senegal and Goree, and of Guadeloupe had given tangible evidence of progress in the war, but at least until the autumn of 1759 general success remained very much in doubt. The talk was more of a patched-up peace than of any prospective triumph, and as late as the end of July 1759 Pitt was speaking of Senegal and Goree as 'good things to make peace with'. The omens at that time by no means foretold the torrent of good news that flowed in during the following three or four months. In Germany Prince Ferdinand's army was in retreat through Hesse, uncovering Hanover again. In Spain, the King was on his death-bed, and there was good reason to fear that his successor, Don Carlos of Naples, to be Charles III of Spain, might join the war on France's side, with consequences incalculable to the favourable balance of naval power on which Britain must depend. As ever, Frederick of Prussia was being pressed hard, and indeed was very soon to suffer the most disastrous of all his defeats, at Kunersdorf. And at home, the threat of invasion was more serious than at any previous period of the war.

Marshal Belleisle's invasion plan as finally approved by Choiseul envisaged, first, a powerful Brest fleet under Admiral Conflans escorting the Duke of Aiguillon's 20,000 troops from Brittany to the Clyde, where they were to make a diversionary landing and occupy Glasgow, Edinburgh and the West of Scotland. Further distraction was to be provided by the privateer François Thurot, who was to break out from Dunkirk with five frigates and a small force and then sail via the North Sea to land in Ireland. Meanwhile the main invasion army was to await the return of Conflans's fleet by way of the north of Scotland, and then to be shielded from sea attack as it was ferried from Flanders to the northern shore of the Thames estuary in some two hundred purpose-built sailing barges, with another hundred or so vessels transporting supplies and stores. This landing was to be on a scale sufficiently massive and militarily overwhelming to make further reinforcement across the Channel unnecessary.

At first Pitt, confident in the navy and having heard Newcastle and Hardwicke cry wolf before, refused to take the threat seriously, although Newcastle's excellent sources of intelligence in Europe gave accounts of 26,000 men encamped in Flanders, many more near Vannes in Brittany, and large numbers of flat-bottomed boats building at Dunkirk, Calais, Rouen, and Le Havre. Newcastle and Hardwicke, always mistrustful of Pitt's militia, were convinced that no more than a few well-disciplined French troops would be able to scatter it, and even doubted its ability to guard 25,000 prisoners of war so far taken. Ligonier, no faint-heart, agreed with Newcastle that forces for home defence were inadequate, the more so since there were no British-based Hessians or Hanoverians to rely on, as there had been (to the nation's shame, Pitt had said) in 1756. He considered that Pitt was now being over-sanguine, and argued for an additional regular corps of six battalions – 10,000 men – to stiffen the militia. Pitt's health, too, worried Ligonier; it was so unreliable, one was never sure during the spring of 1759 of being able to find him for consultation. 'That vile gout', he wrote, 'destroys him'. However, Pitt did accept Ligonier's advice, and suddenly ordered the Under-Secretary at the Admiralty to prepare 5000 tons of troop transports. Anson and Newcastle took fright. Unconsulted, they were afraid Pitt was contemplating another coastal raid; but it transpired that he was ensuring the mobility of Ligonier's anti-invasion force, to be assembled in the Isle of Wight.[41] Meanwhile, efforts to gain more recruits, by bounty or impressment, for land and sea, were redoubled. An amnesty was offered for naval deserters surrendering for service. Citizens of the bigger towns vied with one another to raise subscriptions to pay for bounties. (Pitt and Ligonier each donated £100 to the Lord Mayor of London's fund.) Some wealthy aristocrats were given permission to raise and equip troops of their own for the King's service. One new regiment of light horse was raised under Colonel George Eliott – the first of the Hussar regiments, soon to distinguish itself mightily in Germany. A second was formed under a young colonel named Burgoyne, one day to command at Saratoga. And by the end of 1759 18,000 militiamen were under arms, causing such strain on Ordnance resources that 10,000 muskets had to be ordered from abroad.

On 30 May Pitt had brought to the Commons, just prior to their prorogation, a royal message which, in view of what was now described as the 'imminent danger' of invasion, had announced the calling-up of the militia, which was to be deployed anywhere within the country 'as occasion shall require'.[42] Briefly the militia did now reach something approaching the stature that Pitt and the Tory gentry had intended for it. 'All the country squires are in regimentals', wrote Walpole. 'There is a great spirit in motion . . . everybody is raising regiments'. It had become almost as fashionable as loo. 'How knights of the shire, who have never shot anything but woodcocks, like this warfare I don't know; but the towns through which they pass adore them', in their 'scarlet faced with black, buff waistcoats, and gold buttons'. To Hester – off for her usual summer stay at Wotton – Pitt wrote that 'nothing could make a better appearance than the two Norfolk battalions' commanded by Walpole's nephew Lord Orford, 'with the port of Mars himself'. The occasion was a grand review in Kensington Gardens, in itself 'of no short duration', and it had been preceded by a long and fatiguing cabinet meeting the night before, and followed by heavy afternoon business – all of which however seemed to have made 'not the least [harmful] impression on my ailments'. The crowd had been so thronging and enthusiastic that they held up the parade for half an hour and made Hyde Park 'hardly pervious to my coach'. A fine spectacle, of a kind whose attraction a popular patriotic leader such as Pitt would not be likely to undervalue; but, as he reminded Hester, the glitter of it could not chase from his mind hopes and fears concerning the outcome of critical battles in Germany awaiting

Prince Ferdinand on the Weser against the French, and the Prussians on the Oder against the Russians.[43]

The Prussians went on to suffer defeat, but not Ferdinand, who soon rated as 'our immortal Ferdinand'. Pitt delightedly posted to Wotton the important news just received; 'I cannot let the groom go without a line to my sweetest love'. At Minden, on 1 August, the French had been heavily defeated. There were 'many prisoners, trophies, and cannon', with 'the main of the French army seen to be flying they know not where'.[44] London celebrated the victory with bonfires and illuminations.[45] It was of course an *allied* success, with Hessians and Hanoverians hotly involved; but it had been notable for the valour and efficiency displayed by the British artillery, and, even more, infantry. 'I never thought', said Contades, the defeated French commander, 'to see a single line of infantry break through three lines of cavalry . . . and tumble them to ruin'.[46] Well before Minden, Pitt had finally committed himself to full-bodied military participation on the German front; after it, he was even readier to reinforce Ferdinand with British regiments. Eventually he would have to set a limit and hold to it, but in preparation for the campaigns of 1760, 10,000 more men were sent to Germany. Pitt had been reluctant to learn the lesson of the continental war but, once he had been taught it, he seemed in no danger of forgetting it.

It was a lesson which at Leicester House they had no wish to learn. A day or two before the news of Minden arrived, the Prince of Wales was still employing the sort of language Pitt had taught the nation to use fifteen or twenty years before; 'that horrid electorate [of Hanover], which has always liv'd upon the very vitals of this poor country'.[47] As it now happened, a notorious affair concerned with the battlefield of Minden served still further to widen the breach between Pitt and 'the succession' at Leicester House. Lord George Sackville, commander of the British contingent after Marlborough's death at Münster, a general appointed and much approved by both Ligonier and Pitt, but essentially a Leicester House man, had at Minden argumentatively and inexcusably asked the 'reason why' when ordered to bring his cavalry into action at the crisis of the battle. ('Would he have me break the line?') His repeated failure to obey Ferdinand's command was reckoned to have prevented the French defeat from becoming a total rout, and Ferdinand's order of thanks to his army after the battle went so far as to state that if the cavalry had been led by the Marquis of Granby* instead, the victory would have been more brilliantly decisive.[48] Insulted and enraged, Sackville wrote to enlist Bute in his defence and asked to be recalled, while the Prince of Wales professed himself 'much hurt' on Sackville's behalf, and considered that 'that little German Prince' Ferdinand had been 'pretty pert'.[49] Bute wrote to Pitt, interceding for Sackville.

Pitt's response was mellifluously negative. Although he had himself strongly promoted Sackville's career, he could promise Bute only that 'that most unhappy man' would receive '*all the offices of humanity* which our *first sacred* object . . . the public good, would allow'.[50] And to Sackville himself, the iron fist unmistakable within the velvet glove, Pitt found himself under the painful necessity of declaring his infinite concern at finding no room to offer support for conduct

> which my incompetence perhaps to judge of military questions leaves me at a loss to account for. I cannot enough lament the subject of a correspondence, so unlike everything I had wish't, to a person for whose advantageous situation my poor endeavours had not been wanting.[51]

Not only was Sackville dismissed but, by the judgement of the court martial which he had himself demanded, he was declared unfit to serve the King in any military capacity; and in order to underline the lesson of the affair, Ligonier obtained approval from Pitt and the King for this judgement to be read to all regiments,

> that officers being convinced that neither high birth nor great employments can shelter offences of such a nature, and that, seeing they are subject to censure much worse than death to a man who has any sense of honour, they may avoid the fatal consequences arising from disobedience of orders.[52]

George II, striking Sackville's name off the Privy Council list and forbidding his appearance at court, would have gone further still, and

---

* Second in command of the British in Germany until the disgrace of Sackville, whom he succeeded. Brave and generous, he was 'made for popularity', Shelburne said. And Horace Walpole, on hearing of Minden, wrote: 'The foreign gazettes, I suppose, will give the victory to Prince Ferdinand; but the mob of London, whom I have this minute left, and who must know best, assure me that it was all their own Marquis's doing'.

urged Pitt to get him expelled from the Commons. This Pitt persisted in refusing, whereupon the King 'turned round to Lord Hardwicke and said: "Then I do wish Pitt *very much* joy upon the company which he wishes to keep" '.[53]

The plans prepared by Pitt and Ligonier for the North American campaigns of 1759 did not differ in broad outline from those of 1758, except that possession of Louisbourg and of Fort Duquesne improved the starting positions. Once again the attack was two-fisted: from the south by the old Ticonderoga-Crown Point route along Lakes George and Champlain, towards Montreal and Quebec; and from Louisbourg up the St Lawrence directly towards Quebec, with the assistance of a superior fleet. Very comprehensive orders had been issued, both to Amherst, commander-in-chief after Abercromby's supersession, and to Saunders, the newly appointed naval chief in American waters. But when news finally reached Pitt on 19 January of Forbes's capture of Fort Duquesne he could not resist opening up fresh suggestions to Amherst for a possible supplementary thrust towards 'the western parts' of Lake Erie 'as far as Cayahoga (Cleveland, Ohio). Neither should any possibility be neglected of attacking, in collaboration with Admiral Saunders, 'the forts and places lying on the rivers Mobille and Mississippi' *after* a successful campaign in the north.[54] Of course all this had to be 'without prejudice to the main and decisive objects of the campaign prescribed by my letter of 29 December'. When from his side Amherst prudently sought prior permission for possible variations within the agreed plan, Pitt showed no inclination to tie him down over-precisely:

> His Majesty, placing great confidence in your judgement and capacity, is pleased to leave it entirely to your discretion by what avenues you will penetrate . . .; and whether you shall judge it most expedient to operate in one body, or by detaching in the manner you mention, a corps to the right to Otters Creek, another to the left towards Swegatchie [Oswegatchie, i.e. La Galette or the modern Ogdensburg], in order to divide the enemy; as, an irruption once effectually made, in whatever part it be, Canada must necessarily fall and with it the French power in North America.[55]

For command of the military share in the St Lawrence enterprise Pitt and Ligonier chose Wolfe, despite his asking to be excused 'from taking the chief direction of such a weighty enterprise'. Pitt had planned to find 11,000 regulars for the St Lawrence campaign, but had to be content with fewer than 9000 – who were however to be supplemented by six companies of long service American Rangers. Under Saunders there served altogether 18,000 men, 12,000 in ships of the Royal Navy, 6000 aboard a fleet more than a hundred strong of transports, ordnance vessels, victualling ships, and auxiliaries of all kinds. To ensure overwhelming naval superiority, Pitt and Anson had provided him with a force exceptionally large for a newly promoted Vice-Admiral; and both to Saunders and to Wolfe Pitt had doubly underlined the injunction that 'the success of this expedition will very much depend upon an entire good understanding between our land and sea officers'. If necessary, he instructed Wolfe, 'soldiers under your command shall man the ships when there shall be occasion for them'. Happily, his exhortations in this respect were, for the time, hardly necessary. All the clashes of personality on the campaign were to come between Wolfe and his three brigadiers, George Townshend, Murray, and Monckton; the co-ordination of military and naval tactics proved excellent. After Wolfe's death, Townshend, silent upon any praise of Wolfe himself, paid handsome tribute to the navy's 'constant assistance and support . . . the perfect harmony and correspondence which has prevailed through all our operations'.[56] But those operations had to surmount formidable obstacles, and for Pitt there was to be another long and anxious wait before any good news was to come from the river command. Unluckily, although with careful foresight he had ordered that there should be left behind at Halifax, from Boscawen's 1758 fleet, a squadron under Rear-Admiral Durell strong enough to close the mouth of the St Lawrence to French reinforcement, a large convoy managed to slip through via the northern strait between Newfoundland and Labrador, Durell having waited over-long to be certain that the estuary was clear of ice after the exceptionally severe winter. The French ships included one carrying the young Bougainville,* who brought with him a copy of an intercepted letter from Amherst disclosing the whole outline of the British

---

* Bougainville and James Cook, to be linked so closely in the history of exploration, were also both engaged in the struggle for Quebec. Cook was sailing master of the *Pembroke* and had a considerable share in the vital work of charting the river channels and shoals.

plan of campaign against Canada. Thus the already very tough task facing Wolfe and Saunders was made tougher still.

From the second, mainland, theatre the reports were, as in the preceding war, initially promising and eventually disappointing; but this time Pitt's confidence in his commander-in-chief remained unshaken. Amherst was to survive his failures to preside over the final conquest of Canada.

He had decided to add muscle to his 'left hook' – those western extensions of his offensive upon which Pitt had agreed to allow him discretion; and accordingly he had dispatched Brigadier-General Prideaux towards Lake Ontario with a mixed force of regulars, Americans, and 900 Indians. By 5 August Amherst was able to send a messenger home to tell Pitt of the capture of Fort Niagara, though Prideaux himself had been killed in a firing accident.[57] There was propitious-sounding news too from the Ohio front, where Forbes's successor, Stanwix, having by now rebuilt 'Fort Pittsburgh' (late Duquesne), went on to strengthen the left hook by forcing the French to evacuate the lower Ohio posts of Venango, Le Boeuf and Presqu'île, and retreat beyond Lake Erie to Fort Detroit.[58]

Amherst meanwhile, having painlessly and methodically overcome Abercromby's stumbling-block of Ticonderoga, received news from his scouts of the enemy's abandoning Crown Point on 1 August, the day of Minden. But 'this makes no alteration in my motions', he reported to Pitt, 'as I am already trying all I can to get forward'. He was setting his chief engineer to 'trace out the ground for a fort' – 'the best situation I have seen in America' – which would secure 'entirely all his Majesty's dominions that are behind it from the inroads of the enemy and the scalping parties that have infested the whole country'.[59] So far, matters seemed to be progressing tolerably well.

Brigadier Gage had been sent to take over at Niagara, with instructions from Amherst to advance to La Galette (Ogdensburg) – 'a post', Pitt observed, 'of the utmost consideration' – and proceed down-river towards Montreal; but Gage soon discovered more difficulties than he relished; made no progress; and harvested in time only some sharp criticism from Amherst and severe disapproval from Pitt for premature abandonment of his pressure.[60] Amherst himself, with the main force of 11,000 – again a mixture of regulars, colonials, and Indians – spent two and a half frustrating months securing his rear and building a naval force strong enough to destroy the French craft patrolling Lake Champlain – a schooner, two sloops, and a brigantine. Then, by the time in early October that he was ready (the crank of his saw-mill having meanwhile broken three times), he judged the season too advanced to justify an attempt to advance that year on Montreal. On 18 October he heard from New York that Quebec had surrendered just one month before; on the 19th he decided to return to Crown Point.

News of the taking of Quebec was published in London on that same day – a London gloomy with Wolfe's last despondent dispatch only just received. 'Mr Pitt, with reason, gives it all over', Newcastle had written a few days earlier, 'and declares so publicly'.[61] In a letter of 2 September Wolfe had confessed to Pitt that he 'was at a loss how to determine'. 'My constitution is entirely ruined', he lamented to Holderness a week later (just four days before his triumph and death), 'without the consolations of having done any considerable service to the state; or without any prospect of it'. To his mother he summed up the impasse the expedition seemed to have reached: 'I can't in conscience put the whole army to risk. My antagonist has wisely shut himself up in inaccessible entrenchments, so that I can't get at him without spilling a torrent of blood, and that perhaps to little purpose'.[62]

His three brigadiers, after conferring with Saunders, eventually persuaded him to attempt a landing up-river beyond Quebec, though the cove he finally chose for the famous operation was very much nearer the city than where they had suggested. In his last tense hours Wolfe managed brilliantly to practise what he had long been preaching – what he had earlier claimed that his superiors at Rochefort had *failed* to practise: the necessity in war of seizing 'the lucky moment'. While the navy staged an imposing feint attack down-river, the hazardous night landing was skilfully managed and the troops established in position to the west of the city. The French made mistakes; the discipline and quality of the British regiments were high; Quebec, already half in ruins from bombardment, was obliged to surrender before troops under Bougainville and de Lévis could come to its relief; and the admirable Saunders, whose great part in the victory was inevitably in some degree overlooked amid the apotheosis of Wolfe, was able, soberly as always, to report, 'This was a very critical operation, and very properly and successfully conducted'.[63]

To Pitt, still in mid-October hoping to hear that Amherst was moving forward towards Montreal, the account of this vital victory made sweet music, and he immediately published Townshend's dispatch from Quebec in a *Gazette Extraordinary*. By chance the news had come almost simultaneously with tardy reports from India of the capture of Masulipatam on the Coromandel coast of the Bay of Bengal, and of the relief of Madras, which Lally had laid under siege between December 1758 and March 1759. Pitt had declined to be drawn by Clive's inviting proposition that national resources should be provided 'to obtain absolute possession' of the rich kingdoms of India which, so Clive flatteringly suggested, 'under the management of so able and disinterested a minister, would prove a source of immense wealth' and serve incidentally to diminish the national debt.[64] Pitt had contented himself with a glowing parliamentary tribute to Clive, 'that heaven-born general'; praise for Admiral Watson and his successor in Indian waters, Pocock; a £20,000 annual subsidy for the East India Company; and the dispatch of one new regiment further to reinforce its activities.

Indian successes could not then match Canadian in importance, but news of them was nonetheless timely and welcome. 'We make a great figure in the East Indies', wrote Walpole to Mann. 'In short, Mr Pitt and this little island appear of some consequence even in the map of the world'. Indeed, from towards the end of 1758, the gradual change of tone in Walpole's comments upon Pitt is striking. The old bantering irony and insinuations of charlatanism make way for acknowledgements of the nation's debt to his 'brilliance', his 'spirit and activity'. 'I give him all the honour he deserves'. With one more as-yet-unknowable big victory still to come before the year closed, Walpole now, in one of the most celebrated of all his letters, gave out a paean of praise to the 'ever-warm and victorious' year 1759 – to its wonderful weather, its fortunate events, its outstanding man:

> Can one easily leave the remains of such a year as this? It is still all gold. I have not dined or gone to bed by a fire till the day before yesterday . . . We have not had more conquest than fine weather: one would think we had plundered East and West Indies of sunshine. Our bells are worn threadbare with ringing of victories. I

believe it will require ten votes of the House of Commons before people will believe that it is the Duke of Newcastle that has done this, and not Mr Pitt.[65]

While the journals deluged elegies in honour of Wolfe and odes in praise of Pitt,* the respects of Frederick the Great were tactfully and handsomely conveyed: '*Il faut avouer que L'Angleterre a été longtemps en travail, et qu'elle a beaucoup souffert pour produire Monsieur Pitt; mais enfin elle est accouchée d'un homme*'.[66]

It happened that at the moment when success overseas was confirming Pitt's position as leader of an applauding nation, the always fragile coalition was in apparent danger of disintegration. There were two immediate causes of this governmental malaise: one, a reopening of the old sore proceeding from the King's persistent refusal to award Lord Temple his Garter; and the other, renewed suspicion on Pitt's part that the Newcastle-Hardwicke camp was intriguing behind his back to negotiate secretly for peace. Pitt, conscious that unlike most high servants of state he had until now begged no honours for himself or his relations, felt that King and country owed him some reward. He was prepared to accept recognition vicariously, but at the same time to make the issue of his brother-in-law's Blue Ribband a trial of strength and test of the genuineness of the King's confidence. He desired, he said, 'nothing but this one outward mark of the King's approbation and it was hard if he could not have it'.[67] In September, before he knew that Quebec had fallen, and while he confessed to being in a state of 'unexampled depression', he decided to raise once more with Newcastle the question of Temple's claim. He would not attend court, pleading his depressed state and 'a slight eruption' upon him, but would leave it to 'others' to judge whether 'the pretension in question had anything in it exorbitant or derogatory to the King's honour'.[68]

Newcastle did his best; enlisted Lady Yarmouth's support; did his best again, and still again. George greeted him 'very crossly'. 'I know you have been tormenting my Lady Yarmouth about it', he grumbled;

* Laurence Sterne, about to put before the public his eccentric and soon vastly fashionable *Tristram Shandy*, seized the opportune moment to dedicate it to the all-conquering minister, daring to hope it might make him smile and perhaps rob him of 'one moment's pain'.

'why do you plague her?'[69] Newcastle was obliged to remind the King of the impossibility of carrying on government if Pitt should resign in umbrage, as Newcastle was genuinely afraid he might. 'For God's sake, Sir', he begged the King, 'let me not carry a positive refusal that will ruin everything'.

'The world shall see how I am used', complained George. 'I will have it known'. 'What good, Sir, can arise from thence?' asked Newcastle. 'Perhaps many may blame Mr Pitt's pushing it; but at the same time they will be sorry to see your affairs in confusion for such an object'.[70]

In mid-October, with Pitt's resolution hardening, the King was still fighting doggedly to avoid honouring the man he so heartily detested. 'My Lord', he threw out at Newcastle, 'I will not be bullied'. Meanwhile a new complication was added. An 'anonymous' amateur of secret diplomacy (who was in fact known to be the Dowager Princess of Anhalt-Zerbst, mother of the Tsarina Catherine II) had approached Hardwicke's son Joseph Yorke, minister at the Hague, concerning the possibility of arranging peace between France and Britain. Yorke had composed for this *'inconnue'* a 'very pretty and very proper' reply, of which Hardwicke, Yorke himself, and even at first Newcastle all seemed excessively proud; Newcastle so much so that, *without any word to Pitt*, he read the correspondence to the King, 'for his amusement' – solely, he later protested under pressure, solely for the King's amusement.

Pitt, informed of the matter through the mischievousness, or perhaps malice, of Holderness ('Pitt's footman', complained the King*), was not amused. He pounced upon the already anguished Newcastle. He had heard, he wrote, in the highest of huffs, of certain 'dapplings [dabblings?] for peace' from a certain lady. Of course the Secretary of State should have been *'instantly'* informed, especially

in a moment so critical that one false step may prove fatal . . . I know not how far your Grace may have had the King's orders for this clandestine proceeding; if such be his Majesty's pleasure, it is my

---

* This had less truth in it than formerly. Holderness, who earlier still might perhaps have been written off as Newcastle's footman, had now largely taken over the role once held by Pitt of Leicester House's chief contact in the cabinet.

duty to receive it with all possible respect and submission; but I must find myself thereby deprived of the means of doing his Majesty any service. I beg the favour of your Grace to lay me at the King's feet and to inform his Majesty that my health requires the air of the country for two or three days.[71]

Newcastle explained as well and apologetically as he could, but nevertheless received on the same day a second letter from a crushingly sarcastic Pitt, who had already taken himself off to Hayes:

I cannot help differing from your Grace in not thinking that any letter, however prettily termed and addressed to the amiable sex, ought to be deemed matter for amusement when it relates to the great subject of peace.[72]

He again acknowledged, with his habitual humble-seeming irony, his 'unfitness for the high station' where his Majesty had been pleased to place him, but

while the King designs to continue me there, I trust it is not presumption to . . . most humbly request his gracious permission to retire, whenever his Majesty thinks it for his service to treat of a peace in the vehicle of letters of amusement and to order his servants to conceal, under so thin a covering, the first dawnings of information relative to so high and delicate an object.[73]

These threats of resignation were made just four days after the arrival of the great news from Quebec. Pitt knew well the strength of his position, and was feeling no need to mince his words (except in his affected epistolatory humilities) with the Duke or anybody else. When Newcastle tried again to reassure him that he promised not to attempt to 'enter into separate negotiations for peace on any account in the world', Pitt told him, 'not very politely', that if he did, he would 'not be able to walk the streets without a guard'.[74]

The 'affair of the Garter', Newcastle thought, was now 'desperate'; Pitt, he was afraid, was waiting 'for a handle to quit'. The King, however, was sure he would not. For one thing, he had already promised Pitt that peace would not be made except 'in concert with him'. And even if he did resign, George considered that Charles Yorke would make a very good Secretary to succeed him. Hardwicke, disconcerted by the blame being thrown upon his son over the peace letters, angry with Holderness, and thinking Pitt's own conduct no less 'insidious', agreed with the King; when it came to it, Pitt would not 'quit his own schemes and measures. He won't quit the vain-glory of appearing in parliament at the head of this great system, crowned with all these laurels'.[75]

Newcastle used all the sweet reasonableness he could muster to persuade the King to give way over the Garter. No, insisted George (with some justice), Pitt was attempting to force him; he refused to be forced. Newcastle's own account of an audience of 26 October shows how well he recognized the acute necessity of retaining Pitt in the fold:

> I asked his Majesty, 'Suppose Mr Pitt should quit, how does your Majesty propose to have your affairs carried on?' He said, 'You can do it; you have the majority in the House of Commons'. I replied ... 'No one will have a majority at present against Mr Pitt. No man, Sir, will in the present conjuncture set his face against Mr Pitt in the House of Commons'.[76]

It was not indeed Pitt who quitted. It was Temple himself – for a couple of days, after which he consented to resume his office of Privy Seal on the understanding that the Blue Ribband would be conceded. He received his prize at last (though not before further threats and manoeuvres) at a ceremony where the King, muttering and turning away his head, took no pains to conceal his aversion.[77] Allan Ramsay was straightway engaged to paint the victorious party in the full fig of his accumulated finery, spindly gartered leg prominently displayed.

Walpole's golden late summer gave way at last to a season of fierce autumnal storms. Under Hawke, the British home fleet had been able to keep Brest, the starting-point of all French invasion hopes, under close blockade for six months; but on 9 November, after dogged attempts to hold station off Ushant in the teeth of vicious weather, Hawke was forced to run for shelter into Torbay. Two days later, seven enemy ships of the line were able to get through to Brest, uniting there with Conflans's main squadron; and on the 14th November, the very day that Hawke managed to put out again from Torbay, Conflans left port, with an apparently very powerful force based on twenty ships of the line, to sail the hundred miles down-coast towards

Quiberon Bay, where he was to make contact with the first of the French invasion armies and its transports. Giving chase to the small scouting squadron which Hawke had left behind, Conflans on the morning of 20 November was concerned to discover his own force being overhauled by Hawke's battle-fleet. Amid the fury of a renewed westerly gale, he made for the protection of the Bay, but was followed by Hawke, who accepted formidable risks from reefs and shoals but was prepared, as it proved justifiably, to gamble on inferior French gunnery and seamanship. In the confused battle that followed in the dying hours of daylight on 20 November, and intermittently during the next two days, seven French line-of-battle ships were destroyed or captured, six more escaped up-river (to remain there impotently for many months to come), while the remaining seven escaped to Roche-fort.

The French naval historian of the Seven Years War judged this engagement to be 'the grave of the French Navy in the reign of Louis XV . . . The troops in the Morbihan had to be dispersed . . . all plans for the Channel and the North Sea had to be abandoned . . . After Lagos and Quiberon, France had no more squadrons either in the Mediterranean or the Atlantic'.[78] The only invading troops that managed to set foot on British soil were those under the freebooter Thurot from Dunkirk, who was not as Walpole supposed 'piddling somewhere on the coast of Scotland', but sailing to Belfast Lough – by way of Göteborg and Bergen. He briefly occupied Carrickfergus before being killed in action, and his three remaining ships surrendered to British frigates off the Isle of Man in February 1760. Hawke's own dispatch from Quiberon had the same sobriety as Saunders's* from Quebec:

. . . When I consider the season of the year, the hard gales on the day of action, a flying enemy, the shortness of the day, and the coast they were on, I can boldly affirm that all that could possibly be done has been done. As to the loss we have sustained [two vessels] let it be placed to the account of the necessity I was under of running all risks to break this strong force of the enemy . . .[79]

* Saunders was off the Lizard, almost arrived home, when he heard that Hawke was out in pursuit of the French, and sent a message to Pitt explaining that he would be sailing directly to Hawke's support. He arrived just too late.

Assuming that the British garrisons could cling on during the winter to their forward North American stations, and above all to Quebec until the ice melted again in May, Pitt's hold upon the naval and colonial war now looked impregnable. After Quiberon Bay Choiseul had to accept that Canada, being no longer reinforcible, must be militarily written off; such hope as remained could only lie in the bargaining of a peace conference following a French triumph in Europe. The British, with Amherst strongly placed to the south and the navy commanding the St Lawrence, did not need any wild optimism to suppose that 1760 must see the final conquest of Canada. Relying confidently on Amherst's judgement, Pitt's intructions to him, dispatched between December 1759 and February 1760, were less detailed than in the previous year; happily enclosing a *Gazette Extraordinary* in honour of Quiberon Bay, he saw the reduction of Montreal as 'evidently the great and essential object remaining to complete the glory of his Majesty's arms in that part of the world'.[80] And already, in this midwinter season of forward planning, he was making dispositions for further enterprises – in the West Indies against, first, Dominica and St Lucia, and then Martinique; in Louisiana against Mobile and the Mississippi forts; and, if it should prove possible, in the Indian Ocean against Mauritius.

Europe, on the other hand, presented a tangle of worries. The French still held a numerical advantage over Ferdinand's army, and Minden could now be seen as having avoided disaster rather than ensuring victory. After the defeats of Kunersdorf and Maxen, Prussia was in deeper trouble than ever; and however lyrically Pitt praised his immortal Frederick, and however constantly (and indeed sincerely) he vowed that Britain would not desert him at the peace, he remained anxious lest British participation in the German war should be exploited for Prussian ends, and he was irritated by Frederick's habit, as Britain increased her proportion of men in the allied army, of withdrawing from it for his own purposes an equivalent number of Prussians.

For Pitt the most disquieting aspect of the European situation arose from the trend of Spanish policy. Back in October, Newcastle had noted how Pitt was 'always harping upon Spain'.[81] Over the main subjects of long-standing Spanish complaint – Britain's taking of 'logwood'* from Honduras, and the aggressions and atrocities of British privateers – he had tried to use every opportunity to conciliate Wall, the Spanish foreign minister of past years. But he was now disturbed by the prospect of a Spain under Charles III much more open to French influence and soon prepared to tease the British further, with a claim to share in the Newfoundland fisheries. The Spanish King now expressed himself as 'unable to see with indifference' British successes in America, and offered mediation between Britain and France, which Pitt rejected without hesitation as 'premature and rash'.[82]

There had been much talk of peace and putting about of peace feelers. Frederick would have been happy to escape on tolerable terms; so too would France. So certainly in England would Newcastle, Hardwicke, and their supporters. Austria, however, saw no reason to cease hostilities while holding such promising prospects of regaining her lost territories from Prussia; and Pitt refused to abandon either Prussia or the hope of more comprehensive victories. He did attempt to secure some agreement with Prussia's other enemies, Sweden and Russia, but without success. While Newcastle for a time believed in the talk of peace with which Pitt made generously free, Hardwicke all along was sceptical: Pitt saw, he wrote, 'that in order to obtain peace, so much of our acquisitions must be given up', and this would so disappoint the public, who had been 'blown up to such an extravagant degree', that Pitt would be afraid of losing his hold over them.[83]

Yet the victories of 1759, once the storm in the Temple teacup had subsided, had looked for a time as though they had brought to the cabinet something like general harmony. Pitt himself at the opening of parliament made the point that success had brought unanimity – not, he observed pointedly, unanimity success.[84] At a long *tête-à-tête* in Grosvenor Square in January Hardwicke found him as 'confidential and friendly as possible' – and moreover 'talking very friendly' too of Newcastle. And Barrington was testifying that same month to 'the union, cordiality, and goodwill which reign at present among the

* The tree whose great profitability gave rise to this old and bitter Anglo-Spanish dispute was the *haemotoxylon campechianum* (popularly 'logwood' from being floated down-river in logs). From it were derived an astringent drug, and, more importantly, a dye for which European woollen industries were greedy customers.

King's servants . . . I could not have said this three months ago'.[85] He might fairly have gone on to guess that in three months' time he would not be able to say it either. It would only need estimates-time to come round in the spring for Newcastle to be recording his annual fracas with Pitt.

—◦◦◦—

CHAPTER FIFTEEN

Problems of War and Peace

'Mr Pitt flew into a violent passion at my saying we could not carry on the war another year; and said that was the way to encourage our enemy'. To be 'thus tutored by this gentleman, who knows little or nothing of the matter', seemed to Newcastle hard indeed. He continued to find 'the monstrous increase' in the national debt 'a terrible consideration';[1] and later, after Canada had been finally won, Pitt was still hammering into him that if he wished for an advantageous peace he must show himself to be ready for further war. The army and navy alone would be costing sixteen millions in 1761 ('without one sixpence for other ordinary expenses', sighed Newcastle) – but Pitt insisted that the country could easily afford it: 'there was such an affluence of money from all parts, East Indies, West Indies, etc., that we might get as many millions as we pleased'. And indeed, indeed, Newcastle was bound to admit, there *was* 'now happily a great deal of money in the kingdom'; but he remained in pain that Pitt should continue 'so very meddling in these affairs'.[2]

The total of troops in British pay at the end of 1759, including nearly 69,000 Germans, was rather over 170,000; but still it was not enough to fight this unprecedentedly expensive war. More men were being called for everywhere: in North America, where Amherst was lamenting that the taking of Quebec, being regarded as a prelude to peace, had had the effect of making the colonies 'slothful' in the levying of their quotas;[3] in India, where the Company was calling loudly for more assistance; above all from Germany, where Ferdinand and Sackville's successor Granby were pressing hard for enough reinforcements to give them something nearer to parity with the French.

In the task of raising recruits, Pitt was prepared to utilize every resource and employ any tactic within the limits set by the social and institutional conservatism of the day. Gentlemen of suitable standing with money and patriotism to spare were encouraged to raise their own companies, and some of these went on to perform notably in Germany. Specially approved regular officers were commissioned to form new regiments, offering between £6 and £10 per recruit. Of four new regiments of light cavalry raised during the winter of 1759-60, one was drawn wholly from the footmen and chairmen of the City of London, enlisted at their officers' expense. Over the same period, Ireland provided the chief reservoir for six new infantry regiments. Altogether, before the end of 1760 there would be over 200,000 troops in the pay of the British exchequer, a tenth of them British redcoats on the German front.[4] Ligonier could point out to Granby that he commanded more British troops than the Duke of Marlborough at Blenheim.

Pitt's conversion to this full-blooded continental commitment did not come easily – contritely and disarmingly though he admitted to the Commons that 'he had unlearned his juvenile errors and thought no longer that England could do all by itself'.[5] In April 1760 he was still resisting the sending of infantry; 'perhaps he wants to be ravished into it', suggested Hardwicke. Yet a little later when Ligonier argued for sending four infantry battalions, Pitt wanted to know why they could not send six – as they then did, after cabinet approval.[6] He needed no telling of the dangers he was running and continued to show a certain defensiveness on the subject. 'Three battalions of Guards embark for Germany, we hope, by Friday or Saturday', he wrote to Temple in July. 'I trust your Lordship will approve this sudden and somewhat bold measure . . . Not a moment was to be lost, and I stand responsible for the event. May Heaven send it prosperous'.[7] As the months went by he increasingly hungered for news of a big victory in Germany, and began to grow restive and despondent when it failed to come.

To begin with, even Canada threatened news to damp the spirits. After Wolfe's death, Admiral Saunders, and Brigadiers Monckton and Townshend, had returned home. Wolfe's remaining brigadier, James Murray, had stayed behind in command of the victors of Quebec. As at Louisbourg earlier, the garrison left to guard the fruits of their triumph suffered wretchedly in the ensuing winter and, by the spring, Murray's scurvied troops were so weakened by cold and disease that a third of them were unfit to fight. Seizing their opportunity, the French in April sailed down-river from Montreal in superior force and, Murray choosing to advance out of the city to meet them, fought a second battle of the Heights of Abraham with the positions now reversed. Losing their guns and a third of their effective strength, the British were for the moment saved only by the inability of the French to follow up their success. Under desperate siege, Murray managed, by sloop, to get a message through, down the still dangerously icy river, and so via Halifax, where the Governor, Lawrence, sensibly conceived it his 'indispensible duty . . . to open the pacquets [addressed to Amherst] and transmit copies of them [to Pitt] without a moment's delay'.[8] Pitt and Anson had already, before the winter, taken such precautions as were open to them by holding behind at Halifax a strong squadron under Admiral Lord Colville to be ready to sail to Quebec at the very first opportunity the ice allowed. In March they ordered further frigates to sail from England in support and in fact it was one of these, the *Lowestoffe*, which was in the end to win the race to relieve Quebec.

Murray had estimated he could hold out until 12 May. Colville left for the river on 20 April. Governor Lawrence, writing to Pitt on 11 May, feared the city might have been lost before his alarming information could even reach London. The gloom when it arrived there on 17 June was all the deeper for following the jubilation of the preceding autumn. Pitt did not fail to publish the grave news in the *Gazette*.

'Who the deuce was thinking of Quebec?' asked Walpole: 'The place, I suppose will be retaken; the year 1760 is not the year 1759'. Armchair critics were not wanting: 'We all here blame Murray', Charles Jenkinson wrote; 'how it has marred all our schemes of peace'.[9]

The *Lowestoffe*, closely followed by Colville's own frigates, penetrated to the Quebec basin on 9 May, three days before Murray's deadline. The naval flotilla of the French was destroyed forthwith, and their land force obliged to abandon its stores and cannon and retreat hastily to Montreal. Almost as satisfactory, a supply convoy of twenty sail from Bordeaux was intercepted and captured in the estuary, Pitt's renewed orders to Colville issued on 20 June proving fortunately redundant: 'Whatever shall happen to be the event of Quebec . . . to continue, with the utmost vigilance, to shut up the River St Lawrence, and to prevent all possibility of succour passing that way'. Thus, for the second time, victorious tidings from Quebec followed hard upon forebodings of disaster. Pitt's own huge relief may be felt in the

273

express he dispatched immediately to Hester: 'Join, my love, with me in most humble and grateful thanks to the Almighty . . . Happy, happy day. My joy and hurry are inexpressible'.[10]

Amherst's armies, with the advantages now of secure supplies and superior numbers, proceeded over the summer months of 1760 to complete the conquest of Canada. They converged on Montreal from three directions: Murray advanced up-river from Quebec; Colonel Haviland led a small force northward from Lake Champlain; and Amherst himself, with the largest contingent and the hardest task, swept round in an enveloping movement from Albany, up the Mohawk valley to Oswego, thence over Lake Ontario in a large flotilla of 'bateaux', and down the St Lawrence rapids to approach Montreal from the south-west and prevent any possibility of the French retiring into the interior.

By 8 September, Governor Vaudreuil was left with no option but to surrender to Amherst, together with the town of Montreal, all Canada (comprising, so the always exact and methodical Amherst reported, 108 parishes and 76,172 souls); and, added Amherst to Pitt on 4 October, 'I can assure you, Sir, this country is as quiet and secure as any other province of his Majesty's dominions'. He professed especial pride in that Sir William Johnson – the American in command of the thousand or so 'savages' – had 'taken unwearied pains in keeping the Indians in humane bounds, and I have the pleasure to assure you, that not a peasant, woman, or child has been hurt by them, or a house burnt, since I entered what was the enemy's country'.[11]

Less happily, there was such serious Indian trouble from the Cherokees in the south that Amherst detached a thousand men under Colonel Montgomery to go to the assistance of Governor Lyttelton and the Carolina settlers. Further south still, where Pitt still set his sights on Mobile and the Mississippi forts, the Louisiana French seemed to be having rather more success than the English of Georgia and South Carolina in enlisting the help of the Creeks, Choctaws, and Chickasaws.

Amherst's detailed and businesslike dispatches, displaying before Pitt's eyes the prize for which above all others he had for the past four years worked and schemed, were brought to London and delivered on 5 October by a Major Isaac Barré, an officer who had fought under both Wolfe and Amherst, and lost an eye at Quebec, acquiring thereby what Walpole called a 'savage glare'. He was at this time, in the then accepted manner of ambitious servicemen and politicians, recommending himself to Pitt for advancement – and, being refused, would soon be abusing him in parliament with a saturnine eloquence worthy of Pitt himself.

There was naturally both in Britain and among the British American colonists general celebration at the submission of Canada. In one important quarter, however, a significantly sour note was privately struck. 'I wish my dearest friend [Bute] joy of this success', wrote the Prince who in another few weeks would be King George III; 'but at the same time I can't help feeling that every such thing raises those I have no reason to love'. And if Pitt was, as the Prince suspected, contemplating yet further military involvement in Germany, 'I hope this nation will open her eyes and see . . . that her popular man is a true snake in the grass'.[12]

The allied army in Germany, having fought far into the preceding winter, did not recommence operations until June. Then, though they were outnumbered by two to one, they assumed the initiative. 'The English dragoons', Pitt told Temple, were 'covered with glory'. Although first reports of the campaign were discouraging, during the second half of July the allied generals won two brilliant tactical successes, at Emsdorf and Warburg. At Emsdorf, Eliott's regiment of light horse (15th Light Dragoons), Pitt's very latest reinforcement, won shining laurels, though at a heavy cost; and it was at Warburg that the Marquis of Granby, losing his wig but not his daring or judgement, so successfully charged the enemy 'bald-headed' that he won simultaneously a new metaphor for the language and a new glory to extinguish unpleasant memories of the Sackville episode at Minden. '*Les Anglais ont fait merveilles*', wrote the commanding general, the hereditary Prince of Brunswick, Ferdinand's nephew; and Pitt enthusiastically passed on these praises of the 'glorious event' as usual to Hester down at Hayes. (By the same express he had to tell her of the very sudden death of Newcastle's daughter-in-law; it had 'thrown a cloud over our joy; who can be happy and not tremble!')

The news from Germany soon began to worsen. The Prussians were beaten at Landshut in Silesia. 'Adieu the King of Prussia', cried Walpole, 'unless Prince Ferdinand's battle . . . can turn the scale a little'.[13] But Frederick the Great continued most skilfully to slip away from complete catastrophe though he did need to borrow cavalry from Ferdinand to help him. And against the allied army, numbers began to tell severely. Once again the French would soon be in possession of Hesse and at the borders of the electorate of Hanover.

Pitt fretted. Twice for several weeks earlier in the year he had been plagued by one or other from his repertory of illnesses. Now he was again depressed; 'uneasy and out of humour on account of the inactivity of the [German] campaign'. 'Without a battle', he declared, he would 'not be for continuing the measures in Germany another year' – which, Hardwicke thought, though it was no way for a great minister to talk, represented an attitude that would be popular with 'nine parts in ten of the people in England'.[14] Hester was aware that perhaps she ought to be by her husband's 'dear side' to divert his thoughts 'from too constant an attention to unpleasing circumstances'; and they were both for a time additionally worried for their two small daughters, whom they had decided to subject to the still risky operation of inoculation against smallpox. Fortunately by mid-October the children were reported to be convalescent.[15]

From Europe, however, no public news came to match this private relief. Pitt had 'waited many a tedious day', he told George Grenville; he tried to solace himself with the reassurance that at least events across the Atlantic spoke 'loud enough to be heard at Paris'. And, fresh from another tiff with Newcastle over the cost of the war, he observed with mischievous relish that the coming Commons Address to the Crown would be 'big with a million in every line'.[16]

In August Ligonier became seriously ill of an inflamed bladder, and was out of action for two months. Why need they worry, asked Holderness cynically, since it was always Pitt who decided everything without bothering to consult Ligonier or, for that matter, anybody else? But of Ligonier that was hardly true, and Pitt let his anger be known when word of Holderness's little jibe came to his ears. Even if he overrode Ligonier on occasions, their relationship was basically harmonious, and he relied heavily on Ligonier's technical knowledge and efficient administration. There was now the possibility, alarming to Pitt, Newcastle, and Hardwicke alike, that if Ligonier should die, the King might either make restitution to his son Cumberland by reappointing him Captain General or even himself wish to take over responsibility for military direction. Ligonier's toughness happily averted the dangers; he survived to be back at his desk in November, a month before his eightieth birthday.[17]

Before then it had become obvious that the allied army in Germany faced stern trouble. Pressed for still more troops, Pitt now refused. Ferdinand must do what he could with what he had; and in fact he did now choose the moment for an audacious diversionary stroke against the French base at Wesel, near the Dutch border on the lower Rhine. Declining to send more reinforcements, Pitt agreed to attempt some assistance for the allied army by mounting another big naval-military expedition – not this time to the French mainland, but against Belle Isle, the island lying ten miles or so off the Quiberon peninsula in Brittany. This, he figured, would not only draw off French troops, but profitably occupy eight to ten thousand of the 22,000 troops kicking their heels in southern England. Success would also give a valuable pawn to set against Minorca in future peace negotiations.

The King, Anson, and a convalescing Ligonier all seemed to favour the enterprise, the King at first, so it was reported, 'violently'. Hardwicke did not relish it, and Newcastle openly opposed it as 'a hazardous, ridiculous measure' coming in any case too late to help Ferdinand. When he watched going south on the Portsmouth road past Claremont, 'wagons, heavy artillery, ordnance stores, etc., etc.', intended for 'upwards of 8000' men, he cried, 'Would to God they were now all at Wesel!' It was a cruel thing, he reflected, 'to be alone, scoffed at by a Lord Holderness or overrun by the torrent of his colleague'.[18]

The allied army had laid siege to Wesel and crossed the Rhine beyond it; but at Kloster Kampen on 16 October they were defeated. The day following, Hawke, who had been sent to reconnoitre for the Belle Isle project, wrote for Anson at the Admiralty a report declaring strongly against it, and advocating instead a landing on the Morbihan mainland between Vannes and Lorient. By this time Hawke could reasonably claim to be a Brittany specialist. What was the point of taking an island, he asked, when we were already masters of the sea? In any case the operation, which might be expensive, would probably not detach many French troops from Germany.

Hawke, a mere serving admiral, had no doubt exceeded his brief; but he convinced Anson, who now resolved to circumvent Pitt. He went straight on his own to the King, and found little difficulty in convincing him too of the superiority of the mainland project. Newcastle, waiting in the ante-room and aware of what was brewing, had the pleasure of being able to keep Pitt informed, as he in turn arrived. When Anson emerged from his audience, Pitt angrily demanded to see Hawke's letter, and read it with mounting indignation. There must have been collusion, he accused, between Hawke and Anson. Indeed, Newcastle joyfully reported, Mr Pitt, 'stung to the quick', was

> more disturbed and full of complaints than I had almost ever seen him. He attacked Sir Edward Hawke most bitterly and dissected his letter from one end to the other . . .; that Sir Edward did not know what use to make of Belle Isle; that Mr Pitt did; that he was a very good sea officer but no minister . . .[19]

Next day George II collapsed and died from a heart attack. That event, so long awaited, was to alter many things, not least for Pitt. One immediate effect, however, was to reopen the Belle Isle enterprise for discussion. The cabinet now included a most important recruit, the young George III's 'dearest friend', Pitt's erstwhile ally Lord Bute. It happened that Bute and his royal pupil had always favoured amphibious expeditions above operations in Germany, and Pitt now managed to persuade a majority of the cabinet after all, at a meeting on 11 November, the day of the old King's funeral, to approve an immediate assault on Belle Isle. Over the next fortnight troops and stores were embarked, and a supporting fleet assembled in St Helen's Roads. Perhaps Newcastle calculated that the advancing season and hostile weather would in any case forbid the folly, and by the end of November even Pitt must have recognized that they were doing no more than keep up a threatening bluff. By 13 December that too was abandoned, and the troops were brought ashore. Newcastle thanked God.

He seemed pleased too to think that both Pitt and Prussia might now really be ready to discuss peace seriously. Pitt showed him a letter just received from Frederick (blushing, Newcastle vowed, at its flattering compliments to *'ce caractère d'un vrai Romain dont vous avez donné des marques si éclatantes'* . . . etc., etc.).[20] Frederick, though he had just won costly but vital relief by his brilliant victories at Liegnitz and Torgau, freely recognized the powerful cards his enemies still held, and Newcastle for his part recognized that of British ministers only Pitt had influence with Frederick. He observed too that Pitt, with apparently 'the best disposition', seemed sincerely ready to discuss which of their conquests the British must be ready to sacrifice for an honourable but still profitable peace. Perhaps they would have to give up Guadeloupe and Goree in order to keep *all* Canada and satisfy the American colonists; or perhaps keep Guadeloupe and Goree and 'give up some Canada and confine themselves to the Lakes, etc.'. In either case he would absolutely insist on excluding the French from the Newfoundland fisheries. 'I pressed him much to set things a-going', Newcastle wrote; and Pitt had taken his leave with a rather doleful comment, accepting that now, in the new reign, he and Newcastle found themselves in the same boat: 'Formerly, my Lord, if you told me that you would answer for the King's consent, that was enough; I was satisfied. Where is that satisfaction to be had now?'[21]

In fact the accession of George III had made less immediate difference to the authority of Pitt and Newcastle than some had forecast, or than Newcastle in particular had feared. He emerged from his sudden panic at the prospect of being displaced at the Treasury by Bute, into something much nearer to his chronic situation of plaintive anxiety. True, he lamented that the young king treated him as 'a cypher'; but all the same it appeared that Newcastle was to continue as First Lord, since Bute proposed merely to 'hold the situation of a private man at the side of the King'. Newcastle was even to be permitted to manage the approaching general election in his own time-honoured fashion, as busy and conscientious as ever in dispensing his loaves and fishes. Pitt, busy with bigger things, indicated that he had no wish to meddle in these delicate electoral transactions, always provided that some of his friends 'were taken care of'.[22]

In the preceding summer, through an intermediary, Bute had attempted to restore the old fraternal union, as he described it, with Pitt, but had received a very dusty answer, which raked up old grievances against Leicester House, complained of the 'hourly indications of an imperious nature' shown by Bute, and declared that he, Pitt, would never be 'rid with a check rein', could bear 'no touch of command', would 'not be dictated, prescribed to, etc.'. In short, *aut Caesar aut nihil*. If Bute were to become chief minister, then emphatically Pitt would never serve under him: 'I will even make way for his greatness ... only I cannot make part of it'.[23] Once more he rehearsed his old rituals – half threat, half dream: he too, like Lord Bute, would wish to be 'a private man, if he could once see his country out of the present plunge'. The difference between them would be that Bute would practise *his* private philosophy as court favourite, Pitt his in village retirement.[24]

Although Bute was not yet prime minister, he was now prime adviser to the Crown, and it was he who composed the new king's accession declaration to the Privy Council. This proved the occasion of an immediate trial of strength between Bute and Pitt. Hearing in the text the epithets of 'bloody and expensive' used to describe the war, together with the expression of a desire for peace unqualified by any mention of loyalty to Prussia, Pitt intervened to insist that there must be a revision for the minute-book, where 'bloody and expensive' was allowed to disappear in favour of 'just and necessary', and the hoped-for peace was to be aimed at 'in concert with my allies'. These revised phrases appeared also at the reopening of parliament in the speech from the throne and the loyal addresses.

During the first half of 1761 prospects for an end to the war looked hopeful, but as the months progressed it began instead to look more and more likely that hostilities would be extended. The issue effectively depended on two nicely balanced triangles of forces: abroad, the movements of French, British, and Spanish policy; and at home, the attitudes and rivalries of Bute, Newcastle, and Pitt.

Newcastle was not for peace at any price, or even among those, like the Duke of Bedford, who advocated it most unambiguously; but he had long been looking for some acceptable exit from a struggle he considered ruinously expensive. Bute reckoned Pitt 'madder than ever' for wishing to continue the continental war, and in the end he was to prove readier than Pitt to compromise on a bargain with the French. But, strong as his position was at court, it was weak in parliament and among the public. He dared not be seen to be less patriotic than Pitt and make an unpopular settlement, and it was not until late in the summer that he sided unequivocally with the peace party in the cabinet.[25] Pitt, for all the earlier talk of peace possibilities which Newcastle had found so promising, became as the months moved on and news arrived of fresh British successes overseas, increasingly determined to hold on for outright victory and an absolute minimum of concessions – even when the danger of a war with Spain loomed near. He knew that if Britain humbled the French in America and the West Indies it must bring her critically face to face with Spain. Such a confrontation, if France could be brought to terms first, might be risked without fear; but Pitt came to a more confident conclusion still, that even if France remained in the fight, her naval and overseas position would be so debilitated that Britain would if necessary be equal to taking on the two Bourbon powers together.

Pitt's preparations had already been made for the 1761 season's combined operations, against the remaining French West Indian islands and against Belle Isle (revived as a late substitution for Mauritius), when in March Choiseul presented a double proposal to London – for a peace congress at Augsburg of all the belligerents, and for a separate Anglo-French peace negotiation. Though Prussia and Britain both accepted the Augsburg congress in principle, it was never to meet; but on 7 April the cabinet authorized Pitt to put Choiseul's other proposal to the test.

It was a cabinet in which Bute sat, not now merely as King's favourite but as Pitt's fellow Secretary of State, Holderness having been painlessly ejected with the help of a pension and rich sinecure. The change, to which Pitt had earlier expressed strong disapproval, at least regularized Bute's standing in the councils of state. Newcastle had helped to contrive it; Bute – which meant the Court – was infinitely more valuable as a friend than an enemy. The Duke's only fear was that 'disobliging Mr Pitt' would upset the governmental applecart. Pitt's popularity, he reckoned, was still essential to the administration. What if he should go into opposition? Pitt would never do that, he was assured; it was far likelier that he would choose to retire, loaded with suitable honours. In any case, so Bute tried to persuade Newcastle (and perhaps himself too), Pitt's popularity was on the wane, and if they were all over-careful about offending him they would find themselves more than ever under his thumb. Bute himself, always fixing his eyes on 'ambition's rocky height' but in his heart deeply fearful of it, characteristically professed to need condolences rather than congratulations upon his elevation. He too confessed to fearing 'the temper and manner of Mr Pitt'. Nobody, least of all Newcastle, fancied the assignment of breaking the news to Pitt that his new colleague was to be his one-time ally but now undoubtedly chief challenger – until Bute found courage to do it himself.[26]

Pitt had recently, during February and early March, been more ill than usual: 'laid up with a dreadful gout in all his limbs', according to

Walpole; 'he did not sleep for fourteen nights, till one of his eyes grew as bad as his hands or feet'.[27] Now, philosophically but icily, he accepted Bute's *fait accompli*, 'in all duty and submission to the King'.[28] 'Our friend [Bute] fended off extremely well', wrote Newcastle, 'and from the beginning treated it as a measure of the King's'. Presumably it was somewhat to sugar the pill that the King had agreed at the same time to promote one of Pitt's little party, James Grenville, who now became Cofferer of the Household with £4000 a year, while at the Exchequer Barrington replaced Legge, who by this time had fallen foul not only of Pitt but of Bute too. He even failed to pick up a peerage. More fortunate was Bubb Dodington, who had once been another of Pitt's associates, if more briefly; his wind-favouring bark had found a final haven and tied up alongside Bute; he became Lord Melcombe.

These latter months of Pitt's war ministry were a time of intense diplomatic activity. The new Spanish ambassador in London, Fuentes, was vigorously renewing his country's three major complaints – the violation of its maritime rights as a neutral, forceful British encroachments into Honduras to carry away the 'Campeachy' logwood, and the denial of Spain's claim to a share in the northern fisheries. Meanwhile Grimaldi, the Spanish ambassador in Paris, dangling before Choiseul the prospect of another Bourbon Family Compact, was striving to dissuade France from concluding a 'premature' peace with Britain. Pitt sent a special mission to Paris in the person of Hans Stanley, to attempt the negotiation of an Anglo-French peace bargain, while Choiseul sent an old hand, Bussy, to London upon the same business. Pitt's dictatorial reputation being well known across the Channel, Choiseul could savour some amusement in telling Stanley of the apprehensiveness with which Bussy faced his assignment: '*le pauvre diable*', he said, '*trembloit de peur en partant*'. According to Stanley, Choiseul actually showed him a letter from Bussy asking for permission to return. Choiseul told Louis XV: '*Apparemment il a déplû à M. Pitt qui l'aura fait sauter par les fenêtres*'.[29]

Batches and counter-batches of proposals for the settlement of territorial claims, permutations and counter-permutations, passed between London and Paris; by the summer of 1761 they had reached the dimensions of ultimatum and counter-ultimatum. In this brisk hypothetical bartering the future ownership of some widely scattered and highly valuable properties was at stake: Minorca, Canada, Cape

Breton Island, Senegal, Goree, Guadeloupe and Marie Galante, various Indian and East Indian territories, and the French-occupied areas of western Germany. After June, Pitt could also throw Belle Isle into the reckoning; Bussy had been in London only a fortnight when news arrived of its capture, and he was civilly advised by Pitt that it would be prudent to allow his landlord to have the house illuminated, as its neighbours would be, in the popular celebration of this further victory. Bussy was perhaps surprised to be able to report that he found the formidable Secretary, though obstinate and even captious as a negotiator, strictly courteous in his personal dealings.

Pitt did not dispute that there must be some limited restitution of conquests, if only to permit the return to Prussia, Hanover, Brunswick, and Hesse of their lost lands. 'Some are for keeping Canada, some Guadeloupe', he said in the Commons; 'who will tell me for which I shall be hanged, for not keeping?' After cabinet meetings on 24 and 26 June, when almost every other minister present had considered Pitt's treaty expectations intransigent, he did in fact instruct Stanley to offer Choiseul Guadeloupe, Marie Galante, and Belle Isle in return for Minorca, the Sumatran post of Bencoolen, and French evacuation of German territories.

This was the nearest he ever came to negotiating peace. As time went by, while the terms he was prepared to accept hardened, Choiseul's too became less accommodating as the likelihood of his enlisting Spain as a fully belligerent ally increased. Pitt's stance was further toughened by a resumption of propitious news from a variety of war fronts. In July it was learned that Pondicherry, the last French possession in India, had fallen to Colonel Eyre Coote the previous January; and that in the West Indies the island of Dominica had been taken in June. From Germany too came reassurance: the allied army had at last regained its touch and defeated the French at Vellinghausen. Once again Pitt and Hester could sing with united voice 'renewed praise and thanksgivings to the Almighty'. 'All is joy . . . happy, glorious success'. (As with Minden two years before, it was thought at first that Vellinghausen was a grander victory than it in fact proved; but at least it was a victory.) Horace Walpole, who had been sure – and much relieved – that peace was imminent, took again to throwing his hat in the air: 'How the deuce in two days can one digest all this? . . . I could beat myself for not having a flag ready to display on my round tower and guns mounted on my battlements'.[30] On the other hand, Newcastle thought these victories 'hurt us, as they make peace more difficult'; and Bedford, convinced that 'whilst Mr Pitt has any weight . . . there will be no peace made', was soon expressing the opinion that 'another victory in either of the Indies would undo us'.[31] Bedford, returned from an inauspicious and stormy tenure of the Lord Lieutenancy of Ireland, was now an important force in a cabinet increasingly disinclined to be forever dominated by Pitt.

It was the issue of the fisheries that made the sticking-point, both for Pitt and Choiseul. The fishing grounds of the St Lawrence estuary and the Newfoundland banks were regarded by both France and Britain as of essentially greater importance than any territorial possessions in Canada itself. Not only did they supply the large and lucrative market for dried and salt fish on both sides of the Atlantic – the French share alone being worth the equivalent of half a million a year sterling, as much as all the rest of Canada's produce together – but they were seen also by both countries as a vital peace-time training area for potential sailors in war. Commercial enterprise and naval power spoke the same language on each side of the English Channel, and in Madrid too, where the Spanish government was now pressing its own claim to share the fishing rights.

For the half century since the Peace of Utrecht, Britain and France had by treaty shared the wealth of the Newfoundland banks; the St Lawrence fishery had of course been wholly French. Pitt now demanded the monopoly of both. To Bedford in particular, and to most other cabinet ministers in a lesser degree, this demand seemed excessive and – at least to Bedford – likely in the end to be self-defeating: 'To drive France [he wrote] entirely out of any naval power is fighting against nature, and can tend to no one good to this country, but on the contrary must excite all the naval powers of Europe to enter a confederacy against us . . .' Bedford was also one of the few at this time to express the opinion that it would be folly altogether to expel French power from America and the West Indies; its continuance there would provide the best guarantee of the continuing loyalty of the British colonists to the Crown. It was to go some way to meet the views of his colleagues, and 'preserve unanimity', that Pitt grudgingly and ill-humouredly agreed at last to offer Choiseul a share of the Newfoundland (but not the estuary) fishing rights – and this only 'in return for some very important compensation' such as the demolition of the Dunkirk fortifications.

Choiseul's preferred choice would have been to agree a treaty with Britain if terms could be found not too unfavourable to France. The information that came to him from diplomatic sources during the spring and summer of 1761 was that such a settlement was impossible so long as Pitt's influence in the cabinet was dominant, but that there were good hopes this might be on the wane. Choiseul too was stubborn on the subject of cod; *la pêche est ma folie*, he told Stanley; and he held out for French rights in *both* the fisheries, with a port of shelter for French vessels in the estuary. In July he dispatched to London a counter-ultimatum whose terms would have been unrealistically demanding if he had not by then been holding some powerful cards up his sleeve. If he could not secure a tolerable peace he would clinch the deal with Spain, which had been for some time on offer. To the high indignation of Pitt, French and Spanish demands had now been concerted, and arrived at Westminster in harness. Choiseul had delayed signing a formal agreement with Spain until he could be sure that the British cabinet would not be prepared for further concession; and when Bussy, personally presenting the papers to Pitt, reported the violence of his reaction, Choiseul's mind was made up. It seemed clear now that Pitt was not about to fall. He had, moreover, read Bussy a very stiff lecture: France was not to presume to *intermeddle* in disputes between Spain and Britain; it constituted an affront to the King's dignity and was 'incompatible with the sincerity of the negotiation'. Although it suited the secrecy of Choiseul's intentions that bargaining should appear to continue, after this it was in reality little more than a façade. Signature of the Franco-Spanish alliance was only a few weeks away.

CHAPTER SIXTEEN

---◦◦◦---

Spain and Resignation

Wall, the Spanish minister, and Fuentes, the ambassador in London, had for some time been convinced that Pitt was only trifling with their country's protests until he had dealt final blows to France. The exasperation of Wall in particular – once an Anglophile – had mounted as the years went by with no redress given to his repeated complaints. As early as 1757 Pitt, while insisting on the British right to cut and take away logwood, had offered to withdraw all *recent* encroachments by British operators in the Bay of Honduras and on the 'Mosquito' (Miskito) Shore of Nicaragua; Wall had rejected the limitations implied in Pitt's undertaking, and his hostility grew as nothing was done to implement even that. For three years more this quarrel stood at deadlock; and when in 1761 Wall might perhaps have been willing to settle for a compromise, Charles III was there behind him to insist on total evacuation of the British encroachments.

The strong-arm tactics of the British navy; the molestation by privateers of Spanish merchantmen; seizures of cargoes within Spanish waters; decisions which the Spaniards thought outrageously illegal by British Admiralty prize courts – all these provided another area of indignant complaint; and Pitt had gone some way to admitting its validity and reducing its justification by his privateers bill of 1759, and by repeated instructions to colonial governors to restrain illegalities. But he was swimming against a powerful tide. Lucrative commercial interests were involved; British naval power was cocksure; neutral maritime rights would have been hard to sustain even if Pitt had been ten times as scrupulously concerned for them as he was.

The Spanish claim to a share in the northern fishery was a non-starter, and Pitt's total rejection of it was supported by even the most pacific of his cabinet colleagues. Over the logwood-cutting Newcastle, Hardwicke, and Bute all thought an accommodation ought to be possible, and at one point even Pitt declared himself ready for 'some expedient', though he told Newcastle in July 1760 that if one were found he, Newcastle, must see that his supporters in parliament – and the King – accepted what might prove to be an unpopular concession. He told Newcastle

> he was not in a situation in the administration to stand either breaking with Spain, or the giving up of any right of this country. He said that the Duke of Newcastle is the person who has the confidence of the King, the Duke of Newcastle has the support of Parliament, and a power which may enable him to stand the one or the other. That his situation was very different.[1]

While Pitt played for time in his quarrel with Spain he had not been without cabinet backing. It was not, for instance, merely because Hardwicke was old and tired, and did not wish to come up to town for consultations during the summer recess of 1760, that he argued the wisdom of delay. 'I think it will be right to gain time', he wrote, 'especially till you see the winding up of this campaign, both in Germany and America'.[2] Thus Pitt replied in fairly conciliatory tones on the subject of privateers, while defending the actions of prize courts and criticizing the 'exaggeration' of the Spanish memorials; but on the logwood and the fisheries he omitted to give any answer at all.[3]

Wall had admitted that the British 'in some shape or other' should be allowed to trade in the dyewoods they had 'been in possession of for near a century', but why as an earnest of good intentions had they failed to destroy 'the forts and establishments the British ministry allowed to be illegal'?[4] To this, Pitt merely regretted (3 July 1761) that Spain still harped on this 'capital point of difficulty . . . not admissable on the part of his Majesty'. By 28 July he was complaining of the 'enormity and extreme offensiveness' of now having Anglo-Spanish disputes made part of *French* demands: it fell little short of 'a declaration of war in reversion . . . held out *in terrorem* on the part of Spain'.[5]

Within three weeks of this the old Bourbon Family Compact was finally reactivated. France was not to make peace until Spanish grievances were remedied; and if peace were not concluded by 1 May 1762 Spain was to declare war on Britain.

Hans Stanley agreed with Choiseul and the French that the haughty

287

and dictatorial style of Pitt's later diplomatic communications was *'peu fait pour la négociation'*. Hardwicke too: 'I remember Sir Robert Walpole used to say', he wrote, 'that two nations might be writ into a war; and so I think they may be into perpetuating a war'. And inside the cabinet also, said Hardwicke, 'Mr Pitt's way of talking is such as I believe was never before known between fellow-ministers in the same service'. The month of August saw 'much altercation'. That Pitt was at this time 'a good deal out of order with a bilious complaint' did nothing to decrease his table-thumping and general belligerence. 'The Duke of Bedford stood by us very manfully', reported Hardwicke, 'and my Lord President [Granville] with much firmness, tho' very improperly interrupted'; 'we rid out the tempest'. At one point, however, Newcastle, Devonshire, and Bedford were so affronted by Pitt's violent behaviour that they agreed to absent themselves for a time in protest.[6]

'Is this country to wage eternal war', demanded Hardwicke, 'upon wild imaginary schemes of conquest?'[7] At least with him and with Newcastle Pitt knew where he stood. With Bute it was not so clear, for Bute was very anxious not to be seen as conceding too much to France or Spain, much as he wished in general for peace. At one point he seemed to be agreeing with Pitt that a war with Spain would soon pay for itself in prizes, but about the middle of August he veered decisively towards the arguments of the peace party. Britain's trade with neutral Spain had indeed been lucrative, and it must certainly be lost in a war. Newcastle at this time was significantly finding some London financiers nervous of providing yet more support for government loans if Spain was now to join the war – stirrings in the City which Bussy did not fail to report to Choiseul.[8]

There is nothing to show that Pitt knew yet of any firm Franco-Spanish military engagements, but he had now come to regard war with Spain as not only inevitable but desirable. He repented the conditional concessions to France that he had acquiesced in under colleagues' pressure, particularly in the matter of the fisheries. Better an expanded war, which he was convinced the country could afford and would profit from, than an imperfect compromising peace, or the existing situation where Spain was waging 'the worst species of war' on France's behalf; 'she covers her trade, lends her money, and abets her in negociation'. Better to grasp at once the nettle and

19. Field-Marshal Lord Amherst, by Gainsborough

20. Colonel Isaac Barré, by G. Stuart

21. George III in 1767, by Allan Ramsay

the initiative. Spain, in any case, was weak. What was to be feared from a nation which disposed of a revenue of less than five millions a year ?[9]

If he could not convince his fellow ministers and take them along with him he was now resolved to quit. Many months earlier he had foreseen that treaty negotiations might present more problems for him than the war itself; 'I wish', he had said, 'I could leave off at the war'. Even before these last disagreements over Spain, he had been speaking, to colleagues and to the King too, of his wish to retire. It was an oft-heard tale, but now some of them began to take it more seriously than before. Hardwicke for one had always prophesied that the triumphant war minister would find the descent from glory a difficult manoeuvre. As Dodington had put it, 'He could never never make such a peace as he had taught the nation to expect'. 'He must push things so desperately', Soame Jenyns considered, 'that no one could follow him, and then would make that an excuse for quitting'.[10]

Even if it were true, as it probably was, that a part of him was already looking for such an excuse, he made great efforts during the third week of September to persuade his colleagues to strike first against Spain, before the treasure convoy could make port. He had no private confirmation of Spanish commitment to declare war, but more than enough straws to show which way the wind was blowing – including an intercepted letter from Fuentes to Grimaldi, speaking of the need to *hold back* until the *flota*'s safe arrival at Cadiz.

Admiral Keppel was then cruising off Cape Finisterre with a fleet of some sixty sail, including twenty-eight of the line; he would have the treasure fleet at his mercy if only sanction could be given for the order to attack. Pitt argued his case earnestly in cabinet meetings between 15 and 21 September, and hoped for support from his two principal technical advisers, Anson and Ligonier. Neither backed him. Anson looked at Spain's total of forty ships of the line and thought them too many for comfort; Ligonier at a Spanish army of 70,000-75,000 men, 'valorous, orderly, and well-disciplined'. But war was coming in any event, Pitt argued; the risk attendant on immediate British aggression must be infinitely smaller than the risk of waiting.[11] He did not convince. Only Temple sided with him. The rest still favoured precautionary but less drastic action – further naval reinforcement for the West Indies and the Mediterranean squadrons; 3000 more troops for the West Indies; an offer to give up Honduras logwood establishments; and dispatch of fresh instructions to Lord Bristol to demand specific reassurances from Madrid – though, as Newcastle saw, an unsatisfactory reply to this last would inevitably give 'Mr Pitt great handle against us'. Hardwicke reckoned Pitt's proposal for immediate war 'precipitate, rash, and dangerous'.[12] The King wrote to Bute of 'Mr Pitt's black scheme', and thanked Heaven that Bute knew its author so well:

> That being the case his venome is not to be fear'd; were any of the other ministers as spirited as you are my dearest friend, I would say let that mad Pitt be dismissed, but as matters are very different from that we must get rid of him in a happier minute than the present one.[13]

Pitt and Temple, outvoted in cabinet, on 21 September presented their case in writing to the King, who 'declined accepting it'. Their advice was that he should immediately withdraw his ambassador from Madrid, and 'take forthwith such necessary and timely measures' as God had put in his hands.[14] It seems that by the time the cabinet met that day Pitt must have already made up his mind upon resignation, for he retracted his earlier acquiescence in the concessions made to Choiseul and declared he was

> determined *now* to abide by his own opinion. He spoke very long, very well, very determined [Newcastle reported] but with great politeness and candour. His brother-in-law was the very reverse. He spoke very long indeed, very pompous, very passionate, very ill-bred but very determined, and shewed plainly that their party was taken to quit, or at least to have no share of any measure but their own.[15]

At the cabinet meeting on 2 October – to be his last for nearly five years – Pitt adduced evidence of a further intercepted letter, this time from Grimaldi to Fuentes[16] (though what it contained still fell short of positively proving Spain's commitment to war) and then proceeded to a sort of apologia for his political career and conduct; declared he would be responsible for nothing he did not 'guide' (other versions have the verb as 'direct'); and ended by wishing success to those who would be carrying on the King's business in future. Lord President

Granville replied with 'a speech of compliment',* whereupon Pitt finally thanked 'the old ministers for their civility to him, seeming by that [Charles Jenkinson thought] particularly to except Lord B[ute]'.[17]

Pitt formally resigned on 5 October, Temple on the 9th, and James Grenville on the 12th. Two of the brothers-in-law thus gave prompt evidence of their family solidarity. The third, however, saw no cause for self-immolation. George Grenville had long been drifting resentfully away from Pitt. There had been a petering-out of the letters that used to flow freely and fraternally between Hayes and Wotton (where however Hester was still a regular summer visitor), with their 'affectionate compliments to Mrs Grenville' or to Wotton's own bosky charms, and with benevolent wishes for the progress of estate plantations or the health of the children – though recently he had written in sympathy upon the death of one of these. Grenville was by this time much less Pitt's dear brother-in-law than Lord Bute's 'dear George, with great affection'.[18] He now turned to warm himself before the rising sun, and only narrowly missed becoming Pitt's successor as Secretary, a post which went to another of his brothers-in-law, Lord Egremont. Grenville, having turned down an invitation to become Speaker, accepted Leadership of the Commons (together with his old office) and a cabinet place. James Grenville, who was richly compensated for his loss of office from Temple's horn of plenty, thought his brother George's conduct 'base'; Temple, when George next met him and asked him how he did, turned his back;[19] while henceforth for the next seven years Pitt was to view him as a political enemy.

In his account in the *Annual Register* of the great minister's surrender of the seals of office to the young king, Edmund Burke denied any attempt to add 'colouring to so exquisitely affecting a picture'. His narrative is broadly corroborated from another source close to Bute, but of course Burke could hardly have known of the extent of George III's relief at being rid of this 'mad Pitt' and his 'venom', and his version of the encounter depicts an ironical reversal of roles, with the still somewhat callow George the convincing actor, and the experienced

* Newcastle's account, Yorke, *Hardwicke*, iii. 280. It was the inventive pen of Burke (reporting for the 1761 *Annual Register*, p. 44) which first presented this polite tribute as an acidly hostile rebuke, as it has commonly and spuriously figured since.

actor Pitt betrayed by his complex and never quite governable emotions:

> His majesty expressed his concern for the loss of so able a servant, and . . . made him a most gracious and unlimited offer of any rewards in the power of the crown to bestow . . . Mr Pitt was sensibly touched with the grandeur and condescension of this proceeding. 'I confess, Sir, I had but too much reason to expect your majesty's displeasure. I did not come prepared for this exceeding goodness. Pardon me, Sir, – it overpowers, it oppresses me'. He burst into tears.[20]

Through Bute, the King offered Pitt upon his departure the non-resident governorship of Canada with £5000 a year, which 'would convey to all the world his Majesty's intentions of never parting with that great and important conquest'; or, if Pitt should prefer, Chancellorship of the Duchy of Lancaster with a like salary. Or perhaps, Bute suggested, Pitt would care to make a suggestion of his own?

By every accepted standard of the day Pitt had earned his golden handshake ten times over. And although he had garnered a great popular reputation as the man who forwent the perquisites of office – whom money could not buy – he was in fact very far from under-valuing either honours or riches. He now begged, therefore, in his most verbose vein of self-abasing grandiloquence, for 'those dearer than myself' to be 'comprehended in that monument of royal approbation and goodness with which his Majesty shall condescend to distinguish me'. Any such mark of approbation to his 'unmeritorious' self would be his 'comfort and glory'.[21]

The outcome was that to Hester and to her issue went a barony, for which the title of Chatham was chosen, and to Pitt an annuity of £3000, to be tenable upon his death by Hester, or upon hers by their eldest son John. Pitt prepared to give up his house in St James's Square, and advertised his carriage horses for sale.

Bute had been left in no doubt that it was he above all others who was being held responsible, especially in the City of London, for the resignation of the *darling minister*. He therefore caused details of the barony and pension to be immediately published in the *Gazette* (a step without precedent) rightly calculating that thereby swift damage would be done to Pitt's reputation for disinterestedness. Succeeding

Pitt was going to be 'difficult and dangerous work', as he said to Dodington; it might become rather easier if the incorruptible hero could be shown to be as frail as the next man.

'I am glad you like the *Gazette*', Hardwicke wrote to his son; 'I hear it operates'. And Bedford congratulated Newcastle on the way news of the resignation had been handled; he was 'truly happy' that this looked as if it must 'cut up all Mr Pitt's ill-gotten popularity'.[22]

It did indeed for a time look so. From the announcement in the *Gazette*, artfully set near a report from Spain indicating pacific intentions in Madrid, it appeared, as it was intended to appear, that Pitt had been bought out. Sir Francis Delaval, M.P., observed that Pitt must be a fool; if he had gone to the City and told them he had a poor wife and children unprovided for and opened a subscription, he would have got half a million, not just £3000 a year.[23] As it was, the City seemed ready to tear him to pieces. He became the victim of what the not generally sympathetic Burke called 'a torrent of low and illiberal abuse'. Hack pamphleteers, some of them creatures of Bute or Fox, were soon venomously in print with *The Patriot Unmasked*, *The Right Honourable Annuitant Unmasked*, and other such instant butchery. Some of Pitt's sincerest champions were shaken. Thomas Gray was swearing 'the very night it happen'd . . . that it was a damn'd lie and never could be'. Alas, he cried, for that 'foolishest of great men, that sold his inestimable diamond for a paltry peerage and a pension'.[24] Horace Walpole was as incredulous and no less shocked. It was 'pitiful, wondrous pitiful'; virtue, it seemed, was an errant strumpet, 'and loves diamonds as well as my Lady Harrington, and is as fond of a coronet as my Lord Melcombe [Dodington]'. 'Don't think me changed lightly about Mr Pitt – nobody admired him more'; but when his disinterestedness could not resist a pension, 'he changed, not I'.[25]

Ann Pitt had in her hands, though she never actually used it, a subtler and indeed juster criticism of her brother. When towards the end of 1760 she had written to tell him that she had been fortunate enough to be at last granted a pension, on the Irish list, through the recommendation of Bute,[26] Pitt had sent back an unpleasantly sarcastic little letter, hoping that she would be happy to be under obligation solely to Lord Bute, and congratulating her on the increase in her income, 'so agreeable to your turn of life, whatever repugnancy I find, at the same time, to see my name placed on the pensions of

Ireland'. He did not doubt she would take care to have it understood that he was 'unmixt in the whole transaction'. To the barely suppressed wrath in this note Ann had returned a soft answer. But now she received a rather formal little communication from Hester, with details of the barony and pension granted 'in consideration of Mr Pitt's services. We do not doubt', Hester added, 'of the share you will take in these gracious marks of his Majesty's approbation and goodness'. It was only the persuasion of her friends that held Ann back from returning to Pitt his own note of the previous year suitably amended. As it was, the story of what she had proposed to do gained sufficient circulation to draw its own small quantity of blood.[27]

Pitt's concern at hostile reaction in the City, and indeed beyond, quickly caused him to take his pen in self-justification. In a letter printed in the *Public Ledger* of 17 October, he presented the facts concerning his resignation and its causes, which had been 'grossly misrepresented'; declared, with truth, that the rewards from the King had been 'unsolicited' (though he would hardly have expected anyone to agree that they were also, as he claimed, 'unmerited'); and recorded that he would 'ever be proud to have received them from the best of sovereigns'.[28]

The letter took prompt effect. As Burke wrote and many more considered on maturer reflection, it was 'a shame' that any defence should have been necessary: it was impossible that the King could let the services of such a minister go unrequited. The pension was modest, measured against either that granted to lesser men or the magnitude of his achievement. He had revived the military genius of the British people: 'no man was ever better fitted to be the minister in a great and powerful nation'.[29]

The City soon turned about. Mr Pitt was allowed to be a hero after all, and the Common Council registered its gratitude to him by 109 votes to 15. To the annual banquet of the Lord Mayor, which the King and his new young queen would be attending, and of course members of the cabinet, and indeed anybody who was anybody, Pitt was naturally also invited. At first he contemplated staying away, but was subsequently persuaded by Beckford to attend – 'as he always declared, both then and after, against his better judgement'.[30] As things turned out, first thoughts would certainly have proved wisest. The banquet became less a social occasion than a political demonstration in favour of Pitt and against Bute, and thus by implication against the King also.

Bute entirely lacked popular support; he was deeply suspect, in the first place as king's favourite (and, as scandal inventively alleged, the Dowager Princess's lover too); second, as interloping Scotsman (the English were disposed to think all Scots thieves or barbarians); and now as the man held responsible for Pitt's overthrow. In the streets he went in physical danger; on the occasion of his banquet the coach bearing Barrington and himself was set upon by a mob and he escaped hurt only by his prudent foresight in hiring a bodyguard of 'butchers and bruisers' led by 'George Stephenson, the one-eyed fighting coachman', to see him safely to Guildhall. Beckford had ensured a markedly friendlier reception for Pitt and Temple – who drove to the City together – by visiting public-houses overnight and appointing cheer-leaders to stand at various points along their route, and by himself raising the shout for his hero and for Temple as they entered the hall.[31]

> To *them* [wrote Walpole] all acclamations were addressed; and the distinctions paid in the Guildhall to Mr Pitt, to the total neglect of the King, bestowed all the honour of the triumph on the former . . . The ambition of drawing to himself the homage of the people was not modest. To offer himself as an incentive to civil tumult, and to how dangerous consequences he could not tell, was not a symptom of very innocent intentions.[32]

Of course his political rivals had no faith whatever in the intentions of such an old hand at the parliamentary game, though Hardwicke was gratified to find him proposing to give no disturbance to ministers unless they should misrepresent his motives for resigning.[33] When parliament reassembled, his speeches did prove temperate and un-provocative, though spirited enough in defence of his policies. The fireworks were provided by the farouche glare-eyed newcomer Barré, playing in the Commons a parallel role to that which Stephenson the one-eyed coachman had recently been playing in the London streets – that of Bute's bruiser-in-chief. Before a generally silent House Barré launched two confidently brutal onslaughts upon 'the profligate minister who had thrust himself into power on the shoulders of the mob'; who stood at the dispatch table 'turning up his eyes to heaven that witnessed his perjuries' and laying upon the table 'that sacrilegious hand that had been employed in tearing out the bowels of his mother-country'. The matter was savage and abusive, the manner and diction classically elegant; it was an exceptional début. Not rising to reply, Pitt merely leaned across to ask Beckford, 'pretty loud', how far 'the scalping Indians cast their tomahawks'; but when Barré went on to accuse him of lacking trust in the King, Pitt did spring up to a point of order, and significantly it was his old enemy Fox who then in Walpole's phrase *hallooed* Barré on. When this 'bravo' of Bute's had resumed his seat and was observed to be eating a biscuit, a member expressed surprise: surely such a one fed on nothing but raw flesh?[34]

When Pitt spoke, he was 'modest, humble, stout, sublime, and pathetic, all in their turns ... in manner and language not to be equalled', judged Sackville; 'Garrick never acted better'.[35] He defended his policy towards Spain; paid compliments to his late colleagues; declared that any minister who surrendered the fisheries would one day be impeached. And whoever should cede to Spain 'but a cockboat ceded all'. If Spain herself should begin hostilities, it would be a case of *felo de se*.[36] As for the German war – upon which Barré had accused him, not altogether unfairly, of changing colour like the chameleon – he had, so he averred,

> been robbed of his sleep for many days and now should be robbed of his honour, if our troops were recalled from Germany ... England was equal to both wars, the American and the German, and if it continued, nothing but conquest would follow – all owing to the German war. If we abandoned our allies, God would abandon us. When we had spent a hundred millions, should we throw away the fruit, rather than spend the twelve more? Let a man so narrow-minded stand behind a counter, and not govern a kingdom. *America had been conquered in Germany.*[37]

It was a reflection on the extent to which family associations had gone sour that in the Commons the task of rebutting this line of argument fell largely upon George Grenville, though he had, as Walpole could not resist pointing out, 'during the last reign avowedly or silently supported every one of Pitt's expensive German measures'.[38] Neither Grenville, however, nor his chief, Bute, was just yet proposing to desert Frederick the Great. Bute remained nervous of Pitt – more especially if he should re-combine, as Bute feared, with the Newcastle Whigs – and he tried by feeding Grenville's vanity with exaggerated praises, to improve his morale in the task of standing up to his redoubtable brother-in-law: 'Millions of congratulations', he sent him, 'upon your very great, very able, and manly performance: this will do, my dear friend, and shows you to the world in the light I want'.[39] Grenville was very far from lacking ambition, but he suffered – and continued to suffer, right into his premiership later – from what he considered to be a 'want of marks of credit and power'. It was the eldest brother, Temple, who bore the family rank and wealth, and the brother-in-law Pitt who carried all the charisma and fame; and Grenville at this juncture added to his consciousness of the enmity of the rest of the family a jealous fear of the superior parliamentary talent of his colleague Fox. Pitt treated him with aloofness – Walpole thought 'with contempt' – but, so far, refrained from particular attack.[40]

Bute had no intention of being thought lily-livered by comparison with Pitt, and his brusque diplomacy in demanding from Spain full details of her engagements to France had the effect of precipitating hostilities. On her side Spain, her treasure fleet safely in port, now showed a belligerent confidence which events were quickly to prove ill-grounded. War was declared in the first week of the new year. Before leaving London, her recalled ambassador Fuentes presented a memorial paying Pitt the highly unusual distinction of arraigning him by name.[41]

Bute and Grenville now pressed inside the cabinet for withdrawing all the troops from Germany, Bute using against Newcastle the Duke's own line of argument, that 'we could not carry on *the whole war* at this immense expence another year' – while Newcastle, as ever, was vowing to Hardwicke that he could not, *would not*, go on any longer 'without original concert, confidence, and communication', and bemoaned the prospect of 'remaining in the Treasury to be baited and perhaps overruled by Mr Grenville'.[42]

Newcastle now came to reflect that perhaps he had been better treated even under Pitt; and in any case, now that the war was to be extended, would they not need Pitt back, 'with all his faults'? 'I know nobody', he admitted, 'who can plan, or push the execution of any plan agreed upon, in the manner Mr Pitt did'. And he pointedly reminded Bute that people said that we had worked Mr Pitt out, and were now following his extravagant measures; (meaning the Continent measures;) and that we had better have Mr Pitt again. And, my Lord, [Newcastle continued] I will tell your Lordship what *they say*, that Mr Pitt went out because we would not declare war against Spain; and as soon as he was out, we did the same thing; and, that being the case, Mr Pitt would carry on his own measures better than anybody.[44]

Hostilities with Spain, while generally popular, were not greeted with quite the chauvinistic excitement that had briefly afflicted the public in the previous Spanish war of 1739. By this time there had been a fill of patriotic triumphs; the land tax would now have to stay up at four shillings in the pound, and the national debt would soar higher than ever. The price of Newcastle's latest loan fell four points in the City when news of war came. Still, there were many for whom the new situation offered enticing prospects; there was, for instance, a prompt revival of the boom in the privateering business.

Although it would have been too much to expect Pitt in the Commons altogether to refrain from pointing out the advantage sacrificed by his late colleagues' failure to adopt his advice, there was nevertheless no self-righteous crowing; 'nothing could be more cool and artful'. Pitt even praised ministers for their *caution* towards Madrid, and asked it to be believed that for five years past he too had strained every endeavour to conciliate the court of Spain. But now that war was come, the nation was equal to its tasks; the government must be trusted; there must be unanimity: 'The moment was come when every man ought to *show himself* for the whole. I do . . . cruelly as I have been treated in pamphlets and libels . . . Forget everything but the public! – for the public I forget both my wrongs and my infirmities'.[45]

For the French the colonial war continued to run badly. In February 1762 they lost Martinique to the combined forces of Rodney and Monckton. St Lucia and Grenada soon followed; and justifiably enough the British public agreed to put down these continuing victories to Pitt's account. As Walpole sang light-heartedly away to George Montagu, the British had managed to 'subdue the globe in three campaigns', whereas the snail's-pace Romans had been three centuries conquering the smaller world of antiquity:

Why, the single eloquence of Mr Pitt, like an annihilated star, can shine many months after it has set. I tell you, it has conquered Martinico. If you will not believe me, read the *Gazette*; read Monckton's letter; there is more martial spirit in it than in half Thucydides, and in all the *Grand Cyrus*. Do you think Demosthenes or Themistocles ever raised the Grecian stocks two per cent in four-and-twenty hours? I shall burn all my Greek and Latin books; they are histories of little people.[46]

Bute and George III, while not averse to presiding over a victory or two, had no ambition to emulate the conquests of Rome. The King wanted to 'knock the German war on the head' immediately – and if that were to make Newcastle resign, 'what if he does?'[47] Bute was using the cost of the Spanish war as an argument for ending the Prussian subsidy and was pressing Frederick to make peace with Austria, even at the price of considerable sacrifices. But Frederick, so often taken to the precipice's brink, had just been snatched back once again from destruction, this time by the purest luck. The Tsarina Elizabeth having died, her half-witted Prussophile successor Peter, in the short time that he had before he was assassinated on the orders of his wife Catherine (the Great to be) reversed previous policies, withdrew from the war, and enabled Prussia to concentrate her attentions against the Austrians and the French. This development, in Pitt's view so fortunate, quite dismayed Bute, who made clear to the Russian ambassador that 'it was not the intention of England to make eternal war to please the King of Prussia' – words which were not slow in carrying via St Petersburg to an incensed Frederick in Berlin.[48] For him Pitt's fall had of course been a blow. He many times tried to convince himself, and those round him, that it was only Bute and Bedford and their shambling crew who wished to betray him. 'The [British] nation with the Chevalier Pitt at its head' would have more sense than to threaten him with financial sanctions. But when through ambassador Knyphausen he approached Pitt directly, Pitt could only advise him that Bute's power with the King was so complete that nothing was to be hoped for there.[49] Relations between London and Berlin were not improved at this time by Frederick's habit of giving his frankest opinions their head in letters to Knyphausen, 'without considering', as Hardwicke observed, 'that we can peep into letters and know how to decypher'. One such peep disclosed that Frederick thought Bute, Bedford, and the rest of them deserved to be sent '*à la petite maison*' – to Bedlam.[50]

It was Russia's retirement from the war that loosened the log-jam on the path towards peace. At last Maria Theresa's tenacity showed signs of weakening; the hope of humiliating Frederick and regaining Silesia faded. Choiseul, although he again prepared an elaborate plan for the invasion of Britain, faced poor prospects in Germany and indicated his readiness to resume the peace negotiations broken off during Pitt's last months in power. Spain was to be persuaded to settle her quarrels with Britain by compromise.

While British land and sea forces prepared to attack Havana in the west and Manila in the east, the Spaniards had invaded the territory of Britain's ally Portugal, and in the Commons Grenville moved for a £1 million subsidy to be earmarked for her assistance. Pitt spoke up for Portugal: 'If you, as a maritime power, cannot protect Portugal, Genoa will next be shut against you, and then the ports of Sardinia. What? ports shut against the first maritime power in the world!' But he spoke too for Prussia, and by implication for Newcastle against Bute: 'he wished the vote of credit had been greater, and knew the Duke of Newcastle wished so too'.[51] He did not think it proper, he observed engagingly, to oppose the King's ministers, but if some other member would propose continuing the Prussian subsidy he would support him.

Ever-suffering and newly diminished, Newcastle – who was, after all, still First Lord of the Treasury – had, in cabinet, actually found himself in the unaccustomed position of advocating greater expenditure, two millions to be divided between Portugal and Prussia; but Bute and Grenville roughly demonstrated to him the new limitations on his power, going behind his back to one of the Treasury Secretaries to get statistics for use against him.[52] They were in no way sorry, at the end of May, to see the Duke treat this indignity as the last straw and resign, after forty years of continuous office. He rejected the Crown's proffered sweetener of a pension to reward his long and honourable service. Thus within eight months Newcastle followed Pitt; Bute, with the King's strong backing, had succeeded in ousting the two chief ministers who for four and a half years had sustained 'the great coalition', that always precarious but wonderfully successful contrivance. Effectively prime minister already, this much-resented court politician whom the King still saw as the sole repository of prudent and prescient statesmanship – 'void of the D-of N-'s dirty arts' – now became First Lord of the Treasury, triumphantly at the summit of his greasy pole, yet always apprehensive of the dangers of a slippery descent.

During the summer of 1762, while Colonel Draper's and Admiral Cornish's expedition made sail for the Philippines, and the Earl of Albemarle and Admiral Pocock prepared the assault on Cuba, the British and French negotiated strenuously to find a mutually acceptable peace – Choiseul finding himself much relieved to be treating with 'Mylords Bute and Egremont' in place of Pitt. '*Quant à moi*', he told the Sardinian ambassador, '*j'aimerois mieux aller ramer aux galères que d'avoir rien de pacifique à démêler avec Mr Pitt*'.[53] By September the two governments were ready for exchanging plenipotentiaries to conduct the final stages of bargaining, in which Britain's representative was 'the little Duke', Bedford, chief among the cabinet doves. 'The old Duke', Newcastle, out of power, a limpet bereft of its rock, made a succession of rather inchoate moves towards creating an opposition to fight Bute, but these were motivated less by any real differences over policy than by the simple and very natural desire to re-establish the natural order of Whig supremacy, and, as he put it, 'in a proper way, and as a gentleman, to relieve the publick and my friends from the haughtiness and power of an absolute Scotch Minister'.[54] The weakness of his situation was that upon the one essential issue, of peace or war, he was *plus royaliste que le roi*. Newcastle was the very man who had been preaching peace for years. It was only Pitt – or rather, as Fox contemptuously put it, Pitt and his 'mob', meaning in particular Beckford and his followers in the City of London* and their 'patriot' counterparts among the trading classes of the provincial cities – who stood unequivocally for a different *policy*: either a Carthaginian peace or, failing that, all-out war and destruction to the Bourbons, French and Spanish alike.

---

* It was exactly at this point that Beckford was elected Lord Mayor, in itself a piece of snook-cocking at Bute and a gesture of support for Pitt. Beckford counted Pitt as personal friend as well as public ally; his baby son William, future author of *Vathek* and builder of the monster 'folly' at Fonthill, was already honoured by having Pitt for a godfather.

Newcastle, in his attempts to assemble an opposition, approached the King's uncle, Cumberland, who was inclined to encourage him, hating Bute as he did; and Cumberland was eventually persuaded to sound out possibilities in a conference with Pitt. This lasted four hours but produced nothing, Pitt 'talking in his usual vague and inconclusive manner'[55] and declaring that he must 'have regard for the Tories' who had acted with him, but apparently standing out for the removal of Bute and insisting on total rejection of the sort of peace Bedford was likely to bring back from Paris. As Newcastle sadly reflected, the only opposition of which Pitt could be a member would be one whose views and policies he dictated.

CHAPTER SEVENTEEN

———◆◆◆———

The Peace of Paris and General Warrants

'Pray God the news of the surrender of the Havannah may come time enough to save the fishery', wrote Temple in September to his protégé John Wilkes. The fall of this vital port and fortress, king-pin of Spanish strategy and trade activity in the Caribbean, had been expected for some time, but there had been frustrating delays, and heavy losses among the attacking forces from disease. At the very least it was assumed that news of its capture – arriving finally at the end of September, with accounts of fourteen Spanish ships of the line taken, and stores and treasure worth altogether £3 millions – must mean that some substantial *quid pro quo* would have to be insisted upon if Havana itself were to be restored at the peace. Already inside the cabinet Grenville and Egremont were expressing exasperation at the apparent readiness of Bute and Bedford to surrender overmuch; in particular Grenville fought hard (but unsuccessfully) for the retention of St Lucia in the Windward Islands, with its excellent harbour and commanding naval position. For Bute and Bedford the capture of Havana was almost more embarrassing than gratifying. It had 'turned the heads of the wisest men and those most inclined to peace', wrote Bute. Inevitably it brought further delay, and the need for still further negotiation; but of course it had to be made use of; Florida ought to be demanded in exchange, or perhaps Puerto Rico, and the French terms 'ought to be screwed up higher'.[1] Bute, already as painfully conscious of hostile popular opinion as Newcastle had been after the national misadventures of 1756, and similarly afraid of possible impeachment – he even hinted at a threat of 'scaffolds' – dared not invite the risk of allowing Pitt a second time to storm the Closet and save the nation. Yet the dangers of this in reality were slight. Even a relatively 'bad' peace could hardly be anything but triumphant in absolute terms.

In the end, for the return of Havana Bedford was able to secure the promise of Florida, an exchange which Pitt was shortly to denounce. Lord Mayor Beckford apparently thought Florida 'as barren as Bagshot Heath'; and Pitt would soon be telling the Commons that it was

> no compensation for the Havannah; the Havannah was an important conquest. He had designed to make it, and would have done it some months earlier, had he been permitted to execute his own plans. From the moment the Havannah was taken, all the Spanish treasures and riches in America lay at our mercy . . . It was no equivalent.[2]

On the fisheries, which Pitt held to be the most capital of capital issues, Bute and Bedford were unable to make Choiseul budge. The Preliminaries of Peace, finally agreed at Fontainebleau at the beginning of November 1762, confirmed to the French the right to fish and cure fish along the coasts of Nova Scotia and parts of Newfoundland (as agreed half a century earlier at Utrecht); it also allowed them fishing rights outside a nine-mile territorial limit in the Gulf of St Lawrence and a forty-five mile limit off Cape Breton Island. Moreover, France was to have the islands of St Pierre and Miquelon, off Newfoundland, as havens to which her vessels could repair in those inhospitable seas.

For Pitt, this was betrayal. When, under pressure from colleagues, he had given ground on the fishery question in the summer of 1761, he had very soon recanted, and the following November had told the Commons that if peace negotiations were to be resumed 'we should make the exclusive fishery in the Gulf a *sine qua non*'.[3] Now, a year later, he roundly claimed that when in office he had been overruled by the 'enemy' within the gates. The fishing rights which Britain was now agreeing merely to share would enable France to re-establish and re-man her navy. Consequently, instead of a secure peace they might now look forward only to a ten-years' truce. Victory was to be thrown away.

It was much the same kind of argument that the French were to use in the peacemaking of 1919. Germany, argued Clemenceau, must be left without the opportunity ever to rebuild her military potential.

France, Pitt considered, must be stripped of the prospect of ever again challenging Britain's naval and commercial supremacy. Many blamed the rise of Nazi Germany upon the vindictiveness of the Treaty of Versailles; many Frenchmen thought its moderation excessive. Pitt was inevitably to see the revival of France's navy and the renewed French challenge as justifying all his strictures upon Bute and Bedford. But the counter-view argued most explicitly by Bedford – it was not radically different from Hardwicke's also or Newcastle's – did not lose its validity. A power of France's size and weight would not remain long in humiliation, and could not indefinitely be held down. A punitive peace could not fail to produce the will to be revenged; and if Britain were to look for a kind of hegemony in Europe maintained by her naval and financial strength, what was to prevent France building against her a coalition of resentful continental states? As for the American colonies, Bedford in at least one respect saw further ahead than Pitt. It was all very well chasing French power altogether from North America, but what if the very fear of it had hitherto been the strongest of motives for maintaining colonial respect for British authority?

Once again that autumn Pitt was ill, confined down at Hayes to his bed or his 'great chair'. A severe cold had pulled him down in October. Gout followed, with an attendant variety of ailments, which one may fairly suppose to have been aggravated by his frustration and nervous irritability. At such times in his life both eating and sleeping became problems. He could not abide the noise of his children near him. His swollen hand not allowing him to write, he had to rely on the ever-ministering Hester to be his amanuensis. Walking was not possible without crutches. Merely standing up presented painful difficulty. In this condition he brooded on the wanton abandonment, as he chose to see it, by Bute's government of the great reward they had only to stretch out their hands a little further to grasp, the trophy *his* work had brought within reach.

It was not a view of the proposed treaty held by most. True, there had been criticism of Bedford's excessive pliability; even the King, avid for peace, was complaining in October to Bute that 'the D. of Bedford seems ready to yield every thing'.[4] Bute himself came under fire not only for his surrender upon the fishery but for his apparent readiness to desert Frederick and abandon rich West Indian prizes –

Guadeloupe and Martinique, as well as St Lucia and two of the smaller islands. In any case, Bute was so unpopular that nothing he did at this time was likely to escape censure. 'I am satisfy'd', wrote Fox, 'better or worse terms would neither lessen or increase it'. The clamour against Bute was directed 'against the man, not the measure'.[5] But when the full settlement was looked at, most men recognized British gains as enormous: Canada, with Nova Scotia, and Cape Breton Island; all French and Spanish American lands lying east of the Mississippi, with the single exception of the town and island of New Orleans; in the West Indies, Grenada and the Grenadines, Tobago, St Vincent, and Dominica; in Central America, the right to cut and trade in the Honduras logwood, though Britain once again undertook to demolish the fortifications; in West Africa, Senegal, though Goree was returned to France; in India, the confirmation of all the British gains made since the end of 1748; in Europe, the recovery of Minorca in return for Belle Isle, as Pitt had always intended; the *restoration* of such of the territories and fortresses of Hanover, Hesse, and Brunswick as were still occupied by French troops, and the *evacuation* by them of Prussian territories – the latter however with no stipulation concerning restoration in pre-war condition.

The King, though still with reservations over Bedford's 'yielding', reckoned it all in all 'a noble peace . . . What thanks ought not to be given' to Bute for 'this great service to his country'.[6] If he had not sometimes been 'rough with his colleagues' it might never have come about. He and Bute had in October enlisted Fox to be 'rough' too, if necessary, with any parliamentary opposition to the proposed terms, but it did not look as if they would face serious trouble. Pitt, the likeliest source of it, was ill at Hayes, and it was thought he would not attend the debates. The position of Newcastle and his following was weak. They would naturally wish to challenge Bute and Fox; yet, as Fox himself put it,

> So many of the leaders on the other side are in their hearts for peace, have declared so, and the comparison between this and that which even Mr Pitt offer'd his consent to last year is so obvious, that they will be embarrass'd to let out all their fury against it.[7]

('I mean', he continued sourly, 'all but Mr Pitt, who like his mob is never embarrass'd by any degree of shame'.)

Hooligans – perhaps hired, but certainly not by Pitt – again assaulted Bute as he was being carried to the opening of parliament on 25 November; which made the King so fearful for the safety, and perhaps even the life, of his chief friend and support, that he suggested tentatively to him that he might consider trying to win Pitt back into the ministry, distasteful as they both found him. 'Put him in any situation', George wrote, 'I will consent to it' – anything to shelter Bute 'from what there is at present too much reason to fear'.[8]

It was obvious, however, that under such leadership Pitt was not to be gained. In any case Bute, worried equally by his own health and the unhealthiness of his public reputation, was privately screwing up his determination to retire from the hurly-burly as soon as peace was ratified. On 9 December he and Lord Mansfield in the Lords each spoke effectively in recommendation of the Preliminaries, against the opposition of Hardwicke and Newcastle's supporters. But it was the outcome in the Commons that was more keenly awaited. There, after Beckford and James Grenville had unsuccessfully attempted procedural manoeuvres of delay, hoping that perhaps Pitt might after all be well enough to attend in a few days' time, the main debate began punctually. It did not look as if Fox had even needed to prepare the ground among the 'doubtfuls' as he had been busy doing. The terms would go through easily enough; he forecast no more than sixty dividing upon Pitt's side.

But the day was not to be without its moment of surprise – or melodrama, or heroics, or pathos, or farce, according to members' varying judgement. Suddenly there was a commotion at the doors:

The House was alarmed by a shout from without! The doors opened, and at the head of a large acclaiming concourse was seen Mr Pitt, borne in the arms of his servants, who, setting him down within the bar, he crawled by the help of a crutch, and with the assistance of some few friends, to his seat; not without the sneers of some of Fox's party. In truth, there was a mixture of the very solemn and the theatric in this apparition. The moment was so well-timed, the importance of the man and his services, the languor of his emaciated countenance, and the study bestowed on his dress, were circumstances that struck solemnity into a patriot mind, and did a little furnish ridicule to the hardened and insensible. He was dressed in black velvet, his legs and thighs wrapped in flannel, his feet covered with buskins of black cloth, and his hands with thick gloves . . . having the appearance of a man determined to die in that cause and at that hour.[9]

After a short interposition on the procedural matter and two speeches from other members he rose to speak, though several times during the next three hours and twenty-five minutes he was obliged to ask the House's permission to continue seated. His usually strong and musical voice was so low and faint that members sitting, as Horace Walpole was, at some distance, could only half hear him. Walpole was one of those who sympathized with his condemnation of Bute's treaty terms and was not one of the majority who found him prolix that day and dull – yet he agreed that it was not an occasion on which Pitt's genius thundered. 'His health or his choice' – again Walpole suggests a conscious exploitation of his physical plight – 'had led him to present himself as a subject of affliction to his country, and his ungrateful country was not afflicted'. Some of his countrymen were indeed very little moved by the pathos of the situation:

> The groundlings cry alas! poor man!
> How ill he is! how pale! how wan!. . .
> At length he tries to rise, a hum
> Of approbation fills the room.
> He bows and tries again; but, no,
> He finds that standing will not do,
> And therefore to complete the farce
> The House cries, hear him on his a-se!. . .
> He may break off by grief o'ercome,
> And grow pathetically dumb!
> He next may *swoon* and shut his eyes;
> *A cordial, else the patriot dies!*
> The cordial comes, he takes it off,
> He lives, he lives, I hear him cough. . .[10]

The compiler of the *Parliamentary History*, nearer to the speaker than Walpole or with sharper ears, succeeded in gathering rather more of the substance of Pitt's words. He 'entirely approved' one thing only – the expulsion of French rule from North America – but these ministers could hardly take the credit for that. Unconvincingly, he claimed that they purchased back Minorca at 'fifty times more than it was worth' by surrendering 'the East Indies, the West Indies, and Africa', whereas Belle Isle alone would have sufficed. He defended the German war at tedious length, and condemned the government for deserting Frederick of Prussia, 'the most magnanimous ally this country has ever had'. (In fact, following the Preliminaries, Bute was busy successfully arranging with the French for the speedy evacuation of occupied Prussian lands.) First explaining how he had himself earlier been coerced by colleagues into accepting the cession of Guadeloupe, he demanded to know why ministers had proceeded with *his* plans for the capture of Martinique if they had been determined to give it back – and now Cuba and St Lucia as well. He accepted that he had agreed under pressure to surrender St Pierre conditionally, but now it was a matter of both St Pierre and Miquelon unconditionally. The fishery arrangements were a disaster. They, and the West Indian cessions, had restored to France the means of recovering her prodigious losses and again threatening Britain's maritime and commercial position. The peace terms had in them the seeds of future war.[11]

He was at pains to stress once again that, independent of party, he spoke for no one but himself. 'Seeming to bid adieu to politics, and to despair of his own health', he told members balanced uncomfortably between awe and boredom that 'he might never come to the House again'.[12] He apologized for his speech's length but, even so, was obliged to end before he had really finished, in physical distress. When Fox rose to reply, either from exhaustion or as a gesture of hostility Pitt left the Chamber, not returning for the division. He knew of course that there was not the slightest hope of winning it. The Preliminary Articles, with Fox up, cantered home by 319 votes to 65. Fox's forecast had not been far wrong. Nobody but Pitt had troubled to put up a fight. Members in general agreed with Bedford that Pitt was 'demanding the impossible'. However fascinated or impressed by the Pitt *phenomenon*, many of them found his arguments spurious; most found them unconvincing. As Wilkes had to admit, 'it was the damn'dest peace for the opposition that ever was made'.[13]

Later generations received this outright condemnation by Pitt of the Treaty of Paris (final terms were signed there in February 1763) with sympathetic approval. France did recover. The Bourbon powers did renew the attack. Was not Pitt justified therefore by the course of history? Was not all that he had said in that heroic fight against Bute's terms and his own physical incapacity borne out by future events – the need to face France again in the midst of the coming American revolt, and again from 1793? Did not the wiser Pitt seem to tower as a stricken giant over his opponents of 1762, corrupt Fox, wavering short-sighted Bute, weak-kneed Bedford? Simply as war minister, as planner and co-ordinator and energiser of campaigns, there can indeed be no doubt of Pitt's commanding genius; his political rivals and long-suffering colleagues were nearly all ready to confirm the popular judgement; however wryly or grudgingly, they accepted that Mr Pitt was nonpareil. But his political judgements concerning the Peace of Paris, his prescience, his 'vision' and its implications, are rather more questionable.

His attack on the peace presupposed that a few more islands taken, or fishing grounds denied, would somehow have removed from France the will to seek revenge or the capability to gain it; that a treaty more oppressive to the French in its colonial and maritime terms would somehow have converted what was still easily the strongest state on the continent of Europe to the status of a second-rate power. Even the collapse in twenty years' time of Britain's American empire, an apparent disaster so cataclysmic that even Pitt in his 1762 Cassandra mood did not predict it, and a severer blow than anything he could have inflicted on France at the close of the Seven Years War, had little effect upon Britain's unrelenting progress during the subsequent half-century towards world pre-eminence. It is hard therefore to believe that a power with France's resources, losing Guadeloupe or Martinique or Goree, would have been unable to find the means to rebuild her navy after 1763, or that depriving her of the Newfoundland fishery would have indefinitely immobilized it for lack of sailors. There was much factiousness in Pitt's determination to find no good in any part of the Peace unmixed with evil; yet even amid some transparent absurdities his criticism had its root in passionate conviction: a genuine fear and hatred of the might of France, a burning desire to humble the Bourbon powers, extinguish their empires, and put beyond challenge the world-wide wealth and authority of Britain. His own ambition had always been, and indeed remained despite his infirmities, to be 'the most illustrious man of the first country of

Europe';[14] and of course for a mid-Georgian Englishman Europe must mean the world. Some measure of the sincerity of Pitt's genuine disgust at the Treaty of Paris is surely to be found in his subsequent refusal to share office with those who had prominently supported it.

Then there is the rocket he fired at his own dutiful supporters the Corporation of Bath. These gentlemen, presided over by Pitt's friend and admirer Ralph Allen, in the spring of 1763 adopted an address to the King's Most Excellent Majesty begging leave to congratulate and humbly to thank him 'for an adequate and advantageous peace'. Pitt went out of his way to protest to Allen against *adequate*, an epithet 'repugnant to my unalterable opinion', and threatened to abjure the future electoral favour of 'gentlemen who are come to think so differently from me on matters of the highest importance to the national welfare'. He regretted, he said, embarrassing friends to whom he owed such obligations; and poor Allen was himself embarrassed at Pitt's taking 'so much offence' at a single word. Though he could not undo the resolution, Allen attempted placation; and Pitt, having been seen by the public to make his point, sent afterwards in an enclosure to *Mrs* Allen the reassurance that no incident would 'make the least change in the honour and love' he bore her husband.[15] With an earldom coming his way in a few years, Pitt as it happened was not to have any future need of the suffrage of Bath's leading citizens; and when Allen died in 1764 his unaltered warm feelings for Pitt, and awareness no doubt too of the chronic pressure on Pitt's income of his casually grandiose life-style, were shown in a thousand-pound legacy.

The probability of a much grander financial prize came within Pitt's sights by his fierce opposition to the Treaty of Paris and his onslaught upon the new tax on cider and perry introduced by Bute's Chancellor of the Exchequer, Dashwood, in the month after the Treaty was signed. Sir William Pynsent was an octogenarian landowner of Burton, near the village of Curry Rivel in Somerset (lying between Langport and Taunton), and a member of parliament worth some £40,000. Upon these two topics, the Treaty and the tax, he burned, it appears, with an indignation more violent even than Pitt's. Fifty years before, he had reacted as strongly against that other Tory peace, of Utrecht; and as a man of the West country he also reflected now the riotous popular resentment against the new impost on cider.

Pynsent's legatee was to have been Lord North's wife, his kinswoman: but North's vote for the cider tax put him beyond the pale for old Sir William, who had second thoughts and redirected his very substantial legacy towards the man who was not only the greatest statesman and patriot of his age, but also now champion of the cider presses of the western counties and defender of the farmer's right to be free from the incursions and exactions of the hated exciseman. Pynsent would live nearly two more years, long enough to have *third* thoughts about the destination of his fortune, especially when during 1764 Pitt seemed to have deserted parliament. But since the old man was as talkative as he was fiery, and had made no secret of the terms of his will, it looks most unlikely that Pitt could have been quite so surprised as he professed to be when on Pynsent's death at the beginning of 1765 he received intimation of his rich windfall. The suggestion,[16] however, that the public tiff with Ralph Allen and the Bath Corporation over the address to the King was staged only to keep on the right side of his prospective benefactor and the prospective milk and honey of the Burton estate is no doubt over-cynical.

It was the cider tax that brought Pitt again scathingly face to face in the Commons with George Grenville. Pitt, now according to Newcastle 'in the highest spirits', saw in this duty on cider and in the corruption of Fox's conduct of the Commons two bull points for successful opposition.[17] His assault on the cider tax, which imposed a duty of four shillings per hogshead on the grower and permitted inspection inside private dwellings, was based on the fact that this was an *excise* – still a word emotive and horrendous to the freeborn Englishman. There would be a dangerous precedent, Pitt proclaimed, in allowing excisemen into private houses. It was bad enough for a *trader* to have to submit to such intrusions, but they would be intolerable to those who 'by their birth, education, and profession [were] very distinct from the trader'.[18] An Englishman's home must remain his castle.

Grenville had earlier stung Pitt by criticizing the profusion of his expenditure in the war, and was explaining how the cider measure was necessary to avoid placing further burdens on the Sinking Fund. Where, if not here, were new taxes to be found? He wished gentlemen would tell him. He was entitled to say, 'Tell me where':

Repeating this question in his querulous, languid, fatiguing tone, Pitt, who sat opposite him, mimicking his accent aloud repeated these words of an old ditty – *Gentle Shepherd, tell me where*! and then rising abused Grenville bitterly. He had no sooner finished than Grenville started up in a transport of rage, and said, if gentlemen were to be treated with that contempt – Pitt was walking out of the House, but at that word turned round, made a sneering bow to Grenville, and departed.[19]

This was the condition of rancour into which relations between the two brothers-in-law had by now fallen. There is no evidence that it disturbed Pitt at all, though it was certainly unfortunate for Hester, the more so as Mrs Grenville had been the closest of her girlhood friends. But wherever the demands of politics carried William, Hester faithfully followed; she would never question the rightness of his judgements. As for the cider tax, neither Pitt's high-flown defence of private liberties, nor his contemptuous scoring off George Grenville had any immediate parliamentary consequence, whatever their effect on Sir William Pynsent. The bill went through. Three years later, however, Pitt did help to restore to the private citizen the right to close his door upon the excise man.

When Bute's ill health and failing nerve finally decided him to resign the premiership in April 1763 it was George Grenville who succeeded him, taking over the chief Treasury offices. At that juncture there was certainly no sign that Pitt was likely to retire from politics, as he was so often threatening, and 'practise philosophy in his village'. After a very bad autumn and early winter his health was at least moderately and temporarily mended, and his spirited part in the debates of March 1764 encouraged the Newcastle Whigs to hope for a working partnership with him. Following their defeat over the peace terms, they had been horribly mauled by Fox, acting as 'Commons minister' for Bute and the King. Scores of them and their dependants had been expelled from their 'places', and four of their greatest magnates, Devonshire, Grafton, Rockingham, and Newcastle himself, deprived of their office of lord lieutenant. The purge had been thorough and the rout apparently complete. In woe even acuter than usual, Newcastle saw that nobody could save him and his party but Pitt; 'nothing effectual can be done', he thought, 'unless Mr Pitt will take an effective part in it, and to a degree set himself at the head of it'.[20] Hardwicke was not quite so sure, for he had sons with a career to further – in particular his lawyer son Charles, whose sights were fixed on the Woolsack that his father had so long graced; and everyone knew that Pitt's intention was that the next Lord Chancellor should be not Yorke but Pratt, Chief Justice of the Court of Common Pleas and a devotee of Pitt. But the case of Hardwicke and the Yorkes was rather special. Many of the other leading Whigs began to court Pitt openly. On March 5, for instance, there was a grand dinner at Devonshire House where the most significant of the guests were Pitt and Temple. Yet with Pitt nothing was ever straightforward. He continued to hold the Whigs at arm's length and declared that he did not wish to seem 'to do the D. of Newcastle's business'; however, when Bute, just before resigning, also made overtures in Pitt's direction, Pitt rebuffed him by telling him that he was in fact committed to co-operation with Newcastle.

It was now that the parvenu gentleman journalist John Wilkes, the squint-eyed, sharp-witted member for Aylesbury (and hence protégé of Temple), suddenly enlivened domestic politics. Issue number 45 of his *North Briton*, attacking the Peace of Paris, his Majesty's ministers, and by implication the King himself, had provoked Grenville's recently formed government to resort to a *general* warrant for the arrest of the paper's authors, printers, and publishers. This gave the gadfly Wilkes an eagerly seized chance to pose as champion of civil liberties and the rights of the common citizen. The dissolute gambler and adventurer became at one impudent bound the alleged victim of arbitrary power and a popular hero.

During the summer months of 1763, while the London mob first learned to shout for 'Wilkes and Liberty', and Grenville's administration took on the contentious issue of general warrants, Pitt continued to thrash out with the Whigs the precise terms on which he would work with them. He much disapproved of the *North Briton*'s libels and scurrilities, but Wilkes's prosecution and imprisonment had brought to the fore the whole question of press liberty, whose inviolability Pitt would insist on. It was Pratt, Pitt's number-one lawyer, who in the Common Pleas had upheld Wilkes's parliamentary immunity from arrest, ordered his release, and pronounced general warrants illegal; and now Pitt, as the price of allowing the Whigs to make Charles Yorke the next Lord Chancellor, insisted that Pratt must at least be given a peerage and a seat in the cabinet. Other stipulations were that foreign policy must pursue the Prusso-Russian alliance; that military establishments should not be allowed to run down; and, not least emphatically, that those most closely associated with the concluding of the Treaty of Paris – notably Bedford – were to be excluded in any future arrangement.

The King, while from time to time repeating that he would not 'put himself into the hands of Mr Pitt', could nevertheless see that steady government would not be possible without him, and on 26 August annoyed Grenville by intimating 'his intention of calling Mr Pitt to the management of his affairs, declaring that he meant to do it as cheap as possible and to make as few changes as was possible'.[21] In fact George had by then already arranged, through intermediaries, to see Pitt, and when Grenville on Saturday 27 August arrived at Buckingham House to see the King, he observed already in the courtyard the unmistakable blue and silver livery of two of his brother-in-law's servants and the even more unmistakable chair built to accommodate Pitt's gout. Grenville was obliged to kick his heels for two hours, and then received an ominously frosty welcome from the King. It looked as if Pitt was 'in'. Pitt himself thought so, confident that the King had accepted his terms. The Newcastle Whigs certainly thought so too, and were already picturing themselves back in office under a second Pitt-Newcastle arrangement (with Cumberland supplanting Bute as special royal adviser). Indeed on the following day Pitt was down at Claremont discussing with Newcastle the make-up of a new ministry to include Temple as First Lord, Charles Townshend (Newcastle's nephew) and Pitt himself as Secretaries, either Newcastle or an ennobled Pratt as Lord Privy Seal, Hardwicke as Lord President',* either Legge or James Grenville at the Exchequer, and young Lord Rockingham at the Admiralty. Not only Bedford, but also Mansfield and Fox, were among those to be specifically excluded. 'When I heard Pitt had been with the King', Fox wrote, 'I knew his demands were, however he should word them, crown or sceptre'.[22]

---

* In the place of Earl Granville, Lord President since 1751, the elder statesman who as John Carteret had been twenty years before vilified by Pitt as 'Hanover troop minister', had lived just long enough to praise on his deathbed 'the most honourable peace', following 'the most glorious war . . . this nation ever saw'.

But over the week-end Bute succeeded in persuading the King to reconsider the virtually clean sweep he had been apparently ready to make. It was hardly surprising that Bute, in view of the excited threats that had been made against him, should fear some form of banishment, or even impeachment, for his part in the Peace, if his enemies were now to return too strongly to power; and much as George longed to be rid of the tiresome Grenville, he proved unready, after thinking things over, to desert Bute or others of his recent servants. By Monday morning, after a flustered week-end of consultations, he was fully convinced that it was his 'honour' that was involved. 'Mr Pitt said he could not abandon those friends who had stood by him: the King asked him, then, how he thought it possible for him to give up those who had served *him* faithfully, and devoted themselves to *him*?' According to Grenville, the King told him that Pitt 'had again rose in his demands' during that second audience;[23] but perhaps this was when he saw that his earlier terms were in any case to be rejected. Pitt himself remained tight-lipped on the various rumoured and often contradictory versions of this abortive negotiation, merely commenting in his own vein of deliberate mysteriousness that if he were examined upon oath, he could not say at what point it broke down, but that if the King were 'to assign any particular reason', he would never contradict it. Three months later in the Commons, however, he did emphatically deny that he had ever 'excommunicated' any of the 'peacemakers or Tories', other than perhaps Lord Mansfield.[24] Whatever the exact truth of that, it is certain that he had striven hard to find an accommodation that would permit his return to power; that he thought he had succeeded but then failed; and that failure brought disappointment and depression.

Newcastle, Devonshire, Rockingham, Charles Townshend, and others among prominent opposition leaders – not least the Duke of Cumberland – continued to make efforts to unravel his objections to them, and to mitigate his 'impracticability'. It was agreed among them that 'the whole machine must be directed by him'. 'If he will be at our head, we are ready', said Devonshire, 'to act with him and under him, and not to desire him to attend the Parliament when it is inconvenient with him'; government business in the Commons might be run by Charles Townshend, Legge, Charles Yorke, and James Grenville.[25] They were all convinced that, with Pitt, they would be strong enough to make an already half-willing King rid himself of Grenville and the Bedford connection – ministers he increasingly resented – and put the reins of government back into their hands. But without Pitt and the popular and parliamentary support which only he could command they were powerless.

Much of Newcastle's weakness arose from the circumstance that after his resignation and his subsequent rout at the hands of Bute and Fox many of his followers had refused to follow him into the wilderness; and chief among these were the Yorkes, the ambitious sons of Lord Hardwicke. In Grenville's ministry, amid the very vitals of the enemy, Charles Yorke remained Attorney General; and when an opinion was required of him upon the legality of Wilkes's claim to parliamentary privilege, he pronounced, in April 1763 – moreover in writing and with an absoluteness which alarmed his more cautious father – that a publication of a libel, being a breach of the peace, could not be protected by parliamentary privilege.

Now although Pitt could hardly condemn Wilkes's notorious attack on the Treaty of Paris in number 45 of his *North Briton*, and although Wilkes had recently been and to some extent remained the friend and protégé of Pitt's chief ally Temple, Pitt detested the scurrilous tone of Wilkes's journalism and deplored the man personally. Indeed he was moved to declare in the House of Commons that Wilkes, as the blasphemer of his God and the libeller of his King, 'did not deserve to be ranked among the human species'.[26] There was enough of the puritan in Pitt for him to be disgusted by Wilkes's light-hearted libertinism and the irreverent bawdiness of the *Essay on Woman*. However, Wilkes was undoubtedly a member of parliament; parliament was the sacred palladium of British liberties; and parliamentary privilege was a pillar of that palladium. Wilkes, however detestable, was entitled therefore in Pitt's judgement to privilege.

For Pitt this issue became a matter of high principle. But, as ever with him, there was introduced a powerful admixture of personal antagonism. Charles Yorke, the blackest of the sheep who had strayed from Newcastle's fold, happened also to be the principle rival of Pitt's friend Chief Justice Pratt in the competition for the Woolsack, and it was of course Pratt who had upheld Wilkes's claim to privilege. All the protracted negotiations during 1763 for a common front, the 'solid union' Pitt professed to desire 'upon Revolution principles'[27] between himself and the Whig magnates, became snagged in the quarrel of Pitt and Pratt versus Yorke and the Hardwicke clan, with Newcastle and the Whig majority regretfully entangled between them. Newcastle persistently courted the inevitable and irreplaceable Mr Pitt, while struggling hard not to fall out too irremediably with his old partner and father-confessor Hardwicke. Hardwicke, confined by long illness and infirmity, supported his son, tried nevertheless not altogether to desert Newcastle, but continued to be 'full of jealousies and condemnation of Mr Pitt',[28] being convinced that he was up to his old tricks, running for popularity, and once again, as Hardwicke bitterly complained, trying to blacken the entire legal profession as he had in the habeas corpus *fracas* of 1758. Pitt eventually agreed to accept Charles Yorke as prospective Lord Chancellor, but only if in return Pratt were given a peerage and a place in the cabinet. Yorke himself, whose professional opinion as Attorney General had given considerable succour to both King and government, was under heavy pressure from his late political associates for having spoken in support of 'prerogative'. If Newcastle's reproaches were more in sorrow than anger, Pitt's were decidedly the reverse. At last, by November 1763, Yorke was worn down. He resigned, but in an emotional parting interview with the King vowed at least to stick to his guns on the subject of Wilkes and privilege.

His resignation procured him a good deal of merit with the Newcastle Whigs. Rockingham, for one, now thought that they were 'obliged in honour and gratitude . . . to support him in his point of privilege'.[29] Thus, when the Commons came to debate the motion that parliamentary privilege did not apply in cases of libel, Pitt found a divided opposition.

Once again so gouty that he arrived on crutches and wrapped in flannels, having to be helped to his seat, he spoke for nearly two hours – it was the occasion of that savage attack on the personal and public writings of Wilkes for which his victim never forgave him – arguing the case against any voting away of parliamentary rights. 'This privilege', he said, 'has never been abused; it has reposed in parliament for ages'; but take it away, 'and the whole parliament is laid at the mercy of the crown'.[30] Again, as after his big attack on the Peace just a year previously, he would not wait for the division – knowing he must lose it – but was glad to crawl off to Hayes, where he was to remain ill and out of action for the next two or three months. It was a period during which the Wilkes saga continued to develop. A London mob riotously interfered with the official burning of *The North Briton Number 45* outside the Royal Exchange; the jury in Pratt's Court of Common Pleas, amid popular jubilation, awarded Wilkes £1000 damages against Under-Secretary Wood; Wilkes removed to France; and on 20 January he was expelled from membership of the House of Commons. Horace Walpole thought Pitt's speech on Wilkes and privilege 'the worst I ever heard him make', and even Temple, whom Pitt had gone out of his way in it to eulogize (they would 'die together'), considered that 'its temper was too apt to be heated'.[31]

For all his passionate defence of parliamentary privilege, the strength of Pitt's feelings against Wilkes and his anger at being misunderstood are underlined in a later exchange of letters with a certain Rev. Paul Shenton, who ventured in tones of the properest humble adulation to suggest that he and his influential friends, 'all sincere partizans of Mr Pitt', would be prepared at the next county elections to promote some candidate of 'the party of honour and virtue' – possibly Mr Wilkes, 'that able statesman'. Alas, poor Shenton! Pitt's reply proved a thunderous snub; it would serve, he hoped, as 'a not un-useful admonition to misguided zeal'. Mr Shenton, Pitt did not doubt, would accept his correction 'in good part', but he would have had to be thick-skinned indeed not to feel mightily put down:

> . . . I cannot defer a moment [wrote Pitt] expressing my astonishment and concern that one of your rank, a clergyman, could so mis-conceive of me as to imagine that I countenanced libels, because I disapproved part of the methods of proceeding relating to them. Let me undeceive you, Sir . . . I have ever abhorred such odious and dangerous writings; and in the late instance of the *North Briton*, no man concurred more heartily than I did in condemning and branding so licentious and criminal a paper.
>
> . . . If you really favour me with your good wishes, you will be glad to understand me aright. Be assured then, Sir, that I disdain and detest faction . . .
>
> P.S. – This letter to you may serve for all who, like you, are so widely mistaken concerning me.[32]

It was particularly Pitt's energetic part in the week-long parliamentary clash upon general warrants, in February 1764, which had sent Mr Shenton and his like down their road of misapprehension. Pitt did not need to approve of Wilkes to disapprove of the means by which he had been first arrested, under a (general) warrant issued by the Secretary of State against all those (unspecified) persons concerned with producing the *North Briton*. Here once again, as in the earlier disputes over habeas corpus and the cider excise, he could do battle for a cause in which he solemnly believed, that of the individual against the state, of the private citizen, whether or not a rogue, against the leviathan of executive power.

In spite of 'gout and fever' and bad nights, he was in his place on 13 February (again with his crutches and flannels), ready for a long tough battle. Over the next five days he spoke many times, losing one division at 4.30 a.m. only by the slender margin of ten votes, after pouring forth 'one of his finest rhapsodies upon liberty'.[33] At 10 a.m. Newcastle who, being a peer, had had the benefit of a night's rest, was sending round a note praising Pitt's 'great and glorious endeavours' to the skies ('I shall just call at your door', he added, 'to inquire after your health some time this forenoon'.)[34] Pitt's reserves of strength were thrown into the struggle for three more days, his last weary intervention coming two hours before the final division at 5 a.m. on Saturday.* His own practice as Secretary had to be explained and defended, for on three occasions he had himself issued a general warrant. He pleaded in exculpation the exigencies of a wartime situation; but now maintained that general warrants were *always* wrong, 'even in case of treason'. 'If his own practice had been faulty he was willing to bear his share of public blame'.[35] From the government benches, at one rash moment of the warm debate, Yorke's successor as Attorney General, Fletcher Norton, committed a notorious blasphemy against the dignities of the House: saying that if he were judge, he would pay no more regard to a Commons resolution against general warrants than to the opinion of a drunken porter.[36] Yorke himself, much more circumspect, claiming that he had never seen this particular warrant 'till Wilkes was taken up', admitted that general

---

* Walpole pictured Pitt as a sort of tourist attraction: 'The foreigners . . . think themselves rewarded by *seeing* Mr Pitt *speak* at five in the morning', even though 'the language is a secret to them'.

22. *right* 3rd Earl of Bute, by Reynolds
23. *below* John Wilkes, caricature by Hogarth

24. *left* 2nd Marquis of Rocking-ham, studio of Reynolds

25. The Earl of Chatham in 1772, after Richard Brompton

warrants issued by a Secretary of State dated from the Star Chamber and must be pronounced illegal. Echoes were strong of the seventeenth century and the old Commons battle against prerogative; and if anything were to unite the disparate forces and incompatible personalities within the opposition it was likely to be regard for 'revolution principles' – a political icon then compelling from politicians as automatic a genuflection as today the image of 'parliamentary democracy'.

In the final division on general warrants the opposition mustered 218, only fourteen fewer than the government. Ringing of bells, lighting of bonfires, and an illumination had been prepared in the City of London, in hopeful anticipation of the majority that did not quite materialize. Even so, 'the world expected that the ministers would resign – at least endeavour to treat'.[37] Newcastle, indeed, could hardly have sounded more joyful if the vote had gone the other way. More than ever anxious to be well with Pitt, he hastened to congratulate him on 'the great and glorious minority'. 'Such a minority, with such a leader . . . must have its weight'. He knew that Pitt had exhausted himself physically, and again, 'with the greatest respect and affection', inquired solicitously of his condition. When he set out for Claremont he proposed, he said, to leave a servant behind, to bring him word how Pitt did.[38]

It was Hester, ever more involved as secretary and personal assistant, who replied on her husband's behalf. He had come back, she told Newcastle, in the most acute pain which had denied him any rest. And soon all Newcastle's busy friendliness was seen to have been wasted. The challenge on general warrants proved to be no harbinger after all of a 'solid union upon Whig principles'; and Pitt relapsed, after a further fortnight in bed, into another of his periods of resentful inactivity – Charles Townshend reported him as 'talking the language of despair'.[39] He seems suddenly to have decided to give the Whigs up as a bad job. Was he in fact going to leave parliament for good, perhaps? – for Townshend noticed also that the removal men were taking out his furniture from the house in Jermyn Street that he had used as a town residence after leaving St James's Square upon his resignation in 1761.

Meanwhile, continuing to drink Mr Pitt's health in their new Albemarle Street Club in the intervals between arguments and quarrels among themselves, the Newcastle Whigs looked towards Hayes in anxious incomprehension. After their lively parliamentary crackle in the big February set piece, they feebly fizzled out during the remainder of the session, not a few of them preferring to satisfy their appetite for faction in the election of a new High Steward of the university of Cambridge to replace Lord Hardwicke, who died at the beginning of March.* The King struck back at them with dismissals of those of his household and army (notably of Walpole's friend and kinsman General Conway) who had supported Pitt in the opposition over general warrants. The budget went unopposed, although it contained Grenville's first important proposals for tightening up and exacting revenue from the regulation of American trade; and when Grenville again attacked Pitt's handling of the recent war and its financing, not a member rose from his seat to contest the argument.

This last rankled particularly with Pitt. Six months later (after a summer spent entirely with his family at Hayes), when Newcastle had again come a-wooing, he wrote:

> Having seen the close of last session, and the system of that great war, in which my share of the ministry was so largely arraigned, given up *by silence* in a full House, I have little thoughts of beginning the world again upon a new centre of union. Your Grace will not, I trust, wonder, if after so recent and so strange a phenomenon in politics, I have no disposition to quit the free condition of a man standing *single*, and daring to appeal to his country at large, upon the soundness of his principles and the rectitude of his conduct.[40]

This obviously was not the letter of a man intending to abandon politics or the hope of again leading the nation. His posture, rather, resembles De Gaulle's during the nineteen-fifties, waiting proud and aloof in his rural retreat to be summoned back to the helm, but insisting absolutely upon his own high terms for the service. There would be no 'bargains', no 'stipulations'; Pitt heavily emphasized and repeated the point three times over. 'Whatever I think it my duty to oppose,

* The ranks of the earlier generation of Whig leaders, already deprived of Granville in 1763, were still further thinned within the next few months by the deaths of Legge and the Duke of Devonshire. Newcastle survived, an increasingly forlorn figure, but leadership of the Newcastle Whigs was transferring gradually to Rockingham and the younger men, who were coming more and more to look towards the Duke of Cumberland as their guide and protector.

or to promote', he wrote, 'I shall do it, independent of the sentiments of others', and he proposed to attend at Westminster 'only as often as I think it worth the while' – which turned out to be not at all for nearly two years.

Gout, or generally poor health, was not the only – probably not the primary – reason for this long parliamentary absence. He was, indeed, frequently laid up; but so by this time he had been for many years during which he had managed, with whatever difficulty, to attend. And there were months during 1764-5 when he was tolerably well and able to undertake journeys or to attend energetically to estate improvements and the affairs of his family. Indeed Temple, writing in October 1764 to the Prussian ex-ambassador – admittedly at a time when parliament was in recess – stresses the '*santé parfaite*' of Mr Pitt at that season.[41]

Pitt was certainly far from any intention of abandoning ship, and potential allies and wary opponents continued alike to watch his movements, or lack of them, in nervous puzzlement. When he was in London to attend a royal levee in July 1764 Grenville, suspicious that Pitt, equally with the King, had designs brewing, was anxiously inquiring of his Treasury Secretary Jenkinson just how the King had behaved. Had there perhaps been something beyond the couple of polite questions customary on such formal occasions? Jenkinson thought Pitt had lowered his sights somewhat, and might well now be ready to settle for nominating 'a majority in the cabinet' merely.[42] Newcastle, his recent advances to Pitt uncompromisingly rebuffed, was unquiet not so much from the thought that Pitt might intend to retire as from the fear that he might finally abandon the Whigs and seek a *rapprochement* with Bute, with whom Beckford had had an interview presumably in the role of Pitt's spokesman. Pitt had 'certainly been treating' with Bute, decided Walpole, who was inclined to blame Pitt above others for the poor shape of the opposition, all 'the great and unexpected progress' that had been made in the battle over general warrants having been thrown away.[43]

Pitt himself gave out on the contrary that, systematic opposition being fruitless or, worse still, likely to throw ministers back into the arms of Bute, energies should be reserved for major issues. As it happened, when what was to prove undeniably such an issue did arise in March 1765 – American expenses, and Grenville's attempt to

shift some of the burden of them across the Atlantic by a stamp bill –
nobody recognized it as such, though Pitt afterwards, with his strong
alibi and the advantages of hindsight, would claim that it was only
prostration on his sickbed that had prevented him from being carried
to his place to challenge this piece of foolishness, so great was his
'agitation of mind'. The only prominent opposition spokesman who
would stand in no need of such exculpation, having spoken forcefully
against the bill, was Barré, who now, together with young Lord
Shelburne, having been dismissed along with General Conway from
the King's service for their anti-ministerial vote in the Wilkes affair,
regarded themselves as recruits to the Pitt camp. The young Duke of
Grafton too, and Fox's old henchman John Calcraft, were others
trying to rally under Pitt's banner, but they were all labouring under
the handicap of Pitt's apparent reluctance to fly it himself.

Grenville's Stamp Act, 'little understood . . . and less attended to',[44]
gained a general assent and went through the Commons with a five to
one majority.

CHAPTER EIGHTEEN

———◆◆◆———

'So Near Engaging'

Through much the greater part of 1764 and until the autumn of 1765 Pitt remained at Hayes. He had finished the building of his new and more elegant Hayes Place in the grounds of the old house. Systematically buying up every available adjacent property, he had greatly expanded his acreage. Where he could not buy he rented, until he controlled most of the land surrounding the little village with its few score inhabitants. His domain extended to lordship of the manor of neighbouring Farnborough. Hayes was now his creation; the world associated it with him as naturally as any other of the stately homes with their aristocrat proprietors. And if Hayes could hardly match Stowe or Woburn or Chatsworth, it was still a considerable establishment. When (having been heavily mortgaged) it eventually came under Christie's hammer in 1789, the catalogue advertised an elegant spacious villa of twenty-four bedrooms, with brewhouse, laundry, dairy, stabling for sixteen horses, standing for four carriages, pinery, peachery, fenced park of sixty acres and one hundred and ten acres beyond. The pleasure grounds were 'disposed with taste, fringed with rich plantations maturely grown', the timber 'scattered with pleasing negligence', the paddock 'refreshed with a sheet of water, and the grounds adorned with seats, alcoves, etc.'.[1]

It was a fine setting for rearing a family in, and Pitt always remained devotedly close to his Hester and their children. His two elder sons were born at Hayes. The two girls, Hester and Harriot, and the youngest son James had been born in London, but all the children were brought up at Hayes, with the aid of the usual obligatory army of servants, nurses, grooms, and a private tutor. They must have become as attached to the place as was Pitt himself. On holiday at Weymouth, at a time when the family's future connection with their old home was in doubt, the ten-year-old Hester wrote to her father: 'About Hayes we all continue of the same opinion. John and Harriot say that

[if] there was a concert of musick at Weymouth every day, still they should prefer the sweet chirping of the nightingales of Hayes'. ('I am very sorry you have got the gout', her letter begins, 'but I hope it will not be a long fit. I am very glad that you like the letters which I writ Mama. I should have writ to you before but I thought it would be inconvenient to you as you have so much business'; and it ends, 'I shou'd have writ this letter in Latin, but Mr Wilson [the tutor] thinks I had better stay until I can writ Latin more elegantly'.)²

Pitt refused to trust his children's education to any school; and with his strong views upon the proper contents of a gentleman's mind, he took an especial conscientious pleasure in overseeing the upbringing of his sons, particularly his second son William whose shining intelligence and prodigious teachability came to constitute one of the chief consolations of his latter years. From his side the boy from the tenderest age looked admiringly upon his brilliant and famous father, and determined to emulate him. 'As to William', writes young Hetty, 'he says . . . he does not intend to be a sailor' – William was then seven – 'but a William Pitt in the House of Commons'; and a few months before this, in April 1766, when it appeared that his father was likely to go to the House of Lords, he told his tutor that he was glad not to be the eldest son, because he was going to 'serve his country in the House of Commons like his papa'.³ Very soon he would be old enough to digest such required reading as Thucydides and Polybius and Barrow's *Sermons*, and to be stood by his father on a wooden mounting-block in the grounds of Hayes, where he was bidden to imagine that the surrounding trees were honourable members of parliament and that he was upon his feet addressing them on various subjects dictated to him.

Pitt and Hester, good and loving parents to all their children, could hardly fail to regard William as an especial blessing, and a signal triumph of their joint hands. 'William, our constant theme', Pitt wrote. 'Was ever such a pen, my dear life, under such command, as this sweet boy's?' Between them upon their prodigy they bestowed a fine variety of adoring sobriquets: the Orator, the Philosopher, the Young Senator; Sweet William, Stout William, Eager Mr William; William the Fourth, William the Great. Pitt would be sending him up to Cambridge (not to his own unloved Oxford) when the boy was fourteen and a half. The powerful and challenging impression upon him of his father's greatness never of course left him or let him rest. Sometimes in these early years the paternal imprint shows amusingly enough; in a letter written by the eleven-year-old William concerning one of his father's coach journeyings there is an unconscious but perfect parody of the playful elegance that the elder Pitt habitually affected in writing to his friends upon matters unpolitical – all cumbersome periphrasis and genteel floridity. Was ever such a dutifully filial pen as 'this sweet boy's'?

I flatter myself [the child wrote] that the sun shone on your expedition, and that the views were enough enliven'd thereby to prevent the drowsy Morpheus from taking the opportunity of the heat to diffuse his poppies upon the eyes of any of the travellers.[4]

In or out of office, Pitt was by now a revered national institution. Whatever had been or continued to be his frailties and idiosyncrasies, he had unquestionably been the architect of victory and conquest, and next to the King himself he remained the most emotive living symbol of the nation's greatness; rather like Wellington in his latter years, or Churchill in his. Even the children found some of their father's quasi-royalty descending now to them. When, for instance, on summer holiday they travelled apart from their parents to Weymouth or Brighton or Lyme they were several times greeted *en route* with the pealing of bells or strewing of flowers. Again, 'a deputation of Mohican chiefs, on passage to London with a petition to the King, waited upon the children of the great Pitt as soon as they arrived'.[5] Such flattering expressions of public regard, however often he might affect to discount them, came not at all amiss to Pitt. He expected deference and he valued ceremony and display. His own turn-out upon journeys, with his coach-and-six, his blue-and-silver-liveried coachmen and outriders, and his train of coaches for himself and his servants, often would not have disgraced a royal duke.

When he accepted the pension and the barony for Hester in 1761 he had reckoned it the least the country owed him. Now, in January 1765, when at last old Sir William Pynsent died and left Pitt his entire estate, worth between three and four thousand a year, he accepted it, again with the feeling that something of the sort was surely due to him. Hayes was a fine place. He loved it and had seen the house and estate grow handsomely under his direction. But now at Burton Pynsent he would be able to spread his wings in a manner befitting him – even though that might mean the awkward decision to sell Hayes.

Pitt had never met Pynsent – according to Lady Chatham never even seen him – and Horace Walpole suggested that before the old man's death his wits had wandered well beyond mere eccentricity; that he had lately played with the idea of substituting Wilkes's name for Pitt's in his will; and that, had he lived only a little longer, he would have left his estate to General Conway.[6] However, when Pynsent's house-keeper produced the will, Pitt was unmistakably named as legatee. Even so, his right to this second of his major windfalls from aged eccentrics did not go unchallenged, since Pynsent's son-in-law claimed 'estate entail' over a large proportion of the property by virtue of the rights of his deceased wife, through whom it had originally come to Sir William. The Master of the Rolls did not decide the matter in Pitt's favour until June 1766. Even after that, Pynsent's son-in-law won his case on appeal, and it was not until six years had passed that Pitt's proprietorship was finally confirmed by the House of Lords. However, he was far from waiting for the outcome of these legal processes before taking possession and putting in hand another batch of new and ambitious improvements.

But before he could get down into Somerset in July (after another protracted spell of illness, 'gout without end, and, to close all, an ague and a fever')[7] he had twice been invited by the King to form a government. Relations between George and his principal ministers had become impossibly strained. After his serious illness in the spring and the unpleasantness over the regency bill that followed, and at last, to heighten tension, alarming weavers' riots in the capital, the King had decided that he could stomach his tedious, pedagogical, self-righteous chief minister no longer. George Grenville may well have been, next to Pitt, the ablest of the politicians still in active business, but the King had come to find his very presence uncomfortable, and his nagging persistence insupportable. 'When he has wearied me for two hours', said George, 'he looks at his watch to see if he may not tire me for an hour more'. This acute antipathy to Grenville was such that two years later he was still saying he would rather see the Devil in his closet than Mr Grenville.

In some desperation he now turned to his uncle Cumberland (whom

he had previously been taught to mistrust and who certainly of late
had been acting as chief patron and would-be coordinator of the
opposition) and asked that the Duke should go to Hayes and try to
persuade Pitt to form a ministry in cooperation with Temple and the
Newcastle-Rockingham Whigs. To clear the ground Cumberland
first sent the Earl of Albemarle to see Pitt and ascertain his terms:
final removal of Bute from the King's counsels; restoration to office
for those who had been dismissed for expressing anti-governmental
opinions in parliament; the outlawing of general warrants, with
'ample justice and favour shown to Chief Justice Pratt'; repeal of the
cider excise; and (most important of all perhaps, and a point Pitt
feared the King might jib at) a sincere attempt to build a Russo-
Prussian alliance against the Bourbon powers.[8]

Three days later the mountain was publicly seen to go to Mahomet.
The Duke of Cumberland, mountainous indeed, painfully lame from
an old wound, one-eyed, asthmatic, apoplectic – he had only a few
more months to live – was driven in state with an escort of Guards to
Hayes; in itself a remarkable gesture. Royal dukes were not in the
habit of thus waiting on Commons politicians in the country, least
of all as plenipotentiaries of the crown. Also taking part in the discus-
sions were Albemarle again, for the main body of Whigs, and Temple,
whom Cumberland had already interviewed and found 'more verbose
and pompous' than Pitt and apparently less ready to agree terms. Pitt,
however, proved also unready, and the Hayes talks came to nothing,
merely confusing an already cloudy situation.

Why had Pitt declined? Everyone had a different answer, and the
nearest he came to providing one of his own was in a remark he made
afterwards to James Grenville, that 'nothing was conveyed that might
have for object or end anything like my settling an administration
upon my own plans'. To head the ministry at the Treasury, 'that
bubble' the Duke of Northumberland, he complained, had been
pressed on him by Cumberland for an hour and a half.[9] Many thought
his lack of health was the true reason for his refusal but, according to
Cumberland, while apologizing for his invalidity he claimed that 'he
had still vigour and strength of mind to undertake business, if he saw a
probability of success'.[10] The general Whig view was expressed by
Lord Rockingham's assistant, Edmund Burke: Pitt's failure to come
in as head of what could have been a strong and long-lived adminis-

tration was just one more instance of his 'intractable temper'. Was it pride or patriotism that was more predominant in his character? asked Burke:

> . . . for you may be assured, that he has it now in his power to come into the service of his country upon any plan of politicks he may chuse to dictate . . . with such strength of power as will be equal to everything but absolute despotism over the King and kingdom. A few days will shew whether he will take this part or that of continuing on his back at Hayes talking fustian . . .[11]

It is true that in 'measures' Pitt's proposed policies hardly seemed to differ from those of the Newcastle-Rockingham party.* The point of friction lay in 'men'. Pitt remained unwilling to head a government where he could not be sure of the complete subservience of all ministers. He was afraid of a repetition of the situation of 1761 and would never again lead where he could not, in his word, *guide*; in that of others, dominate.

Horace Walpole's interpretation of events added a further complication, which if not already relevant was certainly soon to be: that it was Temple, already on deteriorating terms with Pitt, who spiked the guns of the negotiation. Pitt had been reckoning that, if he did accept office, Temple would be ready to stand by him as he had in 1761, and take over at the Treasury the nominal headship of what would be a *Pitt* ministry. But Temple, lord of Stowe and first of the Grenvilles, had little relish for the prospect of returning to office in any way subordinate to his brother-in-law. He now began seeking an accommodation with his brother George, and appears to have been setting his sights on a *Temple* ministry, perhaps with Pitt and George Grenville as Secretaries of State. From his side Grenville worked to detach his brother from Pitt's interest, and when one day in May Lord Lyttelton called at Temple's town house intending to go with him, as arranged, to consult Pitt at Hayes – Lyttelton had buried his quarrel with Pitt and was yet another of those suggested at this time for the Treasury – he was made to wait for two hours chatting with

---

* Newcastle was now an old man of seventy-two. The Yorkshire magnate, Marquis of Rockingham, aged now thirty-five, was generally accepted as his successor, and the heirs of the 'Newcastle Whigs' are conveniently referred to from about this time as 'the Rockinghams'.

Lady Temple while her husband was privately closeted with Grenville. The alliance was purely personal, so Temple assured a sceptical Duke of Cumberland; but the Grenville diary for 22 May reports, 'the most perfect reconciliation'; Lord Temple 'afterwards came upstairs to see Mrs Grenville and the children'.[12] A week later all three Grenville brothers, with Mrs George Grenville, went down to Hayes to dine with Pitt and Lady Chatham. It must have proved a somewhat stressful and artificial occasion, and when George Grenville broached political matters, Pitt straightway silenced him. He wished (so Mrs Grenville's diary demurely recounts) that their intercourse 'might be of a friendly domestic nature' merely; 'Mr Grenville . . . said he sincerely thought it best, and each kept strictly to it'.[13]

When the King heard of the Temple-Grenville *rapprochement* he realized that he had no immediate alternative to continuing with the existing ministers so distasteful to him. However, over the next few weeks he was made to suffer such hostile and humiliating treatment from Grenville and Bedford, that by mid-June he was asking his uncle Cumberland once again to sound out Pitt, or failing him the Rockinghams – anybody rather than the 'low men' who were trying to dictate to him by their 'insolent' demands:[14] that Bute should be put incommunicado to the King, that Bute's brother Stuart Mackenzie and Lord Holland (Henry Fox) should both be dismissed, and that Granby should be appointed Captain General instead of Cumberland. The King was obliged to accept all these terms except the last, but redoubled his efforts to gain Pitt. At last on 17 June the Duke of Grafton was asked to deliver to Hayes the message that the King could not do without Pitt – who returned the reply that he was ready to come to Buckingham House if his Majesty 'would graciously condescend, in consideration of his lameness, to see him on the ground floor'. Cumberland, on the King's behalf, and 'with the utmost joy', responded immediately. George would receive Pitt 'below stairs. He allows for the infirmities of the gout, and also knows where merit is'.[15]

At meetings on 19 and 22 June the shape of a new government was agreed in outline between Pitt and the King. Even on the tricky subject of the alliance with Prussia and Russia, pursuit of which Pitt firmly insisted on, the King gave way, against his own judgement that this would merely mean 'ramming Austria deeper with France and kindling a new war'.[16] It was agreed that Temple should be offered

331

the Treasury, with Grafton and Pitt himself as Secretaries. On 24 June, however, Temple drove to Hayes and 'most peremptorily and determinately refused bearing a part in any shape, great or small'.[17] The next day he repeated his refusal to the King, proffering obscure reasons of 'delicacy' – presumably in respect of his agreement with Grenville.

Without Temple's backing, Pitt in his turn refused to engage, despite an almost desperate cry from the King:

> My friend for so the part you have acted deserves from me, think it not strange if in my present distress I wish to see you again, and have your advice; many things have occur'd since you left me I much want to have your opinion about, and I will answer for you, you will give it without hesitation . . .

Pitt answered in his high courtier style:

> Sir – With a heart overflowing with duty and gratitude to the most gracious of Sovereigns, I will punctually attend your Majesty tomorrow morning according to your commands. Too happy and too glorious the remnants of a poor life, cou'd I have been seconded in my unavailing zeal, and devotion to your Majesty's service, honour, and happiness . . .[18]

But *un*seconded, he still answered no. For the third time in two years, George's efforts to enlist Pitt as his chief minister had come to nothing, and upon this occasion at least, not apparently from any intransigence on the part of the two principals to the negotiations. Yet doubts remain. Temple did not have a large following, and his defection need hardly have crippled a Pitt ministry in 1765, supported as it was likely to have been by the King and the party of the Court, by 'Bute's friends', and by a large majority of independents. Was it rather that Pitt's mistrust of the Whig magnates and the Duke of Cumberland (now become a sort of player-manager to them) was so deep-seated that he had already come to view the enterprise of forming a government with misgiving, and Temple's desertion merely provided the last straw?* As for Temple's decision, it did him little good.

* John Brooke (*King George III*, 121–2) has no doubts on this matter: 'Pitt would have no mediator between himself and the throne. Had he taken office in August 1763 he would have been obliged to Bute; had he taken office in June 1765 he would have been

His ambitions did not lessen, but he was never again to come so close to becoming titular head of the King's government. Neither was Grenville's interest served. On 10 July he was dismissed, and the King was able to feel for the time being relieved of his servitude. His uncle Cumberland succeeded in fathering, and during the last few remaining months of his life unofficially leading a Whig administration with Lord Rockingham at the Treasury, the Duke of Grafton and General Conway as Secretaries, and as Lord Privy Seal the old Duke of New-castle putting in his positively final ministerial stint; not wishing for responsibility any more, but still unwilling to be left altogether out in the cold. Out of loyalty to Pitt, Shelburne and Barré declined to serve. Pratt however was given his peerage (a gesture towards Pitt), and became Lord Camden. Pitt's own lawyer, too, was made Treasury Solicitor, and his follower Cooke Joint Paymaster-General. Every-thing possible should be done, Newcastle continued to insist, to attach Pitt's approbation and prestige to the ministry. As for the Duke of Grafton, he only wished for that hour, he told Pitt, in which he could resign the seals to 'you, my successor', whose friendship he had ever valued as 'the first honour' of his life.[19]

Soon after the formation of the Rockingham government, from any approval of which Pitt was quickly at pains to dissociate himself, the new owner of Burton Pynsent went down to Somerset to take possession of his estate, 'where I propose', he wrote, 'to pass not a little of the rest of my days, if I find the place tolerable'. The mansion was already large, situated above the 300-foot escarpment of a wooded ridge of hills overlooking the levels and dykes of Sedgemoor, and beyond them the Somerset farmlands that stretched away beyond Bridgwater to the Bristol Channel coast. It was a fine inheritance, but ripe too for Pitt's imaginative projects, and he was very soon putting in hand extensions and developments, as he had always previously been busy doing at Hayes. 'You see, my dear Lord', he wrote to Temple in October, 'how the passion of dirty acres grows upon a West Saxon of yesterday, and that I meditate laying rapacious hands on a considerable part of the county of Somerset . . . I advance apace in brick and mortar'.[20]

All that is today left of the house is the substantial new wing Pitt

obliged to the Duke of Cumberland. And Pitt would be obliged to no man. With him it must be *ego et rex meus*'.

333

now added, housing among its other accommodation his library, and what is described as a 'bird room' for Lady Chatham. The children's and servants' quarters remained in the older main part of the house. Pitt's nerves increasingly demanded an option on privacy; indeed there was always war within him between the public figure who required popular approbation and found invigoration in the political rough-and-tumble, and the altogether more introverted man longing for escape from the *profanum vulgus* – often too from the family hubbub – and indulging private reflections frequently sombre and misanthropic. At Burton Pynsent one of his innovations, to safeguard his seclusion, was to sink between deep banks a public way which ran through the estate.

As proprietor Pitt could never sit still, or refrain from overspending – though his income by now can hardly have been less than a handsome £7000 a year. As Secretary of State he had always tended to view finance as a subject for lesser minds like Newcastle's or Legge's. In his private affairs Hester's restraining common sense seems to have had little success. Extravagance, beginning as a luxurious gesture to his own position, became an ineradicable habit, and was to end in his old age with irrationality and obsession. He was 'naturally ostentatious', wrote Shelburne, 'to a degree of ridicule; profuse in his house and family beyond what any degree of prudence could warrant'.[21]

At Burton he was before long envisaging princely improvements, raising money to pay for new buildings and farm experiments, for park landscaping and for road-building towards the neighbouring towns of Langport and Taunton. Ever since he took South Lodge at Enfield, thirty years back (and then hardly ever stayed there), he had been 'immersed in the amusing cares of building and gardening'.[22] As well as his new wing to the house at Burton, some at least of the trees he now began planting still survive, his cedars conspicuously. These, together with a quantity of cypresses, he ordered to be brought down from London when (declared his gardener) all the nurseries in Somerset 'would not furnish a hundredth part' of his demands;[23] and within a year or two the conqueror of Canada was receiving from Nova Scotia, via Plymouth, an impressive selection of North American trees for the adornment of his Burton grounds. 'Burton Steeple' also survives, the memorial he erected in honour of his latest benefactor. For this he employed the celebrated Lancelot Brown, to design and construct a massive stone column, 140 feet high, with internal spiral stairs and lofty viewing platform, overlooking Sedgemoor from the hill's edge, half a mile from the house.

If he were to launch out as he meant to in Somerset it would involve raising money. After only a month or two at Burton, Hester and he found themselves 'quite agreed' that they must part with their 'dear Hayes'; and by early November he had found a prospective buyer in Horace Walpole's cousin Thomas (son of Sir Robert's brother the elder Horace), a wealthy merchant and banker, member of parliament and political admirer of Pitt.[24]

For a time now Pitt practised hard – or perhaps it was only fairly hard – to see himself as 'a Somersetshire bystander'. 'All is now over as to me', he wrote to Lady Stanhope (his cousin by marriage whose son one day would be marrying Pitt's daughter Hester); and he resolutely laboured to convince others, and perhaps even himself, that Temple's desertion had saved him from taking on what he would have been physically unfit to perform; his gouty hand admonished him, he wrote, 'how ridiculous a *Secretary* I should have proved . . . where I was so near engaging'.[25]

He was well enough during August to enjoy his horse-riding; but a fall had him back on crutches again by September, 'extremely lame . . . I make a shift notwithstanding', he wrote, 'to enjoy the fine weather, and a pleasing scene about me, in a one-horse chair, and trust I shall soon be able to try my luck again upon a horse'. He claimed to be 'not in the least curious' about the political scene, but at the same time did not fail to remind Hayes' prospective purchaser how he had been frustrated in his 'views for the public good', and would nevertheless continue to stand for the causes of liberty ('true Revolution-principles') and national honour: 'all I can say is this, that I move only in the sphere of measures. Quarrels at court, or family reconciliations, shall never vary my fixed judgement of things'.[26]

These proud words had a fine ring, and doubtless they sounded true metal to Thomas Walpole. Perhaps also to Pitt himself; there was even an element of truth in them. 'Measures' did mean more to him than 'men'; but the well-studied pose of standing on a plane of political existence high above merely personal prejudices and jealousies rests not quite convincingly upon one who had not long before admitted 'excommunicating' Mansfield, if no others, and within a month or two would be telling the King that he refused to enter any government containing the Duke of Newcastle, or indeed *any* government containing past prime ministers.[27]

The death on 31 October of the Duke of Cumberland, who had been nothing less than *de facto* head of the Rockingham administration, removed at least one obstacle to Pitt's return to government. The event, long expected but finally abrupt, found the Somerset bystander already *en route* for Bath, ostensibly to 'try once again to prop up a little a shattered tenement' with the help of the waters.[28] (He still of course had his house in the Circus.) Politically if not geographically Bath was much nearer to Westminster than to Burton Pynsent. Pitt remained there for two months, his family joining him towards the end; not quite the contented back number he had played at being in the wilds of Somerset, but still pretending an aloofness from the political scene that he could never honestly feel for many days at a time. 'The great of this world', he noted to Hester with amused satisfaction, 'seem not to have forgotten the Somersetshire hermit, if the mighty names of Newcastle, Norfolk, Bedford, Rockingham etc., are flattering to the pride of man . . . How I shall sustain these honours, I know not; but while I am relating them to my love, the spirits flow, and the [gouty] hand obeys'.[29] It seems that both Newcastle and Rockingham were circumspectly wooing him at this time through their respective wives, who happened both to be in Bath. 'If a *Real Great Man* comes there', Rockingham had written playfully to his lady, 'I would have you consider him as such and am not afraid of your conversation with him as I don't believe it will be *criminal*'.[30]

His mere presence in Bath was news. 'It rains civilities upon me here from various quarters', he told Hester. 'Many I find are enough dispos'd to take a view of me; whether from curiosity to see a strange new creature, viz., a leader whom nobody follows, or any other reason why, I do not conjecture'. The state of his health, of course, was news too – first of all for Hester:

November 17 . . . I passed a much better night for my fatigue . . . foot much swelled, hand less weak . . .
November 18 . . . I am able to hold a pen, and tell my love the feats I have this day performed. I have visited the fair down of Claverton . . . and have drunk one glass of water as I returned,

sitting in my coach of state, in Stall-street . . . I have no pain worth mentioning, but that of being separated from my kind love, and not seeing five little faces, which form round her a group which sums all delight . . .

November 24 . . . I write, sitting in my great chair by my friends, like an alderman of Bath. My importance in my own eyes does not stop here; for they have this morning beheld by my bed-side the Duke of Bedford, sitting like any brother alderman . . . talking very placidly (and, to be serious, very politely) of houses in the Circus, pleasant airings, Somersetshire prospects, etc.; fitting discourse for such *emeriti* as we are . . . Tenderest blessings from papa to all the pretty, affectionate inquirers.

November 28 . . . I have been airing in the coach today. for the second time, nearly three hours, and came home untired; wanting nothing but dinner, and the sight of my love and of my children. I can stand with the help of crutches . . . My left hand holds a fork at dinner with some *gentilesse* [sic], and my right holds, as you see, a pen inferior to that of few writing-masters, excepting always those two famous scribes, Hester and John . . . I am full of the beauties of our scenes around here.[31]

CHAPTER NINETEEN

———◄◊►———

America and the Rockinghams

By the time parliament met on 17 December two main questions dominated the political scene. What was to be done about America, where Grenville's Stamp Act had set the colonies alight? – and could Pitt be prevailed upon to come once more into the King's government? Rockingham's ministers were unanimous that *something* must be done about the Stamp Act: it must be amended, or suspended, or repealed outright, or repealed with an accompanying declaration of the home government's *right* to tax. Before the ministry's considered proposals were laid before parliament, where they expected a stiff fight, they now badly wanted to have the benefit of Pitt's support. 'G. Conway . . . showed great apprehensions lest Mr Pitt should join in opposition', the King noted; and as for the Duke of Grafton, he made a negotiation with Pitt a condition of his remaining a minister.[1] Newcastle, too, persistently advocated an accommodation with Pitt, and 'wondered at it' when Rockingham appeared to be tardy in offering to grasp this necessary nettle.[2] Rockingham at first seemed willing to try everybody else – Barré and Shelburne (without result), Charles Townshend, even Sackville (which Newcastle was sure would 'quite alienate Mr Pitt', as indeed it emphatically did, when Sackville was made Vice-Treasurer for Ireland); but for a long time he jibbed at approaching Pitt.

It took some time before Englishmen became aware of the fury with which Americans had greeted the Stamp Act. News of organized opposition and rioting was disturbing enough; more immediately alarming in some quarters were the American boycotts upon British imports. Strong pressure for repeal built up from merchants and manufacturers. Newcastle judged quite rightly that majority opinion inside the cabinet, also in favour of repeal, coincided with Pitt's own. In other respects, moreover, the government was pursuing intentions that Pitt surely ought to approve – removing the objectionable excise nature of the cider tax, declaring the illegality of general warrants, but at the same time refusing to encourage the return of Wilkes from his French refuge. Newcastle therefore judged the season appropriate for an indirect approach of his own in the direction of the Bath invalid, via one of Pitt's faithful, George Cooke, a member for Middlesex. Cooke, wary of being thus thought 'connected' with the administration, first sought guidance from Pitt, quoting as Newcastle's opinion what was certainly his own, that the ministry's views on America were 'exactly conformable' with Pitt's.

This brought down fire and brimstone from the hills of Bath. Pitt's animus against a supposedly maleficent Newcastle seems by this time to have become as exaggerated as his estimate of the old man's current influence. Too often in the past, he alleged, he had been 'sacrificed' to Newcastle, who now was proposing 'nothing but a little artifice to hold out to the public an appearance of connection where he knows he has none'. As for 'exactly conformable' ideas, 'whenever my ideas, in their true and exact dimensions, reach the public, I shall lay them before the world myself'. This world, so he lamented tragically to his solicitor Nuthall, 'is fallen into the Duke of Newcastle's hands; the country is undone'; the Duke's influence 'coloured and warped everything'. 'For God's sake, Sir, how is all this to end?' Nuthall faithfully echoed. 'Distraction increases every day, and ruin must follow. You, and only you, can withstand and prevent it . . . I wish you were now in or near this city'.[3]

Pitt, however, though 'much better', was not at Westminster for the preliminary round in December of the important deliberations upon the Stamp Act. 'I crawl to the pump', he wrote, 'and drink water with success. When I shall crawl to London I cannot yet fix'.[4] But by the beginning of the new year ministers had persuaded both Rockingham and the King that it was imperative at least 'to get Mr Pitt's opinion on the American question'.[5] Thomas Townshend, it was agreed, should go as emissary to Bath to attempt a penetration of the great man's mind. He hardly got past its outer defences, Pitt unhelpfully insisting that he would give his opinion to no one but the King or the public. He did, however, venture to Townshend that if he were to accept office, Newcastle must be dismissed and Temple head the Treasury, at the same time throwing out with teasing perversity that if Temple came to see him, 'he should insist on not talking politics'. As Lord Chancellor Northington interpreted all this to the King, Pitt would not come in without Temple; Temple would not come in without George Grenville. And if *that* union were ever achieved, wrote the King to Bute, 'he [Northington] looks on me as a slave for life, which I think also'. In any case, after his three previous attempts to gain Pitt, the King did not relish a fourth; to have to 'entreat' him to form a government would be both demeaning and 'impolitick'. Instead he asked Rockingham to stand firm.[6]

By now it was known that Pitt intended to be present when parliament reassembled in mid-January; and ministers, after a week of anxious discussion, decided to weather the expected storms without further attempts to take him on board.

Pitt's doctrine upon the American question was based upon a distinction which seemed valid when he first made it, but which proved to hold no answer to the pressures which were carrying the Americans forward towards economic and political independence. His thesis was basically simple. 'External' taxation was one thing: Britain had every right to control the colonial economy in her own interests, to impose duties, to forbid manufactures (he would not allow the Americans, he said, to make 'a hobnail or a horseshoe'); but 'internal' taxation was altogether different. And this was a matter, not of expediency, but of constitutional principle. The British parliament could not legally claim to extract revenue from Americans who were not, and could not be (either actually, or through the fiction of 'virtual representation') represented in it.

His magnetic presence, and a sequence of powerful and vivid speeches countering those of Grenville and the Stamp Act's supporters, dominated proceedings in the reassembled parliament. He began by defining his situation there, emphasizing once again how he was 'unconnected and single'. For the late ministry, he proceeded – bowing towards Grenville – he had not a good word. 'As for the present gentlemen . . . their characters are fair. Some of them have done me the honour to ask my opinion . . . But notwithstanding – I love to be explicit – I cannot give them my confidence: pardon me, gentlemen' – bowing towards the Treasury Bench – 'confidence is a plant of slow growth in an aged bosom . . .'

After an oblique reference to the 'overruling influence' he still suspected – that of Bute – which led him on to the Scots, and a ranging testimonial to his own earlier part in bringing the Highlanders into the

King's loyal service, he turned to America, 'a subject of greater importance than ever engaged the attention of the House, that subject only excepted when nearly a century ago it was the question whether you yourselves were to be bound or free . . . It is my opinion', he said,

> that this kingdom has no right to lay a tax upon the colonies. At the same time, I assert the authority of this kingdom over the colonies to be sovereign and supreme, in every circumstance of government and legislation whatsoever.

While emphatically asserting the sovereign authority of Britain in government and legislation, he claimed that taxation was a purely voluntary gift of the Commons; and the Commons of America, represented in their several assemblies, 'would have been slaves' if they had not in this always enjoyed rights like those of the Commons of England. The Americans were the sons, not the bastards, of England.

He seemed to have ended, upon a Latin quotation, and sat down, whereupon first Conway spoke and then Grenville replied at length, ingeniously *inter alia* discovering the right to tax America in Magna Carta. This brought Pitt to his feet again ('I do not speak twice; I only finish'), and members by acclamation allowed him to continue, though he was breaking the rules of debate. The less prepared and more trenchant expression of his views and emotions was now to come:

> Gentlemen – Sir – I have been charged with giving birth to sedition in America . . . Sorry I am to hear the liberty of speech in this House imputed as a crime. It is a liberty I mean to exercise . . . It is a liberty by which the gentleman who calumniates it [Grenville] might have profited . . . The gentleman tells us America is obstinate; America is in almost open rebellion. I rejoice that America has resisted. Three million of people so dead to all feelings of liberty as voluntarily to submit to be slaves would have been fit instruments to make slaves of the rest. I come not here armed at all points, with law cases and acts of parliament, with the statute-book doubled down in dog's ears, to defend the cause of liberty . . . but upon a general principle, upon a constitutional principle . . .
>
> The gentleman boasts of his bounties to America. Are not these bounties intended finally for the benefit of this kingdom? If they

are not, he has misapplied the national treasures. I am no courtier of America; I stand up for this kingdom . . . When two countries are connected together like England and her colonies, without being incorporated, the one must necessarily govern; the greater must rule the less; but so rule it, as not to contradict the fundamental principles that are common to both. If the gentleman does not understand the difference between external and internal taxes, I cannot help it; but there is a plain difference between taxes levied for the purpose of raising a revenue, and duties imposed for the regulation of trade, although in the consequences some revenue might incidentally arise from the latter.

The gentleman asks, when were the colonies emancipated? But I desire to know when they were made slaves . . . I will be bold to affirm that the profit to Great Britain from the trade of the colonies, through all its branches, is two millions a year. This is the fund that carried you triumphantly through the last war . . . You owe this to America; this is the price America pays for her protection . . . And shall a miserable financier come with a boast that he can bring a peppercorn into the exchequer, to the loss of two millions to the nation?

A great deal has been said without doors of the power, of the strength, of America. It is a topic that ought to be cautiously meddled with. In a good cause . . . the force of this country can crush America to atoms . . . But . . . America, if she fell, would fall like the strong man. She would embrace the pillars of the state, and pull down the constitution along with her . . . Is this your boasted peace? Not to sheathe the sword in the scabbard, but to sheathe it in the bowels of your countrymen? Will you quarrel with yourselves, when the whole house of Bourbon is united against you? . . .

The Stamp Act should be repealed absolutely, totally, and immediately . . . At the same time let the sovereign authority of this country be asserted in as strong terms as can be devised . . .; we may bind their trade, confine their manufactures, and exercise every power whatsoever – except that of taking their money out of their pockets without their consent.[7]

The various references to 'the gentleman' and 'the miserable financier' to be found amid these few discontinuous extracts from what amounted to a long and passionately argued speech give at least a hint of the personal overtones sounding through it. Burke, awaiting the moment to make his own maiden speech, flatly describes these Pitt-Grenville exchanges as 'an altercation of several hours', with both men 'heated to a great degree; Pitt as much as contempt, very strongly marked, would suffer him'.[8] And Temple, it seems, attending as onlooker beyond the Bar of the House, in no way lowered the temperature by conspicuously 'smiling and condemning everything Mr Pitt says and applauding the sentiments and behaviour of Mr Grenville'. 'I am sorry to say', Pitt wrote to Hester of her brother, 'Lord Temple rises in passion, and sinks in consideration'.[9]

During the six or seven weeks of American debate which followed, Pitt's influence and prestige stood almost as high as during his triumphant years of victory. Once again the Great Commoner, he towered over the deliberations. Indeed during the first week of February, Sackville reported, Pitt not only 'acted openly in favour of the ministers, but took direction of the proceedings upon him as if he had been in office'.[10] It was 'much too apparent to be disguised', Rockingham told the King, that without Pitt 'your Majesty's present administration will be shook to the greatest degree'; events in the Commons had once again shown 'his amazing powers and influence'. 'What a fellow this Pitt is', wrote Lord Charlemont (who was present); 'I had his bust before, but nothing less than his statue shall content me now'.

He himself, though fatigued when debates ran on into the early hours, was again full of the zest of battle. To Hester, back with 'the dear, dear boys' at Hayes (where they were in what they naturally expected to be their last few months of occupation), he wrote regretting he would have no chance of seeing her 'till Thursday. Business in the House swarms, but the bees never settle . . . All is confusion, as usual'. And a week or two later, to a typical outpouring of Hester's congratulation, he replied to tell of his 'delight, heartfelt and solid' at the result of a vital Stamp Act division, and of the 'applauding joy' of the merchants crowding the lobby, 'saved from despair and bankruptcy . . . Send the saddle-horses if you please', he added, 'so as to be in town early tomorrow morning. I propose and hope to execute my journey to Hayes by eleven'.[11]

On 18 January, the King commissioned Rockingham to approach Pitt with two straight questions: was he willing to serve, and if so would he make Temple's acceptance a condition of his own? Again, Pitt's protestations of willingness were accompanied by stipulations that amounted to refusal. He would serve with Rockingham, Grafton, Conway, and 'those who had stood for the liberties of the country', but there must be 'many removals', led by that of the 'meddling and irksome' Newcastle, and provision must be made also for his own supporters; he named Lords Bristol (Hervey's son), Shelburne, and Camden (Pratt), 'and said he must make an offer to Ld. Lyttelton, yet smil'd on naming him'. As for Temple, they would have to ask him themselves; and if Temple would serve only with his 'new associates' – meaning Grenville and Bedford in particular – Pitt would in that case decline.[12]

It would have been almost impossible for ministers to have avoided a full repeal of the Stamp Act, even if they had wished to (as at least some of them did). Two old alliances were now riding high: it was not only 'Pitt and Liberty', but also the more mundane but very powerful association of 'Pitt and the Prosperity of Trade'. Once again he was the hero – and Grenville now the villain – of the merchants, hard hit as they were by the American boycotts. Profits were depressed and unemployment soaring in the manufacturing districts. Shipping interests and the textile trade were particularly affected, and there were many plans to send delegations to Westminster to put pressure on the politicians. After the vote at 1.30 a.m. on 22 February upon the committee stage of the act of repeal – the vote was 275 to 167 in favour – the crowd waiting outside, having first given three cheers for the leader of the House, Conway, awaited the emergence of their greater champion:

> When Mr Pitt appeared the whole crowd pulled off their hats, huzzaed, and many followed his chair home with shouts and benedictions. The scene changed on the sight of Grenville. The crowd pressed on him with scorn and hisses. He, swelling with rage and mortification, seized the nearest man to him by the collar . . .[13]

In these winter debates of 1766, seven years before the Boston Tea Party and a full decade before the Declaration of Independence, Pitt stood out as the most whole-hearted of pro-Americans. When the Rockingham government coupled their Stamp Act repeal with a statutory declaration insisting on Britain's legal right (though she had for the time being considerately waived it) to what Pitt called internal taxation, it was he who fought the most vigorously against it, but with only small assistance, from Barré and Beckford in the Commons, from Camden in the Lords. Passed by massive majorities, this Declaratory Act was to be named by the Congress nine years later as one of its justifications for taking up arms against King George. He was sorry, Pitt said, that some members seemed to regard him as 'an overheated enthusiastic leveller', ignorant of the civil law and the constitution. He based his objection not on civil but on common law. If liberty were not countenanced in America, it would sicken and die in Britain too. And in any case they ought not to be cavilling over technicalities of law: 'the colonies', he claimed, 'are too great an object to be grasped but in the arms of affection'.[14]

When accounts of Pitt's passionate advocacy of their cause reached the Americans they soon made a hero of him. Statues were to be erected in his honour in New York, in Charleston ('in the Ciceronian character and habiliment'), and at Dedham in Massachusetts. 'Time shall sooner destroy this mark of their esteem', proclaimed the representatives of South Carolina on their statue, 'than erase from their minds the just sense of his patriotic virtue'. Crowds who had recently been making bonfires of the hated stamps turned to drinking toasts to 'Pitt and Liberty'; and at New York on the King's birthday to 'George, Pitt, and Liberty' – with a roasted ox, and free beer for the commonalty, to add festival to the occasion. The time had not yet arrived for a more sober consideration of what was implicit in Pitt's firmly mercantilist views on the regulation of trade and navigation, on his rejection of any colonial rights to manufacture, on his insistence upon the absolute sovereignty of the British crown and parliament.

As on America, so on other matters during the parliamentary spring of 1766, Pitt steered his own entirely independent course, sometimes backing the government, more frequently not. He seconded a ministerial motion for ending the cider excise, but furiously attacked another to economize on the militia. He argued for going further than the ministry intended upon general warrants, again urging that they should be always and everywhere illegal, not merely in cases of libel. When this actually gained support from Grenville, the Rockinghams were quick to smell a rat. Was the amity of the Family being recemented? Similarly, when Pitt made some friendly noises in the direction of the Bute following, there was nervousness lest a détente should be brewing there too.

In French political circles there was meanwhile apprehensive expectation of Pitt's return to power. Horace Walpole was in Paris from October 1765 till April 1766 and was merry enough reading of Pitt's odd foibles and invalid's eccentricities, his 'hopping, crawling, and dressing', as pictured by George Selwyn. 'I laughed till I cried', he replied to Selwyn, 'but I took care not to publish it *here*, where they believe he is more alert and has longer talons than the beast of the Gevaudan . . . You see how true the saying is that nobody is a hero in the eyes of his own *valet de chambre*! In England you are all laughing at a man whose crutch keeps the rest of Europe in awe'. 'I could not have believed it, if I had not come hither', he wrote to Mann, 'how much they dread him'.[15]

When Rockingham again made advances through Nuthall, Pitt's response was returned politely but stonily as before. He would be sent for by the King or not at all. Rockingham persuaded himself that he would be able to soldier on regardless; but both his Secretaries were less sanguine, and his position was drastically weakened when the more positive of them, Grafton, finally decided to resign. As a man of honour, he told the King, he would not continue in a ministry that 'set Mr Pitt at defiance', and humbly counselled that that paragon should be sent for and offered his own terms.[16]

Only four days before this Pitt had given the Commons what Rigby described to his chief the Duke of Bedford as 'a kind of farewell':

> He told us he was going, on account of his health, first to Bath, and then to a place still farther off [it seems that merely Burton Pynsent was meant, though the phrase has a ring of Arthur embarking for Avalon]; he wished for the sake of his dear country, that all our factions might cease . . . that if ever he was again admitted, as he had been, into the royal presence, it should be independent of any personal connections whatsoever . . .

'with plenty of recommendations', Rigby sarcastically added, 'to unanimity, virtue, etc.'.[17]

In early May, well before the session ended, Pitt was off to Bath, leaving Hester to supervise the final clearing-up at Hayes. The green Maytime countryside on the journey down had been lovely, he wrote to her, but 'nothing so pleasing to my eye as poor old Hayes; perhaps not Hayes itself', he amended, 'but what I left there. When will you come? Not till business is done, but the sooner after that, the happier for the wanderer . . .' He still wrote to his wife with all the old demonstrative devotion. However ponderously playful or stiffly high-flown he sometimes sounds – and no less she – there is no mistaking the genuineness and sense of family harmony in these letters. 'My dearest Life', he writes two days after arrival, 'the sight of your hand and the contents of your wished-for letter have made my day happy, absence excepted, and some anxiety for William [who was not well] . . . I am quite delighted with the first fruits of little Mr Secretary's pen. Pray tell him so, and encourage all to write to me; it will do them good, and give papa pleasure . . . I am ashamed to find myself so well, and not sweating in St Stephen's Chapel. I never bore a journey so well'; and then, to end, a touch of the so often repeated self-deception – or perhaps, rather, attempted self-persuasion: 'Was it that I turned my back upon the little tricks of childish men? . . . I could with ease post all the world over, provided it was to fly from such a world'.[18]

Soon Hester joined him at Burton Pynsent, a troublesome cough, brought on he declared by 'an incautious use of the waters', having hastened his departure from Bath.* But 'buried deep in Somersetshire' he quickly grew hungry for the political news that Nuthall could send him – since, as he said, he was 'not *dead*'. He was grateful and honoured to read of Grafton's explanation to the Lords of the reason for his resignation: and now worried again at the machinations of the French. 'Your Ladyship sees', he wrote to Lady Stanhope, 'how the old surly English leaven works still in a retired breast. Farming, grazing, haymaking, and all the *Lethe* of Somersetshire cannot obliterate the memory of days of activity. France is still the object of my mind whenever a thought calls me back to a public world infatuated, bewitched . . .'[19]

Meanwhile the Rockingham administration, having managed to survive the session, was falling apart. The King's men Northington (the Chancellor) and Egmont (First Lord of the Admiralty) had no

---

* 'The people who think everything right that he does, or does not, and who, as often as he changes his mind backwards and forwards, think that right too, take all the pains they can to indulge his pride . . . They stood up all the time he was in the Rooms, and while he drank his glass of water' (Walpole to Mann, 9 June 1766).

confidence in it. Conway was unhappy at its failure to recruit Pitt. Rockingham was displeased at his own lack of credit with the King yet at the same time strangely complacent and insistently unwilling to 'broaden his bottom' by taking in any of the Bute party. The King resented being forced to accept the Duke of Richmond in Grafton's place, and was angry at his ministers' refusal to go through with the financial provision for his brothers which he thought had been agreed. At last Northington indicated his wish to resign from a government that had not the strength to stand up. This heralded its end. He had come to a private understanding (the King later called it an infamous bargain) with his probable successor as Chancellor in a Pitt ministry, Camden – and now Camden advised the King to use Northington's services to approach Pitt. When George decided to act accordingly and informed his ministers so, they seemed, he said, 'thunderstruck'.[20]

CHAPTER TWENTY

Ministry and Collapse of Chatham

Between George III's accession and April 1763 there had been two
and a half years of ministerial tension, though always at that stage the
King had had Bute to turn to. Then, after April 1763 when Bute
resigned, there had been over three years of continual governmental
instability with, for the King, maddeningly frequent crises. Maddening
almost literally: if things continued so, George burst out in a letter to
Bute, 'next year there will be a council of regency'. But Bute, when
secretly appealed to, returned little encouragement beyond advocating
yet another approach to Pitt. The King felt near the end of his tether.
'My prudence is exhausted', he told Egmont on 28 May. 'I am inclined to take any step that will preserve my honour' – and the only
step left to him seemed to be a last desperate bid for Pitt's service.[1]

It was a propitious moment. Pitt was finding the waters of Lethe
at Burton Pynsent no more healing than the waters at Bath. Neither
the 'little tricks of childish men' at Westminster nor the knavish tricks
of the King's enemies abroad would consent to be banished from his
mind. He had never departed from the opinion he had delivered to
the Duke of Devonshire ten years before, that he alone could save the
country. He had put behind him now any idea that he might lead a
revitalized Whig party. Over and over again he had claimed to stand
politically 'single', independent, solitary; 'like a primeval parent,
naked, because innocent; naked, because not ashamed'.[2] If the summons
came to him now, he would stand as the enemy of all parties.

This consorted well with the King's own views. A party was only
a more respectable name for a faction, and for the King it was the
spirit of faction which all along had been the nation's curse. Bute was
now taboo to the Whigs and the public. The Rockinghams were
'weak boys' who had lost the power to govern since Pitt had rebuffed
them. The Bedfords were few in number, and in any case associated
with Grenville, who was taboo to the King. The moment was made

for Pitt, the only man with the authority 'to extricate this country out of faction'.[3] The King dared not now fail to come to an arrangement with him; and Pitt, still only fifty-seven, but aged beyond his years by chronic disease, must have realized that for him it was now or never.

In view of his shaken constitution, he had resolved, while fully intending to remain director-general of policy, to propose for himself no office which would require constant attendance in parliament; and this, he finally decided, ruled him out from his old post of Secretary of State. However, it did conform well with the idea, which was growing on him, of asking for a peerage. The suggestion was not wholly novel. Temple had hinted to Sackville that Pitt might do it. In June 1765 Bedford had reckoned that 'a peerage, with a profitable reversion to his family', would be a bait not lightly to be refused, and might well prove a satisfactory means of buying off Pitt's hostility to a possible Grenville-Temple ministry backed by the Bedfords.[4] On the evidence of their tutor Edward Wilson, Pitt's children were plainly discussing the implications of their father's possible ennoblement three months or so before the event.[5] The disadvantages of such a move must have been obvious to Pitt, though he does seem to have under-estimated its extent: he must thereby lose his uniquely commanding position as the Great Commoner. But the attractions too were immense. His lands and income, further enhanced by a ministerial sinecure, would now at last sustain the weight of honour and magnificence; and if, as he hoped, Temple could be persuaded to take the Treasury, he and his brother-in-law would stand together at the head of a ministry upon a plane of equal social status. There seems no need to invent an inferiority complex for Pitt – underdog at Eton, under-privileged younger brother and impoverished brother-in-law, over-compensating with his famous arrogance – in order to explain his longing for social grandeur, though there has been no shortage of amateur psycho-historians jumping to this explanation. Pitt's regard for honours and status was no less than the next man's; and it was the rule rather than the exception for the outstanding Commons men of his day – including of course those like Carteret who were heirs to a peerage already – eventually to proceed to the Lords. Of his two greatest Commons rivals of the previous decade Murray had long been Lord Mansfield and Fox for three years Lord Holland – only a baron certainly, badly as he had wanted an earldom. It was in the Lords that the heads of the great ruling families were to be found. The Commons was a place for dependants and younger brothers – 'a parcel of younger brothers', Pitt himself once called it.

He intended to establish his own as one of those great families. It had been the dream of his turbulent old grandfather, who once, before things turned finally sour with him, hoped that his diamond might serve to do the trick. But an earldom, more reliably than a diamond, was for ever. Pitt could hardly fail to know that his own fame was already secure. He might now ensure the standing of Pitts for futurity. (As matters purely political were to turn out, for him as for Fox, it was of course to be a *younger* son who would most brilliantly carry forward the family name into the next generation; but Pitt had already in his mind engaged a place on the Commons Front Bench for young William, 'little Mr Secretary'.)

He certainly could not think of figures such as Hardwicke or New-castle as having been in any way deprived of power by being peers, and so long as his own projected ministry could find the men to marshal support in the Commons he did not expect to be diminished himself by his elevation. Because we can now see that the five strongest eighteenth-century prime ministers from the time of Walpole were commoners, at least during their heyday – Walpole himself, Pelham, North, both Pitts – it is perhaps too easy to view the Georgian House of Lords through the wrong end of the historical telescope. As well as dignity and prestige, it still had very significant political power – and after all a majority even of nineteenth-century prime ministers were peers.

When Northington transmitted to Pitt the royal invitation, he lost not a moment in hastening to London (*Lord a mercy*, Hester was told by Smith the bailiff, who had passed him four miles from Marlborough, *going at such a pace*!) – and next day, 12 July, he was received at Rich-mond Lodge. A mutually wary but constructive interview followed, as the King's own draft memorandum records:

> . . . an ardent desire of serving me . . . he wish'd as far as it was possible to dissolve all factions and to see the best of all partys in employment . . . no man was an honest man that recommended none but his own friends . . . he should recommend taking the

351

subsisting administration as the basis . . . he ardently wish'd the assistance of Lord Temple and that he might be 1st Commissioner of the Treasury [but that without Temple's assistance he] should think himself at all events oblig'd to proceed . . . I then enter'd on the subject of Ld Bute. Mr Pitt said my declarations of last year that Ld Bute should not interfere in political matters made him quite easy on that head . . . hop'd I should frequently have the comfort of [Bute's] conversation . . .[6]

Pitt further agreed to restore Bute's brother Mackenzie to his Scottish sinecure (which would satisfy the King's bruised honour) and though he did not altogether approve of all the King's Friends whose names George advanced, he would 'try to shape something agreeable'.

On 15 July the King received Lord Temple, 'who made many professions of duty' but 'flew out into the strongest invectives against all now in office and thus we parted'[7] – with little optimism on the King's side. The following day's meeting between Pitt and Temple turned out unexpectedly sour. Temple wished to insist on a clean sweep of the Rockinghams; on Lord Gower (a Bedford) as Secretary; on Lyttelton as Lord President; and on safeguarding his own position as '*at least equal*' to Pitt's own. He knew it was futile even to suggest a post for Grenville. As for Lyttelton, Pitt was willing to see him in a subordinate post, even as 'nominal cabinet counsellor', but was 'astonished' to hear Temple put him forward for major office.[8] He was ready to let Temple nominate the Exchequer Board, including the Chancellor, but flatly negatived his other demands. Temple, unwilling (as he put it next day to the King) 'to come in as a child and go out as a fool', drove straight back to Stowe in a huff and explained to his brother George in indignant sarcasm how he had declined membership of 'the new, virtuous, patriotic administration' at the head of which 'I might have stood like a capital cypher, surrounded by cyphers of quite different complexion, the whole under the guidance of that great luminary, the great Commoner'.[9]

Pitt at first tried to conceal from Hester (who had rushed up from Somerset to be with him, his pulse having 'quickened towards evening') the stormy differences he had had with her brother, even telling her of Temple's 'kind and affectionate behaviour' – which so pleased Hester that within a few days she was writing to Stowe to express her 'sensible joy' and suggesting a renewal of family visits: 'I long to show you Burton Pynsent'.[10] Unhappily this merely elicited from Temple a lengthy, pompous, self-justifying farrago stiffly declining any renewal of 'our reciprocal country visits'. 'The contents of your letter', he replied, 'make it indispensably necessary for me not to leave you a stranger to the indignation with which I received the proposition of being stuck into a ministry as a great cypher at the head of the Treasury'.[11]

Pitt, though like everyone else he entertained no doubt who was to be 'prime minister', did not wish to head the Treasury himself – and indeed holding the First Lordship of the Treasury by no means yet necessarily implied effective ministerial premiership. It was Carteret, not the First Lord, Wilmington, who plainly had been 'prime minister' in 1742–3; similarly Pitt rather than Devonshire in 1756–7. Even in 1783, or as late as 1807–9, the Duke of Portland, though he headed the Treasury, was only in a very attenuated sense prime minister. With Pitt in 1766 there was also another consideration – his distaste for dealing with finance. As Horace Walpole said, 'the multiplication table' was not for him. He willed ends but left it to others to find means. The office he was now expected to take was again one of the Secretaryships, but instead – keeping the decision to himself – he opted for the Privy Seal, where his purely ministerial burden would be comparatively light.

Pitt's feverishness, whether attributable to London's July heat, to high words with Temple, or simply to fatigue, made him all the happier to accept the lease of a house on the cooler heights of Hampstead – North End – which a friend, Charles Dingley, a rich speculator and sawmills proprietor, had made available. For some time now this became his substitute for his lost Hayes, and thither hurried Hester (leaving the children at Weymouth with their tutor and *fifteen* servants) to support her lord as he worked at building his new administration of 'the best of all parties and exclusion of [almost] no descriptions'.[12] First, the young and rather reluctant Grafton was persuaded to accept the Treasury refused by Temple. Of Pitt's other closest adherents, the intellectually inclined Lord Shelburne took over from Conway the Southern Secretaryship, which included American affairs. Barré and James Grenville became joint Vice-Treasurers of Ireland (this involved sacking Sackville again, which Pitt was very happy to do), while

Camden took the Woolsack which Pitt had always intended for him. Northington was eased into the Lord Presidency, with inordinately handsome financial compensation. Most of the minor as well as some leading members of the Rockingham government retained their places, the principal exceptions being Rockingham himself, Dowdeswell, Charles Yorke, and of course Newcastle, who with dignity denied himself a retirement pension of £4000 a year offered him by Pitt. Rockingham, piqued by Pitt's treatment of him over past months, gave him the snub direct when Pitt called at his house, sending a servant to say he was 'extremely busy, and could not possibly see him'.[13] The Chancellorship of the Exchequer was accepted, after much havering and haggling, by Rockingham's Paymaster, Charles Townshend,* though the appointment was much against Pitt's inclination and judgement. He was talked into it by Grafton, and was soon to learn the unhappy pertinence of Horace Walpole's observation that Townshend possessed all the gifts – except 'common truth, common sincerity, common honesty, common steadiness, common courage, and common sense'.[14] Conway, regarded by the Rockinghams as their key man inside the new camp, became Northern Secretary and was to continue leadership of the Commons. When, very soon, Egmont resigned (not liking the look of his colleagues), a gesture at least was made in the direction of the Bedfords by an offer of the Admiralty to Lord Gower; the 'evident purpose of this', as George Grenville observed, 'is to break and divide us if possible'.[15] And when Gower eventually stood fast by his clan and refused the offer, Pitt was glad to be able to put a *sailor* in instead (the first since Anson's death), and one moreover connected closely with the old days of wartime triumph, Sir Charles Saunders. He happened also to be a Rockingham Whig. The veteran of veterans from those days, Ligonier, now eighty-six, was pensioned off at last, with an earldom but not without protest, and his post of Commander in Chief given to the Marquis of Granby.

By the end of July Pitt, taking for himself the very lightly burdened office of the Privy Seal, had been created 'Viscount Pitt of Burton

* 'C. Townshend took twenty turns and play'd twenty tricks before he was finally kicked up into the Chancellor of the Exchequer' (Burke to O'Hara, 29 July 1766). The Paymastership was worth £7000 a year, against the Exchequer's £2500; but he was angling for a place in the cabinet and a peerage for his wife.

Pynsent and Earl of Chatham in the county of Kent'. He had told no one, and it was with understandable misgiving that his principal ministers first learned of his elevation as they waited in Buckingham House on 28 July to kiss hands on their own appointment. Who, they wondered – not least Conway, on whom the burden would fall heaviest – who would there be in the Commons to fire the big guns when the battle grew tough? And what would 'opinion out of doors' – Pitt's *constituents* the public – have to say when they heard the news?

> How like you Pitt's new title? [Burke asked his friend O'Hara]
> As to the step itself, I think it not a good one. He ought to have kept
> the power of superintendency, if not direct management of the H.
> of Commons, in his own hands, for some time at least. But imprudent
> as it is, I do not see any thing so fatal in it, as is commonly imagined.
> His popularity may suffer something; but he stands on the Closet
> ground, I mean the Bute ground, which is better.[16]

Burke, like most of his fellow Rockinghams still convinced of the Favourite's secret influence, was wide of the mark in respect of Bute, who was in fact feeling aggrieved at being left out in the cold and treated by the King as just another politician like the rest; but he was right in seeing 'the Closet ground' as crucially important. Chatham had thrown in his lot with the Crown against the factions, and the King's backing for him over the coming months was to remain absolutely firm. There had indeed been a strange turn of the wheel. Popularity with the public had always been Pitt's strongest card, and his standing with the monarch his weakest. Suddenly the reverse was true. No doubt the chorus of disapproval that greeted his acceptance of an earldom was orchestrated and amplified by political enemies and party hacks, in pamphlets, newspapers, magazines, cartoons, doggerel verses, lampoons and squibs of every kind; but there *was* a genuine loss in public esteem. Not only the mantle of the Great Commoner, but some sort of cloak of virtue seemed to many admirers to have slipped from his shoulders. 'It was the weakest thing', wrote Gray, 'that was ever done by so great a man'. He immediately lost much popularity in America. 'Numbers of the first people here', a retired army major from Ireland, a veteran of the wars, wrote directly to Chatham, 'are displeased at your accepting of a peerage, as you could not be more honourable than you were'. The popular majority in the City of London were preparing celebrations to mark their hero's re-assumption of power; when they learned of the peerage, they cancelled them. 'Pitt was adored', according to the *Whitehall Evening Post*, 'but Chatham's quite unknown'.[17]

Across the Channel, Choiseul echoed these sentiments, finding in Pitt's sudden loss of popularity an occasion for a certain amount of fear – that he might recompense himself for it by planning further projects of conquest – but of rather more pleasure: '*Nous ne pouvons comprendre ici quel a été le dessein de My lord Chatham en quittant la Chambre des Communes*'. He might well find himself '*comme Sampson après qu'on lui eût coupé les cheveux*'.[18]

Even before the royal warrant for his earldom was signed or the Privy Seal put into his hands, Chatham set out energetically on an attempt to counter the threat, never absent in his fears, of a revival of Bourbon power. Only the circumstances were new; the policy itself was one he had long advocated – and indeed his predecessors of the Rockingham government had tried to follow it too – a northern triple alliance of Britain, Prussia, and Russia. One of his first moves now as prime minister was to call in Hans Stanley (who had acted as his peace terms negotiator in 1761) to go on a special mission to Berlin and St Petersburg, with the credentials of ambassador plenipotentiary to the court of the Tsarina Catherine.

Cold winds from the east, however, nipped this project in early bud. Frederick the Great, confident that he was in no danger now from France and with his eyes fixed rather on the promising weakness of Poland, had no inclination to become involved in any new quarrel between Britain and France or – Chatham's most immediate concern – in any support for Britain's claim against Spain for the unpaid ransom for Manila, agreed in the Peace of Paris. Similarly, the Anglo-Spanish dispute over rights to the Falkland Islands (where Chatham was now sending a naval detachment to protect British interests) seemed happily remote in Potsdam. Frederick was himself trying at this time to conclude a commercial treaty with Spain, in the furtherance of which he managed to use the threat of a Prusso-British alliance, which he had not the least intention of concluding, as a means of exerting pressure on Spain. When from their side the Spaniards artfully suggested Prussian arbitration upon the Manila ransom, and Britain turned this down,

Frederick actually obtained from Chatham's government an apology for the apparent slight upon him. This was in October, when Chatham still clung to hopes of a Prussian alliance, and tact towards Frederick remained desirable. By November Prussian refusal was final; Stanley never sailed on his mission. As Sir Andrew Mitchell set it down:

> His Prussian Majesty answered that at present he saw no likelihood of war; that France could not make war; that Spain was less in a condition to do it; that he therefore made no doubt the Spaniards would pay the Manilla ransom . . . [He] is diffident and backward to enter into engagements with us, and afraid of being drawn into new wars . . . he seems to think himself secure on his own bottom.[19]

Mixing some undiplomatic salt with the honey of his ambassadorial prose, Mitchell told Chatham that Frederick had been impressed by the 'clamour and abuse' arising from his acceptance of a peerage, and was afraid that his 'friend' had thereby 'hurt himself'. Further, there was suspicion in Potsdam of Chatham's *rapprochement* (as Frederick saw it) with the perfidious Bute, who had betrayed Prussia in 1762. In the light of these mistrustful and abortive exchanges of 1766, it is easier to explain Chatham's surprising later verdict on his once so lavishly eulogized ally: 'The King of Prussia', Chatham finally decided, 'is a mischievous rascal, a base friend, a bad ally, a bad relation, and a bad neighbour; in fact the most dangerous and evil-disposed prince in Europe'.[20]

The northern alliance, that '*great cloud of power*' Chatham dreamed of, met with a reception in St Petersburg no more helpful than in Berlin. Catherine the Great had nothing to gain from the project, unless it should bring with it subsidies for Russia and a promise to support her in a war against the Turks. And Macartney, the British ambassador, who had just successfully concluded a commercial treaty with the Russians, was outraged when he learned that Hans Stanley had been appointed by Chatham over his head; he asked to be recalled. When he finally returned to St Petersburg, he too, to satisfy Catherine, had to be accredited as *minister plenipotentiary* with the status designed for Stanley.[21]

When in October Chatham paid a two hours' social visit to Horace Walpole in Bath and the conversation turned to foreign affairs, Chatham had to lament 'that we could get no allies; that he saw no daylight'. However, Walpole reported him as looking well and walking well, 'taking the air', and being 'in excellent spirits'.²²

The threat abroad lay in the Bourbon powers; at home, in the 'factions' from which Chatham always emphasized himself as separate. No doubt the King did honestly believe in the 'great comprehensive and conciliating plan', an administration that might succeed in 'destroying all party distinctions and restoring that subordination to government which alone can preserve that inestimable blessing liberty from degenerating into licentiousness'.²³ If Chatham had cherished similar hopes, they could not have lasted long. The Rockingham Whigs, who had provided the foundation upon which the Chatham ministry was constructed, continued jealously to guard their own party solidarity. Conway, regarded by Rockingham almost as a spy within an enemy camp, yet attempting at the same time to do the right thing by his new chief, soon found himself in an almost impossible position, which the prime minister showed no sign of appreciating. When in November Chatham decided to demote one of the Rockinghams, Lord Edgcumbe, from his place as Treasurer of the Household, in order to put in his stead John Shelley – a nephew of Newcastle but a renegade from the party of his uncle and Rockingham – Conway was not even informed until the decision was made; took understandable umbrage; and came very near then and there to throwing in the towel. Then when it seemed that Lord Bessborough had extricated everybody from trouble by offering to resign his own post to make room for Edgcumbe, Conway 'in a little hour received from Lord Chatham a haughty and despotic answer, *that he would not suffer connections to force the King*. Mr Conway, losing all patience, wrote to the Duke of Grafton, *that such language had never been held west of Constantinople*'.²⁴ Seven of his Rockinghamite colleagues did in fact resign at this juncture, including Saunders from the Admiralty; and a second Rockinghamite admiral, Keppel, was dismissed. (Chatham replaced Saunders with another sailor, Hawke.) It was from this moment that the Rockingham group – except the relatively few retaining ministerial places under Chatham – went into open opposition, in which frustrated and unrewarding situation they were to continue for the next decade and a half.

Of the other three principal connections, the Grenvilles (who numbered among them Pitt's nephew Thomas, hostile now to the uncle who had once been his guardian and mentor) would unquestionably be in opposition. The Bute party was conciliated by a judicious allocation of honours and places. But the Duke of Bedford, after at first seeming to have come to an amicable understanding with Chatham, then asked for *eleven* of his party to be looked after, either with offices or honours. Chatham straightway referred these demands to the King, who not unnaturally declared them extravagant and rapacious. Chatham and he together, said the King, must show the Bedfords 'of what little consequence' they were and, by engaging 'able men be their private connections where they will . . . rout out the present method of banding together'. The idea was still an *anti*-party government; but the great conciliating plan was dead.[25]

Chatham, relying upon royal and public backing, wrote off, or pretended to, the prospects of factional opposition: 'Unions with whomsoever it be give me no terrors: I know my ground: and I leave them to indulge their own dreams. If they can conquer, I am ready to fall . . . Faction will not shake the Closet, nor gain the publick'.[26] It was the same tone that he had adopted when a few weeks earlier Grafton had warned of 'a strong phalanx of able personages' in the Commons likely to give trouble unless their discontents were attended to. 'As to the phalanx your Grace mentions', Chatham replied, 'I either am full of false spirits infused by Bath waters or there is no such thing'.[27] (Chatham had again repaired to Bath during October following more gout in August and September.)

This sanguine-sounding attitude towards potential opposition – and by December that included all three of the main Whig groups, Rockinghams, Bedfords, Grenvilles – might have shown more convincingly if the administration had itself shown some unity, but it lamentably did not. Conway was already full of grievances, and only his conscientiousness and unwillingness to appear personally ambitious kept him with Chatham. Grafton's high regard for his hero was already being seriously qualified, and like Conway he was beginning to realize how little his difficulties were taken into account by the man in command. Of leading ministers, Grafton, Camden, and Shelburne remained closest to Chatham's thinking, but the sharp-minded and somewhat arrogant Shelburne, in addition to being *persona non grata* with the King, was soon at loggerheads with the equally clever, hardly less arrogant, and much more unscrupulous Charles Townshend;

and there was conflict between these two on the most important of the problems that the government was immediately faced with.

This was India. The charter of the East India Company, to whom war and successful intrigue had brought enormous accessions of territory and wealth, was due for renewal. The Company was now master of an empire considerably more extensive and more populous than the country from which it had obtained its original monopoly. It was now in control of the revenues of Bengal, Bihar, and Orissa. Its leading servants had made great fortunes, some by straightforward trading, some by bribery and extortion, many by a mixture of both. At home shareholders pressed for higher dividends. Speculators worked the market. It was Chatham's own grandfather who had once touted his diamond round the courts of Europe and with his Indian riches schemed fretfully to lay the foundations for a house of Pitts who should count in the world. Now indeed his grandson counted, but 'Diamond' Pitt's spiritual descendants, the returned 'nabobs', notorious for the weight of their loot and ostentation of their life-style, were not among those whom Chatham could admire. He had a host of supporters, a few of whom like Beckford might even properly be called his friends, among men whose wealth derived from overseas trade. It did not occur to him to question the morality of fortunes made in the slave and sugar trades. But the 'nabobs', the 'Asiatic plunderers of Leadenhall Street', represented a species he resented. Like Horace Walpole, he was convinced of the 'horrid treachery, fraud, violence, and blood [by which] the Company's servants had stridden to such aggrandizement'. Walpole saw – and wrote that Chatham also saw 'with indignation' – 'three Indian provinces, an empire in themselves, in the hands of a company of merchants who, authorized by their charter to traffic on the coast, had usurped so mighty a portion of his dominions from the Prince who permitted their commerce with his subjects'.[28] This 'too vast' and monopolistic Company – Chatham always hated monopolies – had moreover won its empire, with the appreciable assistance of the Crown's army and navy. It had come to possess much more than what 'by any colourable pretence' constituted rightful property. Before the charter was renewed, at least there must be a full parliamentary inquiry into this question of right.[29]

His own views upon the matter moved somewhat over the years. During the war, in 1757–8, he seemed to be allowing basic right, as well as immediate responsibilities, to the Company; and by 1773 he was to speak of 'a mixed right', with the state 'entitled to the larger share as largest contributor to the acquisition, by fleets and men'.[30] But in 1766 there seems no doubt – and his choice of Beckford in the Commons to move for the inquiry confirms it – that he wished parliament to decide that the fundamental right to the Indian revenues collected by the Company lay with the Crown, which should then re-assign, *ex gratia*, a portion of them to the Company in return for its administrative responsibilities, and 'for the public purposes of defence of India and the extension of trade'.[31] He never of course envisaged governmental interference in India itself, or harboured (as some later claimed for him) a vision of any imperial *raj*. It was rather that he wished to ensure that the state should get a fair return for its investment in Indian conquest.

Speculators, of whom Charles Townshend was one, were en-couraged when in September 1766 the East India Court of Proprietors over-ruled the Directors and increased the dividend from 6% to 10%. It was at this stage that Chatham announced that the forthcoming session of parliament would include an inquiry into the Company's finances. Beyond that, he put forward no clear plan; but it seemed obvious that he intended to meet the Company head on, and obtain and unequivocal parliamentary declaration of the Crown's right. Once that was done – what? All he would say later, in February, was that 'the ways to ulterior and final proceedings upon this transcendans object' would 'open themselves naturally and obviously enough" 'Lord Chatham never did open to us', Grafton wrote, 'what was his real and fixed plan'.[32]

Charles Townshend's secret dabbling in East India stock (he cleared over £7000 profit by April 1767) had given him a strong financial interest in defeating Chatham's intentions. He and his friends, both in the Company and in the cabinet, had no objection to the Exchequer taking a share in the Company's profits, but did everything in their power to frustrate the parliamentary inquiry. Thus within a few weeks of the government's formation, a wide split had opened within it. Townshend in general had backing from Conway, Chatham from Grafton, Shelburne, and Camden. Outside the cabinet, Beckford and the 'popular' anti-monopolistic party in the City of London were of course loud in Chatham's support.

To begin with, it was widely reported with what a rod of iron the new Earl was ruling his ministers. The Prussian ambassador, for instance, reported home how in the ante-room at the King's levee he witnessed a remarkable 'symptom of the subordination' in which Chatham held his colleagues, 'in the style of a commander to his inferior officers'. 'All the ministers in office came and paid their respects to him, and to each as he took leave the Earl handed a little note, with which the minister retired into a corner of the room, to read it and to note down what Pitt had said to him'.[33] 'You will know', wrote the resentful and treacherous Townshend to the dismissed and disgruntled Sackville, 'how entirely everything proceeds from Lord Chatham to the King . . . No other man has the least previous knowledge or influence'.[34] This was never quite true; and the fact that it became less and less so was partly because of the increasing absenteeism of Chatham as his illness grew upon him and paralysed his resolution, but in large measure because of Townshend's own machinations.

1766, with a disastrously wet summer and corn supplies speculatively held back, proved a year of dearth. The poor suffered greatly; there was widespread food rioting; and the government, by Order in Council, decided in October (with parliament still in recess) to put an embargo on the export of corn and flour. This action having been challenged by the opposition groups as extra-parliamentary and therefore arbitrary, Chatham was obliged to concentrate, both in the King's Speech and in his only two speeches as prime minister in the Lords, not upon his principal concern of India, but upon defending himself and his government against an alleged infraction of constitutional liberties. In such an emergency, he claimed – with a resourceful quotation from Locke – the Crown must be the sole judge of necessity. While the Lord Chancellor, Camden, excused in an unfortunate phrase this 'tyranny' of but forty days, in the Commons the unsubtle Beckford blundered into talking of the Crown's right in time of peril to *dispense* with the law. This gave opponents of 'prerogative' – among whom Pitt of old had ever been first in the fray – a weapon with which to beat the administration, who were obliged to bring in a bill to indemnify themselves. When however this measure came before the Lords, Chatham was unrepentant, indeed defiant, once again taking up his old stance of man of the people, above the pettiness of party: 'When the people condemn me', he said, 'I shall tremble; but I shall set my face against the proudest connection in the country'. The young Whig Duke of Richmond thereupon accusing Chatham of insolence, there followed so hot an exchange between the two that the House – which was accustomed to a certain decorum of debate and to eschewing 'inflammatory eloquence' – insisted on withdrawals and mutual apologies.[35]

Already, by the time of this altercation, Chatham was beginning to despair of getting his own way upon the East India question. With every apparent prospect of success Townshend was manoeuvring to negotiate a deal which would bypass the question of right and permit the Company to be left alone on payment of an agreed sum to the nation. On 7 December Chatham wrote to the First Lord, Grafton, with a kind of furious despondency:

> I grieve most heartily at the report of the [ministers'] meeting last night. If the [East India] inquiry is to be contracted within the ideas of Mr Chancellor of the Exchequer . . . the whole becomes a *farce*, and the *ministry a ridiculous phantom* . . . Mr C. Townshend's fluctuations and incurable weaknesses cannot comport with his remaining in that critical office . . . In case this question be not fully supported and carried . . . I shall wash my hands of the whole business.[36]

A month later, from Bath on 10 January, he was sending Grafton further signals of frustration and something like surrender: 'My only hope centres in the justice of parliament, where the question of right can alone be decided . . . I hope soon to be at your Grace's orders in town, though I see not the least use I can be in this matter; possibly rather in the way of others . . .'[37] He had exhibited this mood of petulant pessimism and quite uncharacteristic weakness earlier to Shelburne, and then merely over a proposal he disapproved of that Lord Hillsborough should change posts: 'This incident . . .', he wrote strangely, 'gives abundant room to think I am not likely to be of much use'.[38]

That was back in October, and yet he had since, erratically enough, on his own initiative switched Lord Hillsborough. Now, by January, his administration was altogether at sixes and sevens. 'Your Lordship must have observed', Grafton wrote to him, 'a *peevish* cast in some of our late councils, the bad effect of which your presence can only prevent'. And Beckford, while commiserating with his leader upon the illness that kept him at Bath, wrote of his own frustration at Townshend's hands, of Conway's indecisiveness, and of the urgent necessity of Chatham's presence and advice on 'what steps to take . . . What am I to move on Friday se'nnight?'[39] 'It is not my absence which affects this business [of the East India inquiry]', Chatham replied to Grafton, 'but an unfortunate original difference of opinions among the King's servants, which . . . has . . . thrown it into confusion inextricable'.[40]

In fact Chatham *had* started out for London on 11 January but turned back on a renewal of his gout. His absence, he was soon telling Shelburne, afflicted him beyond expression, but he was just now beginning to be 'lifted into a coach for a little motion and air', and hoping the beneficial effect of the waters would let him be in London within a fortnight. But his remarks on the Indian issue were disappointingly verbose and cloudy. Delay would be necessary to 'give room for the present entangled state of this business to develope itself'.[41]

Shelburne was troubling him with the news from America too, where various assemblies had defied the mutiny act requiring billeting of troops, and New York merchants had petitioned against the whole system of trade regulation, the very ark of the covenant for one holding Chatham's convictions. He could only 'foresee confusion':

A spirit of infatuation has taken possession of New York: their disobedience to the mutiny act will *justly* create a great ferment here . . . The petition of the merchants . . . is highly improper . . . most absurd . . . most excessive . . . most grossly fallacious and offensive. What demon of discord blows the coals in that devoted province I know not; but they are doing the work of their worst enemies themselves . . . The stamp act, of most unhappy memory, has frightened those irritable and umbrageous people quite out of their senses . . .[42]

Coming from one so notoriously masterful, Chatham's helpless-sounding defeatism at once exasperated and alarmed his lieutenants in London. The King, too, hoping that the East India proposals would not be 'whittled to a mere nothing', professed himself by now 'greatly mortified' by his minister's non-appearance. He had clung on to Chatham as his life-line and was not proposing to let go. But his message showed a kindly solicitude. He begged Chatham would not worry unduly about his confinement, and offered sympathy for 'what his mind as well as his body' must be suffering.[43]

Therein lay the hint of a true explanation of Chatham's mysterious weakness, though it was as yet not guessed at, and even now it is well to be chary of dogmatic pronouncements. It has always been hard to decide the relative seniority of chickens and eggs; never more so than with this strange collapse. Discouragement from every direction; awareness of failure; persistent recurrence of pain and the frustration of physical immobility – were these the causes which rendered him unable to face problems or people, and sink increasingly under the weight of depression? Or was it the inherent constitutional flaw, an inescapable biochemical curse, which paralysed body and will, and eventually the mind too, and reduced him to a shadow of himself? Susceptibility to manic-depressive attacks is genetically innate, but they are also admittedly liable to 'be precipitated by environmental circumstances'.[44]

Chatham's environmental circumstances in 1767 could not have been much worse. His gout was painful, persistent, and disabling. Politically nothing had gone well. His foreign policy had failed. The 'conciliating plan', always a sickly child, had been abandoned. The Whig factions, though hostile to one another, were at least united in their opposition. The first minister in the Commons, Conway, was disgruntled and antagonized; he openly described himself as 'a passenger', and might at any minute revert to the Rockinghams. Townshend, the next leading Commons minister, was successfully engaged in schemes to defeat Chatham's intentions. The reports from America were ominously discouraging. As a lapsed commoner, Chatham's own standing with the public was now in doubt. He had offended many of his most faithful supporters; Walpole put it with studied elegance:

> Like oracles and groves, whose sanctity depended on the fears of the devout, and whose mysterious and holy gloom vanished as soon as men dared to think and walk through them, Lord Chatham's authority ceased with his popularity; and his godhead when he had affronted his priests.[45]

Before the end of January 1767, after six months of office, he was very near to abdication. But he summoned his weakening resources for an effort on 10 February, reached Marlborough, again collapsed, and spent the next nearly three weeks in the Castle Inn there, 'still inaccessible and invisible, though surrounded by a train of domestics that occupied the whole inn and wore the appearance of a little Court'.[46]

The decision whether to make a settlement with the East India Company or press the parliamentary inquiry could hardly be delayed longer. While Lord President Northington did his best to hold the divided cabinet together, a fretful and uncomprehending, but still loyal, Grafton sent down to Marlborough urgent cries for help: Chatham's presence was 'absolutely necessary to give dignity to the administration'. Might he perhaps drive down 'to talk this whole matter over'? No, replied Chatham, he was not well enough. Almost incredibly, he wrote now that he was no 'proposer of plans', merely 'an unbiass'd judge of them'; parliament was 'the only place' where he would declare himself finally.[47]

However, by painful stages, a few miles a day, he crawled up to London, just at the time when the opposition parties were in high fettle, tasting the honey of a little popularity by uniting to defeat the government on the budget; they reduced the land tax by a shilling. On 2 March Chatham at last arrived at his house in Bond Street, receiving a not intentionally ironical welcome from the King, which expressed reliance upon the 'firmness' which would 'withstand that evil called connection'. 'Now that you are in town', George believed, 'every difficulty will daily decrease'. He met no matching optimism: Chatham could not yet see 'the preposterous union of clashing factions' giving way before the honest sense of the nation; and, pouring out 'a heart overflowing with the most reverential and warm sense of his Majesty's condescension', he regretted that he was 'out of a condition to attend his Majesty's most gracious presence'.[48] (He did eventually see the King once, on 12 March.) Every kind of rumour was soon circulating about his health, while Chatham's friend Lord Bristol and the Duke of Grafton relayed such reassurance as they could to Buckingham House. Perhaps it was partly an attempt to counter some of the more alarming stories that Chatham, that 'master dissembler', 'scarce lame . . . even paraded through the town in a morning to take the air', at least according to a suspicious Walpole.[49] But certainly he remained ill, inactive, and mostly incommunicado. After his return from Bath he did not attend a single cabinet meeting. When someone remarked to

Lady Temple that he had seen Lord Chatham out in his chariot, with a servant sitting beside him, he had appeared 'very grave and sadly'. 'This looks as if they would not let him go out by himself', wrote Lady Temple to her husband, 'for he certainly does not like the company of servants'.[50]

Two days after his arrival in London, on 4 March, he had made one last effort to rid himself of Townshend, authorizing Grafton, with the King's approval, to make an offer of the Exchequer to Lord North. It was refused. Parliament then, while conceding to the East India Company that it need not reveal its correspondence or accounts, accepted nevertheless that there should be an inquiry, which lumbered uselessly forward over the ensuing weeks with no effective forces pressing what had been Chatham's principal intention, to settle the question of 'right'. Negotiations with the Company, and rival intrigues within both Company and cabinet, continued long past the time when he was capable of taking any active interest in the subject.*

Chatham removed to North End and remained there throughout the summer, while Grafton and Northington laboured to keep the ship of administration afloat, and Conway continued *almost* to resign, and Shelburne struggled to square the circle of American policy by proposing a comprehensive set of resolute but conciliatory measures such as Chatham might well have sanctioned had he been in control. (He tried to submit them by letter and via Grafton, but there was no response.) It was Charles Townshend, however, the unabashable, who now elbowed his way to the centre of the stage, exasperating his colleagues, leaking cabinet secrets to the opposition,[51] openly relishing the absence of Chatham, whose brilliance he at once envied, resented and designed to eclipse. While this weathercock politician's flippant lack of principle shocked and disgusted, his bubbling eloquence and impudent wit delighted. His most scintillating and outrageous performance came in the so-called 'champagne speech' on 8 May, in which opponents and fellow-ministers were impartially put to the rapier. It demonstrated, declared Walpole, that Townshend's abilities rose above, and his judgement fell below, all other men's.[52] Bigger with consequences was his introduction a few days afterwards of the 'Townshend duties', including the tea tax which later was to provoke

* An eventual settlement, short-lived, allowed the Treasury £400,000 a year from the Company, while parliament prohibited the dividend from rising above 10%.

the party in Boston harbour. The measure was designed to please as many and offend as few as possible, either at home or in America. Unlike the Stamp Act, it certainly satisfied Chatham's criterion of 'external taxation'. But as Burke commented, witty as well as wise after the event, 'to tax and to please, no more than to love and be wise, is not given to men'; 'this fine-spun scheme had the usual fate of all exquisite policy'. Townshend's opportunities for fiscal ingenuity, oratorical display, or sabotage of his colleagues' policies were, however, to be cut suddenly short. Intriguing almost to the end, and 'joking on death as naturally as he used to do on the living', he succumbed in September to a 'putrid fever'.[53]

Sinking gradually deeper into melancholia, with little appetite, no strength, a recurrent fever, no ability to concentrate, no power of will or command of himself, Chatham was physically and mentally shipwrecked. Hester did her utmost to protect him from business and from all visitors. Rumour was rife that he was mad, a supposition that was strengthened by the knowledge that mental derangement was common among the Pitt family, and that he was being attended by Dr Addington (father of the future prime minister), a well known practitioner in 'the mad business'. Letters from him went mostly in Hester's hand. In a style extreme with every elaboration of florid artificiality, these communications tell their tale of humiliating helplessness. They beg that Lord Chatham may be left alone. 'Lord Chatham's state, I doubt', wrote Walpole, 'is, too clearly, the gout flown up into his head'.[54]

Unfortunately the leaderless government was in so tattered a condition by the end of May that its majorities in the Lords dwindled to between six and two, with two of the King's brothers press-ganged to help save the day, and 'some lords brought down from their very beds'. Grafton felt that he absolutely must consult Chatham, but on 27 May Hester was under 'the painful necessity of most earnestly entreating his Grace' not to come.[55] This sent Grafton off to the King, who rather than surrender before 'the hydra faction', had a desperate need to cling on to him, and of course to Chatham too, even to a helplessly invalid Chatham. From Grafton on 29 May a second cry for rescue met a second agonized refusal from Chatham in Hester's hand. A meeting was impossible; *'impossible'*; whereupon an urgent appeal arrived from the King, who up till now had behaved with the most tactful consideration for Chatham's troubles – and indeed continued so, but he *had* to bring home to him the severity of the crisis. He begged him to see Grafton, if only for five minutes; or he was ready to come out to North End himself. Uncomprehendingly he desired Chatham to be as firm as his royal self.

'Penetrated and overwhelmed with . . . the boundless extent of your royal goodness', Chatham replied, 'totally incapable as illness renders me, I obey your royal commands'. He would see Grafton, but begged the King not to come; 'the honour and weight of such an audience' would crush him in his enfeebled state.[56]

Grafton went to North End on 31 May expecting to find Chatham very ill indeed, but he was shocked by what he confronted, 'nerves and spirits . . . affected to a dreadful degree . . . his great mind bowed down'. Grafton had to struggle to make his chief aware of the political crisis, but did succeed in getting his permission to open 'a negotiation with the Bedford or Rockingham party – though he preferred the former'.[57]

The King was relieved, if prematurely. A crippled lion was better than a troop of jackals. 'I already look on all difficultys overcome', he wrote. Alas, they were not, or not yet. It looked as if Conway and Northington would resign, and hence the ministry 'infallibly fall into pieces in less than ten days' unless Chatham pointed out the proper persons to fill up the vacancies. 'I earnestly call upon you', George wrote, 'to lay before me a plan, and also to speak to those you shall propose'. The alternative – it was vague, but threatening: 'the necessity of taking steps that nothing but the situation I am left in could have obliged to'.

Chatham's – that is to say Hester's – reply to this was pitiful: 'totally incapable . . . increase of illness . . . unspeakable affliction . . . *utter disability* . . . implore compassion and pardon . . . unfeigned zeal rendered useless'.[58]

Grafton went to see Chatham again on 4 June, in an atmosphere of rather less immediate crisis. Government majorities improved some-what. Conway again deferred his resignation and did not after all desert to the Rockinghams who, while themselves turning down the opportunity of joining the administration in July, saw their rivals the Bedfords drawn into it before the year was out – thereby breaking their alliance with the third Whig connection, the Grenvilles. Conway, in fact, no longer Secretary, remained in the cabinet. The administration, moreover, was considerably more comfortable for having Lord North at the Exchequer in place of the maverick Townshend, and it proved eventually capable of hobbling along. It had of course long ceased in any true sense to be Chatham's ministry. This by any realistic reckoning had come to end, perhaps by January 1767, certainly by March.

Throughout June Chatham and Hester continued to fend off the King, who persisted in trying to instil spirit and optimism where it was so plainly lacking, and in persuading himself as well as Chatham that all political difficulties would melt away as soon as he recovered. Would he not consider consulting the royal physician Sir Clifton Wintringham? None of the King's well-meaning suggestions or hopeful inquiries elicited any cheer. Chatham professed 'entire confidence' in Dr Addington. Replies, some in Chatham's own hand, harped dutifully on his Majesty's infinite goodness and condescension, but continued in the same vein as before: 'utterly incapable of the smallest effort . . . health broken . . . application of mind totally impossible'.[59]

As summer proceeded he grew worse rather than better; sometimes in bed for days on end, sometimes able to go about a little, mostly sitting bowed and brooding, liable to overmastering tears, unwilling to talk, subject to giddiness, palpitations, tremors, frequently refusing food and insisting on a darkened room, unable to bear the presence of others. Special arrangements were contrived for keeping him apart from servants – meals were left at a hatch which could be shut off from his room. His children were kept away from him, in the Bond Street house. Always subject to grandiose fancies, he now became possessed by some of grotesquely irrelevant extravagance. North End was not big enough. He must enlarge it, refurnish and refit it in better style, add a children's wing. In all, he calculated that thirty-four new bedrooms would be needed; and the complaisant Dingley, the proprietor, at one stage actually agreed to this undertaking.* Then the privacy of his northward prospect was ruined by other people's houses. Chatham therefore schemed to do as he had at Hayes, rid himself of immediate neighbours: 'he took four or five houses', reported Horace Walpole, 'as fast as Mr Dingley, his landlord, went into them'. In any case he

---

* These inflated bubbles of a disturbed mind are strangely paralleled by George III's in 1804, when he planned crazily extravagant new palaces.

did not *like* North End, and Burton Pynsent was too distant. He was seized with a yearning to be back at Hayes. Thomas Walpole, who had been in residence little over a year, showed his cousin Horace 'letters he had received from Lady Chatham, begging in the most pathetic terms that he would sell them Hayes again. She urged that it would save her children from destruction; and that her children's children would be bound to pray for him, requesting that he would take some days to consider before he refused'.[60] At first, however, while consenting to let the place to Chatham temporarily, he did refuse. Renting would not do; Chatham must be the owner. Hester and her brother James accordingly enlisted the powerful persuasions of Lord Camden; and eventually Thomas Walpole, apprehensive of being held responsible for an irreversible collapse, capitulated. At least he did not lose financially; he had bought Hayes for £11,780 and he sold it back for £17,400.* The difference between the two sums should have rather more than taken care of his expense on repairs to make the place 'safe and healthy, both which essential qualities' he claimed it lacked when he took possession.[61]

Chatham was in no condition personally to attend to such matters of business, and in August he agreed to Hester taking power of attorney. Thenceforth she was in law what she had for some time been in fact, master as well as mistress of the household. She did not need long to conclude that they could not afford to buy Hayes without selling off a substantial part of the Burton estate, which was now done. Two or three times during July and August it was naturally necessary for Nuthall to be at North End on various such legal matters, and a letter from him to Camden, reporting what he had seen of Chatham's condition, was passed on by Camden to the King, who was thus brought to grasp for the first time the depths into which his prime minister had sunk. He was shocked; to see 'a man that has appeared in so very great a light fall into such a situation is an abasement of human nature; I think it most prudent', he told Camden, 'that this should not be communicated'.[62]

---

* Chatham claimed later that he had paid even more: 'I gave Mr Walpole 2000 *l.*, besides 3000 *l.* more, upon valuation of stock, utensils of farm, etc.' (Chatham to Temple, 9 June 1772, *Grenville Papers* iv. 537).

I think I see a visible alteration for the worse, his hands tremble more, he is paler and thinner in the face, and I am persuaded much emaciated in his body and thighs . . . and in talking over some particulars of his estate he was more than once bewildered . . . there were two or three things I could not make him understand, wch her ladyship cut short by saying she did, and would explain to him another time . . . When we were alone, he . . . say'd he now saw it was impossible he should be well, that he was in a fever all over him; he desired me to feel his hand, wch was very hot and dry indeed. Upon the whole I am satisfied he is . . . dangerously ill. He is miserable beyond conception . . .[63]

In September, Dr Addington advising a change of air and scenery, the King's permission was given for Chatham to go to Burton Pynsent. Every kind of rumour circulated. He had recovered. He was mad as a hatter. 'In his way down to Somersetshire', so Temple was informed, 'he walked ostentatiously before the door of almost every inn in which he stopped, and a servant who went with him into the country is returned, who says he never remembers to have seen his Lordship better in his whole life'. A rather more reliable version of events reached George Grenville: 'Dr Addington contradicts the accounts of Lord Chatham's health, represents him in a very shattered condition, but able to go about a little, and even to be amused by being read to'.[64]

After only a few weeks at Burton Pynsent, he and Hester moved on to Bath, receiving no company, and waiting impatiently for the completion of legal formalities and building repairs which would allow them to get back to Hayes. Before Christmas they were re-installed there, he little changed in condition, still awaiting that 'regular fit of gout' which Dr Addington was convinced would be nature's method of eventually expelling the maleficent humours. On the journey from Bath to Hayes they took care to avoid London, and thus society; instead they stayed overnight at the house of Chatham's sister Catherine and her husband, the Nedhams, thus unknowingly ruining an attempt by Lord Shelburne to snatch a consultation with Chatham as he passed through Bromley. Shelburne's need for help was urgent. He was worried both on the nation's account and more particularly his own. The Bedford party, newly accommodated within the government, were hostile both to him personally and to his American policies of compromise and conciliation. The Bedfords were the tail who would soon be wagging the dog, and Shelburne might reasonably feel that of leading ministers he was the last who would fight hard for the policies of a *Chatham* administration. Earlier in December he had tried, through Hester, to get advice and backing, following a decision he had unsuccessfully resisted to split the Southern Department into two. This had hived off the affairs of America from Shelburne to a Third Secretary, Lord Hillsborough, a hard-liner. Hester had done as Shelburne asked, and told her husband of what was brewing; but his wan and helpless reply came back through her: he was too ill to give an opinion. At Bromley Shelburne waited in vain for a last chance to make some brief contact with his lost leader. The process of elbowing him out of the ministry had in fact begun. Mistrusted by his colleagues, and actively disliked by the King – he was thought 'jesuitical', over-assertive, and rather too clever – he soon began absenting himself from cabinet meetings.

Settled again at 'dear Hayes', Chatham remained in sad plight, low, weak, and at times confused. The children were kept at Bond Street still. Grafton and the King tried to trouble him as little as possible, but when they were obliged to, they now began to strike a note of some exasperation. Grafton, a patient and hitherto generally mild young man – he was still only thirty-two – was irritated into pointing out 'the obligation (the word is not too strong) you are really under to us all', and reminding Chatham of the 'difficulties inexpressible' he was causing to one who took over the Treasury 'solely at your instigation'. The King too sounded increasingly stern:

I am thoroughly convinced . . . your name has been sufficient to enable my administration to proceed. I therefore, in the most earnest manner, call on you to continue in your employment. Indeed, my conduct towards you since your entering my service gives me a double right to expect this of you, as well as what you owe to your country and [your colleagues, especially Grafton and Camden].[65]

The immediate occasion of these pressures was a troublesome peer, Lord Botetourt, a sort of second-class court favourite, who, unable to get the Lord Privy Seal to approve a charter of incorporation he was seeking to protect his private money after the failure of his copper works at Sutton Coldfield, was proposing to move against Chatham in the Lords, alleging unreasonable delay; and to satisfy Lord Botetourt it had been found necessary to put the Privy Seal temporarily in commission and afterwards to hold a Privy Council at Hayes formally to restore it to Chatham. He professed himself 'grieved to occasion so much trouble to his friends', but doubted whether 'he might ever be of the smallest use again', pleading yet again his extreme weakness. He implored royal compassion.

As the year 1768 proceeded it grew increasingly obvious that the genuine Chathamites within the 'Chatham' administration had become a mere remnant. 'I find myself', wrote Camden, 'surrounded by persons to whom I am scarce known, and with whom I have no connection'.[66] Even worse was the situation of Shelburne, now quite isolated. Ill as Chatham was, he was not too incapacitated to appreciate the turn events were taking. 'Lord Chatham is at Hayes', Camden told Grafton in September, 'brooding over his own suspicions and discontents . . . under a persuasion . . . that he is given up and abandoned'.[67] Early in October Grafton, having finally decided to be rid of Shelburne – a course the King had been urging no less than the Bedford group – and aware of likely difficulties at Hayes, tried once more to obtain an interview with Chatham, whom he had not seen for sixteen months. However, he was admitted no further than to Lady Chatham, to whom he explained the Shelburne situation and also the cabinet decision to replace the existing absentee governor of Virginia by one who was willing to reside there, as the Virginia Assembly was demanding. This last move begins to appear a shade less uncomplicatedly prudent and virtuous when names are supplied. The new governor was to be the entrepreneurial Lord Botetourt who had only recently made such trouble for the Lord Privy Seal; and the non-resident (and very indignant) governor to be superseded was one of Chatham's most esteemed generals, the conqueror of Canada, Amherst. Grafton would certainly have needed to use some skilful persuasion, even if he had been allowed to penetrate the Hayes defences, in order to convince Chatham that the government was proceeding on lines acceptable to its nominal leader.

Chatham made up his mind at last that he should 'ask permission' to resign, and wrote to Grafton giving his reasons – his 'broken state of health', and the removal of Shelburne and Amherst. The King, who had earlier brushed aside warnings that Chatham might go if Shelburne were dismissed, now admitted he 'could not conceal the not having expected this development'. In particular, he had not bargained for Chatham making anything other than his health into a resignation issue; but he miscalculated and was annoyed at what he described as desertion. He still looked forward stubbornly to a recovered Chatham lending his weight to the government's standing. 'I think I have a right *to insist* on your remaining in my service', he wrote. But all the comfort he could obtain from Chatham's abject but firm reply was that it omitted to mention the issues of Shelburne and Amherst. Bad health might thus be proffered publicly as the sole reason.[68] This was despite the fact that Chatham, though he still had his bad days, was on the whole improving. An architect named Taylor going down to Hayes in July to consult upon further alterations Chatham was planning to make, had published abroad – and thus considerably annoyed Lady Chatham – how clear-headed and physically alert he had found him, while the following month Sir Robert Bertie was surprised to come upon him one evening out on horseback and seeming 'as well as ever . . . cheerful and alive'.[69]

Chatham's letter of resignation, the last he would ever write to the King, is uncomfortably typical of the extravagantly artificial humility of his pretentious 'courtier' style – and in its penultimate sentence pregnant with irony for the future:

> Penetrated with the high honour of your Majesty's gracious commands, my affliction is infinite to be forced by absolute necessity from illness to lay myself again at your Majesty's feet for compassion. My health is so broken, that I feel all chance of recovery will be entirely precluded by my continuing longer to hold the Privy Seal, totaly disabled as I still am from assisting in your Majesty's councils.
>
> Under this load of unhappiness, I will not despair of your Majesty's pardon, while I supplicate again on my knees your Majesty's mercy, and most humbly implore your Majesty's royal permission to resign that high office.
>
> Should it please God to restore me to health, every moment of my life will be at your Majesty's devotion. In the mean time, the

thought your Majesty deigns to express of my recovery is my best consolation.[70]

Barré went out with Chatham and Shelburne but, of the old faithful, neither James Grenville nor, just yet, Lord Camden. Chatham's own office of Privy Seal was handed to his friend Lord Bristol, who as Lord Lieutenant had for the previous two years been 'governing' Ireland from his London residence.

CHAPTER TWENTY-ONE

A Fury of Opposition

Whether from relief at relinquishing office, or by 'a regular fit of the gout after so long an intermission' (as was generally thought), or from more mysterious natural processes of recovery, Chatham's health improved notably during the autumn of 1768. Walpole thought it must be the gout – or 'gout and the smell of war', two sovereign restoratives for a man such as Chatham. Not that the smell of war was as yet very strong. What there was of it arose from the French seizure of Corsica, which Grafton's ministry had no serious intention of making a *casus belli* – as indeed Lord Mansfield had been obliging enough to tell the French while he was in Paris.[1] The war that was already raging was not foreign but domestic, between crown, government and parliament on the one side, and on the other John Wilkes, 'liberty', and 'the people'.

Another war was brought to a close that same autumn, the complicated family feud between Chatham and the two oldest of the Grenville brothers. (James, the third of the four still surviving, had always remained within the Chatham camp.) John Calcraft, already on his way to becoming Chatham's chief 'man of business', played some part in promoting this reconciliation.[2] Much of the credit, however, must go to Lady Chatham, even though, with such intensely political animals to deal with as her husband and brothers, parliamentary calculations necessarily played their part. Temple admitted that his sister had always 'behaved well' to him and 'the affection he bore to her induced him to renew it' now that she resumed overtures in his direction. Whither Temple went, George Grenville (dissociated from the now ministerial Bedfords) inclined to follow, from the affection he protested he too bore his brother and, as he added mistily, 'from many other motives'.[3] It appeared that once again 'the Family' might be preparing to run in harness together, and Temple entertained optimistic visions of 'a triumvirate' – though he was still nervous of any restoration of Chatham to his old dominance. How on earth were Chatham and George Grenville to marry their incompatible policies together? wondered Horace Walpole. Walpole, like many others intrigued and suspicious, did not know what to think. Surely Chatham could not have been 'acting madness for two years together'? But then what if he had? 'Suppose he is mad – is he a worse politician for that? *Nullum magnum ingenium sine mixtra dementiae.* A mad minister and a mad people must conquer the world'.⁴

Temple was on cordial visiting terms at Hayes from the end of November – a month which saw the death of the old Duke of Newcastle, long slighted, and now little lamented – and he was pleased to observe Chatham's 'mind and apprehension perfectly clear'. He found him in and out of bed, 'better when up'.⁵ A few weeks later the proprietor of Hayes was busy at his old game, personally negotiating for the purchase of a contiguous estate, and entirely well enough to follow the exciting but to him distasteful dénouement of the Wilkes affair. Impudently impenitent, the outlaw, returned from exile, had been three times re-elected for Middlesex as member for a House of Commons which as many times refused to re-admit him and was soon to declare his defeated opponent elected in his stead – all this to the accompaniment of prolonged uproar as the mob ran riot for Wilkes and Liberty, and their hero held court amid the considerable comforts available to him in the King's Bench Prison.

Perhaps Chatham in 1766 before his breakdown – and Grafton too – had made a tactical error when Wilkes had reappeared in England pleading for permission 'to continue in the land and among the friends of liberty'. Grafton, after all, like Temple, had been among those who had visited him when he had first been imprisoned in the Tower; and Chatham, though he detested and vilified Wilkes, had at least championed his cause on parliamentary privilege and general warrants. From neither Chatham nor Grafton, however, nor from Rockingham earlier, did Wilkes receive any crumb of encouragement. He was a demagogue and mischief-maker of rare gifts, but not a radical of any deep convictions, and perhaps the best way of dealing with him (as even the King decided rather late in the day) would have been to defuse his explosive potential by an act of calculating clemency. As it was, Wilkes was never to forgive 'flint-hearted Chatham, that proud, insolent, overbearing, ambitious man' who was at once hypocrite and 'first comedian of our age'.[6]

When Barrington's motion for expelling Wilkes was carried in the Commons in February 1769, significantly it was George Grenville who made the most cogent speech against expulsion, although six years earlier it had been he and his fellow ministers who had been made to bleed most copiously in the *North Briton* affair. It was not just that Grenville had profited by harsh experience. He was now again one of the reunited brothers-in-arms, and they were all agreed that to expel Wilkes was both foolish and unconstitutional. 'My brother made what was universally deemed the best speech he ever made', Hester was told by that 'warm and affectionate brother of Hayes', Lord Temple. In March he was already looking forward to Chatham's 'arrival at court, and in the closet'.[7]

By April 1769, when the Commons voted Wilkes's defeated opponent Colonel Luttrell the lawful member for Middlesex, Chatham – having in the meantime suffered a few more gouty setbacks, and 'though still extremely lame' – was being driven out in his carriage in the fine spring weather; and by midsummer he had 'recovered so much strength and general health', so he told Temple, that he was able to be out riding 'six or seven hours a day, without the least fatigue'.[8] By early July he felt ready enough for the political fray to present himself at the King's levee, where he acknowledged Grafton 'with cold politeness' and was afterwards given a twenty minutes' private audience with the King. Grafton he was henceforth to regard as the weakling who had sold the pass inside the cabinet, the political incompetent who had cared more for Newmarket races and the charms of Nancy Parsons than proper policies towards India and America and Wilkes. From his side Grafton, no great statesman but no mere idler or libertine either, ('thinking the world should be postponed to a whore and a horse-race') felt piqued at what he thought was a shabby deal from Chatham; even thirty-five years later, in his piously Unitarian old age, when his memoirs were set soberly down, he still thought that after his difficult labours during his quondam hero's long illness, he 'surely had a claim to some notice, on his recovery'.[9]

Chatham's resurrection created a general sensation. 'It has opened all eyes and mouths from hence to Madrid', Walpole wrote; '*venit, vidit*, the *vicit* is to come . . . That the moment of his appearance, i.e.

so immediately after the petition of the Livery of London, set on foot
and presented by his friend Alderman Beckford,* has a hostile look,
cannot be doubted'.¹⁰

Probably the King did not doubt it either as he listened during
their brief conversation to Chatham's complaints against Grafton and
his ministry, and to his uncertainties 'whether his health would ever
again allow him to attend parliament; but if it did, and if he should
give his dissent to any measure, that his Majesty would be indulgent
enough to believe that it would not arise from any personal consideration'.¹¹ Decoded from its courtly Chathamese, the message was
no doubt plain enough. It would be opposition, *vi et armis*.

At the end of July the Chathams undertook a sort of ceremonial
ratification of the renewed family treaty, visiting the Temples at
Stowe in high style. 'Lord Chatham passed my door on Friday
morning', wrote Burke to Rockingham, 'in a jimwhiskee drawn by
two horses, one before the other. He drove himself; his train was two
coaches and six, with twenty servants male and female'.¹² George
Grenville completed the Stowe company, in a state of perhaps somewhat
modified amity. It was a good deal less than a twelvemonth since in
the Commons he had been acrimoniously attacking Chatham's part
in the repeal of the Stamp Act.¹³ However, the Chathams now accepted
an invitation to stay at Wotton for a couple of days before leaving
Grenville-shire, a further indication of the ceremonial smoking of
pipes of peace.

Lord Lyttelton, that other survivor from the days when the Cousin-
hood had flourished in pristine patriot purity, wrote to Temple to
convey his congratulations from Pitt territory down at Boconnoc, in
Cornwall, where he was staying with Chatham's nephew Thomas† –
though his good wishes for 'this auspicious league' were mixed with
some barbed and rather un-Lytteltonian jocularity:

> If you don't use me very civilly I will set up against you, and have
> you and Lord Chatham mobbed by my friends in the City, for

---

* One of a spate of petitions protesting against the unconstitutional treatment of
Wilkes.

† 'A creature of Grenville', wrote Walpole contemptuously, though he had earlier
been on familiar and friendly terms with him as a neighbour and fellow cognoscente.
But Walpole's hatred of Grenville spilled over towards anyone associated with him.

joining that oppressor of the colonies, and defender of general warrants, George Grenville. However, since you are so wickedly got together, I advise you to stick close to one another, and then if this country can be saved, your joint efforts will save it. Thomas desires me to join his congratulations to mine . . .[14]

While Temple in particular negotiated strenuously for 'a band of union' with the Rockingham opposition, the Chathams were spending the summer of 1769 in temporary exile from Hayes as guests of yet another, but at this stage less political, branch of 'the Family'. The second Earl Stanhope, Chatham's cousin, scientific dilettante and distinguished mathematician, had seldom involved himself deeply in politics, though on occasions he had come to the Lords to support some line of Pitt policy – against the Hanover connection in the 'forties, or for a militia in the 'fifties. In the crisis of 1759 he had even asked Pitt (apparently without result) to accept the family silver for melting down into coin. Now, ten years later, he was able to show his loyalty and generosity by offering his cousin the use of Chevening House while the not far distant Hayes was being rendered uncomfortable by more of Chatham's endless improvements. Chevening had lain unoccupied, though scrupulously maintained, for a long time while the Stanhopes lived in Geneva, where they had originally gone in a desperate but vain attempt to save the life of their consumptive eldest son; and for many years there had been – and for many more was still to be – an intimate and prolific correspondence between Lady Stanhope and Lady Chatham.

It was inevitable that Chatham, during his months at Chevening, would wish to make his mark on the place. Summer not being the planting season, he contented himself with planning what was to become 'Lord Chatham's Ride', designed to give the visitor arriving from London 'the most beautiful approach of any place in England'. Chatham wrote gratefully and enthusiastically to Stanhope in Geneva, 'The place is in high beauty', and reported his son 'Pitt' (that is, John, Lord Pitt, heir to the earldom) to be awestruck 'at the sight of so much learning' on the Chevening library shelves. The ladies had consulted between themselves where 'my lord' was to sleep, quiet being so essential. 'The quietest room in the house is what is called the Satin Room', wrote sensible Lady Stanhope, 'but leave it if he is well, I don't wish him to be too quiet. The satin bed was a present from Governor Pitt . . .'¹⁵

Besides 'Pitt', among Chatham's children who spent that summer at Chevening was his daughter Hester, now eleven. She would be returning to the place many times, and become its mistress when at sixteen she married the surviving Stanhope son, her cousin Lord Mahon, the future third Earl Stanhope, that maverick radical and political oddity of the younger Pitt's day.*

Chatham was returning to the political scene at a critical moment. Grafton, his disillusioned acolyte, himself described the internal state of the country as 'really alarming'.¹⁶ The Wilkes furore not only refused to die down; it had now become inextricably linked with discontents arising from difficult economic times (not least for merchants with American business), from a number of violent industrial disputes among weavers, seamen, coal-heavers and others, and from a widespread conviction that the nation's government was worm-eaten with corruption. Petitions were in fashion again – Chatham vehemently approved of them – from counties and cities inveighing not only against Grafton's shaky administration but more vaguely and rhetorically against 'prerogative' and 'the iron hand of arbitrary power'. The anonymous 'Junius' (whose style Chatham offered to his son William as a model)† brought a new and brilliantly accomplished savagery into the attacks on Grafton and his ministry, and eventually on the King himself. Most important of all, the American situation had deteriorated during 1768. The Townshend duties had rekindled the sparks of rebellion. There had been more menacing of customs officers, boycotts of British goods, protests against the powers and practices of state governors, resentment at the presence of troops, together with sporadic rioting, in Boston especially. In much the same way as the Rockinghams had qualified their concession of Stamp Act repeal by passing the Declaratory Act, so now the Grafton government (against the wishes of its leader) limited its withdrawal of the detested

* Among the three daughters of this marriage was the very strange Lady Hester Stanhope – traveller, voluntary exile, transvestite, author, 'mystic' – who eventually paralleled and even outdid her grandfather's derangement of seventy years before, walling herself up in her disused-monastery retreat in Lebanon. There had been difficulty in 'making the Queen [Victoria] understand that a Pitt is a unique race'.

† Returning the compliment, Junius frequently used the precise phraseology of Chatham's speeches of 1770-71.

Townshend duties by retaining, singly, the tax on tea. In cabinet Camden, Conway, and Granby had joined Grafton in arguing for total repeal, but five had voted against them. Like Robert Walpole in 1739, unlike Pitt in 1761, the chief minister overruled by his own cabinet saw no cause to resign.[17]

Behind the government of Grafton stood, of course, the determined King, straining every nerve to sustain his servants in office, ready to plug any new leak in the holed ship. It was inevitable, therefore, now that Chatham prepared (in Mansfield's phrase) to 'throw fireballs into the enemy camp', that the enemy would be not merely Grafton and his fellow-ministers, but in some degree and increasingly the King himself. For his part, George was more than ready to reciprocate. The Chatham of 1766 and the great 'conciliating plan', Chatham the ally to help defeat the factions, was by now a memory. *This* Chatham, allied to his odious Grenville relations, trying to unite, and doubtless lead, the opposition, determined to bring down the government even if it meant his being carried to parliament and speaking in a 'horizontal posture',[18] had himself become the least acceptable of all the factions. The King would have no further truck with him.

Before the end of 1769 Chatham was busily burrowing away to undermine the Grafton administration where Camden (Chancellor) and Granby (Commander in Chief) were among the leading figures most susceptible to his influence. There was strong 'bring back Chatham' sentiment too among leading admirals (Saunders, for instance, and Keppel, and Sir Peircy Brett), which he was very far from discouraging. The Navy was particularly worried at this time by reports of the speed and extent of French rebuilding, and by British inaction upon the annexing of Corsica. Upon Granby Chatham set John Calcraft to work, the renegade Foxite who like Fox had made a great fortune in army business and was now Chatham's fellow Kentish landowner at Ingress. Calcraft had useful connections with the Rutland/Granby family; significantly he had lent Granby a very large sum of money. Furthermore, though according to Walpole (and not a few others) 'he had not the reputation of common honesty, or pretended to be actuated by any principle but self-interest and revenge', Walpole also allowed him 'the best head for intrigue' of all Chatham's followers.[19] As for Camden, that long-established if now somewhat shaky Chathamite, he was known to be unhappy in the cabinet, and was honestly convinced that government policies towards America and the Wilkes case were mistaken. 'The lord chancellor', wrote the Bedfordite Rigby, '. . . is affectedly hostile every day to the ministry and has a pride in showing it'.[20] (He was, for instance, the only minister to attend the lord mayoral celebrations in November of Beckford, still Chatham's strongest ally in the City.) Chatham now arranged with Camden that he should hold on to the Chancellorship for the time being on the principle that he could embarrass Grafton's government better by not resigning – or at least not until after parliament had reassembled and Chatham had made his own frontal assault. The Chancellor was 'firm, and in the rightest resolutions', Chatham hopefully told Calcraft on the eve of parliament's opening on 9 January. So, happily, was Granby: 'the expectation of the public was never more fixed upon two great men'.[21]

On 9 January, after three years' absence, Chatham once again rose to speak in parliament, moving an amendment to the Lords' Address urging consideration of the causes of the prevailing discontents and particularly the action of the Commons in 'depriving the electors of Middlesex of their free choice of a representative'.[22] His first speech was not impressive, and he sat down dissatisfied with his own performance. Camden however did what Chatham expected of him, admitting that he had 'for some time beheld with a silent indignation the arbitrary measures' of the ministry, and had 'often hung his head in Council'. This certainly sounded like either a prelude to resignation or an invitation to dismissal.

After Mansfield had replied learnedly and legalistically, proffering no view *of his own* on Wilkes's expulsion beyond accepting that 'a question touching the seat of a member of the Lower House could only be determined by that House',[23] Chatham rose a second time. As on his last great parliamentary occasion, in the debates on Stamp Act repeal, the better bite at the cherry came second. The old fire was there again; the same elegant sarcasm – as so often over the past thirty years, at Mansfield's expense; the stirring rhetorical appeal, as in his best days, to those principles of liberty on which the constitution had been based since Magna Carta:

Those iron barons . . . were never engaged in a question of such importance as the present. A breach has been made in the constitution

384

– the battlements are dismantled – the citadel is open to the first invader . . . the walls totter . . .

Must it be concluded, he demanded, that instead of the divine right of a king, they must now submit to the divine right of an easily corruptible Commons?

> My Lords, five hundred gentlemen are not ten millions . . . If this question be given up, the freeholders of England are reduced to a condition baser than the peasantry of Poland . . . My Lords, this is not the cold opinion of my understanding . . . It is my heart that speaks . . . I am neither moved by [Wilkes's] private vices nor his public merits . . . I am not now pleading the cause of an individual, but of every freeholder of England . . .[24]

For a few weeks it did look as if the government, and therefore the King too, would be in serious trouble. Granby, 'regretting' his earlier vote for the expulsion of Wilkes, finally resigned. So now did James Grenville, Dunning the Solicitor General, and from their Household appointments the Dukes of Manchester and Beaufort and the Earls of Coventry and Huntingdon. Camden was dismissed.* For the opposition the prospects looked favourable enough to encourage Rockingham to receive a visit from Chatham, which seemed to advertise a burial of old hatchets. Temple was as belligerently optimistic as ever, and assured his sister that everything had 'passed very amicably betwixt Lord Rockingham, the Duke of Richmond, and me'.[25]

The unity was rather apparent than real, however. Rockingham had been reluctant to be seen too closely involved with Chatham, and had anyway decided that a personal visit must be 'to him, not by him'.[26] While Chatham strenuously insisted that 'the state of the nation' was such that 'all private animosities must subside', these friendly sentiments left the Rockinghams only moderately impressed; they did not forget or forgive Chatham's uncooperative tactics between 1763 and 1766. Burke wrote with mistrustful distaste of the 'Chathamic language', at once pompous, creeping, and ambiguous; he expected the old hawk

* Whereupon his old rival, Hardwicke's son Charles Yorke, torn and tortured between his own ambition and the King's persuasions on the one side, and the condemnation of his family and party on the other, accepted the Woolsack and worried himself to death within three days. Suicide, though probable, was never proved. 'It was Semele', wrote Walpole, 'perishing by the lightnings she had longed for'.

'to keep hovering in the air over all parties, and to souse down where the prey may prove best';[27] and in his celebrated manifesto for the Rockingham Whigs (*Thoughts on the Present Discontents*, published April 1770), though he did not mention Chatham by name when castigating 'the cant of "not men but measures", a sort of charm by which many people got rid of every honourable engagement', it was obvious whom he was principally aiming at. None of the leading Rockinghams – Burke, Savile, Richmond, Rockingham himself – trusted Chatham to be content with anything less than leadership in the 'cordial union' he now professed so ardently to desire in the cause of liberty and the British constitution, and of awakening the King 'into a just sense of this perilous moment'.

Perilous possibly, though the real peril lay less in disfranchised Middlesex than in smouldering America. Unluckily for the opposition, they were to prove unable to agree on their American policy, and in the Wilkes affair they would be finding themselves on an ebb tide. However, it was an ostensibly united opposition that attacked the government in the Lords debate of 22 January, when even those who thought Chatham's manner 'wild', conceded at least that he spoke in his old brilliant style – a contrast with Rockingham's lame 'hobbling'.[28]

Having first, as was now routine with him, reminded the House of his age and infirmities ('I am now in some pain'), he touched upon Corsica and the French menace: 'I fear, my Lords, it is too much the temper of this country to be insensible to the approach of danger until it comes with accumulated terror upon us'. Next he turned to the state of the army, where the government had done well by increasing the force in Ireland from 12,000 to 15,000, but ill in tying their hands by a promise *always* to keep 12,000 men there, short of the supreme emergency of an invasion. In the disposing of regiments he would never limit prerogative, 'nor pull a feather from the master wing of the eagle . . . The army is the thunder of the Crown. The ministry have tied up the hand that should direct the bolt. My Lords, I remember that Minorca was lost for the want of four battalions'.

But the capital mischief was domestic; the constitution had been violated; the Commons had become corrupt. And here he spoke as if this corruption was a foreign novelty recently imported by new-rich 'nabobs', 'without connection, without any interest in the soil, importers of foreign gold', lavishing their ill-gotten wealth on the purchase of parliamentary boroughs. (This of course was just what sixty or seventy years earlier his own grandfather was doing, and what his own political career had been originally founded upon.) To a degree in this speech he appears to have been fighting over again the battle with the East India Company which his health had made him break off three years before: 'The riches of Asia', he declaimed, 'have been poured upon us, and have brought with them not only Asiatic luxury, but, I fear, Asiatic principles of government'. The nation's 'present discontents' stemmed from the evil of corruption. Until corruption was removed, there could be, and there ought to be, no national harmony. 'If the breach in the constitution be effectually repaired, the people will of themselves return to a state of tranquillity. If not, *may discord prevail for ever!*'

These were wilder words than the House of Lords was used to, but his one constructive suggestion was sober and cautious. Something like it was to be the basis fifteen years later of his son's early abortive attempt at parliamentary reform. 'The boroughs of this country', said Chatham,

> have, properly enough, been called the rotten part of the consti-
> tution . . . But in my judgement, my Lords, these boroughs, corrupt
> as they are, must be considered as the natural infirmity of the con-
> stitution. Like the infirmities of the body, we must bear them with
> patience, and submit to carry them about with us. The limb is
> mortified, but the amputation might be death. Let us try . . . whether
> some gentler remedy may not be discovered . . . The representation
> of the counties is, I think, still preserved pure and uncorrupted . . .

He suggested therefore that every county – and rather tenuously half-suggested that every big city and 'larger trading town' – should be allowed to return three members instead of two; and 'let the shires of Scotland be allowed an equal privilege'.[29] The following year he agreed to add to this reform programme a demand he had previously resisted, to shorten the duration of parliaments from seven years to three. 'Could Lord Lyttelton's caution be brought to taste these ideas', he then wrote to Temple, 'we should take possession of strong ground, let who will decline to follow us' – a reference to the unenthusiastic Rockinghams, happily wedded to their rotten boroughs. 'One line of men, I am assured', he added – he meant the City merchants – 'will zealously support, and a respectable weight of law'.[30]

The nearest the Chatham-Rockingham entente approached to overthrowing the government came when Grafton resigned at the end of January 1770. Only his loyalty, first to Chatham and then to the King, had kept him in office even thus long. Outvoted and deserted by colleagues in the cabinet, battered by Wilkes and Junius, secretly undermined and then openly attacked by Chatham, he had had enough. The day of his resignation he counted the happiest of his life.

The opposition's triumph failed to materialize. Instead, North answered the royal call to take over the Treasury, revitalized the tottering administration, and survived. Rather than yield to Chatham or Rockingham at this moment, so the King told Conway, he would have abdicated, or 'had recourse to the sword'.[31] North was abler than Grafton, harder-working, and more determined; he also had the advantage of being a commoner, and soon showed he possessed the gift of handling the House. Within a few weeks government majorities improved from forty to nearly a hundred, while the opposition over-played its hand in the long-drawn affair of Wilkes and the Constitution, and rapidly lost cohesion as the Rockinghams fell away from Chatham and his radical City supporters.

These dwindling prospects and continuing intermittent illness did not however succeed in silencing Chatham's campaign of frontal assault on the government and calculated insinuation against the Crown. His demand for an inquiry into the civil list expenditure brought from him the sort of rhetorical harangue which might have gone down better in the Commons, or even on the Brentford hustings;

> Does the King of England want to build a palace equal to his rank and dignity? Does he want to encourage the polite and useful arts? Does he mean to reward the hardy veteran? . . . Or does he mean, by drawing the purse-strings of his subjects, to spread corruption through the people, to procure a parliament, like a packed jury, ready to acquit his ministers at all adventures?[32]

He went out of his way to eulogize 'the late good old king' (with whom of course he had ever been the object of intense dislike) for his 'manly virtues of justice, truth, and sincerity' – implying clearly enough the want of these qualities in his successor. When in the same speech he went on to observe that Camden had been dismissed 'for the vote he gave in favour of the right of election in the people', there was uproar, with demands that his words be taken down, and shouts of 'To the Bar'; but he reaffirmed his accusation, and then defiantly demanded to know whether he was to be 'condemned or acquitted'.[33]

He did not scruple to play his own variation on the old theme of the alleged hidden power behind the throne. When he had come from Somerset in 1766, he said, 'on wings of zeal' to be chief minister, he was credulous, he was duped; for he soon found that the same secret influence prevailed which had put an end to the previous administration. If this was intended to refer to Bute, it was not true; if, as most thought, to the King's mother, it was malicious nonsense.* George III might be fairly charged with many errors, prejudices, and obstinacies, but in 1766 he had unquestionably given Chatham the fullest possible backing. These accusations now, self-deceiving or dishonest, provoked Grafton to rise in the King's defence. 'If I understand rightly the words which have been spoken', he said, 'they are only the effects of a distempered mind brooding over its own discontents' – to which Chatham waspishly returned that at no point in his illness had his mind been insufficiently vigorous to see the snares which had been laid for him, of which he had 'a drawer full of proofs'.[34]

The old war between the City of London and the parliament of Westminster, refreshed as it had been by the Middlesex elections, now touched the sort of pitch it had reached in 1733 during the Excise Bill crisis. While the Rockinghams' ardour cooled, Chatham's most vociferous supporters were to be found in the Common Council of the City, led by its two Sheriffs, James Townshend and John Sawbridge, by the Rockinghamite Alderman Trecothick, and – ending his career at a peak of belligerence – the Lord Mayor, Beckford. One remonstrance to the Crown in 1769 having been ignored, the City came again in March 1770, calling for a new parliament, condemning the corruption and backstairs influence, protesting against the disfranchisement of Middlesex and Camden's dismissal, and threateningly reminding the

---

* But with strong demagogic appeal. 'In consequence of this denunciation, papers, to which the *North Britons* were milk and honey, have been published in terms too gross to repeat . . . Every blank wall at this end of the town is scribbled with the words, Impeach the King's Mother; and, in truth, I think her person is in danger' (Walpole to Mann, 15 March 1770).

King, as Junius had earlier, of parallels with certain unhappy events of the reigns of Charles I and James II. George reacted spiritedly, declaring the remonstrance 'disrespectful to me, injurious to my parliament, and irreconcileable to the principles of the constitution'; but, according to Chatham, this royal reply merely '*counterfeited* firmness', under which lay 'real *despair*, convicted guilt, and conscious weakness and incapacity'. The Commons reprobated the City remonstrance by 248 votes to 94. However anxious to make the most of 'secret influence' and the parliamentary corruption inherent in court favours, many of the Rockinghams drew back from the violent demagogic language adopted by Chatham and the London politicians. But Chatham for one was in no mood for retreat. If any should be found 'base enough or silly enough to turn tail in this great moment, a good riddance', said he, 'of such miserable company'.[35]

On 1 May he presented a bill in the Lords (rejected by 89 to 43) to reverse the exclusion of Wilkes by the Commons, that corrupt Commons where the majority had become 'a minister's state engine'. 'I am afraid, my Lords', he said, 'this measure has sprung too near the throne – I am sorry for it; but I hope his Majesty will soon open his eyes'. Labouring away with an energy that belied the infirmities he so often advertised, he moved another resolution (negatived), that the King had been the victim of dangerous advice in spurning the City's remonstrance. Ten days later he was on his feet again, moving this time for the dissolution of parliament ('negatived by a large majority').[36]

During the same month the City presented its third remonstrance to the King, and this time Beckford was bold enough to spring a little surprise and lecture his monarch in person at the levee – though by his own account 'properly and decently' – when his petition was rejected. Chatham was so delighted at what most thought something of an outrage (the Lord Mayor's 'speech' was promptly printed in *The Public Advertiser* and engraved on his memorial when he died next month) that straightway he wrote to Beckford in a rapture of enthusiasm:

In the fulness of heart the mouth speaks; and the overflowing of mine gives motion to a weak hand . . . The *spirit of Old England* spoke, that never-to-be-forgotten day . . . My mind is big only with admiration, thanks, and affection. Adieu, then, for the present . . .

true Lord Mayor of London, that is *first* magistrate of the *first* city in the world.[37]

Chatham, forgiven his peerage now, was acclaimed once again a hero in the City. On 1 June a deputation from the Common Council waited upon him to offer thanks for his zeal in defence of their liberties, and for his labours to purify parliaments 'by shortening their duration and introducing a more full and equal representation'.[38] However, when parliament went into recess Horace Walpole was inclined to think they had heard the last of the Middlesex election, 'which my Lord Chatham has heated so often over, that there is scarce a spark of fire left'.[39] But if Walpole thought that 'miscarriages and derision' was all Chatham had gained from his five months' fury, Chatham himself was unrepentantly rampageous. 'Moderation, moderation', he lamented, seemed to be the burden of the Rockinghams' song. His mood at the moment was to be *im*moderate, intemperate, 'a *scarecrow of violence*' to those timid birds the moderate Whigs, those 'gentle warblers of the grove'.[40]

Thus happily reckless he wrote to Calcraft upon setting out for a summer visit, together with his thirteen-year-old son and heir 'Pitt' and his tutor, to Burton Pynsent and then to his Grenville relations. The consequent exchange of domestic letters, with their sometimes quaintly stilted sincerity and sometimes very unChathamic immediacy, witnesses attachments and intimacies as close and demonstrative as ever. News from Hayes: 'We drive out in the little chaise and the two boys [William and James] squire us . . . We saunter in the high fields . . . The scrubby elm is down and the lawn looks much better, as you knew it would'. News from a Burton 'replete with rural delights': 'Dairy enchanting, pillar [the Pynsent memorial] superb, terrass ravishing . . . I had almost omitted the portico, by day and night; such a silver mantle thrown last night over Troy hill was never seen by youthful poet'. Compliments for 'my inimitable [juvenile] correspondents . . . Pray tell all at Athens, professors and scholars, how truly charmed I am at their performances'. Favourable report upon son and travelling companion from president of mutual admiration society to other members: 'Pitt is everything that can please: he is a sweet idle boy; he is a sensible, conversable, discreet man: sense or nonsense, verse or prose . . . all draw perpetual applauses from papa and Mr

Wilson'. Physically, Chatham seemed delighted with his ability to get about: 'Don't I go on gallantly? When I shall get home at this rate I know not; but sure I am, that my thoughts are at Hayes some part of every hour in every day. I write this just returned from our hills . . . Supper enters. Good night'.[41]

Before parliament met again in November Beckford and Granby were dead; on the very day it reassembled George Grenville died. Of these three Beckford had been Chatham's strongest link with the mercantile community, Granby his most popular and Grenville recently his ablest support in the Commons. Grenville's death was especially damaging to him, for within a month or two, without their leader, some of the chief Grenvillites – Wedderburn, Whately, Lord Suffolk, Augustus Hervey – went over to North and the Court, and were accommodated within the government fold. Lyttelton did not, but remained inactive and lukewarm. He disapproved of scarecrows of violence. Temple, too, from the moment of his brother's death, without ever breaking with Chatham, tended to drift away from active politics. There remained faithful the thrusting Calcraft, Chatham's eyes and ears; the able but much disliked Shelburne and his followers Barré and Dunning (one of the two or three lawyers for whom Chatham ever found a good word); but Camden's presence in parliament was no longer to be relied on, and by and large Chatham was left 'without troops or generals . . .; he must lean on Lord Rockingham, and God knows! that is a slender reed'.[42] Moreover, some of Rockingham's gentle warblers, seeing after a time little to keep them at Westminster, succumbed to their migratory instincts: 'seven or eight peers at least', wrote the Duke of Richmond, 'have taken the opportunity of the thaw for a fortnight's holydays, and are gone into the country to get the little remainder of fox-hunting which the season allows of'.[43]

Two issues dominated the business of the winter. One concerned the ancient conflict between the rival provinces of judges and juries. Lord Mansfield, in the case of the printer Woodfall, who published Junius, had ruled that it was for judge, not jury, to decide a libel's criminality; and for Chatham, as for the Rockinghams, Mansfield's ruling seemed to impose an unacceptable limitation not only on juries' rights, which was to say the people's rights, but also on the freedom of the press. While the Rockinghams contented themselves with promoting a bill, introduced by Dowdeswell, to safeguard the *future* rights of jurors,

Chatham and his followers wanted to go much further – and in the process rout the enemy of old, Mansfield – by securing a measure which would have declared the judgement upon Woodfall itself erroneous. Chatham's language on Dowdeswell's bill was in private bitterly and immoderately contemptuous – 'this dangerous bill', 'this compound of connection, tyranny, and absurdity, not to say collusion' – but in the end he grudgingly consented to support it on the grounds that he proposed amending it in committee.[44] Unsurprisingly it never succeeded in progressing thus far; a parliamentary declaration of juries' rights in libel cases was not passed for another twenty-one years.

'A sort of sullen discontent on both sides' was Burke's description of relations between the two groups in the 'united' opposition after the jury bill had failed. 'The ministerial people looked on, as if they were in the boxes of the opera' while Lord Chatham and his friends 'thought proper to show themselves in a sort of systematick hostility'. Burke continued, 'It does not require a great deal of attention or sagacity to discover their perpetual endeavour to disconcert or disgrace us'.[45]

The second and more dangerous matter dominating the 1770–71 session concerned Spain and the risk of a new conflict, which by December had become serious enough to provoke discussion of the possibility of bringing back the man above all others who had earned some right to direct the nation's affairs in war.

Since the mid-century, the inhospitable barrenness of the Falkland Islands in the South Atlantic, undisturbed before, had begun to attract three rival predators looking for strategic advantage, Britain, France, and Spain; and early in 1770 the Spanish governor of Buenos Aires, on his own initiative, arrived in decisive force to expel the British from their station at Port Egmont. On the return home of Captain Hunt of the frigate *Tamar*, the British government replied by demanding Spanish withdrawal, and reparation for injury. This presented Chatham with familiar ground. This was territory on which he had fought his first big battles in the 'thirties: the Bourbon menace, the infamous Spaniards ('as mean and crafty', he now thundered, as they were 'proud and insolent'), the wrongs suffered by honest British merchants – 'our merchants have been plundered', he cried; 'no protection given them – no redress obtained for them'. In 1738 it had been Captain Jenkins; now it was Captain Hunt, whom he wished to bring before the bar of the House to testify.[46] The nation's condition was as deplorable at home as it was despicable abroad; it was 'injured, insulted, undone'; ministers were guilty of 'ignorance, neglect, or treachery'. If they were forced into a war they 'stood it at the hazard of their heads'.

It was indeed true that since 1763 the Royal Navy had been run down, and so long as France, despite her own shaky finances, seemed prepared to fight alongside her Bourbon ally – that is, until the fall of Choiseul at the end of December – prospects in a new war might have been very doubtful. Even so North and his fellow ministers, though they had set their course upon financial retrenchment, were belligerent enough to reverse engines, raise taxes, impress more sailors, prepare every available ship for war if the Spaniards gave no satisfaction; and even after Choiseul's fall Chatham professed himself 'certain' it was imminent, 'be the ministry what it may at Versailles'.[47]

Protesting that he was neither a warmonger nor 'running the race of popularity', he lambasted the government in one highly coloured speech after another. A long and powerful one on 22 November mingled philippics aimed openly at bringing the government down with a pessimistic analysis of the strategic situation. The army, he alleged, had been allowed to fall shamefully below establishment. Wide open to invasion, the nation should still not humiliate itself by employing foreign auxiliaries in Great Britain, though it could profitably employ 20,000 German Protestants against any invasion of Ireland receiving help from the Irish Catholics. A purely naval war he ruled out as impracticable. The British, a mere seven millions against twenty-five millions of the enemy, must have European allies, but they must be careful to avoid the trap of continental commitments. The continental part of the Seven Years War ('which it has been the fashion to call *my* German war') had been pursued by him – so he claimed, anticipating an obvious charge of inconsistency – only because his predecessors had committed the nation to it: 'it was a weight fastened upon my neck'. As for the navy,

> the first great and acknowledged object of national defence . . . is to maintain such a superior naval force at home that even the united fleets of France and Spain may never be masters of the Channel . . . The second naval object . . . should be to maintain at

all times a powerful western squadron . . . The third object . . . is to maintain such a force in the Bay of Gibraltar . . . to cover that garrison, to watch the motions of the Spaniards, and to keep open the communication with Minorca.

Yet the fact was, he accused, that the navy could not at that moment send out eleven ships of the line* properly manned and equipped to meet the Spaniards waiting at Ferrol. And what of the national unity which the dangers demanded? How could there be unity when the country's rulers and institutions were rotten with corruption – not just government and parliament, but men in the City of London living on their plunder of the helpless; the 'miserable jobbers of Change Alley'; East Indian nabobs; 'what is vulgarly called the *monied interest*: I mean the bloodsucker, that muckworm which calls itself the friend of government . . . the whole race of commissaries, jobbers, contractors, or remitters . . .' but not, he hastened to qualify, 'the honest industrious tradesman, who holds the middle rank, and has given repeated proofs that he preserves law and liberty to gold. I love that class of men'.[48]

Three weeks later the decorum of the House of Lords was disturbed in highly unusual fashion. Lord Gower for the government attempted to prevent the Duke of Manchester (in the presence of 'strangers', including several Commons members) from disclosing details of the nation's allegedly defenceless condition; Gower contending that the debate must be secret. Upon this,

prodigious confusion ensued; and Lord Chatham, in a violent emotion of rage, insisted on being heard, which was impossible from the tumult . . . The servants of the House of Lords were forced to thrust out the Commons by violence, while Lord Chatham, roaring in vain and unregarded, walked out of the House . . . as did [fifteen other peers] . . . The members of the Commons went down in a fury to their own house.[49]

---

* The condition of some ships was undoubtedly rotten, but this figure of Chatham's exaggerated the naval unreadiness. By October the mobilization of the fleet was strongly under way, with impressment proceeding under Order in Council (which Chatham supported *against* his City friends); and by 12 December Hawke, First Lord of the Admiralty, assured the Commons that twenty ships of the line were manned and fit, and twenty more in commission.

When in January 1771 details became available of the convention under which war with Spain was avoided – the Spanish withdrew from Port Egmont, with the question of Falkland Islands sovereignty left open – Chatham still maintained the fury of his attack. He appeared to be seeing Walpole's 1739 Convention of the Pardo over again, and setting himself once more at the head of 'the patriot band'. He continued to make wild assertions of governmental iniquity. There should have been acceptance of British sovereignty without reserve. France had been allowed to interfere in the negotiations; there had even been 'ignominious collusion with the present views of France'.[50] It was perhaps not surprising that some Whig lords should have preferred a little February fox-hunting to listening to this kind of thing.

Next month the hostilities between the House of Commons and the Common Council of the City of London reached a violent climax. A printer and liveryman of the City who had offended – one of several – by publishing an account of a Commons debate, and then refused to answer a summons to appear at the bar of the House, was arrested within the City boundaries on a Speaker's warrant. Three City magistrates promptly released him and imprisoned in his stead, tit for tat, the Speaker's messenger; for which, of the three, Crosby and Oliver (but in the end *not* Wilkes) were hauled before the Commons and committed, if only briefly, to the Tower. The accompaniment of these proceedings was a renewal of riot and disturbance. Government supporters were pelted and manhandled by the mob. Many of them, together with Bute and the Princess Dowager, were burned in effigy. North had to be rescued from an attack upon him in his carriage, which the rioters demolished. The King was hissed and hooted in the streets, and in the Commons Alderman Townshend demanded an inquiry into the conduct of the Princess, who he claimed had been 'the real cause of all the calamities of the past ten years'.

Chatham over the period of these alarums was confined by illness again – with what he variously described as 'an obstinate complaint in consequence of a violent cold' and an unpleasant combination of 'headach and winter' – perhaps a persistent neuralgia.[51] 'In bed and blistered' or from his 'great chair', he kept in touch with his lieutenants – Calcraft, Shelburne, Barré; deplored the inactivity of Temple; suspected Camden of backsliding; considered James Townshend's attack on the Princess Dowager counter-productive (though he had recently indulged in one of his own only slightly less outspoken), but continued to advise 'firmness and vigour by the friends of liberty' on behalf of the injured City officers. The behaviour of the House of Commons was 'rank tyranny'; the Lord Mayor had been committed to the Tower 'for discharge of his duty'. And in respect of the original offence which had sparked off the whole turbulent brouhaha, what objection would an *honest* parliament possibly have to the printing of its debates?[52]

Once he was well enough to be abroad again, he was resolved to make one more attempt to secure the dissolution of this *dis*honest and discredited parliament, despite being discouraged by 'unseasonable refinements in some and tergiversations in others', which had left him 'not a little wounded'. (He meant in particular Camden and Lyttelton.) He knew he could now expect no more support from the Rockinghams; and there were times when he wondered whether to give the game up and leave it to 'the honest demand of the people without doors'.[53]

He was indeed about to give the game up; but not quite yet. By the end of April he was ready to make a last effort as opposition spokesman – though it could be little more than an oratorical gesture. On consecutive days he spoke in support of a motion to expunge the previous year's Commons resolution on Wilkes, and then himself moved to request the King for new elections. But this was by now an old bone he was worrying, and although he growled long and ferociously, there was no meat left on it. On 1 May he rehearsed grievance after grievance against the King's ministers – even harking back once more to 'the last inglorious peace, the origin of our evils' – but finally managed to command only twenty-three votes. By the time a new general election did come round in three years' time, Wilkes was indeed to be unobtrusively allowed back in the Commons, but it was a tamer Wilkes than the rabble-rouser of old; and by that time Chatham had become a stranger to parliament. After the spring of 1771 he was to allow a second period of three years to elapse without coming to Westminster – except on a single occasion in May 1772 when he attended to support a bill aiming to give dissenters the toleration in law that they already largely enjoyed in practice. Dissenters were then attempting to be relieved of the legal requirement, not consistently enforced, to accept the Thirty Nine Articles before taking up public office, and Shelburne and his philosopher friend, the Unitarian Dr

Price, managed to persuade Chatham to come up from Somerset and speak in the cause. This he did with eloquence and some sarcasm against the bishops opposing the bill – those 'interested and aspiring' prelates so remotely distanced from the apostle fishermen who were their humble precursors. 'I am for this bill, my Lords', he said, 'because I am for toleration, that sacred right of nature and bulwark of truth'. The Lords spiritual and temporal proved decisively of a contrary opinion.

His failure to make any significant impact upon men or events after his come-back in 1769 resolved him upon a renewed retreat to the country. Henceforth, until the crisis in America brought him back again, he would content himself with offering advice to the small group of parliamentarians who continued to look to him – a company diminished by the death of Calcraft in August 1772. 'I do not see that the smallest good can result to the public', he wrote to Shelburne, 'from my coming up to the meeting of parliament . . . The narrow genius of "old corps" connection has . . . rendered union on revolution principles impossible . . . In this deplorable conjuncture, it is a species of happiness to be resolved what *not* to do'. Even the City of London disappointed him. The 'popular' party there was splitting into weak squabbling factions; 'a headlong, self-willed spirit' had 'sunk the City into nothing'. *O tempora! O mores!* became his steady refrain: national 'infatuation and degeneracy'; 'contemptible little intrigues'; 'our country so fatally divided against itself'. The farthest possible from the centre of affairs was 'best for a man who is sure he can do no good'.[54]

CHAPTER TWENTY-TWO

At Burton Pynsent

Chatham at Burton Pynsent was by no means as gloomy as he so often sounded or professed. For one thing his health held up well: it was better through the summer of 1771 than he had known it for twenty years; for the whole of 1772 he managed to report 'amazing good health, slight gout excepted'; and in May 1773, though 'held fast' by gout in feet and hands, he still reckoned his physical condition, 'thank God, tolerable for my time of day' – demonstrating the fact by going off the following month with his two eldest sons for a holiday at Lyme Regis.[1] From within his happy Somersetshire horizons it even proved possible sometimes, for all his routine opposition-politician talk of corruption and folly and threatening ruin, to sound almost cheerful for the nation's future. Thus, when another storm blew up over East India Company finances, he 'inclined to think' it would 'roll off';

> for, compared with the rest of Europe, credit in England, though somewhat shaken, is still the pillared firmament, *relatively to others' rottenness*. You see, my dear Lord [Shelburne], how much more tranquil and full of hope a farmer's chimney-corner is, than the Royal Exchange, or the palace of a nabob![2]

And although the parliamentary fuss over what he called the 'new-fangled and impudent . . . wanton and tyrannical' bill 'for abridging the facility of princely nuptials' – George III's Royal Marriages Act – struck him as straining at a gnat after the camel of Wilkes's expulsion had been so tamely swallowed, 'who knows', he wrote, 'but the foul feeder may throw up the camel too, and England enjoy its own again'.[3]

'England's own': there is little difficulty in seeing what he understood by that in European and colonial terms – the whip hand over France and Spain. In domestic terms, his amalgam of opportunism and principle, his descents into factiousness and readiness to paint the greyness of his opponents double-dyed black, his own compromises with 'corruption' (as with rotten boroughs), his willingness to warp facts or re-tell recent history to bolster his arguments or defend his own reputation, all tend to obscure the basic sincerity of his passion for the beauties of the British constitution. Certainly his picture of history was partially and conventionally constructed after the Whiggish fashion of the age, with classical forms dominating the distant landscape and the air heavy still with Roman gravitas and grandeur; with the barons of Magna Carta standing nobly in the middle ground; and prominent in the foreground the leaders of the battle against Stuart prerogative, apotheosised in the figures of the philosopher Locke and the statesman William III. But when Chatham spoke as he so frequently did of 'revolution principles', he was not mouthing a hollow phrase. He knew what constituted the 'liberty' he championed: not of course any sort of democracy, for all his ready talk of 'the people'; equality only in the important sense of equality before the law; a protestant monarchy of severely limited powers; a dominant parliament with each house checking and balancing the other and the executive arm both recruited from and ultimately subordinate to the legislative; revenues under the command of the Commons; habeas corpus and the rule of law (though emphatically not of lawyers); and religious toleration, with a vigilant mistrust of Anglican zealotry but strong safeguards against Catholicism.

Evidence of the genuineness and nicety of this regard for constitutional principles comes particularly in some considered 'meditation' from his 'farmer's chimney-corner' in the autumn of 1773, when he was advising Shelburne on the proper attitude to adopt at Westminster towards a tax intended by the Irish parliament upon absentee landlords. The proposal was eventually dropped but, while it threatened, the heavily interested Rockinghams were for advising the King to use his prerogative of veto. Shelburne, also with Irish estates, at first inclined similarly. Chatham himself confessed that his own mind was 'not quite free from bias in favour of absentees, having . . . a nephew and a cousin-german' with lands in Ireland, and moreover he considered the suggested imposition 'excessively severe', even though it was true that England sucked income out of Ireland to spend at home. Nevertheless, he told Shelburne, after 'attentive consideration',

26. Charles Pratt, Lord Camden, by Nathaniel Dance

27. 3rd Duke of Grafton, by Pompeio Battoni

28. Lord Shelburne, after Reynolds

29. Charles Townshend, wax medallion attributed to I. Gosset

30. Collapse of the Earl of Chatham in the House of Lords. Temple and

Chatham's son William are among the group immediately around him.

31. *above* Hayes Place, Kent

32. Burton Pynsent, Somerset, by T. Bonnor

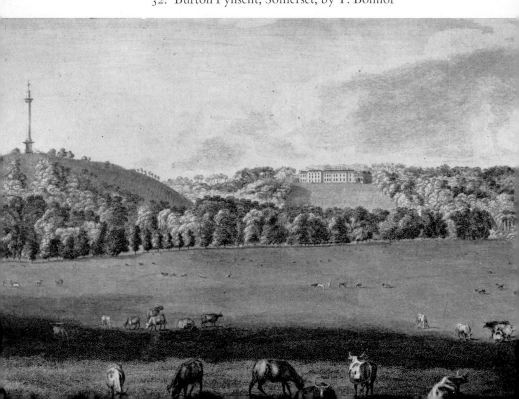

At Burton Pynsent

I could not, as a peer of England, advise the King . . . to reject a tax on absentees, sent over here as the genuine desire of the Commons of Ireland . . . exercising their inherent, exclusive right by raising supplies in the manner they judge best. This great principle of the constitution is so fundamental, and with me so sacred and indispensable, that it outweighs all other considerations . . .

I have . . . sent your Lordship an insignificant, solitary opinion: it is pure in the source, flowing from the old-fashioned Whig principles.[4]

With politics at long range, his attentions centred now upon his estate and his family. Burton Pynsent had come to mean a great deal to him, and he liked to picture himself there, tasting

> . . . the simple life of patriarchs old
> Who, rich in rural peace, ne'er thought of gold

– though his taste for grandeur did soon dictate some hard thinking in the matter of gold. These, his own pastoral strains, pipe forth from the heroic couplets of an *Invitation* he sent to Garrick, hearing that that other great actor was within visiting distance of Burton. The conventionally idyllic little composition (Garrick never came, but replied in kind) offers a nicely idealized self-portrait of the 'unpassion'd' elder statesman under the plain roof of his 'primeval seat' – upon whose ambitious improvement the already overburdened Chatham finances were nevertheless soon staggering:

> A statesman without power, and without gall,
> Hating no courtiers, happier than them all,
> Bowed to no yoke, nor crouching for applause;
> Vot'ry alone to freedom, and the laws.
> Herds, flocks, and smiling Ceres deck our plain,
> And, interspersed, an heart-enlivening train
> Of sportive children frolic o'er the green;
> Meantime pure love looks on, and consecrates the scene.[5]

There was a fair proportion of reality in this prettified *tableau*. Away at Lyme Regis in the summer of 1773 with his friend Thomas Hollis and his sons John and William and only a *certain* amount of gout (one crutch), he longed to be back at Burton, with his 'sweet love' and the

401

'dear girls' and 'little tar' – James, the youngest boy. Especially after Hollis went home, and although the sea was 'nobly beautiful' and there were fine sights to see, he felt in 'exile'. This Thomas Hollis, a wealthy Dorset landowner and politically a Chathamite, was a friend who was likely to have become yet another to bequeath Chatham a fortune, if too sudden death had not anticipated his will-making. It was Hollis who eventually persuaded Chatham that the splendid new dairy farm that he – or more particularly Hester – was running at Burton would stand a better chance of solvency if in the hands of a knowledgeable bailiff; for, though the Chathams' farming was enthusiastic, it proved extravagantly unprofitable. But whatever the profit and loss account, everything at Burton had to be of the best, the cattle and sheep of prize quality, the brood mares the finest money could buy, the sows 'an incomparable race' who must be found 'a proper paramour'. Then there were the riding horses, for whom there was much loving and discriminating attention, the coach horses with their demands upon stabling and attendant household, and the 'smaller families' of Burton – dogs, poultry, 'gallinas', and of course peacocks preening over the lawns. Chatham's old love of landscape gardening could now be indulged in the sort of style of which Hagley* or even Stowe might not be ashamed, and the house itself suitably enlarged and refurbished.

Towards his children Chatham was frankly, in his own description, 'an old doting daddy'. All collectively, and each separately, came in for papa's repeated praise and admiration. The youngest, James, is 'the flower of schoolboys'. When he was nearly eleven, Chatham writes of him fondly to Hester, who was then with the elder children for a season at Hayes:

Little James yesterday riding alone in White Cross, while I planted the other side of the lane, was encountering bravely, but in vain,

* His old friendship rusty but in some degree restored, Lyttelton came to see Chatham at Burton, 'a place which . . . I do not wonder you love at all seasons of the year'. He tried in 1772 to get Chatham to return the visit and look again upon the park at Hagley, 'in a higher degree of beauty than I ever beheld it'. It would be like seeing 'the maturity of a fine child whom you had been fond of in his infancy and had partly formed yourself'. If Chatham delayed, a chance might be lost for ever; Lyttelton was afraid he had not long to live. Chatham corresponded amiably, but did not go, and Lyttelton died in the following summer.

an obstinate and violent fit . . . in that *varmin*, Long Sutton, when farmer Cable of Curry came by and interposed. Our little hero scorned to call for aid, or to quit the saddle, though his danger was not small, the little devil of a mare attempting to rise at the field-gate.[6]

He confessed to *trembling* when he expected James to be sent off to sea at the age of twelve with Alexander Hood, the naval captain who had married Gilbert West's sister Molly, and was to prove the most loyal of friends (and long-suffering of creditors) to Chatham. In the event James Pitt was fifteen before he joined the navy, and then it was with Alexander Hood's later more famous younger brother Samuel. James was to see action in the West Indies in the forthcoming war, and die of fever only two years after his father, at the age of nineteen.[7] (Both Chatham's daughters, Hester and Harriot, after marrying and continuing the line, would also die young, in their twenties.)

All three Pitt boys received much of their education, formal and informal, from their father, who regularly assisted the admirable and admiring tutor, the Rev. Mr Wilson. (Wilson taught the girls too.) The attentions of Chatham, though he gave a good strong grounding of Latin and Greek, of literature and history, and of speech-making in English, were by no means all heavily academic. In charge, for instance, of William and James when the rest of the family were at Hayes, he reports: 'Sleep perfectly good last night without the drops, and little James dreamed of no demons, though our *Contes Arabes* treated horribly of one'.[8] And somewhat earlier than this, he writes to the absent Hester of their boy William, who remained worryingly under-weight and extremely delicate throughout childhood and adolescence:

> My account is happy, dearest love. Our sweet little boy passed the night well, and is quite easy this morning, having had, before going to bed, a copious motion. The discreet Pam [Mrs Sparry, the housekeeper] and I agreed to give but four grains of rhubarb this morning . . . I have seen the maid who sat up in his room, she says his sleep was perfectly quiet.[9]

As they grew old enough and whenever he himself was well enough, Chatham delighted in nothing more keenly than to be out riding with his boys. Of the three, William naturally had least of an outdoor

character, most of a 'contemplative constitution'.[10] As his tutor Wilson
said of him, he never learned but merely seemed to *recollect*; and both
Chatham and Hester were intoxicated with pleasure at the thought of
their '*Philosopher*'.

At Lyme Regis, in William's last summer before being sent to
Cambridge at the age of fourteen, Chatham gazed in grateful satisfaction upon this apple of his autumnal eye: 'It is a delight to see
William see nature in her free and wild compositions; and I tell
myself, as we go, that the *general mother* is not ashamed of her child'.
The particular mother was no less proud: Hester when her boy was
still not thirteen was writing in raptures of 'the fineness of his mind'.[11]
In the room at Lyme Regis as he was writing, Chatham lovingly
contrasted the natures of these two elder sons. There had been a sharp
thunderstorm: 'William was reading to me, and no more moved his eye
out of the book than Archimedes left his geometry when the town was
stormed. Pitt looked round, but rather as an engineer, to consider if
the breach was practicable'. And when the day came for William to
be off to Pembroke Hall at Cambridge – in the protective company
of his tutor, for he was still almost absurdly young and fragile –
Chatham poured out his heart with a most un-English abandon:

How happy, my loved boy, is it that your mamma and I can tell
ourselves, there is at Cambridge *one* without a beard, 'and all the
elements so mixed in him that Nature might stand up and say,
This is a man!' . . . Adieu, again and again, sweet boy; and if you
acquire health and strength every time I wish them to you, you
will be a second Samson . . .[12]

The depth of William's veneration of his father was never in doubt,
and his reply must have brought all that a susceptible father could wish:
'I hope', he wrote, '. . . that I may be, on some future day, worthy to
follow, *in part*, the glorious example always before my eyes'. When
William was immediately ill upon arrival at Cambridge – continuing
so for two months – Chatham, though cheered by a 'comfortable'
letter from Wilson, could not help

being a little in pain lest you should make more haste than good
speed to be well . . . All you want at present is quiet . . . How happy
the task, my noble amiable boy, to caution you against pursuing

too much all those liberal and praiseworthy things to which less happy natures are perpetually to be spurred and driven . . . Your mamma joins me in every good word . . .[13]

For the eldest son John, 'our cavalier', it was arranged that he should go as aide-de-camp to General Carleton, the newly appointed Governor of Canada. Chatham had first thought of sending him to learn the trade of war with the Prussians, but decided he was as yet too young 'for the large and obnoxious intercourse of a foreign army'. 'The time draws nigh for our dear Pitt joining his regiment in Quebec', he wrote to Lady Stanhope in March 1774. 'What pain to part with him! and what satisfaction to see him go in so manly a manner – just in the age of pleasures!'[14] Thus John Pitt came to be soldiering in Canada at the outbreak of the American revolution, and chanced only just to escape capture along with Carleton himself early in 1776. Thereupon he was sent home – capture would perhaps have been as embarrassing to the Americans as to the British authorities. Following then the advice of his father and mother, he resigned from military service until the prospect of renewed war with France permitted him to rejoin his regiment, by then in Gibraltar, with the full-hearted parental blessing which earlier could not be given to participation in a war against 'fellow-Englishmen'.

Although Chatham had by now sold his house in Bath (to Clive) he was still running two expensive country establishments, and by the early 1770s his affairs were deeper than ever in debt. As the remainder of his years ran by, it fell increasingly to Hester, always the greater realist, to try to introduce some prudence into the conduct of the family finances; and when in 1775 he was once again to lose grip and become seriously ill, it was she who became sole manager of business.

By 1772 they had, for the second time, decided that they ought to sell Hayes, and had no compunction in again approaching Thomas Walpole as prospective purchaser. Not surprisingly, however, it was a role he had no wish to fill; 'a disappointed passion', he pointedly observed, 'does not quickly return'.[15] For a time Alexander Hood rented the property – something of an act of charity in itself – and meanwhile, though not in residence there, he busied himself as estate overseer and selling agent on Chatham's behalf. Unfortunately Chatham's notion of what the place ought to fetch, between £22,000 and £24,000, was well above the market price in a year of financial upset and depressed stocks; though, to justify his expectations, he had (as he rather ruefully informed Temple) 'bills to produce of £9000 spent on the premises' since 1768.[16] Temple, the surviving trustee of Chatham's marriage settlement, was trying to help by raising the wind on the trust funds. Hayes had already had one mortgage raised on it, but now Chatham succeeded in persuading Alexander Hood to lend him, first, another £1000 on Hayes, and then £6000 on Burton. For a time there were even thoughts of selling up Burton, but in the outcome only some of the outlying farms were disposed of.

Hood's £7000 proved not enough. The Chathams seemed more than willing to treat him as a milch cow, and though even he began to utter cries of some alarm ('I thought it right to . . . show your Lordship that my powers are limited'), he managed to increase his loan to £8000 at 4½% – 'going to the utmost of his credit' to raise the wherewithal at 5%. Even that did not suffice. In 1775 Molly Hood was assuring Hester that her brother and brother-in-law would be 'proud and ambitious' to raise further money; and by 1776 with help from his West relations, Alexander Hood brought the total sum up to £10,000, most of it secured upon Burton – which last point he was anxious should be fully understood by Chatham's heir, John. The banker through whom this delicate business was transacted was Thomas Coutts, who himself lent Chatham an additional £1000, a transaction kept most carefully secret. One Jouvencel, a free tenant on the Hayes estate who was also a Privy Council clerk, lent £500. Coutts incidentally learned to have the utmost respect for the business abilities of Hester – 'the cleverest *man* of her time'. He and Jouvencel proved good friends to Chatham in another respect, pressing the Treasury to practise better punctuality in the payment of his £3000-a-year pension, which was worth something like an annual *net* £2000, and which had fallen, by 1777, a full year in arrears. Lord North, with a fellow debtor's sympathies and the wish to be generous to a political enemy fallen on hard times (Chatham was by then – 1775 – desperately ill), suggested to the King that the pension might be raised to £3000 *after* payment of fees and expenses, with an additional adjustment to protect the future interests of the second son. But the uncompromisingly hostile tone of the royal refusal illustrates just how deeply Chatham had offended by his political opposition since 1768. In particular his

1774 speeches on America totally undid 'the merit of his former conduct.' The King was afraid lest any concession from him at that time would be wrongly construed as arising from fear, and added:

> As to any gratitude to be expected from him or his family, that would be absurd, when the whole tenour of their lives have shown them void of that most honourable sentiment; but when decrepitude or death puts an end to him as a trumpet of sedition, I shall make no difficulty of placing the second son's name instead of the father, and making up the pension £3000.[17]

Meanwhile Hester was left to juggle as well as she might with mortgage and loan repayments, to wrestle with Coutts's accounts and supervise the household and estate management. By the time of her husband's death, though she had gone a long way to repaying the loans of friends, debts of some £20,000 were still outstanding, which parliament as part of its obituary tribute voted to pay.

CHAPTER TWENTY-THREE

---◆◆◆---

Prophet of Ruin

In America the uneasy three years' truce which had followed North's removal of most of the Townshend duties in 1770 was deceptive. The colonies lapsed for a while into their habitual quarrelsome disunity, but the hostility to Britain which had developed so markedly since 1763 was far from disappearing, as isolated incidents like the burning of the revenue ship *Gaspée* in 1772 served to remind. None of the fundamental issues had been resolved, and it needed only the tea boycott of 1773 to set them alight again. North's ingenious scheme for simultaneously helping the hard-pressed East India Company and undercutting the smugglers by allowing direct exports of cheap Company tea into America was seen there by vested interests and radicals as a challenge too dangerous to ignore. News of the notorious outcome in Boston harbour reached England early in 1774, and North's government replied swiftly by closing the port of Boston, compelling the quartering of troops there, allowing the transfer of Massachusetts trials if necessary to England, and removing the right of election to the upper house of the Massachusetts assembly. Chatham, still at Burton, was in no doubt that the violence upon the tea-cargo was criminal, or that Boston owed reparation; but, he thought, there had been 'a fatal desire to take advantage of this guilty tumult of the Bostonians'. The punitive counter-measures had been too severe, and too sudden; Boston should first have been given time to 'make reparation for a heinous wrong'.[1]

It was Chatham, ironically, who by conquering Canada and removing the French threat to the colonies, had done as much as any man to promote their demand for independence. Independence was a spirit already bred in the American bone of farmer or merchant, of shop-keeper or lawyer or frontiersman. State governments had already had wearisome experience of the difficulty of ruling communities where love of freedom slid easily into ungovernability. It needed only the annihilation of the French menace to set before the colonists'

eyes the expendability of the British connection. The new sense of
national identity would take some time to struggle over the rough
ground of inter-state jealousies and rivalries, of sectional quarrels
within states – primary producers versus middlemen, coastal merchants
and settled farmers versus pioneers of the interior – and of lingering
traditions of Englishness. But Chatham's picture of the colonists, as
Englishmen loyal to English ways, wishing to enjoy English liberties
and respect English laws, frustrated only by the follies and tyrannies of
a corrupt home government, was already unreal and outdated. During
his ministry of 1766 he had been shocked by the 'umbrageousness' of
the radicals and resisters of New York and Boston who had refused to
maintain and supply troops under the terms of the Mutiny Act, but
he could never persuade himself that such people were representative
of honest American opinion. Almost to the end he remained convinced that the colonies, approached in a proper conciliatory manner
and guaranteed freedom from 'illegal' taxation and arbitrary government, would be ready voluntarily to contribute to the costs of defence
and administration. Though he repeatedly harked back to the valiant
part played by colonial volunteers in the wars with France, he found
it easy to forget that during the Seven Years War, *his* war, Britain had
had the utmost difficulty in raising American provincials, and had
wrung sufficient assistance from several of the colonies only by promises
to pay back their expenses. He was unable to see the various anti-
British importation embargoes and the sequence of disorderly episodes
that culminated in the Boston Tea Party as anything but lamentable
consequences of British provocation. He could not imagine that a
population which had long enjoyed a high degree of political autonomy,
and had by the inertia of long usage won itself a sort of fiscal immunity,
would be unpatriotically stubborn in defence of its privileges. He
refused to contemplate the dire possibility – indeed it was fact – that
most Americans were already psychologically dissociated from the
'home country'; that even where lip-service was paid to an old-
fashioned loyalty, England had become a distant irrelevance.

It was not the *absence* of a French menace that was in Chatham's
mind now, but the looming presence of it at home. The situation in
America was inevitably linked with the permanent danger from across
the Channel, which never ceased to worry him. If resistance grew
general in America, France would seize her chance, and England would

be 'no more'. When he learned that Louis XV was seriously ill (in fact he was dying) he wrote, 'I little thought once I should form daily wishes for the health and life of his Most Christian Majesty . . . I consider the peace as hanging on this single life . . . and England undone, if war comes'. By April 1774 he had decided, in view of 'these times ripe to embrace destruction', to go to Hayes in readiness for a return to parliament, though he was still protesting conventionally to Shelburne his unimportance and 'no-weight'.[2] After travelling from Somerset to Kent, he was held back by illness for another month before finally appearing in the Lords, on 26 May. To allow him to speak, ministers had postponed for nine days the third reading of the bill for quartering troops in Boston. Leaning on his crutch, and with 'his legs wrapped in black velvet boots, as if in mourning for the King of France', he made his speech in the low voice of an invalid.

It was a plea for understanding and moderation. Certainly, *if* Bostonians refused to make reparation for their misdeeds, they ought to be punished; but, that aside, there should be an amnesty for offenders. The government should 'proceed like a kind and affectionate parent over a child whom he tenderly loves . . . You will find them children worthy of their sire'. And perhaps to contradict the view of the colonists being put about by less well-informed friends of the administration, he asked it to be remembered that Americans were not rude colonials: 'the principal towns in America are learned and polite, and understand the constitution of the empire as well as the noble lords who are now in office'. It was a constitution which must deny Britain's right to tax the colonies. This conviction he would 'carry to the grave'.[3]

After delivering his speech, he retired home to bed, where Thomas Walpole, visiting him two days later, found him sitting up

> with a satin eider-down quilt on his feet. He wore a duffil cloak without arms, bordered with a broad purple lace. On his head he had a night-cap, and over that a hat with a broad brim flapped all round. It was difficult not to smile at a figure whose meagre jaws and uncouth habiliments recalled Don Quixote when he received the Duenna . . . and was wrapped up in serecloths.[4]

Next month came the Quebec Act, embodying arrangements for Canada which North's government had prepared long before the latest flare-up in Boston. But in the inflamed state of American public opinion, no actions of a British government were likely to escape suspicion. If Britain established French civil law, without juries, in a land where Frenchmen outnumbered Englishmen by thirty to one, that indicated a plain intention that juries, and no doubt habeas corpus too, were to be abolished throughout the old English colonies. If the Catholic religion was given official status in overwhelmingly Catholic Canada, it was clear evidence to puritan New Englanders that Lord North was in league with the Pope and the Devil. If a military government was to be set up with a *nominated* council, it was a sign that Britain was bent on abolishing American representative institutions. If Canadian boundaries were to be extended to the Ohio, it was further proof of the old British aim of blocking American westward expansion and denying manifest destiny. And if Canada was now, as it seemed, to be cosseted, it could only be because the British government was looking at the matter strategically, searching for security in a future war against France and, more ominously, for a friendly base in future operations against Americans. (Some pro-government opinions and speeches certainly lent colour to this last.)

Chatham rushed to embrace these hostile interpretations of what, given a happier atmosphere to the southward of Canada, might have been accepted on balance as a realistic and statesmanlike act. Ministers, he declared, had produced 'a plan of despotism', 'cruel, oppressive, and odious'. Popery was to be established and the veil of the temple of Protestantism rent. Woe to 'those scandalous tools, the bishops'![5] It was a rousing tirade, with no sign of the moderation he had recently been preaching to the government, but a good deal to encourage Americans in the belief that Lord North was aiming to 'enslave them by inches'. In the Lords Chatham enlisted only six supporting votes for his denunciation.

During the long parliamentary recess he worked steadily to inform himself upon American affairs. One of the London sheriffs, Stephen Sayre, who had contacts across the Atlantic, plied him with the news and views of his American correspondents.[6] Among the Americans he talked with was Mehetabel Wright, an artist in wax who, in addition to providing him with a perspective of American affairs as she and her friends saw them, was given sittings to model the effigy of Chatham later to be housed in Westminster Abbey. He made a sympathetic study of various schemes which aimed to overcome the objection of 'no taxation without representation' by establishing a grand imperial federal parliament, with representatives attending from Ireland and all the British colonies, and he discussed this project, and the whole range of American problems, with Benjamin Franklin, who was invited to Hayes in August and again in December. In February Franklin had been examined before the Privy Council for his part in the exposure of Governor Hutchinson of Massachusetts; had been gratuitously and foolishly insulted there by Wedderburn; and had been dismissed from his deputy-post-mastership. This extraordinary man who had devoted much of his inventive and supple intelligence to guiding America along lines of development *within* the British empire had already, by the time Chatham conferred with him, written his disillusioned and satirical *Rules for Reducing a Great Empire to a Small One*.[7] He closely explained and interpreted American shades of opinion, arguing the impracticability in existing conditions of the imperial federal parliament, and trying to reassure Chatham on the navigation acts and American willingness to accept the regulation of trade. In December he brought down to Hayes copies of the First Continental Congress's address to the British people and petition to the King. Chatham considered that that historic assembly had conducted its 'arduous and delicate business with manly wisdom and calm resolution'. He hardly needed Franklin to persuade him that Americans would never come to a settlement 'while the bayonet was at their breasts'. It would be *impossible*, as he wrote to Sayre, 'for freemen in England to wish to see three millions of Englishmen slaves in America'.[8]

The crisis in America did nothing to lessen the breach between Chatham and the Rockinghams. Chatham feared that they were unsound on the principle of regulating trade and navigation, for him an essential gear in the machine of empire; and he insisted that the Rockinghams' Declaratory Act of 1766, asserting the fundamental British *right* to tax the colonies, was constitutionally erroneous and damaging to good relations.[9] Thus the two main opposition groups, each claiming to be friends of true liberty and of conciliation with their fellow citizens across the Atlantic, viewed one another, as the new session approached, with a hampering mistrust. Burke for one was convinced that Chatham would never cooperate fully with the Rockinghams 'as long as he thinks that the Closet door stands a jarr to receive him. The least peep' into the Closet, he wrote, 'intoxicates him and will to the end of his life'.[10] For his part, Chatham expressed fear of others' 'jockeyship', and was anxious to keep the nose of his own horse, a dark one, in the lead. He wished that everyone should be informed that he was going to 'make a motion relative to America' on 20 January, but was determined to conceal its terms from both 'court' (government) and 'faction' (Rockinghams). He was planning one of his *coups de théâtre*. Two days before his promised speech, Hester reported to him strong rumours flying round town that he would be too ill to attend. 'Let me recommend to you', she wrote, 'to have great attention to yourself; and pray let Wielbier and sage Pam join in examining that windows are down, doors shut, etc., that you may not be *made* to catch cold'. Chatham replied:

> For God's sake, sweet life, don't disquiet yourself about the impudent and ridiculous lie of the hour . . . Be of good cheer, noble love –
> 'I am proud – I must be proud – to see
> Men not afraid of God afraid of me.'
> Look fresh and merrily tomorrow,* and I will look to doors and windows. So to my dear Secretary! I wish *somebody* [the King] had as good and as honest an one.[11]

He arrived at the House of Lords on 20 January accompanied by his son William, now fifteen, and Benjamin Franklin, whom he wished to introduce by a door near the throne, but was told that no one entered that way except eldest sons or brothers of peers – upon which he limped back with him to the door near the bar saying loud enough for all to hear and take note, 'This is Dr Franklin, whom I would have admitted'. Chatham's appearance in the House, Franklin observed, 'caused a kind of bustle among the officers . . . something of importance being expected when that great man appears'.[12]

The motion turned out to be for the withdrawal of Gage's troops, that 'army of impotence, irritation and vexation' then penned up in Boston; this to be a prelude to the retraction of 'those violent acts and declarations' which had produced the crisis. He gave 'no tolerable

---

* Hester was staying with the Hoods in Harley Street, ready for presenting her daughter Hester at the Drawing Room, upon her marriage to Lord Mahon. 'His Majesty was very gracious, for *him*', she told Chatham. '. . . You was in general expected to be there . . . Our girl acquitted herself well' (Lady Chatham to Chatham, 20 January 1775).

reason for so precipitate and premature a step', complained Walpole, 'but that it would be an earnest of good intentions'[13] – a criticism which missed Chatham's (as it proved) all too valid point: that Britain was left with no alternative, except to enter upon a civil war she could not win:

> What though you march from town to town, and from province to province; though you should be able to enforce a temporary submission . . . how shall you be able to secure the obedience of the country you leave behind you . . . to grasp the dominion of eighteen hundred miles of continent, populous in numbers, possessing valour, liberty, and resistance?
>
> This resistance to your arbitrary system of taxation might have been foreseen: it was obvious . . . from the Whiggish spirit flourishing in that country . . . the same which formerly opposed loans, benevolences, and ship-money in England, and by the Bill of Rights vindicated the English constitution . . . This glorious spirit of Whiggism animates three millions in America . . .
>
> To such united force, what force shall be opposed? – What, my Lords? – a few regiments in America, and seventeen or eighteen thousand men at home! – The idea is too ridiculous to take up a moment of your Lordships' time . . . We shall be forced ultimately to retract: let us retract when we can, not when we must . . . These violent oppressive acts must be repealed; you will repeal them; . . . I stake my reputation upon it. I will consent to be taken for an idiot if they are not finally repealed. Avoid, then, this humiliating, disgraceful necessity . . . Make the first advances to concord, to peace, and happiness . . .[14]

And the Bourbon powers were watching, 'waiting for the maturity of your errors'. The sword hung over the nation's head by a brittle thread.

As Burke informed his constituents the citizens of Bristol, 'The division was against the question 68, for it 18. More would have been in the minority if Lord Chatham had thought proper to give notice of his motion to the proper people'.[15]

Things began to look not quite so simple when he came in his next speech to commit himself to more detailed proposals; but the initial simplicity of this enlightened defeatism (which Walpole found 'crude and absurd', and the King seditious) looks a great deal more realistic and respectable from two centuries' distance than the contemptuous dismissal of the colonists' qualities which came from several government supporters and even from some ministers – Sandwich for one, with his expressed wish to see a rebel army big enough to make it worth beating.

Over the last days of January Chatham had three further sessions with Franklin and a consultation with Camden. On 31 January Lady Rockingham informed Burke that her husband had received a letter from 'the *greatest* of all Earls . . . There will be a *plan offer'd*, but there are *no explanations* of that plan'.[16] The following day Chatham put his 'poor thoughts' before the Lords in a bill 'for settling the troubles in America and for asserting the supreme legislative authority and superintending power of Great Britain over the colonies'. They were to enjoy the jury system, a fully independent judiciary, and freedom from taxation except by consent, but that consent would be *requested* for a perpetual revenue to the Crown in recognition of burdens borne by the mother country. The Continental Congress of American states would be given constitutional standing and charged with assessing each state's contribution. No accused person would be removed from his colony for trial. The Quebec Act and all the punitive measures against Boston and Massachusetts would be repealed. But the Crown was to retain the right to maintain an army and deploy it wherever it deemed necessary, in any British dominions 'whether in America or elsewhere'.[17]

Franklin was 'filled with admiration' for Chatham, but though he was consulted he could not give the bill unqualified approval, and he later disclaimed having any share in its framing. During a four-hour visit to Hayes on the day before its presentation, he found Chatham so 'full and diffuse' in explaining and defending it that his own objections largely went by the board; but he was willing to give his blessing on the understanding that it would be susceptible to later negotiation and amendment.[18] However, it is very improbable that Chatham's insistence on British parliamentary sovereignty and 'superintending power' could by this time have proved acceptable to the increasingly radical temper and coordinated resistance of Americans. The 1774 Continental Congress did not demand independence, but those who did were every month gaining greater influence; and it was of course for Chatham a notion so abhorrent that he had never, and would never, come within a mile of contemplating acceptance of it.

Shelburne, Camden, and Richmond spoke in favour of Chatham's bill. Grafton objected to its unparliamentary 'hurry'. Temple* was against it, though sorry 'to differ with the only person with whom I ardently wish to agree'.[19] Grafton later repented his attitude and apologized for his errors. In opposing for the ministry, Sandwich 'fancied he had in his eye the person who drew it up' – looking straight at Franklin, again present, in company with Lord Stanhope – 'one of the bitterest and most mischievous enemies this country has ever known'. He was mistaken: the bill was entirely Chatham's; and though it was defeated, perhaps the surprising thing is that it enlisted thirty-two votes. Chatham had wished, he told Stanhope, 'to try the *impossible thing*', when he saw 'the country running upon perdition'.[20] Within a few weeks Lord North, who believed as little as anyone in a war with Americans, began attempts of his own at reconciliation, accompanied though they were with war preparations. Their chances of success looked slim; and though Chatham was ready to accept that North was not one of the '*butchers*' in the government, he wrote off his eleventh hour conciliation moves as 'a mere verbiage, a most puerile mockery'.[21] The shots at Lexington that went round the world were only two months away.

Some time however before those fateful hostilities had begun, Chatham was once more back in the shadows, where he was to remain, with only rare intermissions, for the next twenty-six months. Again it was a great deal worse and more complicated than gout, though the old euphemism was freely passed round. His mental sickness was linked with multiple physical afflictions. His rheumatic condition was of course by now chronic, though the family still prayed for another of those good strong doses of 'regular' gout held to be so curative of the 'flying' sort. It seems very likely that he now had a heart condition too. His kidneys had become diseased. He had digestive trouble. He suffered a rupture and from towards the end of 1776 had to add a truss to his long-established paraphernalia of crutches and flannel and big

* Mostly retired, and dividing his days between Pall Mall and Stowe, where he was engaged in 'Herculean labours of magnificence and taste', he still attended occasionally in the Lords, and continued to maintain friendly relations with Chatham, if at some distance.

boots and 'great chairs'. Dr Addington's letters to Hester[22] mention tremblings, palpitations, and attacks of giddiness, though these might partly be attributed to the nervous, or as Addington called it 'hypochondriacal', aspect of his disorders.

As in his previous severe depressions, although physical debility and melancholia prostrated him for months on end, there would be days, or even weeks, when he decided he was well enough to go riding. But it was a 'cruel illness', as William wrote from Cambridge in July 1775.[23] His life, so Burke thought in the following month, was 'in effect over. It is, I believe, impossible he should recover'. (He noted unenthusiastically that Chatham was still the idol of the Congress in America; and added, after very unfairly holding Chatham half responsible for the Townshend duties, that he could not 'give a guess whether his death would be serviceable or mischievous'.) Yet in September he learned that the patient had 'perfectly recover'd', which, acquainted as he was 'with the astonishing changes of Lord Chatham's condition (whether natural or political)', was indeed amazing. The reprieve was in fact short-lived. 'Lord Chatham continues in the same melancholy way', Camden told Grafton in January 1776, 'and the house is so shut up that his sons are not permitted to receive visitors'.[24]

'In case he should not recover', Chatham in July 1775 gave to Addington 'A Memorandum of a Declaration concerning America', intended to convey to the world that he carried his convictions to the grave unaltered. Without reconciliation, within 'a very few years' France would 'set her foot on English ground'. Copies of this testament were made later by Hester for dispatch to Camden and Shelburne. Addington, who was first entrusted with it, was always something rather more than the Chatham family's chief physician. He became also a personal friend, and politically too he was a Chathamite.* Once it seemed likely that his patient was not dying, he obviously entertained hopes that Chatham might recover sufficiently to lead the country once more. To a modern eye some of his diagnoses and dietetic recommendations appear somewhat bizarre; but he under-

---

* His son was of course to succeed Chatham's son as prime minister. Another who worked rather more than merely professionally in Chatham's interest was Lancelot Brown the landscapist, who during 1777 trod the 'tender ground' of trying to persuade the King himself of the capability of national improvement inherent in another Chatham ministry (Chatham *Correspondence*, iv. 430–1).

stood well enough that, gout and kidney degeneration and rupture and the rest of it notwithstanding, Chatham's psychological sickness was best cured by making him *think* it curable. Thus, for instance, to have a second doctor always sleeping in the house would only, by persuading the patient to believe himself worse, make him so.

Throughout 1776 Chatham remained in a wretched condition of body and mind. In May, William wrote from Cambridge, 'It is some relief that Dr Addington still comforts us with confident hopes; though I cannot but feel it cruel that that is all we have to support us, without any amendment hitherto'. In July there was still 'no consolation' to be found, 'only melancholy comparison'; in October again, 'nothing satisfactory . . . on that affecting subject'. In January 1777 James Grenville received his sister's latest medical bulletin with 'very great concern': in the last attack, 'Lord Chatham's sufferings . . . must have been uncommonly violent'. It was not till April that he could join 'willing responses of joy' to Hester's own at better news. By 26 May Chatham indeed felt himself sufficiently restored to have Hester ask Camden on his behalf for the convening of the Lords to receive a motion in favour of an end to the war in America.[25]

His speech included some trifling criticism of American behaviour ('I do not', he said, 'mean their panegyric'), but was in the main an even more urgent repetition of his old condemnations of all British policy since 1763, coupled now with desperate warnings of the menace from France. Britain, he argued, was left with no intelligent alternative to a cessation of hostilities, and a withdrawal of every one of the 'oppressive' measures of the past fourteen years. 'You may ravage – you cannot conquer'. And even if victory had been possible,

> What then? You cannot make them respect you: you cannot make them wear your cloth: you will plant an invincible hatred in their breasts against you . . . We are the aggressors. We have invaded them . . .

He hammered away at the commercial advantages being thrown away by the government's folly. America was

> the source of all our wealth and power . . . a double market – the market of consumption and the market of supply. This double market, with naval stores, you are giving to your hereditary rival.

France, he said, was already stealing Britain's American trade. Of course she had not *yet* made a treaty with the Americans. Why should she, when Britain was destroying herself without French intervention? But France was merely awaiting her moment. If Britain did not secure peace by giving 'unconditional redress', her fate was decided; 'England, old England', was ruined.[26]

His motion was inevitably lost (by 28 to 99) – treated, wrote Franklin, 'with as much contempt as they could have shown to a ballad offered by a drunken porter'.[27] Walpole thought that 'little remained of his former fire'; but William the younger, present to listen and admire, was 'happy beyond description' at his father's vigour and vivacity and eloquence: 'I only regretted that he did not always raise his voice enough for all the House to hear everything he said'.[28] The King's verdict was no less predictable than Chatham's own views and sentiments: 'like most of the other productions of that extraordinary brain', it amounted to nothing but 'specious words and malevolence'; anyone reading the speech, George wrote, 'if unacquainted with the conduct of the mother country and the colonies, must suppose the Americans poor mild persons who . . . had no choise but slavery or the sword'.[29]

A short time after this, Chatham was out riding when he suffered a seizure, fell from his horse, and for some minutes lay unconscious. Again he recovered. By September he was eating like a farmer, so he wrote to William – 'dear William, the hope and comfort of my life'.[30] 'Emerging out of a long silence', he sent warm remembrances to Temple, who had also recently been through a period of illness. (' "For we were bred upon the selfsame hill" ', he reminded Temple, ' "Fed the same flock, by fountain, shade, and rill" '.) Even into this amicably reminiscent and personally cheerful letter there obtruded gloom for the political future. Whichever side won in America, the result would be ruin: 'poor England will have fallen upon her own sword'.[31]

Temple no doubt sensed a party-political purport in this brotherly approach. There was probably some sort of sisterly approach to him too. Replying to Hester, Temple (physically fine, he assured Chatham; a cold bath every day performed wonders) hoped 'somehow or other' that circumstances might 'bring two friends to be able to act or think together', but he was obliged to declare that he thought the British cause in America just. 'Reconciliation, founded in the independence of

America, makes me rather choose to treat with a beaten enemy'.[32]

To most Englishmen the prospects of this still appeared fairly good at the time Temple was writing. He could not know that, just four days before, Burgoyne had surrendered at Saratoga. After that psychologically decisive event, optimism was to become much harder to sustain. The French took their cue and proceeded to sign treaties with America, commercial and military, by early February. The spirit went out of Lord North, who was kept going politically only by a kind of artificial respiration periodically applied by George III.

News of Saratoga had not yet reached London when the new session of parliament opened. Even so, Chatham reminded the Lords, they faced a 'rugged and awful crisis'. He rose on 20 November to instruct the throne, he said, 'in the language of truth'.

The four speeches he delivered over the next three weeks were among his most impressive. The Duke of Grafton (now after his ministerial comings and goings received back into the Chathamite fold) declared himself incapable of giving 'more than a faint idea' of 'Lord Chatham's powers as an orator, on this memorable occasion' (20 November).[33] But events had deteriorated so far that much of what he had so pungently and passionately to declare could amount to little more than crying over spilt milk. When news came of Saratoga, Rockingham was able to say 'My heart is at ease'; and Burke by then thought that 'we had much better be rid' of the colonies, if they wished to go.[34] But for Chatham what was happening was an unmitigated catastrophe; one, moreover, which statesmanship, he was sure, might have avoided; which he, given authority and health, *would* have avoided.

From this distance it can hardly appear so, though his sympathetic attitude might well have helped delay the decisive break. His predisposition in the colonists' favour often in fact led him to overestimate their loyalty to Britain, and in these all but final speeches of his there was much wishful thinking. 'The freemen whom you call rebels', he declared, would 'cheerfully bleed for you' and 'carry your arms triumphant to every corner of the globe'. Had it not been these 'rebels' who 'raised four regiments on their own bottom and took Louisbourg [in 1745] from the veteran troops of France?' He again reminded his audience, too – a favourite theme – of how successfully he had brought into the late war Highlanders who were also then thought of as rebels, and once 'advocates for popery, slavery, and arbitrary power'.

Again, though Chatham never granted any flaw in his distinction between lawful internal taxation and unlawful external taxation, experience had shown it to be hardly useful. Townshend's 'external' duties had been the occasion of little less agitation than Grenville's 'internal' stamp tax. Then, Chatham's insistence upon Britain's right to ask for an American defence contribution, to regulate colonial trade and navigation in the interests of domestic merchants and manufacturers, and to assert the ultimate sovereignty of the British parliament,* must surely in the end have proved unacceptable to too many Americans for any lasting harmony between *parent* and *children*. (This was Chatham's metaphor as well as George III's.) It was a much idealized America that he so vigorously and eloquently defended. Even during the wars of the 'forties and 'fifties it had never existed quite as he liked to picture it; and certainly it did not so exist by 1777.

However, mournfully and scathingly he could paint a damning picture of the dead end North's government was heading for across the Atlantic, and of the disaster looming from across the Channel. Only once or twice did the note of passion become shrill, as when he tore furiously into Secretary Lord Suffolk, who had ventured to defend the employment of Indians in the fighting as part of 'the means that God and nature put into our hands'. '*Hell-hounds, I say, of a savage war!*' declaimed Chatham in a fierce diatribe. 'Spain armed herself with bloodhounds to extirpate the wretched natives of America; . . . and we turn loose these savage hell-hounds against our brethren and countrymen . . . of the same language, laws, and religion'; he could not, he said, have slept that night without expressing his 'eternal abhorrence'. He returned to this outrage in a later speech: we had set against our fellow countrymen the scalping-knife and the tomahawk wielded by 'the most brutal and ferocious of the human species' – a stigma which all the waters of the Delaware and the Hudson would never wash away. When it was alleged against him that he had himself used Indians in the late war, he at first denied it, appealing for support to Amherst. Amherst, however, and subsequently Chatham too, had

*'I will as soon subscribe to Transubstantiation as to Sovereignty (by right), in the Colonies' (Chatham to Shelburne, 18 December 1777).

to admit that, since the French employed them, the English had followed suit – but only for scouting and tracking.*

Before this outburst, he had reiterated the essential justice of the American cause, and begged members to believe that a friendly disposition still prevailed in the 'principal and sound part of America'. 'Let us escape from the fatal effects of our delusions', and so be able 'again to awe the house of Bourbon, instead of merely truckling, as our present calamities compel us, to every insult of French caprice and Spanish punctilio'. In a debate on the strength of the armed forces a fortnight later, he lambasted the First Lord, Sandwich, on alleged ill-preparedness in the navy – twenty ships of the line fit and ready, against the thirty-five there should be for the Mediterranean alone – and exposed the precarious situation of Minorca and Gibraltar, where Hanoverian troops had had to be stationed, and the second-in-command was a foreigner! The use of German and Swiss hirelings in America fetched from him even angrier bitterness. 'My Lords, if I were an American as I am an Englishman, while a foreign troop was landed in my country I never would lay down my arms – never – never – never!'

By 5 December news of Saratoga had arrived, to intensify his lament. The nation was 'undone, disgraced'. As for General Burgoyne, he would not incline to blame him: 'he might have received orders it was not in his power to execute' – as it happened no bad guess. The fault must lie solely with ministers who had sacrificed 'for the pursuit of a peppercorn' the millions which America meant to British traders and manufacturers.[35]

The chief of those ministers, North, was only too anxious to resign, but meanwhile prepared a plan of reconciliation which proposed enabling peace commissioners to concede to America much of what Chatham had been demanding, including an end to internal taxation and repeal of the measures taken since 1763. It was of course much too late. The first July the Fourth was by now eighteen months into the past, and the French treaties included a recognition of the colonies' independence. At home, independence for America had already been

---

* Although a natural scepticism intrudes, it is true that Amherst in 1762 had been proud to have kept his Indians 'within humane bounds', and Pitt had then written to congratulate him on it (v. *supra*, p. 274).

accepted by the Rockinghams as a necessary price to pay for getting the troops home to confront the French.

In the critical situation following Saratoga, North looked to Chatham as the obvious man to replace him, and told the King so. But George refused to release him, and was fortified to learn of the persisting disagreement between the Rockinghams and Chatham. Among the leading Rockinghams, however, the Duke of Richmond was now doing his best to heal the breach and find common ground; he for one would be ready to cooperate with Chatham, demand for whose return was becoming loud and widespread as confirmation arrived of news of the French treaties, and with it something approaching panic.

Only a few months previously he had been reported near to death. He was known to be still most unwell. But everyone now was looking towards him to save the country a second time: many government supporters besides North himself; the public press; George Grenville's son, George, in a Commons speech; Bute and the Duke of Northumberland; even Lord Mansfield. Dr Addington, Lancelot Brown ('piping hot from Lord Bute'), and Thomas Coutts were all enlisted to use their personal persuasions at Hayes – and Addington at least (an emissary of an emissary of Bute) was given a very dusty answer to take back to the 'courtly insinuation' that Bute's spokesman had put forward: 'Let him remember . . . that his great patron and your village friend differ in this: one has ruined the King and the kingdom; the other still endeavours to save it'. Bute's suggestion, it was reported, was that Chatham should be prime minister with a dukedom, and Bute one of the Secretaries of State. 'Tell the fellow', Chatham was supposed to have said, 'that if he dares to come out I will impeach him'. To the end, Chatham was running true to form.[36]

So too was George III. By mid-March he had given his reluctant consent for positive negotiations to be undertaken through William Eden for the return of Chatham. But he was still adamant that North must continue as prime minister and act as intermediary between him and Chatham, whom he absolutely declined to meet. He was ready to admit Shelburne as Secretary and allow some other Chathamites into the government (Barré preferably in an office not necessitating *seeing* him); and Chatham himself should have the dispensation of honours and a seat in the cabinet, but no more. As for the Rockinghams, they were no more acceptable than 'Lord Chatham and his crew'. He could 'write volumes', he told North, on the state of his feelings towards all of them; he would rather lose his crown than wear it under 'the ignominy of their shackles'.

Hardly surprisingly, Chatham insisted that he must be seen to have direction of affairs; and when Eden saw Shelburne, Chatham's mouthpiece, he was told that 'Lord Chatham must be the dictator', and must also be allowed to bring in Rockingham and Grafton, and to exclude Mansfield, Germain (Sackville), and Gower. North begged the King to yield; Chatham's terms would humiliate him less than those of the Rockinghams, and could only be raised if left unaccepted. George would not be convinced; he had no wish to be 'a slave for the remainder of his days'. And he was unimpressed when North told him, rather misleadingly, that Granby had been sent off to Hayes with the Rockinghams' consent to accepting Chatham's leadership unreservedly; he was, he said, 'extremely indifferent whether Lord Granby goes or does not go with the abject message of the Rockingham party this day to Hayes; I will certainly send none to that place'.[37]

In fact, important differences persisted between Chatham and the Rockinghams. Both wished to extricate British troops from America to be ready to confront the French, but Chatham clung to his desperate hope that this might somehow be done without finally losing the allegiance of the colonists. Many times and woefully he repeated that it was probably too late, but still he would not, could not, accept the idea of severance. It gave him 'unspeakable concern', he told Richmond, to differ with him so profoundly; still, he promised him to do his best to come to Westminster for a motion down in the Duke's name for 7 April.

Supported by his human crutches, his son William and son-in-law Mahon, he struggled to the House of Lords on that day. His son James was there too. Richmond proposed his motion. Weymouth replied for the government. Then Chatham spoke, falteringly, with obvious difficulty and more even than usual references to his infirmities, but at least making clear that he would never 'consent to deprive the royal offspring of the House of Brunswick . . . of their fairest inheritance'.[38] And if peace with the House of Bourbon could not be preserved with honour, why could not war be declared without hesitation? 'Any state is better than despair; . . . and if we fall, let us fall like men'.

Richmond spoke again, pointing out that even the great name of Chatham was hardly sufficient in itself to guarantee victory 'without an army, without a navy, and without money'. It would now be France, Spain, *and America* against Britain; a situation disastrously changed since 1756. Chatham, in some turmoil, struggled to raise himself again to answer the Duke, succeeded at last in getting to his feet, but was unable to stay on them, pressed his hand to his heart, swayed alarmingly, sank back, and was prevented from falling to the floor only by the rescuing arms of neighbouring peers, one of them Lord Temple.[39]

They carried him to the Prince's Chamber, where a doctor present, Richard Brockleby, and then, as quickly as he could arrive, Dr Addington, attended him. He regained consciousness, and after an attack of vomiting seemed sufficiently better to make Addington hopeful of recovery. Two days later they took him to Hayes where, surrounded by his family, he lingered for nearly five weeks. His heir John was under immediate orders to sail with his regiment to Gibraltar (where he was to serve throughout the great siege), and Chatham would not have him delay. William he asked one day to read to him the passage from the *Iliad* telling of the death of Hector. He died on 11 May.

The Commons voted unanimously to give him a funeral and a monument in Westminster Abbey, to pay his considerable debts, and ask for fitting provision to be made for his family. When North reminded the King of his earlier promise to raise the pension and extend its scope beyond the lives of Hester and the eldest son, he readily agreed, but as for the public funeral and monument, he hoped that that would be taken merely as a testimony to Chatham's 'rousing the nation at the beginning of the last war', and *not* to his 'general conduct'. Otherwise he must regard the gesture as a measure offensive to him personally.[40] The death of so assertive a character could hardly be expected to pass without a few such jarring notes. The House of Lords failed to pass a motion of Shelburne's that they should attend the funeral. The attendance there would be 'respectable', wrote William Pitt, 'but it will not be from the encouragement of the Court, who do everything with an ill grace'.[41] Burke's immediate reaction to Chatham's death was that he had 'spit his last venom'. But Burke at least made some considered amends. It was he who inscribed the tribute on the City's Guildhall memorial to 'the principal instrument' in the Supreme Disposer's plan to advance the nation to 'an high pitch of prosperity and glory . . . by commerce for the first time united with, and made to flourish, by war'.[42] And with his fellow Rockinghams Sir George Savile and Thomas Townshend, and the Chathamite Dunning, he was a pall-bearer at the funeral on 9 June.

The City had requested the King for a burial in St Paul's, but it took place at Westminster, with a high pomp which Chatham would have found fitting. After two days lying in state in the black-draped Painted Chamber, attended by eight halberdiers and ten torch-bearers, the body was taken in a procession which included seventy of the poor, one for each year of the statesman's life, from Westminster Hall to the Abbey, with Barré bearing a banner, supported by Rockingham and the Dukes of Northumberland, Richmond, and Manchester. The only members of the Court present were Lord Townshend and Lord Amherst.

Upon a marble urn at Burton Pynsent, later transferred to Stowe, Hester inscribed her own 'witness of unceasing grief for him who, excelling in whatever is most admirable . . . bestowed felicity inexpressible on her whose faithful love was blessed in a pure return that raised her above every other joy but the parental one, and that still shared with him' – words closer to truth than those of many epitaphs.[43] She was to survive her husband for a quarter of a century, spent largely at Burton Pynsent, and experience the further griefs of losing in quick succession three of her five children, but also the triumphant consolation of seeing her remarkable second son prime minister at twenty-four, a sight to make surrounding kingdoms stare as her husband had made them tremble.

'Posterity, this is an impartial picture', wrote Horace Walpole of his presentation of Pitt. 'It is a man I am describing, and one who will bear to have his blemishes fairly delivered to you'. Catching history on the wing, he was always conscious of his own shifting judgement of the man whose great talents seemed matched only by his flaws and follies; who defied pat opinions. Walpole laboured conscientiously to be fair, in the Memoirs at least if not always in the more impromptu and often skittish letters. His panegyric always contained careful qualification: 'whether his qualities were real or fictitious, his actions were so illustrious that few names in the register of Time will excite more curiosity than that of William Pitt'. It was always the eloquence of the man that most of all impressed, even when the panache seemed over-contrived and the wisdom of the speeches' content debatable: 'the memory of his eloquence . . . will remain, when the neglect of his contemporaries, and my criticisms, will be forgotten'. And it was of course the one quality which Walpole despaired of getting on to paper; however, what he wrote was at least 'faithfully taken from his own mouth in the House of Commons; and unless better transcripts appear, this rude sketch may be welcome to posterity'.[44]

One might appraise Pitt, as Walpole attempted; admire him, as most of the nation and even his political enemies learned to; idolize him, like Beckford or the young Grafton; detest him, like Mansfield or George II or, for most of the time, George III. But Pitt would have agreed with Lloyd George that politics was about 'piracy, broadsides, blood on the deck'; and where he was involved the deck was seldom unbloody. For all his erratic tactics, his fighting ambition was as single-minded as his fighting patriotism. His political style allowed, no more than his proud and prickly personality, of secure friendships, whether public or, outside his immediate family, private.

'He depended', wrote Shelburne, 'on taking quick turns, which was his forte'. It was not simply his physical and mental vulnerability that made him, as Grafton, Camden, Shelburne and many more discovered, an exasperating leader to follow. His gifts were great, but they did not include those attributes necessary to the leader of a political party; neither was this because he stood above intrigue, as he constantly claimed. Surprisingly, Shelburne, his disciple and political heir, thought Newcastle at bottom an *honester* man. Indeed, Shelburne's observations as the candid friend are generally more telling than those of avowed adversaries. He was of course a much younger man and never a close personal friend – but then, as he said, who was? Like almost everybody else he found it impossible to establish easy intimacy with this lofty, intimidating figure, with his 'eye that would cut a diamond' and his 'high, pompous, unmeaning language'.

Lord Chatham 'acted the part so well', wrote Shelburne, 'that everybody was persuaded that he had a perfect contempt of both patronage and money, though those that lived to see him near . . . saw plainly the contrary'. 'He knew the value of condescension, and reserved himself for the moment when he was almost certain of gaining his point by it; till then he pranced and vapoured'. To Shelburne he seemed to be *always* acting, 'always made up, and never natural'. 'Very well-bred', with 'all the manners of the *vieille cour*', he 'never escaped a degree of pedantry' in his conversation, 'especially when he affected levity'.[45]

During Britain's great imperial epoch in the century and a half following Chatham's death it was inevitable that, as inaugurator of those triumphs of empire, he should have the warts upon his portrait painted out, and that his rivals and opponents should be seen as little men, short-sighted carpers or self-seeking intriguers, friends of lethargy or crookedness. Newcastle in particular was by nature marked out only too clearly to play Beckmesser to Pitt's noble Hans Sachs. Pitt the superlative orator, the enemy of corruption, champion of freedom in Britain and America, saviour and builder of empire, could always reckon on being given the benefit of any residual doubt in an era when British civil liberties and parliamentary government were everywhere admired and envied, and the British Empire was planting ever wider dominion over palm and pine. His arrogance was indeed conceded, but only as the sort of venial failing commonly associated with genius; and what giant need be criticized for despising pygmies? If other politicians shifted their ground it was because they were shifty. If Pitt changed his, or turned somersault, he was 'inconsistent perhaps, but with the inconsistency of the man who casts off the evil trappings of the past as he advances'.[46] Other politicians intrigued because they were natural intriguers. When Pitt did so, it merely showed that he was 'the veriest amateur in political intrigue and with a profound contempt for move and countermove in the chicanery of party manoeuvres'.[47]

A modern view of Pitt cannot avoid being post-imperial, though by being that it ought not to belittle him. But it will approach nearer, perhaps, even in its confusions, to the views of his contemporaries. They saw a Pitt of paradoxes and contradictions, a Whig whose strongest appeal was to Tories and independents, an enemy to all parties because constituting a party in his own person; venerator but scourge of the monarchy; a leader gifted with genius but liable unaccountably to throw everything aside; an enigma, never predictable; a brilliant parliamentarian when he gave his mind to it; an unmatched orator; according to taste, either a heroic patriot or an unscrupulous demagogue; and – this at least being universally agreed – a supremely able and successful war minister.

A tangled picture, still puzzling and mystifying. It is perhaps fitting that the *same* distinguished modern historian who sees Pitt as bearing 'a heavy share of responsibility for the political confusion of the early years of George III's reign', as 'always proof against the call of duty when he saw nothing to his own advantage', as a political 'bully', as 'the subtle politician, strengthening his hand from every quarter and exploiting every weakness of his opponents', should also write that he was 'incomparably the greatest British statesman of the eighteenth century: none could match him in boldness of purpose or extent of achievement. Almost alone among his contemporaries he saw the vision of Britain expanded across the world, and set her feet firmly on the path of imperial greatness'.[48]

Select Bibliography

Of documentary sources for the life of Pitt many have by now been assembled in various printed collections. Probably the most substantial of these, though very deficient on the earlier years, are the four volumes of correspondence extracted by the statesman's great-grandsons W. S. Taylor and J. S. Pringle from the Public Record Office manuscripts which comprise the largest single assemblage of papers relating to Pitt and his affairs ('Chatham MSS'). For the period of the Seven Years War the two volumes of state papers edited by G. S. Kimball are indispensable. Extensive use of the Prussian state archives was made in A. von Ruville's biography (1907). Lord Rosebery printed much of what survives of the family correspondence of Pitt's early years; Lord Grenville, Lady Chatham's nephew, published separately Pitt's letters to his nephew Thomas; and E. A. Edwards collected those written by him to Hester Grenville before their marriage. Both P. C. Yorke's selection, in his *Hardwicke* (1913), from the Newcastle and Hardwicke papers in the British Museum (Add. MSS. 32679–33201 and 35349–36278) and W. J. Smith's four volumes of the Grenville family papers contain a great deal of important Pitt material. The enormous storehouse of Newcastle's letters and memoranda provide of course inexhaustible fodder for all political history of this period. Relatively recently the letters of Pitt to Bute have been edited by Romney Sedgwick. The Bridport (Hood family) papers in the British Museum (Add. MSS. 35191–35202) contain material relating especially to Chatham's private finances, as do the Record Office letters from the Hoods and Thomas Coutts to Lady Chatham. Also in the Record Office are many of Dr Addington's letters concerning Chatham's later illnesses. Further correspondence to and from Pitt is to be found in the volumes listed below under Fitzmaurice, Fortescue, Gambier, Grafton, Mahon, Miller, Namier, Phillimore, Thackeray, and certain of the collections of the Historical Manuscripts Commission.

A fuller bibliography is printed in Basil Williams's *William Pitt Earl of Chatham* (1913), a book to which, however its interpretation of character and events may be quarrelled with, every biographer of Pitt still remains under heavy obligation.

Bibliography

Printed Documentary and Contemporary Sources
(In italics, the relevant abbreviation used in the References.)

Adolphus, J.: History of England from the Accession of King George III (1803).

Albemarle, Lord: Memoirs of the Marquis of Rockingham (2 vols., 1852).

Almon, J.: Anecdotes of the Life of William Pitt, Earl of Chatham (3 vols., 1797) (*Almon*).

Annual Register (1759–1778).

Barnes, G. R. and Owen, J. H. (eds.): Private Papers of John, Earl of Sandwich (4 vols., 1932–8).

Bateson, M. (ed.): Newcastle's Narrative of Changes in the Ministry 1765–7 (1898).

Bedford, Duke of: Correspondence (ed. Lord J. Russell) (3 vols., 1842–6).

Bisset, A.: Memoirs and Papers of Sir Andrew Mitchell (2 vols., 1850).

Burke, E.: Correspondence (vols. 1–3, general ed. T. W. Copeland 1958–61). Thoughts on the Causes of the Present Discontents (1770).

Carlisle Papers (Historical Manuscripts Commission, 15, App. 6).

Cavendish, Sir H.: Debates of the House of Commons 1768–71 (ed. J. Wright, 2 vols., 1841).

Chandler, R.: History and Proceedings of the House of Commons to the Present Time (14 vols., 1742–4).

Chatham Correspondence (eds. W. S. Taylor and W. H. Pringle, 4 vols., 1838). (*Chat. Corr.*)

Chesterfield, Lord: Letters (ed. B. Dobrée, 6 vols., 1932).
    Old England, or the Constitutional Journal ('Jeffrey Broadbottom', 1743).

Coxe, W.: Memoirs of Sir Robert Walpole (3 vols., 1800). (*Coxe, Walpole*)
    Memoirs of Horatio Lord Walpole (2 vols., 1808).
    Memoirs of the Administration of Henry Pelham (2 vols., 1829).

Cradock, J.: Literary and Miscellaneous Memoirs (ed. J. B. Nichols, 4 vols., 1828).

Dodington, G. Bubb: Diary (ed. H. P. Wyndham, 1784).

Dropmore Papers: Manuscripts of Sir J. B. Fortescue preserved at Dropmore (Historical Manuscripts Commission XIII. App. 3, vol. I, 1892). (*HMC Dropmore*)

Edwards, E. A.: Love Letters of William Pitt, 1st Lord Chatham (1926).

Egmont, Lord: Diary (Historical Manuscripts Commission, 3 vols., 1920–4). (*HMC, Egmont*)

Elliott, G. F. S.: The Border Elliotts and the Family of Minto (1897).

Ellis, Sir H.: Original Letters (vol. 7, 1827).

Fitzmaurice, Lord: Life of William, Earl of Shelburne (2nd ed, 2 vols., 1912).

Fortescue, Sir J.: Correspondence of King George III from 1760 to 1783 (vols., 1–4, 1927–8). (*Fortescue CG3*)

Fox, H., Lord Holland: Memoir, in Life and Letters of Lady Sarah Lennox (2 vols., 1901).

Franklin, B.: The Life of Benjamin Franklin Written by Himself (ed. J. Bigelow, Philadelphia, 2 vols., 1875).

Writings (ed. A. H. Smyth, New York, 10 vols., 1905–7).

Gambier, Lord: Memorials Personal and Historical (ed. Lady Chatterton, 2 vols., 1861).

Gentleman's Magazine.

Gibbon, E.: Memoirs of My Life (ed. G. A. Bonnard, 1966).

Glover, R.: Memoirs of a Celebrated Literary and Political Character (1813).

Grafton, Duke of: Autobiography and Political Correspondence (ed. Sir W. R. Anson 1898).

Grattan, H.: Memoirs of the Life and Times of . . . (vol. 1, 1839).

Gray, T.: Letters, ed. P. Toynbee and L. Whibley (3 vols., 1935).

Grenville, Lord: Letters Written by the late Earl of Chatham to his Nephew Thomas Pitt Esq. (2nd ed., 1804).

Grenville Papers (ed. W. J. Smith, 4 vols., 1852–3).

Hasted, E.: The History and Topographical Survey of Kent (1797).

Hedges, W.: Diary (ed. H. Yule, 3 vols., 1887).

Hervey, Augustus: Journal (ed. D. Erskine, 1953).

Hervey, Lady: Letters of Mary Lepel, Lady Hervey (1821).

Hervey, Lord: Some Materials for the Memoirs of the Reign of George II (ed. R. Sedgwick, 3 vols., 1931).

Hoare, R. C.: History of Wiltshire (6 vols., 1822–4).

Ilchester, Lord: Henry Fox, 1st Lord Holland (2 vols., 1920).

Letters of Henry Fox, Lord Holland.

Johnson, S.: Thoughts on the Late Transactions respecting Falkland's Islands (1771).

Taxation No Tyranny (1775).

Journals and Newspapers: The Public Advertiser, The Public Ledger, The St James's Chronicle, The Morning Chronicle and London Advertiser, The Gazetteer and New Daily Advertiser, The North Briton, The London Magazine, The London Evening Post, The Whitehall Evening Post, The Test, The Contest, The Monitor.

Jenkinson Papers, 1760–1766 (ed. N. S. Jucker, 1949).

'Junius': Letters (various editions).

Bibliography

Kimball, G. S.: Correspondence of William Pitt with Colonial Governors (New York, 2 vols., 1900). (*Kimball*)

Lansdowne House Papers (Historical Manuscripts Commission, Reports 3, 5, 6).

Mahon, Lord: (5th Earl Stanhope): History of England . . . (7 vols., 1854).

Marchmont Papers (ed. G. H. Rose, 3 vols., 1831).

Miller, Sanderson: An Eighteenth Century Correspondence: Letters to Sanderson Miller (eds. L. Dickins and M. Stanton, 1910). (*Sanderson Miller*)

Parliamentary History (eds. W. Cobbett and J. Wright, 36 vols., 1806–20). (*Parl. Hist.*)

Parliamentary Register (ed. J. Almon, 1774–80).

Phillimore, Sir R.: Memoirs and Correspondence of George, Lord Lyttelton (2 vols., 1845). (*Phillimore*)

Rutland Papers (Historical Manuscripts Commission, Reports 12 and 14).

Sedgwick, R. (ed.): Letters of Pitt to Lord Bute, in Essays Presented to Sir Lewis Namier (eds. R. Pares and A. J. P. Taylor, 1956). (*Sedgwick LPB*)

Sedgwick, R. (ed.): Letters from George III to Lord Bute (1940). (*Sedgwick LGLB*)

Stopford Sackville Papers (Historical Manuscripts Commission, vol. 1, 1904; vol. 2, 1910).

Suffolk, Lady: Correspondence (ed. Croker, 2 vols., 1824).

Thackeray, F.: History of William Pitt, Earl of Chatham (2 vols., 1827). (*Thackeray*)

Tomlinson, J. R. G. (ed.): Additional Grenville Papers (1962).

Torrens, W. M.: History of Cabinets (2 vols., 1894).

Trevor, Hare, Round Papers (Historical Manuscripts Commission, 11, App. 9).

Waldegrave, Lord: Memoirs of the Years 1754 to 1758 (1821).

Walpole, H.: Letters (ed. P. Toynbee, 16 vols., 1904; Yale edn. eds. W. S. Lewis and others, in progress).

Memoirs of the Last Ten Years of George II (ed. Lord Holland, 2 vols., 1822 edn.). (*Walpole G2.*)

Memoirs of the Reign of George III (ed. G. F. R. Barker, 4 vols., 1894). (*Walpole G3.*)

Last Journals (ed. J. Doran, 2 vols., 1859).

Weston Underwood Papers (Historical Manuscripts Commission, 10, App. 1).

Bibliography

Wraxall, Sir N. W.: Historical and Posthumous Memoirs (ed. H. B. Wheatley, vol. 1, 1884).
Yorke, P. C.: Life and Correspondence of Lord Chancellor Hardwicke (3 vols., 1913). (*Yorke*)

Secondary Sources

Anson, W. V.: Admiral Lord Anson (1912).
Andrews, C. M.: The Colonial Period in American History (vol. 4, 1937).
Ayling, S. E.: George the Third (1972).
Beer, G. L.: British Colonial Policy, 1754–65 (1907).
Beeson, P. B. and McDermott, W. (eds.): Textbook of Medicine (13th edn., 1971).
Bence-Jones, M.: Clive of India (1974).
Brooke, J.: The Chatham Administration of 1766–68 (1956).
  King George III (1972).
  (See also under Namier.)
Brown, P. D.: The Chathamites (1967).
Browning, R.: The Duke of Newcastle (1975).
Butterfield, Sir H.: Enquiry into the Origins of the Seven Years War, in Man on his Past (1955).
Carswell, J.: The Old Cause, Three Biographical Studies in Whiggism (1954).
Chenevix-Trench, C.: George II (1973).
Christie, I. R.: Crisis of Empire: Great Britain and the American Colonies, 1754–83 (1966).
Climenson, E. J.: Elizabeth Montagu, Queen of the Blue Stockings (2 vols., 1906).
Coleridge, E. H.: Life of Thomas Coutts (2 vols., 1920).
Corbett, Sir J. S.: England in the Seven Years War (2 vols., 1907). (*Corbett*)
Dickerson, O. M.: The Navigation Acts and the American Revolution (1951).
Dickinson, H. T.: Bolingbroke (1970).
  Robert Walpole and the Whig Supremacy (1973).
Dictionary of National Biography.
Dorn, W. L.: Frederick the Great and Lord Bute (Journal of Modern History, i. 529–60).
Ehrman, J.: The Younger Pitt, The Years of Acclaim (1969).
Eyck, E.: Pitt versus Fox, Father and Son (1950).
Foord, A. S.: His Majesty's Opposition, 1714–1830 (1964).
Fortescue, J. W.: History of the British Army (vol. 2, 1899).

George, M. D.: English Political Caricature (vol. i, 1959).

Guttridge, G. H.: English Whiggism and the American Revolution (Berkeley and Los Angeles, 1963).

Horn, D. B.: The Duke of Newcastle and the Origins of the Diplomatic Revolution, in The Diversity of History (1970).

    Sir Charles Hanbury Williams and European Diplomacy, 1747–58 (1930).

Hotblack, K.: Chatham's Colonial Policy (1917). (*Hotblack*)

Hunter, W. W.: History of British India (2 vols., 1900).

Keppel, T.: Admiral Viscount Keppel (2 vols., 1842).

Knollenberg, B.: Origin of the American Revolution (New York, 1960).

Lacour–Gayet, G.: La Marine Militaire sous Louis XV (Paris, 1902).

Langford, P.: The First Rockingham Administration 1765–6 (1973).

    The Excise Crisis: Politics and Society in the Age of Walpole (1975).

Lever, Sir T.: The House of Pitt (1947).

Lewis, M.: The Navy of Britain (1948).

Lloyd, C.: The Capture of Quebec (1959).

Macaulay, Lord: Essays on Pitt (1834) and Chatham (1844).

Mackay, R. F.: Admiral Hawke (1965).

Malcolm, Sir J.: Life of Robert Lord Clive (3 vols., 1836).

Marshall, D.: Eighteenth Century England (1962).

Miller, J. C.: The Origins of the American Revolution (New York, 1945).

Morison, S. E. and Commager, H. S.: The Growth of the American Republic (2 vols., 1962).

Namier, Sir L.: The Structure of Politics at the Accession of George III (2nd edn., 1957).

    England in the Age of the American Revolution (2nd edn., 1961). (*Namier, EAAR*)

Namier, Sir L. and Brooke, J.: Charles Townshend (1964). (eds.) The History of Parliament; The House of Commons 1754–90 (3 vols., 1964).

New Cambridge Modern History: vol. 7, The Old Regime, ed. J. O. Lindsay (1957); vol. 8, The American and French Revolutions, ed. A. Goodwin (1965).

Newman, A. N.: Leicester House Politics, 1748–51, in E.H.R., October 1961).

    The Stanhopes of Chevening (1969).

Norris, J.: Shelburne and Reform (1963).

O'Gorman, F,: The Rise of Party in England . . . 1760–1782 (1975).

Bibliography

Owen, J. B.: The Rise of the Pelhams (1957). (*Owen*)
Pajol, C. P.: Les Guerres sous Louis XV (7 vols., Paris, 1881–91).
Pares, R.: War and Trade in the West Indies (1936).
    Colonial Blockade and Neutral Rights 1739–63 (1938).
    King George III and the Politicians (1953).
Parkman, F.: Montcalm and Wolfe (1884).
Peach, R. E. M.: Life and Times of Ralph Allen (1895).
Plumb, J. H.: Sir Robert Walpole (vols. 1 and 2, 1956–60). Chatham (1953).
Postgate, R.: That Devil Wilkes (2nd edn., 1956).
Richmond, Sir H. W.: Statesmen and Sea Power (1946).
Robertson, Sir C. G.: Chatham and the British Empire (1946).
Rosebery, Lord: Chatham, his Early Life and Connections (1910). (*Rosebery*)
Rudé, G. F. E.: Wilkes and Liberty (1962).
    Hanoverian London (1971).
Ruville, A. von: William Pitt, Earl of Chatham (3 vols., transl. 1907). (*Ruville*).
Salmon, E.: Admiral Sir Charles Saunders (1914).
Shellaberger, S.: Lord Chesterfield (1935).
Sherrard, O. A.: Lord Chatham (3 vols., 1952–8).
Spear, T. G. P.: The Nabobs (1932).
Stroud, D.: Capability Brown (1950).
Sutherland, L. S.: The East India Company in Eighteenth Century Politics (1952).
    The City of London in the Devonshire–Pitt Administration, 1756–7, in Proceedings of the British Academy, 1961.
Thomas, P. D. G.: The House of Commons in the Eighteenth Century (1971).
    British Politics and the Stamp Act Crisis (1975).
Thompson, H. P.: History of Hayes in the County of Kent (1935).
Tunstall, W. C. B.: William Pitt, Earl of Chatham (1938).
    Admiral Byng and the Loss of Minorca (1928).
Turberville, A. S.: The House of Lords in the Eighteenth Century (1927).
Van Doren, C.: Benjamin Franklin (1939).
Warner, O.: With Wolfe to Quebec (1973).
Watson, J. S.: The Reign of George III, 1760–1815 (1960).
Waugh, W. T.: James Wolfe, Man and Soldier (1928).
Whitworth, R.: Field Marshal Lord Ligonier (1958).
Wiggin, L. M.: The Faction of Cousins: a Political Account of the Grenvilles, 1733–63 (New Haven, 1958).

Bibliography

Williams, B.: William Pitt, Earl of Chatham (2 vols., 1913).
 Carteret and Newcastle (1943).
 The Whig Supremacy (2nd edn., revised C. H. Stuart, 1962).
Winstanley, D. A.: Lord Chatham and the Whig Opposition (1912).
 Personal and Party Government in the Reign of George III (1910).
Wyndham, H. A.: A Family History, 1688–1837 (1950).

References

CHAPTER ONE: GOVERNOR PITT AND HIS FAMILY

1 Hedges' Diary, iii. 131
2 G. Rudé, *Hanoverian London*, 41
3 HMC, Dropmore, i. 141
4 Ibid., i. 37–8
5 Ibid., 35
6 Ibid.
7 Ibid., 18–19
8 Ibid., 31
9 Ibid., 21–4
10 Hedges' Diary, iii. 93
11 HMC, Dropmore, i. 35–6
12 Ibid., 39
13 Ibid., 52
14 HMC, Egmont, i. 400–1
15 HMC, Dropmore, i. 42, 59, 62
16 Ibid., 76–80
17 Ibid., 31
18 Hedges' Diary, iii. 94
19 HMC, Dropmore, i. 10, 17, 19
20 Ibid., 9
21 Ibid., 37
22 Ibid., 34
23 Ibid., 42
24 Hedges' Diary, iii. 131; HMC, Dropmore, i. 6
25 Hedges' Diary, iii. 131
26 HMC, Dropmore, i. 50
27 Ibid., 66
28 J. H. Plumb, *Sir Robert Walpole*, i. 335–8
29 HMC, Dropmore, i. 5

CHAPTER TWO: BEGINNINGS

1 HMC, Dropmore, i. 66–74
2 Fitzmaurice, *Shelburne*, i. 56

3   Cowper, *Tirocinium*
4   Rosebery, 28
5   Ibid.; Ruville, i. 72
6   Rosebery, 29
7   Ibid., 28, 30
8   Ibid., 80
9   Ibid., 27
10 H. Walpole to Montagu, 31 July 1767
11 Almon, 22
12 Sherrard, *Lord Chatham*, i. 18
13 Beeson and McDermott, *Textbook of Medicine*, 1682–96
14 H. Walpole to Cole, 5 September 1765
15 T. Potter to Pitt, 4 June 1756
16 Chat. Corr., i. 66
17 Ibid., 118
18 Ruville, i. 89–90
19 HMC, Dropmore, i. 74
20 Ibid., 76
21 Ibid., 86
22 Ibid., 79–85
23 Rosebery, 31
24 Ibid., 35–6
25 E. Eyck, *Pitt and Fox, Father and Son*, 17
26 Macaulay, *Essays* (Everyman ed.), i. 369
27 Rosebery, 39
28 Ibid., 58–9
29 Ibid., 62
30 Ibid., 63–4
31 Fitzmaurice, *Shelburne*, i. 55
32 Rosebery, 57–8
33 Ibid., 65–6
?4 Ibid., 71
35 Sedgwick, *The Commons 1715–54*, ii. 355

CHAPTER THREE: CORNET OF DRAGOONS

1   Rosebery, 64
2   Phillimore, *Lyttelton*, i. 34–41
3   Rosebery, 67–8

4   Ibid., 74–5
5   Ibid., 77
6   Ibid., 78–9
7   HMC, Egmont, ii. 171
8   Ibid., 255–6
9   HMC, Carlisle, 72
10 Rosebery, 80
11 Ibid., 79
12 HMC, Egmont, ii. 307–8
13 Ibid., 299
14 Hervey, *Memoirs*, 553
15 Almon, i. 33
16 HMC, Carlisle, 172
17 Hervey, *Memoirs*, 553
18 Pitt to G. Berkeley, 7 June 1736; Lady Suffolk, *Letters*, ii. 150–1
19 Chatham MSS, 27
20 Hervey, *Memoirs*, 613
21 Phillimore, *Lyttelton*, i. 74–8
22 Almon, i. 37
23 HMC, Dropmore, i. 101

CHAPTER FOUR: THE CAMPAIGN AGAINST WALPOLE

1   Almon, i. 55–6; Thackeray, i. 37
2   Almon, i. 57
3   Ibid., 41; Thackeray, i. 23–5
4   Fitzmaurice, *Shelburne*, i. 34–5
5   Almon, i. 44; Thackeray, i. 28
6   HMC, Egmont, iii. 24–5
7   Ibid., 28
8   Coxe, *Walpole*, iii. 607
9   HMC, Egmont, i. 32
10 Almon, i. 42–50; Thackeray, i. 27–32
11 Chatham MSS, 33
12 Coxe, *Walpole*, iv. 202
13 Almon, i. 59–70; Thackeray, i. 40–4
14 Namier, *Structure of Politics . . .*, 299, 343
15 Chatham MSS, 83
16 Sedgwick, *The Commons 1715–54*, ii. 353

17 Chat. Corr., i. 1–2
18 Lady Suffolk, *Letters*, i. 189–90
19 Williams, *Pitt*, i. 94–5
20 Lady Suffolk, *Letters*, i. 196
21 H. Walpole to Hertford, 7 April 1765
22 Rosebery, 89–90
23 Ibid.
24 H. Walpole to Mann, 10 December 1741, 9 February 1742
25 Owen, 29, 79 and n.
26 H. Walpole to Mann, 22 January 1742
27 R. Walpole to Devonshire, 2 February 1742; Owen 34–5 and 87n.
28 Chesterfield to Dodington, 8 September 1741; Coxe, *Walpole*, iii. 579–81
29 HMC, Egmont, i. 251
30 Owen, 80
31 Marchmont Papers, i. 80
32 Almon, i. 88; Parl. Hist., xii. 488
33 Almon, i. 101; Thackeray, i. 63
34 Yorke, i. 277
35 H. Walpole to Mann, 14 June 1742
36 Marchmont Papers, i. 72, 74

CHAPTER FIVE: THE ASSAULT ON CARTERET

1 Ilchester, *Fox*, i. 93
2 Williams, *Pitt*, i. 103–4
3 Grenville Papers, i. 18–20
4 Add. MSS 33004, f.55 quoted Owen, 134
5 Parl. Hist., xii. 1036
6 Ibid., 1053
7 Almon, i. 116–24; Thackeray, i. 90–4; Williams, *Pitt*, i. 105–6
8 Foord, *His Majesty's Opposition*, 247–8; H. Walpole to Mann, 9 December 1742
9 Yorke, i. 319
10 Thackeray, i. 112–13
11 H. Walpole to Chute, 30 June 1743
12 H. Walpole to Mann, 19 July 1743
13 Newcastle to Orford, Add. MSS, 32700, f.34
14 Orford to Pelham, 20 October 1743; Coxe, *Pelham*, i. 103–6
15 Ilchester, *Fox*, i. 352

References

16 H. Walpole to Mann, 30 November 1743
17 Same to same, 6 January 1743
18 Pelham to Devonshire, 1 December 1743, quoted Owen, 193
19 H. Walpole to Mann, 12 October 1743
20 Thackeray, i. 108
21 Ibid., 126–7
22 Thackeray, i. 117–22; Williams, *Pitt*, i. 113–14
23 HMC, Egmont, i. 286
24 H. Walpole to Mann, 16 February 1744
25 Thackeray, i. 135

CHAPTER SIX: MANOEUVRES AND ACCOMMODATIONS

1 F. H. Garrison, *History of Medicine*, 99, 270–1; Beeson and McDermott, *Textbook of Medicine*, 1682–96
2 Tunstall, *Pitt*, 68
3 Beeson and McDermott, *op. cit.*, 113–16
4 Williams, *Pitt*, i. 120
5 Grenville Papers, i. 32
6 Marchmont Papers, ii. 220
7 Thackeray, i. 137–8
8 Marchmont Papers, i. 67–72
9 Ibid., 74–5
10 Ibid., 84
11 Ibid., 91
12 Add. MSS, 35870, f.90, quoted Owen, 250
13 H. Walpole to Mann, 24 December 1744
14 Marchmont Papers, i. 97
15 G. to Sir T. Lyttelton, M. Wyndham, *Chronicles* . . . i. 192
16 H. Walpole to Mann, 1 February 1745
17 Parl. Hist. xiii. 1054–6
18 Ibid., 1177
19 H. Walpole to Mann, 29 March 1745
20 Add. MSS, 9224 f.2, Devonshire MSS, quoted Owen, 279–80
21 Richmond to Newcastle 16 September 1745, Owen, 283
22 Owen, 284
23 Thackeray, i. 142
24 Chesterfield to Newcastle, 25 November 1745
25 H. Walpole to Mann, 22 November 1745
26 Devonshire MSS, quoted Owen, 290

27 Fox to Ilchester, 21 December 1745, Ilchester, *Fox*, i. 121–2
28 Yorke, i. 481
29 H. Walpole to Mann, 4 November 1745
30 HMC, Egmont, iii. 315
31 Marchmont Papers, i. 181
32 Ibid., i. 171
33 Ilchester, *Letters to Fox*, 12–13
34 H. Walpole to Mann, 15 April 1746
35 H. Walpole to Conway, 8 June 1747

CHAPTER SEVEN: THE PITT STYLE

1 Grenville Papers, i. 67
2 Sanderson Miller, 194
3 Pitt, *Letters to T. Pitt*, 80; Phillimore, ii. 436
4 Grenville Papers, i. 93
5 Chatham MSS, 31, 71; Climenson, *Mrs Montagu*, ii, 9; Williams, *Pitt*, i. 193
6 HMC, Dartmouth, viii. 167
7 Phillimore, i. 287; Grenville Papers, i. 68–9
8 M. Wyndham, *Chronicles . . .*, i. 178–81
9 Graves, *Shenstone*, quoted Williams, *Pitt*, i. 192
10 Sanderson Miller, 348
11 Gambier, *Memorials*, i. 53, 56, 62
12 Climenson, *Mrs Montagu*, ii. 35
13 Walpole G2, ii. 391n.
14 Waldegrave, *Memoirs . . .*
15 Camelford, quoted Rosebery, 496
16 Chat. Corr. ii. 188
17 Ibid., 184–5 and n.
18 W. to A. Pitt, 10 August 1758, Rosebery, 105
19 Pitt, *Letters to T. Pitt*, 91–2
20 Sanderson Miller, 239
21 Pitt, *Letters to T. Pitt*, 34–5
22 Ibid., 100
23 Ibid., 7, 13, 32, 37–9, 58

References

CHAPTER EIGHT: THE PELHAMS' PAYMASTER-GENERAL

1   Phillimore, ii. 454–5
2   Chatham MSS, 48, 51; Williams, *Pitt*, i. 159–62
3   HMC, Dropmore, i. 120, 131
4   Climenson, *Mrs Montagu*, ii. 51–2
5   Parl. Hist., xiv. 202–46; Rosebery, 271–6
6   Grenville Papers, i. 80–9
7   Sedgwick, *The Commons 1715–54*, i. 350–1; Walpole G2, ii. 273
8   Walpole G2, i. 79
9   Chatham MSS, 27, 52; Fitzmaurice, *Shelburne*, i. 56
10 Bedford Correspondence, i. 54
11 Bedford to Newcastle, 24 March 1746; Chatham MSS, 95
12 Parl. Hist., xiv. 695–6
13 Marchmont Papers, ii. 170–1
14 Coxe, *Lord Walpole*, ii. 166
15 Parl. Hist., xiv. 703–4
16 Ibid., 694
17 Ibid., 801
18 Yorke, i. 669
19 Parl. Hist., xiv. 803, 967
20 A. Stone to Newcastle, 22 February 1751, Add. MSS, 32724
21 Almon, i. 254
22 Coxe, *Pelham*, ii. 370
23 Chat. Corr., i. 49
24 Parl. Hist., xv. 154; Williams, *Pitt*, i. 176
25 Walpole G2, i. 10–11, 15–16
26 Ibid., 15
27 Ibid., 19
28 Ibid., 50
29 e.g., Tunstall, *Pitt*, 104
30 Walpole G2, i. 82, 95; HMC, Round, 313

CHAPTER NINE: AN INDELIBLE NEGATIVE

1   W. to A. Pitt, 5 April 1753, Rosebery, 95
2   Lady Suffolk, *Letters*, ii. 232–5, 244, 247
3   Ibid., 250
4   Rosebery, 93

5 Ibid., 94–5
6 Ibid., 97
7 Climenson, *Mrs Montagu*, ii. 31
8 Lyttelton to Miller, 7 July 1753, Sanderson Miller, 224
9 Climenson, *Mrs Montagu*, ii. 40
10 Gambier, *Memorials*, i. 61–2
11 Climenson, *Mrs Montagu*, ii. 38
12 Phillimore, ii. 448; Grenville Papers, i. 105
13 Phillimore, ii. 449, 477; Yorke, ii. 201–2
14 Grenville Papers, i. 112–14
15 Phillimore, ii. 453–5
16 Ilchester, *Fox*, i. 205–9
17 Dodington, 304
18 Grenville Papers, i. 116
19 Phillimore, ii. 468–70
20 Grenville Papers, i. 114
21 Sanderson Miller, 230
22 Add. MSS, 32734 f.322; Rosebery, 329–36
23 Yorke, ii. 215
24 Chat. Corr., i. 105–6; Phillimore, ii. 473; Yorke, ii. 214–15; Grenville Papers, i. 118
25 Add. MSS, 32735 f.21; Chat. Corr., i. 95–100
26 Phillimore, ii. 467
27 M. Wyndham, *Chronicles*, i. 194
28 Phillimore, ii. 477–8; Dodington, 304–5
29 Grenville Papers, i. 122

CHAPTER TEN: HESTER GRENVILLE

1 Gambier, *Memorials*, i. 73
2 M. Wyndham, *Chronicles*, i. 246
3 Climenson, *Mrs Montagu*, i. 167
4 Walpole G2, i. 65–6
5 T. to H. Grenville, 29 August 1742, Chatham MSS, 38
6 J. to H. Grenville, Chatham MSS, 35
7 G. to H. Grenville, 31 July 1746, Chatham MSS, 34
8 E. A. Edwards, *Love Letters of Pitt*, Chatham MSS, 5, 7, 8, 9
9 Rosebery, 355
10 Grenville Papers, i. 125, 131–2
11 Ibid., 124–5

References

12 Climenson, *Mrs Montagu*, ii. 60–1
13 Gambier, *Memorials*, i. 75
14 Rosebery, 101
15 Climenson, *Mrs Montagu*, ii. 63–4

CHAPTER ELEVEN: STRUGGLE FOR POWER

1   Williams, *Carteret and Newcastle*, 197
2   Ibid.
3   Dodington, 317–18
4   Yorke, ii. 216–20
5   Ibid., 219
6   Walpole G2, i. 353
7   Yorke, ii. 218
8   H. Walpole to Mann, 1 December 1754
9   H. Walpole to Bentley, 13 December 1754; Walpole G2, i. 354
10 Walpole G2, i. 358
11 Ibid., 357
12 Ibid., 361
13 H. Walpole to Bentley, 24 December 1754
14 Ilchester, *Fox*, i. 237–8; Walpole G2, i. 364
15 Dodington, 319–20
16 Chesterfield to Dayrolles, 4 February 1755
17 Walpole G2, i. 372
18 Dodington, 370
19 Anson Correspondence, quoted Corbett, i. 58
20 Yorke, ii. 244
21 Dodington, 339
22 Yorke, ii. 229
23 Ibid., 232
24 H. Walpole to Mann, 1 December 1754
25 W. to H. Pitt, 25 September 1755, Chatham MSS, 5
26 Yorke, ii. 234
27 Ibid., 237
28 Ibid., 240
29 Sedgwick LPB, No. 5
30 Dodington, 370–7
31 Newcastle to Lady Lincoln, 26 September 1755; Tunstall, 142
32 Hillsborough to Fox, 13 October 1755; Ilchester, *Fox*, i. 277
33 W. to H. Pitt, 5 January 1756

34   Grenville Papers, i. 168–9
35   Sanderson Miller, 255
36   Walpole G2, i. 412, 416
37   Sedgwick LPB, No. 10
38   Grenville Papers, i. 149–52
39   Walpole G2, i. 491; H. Walpole to Bentley, 17 December 1755
40   Torrens, *Cabinets*, ii. 273
41   Walpole G2, i. 459–61, 470–1
42   Ibid., 424–5
43   Ibid., 427–8
44   Ibid., 429–30
45   Butterfield, *Man on his Past*, 142–70
46   Yorke, ii. 285–7; Corbett, i. 84–95
47   Parl. Hist., xv. 702
48   Thackeray, i. 256
49   Yorke, ii. 289–90
50   Thackeray, i. 258
51   Ilchester, *Fox*, i. 335
52   H. Walpole to Mann, 11 July 1756
53   Add. MSS, 32866, f.210; Yorke, ii. 306
54   Grenville Papers, i. 164–5, 167–9
55   Ibid., 170–1
56   *Public Advertiser*, 19 August 1756
57   Chat. Corr., i. 185–6
58   Ilchester, *Fox*, i. 357–8
59   Yorke, ii. 331
60   Ibid., iii. 334
61   Ibid., ii. 310
62   Grenville Papers, i. 178
63   Yorke, ii. 332
64   Fitzmaurice, *Shelburne*, i. 64–5; Walpole G2, ii. 94
65   Yorke, ii. 221
66   Bedford Corr., ii. 205
67   Devonshire to Fox, 20 October 1756; Torrens, *Cabinets*, ii. 314–15
68   Bedford Corr., ii. 206–9

CHAPTER TWELVE: THE PITT–DEVONSHIRE MINISTRY

1   H. Walpole to Mann, 4 November, 13 November 1756; to Montagu,
    6 November 1756

References

2 Quoted Sherrard, *Chatham*, ii. 153–4
3 Phillimore, ii. 535
4 Sedgwick LPB, Nos. 16, 17
5 Ibid., No. 16
6 Williams, *Pitt*, i. 287–9; Tunstall, 167
7 Phillimore, ii. 543
8 G. F. S. Elliot, *The Border Elliots*, 353
9 Gibbon, *Memoirs*, 111–17, 138
10 C. Barnett, *Britain and Her Army*, 199–200
11 Speech, 14 January 1766; E. M. Lloyd, E. H. R. xvii. 466; Corbett, i. 52n.
12 Hotblack, 32–5
13 Chat. Corr. i. 221–2
14 Pitt to Devonshire, 30 January 1757, quoted Sherrard, *Chatham*, ii. 175
15 Kimball, i. 71
16 Thackeray, ii. 416
17 Chatham MSS, 5
18 Quoted Richmond, *Statesmen and Sea Power*, 130
19 Walpole G2, ii. 141
20 Bute to Pitt, 18 February 1757, Chat. Corr., i. 223–4 (misdated)
21 Sedgwick LPB, No. 22
22 HMC, Weston Underwood, i. 312; Walpole G2, ii. 170
23 Bedford Corr., ii. 229
24 Thackeray, i. 272
25 Bedford Corr., ii. 239; Phillimore, ii. 596; Waldegrave, *Memoirs*, 95
26 18 February 1757, Chat. Corr., misdated
27 Walpole G2, ii. 172; Thackeray, i. 274, 277
28 Walpole G2, ii. 152
29 Thackeray, i. 275; Walpole G2, ii. 157
30 Walpole G2, ii. 191
31 Add. MSS, 32869, Barrington to Newcastle, 21 December 1756
32 Sedgwick LPB, No. 16
33 Add. MSS, 32870, Newcastle to Hardwicke, 4 January 1757
34 Waldegrave, *Memoirs*, 95
35 Ibid., 99–105
36 Ibid., 106

CHAPTER THIRTEEN: THE WAR: JUNE 1757 – JANUARY 1759

1 Torrens, *Cabinets*, ii. 373
2 Sedgwick LPB, No. 31
3 Glover, *Memoirs*, 86
4 Add. MSS, 32871, 6 June 1757
5 H. Walpole to Mann, 5 May 1757
6 Sutherland, *Proceedings of the British Academy* (1960), 147–93
7 Sedgwick LPB, Nos. 33, 34
8 Ibid., No. 38
9 Corbett, i. 189
10 Bute to Pitt, 1 July 1757, Chat. Corr., i. 241 (misdated)
11 Grenville Papers, i. 206
12 Chat. Corr., i. 244
13 Grenville Papers, i. 431–9
14 Bute to Pitt, 13 August 1757, Chat. Corr., i. 301 (misdated); Sedgwick LPB, No. 38
15 Sedgwick LPB, No. 41
16 Ibid., No. 42
17 Walpole G2, ii. 249; Bedford Corr., ii. 277–8
18 Corbett, i. 200
19 Mackay, *Hawke*, 168
20 Sedgwick LPB, Nos. 45–7
21 Walpole G2, ii. 265
22 Williams, *Pitt*, i. 343; Corbett, i. 227n.
23 Sedgwick LPB, No. 44
24 Grenville Papers, i. 209; W. T. Waugh, *Wolfe*, 134–7
25 Chatham MSS, 86
26 Cumberland Papers, quoted Whitworth, *Ligonier*, 216
27 Sedgwick LPB, No. 47
28 Ibid., No. 49
29 Ibid., No. 57
30 Whitworth, *Ligonier*, 215
31 Chat. Corr., i. 200–6
32 Ibid., 247–56
33 Ibid., 263–77
34 Kimball, i. 93–4, 160–1
35 Add. MSS, 32882, Pitt to Bristol, 1 August 1758
36 H. Walpole to Mann, 9 February 1758
37 Sedgwick LPB, No. 50

38 Grenville Papers, i. 230
39 Add. MSS, 32877, Pitt to Newcastle, 28 January 1758
40 Add. MSS, 32878, Holderness to Newcastle, 25 February 1758
41 Add. MSS, 32876, Pitt to Newcastle, 27 December 1757
42 Yorke, iii. 31
43 Ibid., 47
44 Ibid., 44–5
45 Add. MSS, 32879, Newcastle to Hardwicke, 26 April 1758
46 Chat. Corr., i. 305–6
47 Ibid., 306–8
48 Sedgwick LPB, No. 66; Add. MSS, 32878, Pitt to Newcastle, 28 February 1758
49 Sedgwick LPB, No. 68
50 Hotblack, 35–7; Grenville Papers, i. 248; Chatham MSS, 30
51 Chatham MSS, 85
52 Mackay, *Hawke*, 194–7; Anson, *Anson*, 151–6
53 Yorke, iii. 47
54 Sedgwick LPB, No. 72
55 Ibid., No. 76
56 H. Walpole to Strafford, 16 June; to Mann, 18 June; to Chute, 29 June 1758
57 Corbett, i. 254–5. See however ibid. i. 303
58 Waugh, *Wolfe*, 185
59 Grenville Papers, i. 244
60 Corbett, i. 285–6; Sedgwick LPB, No. 81; Chat. Corr., i. 327–30
61 Chat. Corr., i. 323; Sedgwick LPB, No. 88
62 Kimball, i. 138, 141
63 Ibid., 223–4
64 Ibid., 203
65 Ibid., 180
66 HMC, Stopford Sackville, ii. 264
67 Add. MSS, 6832, Newcastle to Mitchell, 12 September 1758
68 Add. MSS, 32883, Newcastle to Hardwicke, 28 August 1758
69 Lady Suffolk, *Letters*, ii. 249
70 Grenville Papers, i. 262
71 Ibid.
72 Kimball, ii. 16–18, 68
73 Whitworth, *Ligonier*, 265
74 H. Walpole to Conway, 19 September 1758
75 Sedgwick LPB, Appendix 1.
76 Sedgwick LGLB, No. 25

References

Ibid., No. 24
78 Sedgwick LGLB, Nos. 35, 43, 44
79 Whitworth, *Ligonier*, 166
80 Hotblack, 40
81 Chat. Corr., i. 353-4
82 Kimball, ii. 200
83 Lansdowne House MSS, quoted Williams, *Pitt*, ii. 2

CHAPTER FOURTEEN: THE YEAR OF VICTORIES

1 Chatham MSS, 78; Williams, *Pitt*, i. 400
2 Bourguet, *Choiseul et l'Alliance Espagnole*, quoted Williams, *Pitt*, i. 389
3 Add. MSS, 32886, Newcastle to the King, 15 December 1758
4 HMC, Stopford Sackville, i. 303-4
5 H. Walpole to Mann, 27 November, 25 December 1758
6 Add. MSS, 32885, ff. 485-6, 490-3
7 Walpole G2, ii. 350-1; Williams, *Pitt*, ii. 53
8 Add. MSS, 32888, Newcastle Memo. for the King, 28 February 1759
9 Devonshire's Diary, 18 April 1759
10 Grenville Papers, i. 280
11 Add. MSS, 32912, f.164
12 Yorke, iii. 55; Add. MSS, 32891, Newcastle to Mansfield, 8 June 1759
13 Add. MSS, 6832, Holderness to Mitchell, 28 May 1759
14 Yorke, iii. 57
15 H. Walpole to Montagu, 16 May 1759
16 H. Walpole to Mann, 10 May 1759
17 Grenville Papers, i. 264
18 Chat. Corr., i. 385-6, 393-4, 400, 410-11
19 Ibid., 413-14
20 Ruville, ii. 236-8
21 Rosebery, 109
22 Ibid., 118
23 Add. MSS, 32892, Newcastle to Hardwicke, 12 June 1759
24 Rosebery, 110
25 Ibid., 117
26 Chat. Corr., i. 457, ii. 1, 2, 7, 45, 54; Chatham MSS, 5, 7, 8
27 Chat. Corr., i. 458
28 H. to W. Pitt, 18 August 1758; Ruville, ii. 214-15
29 Rosebery, 111-12
30 Walpole G3, iii. 30

References

31 Fitzmaurice, *Shelburne*, i. 60
32 Burke, *Correspondence*, i. 265n.
33 Fitzmaurice, *Shelburne*, i. 55–6
34 Climenson, *Mrs Montagu*, ii. 53
35 Rosebery, 104
36 H. to A. Pitt, 29 August 1758 (misdated 1759 in Rosebery, 112–13)
37 Rosebery, 107
38 Williams, *Pitt*, i. 206
39 Rosebery, 120–1
40 H. Walpole to Hertford, 24 February 1764; to Lady Hervey, 11 June 1765; to A. Pitt, 25 December 1765; to Mann, 24 February 1774, 30 October 1778, 9 May 1779
41 Whitworth, *Ligonier*, 283
42 Thackeray, i. 397
43 Chat. Corr., ii. 4–6; Grenville Papers, i. 308
44 Chat. Corr., ii. 8–9
45 H. Walpole to Mann, 8 August 1759
46 Fortescue, *British Army*, ii. 495–6
47 Sedgwick LGLB, No. 36
48 *Annual Register*, *1759*, 233
49 Sedgwick LGLB, No. 37
50 Chat. Corr., i. 417
51 HMC, Stopford Sackville, i. 315
52 Whitworth, *Ligonier*, 323
53 Fitzmaurice, *Shelburne*, i. 246
54 Kimball, ii. 37–8
55 Ibid., 65
56 O. Warner, *With Wolfe to Quebec*, 182
57 Kimball, ii. 146
58 Ibid., 148
59 Kimball, ii. 187
60 Ibid., 217
61 Add. MSS, 32897, Newcastle to Hardwicke, 15 October 1759
62 Chat. Corr., i. 425–30; Warner, op. cit., 144
63 Warner, op. cit., 153
64 Clive to Pitt, 7 January 1759, Chat. Corr., i. 390
65 H. Walpole to Montagu, 21 October 1759
66 Chat. Corr., i. 444–5
67 Yorke, iii. 59
68 Chat. Corr., i. 433–4
69 Yorke, iii. 61

70 Ibid., 62
71 Add. MSS, 32897, Pitt to Newcastle, 23 October 1759, partly in Yorke, iii. 68
72 Yorke, iii. 69
73 Ibid., 69–70
74 Add. MSS, 32897, Newcastle to Hardwicke, 31 October 1759; Yorke, iii. 78
75 Yorke, iii. 74–5, 82
76 Ibid., 74
77 Wraxall, *Memoirs*, i. 129
78 Lacour–Gayet, quoted Mackay, *Hawke*, 253
79 Ibid., 254
80 Kimball, ii. 216–19
81 Add. MSS, 32897, Newcastle to Hardwicke, 15 October 1759
82 Pitt to Bristol, 20 November 1759, Thackeray, i. 459
83 Yorke, iii. 244–5
84 Debate on the Address, November 1759
85 Ellis, *Original Letters* Series 2, iv. 415–17; Yorke, iii. 242–3

CHAPTER FIFTEEN: PROBLEMS OF WAR AND PEACE

1   Yorke, iii. 244, 248–9
2   Ibid., 248–9
3   Kimball, ii. 280, 288, 305
4   Whitworth, *Ligonier*, 317n.
5   Walpole G2, ii. 390
6   Whitworth, *Ligonier*, 320
7   Grenville Papers, i. 347
8   Kimball, ii. 283–6
9   Walpole to Mann, 20 June 1760; Grenville Papers, i. 343–4
10 Kimball, ii. 305; Chat. Corr., ii. 45
11 Kimball, ii. 329–33, 335–41
12 Sedgwick LGLB, No. 60
13 H. Walpole to Mann, 7 July 1760
14 Yorke, iii. 247
15 Grenville Papers, i. 355
16 Ibid.
17 Whitworth, *Ligonier*, 329–32
18 Mackay, *Hawke*, 268
19 Ibid., 272

References

20 Chat. Corr., ii. 77–9
21 Yorke, iii. 313–15
22 Namier, EAAR, 121, 125
23 G. F. S. Elliot, *The Border Elliots*, 362–5; Namier, op. cit., 105–7
24 Minto Papers, quoted Namier, op. cit., 121
25 Pares, *War and Trade in the West Indies*, 580
26 Namier, op. cit., 161–7
27 H. Walpole to Mann, 3 March 1761; Add. MSS, 32920, Hardwicke to Newcastle, 17 March 1761
28 Add. MSS, 32920, Newcastle to Devonshire, 13 March 1761
29 Grenville Papers, i. 371n.
30 H. Walpole to Montagu, 22 July 1761
31 Add. MSS, 32928, Bedford to Newcastle, 14 September 1761

CHAPTER SIXTEEN: SPAIN AND RESIGNATION

1 Add. MSS, 32908, Newcastle Memo., 4 July 1760; Pares, op. cit., 570
2 Add. MSS, 32911, Hardwicke to Newcastle, 14 September 1760; Pares, op. cit., 571
3 Pitt to Bristol, 5 September 1760, Thackeray, i. 484–7
4 Bristol to Pitt, 20 May 1761, Thackeray, i. 501–4
5 Thackeray, i. 560–2, 570–2
6 Grenville Papers, i. 385; Yorke, iii. 317–21
7 Yorke, iii. 317
8 Pares, op. cit., 582 and n.
9 Walpole G3, i. 94; Yorke, iii. 280
10 Adolphus, *History of England*, i. 573; Albemarle, *Rockingham*, i. 47
11 Yorke, iii. 278
12 Ibid., 328
13 Sedgwick LGLB, No. 87
14 Yorke, iii. 275
15 Ibid., 326
16 Chat. Corr., i. 141–4
17 Grenville Papers, i. 391
18 Ibid., 416
19 Ibid., 409, 415
20 *Annual Register, 1761*, 44–5
21 Chat. Corr., ii. 146–53
22 Add. MSS, 35352, Hardwicke to Royston, 12 October 1761; 32929, Bedford to Newcastle, 11 October 1761

455

23 H. Walpole to Conway, 12 October 1761
24 Gray, *Letters*, ii. 771
25 H. Walpole to Lady Ailesbury, 10 October 1761; to Mann, 14 October 1761
26 Chatham MSS, 52
27 Rosebery, 121–4
28 Chat. Corr., ii. 158–9
29 *Annual Register*, *1761*, 45–8
30 Chat. Corr., ii. 165 and n.
31 Ibid., 166–8; *Annual Register*, *1761*, 237
32 Walpole G3, i. 70
33 Phillimore, ii. 630; Yorke, iii. 332
34 Walpole G3, i. 86, 94–6; Williams, *Pitt*, ii. 133–4
35 HMC, Stopford Sackville, i. 86
36 Walpole G3, i. 193
37 Ibid., 75–6
38 Ibid., 81
39 Grenville Papers, i. 418,
40 Namier, EAAR, 301; Walpole G3, i. 81
41 Walpole G3, i. 98
42 Namier, EAAR, 314
43 Ibid., 306–7
44 Add. MSS, 32937, Newcastle to Devonshire, 13 April 1762; Namier, EAAR, 314
45 Walpole G3, i. 104–5
46 H. Walpole to Montagu, 22 March 1762
47 Sedgwick LGLB, Nos. 108, 125
48 Add. MSS, 6809, Mitchell to Bute, 3 May 1762
49 Prussian Archives, quoted Corbett, ii. 330–1
50 Add. MSS, 32935, Newcastle to Hardwicke, 22 February 1762
51 Walpole G3, i. 128–31
52 Namier, EAAR, 313–18
53 Bedford Corr., iii. 84
54 Quoted in Namier, EAAR, 343
55 Walpole G3, i. 173

CHAPTER SEVENTEEN: THE PEACE OF PARIS AND GENERAL WARRANTS

1 Bedford Corr., iii. 136
2 Parl. Hist., xv. 1264

References

3 Yorke, iii. 338
4 Sedgwick LGLB, No. 202
5 Fox Memoir in Ilchester, *Lady Sarah Lennox*, i. 77; Ilchester, *Fox*, ii. 185
6 Sedgwick LGLB, No. 222
7 Fox Memoir in Ilchester, *Lady Sarah Lennox*, i. 77.
8 Sedgwick LGLB, Nos. 233–4
9 Walpole G3, i. 176–8
10 H. Dalrymple, *The Rodondo*, quoted Williams, *Pitt*, ii. 149
11 Parl. Hist., xv. 1259–71
12 Walpole G3, i. 181
13 Bedford Corr., ii. 168–9, 202
14 Walpole G2, ii. 273
15 Peach, *Ralph Allen*, 175–80
16 Ruville, iii. 114–15
17 Yorke, iii. 456
18 Parl. Hist., xv. 1307
19 Walpole G3, i. 198
20 Yorke, iii. 454
21 Grenville Papers, ii. 194–5
22 Ibid., 198; Chatham MSS, 74; Ilchester, *Fox*, ii. 269
23 Grenville Papers, ii. 201
24 Walpole G3, i. 253
25 Namier and Brooke, *Charles Townshend*, 109
26 Thackeray, ii. 44
27 Chat. Corr., ii. 260
28 Yorke, iii. 532
29 Add. MSS, 32952, Rockingham to Newcastle, 31 October 1763
30 Parl. Hist., xv. 1363
31 H. Walpole to Hertford, 25 November 1763; Yorke, iii. 557
32 Chat. Corr., ii. 299–302
33 Walpole G3, i. 290
34 Chat. Corr., ii. 287–8
35 Ibid., 293
36 Ibid., 298; Yorke, iii. 564
37 H. Walpole to Hertford, 19 February 1764; Walpole G3, i. 302
38 Chat. Corr., ii. 288–9
39 Add. MSS, 32958, Townshend to Newcastle, 28 April 1764
40 Chat. Corr., ii. 296–8
41 Grenville Papers, ii. 441
42 Ibid., 386

References

43 H. Walpole to Hertford, 27 March 1764
44 Walpole G3, ii. 49

CHAPTER EIGHTEEN: 'SO NEAR ENGAGING'

1   Christie's Sale Catalogue, 7 May 1789, quoted Ehrman, *The Younger Pitt*, i. 7–8
2   H. P. Thompson, *History of Hayes*, 44
3   Chat. Corr., iii. 27
4   Quoted Ehrman, *The Younger Pitt*, i. 5
5   Ibid.
6   Walpole G3, ii. 32
7   Mahon, *History of England*, v. Appendix iv
8   Albemarle, *Rockingham*, i. 193
9   Walpole G3, ii. 131; Williams, *Pitt*, ii. 173
10 Albemarle, *Rockingham*, i. 202
11 Burke to Flood, 18 May 1765, *Correspondence*, i. 194
12 Grenville Papers, iii. 183
13 Ibid., 191; Walpole G3, ii. 132
14 Fortescue CG3, i. Nos. 88, 100
15 Chat. Corr., ii. 312–13
16 Fortescue CG3, i. No. 100
17 Chat. Corr., ii. 315
18 Fortescue CG3, i. Nos. 94, 95
19 Chat. Corr., ii. 317, 320
20 Grenville Papers, iii. 102–3
21 Fitzmaurice, *Shelburne*, i. 59
22 Grenville Papers, iii. 102
23 Walpole G3, iii. 31
24 Grenville Papers, iii. 102; Chat. Corr., ii. 328, 333
25 Chat. Corr., ii. 323; Mahon, op. cit., v. Appendix, iv, vii
26 Chat. Corr., ii. 326–9
27 Sedgwick LGLB, No. 337
28 Pitt to Temple, 29 October 1765, Grenville Papers, iii. 101
29 Chat. Corr., ii. 330–1
30 P. Langford, *First Rockingham Administration*, 105
31 Chat. Corr., ii. 330–7

References

CHAPTER NINETEEN: AMERICA AND THE ROCKINGHAMS

1   Fortescue CG3, i. No. 176
2   Add. MSS, 32972, Newcastle to Rockingham, 1 December 1765
3   Chat. Corr., ii. 338–46
4   Pitt to Nuthall, 10 December 1765, Chat. Corr., ii. 345
5   Sedgwick LGLB, No. 337
6   Ibid.; Fortescue CG3, Nos. 175–83
7   Chat. Corr., ii. 364–73
8   Burke to O'Hara, 18 January 1766, Correspondence, i. 231–2
9   HMC, Stopford Sackville, i. 106; Chat. Corr., ii. 376
10 HMC, Stopford Sackville, i. 107
11 Chat. Corr., ii. 373, 391–3
12 Fortescue CG3, i. Nos. 206–10
13 Walpole G3, ii. 212
14 Ibid., 215; American Hist. Review, xvii. 3
15 H. Walpole to Selwyn, 7 March 1766; to Mann, 21 March 1766
16 Chat. Corr., ii. 398–401; Fortescue CG3, i. No. 299
17 Bedford Corr., iii. 333
18 Chat. Corr., ii. 416–17
19 Ibid., 423; Mahon, Hist. of England, v. Appendix, vii
20 Sedgwick LGLB, No. 339

CHAPTER TWENTY: MINISTRY AND COLLAPSE OF CHATHAM

1   Fortescue CG3, i. No. 319
2   Walpole G3, ii. 201
3   Sedgwick LGLB, No. 339
4   Bedford Corr., iii. 301
5   Chat. Corr., iii. 27
6   Fortescue CG3, i. No. 143, misdated 'August 1765'
7   Ibid.
8   Ibid.
9   Grenville Papers, iii. 267–8
10 Chat. Corr., ii. 448; Grenville Papers, iii. 279–80
11 Chat. Corr., ii. 467–70
12 King to Bute, 12 July 1766, Sedgwick LGLB, 251
13 W. G. Hamilton to Temple, 30 July 1766, Grenville Papers, iii. 287
14 Walpole G3, iii. 72

References

15 Grenville Papers, iii. 305
16 Burke, *Correspondence*, i. 263
17 Gray to Wharton, 26 August 1766; Major Corry to Chatham, 31 October 1766, Chatham MSS, 27; *Whitehall Evening Post*, 7 August 1766
18 Fitzmaurice, *Shelburne*, i. 282
19 Chat. Corr., iii. 67–70
20 Quoted in Richmond, *Statesmen and Sea Power*, 132; Ruville, iii. 193–4
21 Ruville, iii. 197–8
22 Walpole G3, ii. 261; H. Walpole to Lady Suffolk, 6 October to Chute, 10 October 1766
23 Fortescue CG3, i. No. 372; Chat. Corr., ii. 21
24 Chat. Corr., iii. 126–30; Walpole G3, ii. 270–2
25 Bedford Corr., iii. 358–9; Chat. Corr., iii. 134–8; Fortescue CG3, i. No. 430
26 Grafton, *Autobiography*, 107
27 Ibid., 108–9; Chat. Corr., iii. 110–12
28 Walpole G3, ii. 276
29 Grafton, *Autobiography*, 111–12; Malcolm, *Clive*, iii. 189
30 Sutherland, *East India Company* . . ., 152
31 Chat. Corr., iv. 264–5
32 Fitzmaurice, *Shelburne*, i. 298; Grafton, *Autobiography*, 110; Namier and Brooke, *Charles Townshend*, 167
33 Prussian Archives, quoted Ruville, iii. 184
34 HMC, Stopford Sackville, i. 13
35 Walpole G3, ii. 291
36 Grafton, *Autobiography*, 110–11
37 Ibid., 112
38 Chat. Corr., iii. 116
39 Ibid., 169, 176–8
40 Grafton, *Autobiography*, 113–14; Chat. Corr., iii. 199–201, misdated
41 Chat. Corr., iii. 181–2, 189
42 Ibid., 188–9, 193–4
43 Ibid., 170–1; Fortescue CG3, i. No. 459
44 Beeson and McDermott, *Textbook of Medicine*, 113–16
45 Walpole G3, ii. 273
46 Ibid., 295
47 Grafton, *Autobiography*, 116–21; Chat. Corr., iii. 194–8
48 Chat. Corr., iii. 227–9
49 Walpole G3, ii. 302
50 Grenville Papers, iv. 9
51 Namier and Brooke, *Charles Townshend*, 166

References

52 H. Walpole, *Letters* (ed. Toynbee), vii. 105–6n.
53 Burke, *Speech on American Taxation*, Parl. Hist., xvii. 1215ff.; H. Walpole to Mann, 27 September 1767
54 H. Walpole to Mann, 26 May 1767
55 Chat. Corr., iii. 256–8
56 Ibid., 262–3
57 Grafton, *Autobiography*, 136–9; Walpole G3, iii. 38–9n.
58 Chat. Corr., iii. 266–8
59 Ibid., 271–8
60 Walpole G3, iii. 30–1
61 Chat. Corr., iii. 289–92; Chatham MSS, 10, 51 (corr. with Nuthall), 66 (with T. Walpole)
62 Fortescue CG3, i. No. 552
63 Nuthall to Camden, 5 August 1767, Brooke, *Chatham Administration*, 311–12
64 Grenville Papers, iv. 159, 163–4
65 Chat. Corr., iii. 312, 318
66 Grafton, *Autobiography*, 214
67 Ibid.
68 Ibid., 218–24; Chat. Corr., iii. 338–43; Fortescue CG3, ii. Nos. 669–71
69 Grenville Papers, iv. 310, 341–2
70 Chat. Corr., iii. 343–4

CHAPTER TWENTY-ONE: A FURY OF OPPOSITION

1 Grafton, *Autobiography*, 203–4; H. Walpole to Mann, 18 November 1768
2 Walpole G3, iii. 184
3 Grenville Papers, iv. 398–9
4 H. Walpole to Mann, 2 December 1768
5 Grenville Papers, iv. 404
6 J. Wilkes, *Letter to the Duke of Grafton*
7 Chat. Corr., iii. 349–50, 353
8 Ibid., 355; Grenville Papers, iv. 426
9 Grafton, *Autobiography*, 236
10 H. Walpole to Mann, 17 July 1769
11 Grafton, *Autobiography*, 237
12 Burke, *Correspondence*, ii. 52
13 Walpole G3, iii. 172
14 Grenville Papers, iv. 436–7

References

15 A. N. Newman, *The Stanhopes of Chevening*, 362–3
16 Grafton, *Autobiography*, 229
17 Ibid., 229–30
18 Walpole G3, iii. 266; to Mann, 19 January 1770
19 Walpole G3, iii. 184, iv. 119
20 Albemarle, *Rockingham*, ii. 155
21 Chat. Corr., iii. 388–9
22 Thackeray, ii. 127–32
23 Ibid., 132–6
24 Ibid., 136–45
25 Chat. Corr., iii. 395
26 Winstanley, *Chatham and the Whig Opposition*, 290
27 Burke to Rockingham, 29 October 1769, *Correspondence*, ii. 103
28 Walpole G3, iv. 39; to Mann, 23 January 1770
29 Thackeray, ii. 162–5
30 Grenville Papers, iv. 534
31 Walpole G3, iv. 41
32 Chat. Corr., iii. 426n.
33 Thackeray, ii. 182–3
34 Ibid., 180–1; Walpole G3, iv. 63
35 Cavendish, Debates, i. 517–18; Chat. Corr., iii. 428
36 Thackeray, ii. 185–93
37 Chat. Corr., iii. 462–3
38 Thackeray, ii. 193–4
39 H. Walpole to Mann, 24 May 1770
40 Chat. Corr., iii. 469
41 Ibid., 469–70; Chatham MSS, 8, 9
42 H. Walpole to Mann, 12 November 1770
43 Richmond to Chatham, 20 February 1771, Chat. Corr., iv. 97
44 Ibid., 100, 104, 108–9
45 Burke to O'Hara, 2 April 1771, *Correspondence*, ii. 210
46 Walpole G3, iv. 139–40
47 Chat. Corr., iv. 65
48 Thackeray, ii. 207–25
49 Walpole G3, iv. 145
50 Chat. Corr., iv. 76–7
51 Ibid., 148, 165
52 Ibid., 131–53, 172n.
53 Ibid., 163
54 Ibid., 187, 230

References

CHAPTER TWENTY-TWO: AT BURTON PYNSENT

1 Chat. Corr., iv. 186, 233, 264
2 Ibid., 242
3 Ibid., 203-4
4 Ibid., 299-302, 305-7, 319-21
5 Ibid., 197n.
6 Ibid., 215-16, 357
7 Tunstall, *Pitt*, 437; Add. MSS, 35192, quoted Williams, *Pitt*, ii. 291
8 Chat. Corr., iv. 206
9 Chatham MSS, 5
10 Chat. Corr., iv. 207
11 Ibid., 207n., 267
12 Ibid., 290-1
13 Ibid., 294, 309-10
14 Lansdowne House MSS, quoted Williams, *Pitt*, ii. 291
15 T. Walpole to Chatham, 6 April 1772, Chatham MSS, 66
16 Grenville Papers, iv. 538
17 Fortescue CG3, iii. No. 1691

CHAPTER TWENTY-THREE: PROPHET OF RUIN

1 Chat. Corr., iv. 336-7
2 Chatham to Shelburne, 6 March 1772, Chat. Corr., iv. 331-3; ibid., 342-3
3 Ibid., 345 n.-8n.; Thackeray, ii. 262-6
4 Walpole, *Last Journals*, i. 370
5 Ibid., 374
6 Thackeray, ii. 273-6
7 Franklin, *Autobiography*, ii. 168-79; *Writings*, vi. 127-37
8 Franklin, *Autobiography*, ii. 289; Chat. Corr., iv. 368
9 Rockingham to Burke, 7 January 1775, Burke, *Correspondence*, iii, 91
10 Burke to Rockingham, 5 January 1775, Ibid., iii. 89
11 Chat. Corr., iv. 370-2
12 Franklin, *Autobiography*, ii. 298
13 Walpole, *Last Journals*, i. 446
14 Chat. Corr., iv. 377-84; Thackeray, ii. 281-90
15 Burke, *Correspondence*, iii. 103
16 Ibid., 108-9

References

17 Thackeray, ii. 291–8
18 Franklin to Stanhope, Chat. Corr., iv. 385; Franklin, *Autobiography*, ii. 304–5
19 Chat. Corr., iv. 395–7
20 Ibid., 391
21 Ibid., 402–3
22 Chatham MSS, 15, 16
23 Chat. Corr., iv. 427n.
24 Burke, *Correspondence*, iii. 186, 195, 210; Grafton, *Autobiography*, 280
25 Chat. Corr., iv. 427–8n., 432
26 Ibid., 432–7n.
27 Franklin, *Writings*, vi. 306
28 Walpole, *Last Journals*, ii. 118; Chat. Corr., iv. 437
29 Fortescue CG3, iii. No. 2006
30 Chat. Corr., iv. 440
31 Grenville Papers, iv. 573
32 Chat. Corr., iv. 445–6
33 Grafton, *Autobiography*, 295
34 Burke, *Correspondence*, iii. 408–9
35 Thackeray, ii. 322–48, 351–9
36 Chat. Corr., iv. 494–5; Thackeray Appendix viii. 633–57
37 G. H. Guttridge, *English Whiggism* . . ., 99–102; Fortescue CG3, iv. Nos. 2221–6, 2228–30, 2234–5, 2240, 2247, 2257
38 Thackeray, ii. 378; Parl. Hist., xix. 1023
39 Fitzmaurice, *Shelburne*, ii. 21–2; Thackeray, ii. 380–1
40 Fortescue CG3, iv. No. 2236
41 W. Pitt to Lady Chatham, 6–9 June 1778, Chatham MSS, 12
42 Chat. Corr., iv. 530
43 Ibid., 531
44 Walpole G2, ii. 349; G3, i. 83–4, 274–5
45 Fitzmaurice, *Shelburne*, i. 59–65
46 Williams, *Pitt*, i. 162
47 Sir C. G. Robertson, *Chatham and the British Empire*, 113
48 J. Brooke, *King George III*, 77, 116; *Chatham Administration*, 385; *History of Parliament*, under *Pitt*.

Index

Abercromby, General James, 217, 226, 229, 231, 233, 234, 258, 260
Adam, Robert, 47
Addington, Dr Anthony, 368, 370, 372, 416, 418, 423, 425
Addington, Henry (Viscount Sidmouth), 417n.
Africa, West, 193-4, 224, 237-8, 306, 309
Aiguillon, Duc d', 227, 254
Aix-la-Chapelle, Treaty of, 122, 124, 152, 197
Albemarle, George Keppel, 3rd Earl of, 329
Aldborough, Yorks, 136, 138, 188
Allen, Ralph, 102, 207, 249, 311, 312
Almon, John, 26, 64, 126
Amherst, Sir Jeffery (Lord Amherst), 217, 226, 229, 231, 234, 258, 259-61, 271, 274, 374-5, 421, 426
Anhalt-Zerbst, Dowager Princess of, 264
Anne, Queen, 12, 18, 19
Anson, Admiral George (Lord Anson), 92, 120, 160, 176, 178, 180, 192-3, 194, 200, 209, 215, 225, 254, 259, 277, 278, 289, 354
Anstruther, Lieut.-General Philip, 129-30
Argenson, Comte d', 197
Army, manpower and organization of, 59-60, 84, 96, 100, 176, 190-2, 198-9, 271-2, 386, 394
'Army of Observation', 198-9, 203, 210
'Asiento' with Spain, 61, 65, 125
Astrop Wells, 103, 133, 144
Augusta (Dowager), Princess of Wales, 53, 130, 133, 134, 137, 138, 165, 295, 389, 396-7
Ayscough, Rev. Francis, 37-8, 114, 116, 128, 136, 150, 188

Baltic trade and diplomacy, 209-10, 240
Barré, Colonel Isaac, 274-5, 295-6, 324, 333, 338, 345, 353, 376, 392, 396, 423, 426
Barrington, General John, 239
Barrington, W. W., 2nd Viscount, 98, 99, 129, 202, 205, 218, 269-70, 282, 295, 379
Barrymore, 4th Earl of, 86
Bath, 24, 27, 37, 83, 145, 251-2; Pitt's visits before his marriage, 36, 89, 103, 132, 134; No. 7, The Circus, 103, 133, 167, 246, 336, 405; corporation of, relations with Pitt, 207n., 311, 312; his stays there 1765-7, 336-7, 339, 346-7, 357-8, 359, 363-4
Bath, Earl of, see Pulteney
Bavaria, 71, 77, 125, 126, 241
Beaufort, 5th Duke of, 385
Beauséjour, Fort, 162
Beckford, William (1709-70), 200, 228, 249, 296, 304, 345, 360, 427; and Jenkins's Ear, 60; and the West Indies, 181, 187, 238, 242; as City representative, 207, 240, 242, 295, 301, 307, 380, 384, 389, 390; Chatham's Commons spokesman, 361, 362, 363-4
Beckford, William (1750-1844), 301n.
Bedford, 4th Duke of, 68, 92, 96, 97, 129, 138, 165, 184, 191, 293, 315, 317, 336, 337, 344, 346, 350; and America, 119-20, 284, 305; and peace-making (1760-2), 280, 284, 288, 299-300, 301, 303-5, 306, 309, 310
Bedford Party ('The Bedfords'), 349, 350, 352, 354, 359, 369, 372-3, 374, 377
Belle Isle, 120, 180, 277-8, 281, 283, 306, 309
Belleisle, Marshal, Duc de, 175, 253

465

Index

Index

468

Index

469

Index

Navy, strength and role of—*cont.*
190, 192-3, 194-6, 197, 209, 225, 240,
259, 261, 383, 394-5
Nedham, Robert, 44, 372
Netherlands (United Provinces), *see*
Holland
Newcastle, Thomas Pelham-Holles,
Duke of, 43, 63, 66, 67, 68, 73, 75, 82,
101, 114-15, 118, 120, 128, 200, 351, 428;
and his brother Henry Pelham (-1754),
81, 97, 98, 116, 125-7; dependence on
Hardwicke, 138, 154n., 156; foreign
policy, and relations with Pitt (-1757),
123, 125-7, 136, 137-43, Chapter 11
passim, 186-8, 197, 202, 203; in coalition with Pitt (1757-61), 204-9, 213,
214, 217, 221-3, 228, 232, 236, Chapters
14 and 15 *passim*, 286-91; after October
1761, 297, 299, 300, 301, 303, 305, 312,
313, 314, 315, 316-18, 322n., 330, 333,
336, 339, 344, 378
Newdigate, Sir Roger, 93
Newfoundland, 259, 269, 284, 304, 310
New Orleans, 122, 152
Newspapers and journals, 54, 99, 181,
207-8, 262, 263, 268, 273, 292-3, 294,
314, 319, 355-6, 390
New York, 195, 229, 345, 364, 409
Niagara, Fort, 155, 162, 260
Nicaragua, 286
Norfolk House, 58, 59
Norris, Sir John, 86-7
North End, Hampstead, 353, 367, 369,
370-1
North, Frederick, Lord, 351, 370, 388,
392, 408, 411, 416, 420, 421, 422, 423,
424, 425
Northington, Robert Henley, Earl of,
205, 339-40, 347-8, 351, 354, 366
Northumberland, Hugh, Duke of, 329,
423, 426
Norton, Fletcher, 320
Nova Scotia, 122, 152, 162, 194, 195,
196, 211, 304, 306, 334
Nuthall, Thomas, 333, 339, 346, 347, 371

Ogdensburg, 258, 260
Ohio river, 122, 153, 162, 230, 234, 260,
411

Okehampton, Devon, 19, 21, 44, 116,
118, 188, 207n.
Old Sarum, 12-14, 20-1, 44, 46, 67, 114,
115, 118, 136, 148, 188
Oliver, Richard, 396
Ontario Lake, 152, 180, 229, 230, 233,
260, 274
Orford, 2nd Earl of, 255
Osborn, Admiral Henry, 226, 232,
234n.
Oswego, Fort, 180, 274
Oxford University, 26, 29, 30-5, 46, 157,
186, 326

Pall Mall, 14, 16, 19, 22-3, 36, 47, 58, 69,
416n.
Pardo, Convention of the, 64-7, 396
Paris, Treaty of (1763), 303-11, 356, 397
Parliament, condition and proposed
reform of, 20-1, 67-8, 95, 386-8, 397
'Patriots', 52-3, 57, Chapter 4 *passim*, 122,
166
Pelham, Henry, before 1744, 43, 82, 83,
85, 87; as prime minister (1744-54), 91,
93, 95-9, 102, 109, 115, 116, 118,
120-1, 124-9, 137, 139, 173, 236, 242,
351
Pembroke, 9th Earl of, 46
Pembroke, 10th Earl of, 145
Pennsylvania, 152, 177
Peter III, Tsar, 299
Philadelphia, 230, 234
Philippines, 300, 301, 356-7
Pitt, Ann, 12; relations with Pitt in
youth, 27, 35-8, 40-2, 45, 49-50, 58,
249; quarrels and reconciliations, 69-70,
250-3, 293-4; ill-health, 109-10, 133-4,
148, 232, 248, 250-3; later years, 253
Pitt, Catherine (Mrs Nedham), 12, 44,
372
Pitt, Elizabeth (Mrs Hannan), 12, 70n.,
135, 250
Pitt, Essex (Mrs Cholmondeley), 13
Pitt, George (of Stratfield Saye), 17
Pitt, Harriot (Lady Corbett), 12, 35, 44,
45
Pitt, Harriot (Lady Eliot), 226, 249, 276,
325, 403
Pitt, Hester, *see* Chatham, Lady

472

Index

Index

Thomas, 2nd
Lord Lyttelton
(1744-79)

Richard Grenville,
1st Earl
Temple
(1711-79)

George
(1712-70)
m.
Elizabeth
Wyndham

James
(1715-83)

Rev. Gilbert
West (1703-56)

William

Temple,
Vice-Admiral
(1713-57)

Maria (Molly)
m.
Alex Hood
1st Viscount
Bridport

3rd Ear

Christian
m.
Thomas
Saunders

Amelia
m.
William
Spry

Thomas Pitt
1st Lord
Camelford
(1737-93)
m.
Anne Wilkinson

John Pitt
2nd Earl of
Chatham
(1756-1835)
m.
Mary, d.
of Thomas
Townshend
Lord Sydney

Thomas Pitt
2nd Lord
Camelford
(1775-1804)

Anne m. William W.
Grenville,
Ld. Grenville
(1759-1834)

(3)
George
2nd Earl
Temple,
1st Marquis
of Buckingham
(1753-1813)

Thomas
(1755-184

Dukes of
Buckingham
and Chandos